RAF AIRFIELDS
OF WORLD WAR 2

IT'S IN THE BAG

RAF AIRFIELDS
OF WORLD WAR 2

JONATHAN FALCONER

RAF Airfields of World War 2
Jonathan Falconer

First published in 2012 by Midland Publishing
Reprinted in 2015 by Crécy Publishing Ltd

ISBN 978 1 85780 349 5

Printed in Slovenia by GPS Group

Crecy Publishing Ltd
1a Ringway Trading Est
Shadowmoss Rd
Manchester
M22 5LH
Tel +44 (0)161 499 0024
www.crecy.co.uk

PREVIOUS PAGE: Flg Off Chas King, RAAF, and his No 196 Squadron crew with their Stirling Mk IV, 'It's in the Bag', at Wethersfield, Essex. Standing from left to right the crew are: Flt Sgt P. Smith, RAFVR, flight engineer; Flg Off Chas King, RAAF, pilot; Warrant Officer J. Corcoran, RNZAF, navigator; Warrant Officer H. McLaren, RAAF, bomb-aimer. Kneeling: Flt Sgt J. Heslop, RAFVR, air gunner; Flg Off D. Hunt, RAAF, wireless op/AG. *(Chas King)*

ABOVE: A Pathfinder Force Lancaster of No 35 Squadron taxis between two bands of flame along Graveley's runway during a FIDO test in 1945. FIDO burner installations were installed at 15 wartime fighter, bomber and coastal airfields in England. They used a staggering total of 30 million gallons of petrol to heat and disperse fog from runways, enabling aircraft to take off and land in safety. *(Imperial War Museum (IWM) CH15271)*

FRONT JACKET PICTURES: See pages 80, 101, 130, 156, 240.

FRONT FLAP PICTURES: See pages 42 and 182.

BACK JACKET PICTURES: See pages 69, 200 and 213.

CONTENTS

ACKNOWLEDGEMENTS

The first editions of RAF Bomber Airfields of World War 2 (1992) and RAF Fighter Airfields of World War 2 (1993)

John Allison; Dick Armstrong for drawing many of the airfield maps; J. Barrien; Owen Baum; Ray Beeforth; Chaz Bowyer; Ron Clark, pilot, No 100 Squadron; Seb Cox of the RAF Air Historical Branch, Great Scotland Yard, for help and guidance with primary research sources; Eric Davey; Mrs Frances M. Davies, for permission to reproduce letters written by her late fiance, Sgt Jim Bowler; John Foreman; Steve Grant; my friend Andy Gray for his chauffeuring duties in Norfolk during September 1991; Colin Hawkesworth of the Construction Industry Training Board, Bircham Newton, Norfolk; Peter Holway; W. Huntley; Z. Hurt; Mrs I.M. Hockin; Bill Johnson, ground-crew, No 1666 HCU; Sqn Ldr W.L.H. 'Johnny' Johnston, pilot with Nos 152, 92, 234 Squadrons 1940–44; Len Manning, air gunner, No 57 Squadron; Ken Merrick in Highbury, Australia, for his customary help and kindness in tracking down photographs; Simon Parry; Bruce Robertson for so kindly providing photographic and documentary material; Alan Thorpe, Company Archivist and Historian, John Laing Plc, for his kind assistance in providing photographs and documentary material relating to the airfield construction programme; Andrew Wadsted, Public Relations Manager, Costain Group Plc; N.D. Welch; Alan White; Clive Williams for help with secondary research sources; Mrs Jean Yeomans, for permission to reproduce letters from Flg Off 'Bunny' Shaw.

Staff of the Commonwealth War Graves Commission, Imperial War Museum, Public Record Office, RAF Museum and the Public Archives of Canada.

These newspapers kindly published my requests for help: *Bristol Evening Post, Cambridge Evening News, Camelford & Delabole Post, Derby Evening Telegraph, Eastern Evening News, East Anglian Daily Times. Grimsby Evening Telegraph, Hartlepool Mail, Leicester Mercury, Lincolnshire Echo, Liverpool Echo, Manchester Evening News, Newcastle Evening Chronicle, Northants Evening Telegraph, Portsmouth News, Sunderland Echo, Yorkshire Evening Post.*

The large airfield plans are reproduced with permission of the Controller of HMSO.

Acknowledgements for this new (2012) edition

From Australia, Kristen Alexander (Canberra) – 'War over the West' and 'Pockley the U-boat magnet'; Chris Taylor (Sydney) – 'War over the West'; Tim and Peter Pockley (Australia) – 'Pockley the U-boat Magnet'; Keith Janes (UK), Lloyd Holland and Ronald Larche (Canada), Dennis Burke (Ireland) – 'Interned in Portugal'. Dr Alfred Price, Sqn Ldr Andy Thomas and Ken Merrick (in Australia) for their help with the supply of photographs; the Australian War Memorial, Canberra; Imperial War Museum, London; The National Archives, Kew; RAF Museum, London; and Nick Grant and Matthew Wharmby at Ian Allan Publishing.

Almost 20 years have passed since publication of the first editions of *RAF Bomber Airfields of World War 2* and *RAF Fighter Airfields of World War 2*. Sad to say, many of the original contributors have since passed on. Three in particular that I'd like to remember are aviation authors Chaz Bowyer and Bruce Robertson, and Spitfire pilot Sqn Ldr Johnny Johnston. All three offered me help and encouragement with the first editions. Chaz and Bruce made their own significant contributions to the world of aviation literature from the 1960s through to the late 1990s. Their books can still be found on the shelves of most enthusiasts.

Author's Note

This book deals specifically with airfields and flying boat bases, squadrons and units in the British Isles under the operational control of RAF Fighter, Bomber and Coastal Commands – the three main frontline commands of the RAF between 1939 and 1945; Air Defence of Great Britain (ADGB) and the 2nd Tactical Air Force (2 TAF). All airfields and flying boat bases are listed within the county boundaries as they were at the outbreak of war in 1939.

On some airfields, squadrons and units took up residence before the outbreak of war; on others they remained after the war's end. With instances such as these, the dates pre-3 September 1939 and post-8 May 1945 have been included for the sake of completeness, even though they fall outside the book's time frame.

Aircraft operated by a squadron or unit are listed in the order in which they served: Spitfire I, VB; Typhoon IB. It does not necessarily mean that the squadron in question operated all of these types at the same time. In the orders of battle to be found in the appendices, where a squadron or a unit's aircraft types are listed thus – Mosquito II/VI or Beaufighter VIF/Mosquito II – this denotes that the squadron or unit was in the process of converting from one mark or type of aircraft to another at that particular time.

Jonathan Falconer

Bradford-on-Avon, *February 1993 and September 2012*

INTRODUCTION

In 1992 Ian Allan published the first of my two books about RAF wartime airfields – *RAF Bomber Airfields of World War Two*. It was followed in 1993 by a similar volume on RAF fighter airfields. Both books were a success and have remained in print for the best part of two decades.

This new, re-illustrated, volume is the result of a complete revision and updating of these two books and the inclusion of fresh material about wartime RAF Coastal Command bases. The result is a full coverage of RAF frontline airfields and air bases in the UK between 1939 and 1945.

Over the past twenty years the status of many of the airfields described has changed: some that had survived as time capsules since their closure after the war, finally fell prey to property developers and industrial re-development; others that had remained in use through the Cold War became victims of the 'peace dividend' of the 1990s and the Strategic Defence Review of 2011, when they were closed or sold off by the Ministry of Defence. These changes in status are recorded here.

Some of the personal stories from the original editions have been retained, but now include accounts from Coastal Command. Since first publication of *RAF Bomber* and *RAF Fighter Airfields* much new information has come to light, which means I have been able to update (and in one case virtually re-write) several of the narrative accounts and personal stories.

The illustrative content has also been revised, with more than 50 per cent of photographs that are new to this book. They feature airfields, aircraft, events and people, and some maps, all of which have been obtained from a variety of different sources, including official archives in the UK and overseas, from personal collections, and are supported by a selection of present-day photographs.

I hope this new volume will become a source of interest, as well as one of reference, to all those with a fascination in Britain's wartime airfields and the great deeds to which they bore witness.

Jonathan Falconer, Bradford-on-Avon, *September 2012*

TL

GIVE US THE TOOLS

'We shall not fail or falter; we shall not weaken or tire. Neither the sudden shock of battle, nor the long-drawn trials of vigilance and exertion will wear us down. Give us the tools, and we will finish the job.'

Prime Minister Winston Churchill, BBC radio broadcast, 9 February 1941

THE RAF'S AIRFIELD BUILDING PROGRAMME

The cult of the bomber was very much a phenomenon of the interwar period. Its new role of mass destruction witnessed during the closing stages of World War 1 strongly affected military thinking in the years that immediately followed. Three men in particular can be credited with the original theories of air warfare: General Giulio Douhet of Italy, Air Marshal Sir Hugh Trenchard of Great Britain, and Brigadier-General William 'Billy' Mitchell of the USA. The early air theorists argued that the object of war was to destroy the will of the enemy as well as his ability to resist, and then to impose one's own will upon him. In the conflict of the future these three men believed naval and ground forces would no longer have the decisive role. With the advent of the aeroplane, the obstacle of the enemy's surface forces could be jumped and attacks could be staged by air to hit at the enemy's population, or at the industry and economy that supported it. Gone were the days of air forces being merely auxiliary to an army or navy.

In Douhet's view, the best way to attain victory was to destroy air bases, supply points and centres of production on which the enemy depended. His strategic bomber force would have two separable functions: it must be able to win command of the skies, and be able to exploit that command. The immediate aim of air warfare, as Douhet clearly saw, was the need to defeat totally the opposing air force.

Trenchard's theory was that the heart of air power lay in strategic bombing of an independent character. He argued that operations in direct support of the Army and Navy were subsidiary and diversionary.

LEFT: On a waterlogged dispersal pan at Linton-on-Ouse, ground crew prepare to start the engines of this Halifax Mk II Series 1 of 35 Squadron in 1941. (IWM D6054)

'Billy' Mitchell also argued for an independent force, but his advocacy of autonomy for the air arm aroused American democracy's strong distaste for the military establishment and its theories of total war. This effectively put paid to any ideas of an independent air force in America for a long time to come.

Throughout the interwar period various international conventions were held with the intention of banning the bomber. In 1922 the Washington Conference on the Limitation of Armaments strongly condemned aerial bombardment. The Hague Rules of Aerial Warfare of 1923, although never ratified, attempted to provide a definition of what constituted a military target, what could be suitably subjected to air bombardment, and what could not. Military targets included: '. . . military forces, works, establishments or depots, factories constituting important and well-known centres engaged in the manufacture of guns, munitions or distinctively military supplies; lines of communication or transportation for military purposes'.

One of the important reasons for the failure to reach an agreement can be attributed to the fact that the Hague Rules saw aerial bombardment as legitimate, but only when directed against military objectives. The difficulty lay in defining and reaching agreement on what constituted a military objective. The rules therefore left it to the discretion of the attacker as to whether a military target was important enough to warrant a bombardment. In 1928 Trenchard produced a paper in which he acknowledged that although bombing of civilians could be contrary to the rules of warfare, 'it is an entirely different matter to terrorise munitions workers (men and women) into absenting themselves from work or stevedores into abandoning the loading of a ship with munitions through fear of air attack upon the factory or dock concerned'.

ABOVE: Ungainly in appearance, the twin-engine Handley Page Heyford was the RAF's last biplane heavy bomber to enter service, in November 1933. Illustrated here is Heyford Mk I, K3490 (the second production Heyford), of No 99 Squadron at Upper Heyford, Oxfordshire, in November 1933. (Author)

During the 1930s it was the predictions of men such as J. M. Spaight (author of the influential Air Power in the Next War) and the dire warnings of a handful of politicians like Winston Churchill, which cajoled the Air Ministry and the British Government into expanding the RAF to meet the emerging threat of the German Luftwaffe.

The politician Harold Macmillan wrote in his memoirs: 'We thought of air warfare in 1938 rather as people think of nuclear warfare today.' Further attempts to restrict air warfare failed in 1932 when a disarmament conference organised by the League of Nations assembled in Geneva. By the time Germany withdrew from the conference in 1933 there had been no significant progress. Despite their decision to increase defence expenditure, it only gradually became obvious to the Prime Minister, Stanley Baldwin, and his Cabinet that Germany, under Hitler, was re-arming at a rapid rate and preparing for war.

Thus, the RAF was the only air force in the developed world prior to 1939 to have given much thought to the defensive capabilities of the fighter – thoughts well placed, as events were ultimately to prove.

In 1935 the RAF was forced by the Government into accepting the Re-orientation Plan, under which a greater emphasis than before was placed on air defence. However, this emphasis on the production of defensive fighters and AA weapons was met with some scepticism by the RAF's advocates of the bomber strategy. In admitting there was a defence against the bomber, the concept of the invincible bomber that would always get through to its target had been undermined and with it the philosophy on which the independent RAF had been created in 1918.

Notwithstanding these arguments, a decision to adopt an expansion programme, known as Scheme 'C', was set in motion which provided for a home-based air force of 70 bomber and 35 fighter squadrons. The scheme presented certain difficulties of administration under the existing RAF organisation and, as a consequence, the Service was completely re-organised into four new commands: Fighter, Bomber, Coastal and Training.

Expansion Scheme 'C' was one of a number of prewar schemes for the RAF that provided not only for an increase in the number of aircraft but also for a comprehensive programme of airfield construction to house the new squadrons and aircraft of the various commands.

In particular, Scheme 'C' emphasised the need for the bomber force to be able to reach Berlin in a latitudinally straight line. The eastern counties of England, notably Lincolnshire and Yorkshire, were therefore the obvious

ABOVE: The rugged Gloster Gamecock typified the single-engine biplane fighter aircraft that served in the RAF's frontline fighter squadrons during the interwar period. Gamecocks equipped five RAF fighter squadrons during the 1920s, and a Mk I of No 43 Squadron is illustrated. (Author)

choice for the construction of these new airfields, sowing the seeds for the rapid growth of what later became known as the 'Bomber Counties' of World War 2.

Such a large scale increase in the size of the RAF would inevitably cause problems with a shortage of suitable airfield accommodation. At the end of World War 1 there had been some 300 military aerodromes in the UK, yet by 1924 this number had diminished to 27. The need clearly existed for a rapid programme of airfield construction to accommodate the growing air force.

Created in 1934, the Air Ministry Works Directorate (AMWD) was formed as the body responsible for the planning and organisation of these new airfields and a subsidiary of the AMWD, known as the Air Ministry Aerodromes Board (AMAB). Its task was to work in close liaison with the Air Ministry Lands Branch (AMLB) in the selection of suitable sites for new airfields. An important part of the AMAB's brief was to create a standard architectural style for both airfield and domestic facilities, and to prepare plans for the modification of existing airfields.

In 1935 the RAF's prewar Expansion Scheme in terms of aircraft and airfields really took off. With a carefully planned airfield expansion programme totalling some 100 new military airfields, it continued unabated up to the outbreak of war four years later in 1939.

The environmental impact of all this new land development, much of it in the heart of the English countryside, attracted the attentions of a number of monitoring groups. All plans for permanent buildings on new airfields had to be approved by the Royal Fine Art Commission, while the siting of airfields in the countryside involved consultations with the Society for the Preservation of Rural England.

The Expansion Scheme stations were characterised by their distinctive and comfortable neo-Georgian headquarters buildings, messes and married quarters. Elevational treatments could vary even around individual airfields, and also from airfield to airfield, offering a discreet mixture of neo-Georgian, Art Deco and Utilitarian styling. Accommodation was centralised and laid out to a roughly circular arrangement; it was not dispersed over a larger area like the hostilities-only temporary stations built during World War 2. Technical buildings were generally located alongside and to the rear of the hangars. Because of the large aircraft they operated, bomber airfields and flying

boat bases needed larger hangars and more technical accommodation than, say, a fighter airfield.

Airmen's quarters were located close to the hangars and technical buildings; the officers' and sergeants' messes generally occupied sites of a more secluded nature. All technical and domestic accommodation was built to a high standard of finish using brick, stone and roofing materials chosen to blend as harmoniously as possible with the hues of the surrounding countryside. With the outbreak of war, comprehensive airfield camouflage schemes were put into operation using paint, netting and other materials to make runways, hangars and other buildings as inconspicuous as possible from the air.

Work on the first of the Expansion Scheme stations – Cranfield, Feltwell, Harwell, Marham, Stradishall and Waddington for Bomber Command; Cranfield, Church Fenton, Tern Hill and Odiham for Fighter Command – was begun in 1935. At the same time a number of existing RAF stations like the bomber airfield at Upper Heyford, and the fighter airfields at Catterick, Hornchurch, North Weald, Tangmere, Turnhouse and Wittering, underwent modernisation programmes.

ABOVE: In October 1938 No 9 Squadron became the first RAF unit to receive the monoplane Vickers Wellington medium bomber. These Mk Is pictured in July 1939 are fitted with their original Vickers front turrets. (Author)

More new permanent stations were started in 1936 like Dishforth, Driffield, Finningley, Hemswell, Leconfield, Scampton, Upwood and Wyton for Bomber Command. The last 'permanent' bomber stations to be built before the outbreak of war included Binbrook, Bramcote, Coningsby, Leeming, Middleton St George, Newton, North Luffenham, Oakington, Oulton, Swanton Morley, Swinderby, Syerston, Topcliffe and Waterbeach. The last permanent fighter stations to be constructed were Middle Wallop, Ouston and West Malling.

Several contracts for permanent airfields were begun late in 1939 and included a number of modifications and economies, which resulted in a considerable speeding up in construction. These were among the last of the so-called permanent airfields to be completed during the opening years of the war and some of the first to include a concrete perimeter track.

Airfield construction

The AMAB selected and inspected sites which were reasonably flat and free from obstructions, and between 50 and 600ft above mean sea level. Reconnaissance engineers were given a few days in which to examine the site in detail with particular attention being given to soil type, drainage and obstructions to flying. If the site was deemed suitable for development, the land was requisitioned under the Emergency Powers (Defence) Act of 1939 and civilian building contractors were invited to tender for the contract.

A number of companies were involved in the airfield construction programme, including John Laing & Son Ltd, Taylor-Woodrow Ltd, Richard Costain Ltd and George Wimpey & Co Ltd – household names in the construction industry today. A greater number of small local contractors were also involved in the programme, and in cases where these firms had insufficient plant of their own, machinery was loaned to them by the AMWD so that all firms could play their fullest part in the huge programme of airfield construction. Once tenders had been accepted and issued, work commenced on clearing and levelling the site. Armies of workmen and heavy plant machinery moved in to transform one of many small corners of the English rural landscape into a home for hundreds of RAF servicemen and women, and a launch pad from which scores of Allied combat aircraft could defend the homeland and strike at the very heartland of Nazi Germany.

At the outbreak of war, Bomber Command was operating from some 33 permanent airfields in England and Scotland. A significant number of large, permanent airfields were nearing completion and formed part of the RAF's prewar Expansion Scheme. As a result of changing requirements, major extensions were undertaken at these semi-completed airfields to provide additional barrack blocks, bomb stores and sundry ancillary buildings.

Runways

Airfields built before World War 2 generally had no paved runways: grass landing strips were the norm, as, for example, at Bircham Newton in Norfolk. With the introduction to service of heavier aircraft, particularly

BELOW: In 1937 the first of the new breed of single-seat monoplane fighters began to replace the comparatively primitive biplanes. Seen at Northolt in early 1938 are Hawker Hurricane Mk Is of No 111 Squadron, the first squadron to equip with the type. (RAF Museum)

ABOVE: The RAF Airfield Construction Branch (RAF ACB) was employed in the UK and overseas for the construction of new airfields, and the maintenance, improvement and expansion of existing ones. This photograph shows a team from an RAF Airfield Construction Squadron (ACS) 'somewhere in Europe' in 1944–5. General construction trade squadrons were numbered from 5001 to 5020; the mechanical plant squadrons were numbered 5201 to 5207. Most of the ACS officers were qualified civil engineers and many of the tradesmen were either ex-civilian tradesmen or trade apprentices. By the war's end some 30,000 men were serving in the RAF ACB. (Author)

bombers, the need for paved runways to allow an unhindered all-weather operational capability became very clear. The grass airfields were generally quite adequate during the summer months, but with the onset of winter and its attendant increase in rainfall, poor drainage of surface water led to waterlogging and serious problems for an airfield's operational status. Generally speaking, the early runways were graded Tarmac coated with asphalt laid over a hardcore base and were not as durable as many built later in the war. However, the necessity for surfaced runways became apparent and work commenced in 1939 gradually to re-equip the majority of Bomber Command's airfields with a new three-runway layout, perimeter tracks and concrete dispersal pans.

Despite pleas for runways at his fighter airfields to improve their operational status, Fighter Command's Commander-in-Chief, Sir Hugh Dowding, had to wait until shortly before the outbreak of war for his wishes to be granted. Then priority was given only to Kenley, Biggin Hill, Church Fenton, Debden, Northolt, Tangmere, Turnhouse and Hendon. There were only three fighter stations known to have had one or more runways before World War 2 and these were Odiham, Aldergrove and North Weald.

Fighter Command airfields equipped with surfaced runways and perimeter tracks generally fared better and suffered less damage than those in Bomber Command, for the simple reason that a fully loaded four-engine Short Stirling bomber weighed considerably less than a single-engine Spitfire. Despite the benefits to be gained from surfaced runways, many fighter airfields retained their grass-surfaced runways throughout the war.

By virtue of the fact that it operated smaller aircraft, Fighter Command's new or updated airfields generally needed fewer large hangars and technical buildings than those of Bomber Command.

From December 1940, all new bomber airfields in the UK were to be constructed with one paved main runway of 1,400yd and two subsidiaries of 1,100yd in length. By 1942

HONILEY – *Ingredients for a fighter station*

Honiley in Warwickshire was a fighter station in No 9 Group that was developed from an intended bomber OTU station. The main contractor was the building and engineering firm of John Laing & Son Ltd of Mill Hill in northwest London. To give an idea of what was physically involved in the construction of a wartime airfield, the following facts and figures make interesting reading:

Contract Value
£588,042

Buildings Contract
Number of bricks used: 3½ million
Length of soil drains: 3½ miles
Length of surface water drains: 2¾ miles
Length of water main: 4 miles
Area of concrete roads, aprons etc: 66,000sq yd

Runways Contract
Area of top concrete laid: 353,000sq yd
Volume of all concrete laid: 60,000cu yd
Volume of excavation of virgin ground: 150,000cu yd
Length of perimeter track: 3¼ miles
Length of surface water drains: 14 miles
Length of French drains: 8½ miles
Tarmac area laid: 7,000sq yd
Area of asphalt surfacing: 338,000sq yd
Volume of ashes used as filling: 75,000cu yd

Other interesting facts
Length of hedgerow uprooted: 1¾ miles
Number of trees uprooted: 5,000
Sectional huts erected: if placed end to end their length would be 1 mile
(Source: John Laing Plc)

the requirements had changed still further, setting the standard for runway dimensions until the end of the war: a main runway length of 2,000yd with subsidiaries of 1,400yd (this also applied to any extensions to existing runways). However, towards the end of World War 2, doubts were expressed about the need for a three-runway layout on heavy bomber stations since, in practice, the subsidiary runways were very rarely used.

The new dispersal pan system allowed squadron aircraft to be scattered around an airfield perimeter to save them from damage or destruction in the event of enemy air attack. Aircraft were only returned to the central maintenance area or hangars for major engineering and repair work. The number of dispersals varied from 50 at parent stations to 25 at satellites.

Flying boat bases

Compared to conventional landplanes, flying boats can operate from an already existing surface – water. Another advantage, particularly during the war years, was that the growth in aircraft size posed little problem from the operating viewpoint, unlike the experience of Bomber Command.

Before the war there was a handful of flying boat bases in the British Isles and overseas, but with the outbreak of war more had to be built. The ideal requirements for the location of a flying boat base were an unobstructed expanse of water in which an area of 4,000yd in diameter could be contained, with a minimum depth of 10ft. For safety reasons when operating heavy flying boats like the Sunderland and Catalina, there could be no surrounding topographical feature, like a hillside or a headland, which would rise above a gradient of 1 in 50 from the outer edge of the landing area. Additional operating precautions and limitations also needed to be observed: the landing area had to be kept free from flotsam, jetsam, boats and other shipping, which could hole a hull and spell disaster to a flying boat taking off or alighting. In addition, the Sunderland could not take off in waves greater than 4ft, nor land if they were more than 2ft. This could also hole the hull or rip wing floats off.

Aircraft moorings needed to be sheltered from the wind, in a minimum of 10 ft of water, and within easy reach of the operational area, slipways and maintenance base. The operational area of water used for taking off and landing usually consisted of two flying strips measuring about 4,000 x 400yd, with a minimum depth of 10ft at all times. Landing strips were marked with pairs of lighted buoys, and leading-in lights were provided for night flying.

To enable flying boats to be brought ashore for repair and maintenance, and to return them again to the water, 150ft wide slipways were constructed. A gentle gradient of 1 in 15 was needed to take into account the flying boat's hull configuration and the location of its beaching gear, as well as facilitating a tractor or a winch in pulling an aircraft out or returning it again to the water. Slipways also needed a load-bearing capability strong enough to handle a 40,000lb aircraft.

Shore-based facilities were very similar to those of landplane airfields having extensive airfield, technical and domestic sites, but specific requirements included hangars large enough to accommodate the 112ft 9½in wingspan of Sunderlands, hardstands and taxi tracks (6in thick concrete

SCULTHORPE – *Ingredients for a bomber station*

The following figures are typical of the quantity of work involved in the building of one RAF bomber airfield in 1942: 603,000sq yd total area of surfacing; 242,000cu yd of concrete; 1,030,000cu yd of excavation; 34 miles of drainage work; 10 miles of cable ducts; and 7 miles of water main.

During 1943, the RAF identified a number of its airfields as suitable for improvement to Very Heavy Bomber (VHB) standard in order to take the Boeing B-29 Superfortress (named 'Washington' in RAF service) and the projected Vickers Windsor (never to enter service). Lakenheath, Marham and Sculthorpe were earmarked to become the first VHB airfields and were closed during 1944–45 for major reconstruction work.

John Laing & Son Ltd began construction work at Sculthorpe in May 1944 on what was to become one of the most extensive RAF airfields in the country. The rebuilt Sculthorpe covered an area of some 750 acres, with a new main runway of 3,000yd in length and all three runways 100yd wide – twice the normal width. In order for the runways to bear the greater weight of the envisaged very heavy bombers, a sub-base of 4in of mass concrete was laid on a specially prepared sub-grade, and finished with 8-12in of high-grade quality concrete paving.

If the figures above are compared with those for the reconstruction at Sculthorpe in 1944, the enormity of the task can be appreciated: 1,100,000sq yd total area of surfacing; 566,300cu yd of concrete; 1,530,000cu yd of excavation; 34 miles of drainage work; and 32 miles of cable ducts. The work required the following materials: 120,764 tons of cement; 159 miles of heavy-duty steel road forms; and 200 miles of sealing compound.

Source: John Laing plc

ABOVE: After the reconnaissance engineers had finished their job and the site had been requisitioned, the first task was to clear and level the ground. Here a 12cu yd scraper drawn by a 90hp tractor works on runway excavation. (John Laing Plc)

ABOVE: Mechanical spreading and compacting machines like this one were used on runway construction. The compacting machine has a front screeding beam with a span of 20ft, a compacting beam capable of working at up to 3,000 impulses per minute, and also a back finishing beam. (John Laing Plc)

blocks 12in square, grouted together, or Tarmac over levelled sand), large dispersal pens, and fuelling points for tenders to refuel aircraft at their moorings.

'Hostilities-only' airfields

As the war progressed so too did the pace of the RAF's airfield construction programme. The need for rapid construction of airfields led to the development of many prefabricated building designs such as the Nissen and Romney hut, and the 'T' Type hangar, all of which combined ease and speed of erection with cost-effectiveness and durability.

Runway construction was speeded up, with an average completion time, from foundations down to receiving the first aircraft, of five to seven months. It would take a total of some 18 months for a labour force of 1,000 men to complete an entire 'A' class (Heavy Bomber) airfield with all facilities.

Gone were the days of comfortable neo-Georgian elegance and centralisation of facilities; here, for the duration of hostilities, were the dispersed utilitarian quagmires that would serve the RAF's frontline commands and many of its squadrons. Such was the rapid rate of construction that in the peak year of 1942 an average of one new airfield was coming into use with the RAF every three days. In this year, some 127,000 men were employed on Air Ministry Works out of a total building and civil engineering workforce of 393,400 nationwide.

By the end of World War 2 over 170 airfields in England and Scotland had seen use by Fighter, Bomber and Coastal Commands. Yet, within months of peace being declared, the RAF had begun to wind down. Its huge arsenal of aircraft and weapons, men and airfields became surplus to requirements almost overnight. Squadrons were disbanded and hundreds of perfectly serviceable aircraft scrapped; air and ground crews were demobbed, returning to the comparatively humdrum life of civvy street. Dozens of airfields were downgraded to Care & Maintenance status before their eventual closure and return to the more peaceable ways of agriculture.

A number of permanent airfields such as Coningsby, Leeming and Waddington, which had played key roles in the wartime air offensives, have survived into the 21st century to see use by the RAF's small force of Typhoons and Tornados – jet-age successors to the legendary Spitfires and Lancasters. An even greater number of these airfields have succumbed to the ravages of time and nature, and to landowners and property developers with little sense of our wartime heritage.

ABOVE: RAF station buildings of the prewar Expansion Scheme featured a high standard of design, construction and comfort. The elegant neo-Georgian façade of the officers' mess at Bircham Newton in Norfolk is typical of the period. (Author)

BELOW: The parade square and airmen's quarters at RAF Upwood, one of a clutch of Expansion Scheme stations started in 1936. (Author)

ABOVE: In contrast to the carefully planned peacetime accommodation, the dispersed sites of the utilitarian 'hostilities-only' airfields like RAF Ludford Magna in Lincolnshire offered little in the way of elegance or creature comforts. The nickname of 'Mudford Magna' needs little explanation. (Peter Holway)

BELOW: Harwell was one of the first pre-war Expansion Scheme permanent RAF stations to be completed. Note the camouflage painting of walls and roofs. (UK Atomic Energy Authority)

ABOVE: This C Type hangar at Upwood is pictured towards the end of the war. (Author's collection)

BELOW: Camouflaged AAP HP Sheds (AAP = Aircraft Acceptance Park; HP = Handley Page V1500 bomber) form the backdrop to Hurricanes of 501 Squadron getting airborne from Hawkinge during the Battle of Britain on 16 August 1940. During World War 1 aircraft were assembled and flight-tested at Aircraft Acceptance Parks (Hawkinge was No 12 AAP). (Author's collection)

HANGAR DESIGNS COMMONLY SEEN AT OPERATIONAL RAF AIRFIELDS IN THE UK, 1939–45

A' Type (1924)
Open span: 120ft; length: 250ft; max door height clearance: 25ft.
With the expansion of the RAF during the 1930s, and the anticipation of larger aircraft entering service, the 'A' Type proved ultimately to be unsuitable and thus a larger hangar was required.

Belfast Truss or General Service Shed (GS) (1917)
One of the most successful of the early designs of hangar, the Belfast was a buttressed structure built of brick and so-called because of its Belfast roof trusses.

Bellman (8349/37) (1937)
Open span: 87ft 9in; length: 175ft; max door height: 26ft.
Of steel construction with steel doors at each end, the Bellman was the most common steel hangar on RAF airfields up until 1940 when it was superseded by the 'T' Types.

Bessonneau (1916)
Temporary structures with wooden frames covered with canvas. Many were produced and a large number were brought out of storage during World War 2 for emergency use.

Blister (1939)
Designed with the dispersal principle in mind, Blisters were small open-ended hangars, all to a standard length of 45ft but in the following three permutations: 'Standard' Blister, with wooden arched-rib construction clad with corrugated iron sheeting (span 45ft); 'Over' Blister, the same basic construction as the 'Standard' but with steel cladding (span 65ft); 'Extra Over' Blister, the same construction as 'Over' Blister but with a 69ft span.
Blister hangars had canvas curtains at each end, although in many cases these were discarded. Some were bricked up at one end.

Butler Combat Hangar and 'Merton' Type (1939–45)
The former was an American-built steel-framed hangar used on only a few RAF fighter airfields. The RAF equivalent was the smaller Merton with tubular steel framework covered with canvas.

Callender-Hamilton (1937, 1940)
Open span: 90ft; length: 185ft; max door height: 25ft.
Transportable steel hangar with steel doors at each end, similar in design and appearance to the Bellman.

B1 and B2 Types (1942)
Open span: 120ft; length: 227ft 6in; max door height: 27ft (B1), 20ft 6in (B2).
A MAP design used at many of Fighter Command's frontline stations and OTUs for the major servicing of aircraft. Steel construction with doors at each end.

C Type (1934)
'C' Type Gabled (1934) – Max door height: 35ft;
'C' Type Hipped (1938) – Max door height: 30ft.
Open span: 152ft; length: 300ft; max door height clearance: 35ft.
The width of the 'C' Type was standard, although the length could vary according to local requirements. It was of brick and steel construction with steel plate doors at each end and came with either a gabled or hipped roof design. Single- or two-storey offices and workshops were built externally along the length of the hangar on either side.

'C1' Type (1939)
The same as the 'C', but making extensive use of asbestos sheeting instead of brickwork to save time and construction costs.

'D' Type (1936)
Open span: 150ft; length: 300ft; max door height: 30ft.
Constructed predominantly from reinforced concrete topped by a curved roof.

'F' Type
One of the earliest of the interwar period hangars, built of steel with side-opening doors.

'J' and 'K' Types (1939)
Open span: 150ft; length: 300ft; max door height: 30ft.
Predominantly of metal and brick construction with a curved roof of 0.25in steel plate. Offices and workshops built externally along the length of the hangar on either side.

'T' Types (1940/41/42)
The main types were the 'T2' and 'T2' (Home).
Open spans of 90ft or 97ft 2in; length: 239ft 7in; max door height: 25ft.
Lengths could vary according to local requirements.
'T' stood for Transportable. The type was a transportable metal hangar which was quick to erect. T2s were by far the most ubiquitous type of hangar to be seen on wartime RAF airfields, superseding the prewar Bellman design.

FIGHTER COMMAND GROUP STRUCTURE

Initially, Fighter Command comprised four principal internal formations: Nos 11 and 12 (Fighter) Groups – the former tasked with all defence south of a line east-west through Bedford, the latter to cover the UK north of this same dividing line – No 22 (Army Co-operation) Group, and the civilian Observer Corps. However, the gradual expansion of Fighter Command in the years leading up to the war necessitated the formation of more groups to further divide the original two into more manageable units of control.

ABOVE: Spitfire PRIG, R7116, 'C', of No 140 Squadron, is seen here in late 1941. Note the rearward-facing oblique camera behind the cockpit. (Alfred Price)

LEFT: Typhoon pilots of 486 (New Zealand) Squadron at Tangmere in 1943. (Author's collection)

On the outbreak of war in September 1939, the following fighter groups were in existence, concentrated at 14 airfields: No 11 Group (Southern England), No 12 Group (Midlands) and No 13 Group (North). The three groups consisted of 31 squadrons, equipped as follows: 14 Hurricane, eight Spitfire, seven Blenheim, one Spitfire/Gladiator, and one Gladiator.

By the early summer of the following year, three more fighter groups had been formed to help tackle the grave threat of invasion posed by the Nazis and to spread the burden of the UK's fighter defence, hitherto the task of the existing three groups. These were No 9 Group (Northwest Midlands) in August, No 10 Group (West) in July, and No 14 Group (Scotland, Orkneys, Shetlands), also in July.

From small beginnings, Fighter Command grew not only into a powerful defensive but also an offensive force. By March 1943 the Command could field some 100 frontline squadrons operating from over 50 airfields across the UK.

Groups, sectors and squadrons

Fighter Command's basic organisational structure can be split up as follows into Headquarters RAF Fighter Command set in overall control above Groups, Sectors and Squadrons. The Fighter Command operations room at Bentley Priory was used mainly for organising reinforcement from one Group to another.

The Groups under the command of an air vice-marshal were arranged in a geographical pattern, each Group covering a particular area of the UK. Each Group was subdivided into Sectors, which comprised a number of fighter stations, satellites and Forward Operating Bases (FOBs), with one station selected as the Sector Station under the command of a group captain. The Group Operations Rooms allocated squadrons to counter a particular raid and generally speaking had a broader picture of events than the Sector Operations Rooms.

Each Fighter Sector was assigned a number of squadrons which it controlled through its Operations Room. Here the Sector Controller could watch the movements of raids in his area and have radio control of his fighters. During the Battle of Britain period this could number between two and four squadrons, while later in the war the numbers increased and could number six or more.

A squadron, commanded by a squadron leader or wing commander, could number some 16 aircraft and 20 pilots, plus ground crew of non-commissioned officers and airmen to maintain the aircraft. Each aircraft had its own dedicated airframe rigger and engine fitter, whilst the other necessary technical trades like armourers, electricians, instrument technicians and wireless mechanics were allocated to each flight and not to any particular aircraft.

Each squadron was split into two Flights, 'A' and 'B', each led by a Flight Commander, usually of flight lieutenant rank. Each Flight was further subdivided (when each Flight was operating at the full strength of six aircraft) into three-aircraft Sections identified by a colour-code as follows: 'A' Flight – Red and Yellow sections; 'B' Flight – Blue and Green sections. For example, Green 1 would be leading the second section of 'B' Flight, with Green 2 to his right and Green 3 to his left.

The organisation of training groups in Fighter Command

At the outbreak of war in 1939, Fighter Command allocated a number of aircraft and crews to two Group Pools, each under the control of an operational Group, for final operational training prior to joining a squadron. These Group Pools were renamed Operational Training Units (OTU) in the spring of 1940, and at the end of the same year the three OTUs had '50' added to their numbers, becoming Nos 55 OTU, 56 OTU and 57 OTU. In December 1940, No 81 (OTU) Group was formed to incorporate the existing fighter OTUs and in May 1943 it was disbanded, control of OTUs being assumed by No 9 Group which then relinquished its frontline duties. In the summer of 1944, No 9 Group was disbanded and control of individual OTUs devolved onto the existing frontline Groups once more.

Restructuring Fighter Command in 1943

With the approach of the invasion of Europe by Allied forces, in 1943 the home-based elements of RAF Fighter Command underwent a major structural reorganisation. On 13 November the Allied Expeditionary Air Force came into being under the command of Air Chief Marshal Sir Trafford Leigh-Mallory and it had three elements: the first was the US 9th AF; the second and third were formed two days later on 15 November with the dissolution of RAF Fighter Command. The tactical elements became 2nd Tactical Air Force (2 TAF), while the remaining squadrons came under the command of a new organisation named Air Defence of Great Britain (ADGB).

The 2nd Tactical Air Force was made up of four groups: Nos 83 and 84 Groups were known as 'composite' groups, which meant that they contained fighter, fighter-bomber and recce squadrons tasked with Continental tactical strike operations; No 2 (Bomber) Group, hived off from Bomber Command on 1 June 1943, came temporarily under the control of Fighter Command until 15 November that same year when it became part of 2 TAF for tactical light bombing operations; and No 85 Group, which was tasked with the air defence of the Allied armies and air forces on the Continent. The remaining fighter squadrons came under ADGB control. However, after D-Day, any 2 TAF flying units which remained in the UK came under the nominal control of No 11 Group ADGB. On 15 October 1944, ADGB was disbanded and Fighter Command came into existence once more.

ADVANCED LANDING GROUNDS

Most airfields constructed for the RAF during the prewar Expansion period were sited in East Anglia but, with the outbreak of war and the eventual plans for the invasion of the Continent in 1944, the handful of airfields in the south and east of England which were closest to the planned invasion area were insufficient in number. Therefore plans were drawn up and work started in late 1942 on the construction of temporary airfields in Hampshire, Sussex and Kent, known as Advanced Landing Grounds (ALGs). From these ALGs the RAF and USAAF fighter and fighter-bomber squadrons operated Spitfires, Typhoons, Tempests, Mustangs and Thunderbolts to help establish a vital foothold in Europe.

Because at this time civilian labour in the UK was largely taken up in the construction of airfields for Bomber Command, much of the building of ALGs was undertaken by RAF and Army Airfield Construction Units. Once completed, ALGs had two metal track runways, one 1,600yd and the other 1,400yd in length, surrounded by a perimeter track running as close to the runways as possible in order to save valuable agricultural land. Initially, all of the RAF's ALGs were surfaced with Sommerfeld Track – basically a mesh of steel rods and bars held on the ground by angle iron pickets. Wear and tear resulted in their replacement by a similar design called Square Mesh Track (SMT). ALGs used by the USAAF were surfaced with Pierced Steel Plank (PSP) and Bar & Rod Track. These different types of tracking all possessed the same requisite qualities of ease of manufacture using available raw materials, speed of laying and dismantling for use elsewhere and durability in use. They also had to be easy to repair and to be inconspicuous from the air.

A maximum of 50 aircraft and four Blister hangars were planned for each ALG, together with tented accommodation and locally requisitioned property for some 100 officers and 2,000 men. No night flying or landing aids were considered necessary but a central bomb store was provided for a cluster of ALGs. Ammunition and fuel was stored on site, with up to 18,000gal of storage capacity for the latter.

Once the beachhead had been consolidated in France and new ALGs established on the Continent, the ALGs in southern England had served their purpose and were abandoned. They were soon all ripped up and, in most cases, by early 1945 the land had been quickly returned to agriculture. Much of the usable PSP was transported to Normandy for re-use on ALGs there.

BOMBER COMMAND GROUP STRUCTURE

At the outbreak of war in September 1939, Bomber Command's frontline force consisted of 29 home-based squadrons divided between four Groups and spread across 17 airfields. Each Group was equipped with a particular type of twin-engine bomber aircraft dedicated to a specific bombing role – light, medium or heavy.

No 2 Group was East Anglia-based and equipped with the elegant Bristol Blenheim light bomber; No 3 Group, also based in East Anglia, was equipped with Dr Barnes Wallis' 'geodetic' medium bomber, the Vickers Wellington; Yorkshire-based No 4 Group's warhorse was the slab-sided Armstrong Whitworth Whitley heavy bomber; and No 5 Group was based in Lincolnshire and equipped with the 'flying panhandle' – the Handley Page Hampden medium bomber. No 1 Group, with 10 squadrons of single-engine Fairey Battle light bombers, had moved to France on 1 September to form part of the Advanced Air Striking Force (AASF) and did not come under Bomber Command's operational control again until June 1940.

From comparatively small beginnings, Bomber Command grew into an awesome Leviathan capable of laying waste to Nazi Germany's cities and industrial might. In September 1939, Bomber Command could muster a daily average of 280 aircraft with crews; in the closing months of the war, Bomber Command could field a daily average of 1,069 aircraft with crews, drawn from 95 squadrons flying from more than 60 airfields and under the control of seven Groups. By then it was a predominantly heavy bomber force.

If we take a look at the disposition of its Groups in 1945, the motif of the picture is little changed from 1939; but what has changed is its sheer size and destructive power. No 1 Group operated from airfields in north Lincolnshire and was an all-Avro Lancaster force; No 2 Group's light bombers had been hived off in May 1943 to join the 2nd TAF, in preparation for the Normandy landings in June 1944; No 3 Group was based in Suffolk and Cambridgeshire and, like No 1 Group, it too was an all-Lancaster Group; No 4 Group's squadrons flew Handley Page Halifaxes from airfields in East Yorkshire. South of the Humber Estuary, No 5 Group was predominantly an all-Lancaster force flying from Lincolnshire, although the Group did operate a number of de Havilland Mosquitoes in the Pathfinder role. No 5 Group was unique in the Command because it

BELOW: A freezing winter scene on a dispersal pan at Mildenhall as a Stirling crew from No 149 Squadron pose for the camera beneath the nose of Stirling Mk I W7455 on 16 January 1942. (IWM TR135)

ABOVE: Woodbridge Emergency Landing Ground (ELG) was the first of three Bomber Command emergency runways specially built for the benefit of damaged Allied aircraft returning from operations over Europe. It was opened in No 3 Group, Bomber Command, on 15 November 1943 and was administered as a satellite of RAF Bentwaters. On the south side of the single large runway (3,000yd long by 250yd wide) eight dispersal loops were built, onto which crashed bombers were taken, and where serviceable aircraft were parked. (IWM HU93009)

RIGHT: Concrete dispersal pans were an innovation in World War 2 airfield design, which allowed squadron aircraft to be scattered around an airfield's perimeter, minimising their vulnerability to damage in the event of enemy air attack. This Halifax Mk VI of No 426 (Canadian) Squadron is pictured on its dispersal at Linton-on-Ouse during the spring of 1945. In the right foreground can be seen a hut typical of those used at dispersals by squadron ground crews, who carried out maintenance on their charges in the open except for major overhauls. (K. Merrick)

possessed its own target-marking element, made up of three squadrons 'on loan' from No 8 (PFF) Group. The decision to amputate a vital part of the PFF's body and transplant it elsewhere in the Command was the source of some considerable displeasure at No 8 Group's Headquarters.

Moving further north to North Yorkshire and Co Durham, the Canadian squadrons of No 6 (RCAF) Group flew a mixed force of Halifaxes and Lancasters. Bomber Command's specialist target marking force was No 8 (PFF) Group – the Pathfinders – which flew a mixed force of Lancasters and Mosquitoes from airfields around Ely in Cambridgeshire's fenlands. Finally, another specialised force existed for bomber support duties in the shape of No 100 (SD) Group, which flew electronic/radio countermeasures and intruder sorties with a mixed force of Mosquitoes, Halifaxes, Lancasters, Stirlings, Liberators and Flying Fortresses from airfields in northern Norfolk.

One point worth bearing in mind when noting the aircraft types allocated to the various squadrons concerns the changing criteria, as the war progressed and new types entered service, for the classification of light, medium and heavy bomber aircraft. In 1940, the twin-engine Armstrong Whitworth Whitley was classed as a heavy bomber. It could fly 1,630 miles with a 3,750lb bomb load at a cruising speed of 165mph; it was withdrawn from frontline service in May 1942. Yet the Avro Lancaster, undisputed queen of the new breed of four-engine heavies, which entered squadron service in January 1942, could carry a 14,000lb bomb load up to 1,660 miles at a cruising speed of 216mph. It, too, was classed as a heavy bomber. Of the same period, de Havilland's twin-engine 'Wooden Wonder' the Mosquito was classed as a light bomber, yet it was capable of carrying a 3,000lb bomb load for up to 1,620 miles at a cruising speed of 265mph. By comparison, its counterpart of 1940, the single-engine Fairey Battle, could carry a 1,420lb bomb load over 1,200 miles at a cruising speed of little over 200mph. These comparisons only go to show how rapid was the development in bomber design under wartime conditions.

The base system

Within each group the next tier of command was at station level, each of which was commanded by a group captain or, from late in 1942 when the base system came into existence, an air commodore. This situation came about as a result of the rapid growth in the number of airfields which began to put a strain on the administrative abilities of individual group headquarters. To ease this strain and to offer greater local control to stations and their satellites, the base system was devised. This comprised a parent station – usually one of the prewar permanent types – which hosted the base administrative apparatus and usually two squadrons, and a number of substations of temporary wartime construction, each commanded by a group captain. Each Base Headquarters was

identified by a two-digit code, the first digit identifying the parent group and the second the base itself. For example, Pocklington in Yorkshire was designated as No 42 Base Headquarters and its four satellite stations – Elvington, Full Sutton, Snaith and Burn – each became known as a No 42 Base Substation. On 16 September 1943, a Bomber Command Directive stated that from henceforth all bases were to be known by number and not their geographical location. This situation pertained until the end of the war.

Stations could house either one or two squadrons and/ or a number of smaller miscellaneous units, such as Beam Approach Training Flights (BAT Flt). Each individual station provided its resident squadrons with technical and domestic housing with facilities, messing facilities, flying control, emergency services and airfield security.

A squadron was normally commanded by an officer of wing commander rank, with a total complement on average of some 24 aircraft, and was responsible for its own aircraft maintenance and administration. At the sharp end, individual aircraft, air crews and ground crews were allocated to a particular flight, of which each squadron had three. Each flight was made up of some eight aircraft, each with its own dispersal pan on the airfield perimeter and with an air crew of seven (generally) and its own dedicated ground crew.

ABOVE: The watchtower at Little Snoring, Norfolk, is now an empty shell and the airfield has long since been returned to agriculture. However, the lonely watchtower and the ploughed earth on which it stands still cradle memories of the momentous events all those years ago, which its squadrons of Lancasters and Mosquitoes helped to carve. (Author)

BELOW: Surviving buildings on some World War 2 airfields have been adapted for agricultural and light industrial uses. This is the parachute store on the former Canadian bomber base at Tholthorpe in North Yorkshire, pictured in 1997. (Author)

COASTAL COMMAND GROUP STRUCTURE

Coastal Command's operational group boundaries were less rigid than those for the other two operational commands. In 1939 Coastal Command operated four groups in the UK – No 15 with bases in South West England, Wales and Northern Ireland; No 16 in East Anglia and Southern England; No 18 in Lincolnshire and north into Scotland and the Orkneys; No 17 was Coastal Command's Operational Training Group and had no operational boundary.

In 1941 No 19 Group was formed with bases in South and South West England and South Wales, with No 15 Group's bases now in Northern Ireland and in the Western Isles. No 106 Group was formed in 1944 and controlled Coastal Command's Photo Reconnaissance squadrons, covering the whole of Northern Europe from its main base at Benson in Oxfordshire, with detachments in the South West of England and in Scotland.

ABOVE: Maintenance for landplanes was carried out on terra firma, but that for flying boats was usually undertaken as they floated at their moorings. In this photograph taken in August 1940 an airman steers an 18ft planing dinghy past Short Sunderland Mk Is of No 210 Squadron undergoing maintenance out in Oban Bay, Argyll. (IWM CH859)

ABOVE: In this oblique aerial view, the Coastal Command airfield at Benbecula in the Outer Hebrides is pictured from west-south-west on 9 May 1941, when the runways were still under construction. The method used was known as 'sand carpet', which consisted of bitumen laid directly over compacted sand, resulting in a flexible surface. (IWM HU92989)

RAF FRONTLINE AIRFIELDS – AN A TO Z

'Airfield construction reached its peak in 1942 when 125 new aerodromes came into use, an average of one every three days.'

David J. Smith, *Britain's Military Airfields 1939-45*

KEY

OPENED: The date on which the airfield officially opened for flying operations during World War 2 (eg: Downham Market, 07/42) or, in the case of an old-established airfield or one which had seen almost continuous use up until then, the date on which it first saw use for flying (eg: Waddington, 11/16).

CLOSED: The date on which operational flying from the airfield ceased (eg: Barford St John, 03/46); or, in the case where the airfield has continued in use since the war's end on a regular or semi-regular basis, its current use in 2011 (eg: Twinwood Farm, concert arena/ museum/agriculture).

ELEVATION: The airfield's height in feet above mean sea level.

PUNDIT CODE: In order to identify airfields from the air a system of two-letter codes was adopted, usually taken from letters making up the airfield's name (eg: 'AY' for Alconbury). However, with the proliferation of airfields during the war years the number of relevant code permutations became exhausted and so new codes with apparently little or no connection to the airfields they represented were introduced (eg: 'AL' for Blyton or 'AC' for Breighton). These were displayed on the ground in 10ft-high white capital letters adjacent to the signals area or in the signals square near the control tower. At night this method of airfield identification was not usable so a mobile beacon situated several miles from the airfield, known as a Pundit, was used to flash in red light the identity letters in Morse code.

MAIN CONTRACTOR: The civil engineers, building contractors and RAF Airfield Construction Squadrons that undertook most of the construction work at an airfield. In some cases this was a consortium of smaller contractors instead of one of the bigger firms like Laing or Costain.

RUNWAYS: The flying surfaces at the airfield were generally made from concrete or tarmac, or a combination of both on a compacted hardcore base. Some runways were also surfaced with wood or rubber chippings or pine needles. They were usually laid to a triangular pattern with the main runway orientated roughly SW/NE to suit the prevailing wind.

HANGARS: Large purpose-built weatherproof structures for aircraft storage and overhaul (see the earlier section on 'Hangar Designs Commonly Seen at RAF Airfields').

USER SQNS/UNITS: The RAF frontline squadrons (sqn) and second-line training units, ie: Operational Training Units (OTU), Heavy Conversion Units (HCU), their parent groups (Gp), and their dates of occupancy.

Notes that follow this entry refer to significant changes in the airfield's status during the war years (eg: Alconbury, became satellite to Wyton 09/39), and to any awards of the Victoria Cross to aircrew of based squadrons (eg: Bardney, Flt Sgt G. Thompson, 9 Sqn, 01/01/45).

LEFT: Armourers winch a 4,000lb 'Cookie' into the bulged bomb-bay of Mosquito Mk IV, DZ637, 'X', of No 692 Squadron in April 1944. Ten months later DZ637 was serving with No 627 Squadron (Woodhall Spa) when she was hit by flak on ops to Siegen on 1/2 February 1945 and crash-landed onto a road in Germany, killing her crew of Flt Lt Ronald Baker (pilot) and navigator Sgt Douglas Betts. (IWM CH12622)

ABBOTSINCH, Renfrewshire

LOCATION: 6m W of Glasgow
OPENED: 1932
CLOSED: 1963. Glasgow Airport (2011)
ELEVATION: 18ft
FORMATION: Coastal Command
RUNWAYS: 3 concrete
HANGARS: Callender-Hamilton (3), Bellman (7)
USER SQNS/UNITS:

309 (Polish) Sqn
07/10–06/11/40
Lysander III

Torpedo Training Unit (TTU)
03/40–09/42
Swordfish; Shark; Beaufort

Merchant Ship Fighter Unit (MSFU)
(formed Speke, 05/05/41)
Sea Hurricane

1441 Combined Operations Development Flight (CODF)
01/42
Anson; Lysander; Tiger Moth

To RN as HMS *Sanderling*, 08/43

ABINGDON, Berks

LOCATION: NW of Abingdon
OPENED: 01/09/32
CLOSED: 1992. Army base (2011)
ELEVATION: 245ft
PUNDIT CODE: AB
FORMATIONS: 6, 91 (OTU) Grp Bomber Command
MAIN CONTRACTOR: Various
RUNWAYS: 2 concrete
HANGARS: C Type (1), A Type (4)
USER SQNS/UNITS:

97 Sqn
16/09/39–02/04/40
Whitley II

166 Sqn
16/09/39–02/04/40
Whitley I, III

10 OTU
02/04/40–10/09/46
Whitley I–III, V, VII; Wellington III, X

Opened in Bomber Command as parent station, 01/09/32

ACKLINGTON, Northumberland

LOCATION: 3m SW of Amble
OPENED: 1938
CLOSED: 1972. HMPs Acklington and Castington/open-cast mine (2011)
ELEVATION: 120ft
PUNDIT CODE: AI
FORMATION: 13 Grp Fighter Command
MAIN CONTRACTOR: Various
RUNWAYS: 3 Tarmac
HANGARS: F Type (2), Bellman (1), Blister (16)
USER SQNS/UNITS:

1 Sqn
08/07/42–09/02/43
Hurricane IIc, I, IIb; Typhoon Ib

25 Sqn
19/12/43–05/02/44
Mosquito II, XVII

32 Sqn
27/08–15/12/40
Hurricane I

43 Sqn
18/11/39–26/02/40
Hurricane I

BELOW: No 111 Squadron pilots are served mugs of tea by a ground crewman beside their dispersal caravan at Acklington, late in 1939. In the background is a Hurricane Mk I wearing the squadron code 'JU'. (RAF Museum)

46 Sqn
10/12/39–17/01/40
Hurricane I
56 Sqn
23/02–07/03/44
Typhoon Ib
72 Sqn
02/03–01/06/40
05/06–31/08/40
15/12/40–08/07/41
Gladiator I, II; Spitfire I, IIa, IIb
79 Sqn
13/07–27/08/40
Hurricane I
111 Sqn
27/10–07/12/39
Hurricane I
130 Sqn
21/12/43–04/01/44
Spitfire Vb
141 Sqn
29/01–23/06/42
Beaufighter If
152 Sqn
02/10/39–12/07/40
Gladiator I, II; Spitfire I
164 Sqn
08/03–11/04/44
Typhoon Ib
198 Sqn
09/02–24/03/43
Typhoon Ia, Ib
219 Sqn
23/06–21/10/42
Beaufighter If
222 Sqn
25/02–10/03/44
Spitfire LFIXb
258 Sqn
17/12/40–01/02/41
Hurricane I
266 Sqn
15–23/03/44
Typhoon Ib
315 (Polish) Sqn
08/01–13/03/41
Hurricane I
316 (Polish) Sqn
22/09/43–15/02/44
Spitfire LFVb

ABOVE: This Wellington Mk I of No 40 Squadron is pictured on a freezing dispersal at Alconbury in 1941. (Andy Thomas)

317 (Polish) Sqn
19/02–29/04/41
Hurricane I
322 (Dutch) Sqn
10/03–24/04/44
Spitfire Vb, Vc
349 (Belgian) Sqn
25/08–22/10/43
Spitfire Va, LFVb
350 (Belgian) Sqn
13/03–08/06/43
20/07–25/08/43
Spitfire Vb
406 (Canadian) Sqn
05/05/41–01/02/42
Blenheim If, IVf; Beaufighter IIf
409 (Canadian) Sqn
23/02–19/12/43
05/02–01/03/44
Beaufighter VIf
410 (Canadian) Sqn
20/10/42–21/02/43
Beaufighter IIf; Mosquito II
1460 Flt 539 Sqn
15/12/41 (02/09/42)–25/01/43
Havoc I, II (Turbinlite); Boston III (Turbinlite)
607 (AAF) Sqn
10/10–14/11/39
Gladiator I
609 (AAF) Sqn
07–17/10/39
21/03–01/04/44
Spitfire I; Typhoon Ib

59 OTU
26/02–01/06/45
Typhoon I
To 13 Grp Fighter Command as satellite to Usworth, 09/39
Closed for reconstruction, 06/44–02/45
13 Grp Forward Sector Station, 05/45

ALCONBURY, Hunts

LOCATION: 5m NW of Huntingdon
OPENED: 17/05/38
CLOSED: USAF base, non-flying (2011)
ELEVATION: 165ft
PUNDIT CODE: AY
FORMATIONS: 2, 3 Grp Bomber Command
MAIN CONTRACTOR: Various
RUNWAYS: 3 concrete
HANGARS: T2 (2)
USER SQNS/UNITS:
15 Sqn
14/04–15/05/40
Blenheim IV; Wellington I
40 Sqn
02/02/41–14/02/42
Wellington I
156 Sqn
14/02/42–07/08/42
Wellington I, III
Opened in Bomber Command as satellite to Upwood, 17/05/38
Became satellite to Wyton, 09/39
To USAAF as Station AAF-102, 08/42

ALDERGROVE, Co Antrim, NI

LOCATION: 13m NW of Belfast
OPENED: 1918
CLOSED: Belfast International Airport (2011)
ELEVATION: 294ft
PUNDIT CODE: JV
FORMATIONS: 13 Grp Fighter Command; 17 Grp Coastal Command
MAIN CONTRACTOR: Various
RUNWAYS: 2 concrete
HANGARS: 18 various
USER SQNS/UNITS:

59 Sqn
11/05–15/09/43
Liberator V

86 Sqn
18/03–06/09/43
Liberator IIIa, V

120 Sqn
14/02–15/04/43
Liberator I, III

143 Sqn
16/12/41–23/04/42
Blenheim IV

206 Sqn
12/08/41–30/06/42
Hudson V

220 Sqn
14/02–20/03/43
Fortress II

233 Sqn
08/12/40–16/08/41
Hudson III, V

245 Sqn
20/07/40–14/07/41
Hurricane I

252 Sqn
04–06/41
Beaufighter

254 Sqn (det)
1940
Blenheim

254 Sqn
29/05–10/12/41
Blenheim IV

272 Sqn
19/11/40–03/04/41
Blenheim IV

311 (Czech) Sqn
28/04–12/06/42
Wellington Ic

502 (AAF) Sqn
15/05/25–27/01/41
Anson I; Whitley V

9 OTU
07/06–09/09/42
Beaufort

Station Flight Aldergrove > 402 Flt > 1402 Met Flt
10/36–02/45
Gladiator; Hurricane; Blenheim

1674 HCU
10–19/10/43
01/02/44–08/45
Fortress; Liberator; Halifax

To 13 Grp Fighter Command as Sector Station, 07/40
To 17 Grp Coastal Command, 07/41

ANDOVER, Hants

LOCATION: 2½m W of Andover
OPENED: 08/17
CLOSED: 1977. HQ Land Forces, British Army/commercial storage (2011)
ELEVATION: 260ft
PUNDIT CODE: Not known
FORMATION: 22 (AC) Grp
MAIN CONTRACTOR: Various
RUNWAYS: Grass
HANGARS: Belfast Truss (7), GS (4), Blister (5)
USER SQNS/UNITS:

No 2 School of Army Co-operation
21/10/39–01/07/41
Blenheim; Anson

To 22 (AC) Grp Fighter Command, 05/39
To Army Co-operation Command, 12/40
To USAAF as Station AAF-406, 03/44

ANDREWS FIELD (Great Saling), Essex

LOCATION: 12m E of Stansted
OPENED: 07/42
CLOSED: 11/45. Agriculture/light aviation (2011)
ELEVATION: 290ft
FORMATION: 11 Grp Fighter Command

PUNDIT CODE: GZ
MAIN CONTRACTOR: US Pioneer Corps
RUNWAYS: 3 concrete/Tarmac
HANGARS: T2 (2)
USER SQNS/UNITS:

19 Sqn
14/10/44–13/02/45
Mustang III

65 Sqn
14/10/44–16/01/45
06–15/05/45
Mustang III, IV

122 Sqn
14/10/44–01/05/45

ABOVE: Spitfire Mk VII, MD159, 'B', and Halifax Met III, LV788, 'R', both of No 518 Squadron, pictured in flight above Aldergrove in late 1945. (Andy Thomas)

Mustang III
129 Sqn
11/10–11/12/44
Mustang III
303 (Polish) Sqn
04/04–16/05/45
Mustang I, IV
306 (Polish) Sqn
10/10/44–10/08/45
Mustang III
315 (Polish) Sqn
10–24/10/44
16/01–08/08/45
Mustang III
316 (Polish) Sqn
24/10/44–16/05/45
Mustang III
616 (AAF) Sqn
28/02–31/03/45
Meteor III
Opened as USAAF Station AAF-485, 04/43
To 11 Grp RAF Fighter Command as Forward Airfield, 09/44

ANGLE, Pembrokeshire

LOCATION: 8¾m W of Pembroke
OPENED: 12/41
CLOSED: 1945. Agriculture (2011)
ELEVATION: 182ft
PUNDIT CODE: AE
FORMATION: 10 Grp Fighter Command
MAIN CONTRACTOR: Various
RUNWAYS: 3 Tarmac
HANGARS: Blister (4), T2 (1)
USER SQNS/UNITS:

ABOVE: Framed by the entrance of a Butler combat hangar draped with camouflage netting, Spitfire LF Mk IXBs of Nos 312 and 313 (Czech) Squadrons undergo engine repair and maintenance at Appledram, Sussex, on 19 April 1944. (IWM CH18720)

32 Sqn
01/06–27/11/41
Hurricane I, IIb

152 Sqn
16/08–27/09/42
Spitfire Vb

263 Sqn
18/04–15/08/42
Whirlwind I

312 (Czech) Sqn
24/01–18/04/42
Spitfire Vb

421 Sqn
26/10–01/11/42
14–30/11/42
04/12/42–29/01/43
Spitfire Vb

615 (AAF) Sqn
27/11/41–23/01/42
Hurricane IIb, IIc

Coastal Command Development Unit (CCDU)
09/43–01/45
Beaufighter X; Wellington; Halifax II; Liberator V

Opened in Fighter Command as Forward Airfield, 12/41
To RN, 05/43
To 19 Grp Coastal Command, 09/43

ANNAN, Dumfries

LOCATION: 2¾m NE of Annan
OPENED: 04/42
CLOSED: 1945. Disused Chapelcross nuclear power station (2011)
ELEVATION: 30ft
PUNDIT CODE: AG
FORMATIONS: 9, 81 (OTU) Grp Fighter Command
MAIN CONTRACTOR: John Laing & Son Ltd
Runways: 2
HANGARS: Blister (8), T1 (3)
USER SQNS/UNITS:

55 OTU > 4 TEU > 3 TEU
28/04/42 (26/01/44) (28/03/44)–17/07/44
Hurricane I, II; Master I; Typhoon

Opened in Fighter Command as parent station, 04/42
To 9 Grp, 06/43
To Maintenance Command, 07/44

APPLEDRAM, Sussex

LOCATION: 1½m S of Chichester
OPENED: 05/43
CLOSED: 11/44. Agriculture (2011)
ELEVATION: 22ft
PUNDIT CODE: AO

FORMATIONS: 83, 84 Grp 2 TAF
MAIN CONTRACTOR: RAF Airfield Construction Service (RAFACS)
RUNWAYS: 2 steel matting
HANGARS: Blister (4)
USER SQNS/UNITS:
175 Sqn
02/06–01/07/43
Typhoon Ib
181 Sqn
02/06–03/07/43
Typhoon Ib
182 Sqn
02/06–02/07/43
Typhoon Ib
302 (Polish) Sqn
28/06–16/07/44
Spitfire IXe
308 (Polish) Sqn
28/06–16/07/44
Spitfire IX
310 (Czech) Sqn
03/04–22/06/44
Spitfire LFIX
312 (Czech) Sqn
04/04–22/06/44
Spitfire LFIXb
313 (Czech) Sqn
04/04–22/06/44
Spitfire IX
317 (Polish) Sqn
28/06–16/07/44
Spitfire IX
Advanced Landing Ground (ALG)
*Known today as Apuldram

ASHBOURNE, Derbys

LOCATION: 9m NW of Derby
OPENED: 07/42
CLOSED: 1954. Industry/leisure (2011)
ELEVATION: 590ft
PUNDIT CODE: AS
FORMATIONS: 38 Wing/38 Grp Fighter Command
MAIN CONTRACTOR: Various
RUNWAYS: 3 concrete
HANGARS: T2 (4)
USER SQNS/UNITS:
42 OTU
26/10/42–20/03/45
Blenheim; Whitley V; Oxford; Anson; Albemarle
Opened in Army Co-operation Command, 07/42
To 38 Wing Fighter Command, 06/43
To 38 (Airborne Forces) Grp, 09/43

ASHFORD, Kent

LOCATION: 2½m SW of Ashford
OPENED: 03/43
CLOSED: 09/44. Agriculture (2011)
ELEVATION: 130ft
PUNDIT CODE: ZF
FORMATION: 83 Grp 2 TAF
MAIN CONTRACTOR: RAFACS/Royal Canadian Engineers
RUNWAYS: 2 steel matting
HANGARS: None
USER SQNS/UNITS:
65 Sqn
05–15/10/43
Spitfire IX
122 Sqn
05–15/10/43
Spitfire IX
Advanced Landing Ground (ALG)
To USAAF as Station AAF-417, 03/44

ASTON DOWN, Gloucs

LOCATION: 3m NW of Stroud
OPENED: 10/38
CLOSED: 1967. Light industry/storage/gliding (2011)
ELEVATION: 600ft
PUNDIT CODE: AD
FORMATIONS: 9, 12, 81 (OTU) Grp Fighter Command
MAIN CONTRACTOR: Various
RUNWAYS: 3 concrete
HANGARS: Various (50)
USER SQNS/UNITS:
4 Sqn
03/01–03/03/44
Mustang I; Spitfire PRVI; Mosquito PRXVI
12 Grp Pool 5 OTU 55 OTU
23/08/39 (15/03/40) (01/11/40)–03/41
Harvard IIb; Gladiator; Blenheim I; Spitfire; Hurricane I, II; Defiant I; Battle; Master I, II, III
52 OTU
08/41–10/08/43
Spitfire II, V; Harvard; Master I, II
Fighter Leaders' School
10/08/43–25/01/44
Spitfire Vb
3 Tactical Exercise Unit (TEU) 55 OTU
14/07/44 (15/12/44)–14/06/45
Typhoon Ib; Hurricane I, II; Master I, II, III; Martinet; Harvard IIb
84 Group Support Unit (GSU)
14/02–13/07/44
Typhoon I; Tempest V; Spitfire IX; Mustang I
To 12 Grp Fighter Command, 09/39
To 81 (OTU) Grp, 12/40
To 9 Grp, 06/43

ATCHAM, Salop

LOCATION: 5m E of Shrewsbury
OPENED: 09/41
CLOSED: 04/46. Industry/public highway (2011)
ELEVATION: 200ft
PUNDIT CODE: AP
FORMATION: 9 Grp Fighter Command
MAIN CONTRACTOR: Various
RUNWAYS: 3 Tarmac
HANGARS: Blister (8), Callender-Hamilton (3)
USER SQNS/UNITS:
74 Sqn
25/03–10/04/42
Spitfire Vb
131 Sqn
27/09/41–09/02/42
Spitfire Ia, IIa, Vb
232 Sqn
10/04–16/05/42
Spitfire Vb
350 (Belgian) Sqn
19/02–05/04/42
Spitfire IIa
Opened in Fighter Command as Group Sector Station, 09/41
To USAAF as Station AAF-342, 06/42
To RAF (non-operational), 03/45

ABOVE: Air and ground crews of No 88 Squadron at Attlebridge stand around a bomb trolley loaded with 500-pounders that are about to be winched into the bomb-bays of waiting Boston Mk IIIs in May 1942. (IWM CH5595)

ATTLEBRIDGE, Norfolk

LOCATION: 8m NW of Norwich
Opened: 06/41
Closed: 1950. Poultry farming (2011)
Elevation: 165ft
Pundit code: AT
Formation: 2 Grp Bomber Command
Main contractor: Richard Costain Ltd
Runways: 3 concrete
Hangars: T2 (2)
User sqns/units:

88 Sqn
01/08/41–30/09/42
Blenheim IV; Boston III

320 (Dutch) Sqn
30/03/43–30/08/43
Hudson VI; Mitchell II

Opened in Bomber Command as satellite to Swanton Morley, 06/41
Closed for rebuilding, 09/43
Transferred to USAAF as Station AAF-120, 03/44

AYR, Ayrshire

LOCATION: 4m SSE of Troon
Opened: 04/41
Closed: 1946. Leisure activity/industry/housing (2011)
Elevation: 50ft
Pundit code. AR
Formation: 13 Grp Fighter Command
Main contractor: Various
Runways: 3 Tarmac/asphalt
Hangars: Bellman (3), Blister (17)
User sqns/units:

1 Sqn
22–29/04/44
Typhoon Ib; Spitfire IXb

3 Sqn
06–14/04/44
Tempest V

56 Sqn
30/03–07/04/44
Typhoon Ib

72 Sqn
12/08–26/09/42
Spitfire Vb

130 Sqn
16–30/11/43
Spitfire Vb

141 Sqn
29/04/41–29/01/42
Beaufighter If

165 Sqn
06/04–15/08/42
Spitfire Va, Vb

169 Sqn
01/10–08/12/43
Mosquito II

186 Sqn
03/08/43–07/01/44
Hurricane IV; Typhoon Ib

222 Sqn
22/10/42–27/03/43
Spitfire Vb

239 Sqn
30/09–10/12/43
Beaufighter If

312 (Czech) Sqn
19/08/41–01/01/42
Hurricane IIb; Spitfire IIa, IIb, Vb

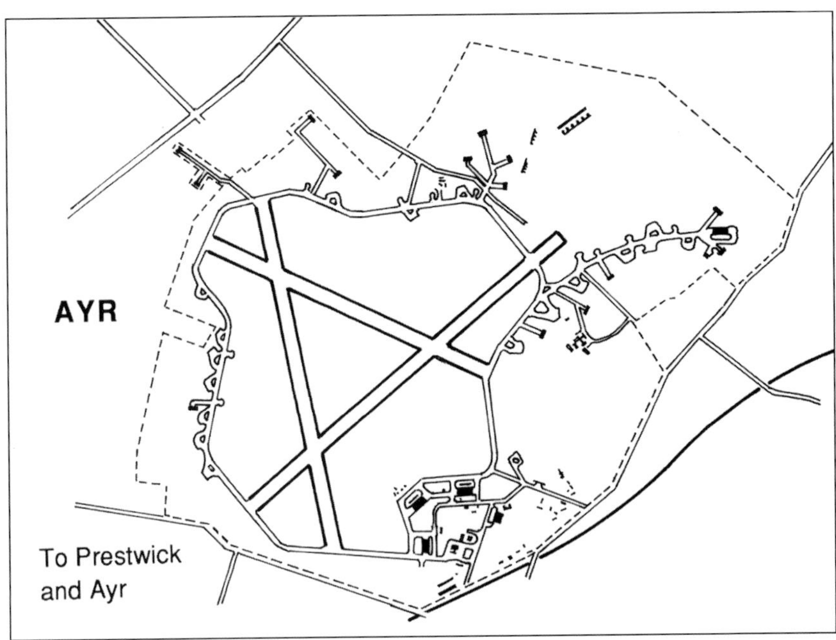

313 (Czech) Sqn
10–20/01/44
Spitfire Vc
322 (Dutch) Sqn
25/02–01/03/44
Spitfire Vb, Vc
329 (French) Sqn
03–22/01/44
16–24/03/44
Spitfire Vb, Vc, IX
340 (French) Sqn
01/01–01/04/42
Spitfire IIa, Vb
345 (French) Sqn
30/01–26/04/44
Spitfire Vb
402 (Canadian) Sqn
10/07–19/08/41
19/12/43–02/01/44
Hurricane IIb; Spitfire Vb, Vc
406 (Canadian) Sqn
01/02–16/06/42
Beaufighter IIf
410 (Canadian) Sqn
30/06–06/08/41
15/06–01/09/42
Defiant I; Beaufighter IIf
438 (Canadian) Sqn
10/01–18/03/44
Hurricane IV; Typhoon Ib
439 (Canadian) Sqn
08/01–18/03/44
Hurricane IV; Typhoon Ib
440 (Canadian) Sqn
08/02–18/03/44
Hurricane IV; Typhoon Ib
486 (New Zealand) Sqn
21–29/03/44
Typhoon Ib
488 (New Zealand) Sqn
01/09/42–03/08/43
Beaufighter IIf, VIf
602 (AAF) Sqn
15/04–10/07/41
Spitfire I, IIa
611 (AAF) Sqn
08–19/02/44
Spitfire LFVb
Opened in Fighter Command as parent station, 04/41

BAGINTON, Warks
LOCATION: 3m SE of Coventry
Opened: 1934
Closed: Coventry Airport (2011)
Elevation: 270ft
Pundit code: NG
Formation: 9 Grp Fighter Command
Main contractor: Various
Runways: 3 grass
Hangars: Bellman (2)
User sqns/units:
32 Sqn
19/10–25/11/42
Hurricane IIb
79 Sqn
24/12/41–04/03/42
Hurricane IIb
134 Sqn
26/03–10/04/42
Spitfire Vb
135 Sqn
15/08–04/09/41
Hurricane IIa
308 (Polish) Sqn
25/09/40–31/05/41
Hurricane I; Spitfire I
403 (Canadian) Sqn
19/02–30/05/41
Tomahawk I, IIa; Spitfire I
457 (Australian) Sqn
16/06–07/08/41
Spitfire I
605 (AAF) Sqn
30/05–04/09/41
Hurricane IIa
No 1 Camouflage Unit
09/39
Reliant; Blenheim; Spitfire
Became Fighter Command Sector Station, 09/40
Downgraded to satellite to Honiley, 08/41

BALADO BRIDGE, Kinross
LOCATION: 2m W of Kinross
Opened: 03/42
Closed: 1957. Agriculture/industry/leisure/aviation (2011)
Elevation: 420ft
Pundit code: Not known
Formation: 81 (OTU) Grp Fighter Command
Main contractor: Various
Runways: 2 concrete
Hangars: Blister (4), B1 (1), Super Robin (1)
User sqns/units:
58 OTU 2 TEU
23/03/42 (17/10/43)–25/06/44
Spitfire I, II, V; Hurricane
Opened in Fighter Command as satellite to Grangemouth, 03/42
To War Dept, 11/44

ABOVE: In the bleak midwinter: the engines of a No 408 (Canadian) Squadron Hampden are run up in the thick snow on its dispersal at Balderton in early 1942. (IWM CH4738)

BALDERTON, Notts
LOCATION: 2¾m SSE of Newark-on-Trent
OPENED: 06/41
CLOSED: 1954. Agriculture/quarrying (2011)
ELEVATION: 67ft
PUNDIT CODE: BL
FORMATIONS: 7 (T), 5 Grp Bomber Command
MAIN CONTRACTOR: W. & C. French
RUNWAYS: 3 Tarmac
HANGARS: T2 (2), B1 (1)
USER SQNS/UNITS:

227 Sqn
21/10/44–05/04/45
Lancaster I, III

408 (Canadian) Sqn
09/12/41–14/09/42
Hampden

25 OTU
06/41–11/41
Hampden

1668 HCU
15/08/43–17/11/43
Lancaster I; Halifax II, V

Opened in Bomber Command as satellite to Finningley, 06/41
Became satellite to Syerston, 12/41
To USAAF as Station AAF-482, 02/01/44
Returned to RAF as 56 Base substation, 10/44

BALLYHALBERT, Co Down, NI
LOCATION: 11m SE of Newtownards
OPENED: 06/41
CLOSED: 1946. Agriculture/caravan park/housing (2011)
ELEVATION: 26ft
PUNDIT CODE: YB
FORMATIONS: 13, 82 Grp Fighter Command
MAIN CONTRACTOR: Various
RUNWAYS: 3 Tarmac
HANGARS: Bellman (2), Blister (12)
USER SQNS/UNITS:

25 Sqn
16/01–17/05/42
Beaufighter If

26 Sqn
19–21/07/43
21/07/43–12/02/44 (det)
Mustang I

63 Sqn (det)
05–08/44
Hurricane IV; Spitfire Vb

125 Sqn (det)
11/43–03/44
Beaufighter VIf

130 Sqn
30/04–05/07/43
Spitfire Vb

153 Sqn
24/10/41–18/12/42
Defiant I; Beaufighter If, VIf

231 Sqn (det)
01–06/43
Mustang I

245 Sqn
14/07–01/09/41
Hurricane I, IIb

256 Sqn (det)
03/41– 04/43
Defiant I, II; Hurricane I, IIb; Beaufighter If, VIf

303 (Polish) Sqn
12/11/43–30/04/44
Spitfire LFVb

315 (Polish) Sqn
06/07–13/11/43
Spitfire Vb
501 (AAF) Sqn
19/10/42–30/04/43
Spitfire Vb
504 (AAF) Sqn
26/08/41–12/01/42
19/06–19/10/42
Hurricane IIb; Spitfire IIa, IIb, Vb
Opened as Fighter Command Sector Station, 06/41
To 82 Grp, 09/41
To RN as HMS *Corncrake*, 04/45

BELOW: An air-to-air view of Liberator GRV, BZ877 '2-Q', of No 86 Squadron, based at Ballykelly, Co Londonderry, during November 1943. (IWM CH11800)

BALLYKELLY, Co Londonderry, NI

LOCATION: 3m W of Limavady
OPENED: 06/1941
CLOSED: 1971. Awaiting disposal by MOD (2011)
ELEVATION: 10ft
FORMATION: 15 (T) Grp Coastal Command
RUNWAYS: 3 concrete
HANGARS: T2 (5), Blister (8)
USER SQNS/UNITS:
53 Sqn (det)
09/44–06/45
Liberator Va, VI, VII
59 Sqn
15/09/43–14/09/45
Liberator V
86 Sqn
06/09/43–24/03/44
Liberator IIIa, V
120 Sqn
21/07/42–14/02/43
24/03/44–04/06/45
Liberator I, II, III
153 Sqn
10/41–12/42
Defiant I; Beaufighter If
220 Sqn
20/06/42–14/02/43
Fortress I, II
Coastal Command Development Unit (CCDU)
01/12/41–18/06/42
Hudson; Whitley

BANFF, Banffshire
LOCATION: 4½m W of Banff
OPENED: 04/1943
CLOSED: 1946. Farmland/industry (2011)
ELEVATION: 250ft
FORMATION: 18 Grp Coastal Command
RUNWAYS: 3 concrete
HANGARS: T2 (3), Double Blister (13)
USER SQNS/UNITS:

14 Sqn
25/05–29/08/45
Mosquito VI

65 Sqn
28/01–01/02/45
Mustang III

143 Sqn
23/10/44–01/06/45
Mosquito VI

144 Sqn
03/09–23/10/44
Beaufighter X

235 Sqn
06/09/44–10/07/45
Mosquito VI

248 Sqn
06/09/44–10/ 07/45
Mosquito VI/XVIII

279 Sqn (det)
02–09/45
Warwick I; Hurricane IIc

281 Sqn (det)
02/44–02/45
Warwick I

333 (Norwegian) Sqn
01/09/44–06/45
Mosquito VI; Catalina IV

404 (Canadian) Sqn
03/09–22/10/44;
03/04–25/05/45
Beaufighter X; Mosquito VI

489 (New Zealand) Sqn
16/06–01/08/45
Mosquito VI

14 (P) AFU
25/05/43–31/08/44
Oxford

1512 BAT Flt
05/43–31/08/44
Oxford

Opened in Flying Training Command, 04/43
To Coastal Command, 09/44

BELOW: De Havilland Mosquito FBVI, PZ446, of No 143 Squadron, is serviced and re-armed with 60lb rocket projectiles at Banff for an anti-shipping strike off Norway in December 1944. PZ446 survived the war. (IWM HU1626)

ABOVE: Wg Cdr Tony Gadd leads 21 Beaufighters of Nos 144 and 404 (Canadian) Squadrons and 11 Mosquitoes of No 235 Squadron in a convoy attack off Stong Fjord on 19 September 1944. The Mosquito in the picture is attacking the lead ship, the 1,367-ton *Lynx*. (Crown Copyright)

BELOW: Fully armed and ready for action, Mosquito FBVI, NE-Y, of No 143 Squadron, is photographed at low level over the sea. (Author)

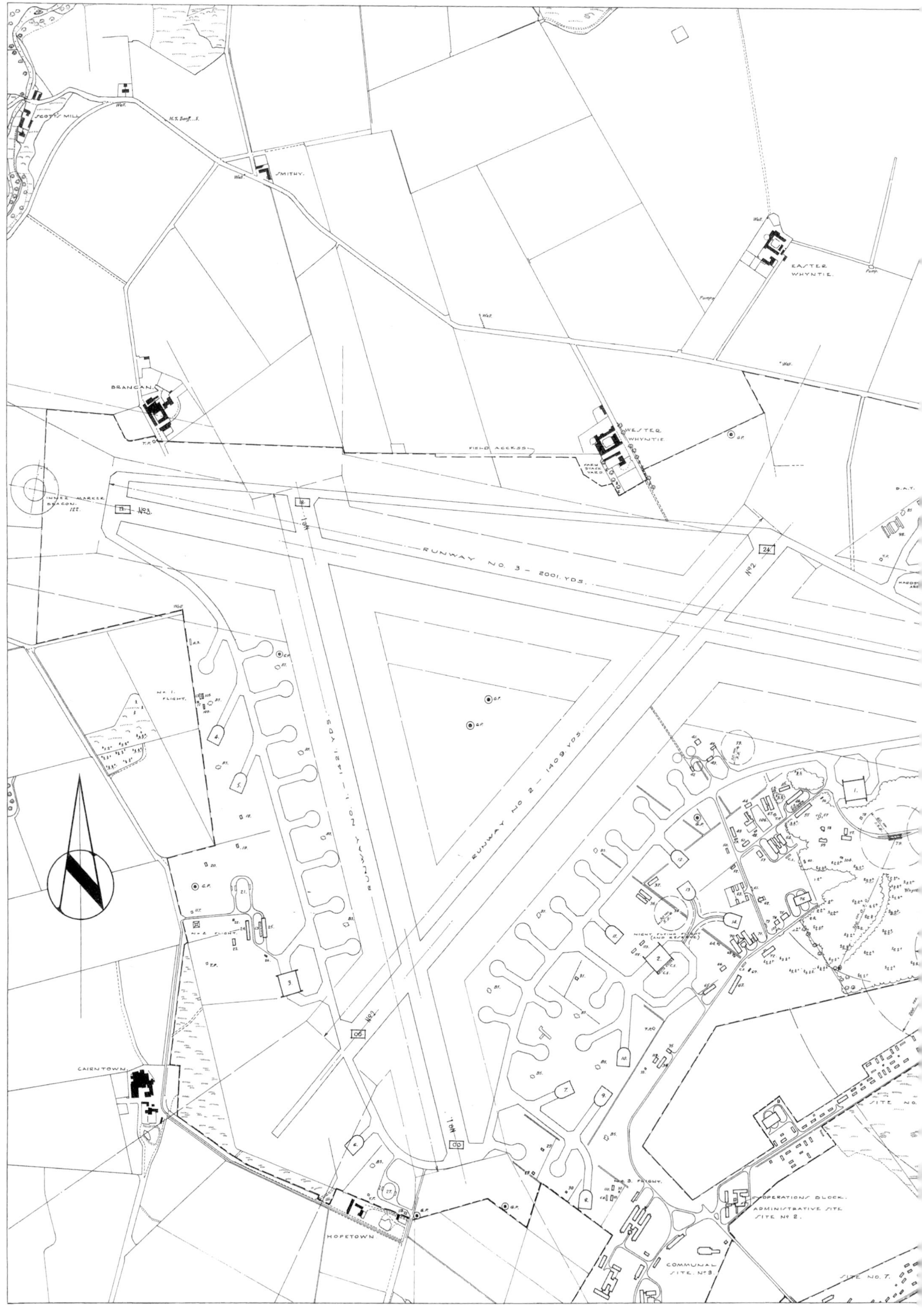
SCOTT'S MILL
SMITHY.
EASTER WHYNTIE.
BRANCAN.
WESTER WHYNTIE.
FIELD ACCESS.
INNER MARKER BEACON.
RUNWAY NO. 3 – 2001. YDS.
RUNWAY NO 2 – 1409. YDS.
RUNWAY NO 1 – 1421 YDS.
No 1. FLIGHT.
No 2. FLIGHT.
NIGHT FLYING FLIGHT (AND RESERVE)
No 3. FLIGHT.
CAIRNTOWN.
HOPETOWN
COMMUNAL SITE. No 3.
OPERATIONS BLOCK.
ADMINISTRATIVE SITE
SITE No 2.
SITE NO. 7.

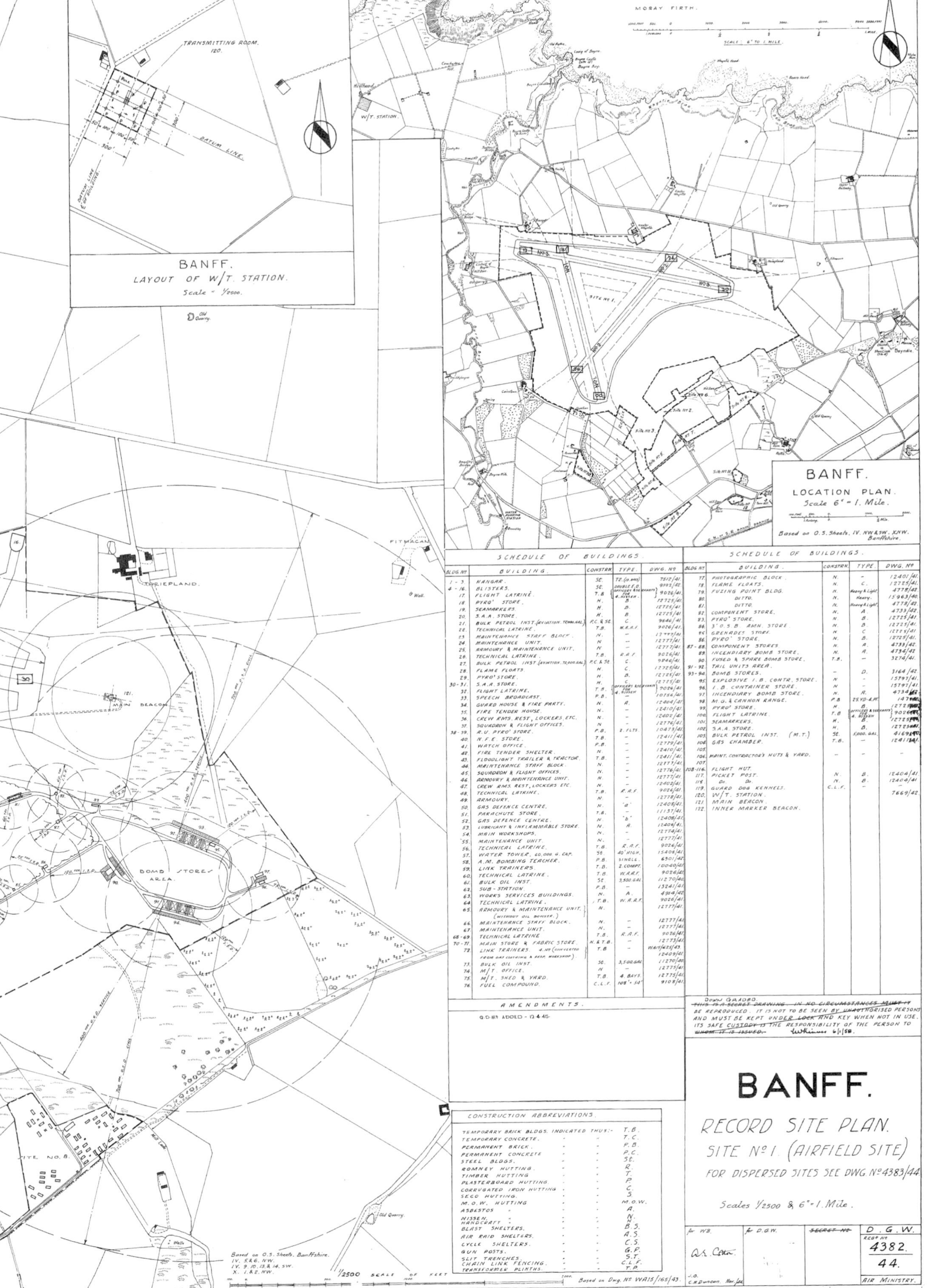

SCHEDULE OF BUILDINGS.

BLDG. No	BUILDING.	CONSTRN.	TYPE.	DWG. No
1 - 3.	HANGAR.	St.	T2. (12 BAYS)	7512/41.
4 - 16.	BLISTERS.	St.	DOUBLE E.O.	9392/42.
17.	FLIGHT LATRINE.	T.B	OFFICERS & SERVANTS FOR 4. NISSEN.	9026/41.
18.	PYRO' STORE.	H.	B	12725/41.
19.	SEAMARKERS.	H.	B.	12725/41.
20.	S.A.A. STORE.	H.	B.	12725/41.
21.	BULK PETROL INST. (AVIATION. 72,000 GAL.)	P.C. & St.	C.	9846/41.
22.	TECHNICAL LATRINE.	T.B.	W.A.A.F.	9026/41.
23.	MAINTENANCE STAFF BLOCK.	N.	–	12777/41.
24.	MAINTENANCE UNIT.	N	–	12777/41.
25.	ARMOURY & MAINTENANCE UNIT.	N	–	12777/41.
26.	TECHNICAL LATRINE.	T.B.	R.A.F.	9026/41.
27.	BULK PETROL INST. (AVIATION. 72,000 GAL.)	P.C. & St.	C.	9846/41.
28.	FLAME FLOATS.	H.	C.	12725/41.
29.	PYRO' STORE.	H.	B.	12725/41.
30 - 31.	S.A.A. STORE.	H.	C.	12725/41.
32.	FLIGHT LATRINE.	T.B.	OFFICERS & SERVANTS FOR 4. NISSEN	9026/41
33.	SPEECH BROADCAST.	P.B.	–	10786/41.
34.	GUARD HOUSE & FIRE PARTY.	N.	A.	12404/41.
35.	FIRE TENDER HOUSE.	N.	–	12410/41.
36.	CREW RMS. REST, LOCKERS, ETC.	N.	–	12402/41.
37.	SQUADRON & FLIGHT OFFICES.	N	–	12776/41.
38 - 39.	R.U. PYRO' STORE.	P.B.	2. FLTS.	10473/41.
40.	N.F.E. STORE.	T.B.	–	12411/41.
41.	WATCH OFFICE.	P.B.	–	12779/41.
42.	FIRE TENDER SHELTER.	N.	–	12410/41.
43.	FLOODLIGHT TRAILER & TRACTOR.	T.B.	–	12411/41.
44.	MAINTENANCE STAFF BLOCK.	N.	–	12777/41.
45.	SQUADRON & FLIGHT OFFICES.	N.	–	12776/41.
46.	ARMOURY & MAINTENANCE UNIT.	N.	–	12777/41.
47.	CREW RMS. REST, LOCKERS ETC.	N.	–	12402/41.
48.	TECHNICAL LATRINE.	T.B.	R.A.F.	9026/41.
49.	ARMOURY.	N	–	12778/41.
50.	GAS DEFENCE CENTRE.	N.	'a'	12408/41.
51.	PARACHUTE STORE.	T.B.	–	11137/41.
52.	GAS DEFENCE CENTRE.	N.	'b'	12408/41.
53.	LUBRICANT & INFLAMMABLE STORE.	N.	A.	12406/41.
54.	MAIN WORKSHOPS.	N.	–	12774/41.
55.	MAINTENANCE UNIT.	N.	–	12777/41.
56.	TECHNICAL LATRINE.	T.B.	R.A.F.	9026/41.
57.	WATER TOWER, 20,000 G. CAP.	St.	40' HIGH.	15408/41.
58.	A.M. BOMBING TEACHER.	P.B.	SINGLE.	6301/42.
59.	LINK TRAINERS.	T.B.	2. COMPT.	10040/41.
60.	TECHNICAL LATRINE.	T.B.	W.A.A.F.	9026/41.
61.	BULK OIL INST.	St.	3,500 GAL.	11270/40.
62.	SUB-STATION.	P.B.	–	13241/41.
63.	WORKS SERVICES BUILDINGS.	N.	A.	4914/42.
64.	TECHNICAL LATRINE.	T.B.	W.A.A.F.	9026/41.
65.	ARMOURY & MAINTENANCE UNIT. (WITHOUT OIL BOWSER.)	N.	–	12777/41.
66.	MAINTENANCE STAFF BLOCK.	N.	–	12777/41.
67.	MAINTENANCE UNIT.	N.	–	12777/41.
68 - 69.	TECHNICAL LATRINE.	T.B.	R.A.F.	9026/41.
70 - 71.	MAIN STORE & FABRIC STORE.	N. & T.B.	–	12773/41.
72.	LINK TRAINERS. 4. No. (CONVERTED FROM GAS CLOTHING & RESP. WORKSHOP.)	T.B	–	WA15/425/43. 12409/41.
73.	BULK OIL INST.	St.	3,500 GAL.	11270/40.
74.	M/T. OFFICE.	N	–	12775/41.
75.	M/T. SHED & YARD.	T.B.	4. BAYS.	12775/41.
76.	FUEL COMPOUND.	C.L.F.	108' × 54'	9108/41.
77.	PHOTOGRAPHIC BLOCK.	N.	–	12401/41.
78.	FLAME FLOATS.	N.	C.	12725/41.
79.	FUZING POINT BLDG.	N.	Heavy & Light.	4778/42.
80.	DITTO.	N.	Heavy.	15963/40.
81.	DITTO.	N.	Heavy & Light.	4778/42.
82.	COMPONENT STORE.	N.	A.	4733/42.
83.	PYRO' STORE.	N.	B.	12725/41.
84.	3" O.S.B. AMN. STORE.	N.	B.	12725/41.
85.	GRENADES STORE.	N.	C	12725/41.
86.	PYRO' STORE.	N.	B.	12725/41.
87 - 88.	COMPONENT STORES.	N.	A.	4733/42.
89.	INCENDIARY BOMB STORE.	N.	A.	4734/42
90.	FUSED & SPARE BOMB STORE.	T.B.	–	3274/41.
91 - 92.	TAIL UNITS AREA.			
93 - 94.	BOMB STORES.	–	D.	3164/42.
95.	EXPLOSIVE I.B. CONTR. STORE.	N	–	15797/41.
96.	I.B. CONTAINER STORE.	N	–	15797/41.
97.	INCENDIARY BOMB STORE.	N.	A.	4734/42.
98.	M.G. & CANNON RANGE.	P.B	25 YD. 4. PT.	147[illegible]
99.	PYRO' STORE.	H.	B.	12725/41.
100.	FLIGHT LATRINE.	T.B	OFFICERS & SERVANTS FOR 4. NISSEN	9026/41.
101.	SEAMARKERS.	H.	B.	12725/41.
102.	S.A.A. STORE.	H.	B.	12725/41.
103.	BULK PETROL INST. (M.T.)	St.	5,000. GAL.	4169/40.
104.	GAS CHAMBER.	T.B.	–	12411/41.
105.				
106.	MAINT. CONTRACTOR'S HUTS & YARD.	–	–	–
107.				
108 - 116.	FLIGHT HUT.			
117.	PICKET POST.	N.	B.	12404/41.
118.	Do. Do.	N.	B.	12404/41
119.	GUARD DOG KENNELS.	C.L.F.	–	–
120.	W/T. STATION.			7669/42.
121.	MAIN BEACON.			
122.	INNER MARKER BEACON.			

AMENDMENTS.

Q.D.M. ADDED - 12.4.45.

CONSTRUCTION ABBREVIATIONS.

TEMPORARY BRICK BLDGS. INDICATED THUS:-	T.B.
TEMPORARY CONCRETE.	T.C.
PERMANENT BRICK.	P.B.
PERMANENT CONCRETE	P.C.
STEEL BLDGS.	St.
ROMNEY HUTTING.	R.
TIMBER HUTTING	T.
PLASTERBOARD HUTTING.	P.
CORRUGATED IRON HUTTING	C.
SECO HUTTING.	S.
M.O.W. HUTTING	M.O.W.
ASBESTOS "	A.
NISSEN. "	N.
HANDCRAFT "	H.
BLAST SHELTERS.	B.S.
AIR RAID SHELTERS.	A.S.
CYCLE SHELTERS.	C.S.
GUN POSTS.	G.P.
SLIT TRENCHES.	S.T.
CHAIN LINK FENCING.	C.L.F.
TRANSFORMER PLINTHS.	T.P.

DOWN GRADED.
~~THIS IS A SECRET DRAWING. IN NO CIRCUMSTANCES MUST IT~~ BE REPRODUCED. IT IS NOT TO BE SEEN BY ~~UNAUTHORISED~~ UNAUTHORISED PERSONS AND MUST BE KEPT UNDER ~~LOCK~~ AND KEY WHEN NOT IN USE. ITS SAFE ~~CUSTODY IS~~ THE RESPONSIBILITY OF THE PERSON TO ~~WHOM IT IS ISSUED.~~ 6/1/58.

BANFF.

RECORD SITE PLAN.
SITE No 1. (AIRFIELD SITE)

FOR DISPERSED SITES SEE DWG. No 4383/44.

Scales 1/2500 & 6" = 1. Mile.

for W.B.	for D.G.W.	~~SECRET No~~	D.G.W.
A.S. Caton. J.O. C.H. Duncan. Nov./44.			REGD No 4382. / 44. AIR MINISTRY.

BARDNEY, Lincs

LOCATION: 10m E of Lincoln
OPENED: 04/43
CLOSED: 1963. Agriculture (2011)
ELEVATION: 40ft
PUNDIT CODE: BA
FORMATION: 5 Grp Bomber Command
MAIN CONTRACTOR: Various
RUNWAYS: 3 concrete
HANGARS: T2 (2), B1 (1)
USER SQNS/UNITS:

9 Sqn
14/04/43–06/07/45
Lancaster I, III

189 Sqn
15/10/44–02/11/44
08/04/45–15/10/45
Lancaster I, III

227 Sqn
07/10/44–12/10/44
Lancaster I, III

Bomber Command Film Unit
10/03–08/04/45
Lancaster

Opened as 53 Base substation, 04/43
*Flt Sgt G. Thompson, 9 Sqn, awarded posthumous VC, Dortmund-Ems Canal, 01/01/45

BARFORD ST JOHN, Oxon

LOCATION: 4½m SSE of Banbury
OPENED: 06/41
CLOSED: 03/46. USAF base, non-flying (2011)
ELEVATION: 380ft
PUNDIT CODE: BJ
FORMATION: 92 (OTU) Grp Bomber Command
MAIN CONTRACTOR: Various
RUNWAYS: 3
HANGARS: T2 (1), B1 (1)
USER SQNS/UNITS:

16 OTU
15/12/42–03/46
Wellington III, X; Mosquito III, X, XVI, XX, XXV, TIII

Opened under Flying Training Command, 06/41
Transferred to Bomber Command as satellite to Upper Heyford, 15/12/42

BASSINGBOURN, Cambs

LOCATION: 3m N of Royston
OPENED: 03/38
CLOSED: Army base (2011)
ELEVATION: 78ft
PUNDIT CODE: BS
FORMATIONS: 3, 6 (T), 7 (T), 92 (OTU) Grp Bomber Command
MAIN CONTRACTOR: John Laing & Son Ltd
Runways: 3 concrete/Tarmac
Hangars: C Type (4)
USER SQNS/UNITS:

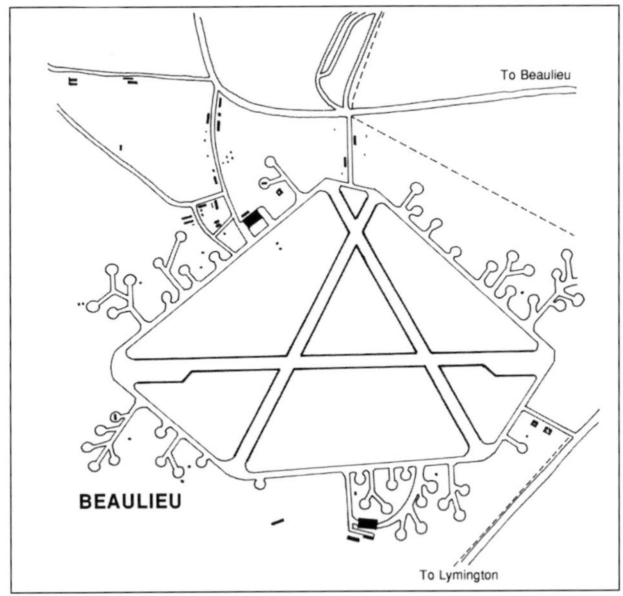

35 Sqn
07/12/39–01/02/40
Battle; Blenheim IV; Anson I

98 Sqn (det)
03/40
Battle

104 Sqn
02/05/38–17/09/39
Blenheim I; Anson I

108 Sqn
02/05/38–17/09/39
Blenheim I; Anson I

215 Sqn
24/09/39–08/04/40
Harrow II; Wellington I

422 (Canadian) Sqn
25/07–04/09/45
Liberator VI, VIII

423 (Canadian) Sqn
08/08–04/09/45
Liberator VI, VIII

11 OTU
08/04/40–02/10/42
Wellington I; Anson I

Opened in Bomber Command as parent station, 03/38
To USAAF as Station AAF-121, 10/42
To RAF, 06/45

BEAULIEU, Hants

LOCATION: 3½m NNE of Lymington
OPENED: 08/42
CLOSED: 09/50. Forestry Commission/ campsite (2011)
ELEVATION: 135ft
PUNDIT CODE: BQ
FORMATIONS: 2 TAF; 10 Grp ADGB
MAIN CONTRACTOR: Various
RUNWAYS: 3 Tarmac
HANGARS: Blister (1), T2 (2)
USER SQNS/UNITS:

257 Sqn
20/01–03/02/44
Typhoon Ib

263 Sqn
23/01–06/03/44
Typhoon Ib

486 (New Zealand) Sqn
31/01–28/02/44
Typhoon Ib; Tempest V

Opened in 19 Grp Coastal Command, 08/42
To 2 TAF, 01/44
To 10 Grp ADGB as Forward Airfield, 03/44
To USAAF, 05/44
To RAF, 09/44

LEFT: A 22,000lb Grand Slam earthquake bomb cradled on its trolley in the bomb dump at Bardney on 8 May 1945 – VE-Day. The corporal in the foreground holds a 40lb general-purpose bomb as a size comparison. In the background can be seen the tail cone of an 8,000lb Blockbuster high-explosive blast bomb. (Australian War Memorial SUK 14593)

BECCLES, Suffolk

LOCATION: 5m SW of Lowestoft
OPENED: 1943
CLOSED: 1945. Private light aviation (2011)
ELEVATION: 50ft
FORMATION: 16 Grp Coastal Command
RUNWAYS: 3 concrete and Tarmac
HANGARS: T2 (2)
USER SQNS/UNITS:

278 Sqn (det)
02–10/45
Walrus; Sea Otter

280 Sqn
30/10/44–03/11/45
Warwick I

618 Sqn
21/08–30/10/44
Mosquito IV

BENBECULA, Hebrides

LOCATION: W side of Isle of Benbecula
OPENED: 08/41
CLOSED: 01/46. Benbecula Airport (2011)
ELEVATION: 19ft
FORMATION: 15 (T) Grp Coastal Command
RUNWAYS: 3 bitumen
HANGARS: ½ T2 (10)
USER SQNS/UNITS:

ABOVE: A No 220 Squadron Fortress Mk IIA is bombed-up with depth-charges at Benbecula in the Outer Hebrides during May 1943. (IWM CH11101)

36 Sqn
09/03–04/06/45
Wellington XIV
179 Sqn
21/09/44–10/44
Wellington XIV
206 Sqn
30/06/42–10/43
Hudson V; Fortress II
220 Sqn
07/42–02/43 (det)
13/03/43–18/10/43
Fortress II
304 (Polish) Sqn
21/09/44–03/45
Wellington XI, XII, XIV
455 (Australian) Sqn (det)
04/42–04/44
Hampden; Beaufighter X
838 NAS
10–11/44
Swordfish II, III
842 NAS
09–11/44
Swordfish II, III

BENSON, Oxon

LOCATION: 1¾m NE of Wallingford
OPENED: 04/39
CLOSED: RAF base (2011)
ELEVATION: 215ft
PUNDIT CODE: EB
FORMATIONS: 1, 6 (T) Grp Bomber Command; 106 (PR) Grp Coastal Command
MAIN CONTRACTOR: John Laing & Son Ltd
RUNWAYS: 2 concrete
HANGARS: C Type (4), O Blister (4), EO Blister (14)
USER SQNS/UNITS:
1 PRU
27/12/40–19/10/42
Spitfire; Blenheim; Mosquito
(disb 10/42 and re-formed as five PR squadrons)
2 Sqn (det)
01–02/44
Mustang I
52 Sqn
18/09/39–06/04/40
Battle
63 Sqn
09/09/39–06/04/40
Battle
103 Sqn
01/04–02/09/39
Battle
140 Sqn
17/09–29/10/41
04/11/41–20/05/42
05/42–10/43 (det)
Spitfire C, I, IV, PRVII, IX; Blenheim IV; Ventura I
150 Sqn
03/04–02/09/39
Battle
207 Sqn
04/40
Battle
540 Sqn
10/42–02/44 (det)
29/02/44–29/03/45
Mosquito VI, IX, XVI
541 Sqn
19/10/42–01/10/46
Spitfire IV, X, XI, XIX; Mustang III
542 Sqn
19/10/42–27/08/45
Spitfire IV, X, XI, XIX
543 Sqn
19/10/42–18/10/43
Spitfire IV, XI
544 Sqn
19/10/42–13/10/45
Maryland; Wellington IV; Spitfire IV, XI; Mosquito IV, IX, XVI, 32, 34
618 Sqn (det)
04–10/43
Mosquito IV; Beaufighter II
12 OTU
06/04/40–09/41
Battle; Wellington

BENTWATERS, Suffolk

LOCATION: 4½m NE of Woodbridge
OPENED: 04/44
CLOSED: 1993. Warehousing/offices/light industry (2011)
ELEVATION: 80ft
PUNDIT CODE: BY
FORMATION: 11 Grp Fighter Command
MAIN CONTRACTOR: Various
RUNWAYS: 3 concrete/Tarmac
HANGARS: T2 (2)
USER SQNS/UNITS:

64 Sqn
29/12/44–15/08/45
Mustang III

65 Sqn
15/05–13/08/45
Mustang IV

118 Sqn
15/12/44–11/08/45
Spitfire IXc; Mustang III

126 Sqn
30/12/44–05/09/45
Mustang III, IV

129 Sqn
11/12/44–26/05/45
Mustang III

165 Sqn
15/12/44–29/05/45
Spitfire IXb; Mustang III

234 Sqn
17/12/44–01/05/45
Mustang III, IV

Opened in Bomber Command, 04/44
To 11 Grp Fighter Command, 12/44

ABOVE: The original wartime watchtower at Bentwaters was extensively modified by the USAAF/USAF who occupied the airfield until 1993. The war-vintage Nissen hut in the foreground looks slightly incongruous in this photograph taken in 2010. (Author)

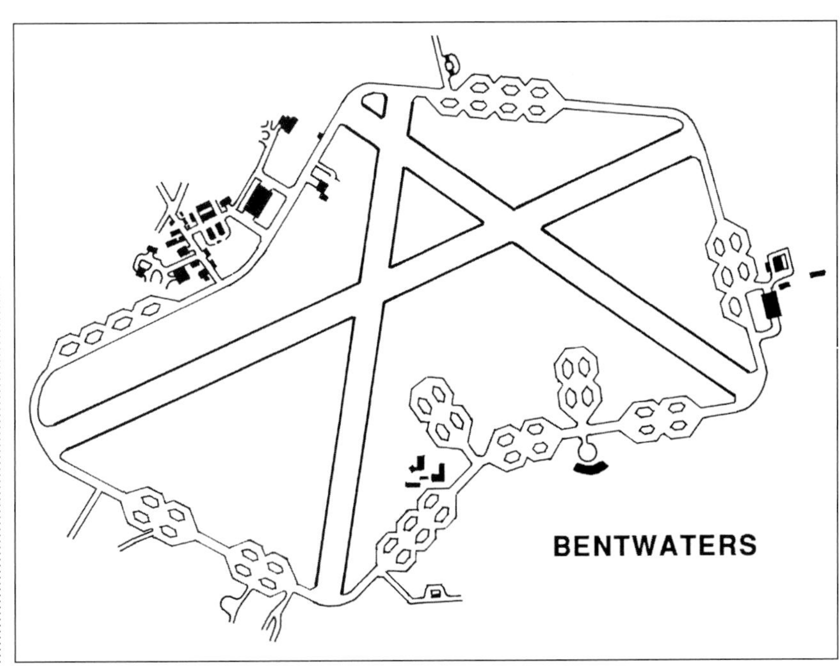

ABOVE: Blenheim Mk Is equipped No 90 Squadron when it was stationed at Bicester between March 1937 and May 1939, after which it converted to the Blenheim Mk IV and moved to West Raynham in Norfolk. (Author)

BICESTER, Oxon

LOCATION: 1¾m NNE of Bicester
OPENED: 1917
CLOSED: 2004. Army base/gliding (2011)
ELEVATION: 271ft
PUNDIT CODE: BC
FORMATIONS: 6 (T), 7 (T), 92 (OTU) Grp Bomber Command; 9 Grp Fighter Command
MAIN CONTRACTOR: Various
RUNWAYS: 3 grass
HANGARS: A Type (2), C Type (2)
USER SQNS/UNITS:

104 Sqn
12/09/39–08/04/40
Blenheim I, IV; Anson I

108 Sqn
12/09/39–08/04/40
Blenheim I, IV; Anson I

13 OTU
08/04/40–12/10/44
Blenheim I, IV, V; Spitfire; Mosquito

1551 Flt
20/11/42–15/04/43
Anson; Oxford; Master

307 FTU
24/12/42–18/03/43
Blenheim V

To 9 Grp Fighter Command, 6/43

BIGGIN HILL, Kent

LOCATION: 5½m SSE of Bromley
OPENED: 02/17
CLOSED: 1992. Biggin Hill Airport (2011)
ELEVATION: 377ft
PUNDIT CODE: GI
Formation: 11 Grp Fighter Command
MAIN CONTRACTOR: Various
RUNWAYS: 3 asphalt
HANGARS: Bessonneau (2), Blister (12)
USER SQNS/UNITS:

1 Sqn
09/02–15/03/43
Typhoon Ib

3 Sqn
01/05–02/09/39
Gladiator I; Hurricane I

19 Sqn
01–07/07/42
Spitfire Vb

32 Sqn
27/03–26/05/40
04/06–27/08/40
Hurricane I

41 Sqn
21–28/05/43
Spitfire XII

64 Sqn
13–15/10/40
Spitfire I

66 Sqn
07/11/40–24/02/41
Spitfire I, IIa

72 Sqn
31/08–01/09/40
12/09–13/10/40
26/07–20/10/41

22/03–30/06/42
07/07–04/08/42
Spitfire I, IIb, Vb, Vc, IX
74 Sqn
15/10/40–20/02/41
Spitfire IIa
79 Sqn
08/03–10/05/40
21–27/05/40
05/06–01/07/40
27/08–08/09/40
Hurricane I
91 Sqn
07–29/10/44
Spitfire IXb
92 Sqn
08/09/40–09/01/41
20/02–24/09/41
Spitfire I, Vb
133 Sqn
03/05–30/06/42
12–31/07/42
31/08–23/09/42
Spitfire Vb
154 Sqn
05/11/44–01/03/45
Spitfire VII; Mustang IV
213 Sqn
09–18/06/40
Hurricane I
242 Sqn
21/05–08/06/40
Hurricane I
264 Sqn
11/01–14/04/41
Defiant I
322 (Dutch) Sqn
31/10/44–03/01/45
Spitfire LFIXe, LFXVIe
340 (French) Sqn
23/09/42–21/03/43
02/11–17/12/44
Spitfire Vb, IXb
341 (French) Sqn
21/03–11/10/43
Spitfire IXb
345 (French) Sqn
28/10–01/11/44
Spitfire HFIX
401 (Canadian) Sqn
20/10/41–19/03/42
03–14/08/42
21/08–24/09/42
13/10/43–08/04/44
Spitfire Vb, IX, IXb
411 (Canadian) Sqn
13/10/43–24/02/44
29/02–16/04/44
Spitfire IXb
412 (Canadian) Sqn
14/10/43–05/01/44
20/01–30/03/44
07–15/04/44
Spitfire Vb, IXb
485 (New Zealand) Sqn
01/07–18/10/43
Spitfire IXb
601 (AAF) Sqn
02/09–30/12/39
Blenheim If
602 (AAF) Sqn
16–20/08/42
Spitfire Vb
609 (AAF) Sqn
24/02–28/07/41
24/09–19/11/41
18/09–02/11/42
Spitfire IIa, Vb; Typhoon Ia, Ib
610 (AAF) Sqn
10–27/05/40
08/07–31/08/40
Spitfire I
611 (AAF) Sqn
23/09/42–01/07/43
Spitfire IX
11 Grp Sector Station, 09/39
To Balloon Command, 07/44
To ADGB, 09/44
To 11 Grp Fighter Command, 10/44

ABOVE: The problems which had dogged the first cannon-armed Spitfires during the Battle of Britain had been ironed out by the time No 92 Squadron received its Mk IBs in November 1940. Pictured at Biggin Hill is R5908, 'F'. (Alfred Price)

BINBROOK, Lincs

LOCATION: 9m SW of Grimsby
OPENED: 06/40
CLOSED: 1995. Agriculture/light industry (2011)
ELEVATION: 373ft
PUNDIT CODE: BK
Formation: 1 Grp Bomber Command
MAIN CONTRACTOR: Various
RUNWAYS: 3 concrete/Tarmac
HANGARS: C Type (5)
USER SQNS/UNITS:
12 Sqn
03/07–08/40
09/40–24/09/42
Battle; Wellington II
142 Sqn
03/07–12/08/40

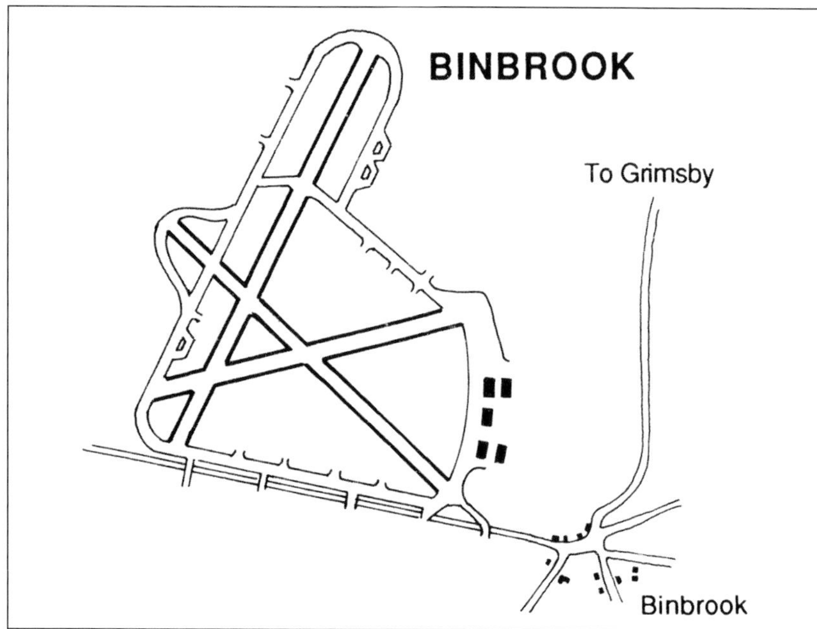

06/09/40–26/11/41
Battle; Wellington II, IV
460 (Australian) Sqn
14/05/43–28/07/45
Lancaster I, III
Opened as parent station, 06/40
Became 12 Base HQ, 01/43

BIRCHAM NEWTON, Norfolk

LOCATION: 8m WNW of Fakenham
OPENED: 1916
CLOSED: 1966. Industry, National Construction College (2011)
FORMATION: 16 Grp Coastal Command
RUNWAYS: 3 steel matting
HANGARS: C Type (3), Bellman (3), Blister (10), Belfast (2)
USER SQNS/UNITS:
42 Sqn
18/08/39–28/04/40
Vildebeeste III
119 Sqn
02/10/44–21/02/45
22/05/45 (disb)
Albacore I
206 Sqn
01/08/36–30/05/41
Anson I; Hudson I
221 Sqn
21/11/40–02/05/41
Wellington I, III
229 Sqn (det)
06–09/40
Hurricane I
233 Sqn (det)
10/39–08/40
Blenheim
235 Sqn
25/04–26/05/40
Blenheim If, IVf
248 Sqn
15/06–09/41
Blenheim If, IVf
254 Sqn
28/01–24/04/40
Blenheim IV
279 Sqn
16/11/41–11/44
Hudson
280 Sqn
02–11/42 (det)
05/11/42–23/09/43
Anson I; Warwick I
320 Sqn
24/04/42–15/03/43
Hudson
407 Sqn
31/03/42–02/02/43
Hudson
415 Sqn
15/11/43–26/07/44
Wellington XIII; Albacore
500 Sqn
30/05/41–22/03/42
Blenheim IV; Hudson V
521 Sqn
31/07/42–22/03/43
Spitfire, Hudson; Gladiator; Mosquito IV
598 Sqn
12/03–03/05/45
Oxford; Martinet; Hurricane IIc, IV; Beaufighter I
608 Sqn
30/06–12/41
Blenheim IVf; Hudson
695 Sqn
31/10/42–11/08/45
Henley; Martlet; Avenger
1401 Meteorological Reconnaissance Flight
29/10/41–31/07/42
Blenheim IV; Gladiator; Hudson; Spitfire V
403 Meteorological Reconnaissance Flight 1403 Flt
11/40 (01/03/41)–31/07/42
Blenheim IV; Hudson
Warwick Training Flight
28/06–21/11/43
Warwick I
819 NAS
09/44–01/45
27/02–07/03/45
Swordfish
855 NAS
06/09–17/10/44
Avenger

BIRCOTES, Notts

LOCATION: 1m W of Bawtry
OPENED: 11/41
CLOSED: 07/48. Agriculture (2011)
ELEVATION: 110ft
PUNDIT CODE: BR
FORMATIONS: 7 (T), 93 (OTU) Grp Bomber Command
MAIN CONTRACTOR: Various
RUNWAYS: 3 grass
HANGARS: T2 (1), B1 (1), Bessonneau (1)
USER SQNS/UNITS:

ABOVE: The life of Lockheed Hudson Mk I, P5120, 'C', of No 206 Squadron was short. It was delivered to the squadron in April 1940 but was written off in a crash-landing at Bircham Newton on 20 June. P5120 is pictured off the English coast. (IWM CH281)

18 OTU
10/43–08/44
Wellington III, X
25 OTU
06/41–07/01/43
Wellington III, X
Opened as satellite to Finningley, 11/41

BITTESWELL, Leics

LOCATION: 2m W of Lutterworth
OPENED: 07/41
CLOSED: 1987. Industrial estate/retail park (2011)
ELEVATION: 420ft
PUNDIT CODE: BT
FORMATIONS: 7 (T), 93 (OTU) Grp Bomber Command
MAIN CONTRACTOR: Various
RUNWAYS: 3 concrete
HANGARS: T2 (1), B1 (1)
USER SQNS/UNITS:
18 OTU
02/42–06/43
Wellington III, X
29 OTU
06/43–11/44
Wellington III, X
Opened as satellite to Bramcote, 02/42
Became satellite to Bruntingthorpe, 06/43
To Transport Command, 11/44

BLACKBUSHE (Hartfordbridge Flats), Hants

LOCATION: 10m SSE of Reading
OPENED: 11/42
CLOSED: 11/46. Blackbushe Airport/ British Car Auctions/business park (2011)
ELEVATION: 320ft
PUNDIT CODE: XB
FORMATIONS: 2, 85 Grp 2 TAF
MAIN CONTRACTOR: Sir Alfred McAlpine Ltd
RUNWAYS: 3 concrete
HANGARS: Bessonneau (2), Blister (6), T2 (3)
USER SQNS/UNITS:
16 Sqn
29/06/43–16/04/44
Mustang I; Spitfire PRXI
21 Sqn
19/08–27/09/43
Ventura I, II; Mosquito VI
88 Sqn
19/08/43–16/10/44
Boston IIIa
107 Sqn
20/08/43–01/02/44
23/10–19/11/44
Boston IIIa
140 Sqn
16/03/43–07/04/44
Spitfire I, IV, PRVII, XI; Blenheim IV; Ventura I; Mosquito IX, XVI
162 Sqn
10/07/45–14/07/46 (DB)
Mosquito XX, XXV

167 Sqn
30/03/45–01/02/46 (DB)
Warwick I, III
171 Sqn
07/12/42–01/02/43 (DB)
Mustang Ia
226 Sqn
13/02–17/10/44
Mitchell II
264 Sqn
07/05–26/07/44
Mosquito XIII
301 Sqn
04/04–02/07/45
Warwick I, II
305 Sqn
23–25/10/44
30/10–19/11/44
Mosquito VI
322 (Dutch) Sqn
4/04–20/06/44
Spitfire XIV
342 Sqn
06/09/43–17/10/44
Boston IIIa, IV
418 (Canadian) Sqn
21/11/44–15/03/45
Mosquito VI
430 Sqn
01–08/01/43
Tomahawk I, III
605 (AAF) Sqn
21/11/44–15/03/45
Mosquito VI
613 Sqn
23–25/10/44
30/10–20/11/44
Mosquito VI
Opened in 70 Grp Army Co-operation Command, 11/42
To 2 Grp, 2 TAF, 08/43
To 85 Grp, 2 TAF, 11/43
Name changed from Hartfordbridge Flats to Blackbushe, 12/44
To 46 Grp Transport Command, 03/45

BLYTON, Lincs

LOCATION: 4½m NE of Gainsborough
OPENED: 11/42
CLOSED: 1954. Agriculture/motorsport (2011)
ELEVATION: 70ft
PUNDIT CODE: AL
FORMATIONS: 1, 7 (HCU) Grp Bomber Command
MAIN CONTRACTOR: Various
RUNWAYS: 3 concrete
HANGARS: T2 (2), B1 (1)
USER SQNS/UNITS:
199 Sqn
07/11/42–03/02/43
Wellington III
1662 HCU
02/43–04/45
Halifax, I, II, V; Manchester; Lancaster I, III
Opened as satellite to Lindholme, 11/42
Became 11 Base substation, 01/43
Became 71 Base substation, 11/44

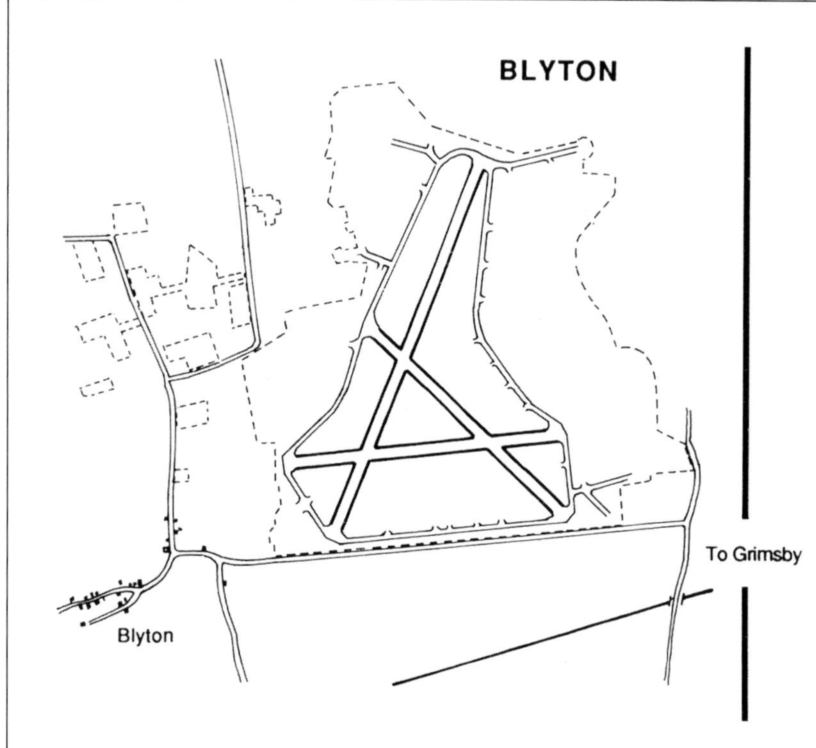

BODNEY, Norfolk

LOCATION: 4½m W of Watton
OPENED: 03/40
CLOSED: 11/45. Agriculture (2011)
ELEVATION: 149ft
PUNDIT CODE: BO
FORMATION: 2 Grp Bomber Command
MAIN CONTRACTOR: Various
RUNWAYS: 3 grass
HANGARS: T2 (2), Blister (5)
USER SQNS/UNITS:
21 Sqn
14/03–31/10/42
Blenheim IV; Ventura I, II
82 Sqn
03/40–04/41
Blenheim IV
105 Sqn
21/05/41–07/41
Blenheim IV
Opened as satellite to Watton, 03/40
Transferred to USAAF as Station AAF-141, 05/43

BOGNOR, Sussex

LOCATION: 2m NW of Bognor Regis
OPENED: 06/43
CLOSED: 01/45. Agriculture (2011)
ELEVATION: 23ft
PUNDIT CODE: OG
FORMATIONS: 83, 84 Grp 2 TAF
MAIN CONTRACTOR: Royal Canadian Engineers

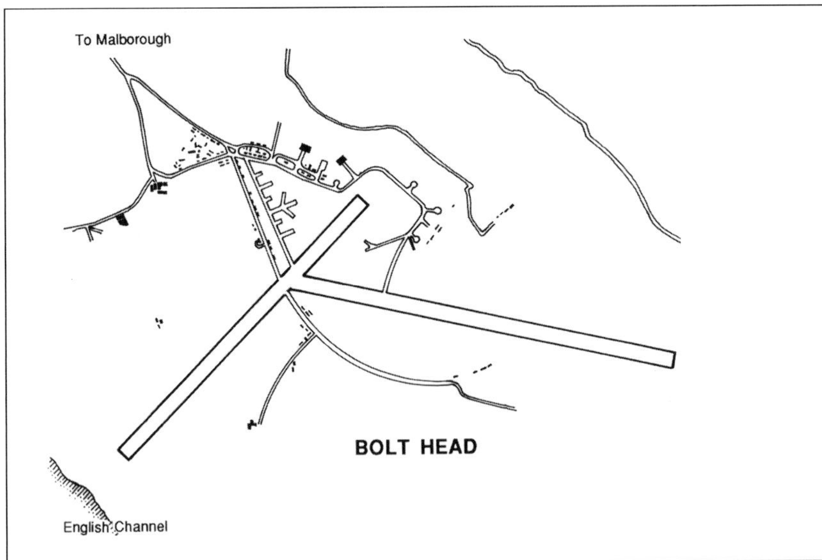

RUNWAYS: 2 steel matting
HANGARS: Blister (4)
USER SQNS/UNITS:

19 Sqn
06/06–02/07/43
Spitfire Vb

66 Sqn
31/03–22/04/44
25/04–08/05/44
14/05–22/06/44
Spitfire LFIXb

122 Sqn
01/06–01/07/43
Spitfire Vb

331 (Norwegian) Sqn
31/03–22/06/44
Spitfire IXb

332 (Norwegian) Sqn
31/03–21/06/44
Spitfire IXb

602 (AAF) Sqn
01/06–01/07/43
Spitfire Vb

83 GSU
21/06–26/09/44
Mustang I; Spitfire IX, XI; Typhoon I

Advanced Landing Ground (ALG)

BOLT HEAD, Devon

LOCATION: 1m W of Salcombe
OPENED: 1941
CLOSED: 1947. Agriculture (2011)
ELEVATION: 420ft
PUNDIT CODE: OH
FORMATIONS: 10, 11 Grp Fighter Command
MAIN CONTRACTOR: Various
RUNWAYS: 2 steel matting
HANGARS: Blister (2)
USER SQNS/UNITS:

41 Sqn
29/04–16/05/44
24/05–19/06/44
Spitfire XII

234 Sqn
18/03–29/04/44
Spitfire Vb

263 Sqn
19/06–10/07/44
Typhoon Ib

266 Sqn
07–12/03/44
Typhoon Ib

610 (AAF) Sqn
26/06–19/12/43
16–24/05/44
Spitfire Vb, Vc, XIV

611 (AAF) Sqn
17/07–30/08/44
Spitfire IX

Opened as Forward Operating Base (FOB) for 10 and 11 Grps, 1941
Upgraded to satellite to Exeter, 04/42
To C&M, 04/45

BOTTESFORD, Lincs

LOCATION: 7m NW of Grantham
OPENED: 10/09/41
CLOSED: 1948. Agriculture/light industry (2011)
ELEVATION: 110ft
PUNDIT CODE: AQ
FORMATIONS: 3, 5, 7 (HCU) Grp Bomber Command
MAIN CONTRACTOR: George Wimpey & Co Ltd

ABOVE: Mechanics work on the Merlin engines of an Avro Lancaster of No 207 Squadron at Bottesford in June 1942. (Crown Copyright)

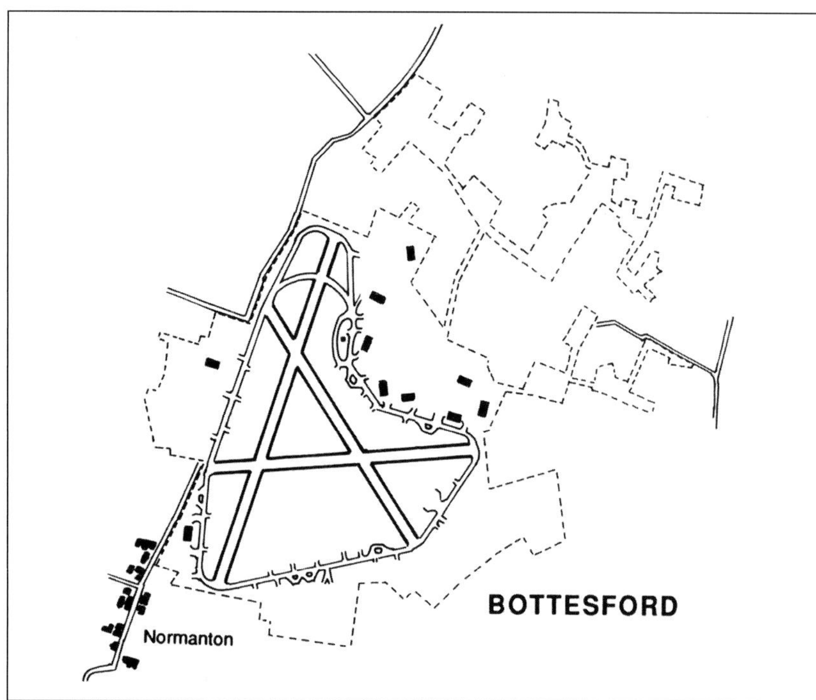

RUNWAYS: 3 concrete
HANGARS: T2 (9), B1 (1)
USER SQNS/UNITS:

90 Sqn
07/11–29/12/42
Stirling I

207 Sqn
17/11/41–20/09/42
Manchester; Lancaster I

467 (Australian) Sqn
22/11/42–13/11/43
Lancaster I, III

1668 HCU
07/44–03/46
Lancaster I, II, III

Opened as parent station, 10/09/41
Transferred to USAAF as Station AAF-481, 11/43
Returned to RAF control, 07/44
Became 72 Base HQ, 11/44

BOULMER, Northumberland

LOCATION: 3½m E of Alnwick
OPENED: 03/43
CLOSED: RAF base, flying (2011)
ELEVATION: 44ft
PUNDIT CODE: BM
FORMATIONS: 9, 81 (OTU) Grp Fighter Command
MAIN CONTRACTOR: Various
RUNWAYS: 3 Tarmac
HANGARS: Blister (4)
USER SQNS/UNITS:

57 OTU
01/03/43–06/06/45
Spitfire; Master

59 OTU
1943–44
Hurricane; Master

Opened as satellite to Eshott, 03/43
Additionally used as satellite to Milfield, 1943–44

BOURN, Cambs

LOCATION: 7m W of Cambridge
OPENED: 04/41
CLOSED: 1948. Agriculture/light industry/light aviation (2011)
ELEVATION: 235ft
PUNDIT CODE: AU
FORMATIONS: 1, 2, 3, 5, 8 (PFF) Grp Bomber Command
MAIN CONTRACTOR: Various
RUNWAYS: 3 concrete
HANGARS: T2 (2), B1 (1)
USER SQNS/UNITS:

15 Sqn
13/08/42–14/04/43
Stirling I, III

97 Sqn
18/04/43–18/04/44
Lancaster I, III

101 Sqn
11/02–11/08/42
Wellington I, III

105 Sqn
23/03/44–29/06/45
Mosquito IV

162 Sqn
16/12/44–10/07/45
Mosquito XX, XXV

609 Sqn
26–30/08/42
Typhoon I

Opened as satellite to Oakington, 04/41
Upgraded to parent station status, 08/42

BRADWELL BAY, Essex

LOCATION: 6m NE of Southminster
OPENED: 11/41
CLOSED: 1946. Agriculture/disused Bradwell nuclear power station (2011)
ELEVATION: 30ft
PUNDIT CODE: RB
FORMATIONS: 11 Grp Fighter Command; 2 TAF
MAIN CONTRACTOR: Various
RUNWAYS: 3 Tarmac/asphalt
HANGARS: Bellman (1), Blister (12)
USER SQNS/UNITS:

3 Sqn
06/03–06/04/44
14–28/04/44
Typhoon Ib; Tempest V

23 Sqn
14–21/08/42
13/10–27/12/42
Havoc I; Boston III; Mosquito II

29 Sqn
13/05–03/09/43
Beaufighter VIf; Mosquito XXI, VI

56 Sqn
23/08–04/10/43
Typhoon Ib

64 Sqn
30/08–29/12/44
Spitfire IX; Mustang III

124 Sqn
23/04–26/07/44
Spitfire VII
126 Sqn
30/08–30/12/44
Spitfire IXb
151 Sqn
01/03–17/05/45
Mosquito XXX
157 Sqn
15/03–13/05/43
Mosquito II
198 Sqn
19–22/08/43
Typhoon Ib
219 Sqn
01/04–29/08/44
Mosquito XVII, XXX
247 Sqn
04/06–10/07/43
Typhoon Ib
310 (Czech) Sqn
29/12/44–27/02/45
Spitfire LFIX
312 (Czech) Sqn
03/10/44–27/02/45
Spitfire HFIX
313 (Czech) Sqn
29/12/44–27/02/45
Spitfire IX
418 (Canadian) Sqn
15/04/42–15/03/43
Boston III
456 (Australian) Sqn
16/03–15/06/45
Mosquito XXX
488 (New Zealand) Sqn
03/09/43–03/04/44
Mosquito XII, XIII
501 (AAF) Sqn
22/09/44–03/03/45
Tempest V
605 (AAF) Sqn
06/10/43–07/04/44
Mosquito VI
611 (AAF) Sqn
30/08–03/10/44
Spitfire IX
Opened in 11 Grp Fighter Command as parent station, 11/41

BRAMCOTE, Warks

LOCATION: 4m SE of Nuneaton
OPENED: 04/06/40
CLOSED: Army base (2011)
ELEVATION: 378ft
PUNDIT CODE: RT
FORMATIONS: 1, 6, 92 Grp Bomber Command
MAIN CONTRACTOR: John Laing & Son Ltd
RUNWAYS: 3 steel matting
HANGARS: C Type (5)
USER SQNS/UNITS:
151 Sqn
28/11–22/12/40
Hurricane I
215 Sqn
10–24/09/39
Wellington I
300 (Polish) Sqn
01/07–22/08/40
Battle
301 (Polish) Sqn
22/07–29/08/40
Battle
304 (Polish) Sqn
22/08–02/12/40
Battle; Wellington I
305 (Polish) Sqn
29/08–02/12/40
Battle; Wellington I
18 OTU
15/06/40–07/03/43
Wellington I, III
Opened as parent station, 06/40
To Transport Command, 04/43

BRAWDY, Pembrokeshire

LOCATION: 9m NW of Haverfordwest
OPENED: 1944
CLOSED: 1996. Industry/Army barracks (2011)
ELEVATION: 350ft
FORMATION: 19 Grp Coastal Command
RUNWAYS: 3 concrete
HANGARS: T2 (2)
USER SQNS/UNITS:
517 Sqn
01/02/44–30/11/45
Halifax III, V
595 Sqn (det)
01/45
Spitfire Vb, XII
8 OTU (det)
02–04/45
Spitfire; Mosquito

BREIGHTON, Yorks

LOCATION: 5½m NE of Selby
OPENED: 01/42
CLOSED: 1946. Flying club (2011)
ELEVATION: 24ft
PUNDIT CODE: AC
FORMATIONS: 4, 5 Grp Bomber Command
MAIN CONTRACTOR: Various
RUNWAYS: 3 Tarmac
HANGARS: T2 (2), B1 (1)
USER SQNS/UNITS:
78 Sqn
16/06/43–20/09/45
Halifax II, III, VI

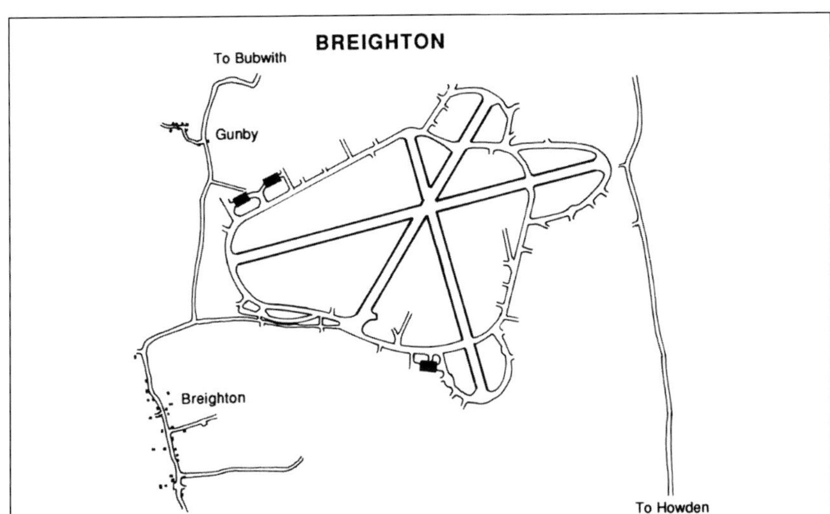

ABOVE: Halifax Mk II Series 1A, LW235, 'B', of No 78 Squadron, based at Breighton, Yorkshire, captured by the camera on 25 September 1943. LW235 went on to serve with No 102 Squadron and No 1666 HCU, but was destroyed in a crash at Nunnington, Yorkshire, while serving with the latter on 20 October 1944. (IWM CH11328)

460 (Australian) Sqn
04/01/42–14/05/43
Wellington IV; Halifax II; Lancaster I, III
1656 HCU
07–26/10/42
Manchester; Lancaster I
Opened as satellite to Holme-on-Spalding Moor, 01/42
Became 44 Base substation, 11/44

BRENZETT, Kent

LOCATION: 3m NW of New Romney
OPENED: 03/43
CLOSED: 12/44. Agriculture/Brenzett Aeronautical Museum (2011)
ELEVATION: 9ft
PUNDIT CODE: ZT
FORMATIONS: 84 Grp 2 TAF; 11 Grp Fighter Command
MAIN CONTRACTOR: RAFACS
RUNWAYS: 2 steel matting
HANGARS: Blister (5)
USER SQNS/UNITS:
129 Sqn
08/07–11/10/44
Mustang III
181 Sqn
02/07– 08/10/43
Typhoon Ib
306 (Polish) Sqn
08/07–10/10/44
Mustang III
315 (Polish) Sqn
10/07–10/10/44
Mustang III
Advanced Landing Ground (ALG)

BRUNTINGTHORPE, Leics

LOCATION: 10m S of Leicester
OPENED: 11/42
CLOSED: 1962. Private airfield/car performance proving ground (2011)
ELEVATION: 450ft
PUNDIT CODE: BP
FORMATION: 92 (OTU) Grp Bomber Command
MAIN CONTRACTOR: Various
RUNWAYS: 3 concrete
HANGARS: T2 (4), B1 (1)
USER SQNS/UNITS:
29 OTU
06/43–19/06/45
Wellington III, X
Opened as satellite to North Luffenham, 11/42
Upgraded to parent station status, 06/43

BRUNTON, Northumberland

LOCATION: 9m N of Alnwick
OPENED: 08/42
CLOSED: 05/45. Disused (2011)
ELEVATION: 80ft
PUNDIT CODE: BN
FORMATIONS: 9, 81 (OTU) Grp Fighter Command
MAIN CONTRACTOR: Various
RUNWAYS: 3 Tarmac
HANGARS: Blister (4)
USER SQNS/UNITS:
56 OTU
15/12/44–21/05/45
Typhoon Ib; Tempest
59 OTU
04/08/42–26/01/44
Hurricane; Typhoon Ib
Fighter Leaders' School
26/01–27/12/44
Spitfire; Typhoon; Hurricane
Opened as satellite to Milfield, 08/42

ABOVE: An unidentified No 578 Squadron crew (but possibly that of Flg Off I. Denley, RAAF) poses for the camera beside Halifax Mk III, NA618, 'N', in late 1944. On ops to Düsseldorf on 20/21 February 1945, NA618, with Denley and crew onboard, was attacked by a Ju88 night fighter. The Halifax exploded in mid-air but miraculously six of the eight-man crew (including Denley) survived to become PoWs. (Author)

BURN, Yorks

LOCATION: 2½m S of Selby
OPENED: 11/42
CLOSED: 1946. Agriculture/gliding (2011)
ELEVATION: 20ft
PUNDIT CODE: AZ
FORMATIONS: 4, 6 (RCAF) Grp Bomber Command
MAIN CONTRACTOR: Various
RUNWAYS: 3 concrete/Tarmac
HANGARS: T2 (2), B1 (1)
USER SQNS/UNITS:

431 (Canadian) Sqn
13/11/42–15/07/43
Wellington X

578 Sqn
06/02/44–15/04/45
Halifax III

1653 HCU
06–10/42
Halifax I

Opened as satellite to Pocklington, 11/42
Became 42 Base substation, 11/44
*Plt Off C.J. Barton, 578 Sqn, awarded posthumous VC, Nuremberg, 30–31/03/44

CAISTOR, Lincs

LOCATION: 5½m SE of Brigg
OPENED: 1941
CLOSED: 1963. Agriculture (2011)
ELEVATION: 100ft
PUNDIT CODE: Not known
FORMATIONS: 9, 81 (OTU) Grp Fighter Command
MAIN CONTRACTOR: Various
RUNWAYS: 4 grass
HANGARS: Blister (1)
USER SQNS/UNITS:

53 OTU
17/05/43–15/05/45
Spitfire

Opened as RLG for Kirton-in-Lindsey, 1941
RLG to Leconfield, 05/42
RLG to Manby, 12/42
To Kirton-in-Lindsey as RLG, 1943

CARNABY, Yorks

LOCATION: 2m SW of Bridlington
OPENED: 26/03/44
CLOSED: 1963. Industrial park (2011)
ELEVATION: 35ft

ABOVE: Sunderland Mk III, EK591, 'U', of No 422 (Canadian) Squadron, alights at Castle Archdale/Lough Erne. Flown by Warrant Officer Frank Morton, RCAF, from Calgary, Alberta, this aircraft sank a German Type VIIC U-boat, U-625 (Kapitänleutnant Hans Becker), on 10 March 1944. It was the Morton crew's first operational patrol. EK591 is pictured here on 15 July 1944. (Andy Thomas)

PUNDIT CODE: KQ
FORMATION: 4 Grp Bomber Command
MAIN CONTRACTOR: John Laing & Son Ltd
HANGARS: None
RUNWAYS: 1 bitumen, 3,000yd x 250yd with undershoots and overshoots of 500yd each
USER SQNS/UNITS:
None. FIDO-equipped Emergency Diversion Runway under control of 4 Grp Bomber Command

CASTLE ARCHDALE (Lough Erne), Co Fermanagh, NI

LOCATION: 10m NW of Enniskillen
OPENED: 02/1941
CLOSED: 1958. Country Park/Museum (2011)
ELEVATION: 138ft
FORMATION: 15 (T) Grp Coastal Command
RUNWAYS: none. Lough Erne alighting area and moorings
HANGARS: T2 (2)
USER SQNS/UNITS:

119 Sqn
16/04–06/09/42
Catalina Ib

201 Sqn
30/09/41–08/04/44
Sunderland I, II, III

202 Sqn
03/09/44–27/06/45
Catalina Ib, IV

209 Sqn
23/03–26/07/41
Lerwick I; Catalina I

228 Sqn
11/12/42–04/05/43
Sunderland I, II, III

240 Sqn
25/08/41–04/07/42
Catalina I, IIa

422 (RCAF)
02/04–30/10/42
13/04–04/11/44
Lerwick I; Catalina Ib; Sunderland III

423 (RCAF)
02/11/42–08/08/45
Sunderland II, III

302 Ferry Training Unit (FTU)
09–12/42
Catalina

CASTLE CAMPS, Essex

LOCATION: 6m NE of Saffron Walden
OPENED: 06/40
CLOSED: 01/46. Agriculture/light industry (2011)
ELEVATION: 417ft
PUNDIT CODE: CC
FORMATION: 11 Grp Fighter Command
MAIN CONTRACTOR: Various and John Laing & Son Ltd
RUNWAYS: 3 Tarmac
HANGARS: Bellman (1), Blister (8)
USER SQNS/UNITS:

25 Sqn
27/10/44–14/07/45
Mosquito XVII, XXX, VI

68 Sqn
23/06–28/10/44
Beaufighter VIf; Mosquito XVII, XIX

73 Sqn
05/09–06/11/40
Hurricane I

85 Sqn
03–05/09/40
Hurricane I

91 Sqn
29/02–17/03/44
Spitfire XII
151 Sqn
08/10–19/11/44
Mosquito XXX
157 Sqn
18/12/41–15/03/43
Mosquito II
307 (Polish) Sqn
27/01–31/05/45
Mosquito XXX
410 (Canadian) Sqn
30/12/43–29/04/44
Mosquito XIII
486 (New Zealand) Sqn
06–21/03/44
29/03–29/04/44
Typhoon Ib; Tempest V
605 (AAF) Sqn
15/03–06/10/43
Mosquito II, VI
Opened in Fighter Command as satellite to Debden, 06/40
Closed for rebuilding, 11/40
Reopened, 12/41
Achieved parent station status, 04/42
Satellite to North Weald, 07/43

CASTLE DONINGTON, Leics

LOCATION: 8m SE of Derby
OPENED: 01/43
CLOSED: 1946. Nottingham East Midlands Airport (2011)
ELEVATION: 290ft
PUNDIT CODE: CD
FORMATION: 92 (OTU) Grp Bomber Command
MAIN CONTRACTOR: Various
RUNWAYS: 3 concrete
HANGARS: T2 (1), B1 (1)
USER SQNS/UNITS:
28 OTU
31/01/43–15/10/44
Wellington I, III, X
Opened as satellite to Wymeswold, 01/43
To Transport Command, 10/44

CASTLETOWN, Caithness

LOCATION: 5½m E of Thurso
OPENED: 05/40
CLOSED: 1945. Disused/agriculture (2011)
ELEVATION: 90ft
PUNDIT CODE: AX
FORMATIONS: 13, 14 Grp Fighter Command
MAIN CONTRACTOR: Various
RUNWAYS: 3 asphalt
HANGARS: Bellman (1), T3 (1)
USER SQNS/UNITS:
1 (RCAF) Sqn
12/12/40–01/03/41
Hurricane I

ABOVE: The big freeze. Nearly all the aircraft on the strength of three Coastal Command squadrons can be seen here, drawn up out of the water at Castle Archdale in Northern Ireland when Lough Erne froze over in January 1945. More than 30 aircraft are visible, including Sunderlands of Nos 201 and 423 (Canadian) Squadrons, and No 202 Squadron's Catalinas. (IWM CH14837)

3 Sqn
03–14/09/40
13/10/40–07/01/41
10/02–03/04/41
Hurricane I
17 Sqn
05/04–16/06/41
Hurricane IIa, I
54 Sqn
17/11/41–02/02/42
Spitfire IIb
66 Sqn
08–14/05/44
Spitfire LFIXb
118 Sqn
19/10/43–20/01/44
Spitfire Vb
123 Sqn
22/09/41–11/04/42
Spitfire IIa, Vb
124 Sqn
10/05–17/11/41
Spitfire I, IIb, Va, Vb
131 Sqn
22/01–26/06/43
Spitfire Vb, Vc
132 Sqn
17/01–10/03/44
Spitfire Vb, VI
167 Sqn
01/06–14/10/42
Spitfire Vb
213 Sqn
18/02–11/05/41
Hurricane I
232 Sqn
18/09–13/10/40
Hurricane I
260 Sqn
22/11–05/12/40
07/01–10/02/41
Hurricane I
310 (Czech) Sqn
26/06–19/09/43
Spitfire VI
331 (Norwegian) Sqn
1/08–21/09/41
Hurricane IIb
504 (AAF) Sqn
21/06–02/09/40
10/03–30/04/44
Hurricane I; Spitfire IXb, Vb
607 (AAF) Sqn
27/07–20/08/41
Hurricane I, IIa, IIb
610 (AAF) Sqn
15/10/42–20/01/43
Spitfire Vb, Vc
Opened in Fighter Command as a satellite to Wick, 05/40

CATTERICK, Yorks

LOCATION: 4½m SE of Richmond
OPENED: 1914
CLOSED: 1994. Army base (2011)
ELEVATION: 175ft
PUNDIT CODE: AK
FORMATION: 13 Grp Fighter Command
MAIN CONTRACTOR: Various and John Laing & Son Ltd
RUNWAYS: 1 asphalt
HANGARS: Blister (8), C Type (2)
USER SQNS/UNITS:
17 Sqn
31/10–10/11/41
Hurricane IIb
41 Sqn
25/09/36–19/10/39
25/10/39–28/05/40
17/06–26/07/40
08/08–03/09/40
23/02–28/07/41
Demon; Fury II; Spitfire I, IIa
54 Sqn
28/05–04/06/40
28/07–08/08/40
03/09/40–23/02/41
Spitfire I
68 Sqn
07/01–23/04/41
Blenheim If
122 Sqn
31/08–06/10/41
Spitfire I, IIa
130 Sqn
18/09–10/11/43
Spitfire Vb
131 Sqn
10/07–06/08/41
Spitfire Ia
134 Sqn
07–30/12/41
Spitfire Va
145 Sqn
28/07/41–11/02/42
Spitfire IIb, Vb
219 Sqn
04/10/39–12/10/40
25/04–14/05/43
Blenheim If; Beaufighter If
222 Sqn
14–25/02/44
Spitfire LFIXb
256 Sqn
23/11/40–04/01/41
Defiant I
306 (Polish) Sqn
30/05–11/08/43
Spitfire Vb
313 (Czech) Sqn
10/05–01/07/41
Spitfire I
331 (Norwegian) Sqn
21/07–21/08/41
Hurricane I
332 (Norwegian) Sqn
15/01–19/06/42
Spitfire Va, Vb
401 (Canadian) Sqn
23/01–29/05/43
Spitfire Vb
403 (Canadian) Sqn
19/06–01/07/42
08/07/42–23/01/43
Spitfire Vb
504 (AAF) Sqn
02–06/09/40
Hurricane I
600 (AAF) Sqn
12/10/40–14/03/41
Beaufighter If
609 (AAF) Sqn
27/08–07/10/39
Spitfire I
Fighter Command Sector Station, 09/39

CHAILEY, Sussex

LOCATION: 9m NNW of Brighton
OPENED: 06/43
CLOSED: 01/45. Agriculture (2011)

ELEVATION: 105ft
PUNDIT CODE: AJ
FORMATIONS: 84 Grp 2 TAF; 11 Grp Fighter Command
MAIN CONTRACTOR: RAFACS
RUNWAYS: 2 steel matting
HANGARS: Blister (4)
USER SQNS/UNITS:
302 (Polish) Sqn
26/04–28/06/44
Spitfire IX, IXe
308 (Polish) Sqn
28/04–28/06/44
Spitfire IX
317 (Polish) Sqn
26/04–28/06/44
Spitfire IX
Advanced Landing Ground (ALG)
Not used for operational flying until 04/44

CHARMY DOWN, Somerset

LOCATION: 3½m N of Bath
OPENED: 11/40
CLOSED: 10/46. Agriculture (2011)
ELEVATION: 690ft
PUNDIT CODE: CH
FORMATIONS: 10 Grp Fighter Command; 23 Grp Flying Training Command
MAIN CONTRACTOR: Various
RUNWAYS: 3 Tarmac
HANGARS: Bellman (1), Blister (12)
USER SQNS/UNITS:
87 Sqn
18/12/40–07/08/41
27/01–02/11/42
Hurricane I, IIc
88 Sqn (det)
08/41–09/42
03–08/43
Boston III
107 Sqn (det)
08/42–08/43
Boston III
125 Sqn
07/08–24/09/41
Defiant I
137 Sqn
20/02–08/11/41
Whirlwind I
234 Sqn
23–30/08/42
Spitfire Vb
245 Sqn
26/10/42–29/01/43
Hurricane IIc
263 Sqn
07/08–19/12/41
23/12/41–28/01/42
Whirlwind I
417 (Canadian) Sqn
27/11/41–26/01/42
Spitfire IIa
421 Sqn
30/11–04/12/42
Spitfire Vb
1454 Flt > 533 Sqn
01/42 (08/09/42)–25/01/43
Havoc I, II (Turbinlite); Boston III (Turbinlite)
Fighter Leaders' School
02–08/43
Spitfire Vb
Opened in Fighter Command as satellite to Colerne, 11/40
To USAAF as Station AAF-487, 12/43
To 23 Grp RAF Flying Training Command, 10/44

CHARTER HALL, Berwickshire

LOCATION: 15m WSW of Berwick on Tweed
OPENED: 04/42
CLOSED: 03/46. Agriculture/light aviation (2011)
ELEVATION: 368ft
PUNDIT CODE: KH
FORMATIONS: 9, 81 (OTU) Grp Fighter Command
MAIN CONTRACTOR: James Miller & Partners Ltd
RUNWAYS: 2 Tarmac
HANGARS: Bellman (4), Blister (7)
USER SQNS/UNITS:
54 OTU
01/05/42–31/10/45
Blenheim I, IVf, V; Beaufort I; Beaufighter I, II, VI; Wellington XVIII;
Mosquito II, III, VI, XII, XIII, XVII, XIX, 30
Opened in Fighter Command as parent station, 04/42
To 9 Grp, 06/43

CHEDBURGH, Suffolk

LOCATION: 6m SW of Bury St Edmunds
OPENED: 07/09/42
CLOSED: 10/52. Agriculture/light industry (2011)
ELEVATION: 410ft
PUNDIT CODE: CU
FORMATIONS: 3, 7 (T) Grp Bomber Command
MAIN CONTRACTOR: John Laing & Son Ltd
RUNWAYS: 3 concrete
HANGARS: T2 (2), B1 (1)
USER SQNS/UNITS:
214 Sqn
01/10/42–10/12/43
Stirling I, III
218 Sqn
05/12/44–10/08/45
Lancaster I, III
620 Sqn
17/06–23/11/43
Stirling I, III
1653 HCU
21/11/43–12/44
Stirling I, III
Opened in Bomber Command as satellite to Stradishall, 09/42
Became 31 Base substation, 06/43

CHEDDINGTON, Bucks

LOCATION: 6¾m ENE of Aylesbury
OPENED: 03/42
CLOSED: 1952. Agriculture/light industry (2011)
ELEVATION: 304ft
PUNDIT CODE: CZ
FORMATIONS: 7 (T), 92 (OTU) Grp Bomber Command
MAIN CONTRACTOR: George Wimpey & Co Ltd
RUNWAYS: 3 concrete
HANGARS: T2 (4)
USER SQNS/UNITS:

26 OTU
15/03–03/09/42
Wellington I
Opened as temporary satellite to Wing, 03–09/42
To USAAF as Station AAF-113, 10/42

CHEDWORTH, Gloucs

LOCATION: 8m SE of Cheltenham
OPENED: 04/42
CLOSED: 05/45. Agriculture (2011)
ELEVATION: 826ft
PUNDIT CODE: YW
FORMATIONS: 9, 81 (OTU) Grp Fighter Command
MAIN CONTRACTOR: Various
RUNWAYS: 2 Tarmac
HANGARS: Blister (2)
USER SQNS/UNITS:
52 OTU > Fighter Command School of Tactics
08/42–02/43
Spitfire I, II
3 Tactical Exercise Unit (TEU)
17/07–18/12/44
Mustang; Typhoon Ib
55 OTU
18/12/44–29/05/45
Typhoon Ib
Satellite to Aston Down, 08/42
To Flying Training Command as satellite to South Cerney, 02/43
To Fighter Command as satellite to Honiley, 10/43
Satellite to Aston Down, 07/44

CHILBOLTON, Hants

LOCATION: 4m SE of Andover
OPENED: 09/40-01/41
CLOSED: 1961. Agriculture (2011)
ELEVATION: 290ft
PUNDIT CODE: CI
FORMATIONS: 9, 10 Grp Fighter Command
MAIN CONTRACTOR: Various
RUNWAYS: 3 concrete/Tarmac
HANGARS: Blister (3), T2 (2)
USER SQNS/UNITS:
174 Sqn
01–11/03/43
Hurricane IIb
184 Sqn
01–11/03/43
Hurricane IId
238 Sqn
30/09/40–00/01/41
01/02–01/04/41
16/04–20/05/41
Hurricane I, IIa
245 Sqn
01/09–17/11/41
Hurricane IIb
308 (Polish) Sqn
31/05–24/06/41
Spitfire IIa
504 (AAF) Sqn
11–26/08/41
Hurricane IIb
507 Sqn
25/06–05/08/41
Spitfire IIa
41 OTU
23/03–26/05/45
Hurricane; Spitfire; Master; Martinet
Opened in Fighter Command as RLG to Middle Wallop, 09/40
Achieved full satellite status, 04/42
To 70 (Training) Grp, 11/42
To 10 Grp Fighter Command, 06/43
To USAAF as Station AAF-404, 12/43
To RAF Fighter Command, 03/45

CHIPPING WARDEN, Oxon

LOCATION: 6m NE Banbury
OPENED: 08/41
CLOSED: 1953. Agriculture/light industry (2011)
ELEVATION: 457ft
PUNDIT CODE: CW
FORMATIONS: 6 (T), 92 (OTU) Grp Bomber Command
MAIN CONTRACTOR: Various
RUNWAYS: 3 concrete
HANGARS: T2 (4), J Type (1)
USER SQNS/UNITS:
12 OTU
07/41–14/06/45
Wellington III, X
Opened in Bomber Command as parent station, 08/41

CHIVENOR, Devon

LOCATION: 4½m W of Barnstaple
OPENED: 1940
CLOSED: 1995. Royal Marines base (2011)
ELEVATION: 16ft
FORMATIONS: 17, 19 Grp Coastal Command
RUNWAYS: 3 concrete
HANGARS: EO Blister (1), Bellman (4), Hinaidi (4)
USER SQNS/UNITS:
3 (C) OTU
01/10/40–07/41
Blenheim; Anson; Beaufort
5 (C) OTU
07/41–05/42
Blenheim; Anson; Beaufort
14 Sqn
24/10/44–25/05/45
Wellington XIV
51 Sqn (det)
06/05–27/10/42
Whitley V
59 Sqn
06/02–27/03/43
Fortress IIa
77 Sqn (det)
06/05/42–05/10/42
Whitley V
172 Sqn
04/04/42–01/09/44
Wellington GRVIII, XII, XIV
179 Sqn
06–21/09/44
23/10–01/11/44
Wellington XIV
235 Sqn
16/07/42–21/01/43
Beaufighter Ic, VIc
252 Sqn
01/12/40–06/04/41
Blenheim If, IVf; Beaufighter Ic
272 Sqn
03/04–28/05/41
Beaufighter Ic
404 (Canadian) Sqn
22/01–02/04/43
Beaufighter IIf
304 (Polish) Sqn
19/02–21/09/44
Wellington XIV

ABOVE: Mosquito NF Mk II, DD750, of No 25 Squadron, was returning to its base at Church Fenton after a cancelled Ranger operation on the evening of 22 March 1943 when it clipped the top of the escarpment at Windgate Nick in low cloud. The Mosquito crashed onto moorland near Silsden, West Yorkshire, killing the pilot Sgt John Staples, RAFVR, from Anglesey, and the navigator, Sgt Ralph Andrews, RAFVR, of Stoke-on-Trent. (Author)

407 (Canadian) Sqn
01/04–03/11/43
02/12/43–29/01/44
28/04–24/08/44
11/11/44–04/06/45
Wellington XII/XIV

547 Sqn
10/12/42–22/01/43
02/04–31/05/43
Wellington VIII

612 (AAF) Sqn
25/05–01/11/43
03/12/43–26/01/44
01/03–09/09/44
Whitley VII; Wellington VIII, XIII, XIV

CHRISTCHURCH, Hants

LOCATION: 1½m E of Christchurch
OPENED: 1935
CLOSED: 1967. Housing/light industry (2011)
ELEVATION: 20ft
PUNDIT CODE: XC
FORMATIONS: 10, 11 Grp Fighter Command
MAIN CONTRACTOR: Various
RUNWAYS: 5 grass/steel matting/concrete
HANGARS: Bellman (1), Bessonneau (1), Blister (3)
USER SQNS/UNITS: No units based
To 10 Grp Fighter Command as satellite to Hurn, 08/41
To 11 Grp as satellite to Ibsley, 11/44
To 46 Grp Transport Command, 03/45

CHURCH BROUGHTON, Derbys

LOCATION: 9m W of Derby
OPENED: 08/42
CLOSED: 06/45. Business park/light industry
ELEVATION: 225ft
PUNDIT CODE: CB
FORMATION: 93 (OTU) Grp Bomber Command
MAIN CONTRACTOR: Various
RUNWAYS: 3 concrete/Tarmac
HANGARS: T2 (1), B1 (1)
USER SQNS/UNITS:

27 OTU
08/42–22/06/45
Wellington III, X

93 Grp Instructors' Pool
04/43–06/45
Wellington III, X

1429 OTF
31/08/42–06/45
Wellington III, X

Opened in Bomber Command as satellite to Lichfield, 08/42

CHURCH FENTON, Yorks

LOCATION: 4m SE of Tadcaster
OPENED: 06/37
CLOSED: RAF base, non-flying/UAS flying (2011)
ELEVATION: 27ft
PUNDIT CODE: CF
FORMATIONS: 11, 12, 81 (OTU) Grp Fighter Command
MAIN CONTRACTOR: Various
RUNWAYS: 3 concrete/Tarmac
HANGARS: Bellman (1), Blister (10), C Type (2), T2 (1)
USER SQNS/UNITS:

25 Sqn
17/05/42–19/12/43
Beaufighter If; Mosquito II, VI

46 Sqn
28/02–01/03/41
Hurricane I
64 Sqn
24/08/39–01/05/40
Blenheim If; Spitfire I
68 Sqn
16/03–20/04/45
Mosquito XXX
71 Sqn
19/09–23/11/40
Buffalo I
72 Sqn
01/06/37–17/10/39
01/11–01/12/39
13/01–02/03/40
Gladiator I; Spitfire I
73 Sqn
18/06–05/09/40
Hurricane I
85 Sqn
05/09–23/10/40
Hurricane I
87 Sqn
24/05–05/07/40
96 Sqn
06/08–04/09/43
Beaufighter VIf
124 Sqn
18/03–23/04/44
Spitfire VII
125 Sqn
24/04–20/11/45
Mosquito XXX
183 Sqn
01/11/42–01/03/43
12–24/03/43
Hurricane I; Typhoon Ia, Ib
234 Sqn
22/05–18/06/40
26/06–08/07/43
31/12/43–28/01/44
Spitfire I, Vb
242 Sqn
30/10/39–21/05/40
Blenheim I; Battle; Hurricane I
249 Sqn
16–17/05/40
08/07–14/08/40
Hurricane I, II; Spitfire I
264 Sqn
18/12/43–07/05/44
Mosquito II, XII
306 (Polish) Sqn
29/08–07/11/40
Hurricane I
307 (Polish) Sqn
06/05/44–27/01/45
Mosquito XII
308 (Polish) Sqn
29/04–05/07/43
Spitfire Vb
456 (Australian) Sqn
31/12/44–16/03/45
Mosquito XVII, XXX
488 (New Zealand) Sqn
25/06–01/09/42
Beaufighter IIf
600 (AAF) Sqn
02/09–18/11/42
Beaufighter VIf
604 (AAF) Sqn
25/04–03/05/44
Mosquito XII, XIII
4 OTU > 54 OTU
16/12/40 (21/12/40)–01/05/42
Blenheim; Beaufighter; Defiant; Master; Havoc; Oxford
13 Grp Fighter Command station, 09/39
To 12 Grp, 08/40
To 81 (OTU) Grp, 12/40
To 12 Grp, 05/42

CLEAVE, Cornwall

LOCATION: 4½m N of Bude
OPENED: 05/39
CLOSED: 11/45. GCHQ satellite ground station (2011)
ELEVATION: 400ft
PUNDIT CODE: Not known
FORMATION: 10 Grp Fighter Command
MAIN CONTRACTOR: Various
RUNWAYS: 2 grass
HANGARS: Bellman (2), Blister (1)
USER SQNS/UNITS: No fighter units based
1 AACU
05/39–10/42
Henley; Wallace
639 Sqn
01/12/43–30/04/45
Henley; Hurricane
Opened in 22 Grp (Army Co-operation), 05/40
To 10 Grp Fighter Command, 06/43

COLEBY GRANGE, Lincs

LOCATION: 5m S of Lincoln
OPENED: 1940
CLOSED: 1963. Agriculture (2011)
ELEVATION: 200ft
PUNDIT CODE: CG
FORMATION: 12 Grp Fighter Command
MAIN CONTRACTOR: Various
RUNWAYS: grass
HANGARS: Blister (15), T1 (1)
USER SQNS/UNITS:
68 Sqn
05/02–01/03/44
Beaufighter VIf
264 Sqn
07/11–18/12/43
Mosquito II
307 (Polish) Sqn
02/03–06/05/44
Mosquito II, XII
409 (Canadian) Sqn
26/07/41–23/02/43
19/12/43–05/02/44
Defiant I; Beaufighter IIf, VIf
410 (Canadian) Sqn
21/02–20/10/43
Mosquito II, VI
Opened as RLG for Cranwell in Flying Training Command, 03/40
To 12 Grp Fighter Command as satellite to Digby, 05/41

COLERNE, Wilts

LOCATION: 6m NE of Bath
OPENED: 01/40
CLOSED: 1974. Army base (2011)
ELEVATION: 577ft
PUNDIT CODE: CQ
FORMATION: 10 Grp Fighter Command
MAIN CONTRACTOR: Various
RUNWAYS: 3 Tarmac
HANGARS: Blister (1), J Type (1), K Type (3), L Type (5), Robin (6)
USER SQNS/UNITS:

ABOVE: It is late in 1941 and Boulton Paul Defiant Mk I, N1801, Coimbatore II, of No 264 Squadron, is serviced on a dispersal at Colerne in Wiltshire. This aircraft was flown by the successful night fighting partnership of Flg Off F.D. Hughes (pilot) and Sgt F. Gash (gunner), and displays a tally of five enemy aircraft 'kills'. Converting to the Bristol Beaufighter, Hughes later increased his score with Nos 125 and 600 Squadrons and by the end of the war he had destroyed 18½ enemy aircraft. (IWM CH4810)

19 Sqn
23–31/07/42
Spitfire Vb

29 Sqn
22/02–11/05/45
Mosquito XXX

87 Sqn
28/11–18/12/40
07/08/41–27/01/42
Hurricane I, IIc

89 Sqn
25/09–19/11/41
Beaufighter If

118 Sqn
07–09/04/41
Spitfire IIa

125 Sqn
16/06–07/08/41
25/01–14/05/42
Defiant I, II; Beaufighter IIf

131 Sqn
10–22/02/44
29/02–24/03/44
Spitfire IX

137 Sqn
02/01–04/02/44
Typhoon Ib

151 Sqn
30/04–16/08/43
17/11/43–25/03/44
Mosquito II, XII, XIII

165 Sqn
10/02–01/03/44
07–10/03/44
Spitfire IXb

175 Sqn
08/04–29/05/44
Typhoon Ib

183 Sqn
24/03–08/04/43
30/05–05/06/43
Typhoon Ib

184 Sqn
01/12/42–01/03/43
Hurricane IId

256 Sqn
06/02–26/03/41
Defiant I

263 Sqn
28/01–10/02/42
15/08–13/09/42
Whirlwind I

264 Sqn
01/05/42–30/04/43
30/11–01/12/44
Defiant II; Mosquito II, XIII

307 (Polish) Sqn
26/03–26/04/41
Defiant I
316 (Polish) Sqn
18/06–02/08/41
Hurricane I, IIa, IIb
317 (Polish) Sqn
26–27/06/41
Hurricane I
402 (Canadian) Sqn
04–17/03/42
Hurricane IIb
406 (Canadian) Sqn
17/09–27/11/44
Mosquito XXX
410 (Canadian) Sqn
28/07–09/09/44
Mosquito XIII, XXX
417 (Canadian) Sqn
26/01–24/02/42
Spitfire IIa
456 (Australian) Sqn
17/08–17/11/43
Mosquito II, VI
488 (New Zealand) Sqn
03–12/05/44
29/07–09/10/44
Mosquito XIII
501 (AAF) Sqn
09/04–25/06/41
Spitfire I
504 (AAF) Sqn
28/03–10/08/45
Meteor III
1454 Flt
04/07/41–00/01/42
Havoc I (Turbinlite)
1457 Flt
15/09–00/11/41
Havoc I (Turbinlite)
600 (AAF) Sqn
27/04–18/06/41
27/06–06/10/41
Beaufighter If, IIf
604 (AAF) Sqn
13–25/07/44
28/07–06/08/44
Mosquito XIII
616 (AAF) Sqn
17/01–28/02/45
Meteor III

Became a 10 Grp Fighter Command Sector Station, 05/40

COLLYWESTON, Northants

LOCATION: 3m SW of Stamford
OPENED: 05/40
CLOSED: RAF base (2011)
ELEVATION: 282ft
PUNDIT CODE: WI
FORMATION: 12 Grp Fighter Command
MAIN CONTRACTOR: Various
RUNWAYS: 4 grass
HANGARS: Blister (4)
USER SQNS/UNITS:
23 Sqn
31/05–16/08/40
Blenheim If
133 Sqn
28/09–03/10/41
Hurricane IIb
152 Sqn
27–30/09/40
Spitfire I
266 Sqn
03–24/10/41
Spitfire Vb
349 (Belgian) Sqn
08–29/06/43
Spitfire Va
1426 Enemy Aircraft Flight
04/43–01/45
Junkers Ju88; Focke-Wulf Fw190; Messerschmitt Bf109; Messerschmitt Bf110; Heinkel He111; Henschel Hs129

Opened in Fighter Command as a satellite to Wittering, 05/40

To 21 Grp Flying Training Command, 04/45

COLTISHALL, Norfolk

LOCATION: 8m NE of Norwich
OPENED: 05/40
CLOSED: 2006. Disused (2011)
ELEVATION: 57ft
PUNDIT CODE: CS
FORMATION: 12 Grp Fighter Command
MAIN CONTRACTOR: Various
RUNWAYS: 3 steel matting
HANGARS: Blister (8), C Type (4)
USER SQNS/UNITS:
1 Sqn
08/04–14/05/45
Spitfire IXb
25 Sqn
05/02–27/10/44
Mosquito XVII, XXX
64 Sqn
15/10–11/11/40
25/09/43–21/01/44
02/02–29/04/44
Spitfire I, Vc
66 Sqn
29/05–03/09/40
Spitfire I
68 Sqn
08/03/42–05/02/44
28/10/44–08/02/45
27/02–16/03/45
Beaufighter If, VIf
72 Sqn
20–30/10/40
02–29/11/40
Spitfire I
74 Sqn
09/09–15/10/40
Spitfire I, IIa
80 Sqn
20–29/09/44
Tempest V
118 Sqn
17/01–15/08/43
Spitfire Vb
124 Sqn
10/02–07/04/45
Spitfire HFIXe
125 Sqn
18/10/44–24/04/45
Mosquito XVII, XXX
133 Sqn
31/07–15/08/41
Hurricane IIb
137 Sqn
08–31/11/41
Whirlwind I
152 Sqn
17/12/41–17/01/42
Spitfire IIa

ABOVE: This intriguing view was taken from inside a blister hangar at Collyweston in Northamptonshire on 22 February 1945. It shows aircraft of No 1426 (Enemy Aircraft) Flight undergoing servicing outside on a hardstanding. In the background, left, is Focke-Wulf Fw190A-5/U8 (c/n 2596), formerly of I/SKG10, serial PM679, which was used as a source of spares for one of No 1426 Flight's other Fw190s – A-4/U8, PN999. In the mid-background is an unidentified Fw190. At background, right, is Junkers Ju88S-1, TS472, a high-altitude bomber version that was captured intact at Villacoublay, near Paris, in September 1944. In the foreground is a Bf109, probably G-2/Trop (c/n 10639), RN228, formerly of JG53. (IWM CH15623)

154 Sqn
12/03–05/04/42
Spitfire IIa, IIb, Va, Vb

195 Sqn
21/08–24/09/43
Typhoon Ib

222 Sqn
11/11/40–06/06/41
Spitfire I, IIa, IIb

229 Sqn
01/07–25/09/44
02/12/44–10/01/45
Spitfire IX, LFXVIe

234 Sqn
28/01–18/03/44
Spitfire Vb

242 Sqn
18/06–26/10/40
30/11–16/12/40
Hurricane I

255 Sqn
20/09/41–02/03/42
Defiant I; Beaufighter IIf

257 Sqn
16/12/40–07/11/41
Hurricane I, IIb, IIc

274 Sqn
20–29/09/44
Tempest V

303 (Polish) Sqn
25/09/44–04/04/45
Spitfire LFVb, IXc, XVI

312 (Czech) Sqn
11/07–27/08/44
Spitfire HFIX

315 (Polish) Sqn
24/10–01/11/44
16/01–08/08/45
Mustang III

316 (Polish) Sqn
28/04–04/07/44
27/08–24/10/44
Mustang III

453 (Australian) Sqn
30/09–18/10/44
Spitfire IXb

602 (AAF) Sqn
30/09–18/10/44

19–23/02/45
05/04–15/05/45
Spitfire IXb, XVI

603 (AAF) Sqn
10/01–24/02/45
05–28/04/45
Spitfire LFXVIe

611 (AAF) Sqn
04/08–06/09/43
13/09–08/10/43
13/10–19/11/43
23/11/43–08/02/44
19/02–30/04/44
Spitfire LFVb

616 (AAF) Sqn
03–09/09/40
Spitfire I

Opened in Fighter Command as parent station, 05/40

CONINGSBY, Lincs

LOCATION: 7½m SSW of Horncastle
OPENED: 04/11/40
CLOSED: RAF (2011)
ELEVATION: 25ft
PUNDIT CODE: CY
FORMATIONS: 5, 8 (PFF) Grp Bomber Command
MAIN CONTRACTOR: Various
RUNWAYS: 3 concrete/asphalt
HANGARS: T2 (3), B1 (1), J Type (2)
USER SQNS/UNITS:

61 Sqn
12/01–15/04/44
Lancaster I, III

83 Sqn
18/04/44–05/11/46
Lancaster I, III; Lincoln 2

97 Sqn
10/03/41–02/03/42
18/04/44–12/11/46
Hampden; Manchester; Lancaster I, III

106 Sqn
23/02/41–01/10/42
Hampden; Manchester; Lancaster I

617 Sqn
30/08/43–10/01/44
Lancaster I, III

619 Sqn
09/01–17/04/44
Lancaster I, III

Opened in Bomber Command as parent station, 04/11/40
Became 54 Base HQ, 08/43

CONNEL, Argyllshire

LOCATION: 5m NE of Oban
OPENED: 1942
CLOSED: 1945. Private flying (2011)
ELEVATION: 18ft
FORMATION: 17 Grp Coastal Command
RUNWAYS: 2 Tarmac
HANGARS: T3 (2)
USER SQNS/UNITS: None based, but used as a landplane annexe to RAF Station Oban, and as an ELG

COOLHAM, Sussex

LOCATION: 6m SSW of Horsham
OPENED: 04/44
CLOSED: 01/45. Agriculture (2011)
ELEVATION: 55ft
PUNDIT CODE: XQ
FORMATION: 84 Grp 2 TAF

ABOVE: Hampden Mk I, P1316, 'P', of No 14 OTU at Cottesmore pictured in July 1940. Behind P1316 is Handley Page Hereford Mk I, L6063. This unit used both aircraft types for operational training. (IWM CH711)

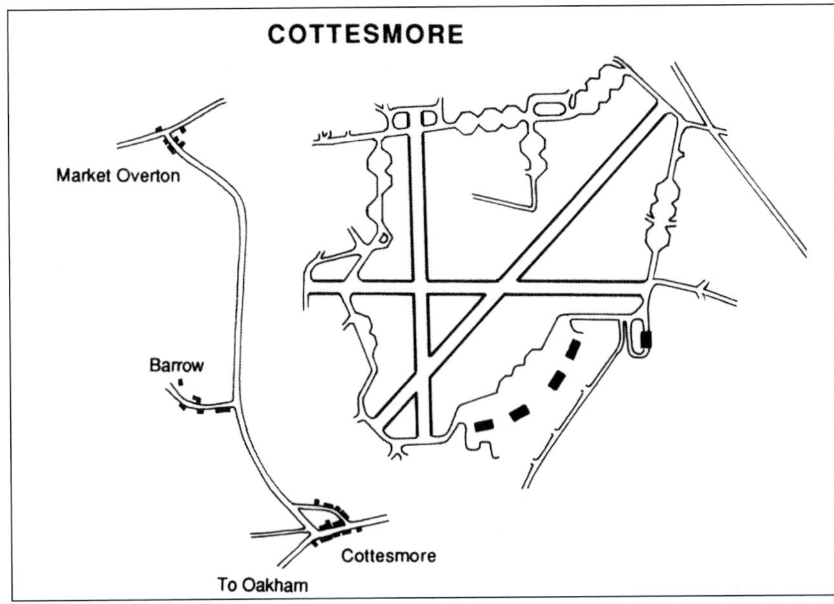

MAIN CONTRACTOR: RAF 5018 ACS
RUNWAYS: 2 steel matting
HANGARS: Blister (5)
USER SQNS/UNITS:
129 Sqn
03/04–22/06/44
Mustang III
222 Sqn
30/06–04/07/44
Spitfire LFIXb
306 (Polish) Sqn
01/04–22/06/44
Mustang III
315 (Polish) Sqn
01/04–22/06/44
Mustang III
349 (Belgian) Sqn
30/06–04/07/44
Spitfire LFIXe
485 (New Zealand) Sqn
30/06–03/07/44
Spitfire IXb, IXe
Advanced Landing Ground (ALG)

COTTESMORE, Rutland
LOCATION: 5½m NNE of Oakham
OPENED: 03/38
CLOSED: RAF (2011), scheduled for closure
ELEVATION: 460ft
PUNDIT CODE: CT
FORMATIONS: 5, 6 (T), 92 (OTU) Grp Bomber Command
MAIN CONTRACTOR: George Wimpey & Co Ltd
RUNWAYS: 3 Tarmac
HANGARS: C Type (4), T2 (1)
USER SQNS/UNITS:
106 Sqn
01/09–06/10/39
Hampden
185 Sqn
24/08/39–08/04/40
08/04–07/05/40
Hampden
14 OTU
08/04/40–01/08/43
Hampden; Hereford; Wellington I; Anson I
Opened in Bomber Command as parent station, 03/38
Closed for runway rebuilding, 08/43
To USAAF as Station AAF-489, 09/43

CRANAGE, Cheshire
LOCATION: 2¾m NNE of Middlewich
OPENED: 10/40
CLOSED: 06/45. Light industry/gas storage (2011)
ELEVATION: 165ft
PUNDIT CODE: RG
FORMATION: 9 Grp Fighter Command
MAIN CONTRACTOR: Various
RUNWAYS: 3 steel matting
HANGARS: Bellman (8), Blister (4)
USER SQNS/UNITS:
96 Sqn
16/12/40–21/10/41
Hurricane I, IIc; Defiant I
307 (Polish) Sqn (det)
1940–41
Defiant I
Opened in Flying Training Command, 10/40
To Fighter Command, 12/40
To Flying Training Command, 10/41

CRANFIELD, Beds
LOCATION: 8m SW of Bedford
OPENED: 06/37
CLOSED: 1952. Cranfield Airport/Cranfield University (2011)
ELEVATION: 340ft
PUNDIT CODE: CX
FORMATIONS: 9, 81 (OTU) Grp Fighter Command
MAIN CONTRACTOR: John Laing & Son Ltd
RUNWAYS: 3 concrete
HANGARS: Blister (9), C Type (4), T3 (1)
USER SQNS/UNITS:
35 Sqn
25/08–07/12/39
Battle
181 Sqn
01–08/03/43
Typhoon Ib
183 Sqn
01–08/03/43
Typhoon Ib
207 Sqn
24/08–09/12/39
05/04–19/04/40
Battle
51 OTU
17/08/41–14/06/45
Blenheim I, IV, V; Beaufighter I, II, VI; Hudson III; Havoc I, II; Beaufort I, II; Mosquito II, III, VI, XII; Wellington XVII, XVIII; Hurricane IIc, IV
Opened in Bomber Command as parent station, 06/37
To 81 (OTU) Grp Fighter Command, 05/41

ABOVE: Air crew from Nos 431 and 434 (Canadian) Squadrons are briefed by Sqn Ldr W.A. Bentley for a raid on Essen in 1944. The two senior officers seated in the foreground are Grp Capt R.S. Turnbull (Station Commander at RAF Croft, and formerly the CO of 427 (Canadian) Squadron) and Wg Cdr A.L. Blackburn, CO of 434 (Canadian) Squadron. (Public Archives of Canada DND/UK 16239)

CROFT, Yorks

LOCATION: 4½m S of Darlington
OPENED: 10/41
CLOSED: 1946. Car and superbike race circuit (2011)
ELEVATION: 182ft
PUNDIT CODE: CR
FORMATIONS: 4, 6 (RCAF) Grp Bomber Command
MAIN CONTRACTOR: Various
RUNWAYS: 3 Tarmac
HANGARS: T2 (2), B1 (1)
USER SQNS/UNITS:

419 (Canadian) Sqn
01/10–10/11/42
Wellington II

427 (Canadian) Sqn
07/11/42–05/05/43
Wellington III, X

431 (Canadian) Sqn
10/12/43–07/06/45
Halifax V, III; Lancaster X

434 (Canadian) Sqn
11/12/43–10/06/45
Halifax V, III; Lancaster I, III, X

1664 HCU
10/05–07/12/43
Halifax V; Lancaster I

Opened in Bomber Command as satellite to Middleton St George, 10/41

Became 64 (RCAF) Base substation, 03/43

CROSBY-ON-EDEN, Cumberland

LOCATION: 5m ENE Carlisle
OPENED: 02/41
CLOSED: 1947. Carlisle Airport (2011)
ELEVATION: 164ft
PUNDIT CODE: KX
FORMATIONS: 81 (OTU) Grp Fighter Command; 17 Grp Coastal Command; Transport Command
MAIN CONTRACTOR: Various
RUNWAYS: 3 Tarmac
HANGARS: Bellman (3), Blister (5), T2 (3)
USER SQNS/UNITS:

9 OTU
08/09/42–11/08/44
Beaufort; Beaufighter

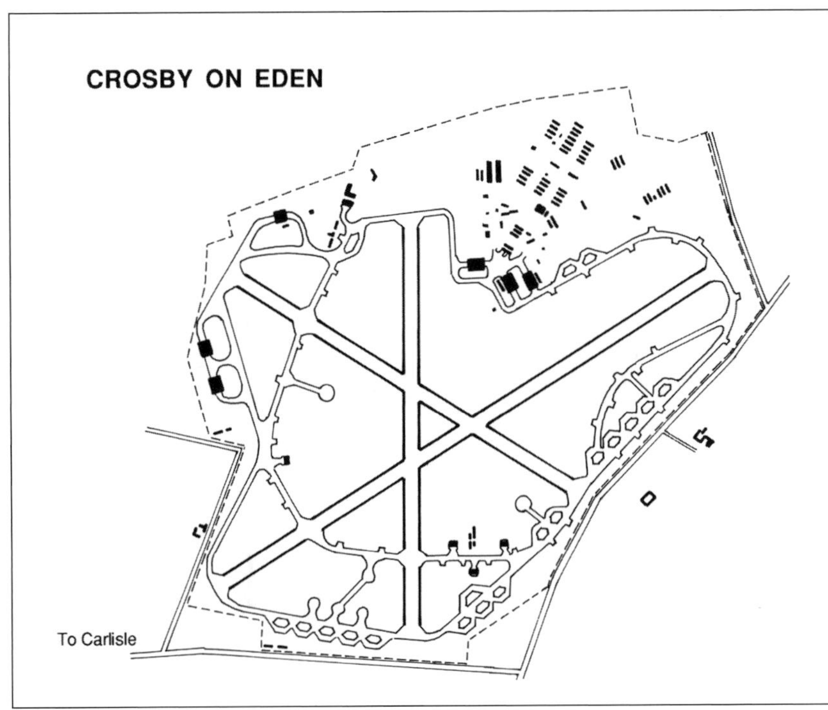

59 OTU
20/02/41–08/08/42
Hurricane I
109 OTU > 1383 TCU
08/44(01/08/45)–05/46
Dakota
Opened in Fighter Command, 02/41
To Coastal Command, 08/42
To Transport Command, 08/44

CROUGHTON, Northants

LOCATION: 3m SSW of Brackley
OPENED: 06/41
CLOSED: 05/46. USAF base, non-flying (2011)
ELEVATION: 450ft
PUNDIT CODE: AW
FORMATIONS: 7 (T), 92 (OTU) Grp Bomber Command
MAIN CONTRACTOR: Various
RUNWAYS: 3 grass
HANGARS: T2 (4)
USER SQNS/UNITS:
16 OTU
06/41–07/42
Hampden
Opened in Bomber Command as satellite to Upper Heyford, 06/41
To Flying Training Command, 07/42

CROYDON, Surrey

LOCATION: 2½m SW of Croydon
OPENED: 01/16
CLOSED: 1959. Housing/retail/parkland (2011)
ELEVATION: 217ft
PUNDIT CODE: CO
FORMATIONS: 11 Grp Fighter Command; Transport Command
MAIN CONTRACTOR: Various
RUNWAYS: 3 grass
HANGARS: Blister (4)
USER SQNS/UNITS:
1 Sqn
07/04–01/05/41
Hurricane I, IIa, IIb
1 (Canadian) Sqn
07–08/40
Hurricane I
3 Sqn
02–10/09/39
17/09–12/10/39
13/11/39–28/01/40
Hurricane I
17 Sqn
02–09/09/39
26/02–01/04/41
Hurricane I, IIa
72 Sqn
01–12/09/40
Spitfire I
85 Sqn
19/08–03/09/40
Hurricane I
92 Sqn
30/12/39–09/05/40
Blenheim If; Spitfire I
111 Sqn
04/06–19/08/40
03–08/09/40
Hurricane I
116 Sqn
12/12/42–02/07/44
Oxford; Anson
145 Sqn
10/10/39–09/05/40
Blenheim If147 Sqn
01/09/44–15/09/46
Dakota; Anson XII
271 Sqn (det)
04/45
Dakota
287 Sqn
19/11/41–03/07/44
Oxford; Hurricane I, IIb, IV
302 (Polish) Sqn
30/06–07/07/42
Spitfire Vb
317 (Polish) Sqn
30/06–07/07/42
Spitfire Vb
414 (Canadian) Sqn
12/08/41–05/12/42
Lysander III; Tomahawk I, II; Mustang I
501 (AAF) Sqn
21/06–04/07/40
Hurricane I
605 (AAF) Sqn
07/09/40–25/02/41
Hurricane I, IIa
607 (AAF) Sqn
14–15/11/39
22/05–04/06/40
Gladiator I; Hurricane I
615 (AAF) Sqn
02/09–15/11/39
Gladiator I, II
Satellite to Kenley in 11 Grp Fighter Command, 09/39
To Transport Command, 03/43

ABOVE: This Spitfire Mk VII, MD172, 'L', of No 131 Squadron, is pictured at Culmhead in the spring of 1944. (Alfred Price)

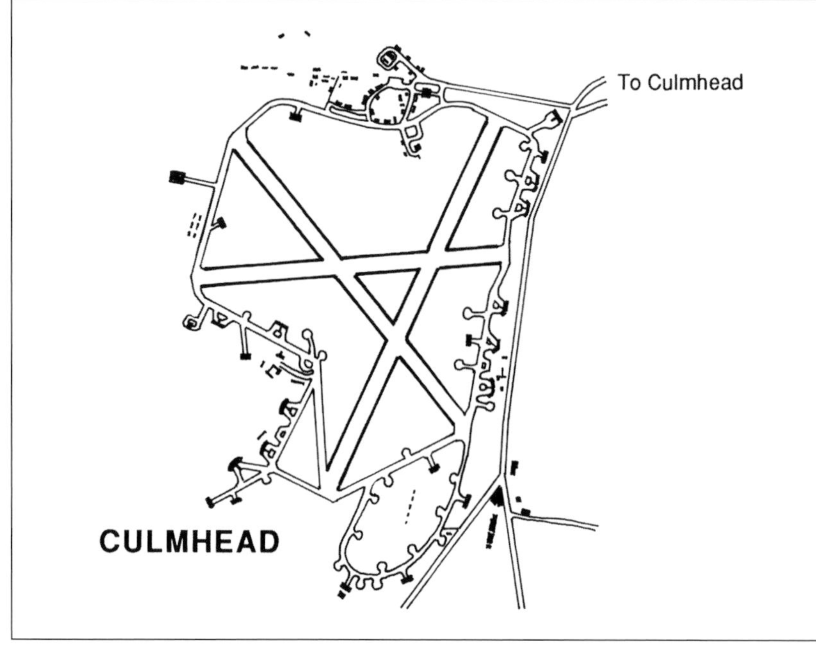

CULMHEAD (Church Stanton), Somerset

LOCATION: 6m S of Taunton
OPENED: 08/41
CLOSED: 08/46. Derelict/light industry (2011)
ELEVATION: 864ft
PUNDIT CODE: UC
FORMATIONS: 10 Grp Fighter Command
MAIN CONTRACTOR: Various
RUNWAYS: 3 asphalt
HANGARS: Blister (10), T2 (1)

USER SQNS/UNITS:

66 Sqn
28/06–10/08/43
Spitfire Vb, Vc

126 Sqn
22/05–03/07/44
Spitfire IXb

131 Sqn
17/09/43–10/02/44
Spitfire IX

154 Sqn
07/05–07/06/42
Spitfire Vb

165 Sqn
17/09/43–10/02/44
Spitfire IXb

302 (Polish) Sqn
07/08–05/09/41
Hurricane IIb

306 (Polish) Sqn
12/12/41–03/05/42
Spitfire Vb

312 (Czech) Sqn
10/10/42–20/02/43
14/03–24/06/43
Spitfire Vb, Vc

313 (Czech) Sqn
08/06/42–28/06/43
Spitfire Vb, Vc

316 (Polish) Sqn
02/08–13/12/41
Hurricane IIa, IIb; Spitfire IIa, Vb

504 (AAF) Sqn
30/06–14/08/43
Spitfire Vb, Vc

610 (AAF) Sqn
07–23/04/44
30/04–16/05/44
Spitfire XIV

ABOVE: Bristol Beaufighter TF Mk X, NE831, 'O', of No 144 Squadron, is photographed on its belly after crash-landing at Dallachy, Morayshire, returning from the costly attack on the German destroyer Z-33 and its escorting vessels in Førdefjord, Norway, on 9 February 1945. Thirty-one Beaufighters of the Dallachy Strike Wing were involved in the operation, of which nine were shot down by German fighters and anti-aircraft defences. Flt Sgt S. Butler (pilot) and Flt Sgt Nicholls (navigator) in NE831 were the last to attack the German vessels, during which they were hit by flak from Z-33, and then by fire from a Focke-Wulf Fw190 of 9/JG5. After manoeuvring violently, Butler managed to escape over the North Sea to make a successful wheels-up landing at Dallachy. (IWM CH17875)

616 (AAF) Sqn
16/05–21/07/44
Spitfire VII; Meteor I
Opened in Fighter Command as Church Stanton, 08/41
Renamed Culmhead, 12/43
To 23 Grp Flying Training Command, 12/44

DALLACHY, Morayshire

LOCATION: 9m E of Elgin
OPENED: 1943
CLOSED: 1945. Disused (2011)
ELEVATION: 250ft
FORMATION: 18 Grp Coastal Command
RUNWAYS: 2 concrete
HANGARS: T2 (2), Double Blister (5)
USER SQNS/UNITS:
144 Sqn
23/10/44–25/05/45
Beaufighter X
404 (Canadian) Sqn
22/10/44–03/04/45
Beaufighter X
455 (RAAF) Sqn
20/10/44–25/05/45
Beaufighter X
489 (RNZAF) Sqn
24/10/44–16/06/45
Beaufighter X
14 (P) AFU
05/43–31/08/44
Oxford
1542 BAT Flt
08/06/43–31/08/44
Oxford
Coastal Command satellite to Banff

DALTON, Yorks

LOCATION: 4m S of Thirsk
OPENED: 11/41
CLOSED: 12/45. Industrial estate (2011)
ELEVATION: 79ft
PUNDIT CODE: DA
FORMATIONS: 4, 6 (RCAF) Grp Bomber Command
MAIN CONTRACTOR: Various
RUNWAYS: 3 Tarmac
HANGARS: T2 (2), B1 (1)
USER SQNS/UNITS:
102 Sqn
15/11/41–07/06/42
Halifax II
420 (Canadian) Sqn
06/11–12/12/43
Halifax III
424 (Canadian) Sqn
3–16/05/43
Wellington III, X
428 (Canadian) Sqn
07/11/42–04/06/43
Wellington III, X
1652 HCU
13/07–31/08/42
Halifax I, II
1666 HCU
15/05–21/10/43
Halifax II
Opened in Bomber Command as satellite to Topcliffe, 11/41
Became 61 (RCAF) Base substation, 03/43
Became 76 Base substation, 11/44

ABOVE: The port underwing rocket rail installation can be clearly seen here on Beaufighter TF Mk X, NE355, 'H', of No 404 (Canadian) Squadron at Davidstow Moor. Armourers will plug the pigtail electrical leads dangling from each rocket projectile into their individual sockets in the wing to arm them before take-off. (Public Archives of Canada DND/UK PL-41048)

DARLEY MOOR, Derbys

LOCATION: 3m S of Ashbourne
OPENED: 07/42
CLOSED: 02/45. Motor racing/ microlight/paragliding (2011)
ELEVATION: 580ft
PUNDIT CODE: DM
FORMATION: 38 Grp Fighter Command
MAIN CONTRACTOR: Various
RUNWAYS: 3 concrete
HANGARS: None
USER SQNS/UNITS:

42 OTU
12/06/43–20/03/45
Blenheim IV; Whitley V; Albemarle I, II; Oxford II; Anson I; Martinet I; Lysander III

Opened in 38 Wing Army Co-operation Command as a satellite to Ashbourne, 07/42

To 38 Grp Fighter Command, 06/43

DAVIDSTOW MOOR, Cornwall

LOCATION: 11m W of Launceston
OPENED: 10/1942
CLOSED: 12/1945. Disused (2011)
ELEVATION: 969ft
FORMATION: 19 Grp Coastal Command
RUNWAYS: 3 concrete
HANGARS: T2 (3)
USER SQNS/UNITS:

53 Sqn
01/01–18/02/43
Hudson V

144 Sqn
10/05–01/07/44
Beaufighter X

269 Sqn
08/01–08/03/44
Hudson IIIa; Spitfire Vb; Walrus

304 (Polish) Sqn
07/06–13/12/43
Wellington XIII, XIV

404 (Canadian) Sqn
08/05–01/07/44
Beaufighter X

524 Sqn
07/04–01/07/44
Wellington XIII
612 (AAF) Sqn
18/04–25/05/43
Wellington XIII
Used by USAAF, 10–12/42
Used by RAF, 01–06/43
To C&M, 09/44
*Highest operational airfield in the UK

DEANLAND, Sussex

LOCATION: 5m E of Lewes
OPENED: 04/44
CLOSED: 01/45. Light aviation (2011)
ELEVATION: 60ft
PUNDIT CODE: XB
FORMATION: 84 Grp 2 TAF
MAIN CONTRACTOR: RAFACS/Royal Engineers Airfield Construction Group
RUNWAYS: 2 steel matting
HANGARS: Blister (4)
USER SQNS/UNITS:

ABOVE: Twenty-two-year-old Flt Sgt Dennis Sims of No 234 Squadron was killed on D-Day returning to Deanland from a beachhead patrol. His Spitfire Mk VB, AA936, may have been hit by flak from either enemy or Allied AA defences and disintegrated in mid-air, or plunged into the Channel. (W. Johnston)

ABOVE: On 12 August 1944, 24 rocket-armed Beaufighter TF Mk Xs of Nos 236 and 404 (Canadian) Squadrons operating from Davidstow Moor attacked the heavily-armed German Sperrbrecher 7 off Royan in the mouth of the Gironde, south-west France. The vessel was badly damaged by the Beaufighters but was finished off by three Royal Navy warships. (Crown Copyright)

64 Sqn
29/04–26/06/44
Spitfire Vc
91 Sqn
21/07–07/10/44
Spitfire XIV, IXb
234 Sqn
29/04–19/06/44
Spitfire Vb
302 (Polish) Sqn
01–12/04/44
14–26/04/44
Spitfire IX
308 (Polish) Sqn
01–28/04/44
Spitfire IX
317 (Polish) Sqn
01–26/04/44
Spitfire IX
322 (Dutch) Sqn
21/07–10/10/44
Spitfire XIV, LFIXe
345 (French) Sqn
16/08–10/10/44
Spitfire Vb, HFIX
611 (AAF) Sqn
30/04–24/06/44
Spitfire LFVb
Advanced Landing Ground (ALG)

DEBDEN, Essex

LOCATION: 3m SE of Saffron Walden
OPENED: 04/37
CLOSED: 1975. Army base (2011)
ELEVATION: 395ft
PUNDIT CODE: DB
FORMATION: 11 Grp Fighter Command
MAIN CONTRACTOR: W. & C. French Ltd
RUNWAYS: 2 concrete/Tarmac
HANGARS: Bellman (1), Blister (11), C Type (3)
USER SQNS/UNITS:
17 Sqn
09/09–16/12/39
24–30/12/39
08–13/01/40
20–30/01/40
11–22/02/40
27/02–05/03/40
12–23/03/40
27/03–05/04/40
13–23/04/40
30/04–07/05/40
22–25/05/40
19/06–19/08/40
02/09–09/10/40
Hurricane I
25 Sqn
08/10–27/12/40
Blenheim If; Beaufighter If
29 Sqn
22/11/37–04/04/40
10/05–27/06/40
Demon; Blenheim If
41 Sqn
08/07–01/08/42
Spitfire Vb
54 Sqn
11–13/06/41
Spitfire Va
65 Sqn
22/12/41–14/04/42
Spitfire Vb
71 Sqn
02/05–14/08/42
20/08–29/09/42
Spitfire Vb
85 Sqn
04/11/38–09/09/39
23/05–19/08/40
01/01–03/05/41
Hurricane I; Defiant I; Havoc I
87 Sqn
07/06/37–04/09/39
22–24/05/40
Gladiator I; Hurricane I
111 Sqn
19/08–03/09/40
01/11–15/12/41
22/12/41–30/06/42
07–28/07/42
Hurricane I; Spitfire Vb
121 Sqn
23–29/09/42
Spitfire Vb
124 Sqn
29/07–25/09/42
Spitfire VI
129 Sqn
01/11–22/12/41
Spitfire Vb
157 Sqn
15–18/12/41
No aircraft
257 Sqn
15/08–05/09/40
Hurricane I
258 Sqn
03/10–01/11/41
Hurricane IIa
264 Sqn
27/11–31/12/40
Defiant I
303 (Polish) Sqn
05–12/03/43
Spitfire Vb
350 (Belgian) Sqn
15/04–30/06/42
Spitfire Vb
403 (Canadian) Sqn
25/08–03/10/41
Spitfire IIa, Vb
418 (Canadian) Sqn
15/11/41–15/04/42
Boston III
504 (AAF) Sqn
09/10–24/12/39
30/12/39–08/01/40
13–20/01/40
30/01–11/02/40
22–27/02/40
05–12/03/40
18–27/03/40
04–13/04/40
23–30/04/40
07–12/05/40
21–22/05/40
Hurricane I
531 Sqn
02–09/10/42
Havoc I (Turbinlite); Boston III (Turbinlite)
601 (AAF) Sqn
19/08–02/09/40
Hurricane I
51 OTU
26/07–17/08/41
Blenheim; Beaufighter; Havoc; Hudson
52 OTU
01/02–15/08/41
Hurricane; Master; Battle

11 Grp Fighter Command Sector Station, 09/39
To USAAF as Station AAF-156, 09/42

DESBOROUGH, Northants

LOCATION: 6m NNW of Kettering
OPENED: 01/09/43
CLOSED: 1946. Agriculture (2011)
ELEVATION: 460ft
PUNDIT CODE: DS
FORMATION: 92 (OTU) Grp Bomber Command
MAIN CONTRACTOR: Various
RUNWAYS: 3 Tarmac
HANGARS: T2 (4), B1 (1)
USER SQNS/UNITS:

84 OTU
15/09/43–14/06/45
Wellington III, X

Opened in Bomber Command as parent station, 09/43

DETLING, Kent

LOCATION: 3½m NE of Maidstone
OPENED: 09/38
CLOSED: 10/59. Kent Showground/light industry/agriculture (2011)
ELEVATION: 530ft
PUNDIT CODE: DQ
FORMATIONS: 11 Grp Fighter Command; 83 Grp 2 TAF
MAIN CONTRACTOR: Various
RUNWAYS: 3 grass
HANGARS: Bellman (1), Bessonneau (1), Blister (14)
USER SQNS/UNITS:

1 Sqn
22/06–11/07/44
10/08–18/12/44
Spitfire IXb

26 (South African) Sqn
21/06/43–28/04/44
Mustang I; Spitfire Vb

80 Sqn
19/05–22/06/44
Spitfire IX

118 Sqn
20–23/01/44
05/02–10/03/44
12/07–09/08/44
Spitfire IXc, Vb, VII, IXc

124 Sqn
26/07–09/08/44
Spitfire HFIXe

132 Sqn
12/10/43–17/01/44
10–13/03/44
19/03–18/04/44
Spitfire IXb

165 Sqn
22/06–12/07/44
10/08–15/12/44
Spitfire IXb

184 Sqn
12/10/43–06/03/44
Hurricane IV

229 Sqn
19/05–22/06/44
Spitfire IX

274 Sqn
19/05–22/06/44
Spitfire IX

453 (Australian) Sqn
19–21/01/44
04/02–13/03/44
19/03–18/04/44
Spitfire IXb

504 (AAF) Sqn
12/07–13/08/44
Spitfire IXe

602 (AAF) Sqn
12/10/43–17/01/44
12–13/03/44
20/03–18/04/44
Spitfire IXb, LFVb

Opened in 6 Grp Bomber Command, 09/38
To 16 Grp Coastal Command, 11/38
To Army Co-operation Command, 01/43
To 11 Grp Fighter Command, 06/43
To 83 Grp, 2 TAF, 11/43
To ADGB, 05/44
To C&M, 01/45

DIGBY, Lincs

LOCATION: 10m SSE of Lincoln
OPENED: 03/18
CLOSED: RAF base, non-flying (2011)
ELEVATION: 67ft
PUNDIT CODE: DJ
FORMATION: 12 Grp Fighter Command
MAIN CONTRACTOR: Various
RUNWAYS: 3 grass
HANGARS: Blister (10), C Type (2)
USER SQNS/UNITS:

19 Sqn
17/05–04/06/43
Spitfire Vb

29 Sqn
27/06–27/07/40
Blenheim If

46 Sqn
15/11/37–10/12/39
17/01–09/05/40
13/06–01/09/40
14/12/40–28/02/41
Gauntlet II; Hurricane I

56 Sqn
31/05–05/06/40
Hurricane I

73 Sqn
09/11/37–09/09/39
Gladiator I; Hurricane I

79 Sqn
27/05–05/06/40
Hurricane I

92 Sqn
20/10/41–12/02/42
Spitfire Vb

111 Sqn
21–30/05/40
Hurricane I

151 Sqn
01/09–28/11/40
Hurricane I

167 Sqn
13–18/05/43
Spitfire Vb,Vc

198 Sqn
07/12/42–23/01/43
Typhoon Ia, Ib

222 Sqn
10–23/05/40
Spitfire I

229 Sqn
04/10/39–26/06/40
Blenheim If; Hurricane I

242 Sqn
01/09–30/10/42
Spitfire Vb

310 (Czech) Sqn
11/07–28/08/44
Spitfire Vb
349 (Belgian) Sqn
16–25/08/43
Spitfire Va
350 (Belgian) Sqn
25/08–07/09/43
19/09–01/10/43
Spitfire Vb
1 (RCAF) Sqn > 401 (Canadian) Sqn
22/02(01/03/41)–20/10/41
Hurricane I, IIa; Spitfire IIa
2 (RCAF) Sqn > 402 (Canadian) Sqn
11/12/40 (01/03/41)–23/06/41
21/03–07/08/43
19/09–19/12/43
02/01–12/02/44
Hurricane I, IIa, IIb; Spitfire Vb, Vc
409 (Canadian) Sqn
16/06–26/07/41
Defiant I
411 (Canadian) Sqn
16/06–19/11/41
30/03–05/06/42
07/06–05/08/42
08/08/42–01/03/43
12–22/03/43
Spitfire I, IIa, Vb
412 (Canadian) Sqn
30/06–20/10/41
Spitfire IIa
416 (Canadian) Sqn
07/06–09/08/43
02/10/43–12/02/44
Spitfire Vb, Vc, IXb
421 (Canadian) Sqn
06/04–03/05/42
Spitfire Va
438 (Canadian) Sqn
10/11–19/12/43
Hurricane IV
441 (Canadian) Sqn
08/02–18/03/44
Spitfire Vb
442 (Canadian) Sqn
08/02–18/03/44
Spitfire Vb
443 (Canadian) Sqn
08/02–18/03/44
Spitfire Vb
504 (AAF) Sqn
27/08–09/10/39
30/04–11/07/44
Gauntlet II; Hurricane I; Spitfire Vb
601 (AAF) Sqn
25/03–10/04/42
Spitfire Vb
609 (AAF) Sqn
19/11/41–30/03/42
Spitfire Vb
611 (AAF) Sqn
10/10/39–13/12/40
Spitfire I, IIa
Fighter Command Sector Station, 09/39

DISHFORTH, Yorks

OPENED: 09/36
CLOSED: Army Air Corps base (2011)
ELEVATION: 117ft
PUNDIT CODE: DH
MAIN CONTRACTOR: Various
FORMATIONS: 4, 6 (RCAF) Grp Bomber Command
RUNWAYS: 3 concrete/Tarmac
HANGARS: C Type (5)

BELOW: Spitfire Mk IIAs of No 411 (Canadian) Squadron at Digby in October 1941. In the foreground WAAF mechanics help the pilot to strap in to DB-R, Venture I. Note the semi-completed C-Type Hangar (centre background) and double blast pen (centre right). (Public Archives of Canada PL-4918)

ABOVE: These Handley Page Halifax Mk IIIs of No 426 (Canadian) Squadron are parked inside and beyond No 2 Hangar at Dishforth, Yorkshire, during March 1945. An Airspeed Oxford of No 1664 Conversion Unit is also visible in the hangar at right. (IWM HU56271)

USER SQNS/UNITS:

10 Sqn
25/01/37–08/07/40
Heyford; Whitley I

51 Sqn
09/12/39–06/05/42
Whitley II, III, IV

78 Sqn
01/02/37–13/12/39
16/07/40–07/04/41
Heyford III; Whitley I, IVa

425 (Canadian) Sqn
25/06/42–16/05/43
06/11–09/12/43
Wellington III, X; Halifax III

426 (Canadian) Sqn
15/10/42–17/06/43
Wellington III, X

Opened in Bomber Command as parent station, 09/36
Became 61 Base substation, 01/43
Became 76 Base substation, 11/44

DOCKING, Norfolk

LOCATION: 10m NW of Fakenham
OPENED: 1940
CLOSED: 1958. Disused (2011)
ELEVATION: 210ft
FORMATION: 16 Grp Coastal Command
RUNWAYS: 3 grass
HANGARS: Blister (8), A1 (1)
USER SQNS/UNITS:

53 Sqn
18/02–18/03/43
Whitley VII

221 Sqn
25/12/41–08/01/42
Wellington VIII

235 Sqn
31/05–16/07/42
Beaufighter Ic

288 Sqn (det)
01–3/44
Hurricane I, Spitfire Vb, IX

304 (Polish) Sqn
02/04–07/06/43
Wellington X

415 (Canadian) Sqn (det)
15/11/43–26/07/44
Wellington XIII

521 Sqn
01/09/43–01/11/44
Ventura V, Hudson III, VI, Hampden, Gladiator II, Spitfire IX, Hurricane IIc,

524 Sqn
01–23/07/44
Wellington XIII

855 NAS
09/44–10/44
Avenger I

1401 Met Flt
01–07/42
04–09/43
Gladiator; Blenheim; Hudson; Spitfire; Hampden

1525 BAT Flt
07/42–05/45
1693 ASR Training Unit
06–07/45
Warwick Training Unit
25/06–03/07/43
Warwick I
Opened in Coastal Command as satellite to Bircham Newton

DONCASTER, Yorks

LOCATION: 1¼m SE of Doncaster
OPENED: 01/16
CLOSED: 1992. Retail/leisure/museum (2011)
ELEVATION: 25ft
FORMATION: 93 Grp Bomber Command
MAIN CONTRACTOR: Various
RUNWAYS: 2 grass, 1 metal sheeting
HANGARS: Bellman (3)
USER SQNS/UNITS:
18 OTU
06/43–01/45
Wellington III, X
Used as Bomber Command satellite to Finningley, 06/43

DONNA NOOK, Lincs

LOCATION: 12½m SE of Grimsby
OPENED: 1940
CLOSED: 1945. Agriculture (2011)
ELEVATION: 13ft
FORMATION: 16 Grp Coastal Command
RUNWAYS: 2 grass
HANGARS: T2 (1), Blister (2)
USER SQNS/UNITS: No squadrons based
Coastal Command satellite and RLG to North Coates

DOWNHAM MARKET, Norfolk

LOCATION: 10m S of King's Lynn
OPENED: 07/42
CLOSED: 24/10/46. Agriculture/ industrial estate (2011)
ELEVATION: 117ft
PUNDIT CODE: DO
FORMATIONS: 3, 8 (PFF) Grp Bomber Command
MAIN CONTRACTOR: W. & C. French Ltd
RUNWAYS: 3 concrete
HANGARS: T2 (2), B1 (1)
USER SQNS/UNITS:
214 Sqn
01/12/43–17/01/44
Stirling III
218 Sqn
10/07/42–07/03/44
Stirling I, III
571 Sqn (LNSF)
07–24/04/44
Mosquito XVI
608 Sqn
01/08/44–24/08/45
Mosquito XVI, XX, XXV
623 Sqn
10/08–06/12/43
Stirling III

BELOW: An engine failure on take-off for its 14th op on 7 May 1943 caused No 218 Squadron's Stirling Mk I, EF353, to swing and then plough into the station Ops block at Downham Market, overturning the station commander's car. (J. McIlhinney)

635 Sqn
20/03/44–01/09/45
Lancaster III, VI
Opened in Bomber Command as satellite to Marham, 07/42
Raised to parent station status, 03/44
*Flt Sgt A.A. Aaron DFM, 218 Sqn, awarded posthumous VC, Turin, 12–13/08/43
*Sqn Ldr I.W. Bazalgette DFC, 635 Sqn, awarded posthumous VC, Trossy St Maxim, 04/08/44

DREM, East Lothian

LOCATION: 4m NNW of Haddington
OPENED: 1917
CLOSED: 03/46. Agriculture (2011)
ELEVATION: 36ft
PUNDIT CODE: DE
FORMATION: 13 Grp Fighter Command
MAIN CONTRACTOR: Various
RUNWAYS: 3 grass
HANGARS: Bellman (3), Blister (14)
USER SQNS/UNITS:

29 Sqn
04/04–10/05/40
01/03–01/05/44
Blenheim If; Mosquito XII, XIII

43 Sqn
12/12/40–22/02/41
01/03–04/10/41
Hurricane I, IIa, IIb

64 Sqn
17/05–06/08/41
04/10–16/11/41
Spitfire IIa

65 Sqn
26/09–02/10/42
11/10/42–03/01/43
10/01–29/03/43
Spitfire Vb

72 Sqn
01/12/39–12/01/40
Spitfire I, Vb, Vc

91 Sqn
17/03–23/04/44
Spitfire XIV

96 Sqn
04/09–08/11/43
Beaufighter VIf; Mosquito XIII

111 Sqn
07/12/39–27/02/40
08/09–12/10/40
Hurricane I

123 Sqn
06/08–22/09/41
Spitfire I, IIa

124 Sqn
29/12/42–21/01/43
Spitfire VI

130 Sqn
30/03–30/04/43
Spitfire Vb

137 Sqn
02–11/08/42
Whirlwind I

141 Sqn
15–22/10/40
Defiant I

145 Sqn
14–31/08/40
Hurricane I

186 Sqn
27/04–03/08/43
No aircraft

197 Sqn
25/11/42–28/03/43
Typhoon Ia, Ib

222 Sqn
10–15/08/42
21/08–22/10/42
Spitfire Vb

232 Sqn
24/10–11/11/40
Hurricane I

242 Sqn
01/06–11/08/42
Spitfire Vb

245 Sqn
12/05–05/06/40
Hurricane I

258 Sqn
04–17/12/40
Hurricane I

260 Sqn
16/04–19/05/41
Hurricane I

263 Sqn
10–28/06/40
02/09–28/11/40
Hurricane I; Whirlwind I

307 (Polish) Sqn
09/11/43–02/03/44
Mosquito II, XII

340 (French) Sqn
20/12/41–01/01/42
30/04–09/11/43
17/12/44–30/01/45
Spitfire IIa, Vb, IXb

410 (Canadian) Sqn
06/08/41–15/06/42
Defiant I; Beaufighter IIf

453 (Australian) Sqn
09/06–25/09/42
Spitfire Vb

488 (New Zealand) Sqn
03/08–03/09/43
Beaufighter VIf; Mosquito XII

600 (AAF) Sqn
14/03–27/04/41
Beaufighter If

602 (AAF) Sqn
13/10/39–14/04/40
22/05–13/08/40
Spitfire I

603 (AAF) Sqn
14/04–05/05/40
13/12/40–27/02/41
07/05–14/06/45
Spitfire I, IIa, LFXVIe

605 (AAF) Sqn
28/05–07/09/40
Hurricane I

607 (AAF) Sqn
08/11–12/12/40
02/03–16/04/41
Hurricane I

609 (AAF) Sqn
17/10–05/12/39
10/01–20/05/40
Spitfire I

611 (AAF) Sqn
12/11/41–03/06/42
Spitfire IIa, IIb, Vb
Reopened in Flying Training Command, 1939
To 13 Grp Fighter Command, 10/39
To RN as HMS *Nighthawk*, 04/45

ABOVE: Merlin-engine Wellington Mk IIs of No 104 Squadron in 1941. W5461, 'R', in the foreground failed to return to Driffield from ops on Berlin on 12/13 August. The six-man crew, skippered by Sqn Ldr H. Budden DFC, survived to become PoWs. (Author)

DRIFFIELD, Yorks

LOCATION: 2m WSW of Great Driffield
OPENED: 30/07/36
CLOSED: 1996. Agriculture/disused (2011)
ELEVATION: 63ft
PUNDIT CODE: DR
FORMATIONS: 2, 4, 6 (RCAF) Grp Bomber Command
MAIN CONTRACTOR: Various
RUNWAYS: 3 concrete
HANGARS: C Type (5)
USER SQNS/UNITS:

77 Sqn
25/07/38–28/08/40
Wellesley; Whitley III, V

88 Sqn
14–23/06/40
Battle

97 Sqn
30/04–20/05/40
Whitley

102 Sqn
11/07/38–25/08/40
Heyford II, III; Whitley III, V

104 Sqn
07/04/41–14/02/42
Blenheim IV; Wellington II

158 Sqn
14/02–06/06/42
Wellington II

196 Sqn
07/11–22/12/42
Wellington III

405 (Canadian) Sqn
23/04–20/06/41
Wellington II

462 (Australian) Sqn
12/08–22/12/44
Halifax III

466 (Australian) Sqn
15/10–22/12/42
03/06/44–06/09/45
Wellington II, X; Halifax II, III, VI

Opened in Bomber Command as parent station, 30/07/36
Became 43 Base HQ, 06/06/43

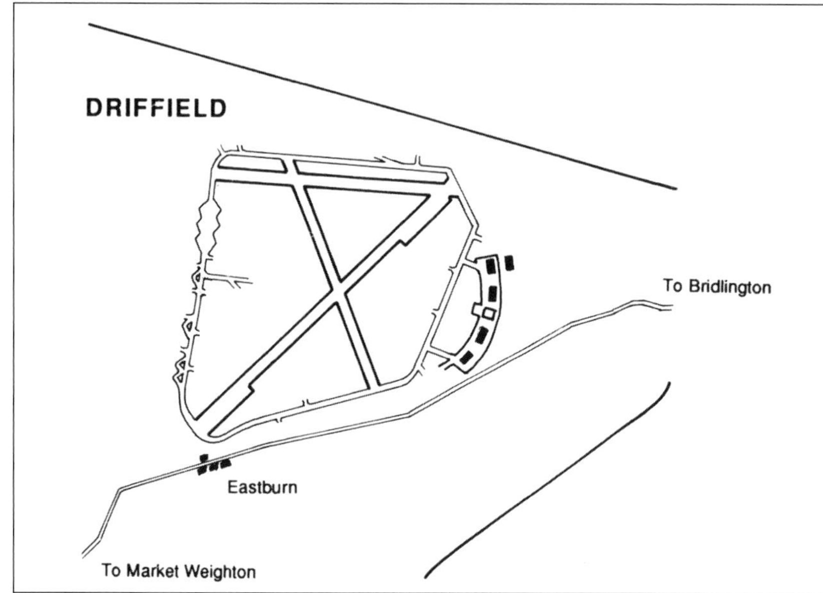

DUNHOLME LODGE, Lincs

LOCATION: 5m NE of Lincoln
OPENED: 05/43
CLOSED: 1964. Agriculture/industry (2011)
ELEVATION: 100ft
PUNDIT CODE: DL
FORMATIONS: 1, 5 Grp Bomber Command

MAIN CONTRACTOR: Various
RUNWAYS: 3 concrete/Tarmac
HANGARS: T2 (2), B1 (1)
USER SQNS/UNITS:
44 Sqn
31/05/43–30/09/44
Lancaster I, III
170 Sqn
22/10–29/11/44
Lancaster I, III
619 Sqn
17/04–28/09/44
Lancaster I, III
Opened in Bomber Command as parent station, 05/43
Closed, 11/44

DUNKESWELL, Devon

LOCATION: 5m NNW of Honiton
OPENED: 1943
CLOSED: 1945. Light aviation (2011)
ELEVATION: 839ft
FORMATIONS: 10 Grp Fighter Command; 19 Grp Coastal Command
Contractor: George Wimpey & Co Ltd
RUNWAYS: 3 concrete/Tarmac
HANGARS: T2 (5)
USER SQNS/UNITS: No RAF sqns based
Opened in RAF Fighter Command
To Coastal Command, 05/42
To USAAF as Station AAF-173, 08/43
To US Navy as Navy Station 804, 09/43

DUNSFOLD, Surrey

LOCATION: 8½m SSE of Guildford
OPENED: 12/42
CLOSED: Private airfield/BBC 'Top Gear' test track/industry (2011)
ELEVATION: 168ft
PUNDIT CODE: DT
FORMATIONS: 11 Grp Fighter Command; 2 Grp 2 TAF; ADGB
MAIN CONTRACTOR: Royal Canadian Engineers
RUNWAYS: 3 concrete
HANGARS: Blister (11), T2 (2)
USER SQNS/UNITS:
98 Sqn
18/08/43–18/10/44
Mitchell II, III
180 Sqn
18/08/43–12/04/44
26/04–18/10/44
Mitchell II
Satellite to Odiham, 01/45

DUXFORD, Cambs

LOCATION: 8m S of Cambridge
OPENED: 1919
CLOSED: 07/61. Imperial War Museum/general aviation (2011)
ELEVATION: 97ft
PUNDIT CODE: DX
FORMATION: 12 Grp Fighter Command
MAIN CONTRACTOR: Various

ABOVE: Lancaster Mk I, R5729, 'A', of No 44 Squadron, awaits the arrival of its crew at Dunholme Lodge before setting out for a raid on Berlin on 2 January 1944. Bomber Command lost 27 aircraft that night. R5729 and her crew skippered by Plt Off L. Curatolo, RCAF, were shot down by a night fighter on ops to Brunswick on 14/15 January. All the crew were killed. (IWM CH11929)

RUNWAYS: 3 grass
HANGARS: Belfast (4), Blister (8)
USER SQNS/UNITS:
19 Sqn
16–25/05/40
05–25/06/40
03–24/07/40
01/11/40–06/02/41
Spitfire I, Ib, IIa
56 Sqn
26/06/41–30/03/42
Hurricane IIb; Typhoon Ia
66 Sqn
20/07/36–16/05/40
Gauntlet II; Spitfire I
133 Sqn
15/08–28/09/41
Hurricane IIb
181 Sqn
25/08–10/12/42
Hurricane I; Typhoon Ia, Ib
195 Sqn
15–19/11/42
Typhoon Ib
222 Sqn
04/10/39–10/05/40
Blenheim If; Spitfire I
242 Sqn
26/10–30/11/40
Hurricane I
264 Sqn
10/05–03/07/40
Defiant I
266 Sqn
29/01–02/08/42
11/08–21/09/42
Spitfire Vb; Typhoon Ia, Ib
310 (Czech) Sqn
10/07/40–26/06/41
Hurricane I, IIa
312 (Czech) Sqn
29/08–26/09/40
Hurricane I
601 (AAF) Sqn
16/08/41–06/01/42
Hurricane IIb; Airacobra I
609 (AAF) Sqn
30/03–26/08/42
30/08–18/09/42
Spitfire Vb; Typhoon Ia, Ib
611 (AAF) Sqn
13/08–10/10/39
Spitfire I
1426 Enemy Aircraft Flight
Junkers 88; Messerschmitt Bf109; Messerschmitt Bf110; Heinkel He111
21/11/41–04/43
AFDU
12/40–03/43
Spitfire; Hurricane; Various
Fighter Command Sector Station, 09/39
To USAAF as Station AAF-357, 04/43

DYCE, Aberdeenshire

LOCATION: 5m N of Aberdeen
OPENED: 07/34
CLOSED: Aberdeen Airport (2011)
ELEVATION: 215ft
PUNDIT CODE: DY
FORMATIONS: 18 Grp Coastal Command; 13 Grp Fighter Command
MAIN CONTRACTOR: Various
RUNWAYS: 3 concrete/Tarmac
HANGARS: Bellman (4), Blister (12), T3 (2)
USER SQNS/UNITS:
111 Sqn
12/10/40–20/07/41
Hurricane I; Spitfire I, IIa
129 Sqn
26/05–10/06/45
Mustang III; Spitfire IXe
141 Sqn
22–30/08/40
Defiant I
145 Sqn

BELOW: Hurricane Mk I, V7462, 'T', of No 111 Squadron, is seen in flight near Dyce on 30 November 1940. (111 Sqn records via Andy Thomas)

31/08–09/10/40
Hurricane I
165 Sqn
29/03–30/06/43 (det)
29/05–15/06/45
Spitfire IXb/IXe; Mustang III
310 (Czech) Sqn
20/07–24/12/41
Hurricane IIa, IIb; Spitfire IIa, Vb
331 (Norwegian) Sqn
22/04–22/05/45
Spitfire IXe
332 (Norwegian) Sqn
22/04–22/05/45
Spitfire IXe
404 (Canadian) Sqn
24/09/42–22/01/43
Blenheim IVf; Beaufighter IIf
416 (Canadian) Sqn
14/03–03/04/42
Spitfire Vb
540 Sqn (det)
11/44
Mosquito VI, XVI, XXXII
602 (AAF) Sqn
14/04–22/05/40
Spitfire I
603 (AAF) Sqn
17/01–14/04/40
15/12/41–14/03/42
Spitfire I, Vb
8 OTU
01/03/43–12/01/45
Mosquito; Spitfire; Master; Anson
Opened in Coastal Command, 10/39
To Fighter Command, 01/40
To Coastal Command, 07/42

EARLS COLNE, Essex

LOCATION: 5m ENE of Braintree
OPENED: 08/42
CLOSED: 03/46. Golf course/light industry/light aviation (2011)
ELEVATION: 227ft
PUNDIT CODE: EC
FORMATION: 38 Grp Fighter Command
MAIN CONTRACTOR: US Army
RUNWAYS: 3 concrete/Tarmac
HANGARS: T2 (2)
USER SQNS/UNITS:
296 Sqn
29/09/44–23/01/46
Albemarle II, V, VI; Halifax V, III, VII
297 Sqn
30/09/44–01/04/46
Albemarle II, V, VI; Halifax V, III, VII
Opened in Bomber Command, 08/42
To USAAF as Station AAF-358, 05/43
To 38 Grp RAF Fighter Command, 09/44

EAST FORTUNE, East Lothian

LOCATION: 4m NNE of Haddington
OPENED: 1916
CLOSED: 1961. National Museum of Flight/motorcycle race track (2011)
ELEVATION: 97ft
PUNDIT CODE: EF
FORMATIONS: 81 (OTU) Grp Fighter Command; 17 Grp Coastal Command
MAIN CONTRACTOR: Various
RUNWAYS: 3 Tarmac
HANGARS: Blister (8), Callender-Hamilton (3), T2 (1)
USER SQNS/UNITS:
60 OTU > 132 OTU
04/06/41 > 24/11/42–15/05/46
Defiant; Blenheim; Oxford; Master; Beaufighter; Beaufort; Mosquito II/VI
(Transferred to Coastal Command as 132 OTU)
Satellite to Drem, 06/40
To Coastal Command, 11/42

EAST KIRKBY, Lincs

LOCATION: 4m SW of Spilsby
OPENED: 20/08/43
CLOSED: 04/70. Agriculture/Lincolnshire Aviation Heritage Centre (2011)
ELEVATION: 40ft
PUNDIT CODE: EK
FORMATION: 5 Grp Bomber Command
MAIN CONTRACTOR: John Laing & Son Ltd
RUNWAYS: 3 concrete
HANGARS: T2 (6), B1 (1)
USER SQNS/UNITS:
57 Sqn
27/08/43–27/11/45
Lancaster I, III
630 Sqn
15/11/43–18/07/45
Lancaster I, III
Opened in Bomber Command as parent station, 20/08/43
Became 55 Base, 15/04/44

EAST MOOR, Yorks

LOCATION: 7¾m N of York
OPENED: 06/42
CLOSED: 06/46. Agriculture/light industry/leisure (2011)
ELEVATION: 91ft
PUNDIT CODE: EM
FORMATIONS: 4, 6 Grp Bomber Command
MAIN CONTRACTOR: Various
RUNWAYS: 3 concrete
HANGARS: T2 (2), B1 (1)
USER SQNS/UNITS:
158 Sqn
06/06–06/11/42
Halifax II
415 (Canadian) Sqn
26/07/44–15/05/45
Halifax III, VII
429 (Canadian) Sqn
07/11/42–13/08/43
Wellington III, X
432 (Canadian) Sqn
19/09/43–15/05/45
Wellington X; Lancaster II; Halifax III, VII
1679 HCU
20/05–13/12/43
Lancaster II
Opened in Bomber Command as satellite to Linton-on-Ouse, 06/42
Became 62 Base substation, 04/43

EAST WRETHAM, Norfolk

LOCATION: 6m NE of Thetford
OPENED: 03/40
CLOSED: 07/46. Army training ground (2011)

ELEVATION: 135ft
PUNDIT CODE: UT
FORMATION: 3 Grp Bomber Command
MAIN CONTRACTOR: Various
RUNWAYS: 3 grass
HANGARS: Bellman (2)
USER SQNS/UNITS:

115 Sqn
08/11/42–06/08/43
Wellington III; Lancaster II

311 (Czech) Sqn
16/09/40–28/04/42
Wellington I

1429 Flt
01–07/42
Wellington; Oxford

1678 HCU
03–08/43
Lancaster II

Opened in Bomber Command as satellite to Honington, 03/40
Closed to C&M, 08/42
Reopened as satellite to Mildenhall, 11/42
Transferred to USAAF as Station AAF-133, 10/43

EASTCHURCH, Kent

LOCATION: 4½m SE of Sheppey
OPENED: 1911
CLOSED: 1946. HMP Standford Hill (2011)
ELEVATION: 47ft
PUNDIT CODE: EA
FORMATIONS: 11 Grp Fighter Command; 83, 84 Grp 2 TAF
MAIN CONTRACTOR: Various
RUNWAYS: 3 grass
HANGARS: Bellman (3)
USER SQNS/UNITS:

65 Sqn
14–20/08/42
Spitfire Vb

122 Sqn
18/05–01/06/43
Spitfire Vb

124 Sqn
30/06–05/07/42
Spitfire Vb

132 Sqn
05/04–18/05/43
Spitfire Vb

165 Sqn
15–20/08/42
Spitfire Vb

174 Sqn
21/01–04/02/44
Typhoon Ib

175 Sqn
24/02–08/03/44
Typhoon Ib

181 Sqn
06–21/02/44
Typhoon Ib

182 Sqn
05–23/01/44
Typhoon Ib

183 Sqn
14–25/07/44
Typhoon Ib

184 Sqn
05/04–31/05/43
11/03–03/04/44
Hurricane IId, IV; Typhoon Ib

245 Sqn
25–30/04/44
12–22/05/44
Typhoon Ib

247 Sqn
01–24/04/44
Typhoon Ib

263 Sqn
23/07–06/08/44
Typhoon Ib

266 Sqn
29/06–13/07/44
Spitfire I; Typhoon Ib

401 (Canadian) Sqn
03–28/07/42
Spitfire Vb

To 16 Grp Coastal Command, 11/38
To Technical Training Command, 06/41
To 11 Grp Fighter Command, as Forward Operating Base (FOB) for Gravesend, 06/42
To 72 Grp Army Co-operation Command, 10/42
To 11 Grp Fighter Command, 04/43
To 54 Grp Flying Training Command (but continued in use as FOB), 05/43

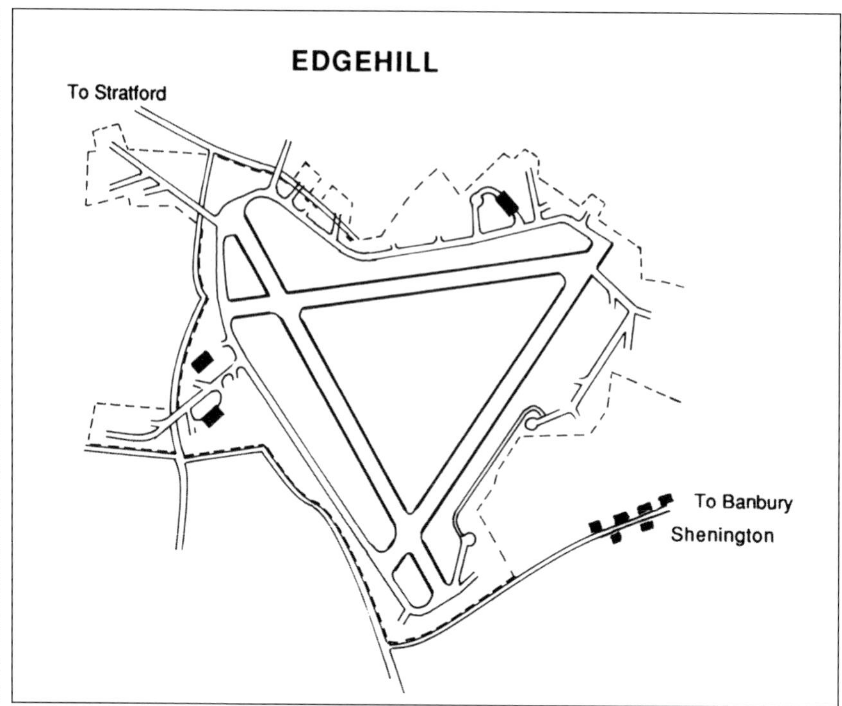

EDGEHILL, Warks

LOCATION: 3m SE of Kineton
OPENED: 10/41
CLOSED: 06/45. Agriculture/gliding club (2011)
ELEVATION: 628ft
PUNDIT CODE: EH

FORMATIONS: 6 (T), 91 (OTU), 92 (OTU) Grp Bomber Command
MAIN CONTRACTOR: Various
RUNWAYS: 3 concrete/Tarmac
HANGARS: T2 (2), B1 (1)
USER SQNS/UNITS:
12 OTU
12/04/43–06/45
Wellington I, III, X
21 OTU
21/10/41–12/04/43
Wellington I
Opened in Bomber Command as satellite to Moreton-in-Marsh, 10/41
Became satellite to Chipping Warden, 04/43

EGLINTON, Co Londonderry, NI

LOCATION: 6½m NE of Derry
OPENED: 04/41
CLOSED: 09/66. City of Derry Airport (2011)
ELEVATION: 26ft
PUNDIT CODE: QN
FORMATION: 13 Grp Fighter Command
MAIN CONTRACTOR: Stewart Partners Ltd
RUNWAYS: 3 Tarmac
HANGARS: Blister (12)
USER SQNS/UNITS:
41 Sqn
22–30/09/42
Spitfire Vb
133 Sqn
08/10/41–02/01/42
Hurricane IIb; Spitfire IIa
134 Sqn
30/12/41–26/03/42
Spitfire Va, IIa, Vb; Hurricane IIb
152 Sqn
17/01–16/08/42
Spitfire IIa, Vb
Opened in Fighter Command as parent station, 04/41
To USAAF as Station AAF-344, 08/42
To RN as HMS Gannet, 05/43

ELGIN, Morayshire

LOCATION: 3m SW of Elgin
OPENED: 06/40
CLOSED: 1947. Agriculture (2011)
ELEVATION: 100ft
PUNDIT CODE: Not known
FORMATIONS: 2, 6 (T), 91 (OTU) Grp Bomber Command
MAIN CONTRACTOR: Various
RUNWAYS: 3 grass
HANGARS: T2 (1), B1 (1)
USER SQNS/UNITS:
21 Sqn
24/06–30/10/40
Blenheim IV
57 Sqn
23/06–14/08/40
Blenheim IV
20 OTU
06/40–06/45
Wellington III, X
Opened in Bomber Command as satellite to Lossiemouth, 06/40

ELSHAM WOLDS, Lincs

LOCATION: 7m N of Brigg
OPENED: 07/41
CLOSED: 1947. Agriculture/industry/A15 link road (2011)

BELOW: No 77 Squadron moved to Elvington on 5 October 1942 and remained there until 15 May 1944, operating Halifax Mk IIs and Vs. Here the squadron's Mk II Series 1 (Special), JB911, 'X', beats up the airfield during July 1943 to the delight of watching ground crew. JB911 went on to serve with No 1658 HCU and was struck off charge on 1 November 1946. (IWM CH10594

ABOVE: 'Watch Office for Night Fighter Stations 4533/42.' The watchtower and several other nearby buildings at Elvington have been restored to their wartime condition and today form part of the Yorkshire Air Museum. (Author)

ELEVATION: 241ft
PUNDIT CODE: ES
FORMATION: 1 Grp Bomber Command
MAIN CONTRACTOR: Various
RUNWAYS: 3 concrete
HANGARS: J Type (1), T2 (5)
USER SQNS/UNITS:

100 Sqn
01/04–03/12/45
Lancaster I, III

103 Sqn
11/07/42–26/11/45
Wellington I; Halifax II; Lancaster I, III

576 Sqn
25/11/43–31/10/44
Lancaster I, III

Opened in Bomber Command as parent station, 07/41
Became 13 Base, 1943

ELVINGTON, Yorks

LOCATION: 5m ESE of York
OPENED: 10/42
CLOSED: Yorkshire Air Museum/ motorsport (2011)
ELEVATION: 44ft
PUNDIT CODE: EV
FORMATION: 4 Grp Bomber Command
MAIN CONTRACTOR: Various
RUNWAYS: 3 asphalt
HANGARS: T2 (2), B1 (1)
USER SQNS/UNITS:

77 Sqn
05/10/42–15/05/44
Whitley; Halifax II, V

346 (French) Sqn
16/05/44–20/10/45
Halifax V, III, VI

347 (French) Sqn
20/06/44–20/10/45
Halifax V, III, VI

Opened in Bomber Command as satellite to Pocklington, 10/42
Became 42 Base substation, 1943

ENSTONE, Oxon

LOCATION: 5m E of Chipping Norton
OPENED: 09/42
CLOSED: 1947. Light aviation (2011)
ELEVATION: 550ft
PUNDIT CODE: EN
FORMATIONS: 6 (T), 91 (OTU) Grp Bomber Command
MAIN CONTRACTOR: Various
RUNWAYS: 3 concrete
HANGARS: T2 (1), B1 (1)
USER SQNS/UNITS:

21 OTU
12/04/43–08/45

Wellington I, III, X
Became satellite to Moreton-in-Marsh, 04/43

ESHOTT, Northumberland

LOCATION: 7m N of Morpeth
OPENED: 11/42
CLOSED: 06/45. Agriculture/light aviation (2011)
ELEVATION: 151ft
PUNDIT CODE: Not known
FORMATIONS: 9, 81 (OTU) Grp Fighter Command
MAIN CONTRACTOR: Various
RUNWAYS: 3 concrete
HANGARS: Blister (8), T3 (1)
USER SQNS/UNITS:
57 OTU
10/11/42–06/06/45
Spitfire
Opened in Fighter Command as satellite to Boulmer, 11/42

EXETER, Devon

LOCATION: 4m E of Exeter
OPENED: 05/37
CLOSED: 1947. Exeter International Airport (2011)
ELEVATION: 100ft
PUNDIT CODE: EX
FORMATION: 10 Grp Fighter Command
MAIN CONTRACTOR: John Laing & Son Ltd
RUNWAYS: 3 asphalt
HANGARS: Blister (10), RAF 7 (1)
USER SQNS/UNITS:
66 Sqn
24/02–27/04/41
Spitfire I, IIa
87 Sqn
05/07–28/11/40
Hurricane I
125 Sqn
15/04–14/11/43
Beaufighter VIf
131 Sqn
26/06–16/08/43
Spitfire Vb, Vc
165 Sqn
30/07–08/08/43
Spitfire Vb, Vc
213 Sqn
18/06–07/09/40
Hurricane I
247 Sqn
17/05–21/09/42
Hurricane I, IIc
263 Sqn
28/11/40–24/02/41
Whirlwind I
266 Sqn
08/01–07/09/43
10–21/09/43
Typhoon Ib
307 (Polish) Sqn
26/04/41–15/04/43
Defiant I; Beaufighter IIf, VIf; Mosquito II
308 (Polish) Sqn
01/04–07/05/42
Spitfire Vb
310 (Czech) Sqn
07/05–01/07/42
07/07–16/08/42
21/08/42–26/06/43
Spitfire Vb, Vc
317 (Polish) Sqn
21/07/41–01/04/42
Hurricane IIb; Spitfire Vb
406 (Canadian) Sqn
15/11/43–14/04/44
Beaufighter VIf
421 (Canadian) Sqn
29/06–08/07/42
Spitfire Vb
504 (AAF) Sqn
18/12/40–21/07/41
Hurricane I
601 (AAF) Sqn
07/09–17/12/40
Hurricane I
610 (AAF) Sqn
04/01–07/04/44
Spitfire Vb, Vc, XIV
616 (AAF) Sqn
17/09–16/11/43
01/12/43–18/03/44
Spitfire VI, VII
Opened in Fighter Command as parent station, 07/40
To USAAF, 04/44
To 23 Grp, RAF Flying Training Command, 01/45

FAIRFORD, Gloucs

LOCATION: 9m N of Swindon
OPENED: 01/44
CLOSED: USAF forward operating base/ NASA Space Shuttle diversion airfield (2011)
ELEVATION: 256ft
PUNDIT CODE: FA
FORMATION: 38 Grp Fighter Command
MAIN CONTRACTOR: Sir Alfred McAlpine Ltd
RUNWAYS: 3 concrete/asphalt
HANGARS: T2 (2)
USER SQNS/UNITS:
190 Sqn
25/03–14/10/44
Stirling IV
620 Sqn
18/03–18/10/44
Stirling IV
Opened in 38 Grp with full station status, 01/44
To 23 Grp Flying Training Command, 10/44

FAIRLOP, Essex

LOCATION: 3m NE of Ilford
OPENED: 11/41
CLOSED: 08/46. Leisure park/sports (2011)
ELEVATION: 85ft
PUNDIT CODE: FP
FORMATION: 11 Grp Fighter Command
MAIN CONTRACTOR: Various
RUNWAYS: 3 concrete/asphalt
HANGARS: Blister (8)
USER SQNS/UNITS:
64 Sqn
08/09–14/11/42
02/01–15/03/43
Spitfire IX
65 Sqn
18–31/05/43
Spitfire Vb
81 Sqn
17/07–01/09/42
Spitfire Vb

122 Sqn
08–29/06/42
06–17/07/42
16/11–09/12/42
Spitfire Vb, IX
154 Sqn
27/07–10/08/42
15/08–01/09/42
Spitfire Vb
164 Sqn
22/09/43–04/01/44
13/01–11/02/44
Hurricane IV; Typhoon Ib
182 Sqn
05–29/04/43
Typhoon Ib
193 Sqn
20/02–16/03/44
Typhoon Ib
195 Sqn
24/09/43–15/02/44
Typhoon Ib
239 Sqn
21–27/06/43
Mustang I
245 Sqn
28/05–02/06/43
Typhoon Ib
247 Sqn
05/04–29/05/43
Typhoon Ib
302 (Polish) Sqn
19/08–18/09/43
Spitfire Vb, Vc
313 (Czech) Sqn
29/04–28/06/42
Spitfire Vb
317 (Polish) Sqn
21/08–21/09/43
Spitfire Vb
350 (Belgian) Sqn
15–23/03/43
Spitfire Vb, Vc
602 (AAF) Sqn
29/04–01/06/43
Spitfire Vb
603 (AAF) Sqn
12/11–15/12/41
Spitfire Va, Vb
Opened in Fighter Command as satellite to Hornchurch, 11/41
To Balloon Command as 24 Balloon Centre, 09/44

FAIRWOOD COMMON, Glamorgan

LOCATION: 5m W of Swansea
OPENED: 06/41
CLOSED: Swansea Airport (2011)
ELEVATION: 268ft
PUNDIT CODE: FC
FORMATION: 10 Grp Fighter Command
MAIN CONTRACTOR: Various
RUNWAYS: 3 Tarmac
HANGARS: Blister (8), Bellman (3)
USER SQNS/UNITS:
33 Sqn
10–18/08/44
Spitfire LFIXe
41 Sqn
16–24/05/44
Spitfire XII
66 Sqn
20/02–16/03/45
Spitfire LFXVIe
68 Sqn
01/03–23/06/44
Beaufighter VIf
79 Sqn
14/06–24/12/41
Hurricane I, IIb
125 Sqn
24/09/41–25/01/42
14/05/42–15/04/43
Defiant I, II; Beaufighter IIf, VIf
127 Sqn
20/02–17/03/45
Spitfire XVI
132 Sqn
13–19/03/44
Spitfire Vb, VI
164 Sqn
29/01–08/02/43
12–26/12/44
Typhoon Ib
193 Sqn
18/09–06/10/44
Typhoon Ib
197 Sqn
25/11–12/12/44
Typhoon Ib
198 Sqn
06–21/11/44
Typhoon Ib
257 Sqn
11–12/04/44
11–30/08/44
Typhoon Ib
263 Sqn
10/02–18/04/42
05–23/01/44
13/01–10/02/45
Whirlwind I; Typhoon Ib
264 Sqn
07–12/08/43
Mosquito II
266 Sqn
25/04–04/06/45
Typhoon Ib
302 (Polish) Sqn
02–19/12/43
30/08–16/09/44
Spitfire IX, IXe
307 (Polish) Sqn
15/04–07/08/43
Mosquito II
312 (Czech) Sqn
01–24/01/42
18–20/04/42
24/02–02/05/42
Spitfire Vb
317 (Polish) Sqn
27/06–21/07/41
Hurricane I
322 (Dutch) Sqn
10–31/10/44
Spitfire LFIXe
331 (Norwegian) Sqn
19/09–06/10/44
Spitfire IXb
332 (Norwegian) Sqn
11–31/12/44
Spitfire IXb
345 (French) Sqn
16/03–02/04/45
Spitfire HFIX
401 (Canadian) Sqn
08–18/04/44
Spitfire IXb
402 (Canadian) Sqn
17/03–14/05/42
Spitfire Vb

403 (Canadian) Sqn
23/09–03/10/44
Spitfire IXb
412 (Canadian) Sqn
08/02–01/03/43
08–13/04/43
13/03–07/04/44
Spitfire Vb, IXb
421 (Canadian) Sqn
03/05–14/06/42
28–29/06/42
08/07–16/08/42
22/08–06/10/42
11–26/10/42
Spitfire Vb
456 (Australian) Sqn
17/11/43–29/02/44
Mosquito II, XVII
504 (AAF) Sqn
21/07–11/08/41
Hurricane IIb
536 Sqn
27/10/42–25/01/43
Havoc II (Turbinlite)
600 (AAF) Sqn
18–27/06/41
Beaufighter If, IIf
609 (AAF) Sqn
06–20/02/44
Typhoon Ib
610 (AAF) Sqn
19/12/43–04/01/44
23–30/04/44
Spitfire Vb, Vc, XIV
615 (AAF) Sqn
23/01–17/03/42
Hurricane IIb, IIc
616 (AAF) Sqn
24/04–16/05/44
Spitfire VII
Opened in Fighter Command as parent station, 06/41
Upgraded to Sector Station, 10/41

FALDINGWORTH, Lincs

LOCATION: 5nm SW of Market Rasen
OPENED: 1943.
CLOSED: 1972.
ELEVATION: 50ft
FORMATION: 1 Grp Bomber Command
RUNWAYS: 3 concrete
HANGARS: T2 (2), B1 (1)
USER SQNS/UNITS:
300 (Polish) Sqn
03/44–01/47
1667 HCU
10/43–02/44
Satellite of Ludford Magna under 14 Base, 12/43

FELTWELL, Norfolk

LOCATION: 10m W of Thetford
OPENED: 04/37
CLOSED: 05/58. USAF housing and containment area (2011)
ELEVATION: 25ft
PUNDIT CODE: FL
FORMATIONS: 2, 3 Grp Bomber Command
MAIN CONTRACTOR: Various
RUNWAYS: 3 grass
HANGARS: C Type (5)
USER SQNS/UNITS:
37 Sqn
26/04/37–13/11/40
Wellington I
57 Sqn
18/11/40–04/09/42
Wellington I, II, III
75 (New Zealand) Sqn
08/04/40–15/08/42
Wellington I, III
192 Sqn
05/04–25/11/43
Mosquito IV, Wellington X
320 (Dutch) Sqn
04–05/43
Mitchell II
464 (Australian) Sqn
15/08/42–03/04/43
Ventura I, II
487 (New Zealand) Sqn
15/08/42–03/04/43
Ventura II
3 LFS
11/43–01/45
Lancaster I, III
1473 RCM Flt
14/09–11/43
Leopard Moth; Wellington; Anson; Whitley
Bombing Development Unit (BDU)
04–11/43
01–06/45
Halifax III, VI; Lancaster I, III; Mosquito IX, XVI, XX
Opened in Bomber Command as parent station, 04/37
*Sgt J.A. Ward, 75 (New Zealand) Sqn, awarded VC, Munster, 07–08/07/41

FILTON, Bristol

LOCATION: 4¾m NW of Bristol
OPENED: 1911
CLOSED: BAe Systems/Airbus UK/Rolls-Royce/MBDA (2011)
ELEVATION: 210ft
PUNDIT CODE: Not known
FORMATIONS: 10, 11 Grp Fighter Command
MAIN CONTRACTOR: Various
RUNWAYS: 2
HANGARS: B Type (2), Various (23)
USER SQNS/UNITS:
25 Sqn
15/09–04/10/39
Blenheim If
118 Sqn
20/02–07/04/41
Spitfire I
145 Sqn
09–10/05/40
Blenheim If; Hurricane I
263 Sqn
02/10/39–24/04/40
10/04–07/08/41
Gladiator I, II; Whirlwind I
501 (AAF) Sqn
14/06/29–27/11/39
17/12/40–09/04/41
DH9A; Wapiti; Wallace; Hart; Hind; Hurricane I
504 (AAF) Sqn
26/09–18/12/40
Hurricane I
To 44 Grp Transport Command, 12/41

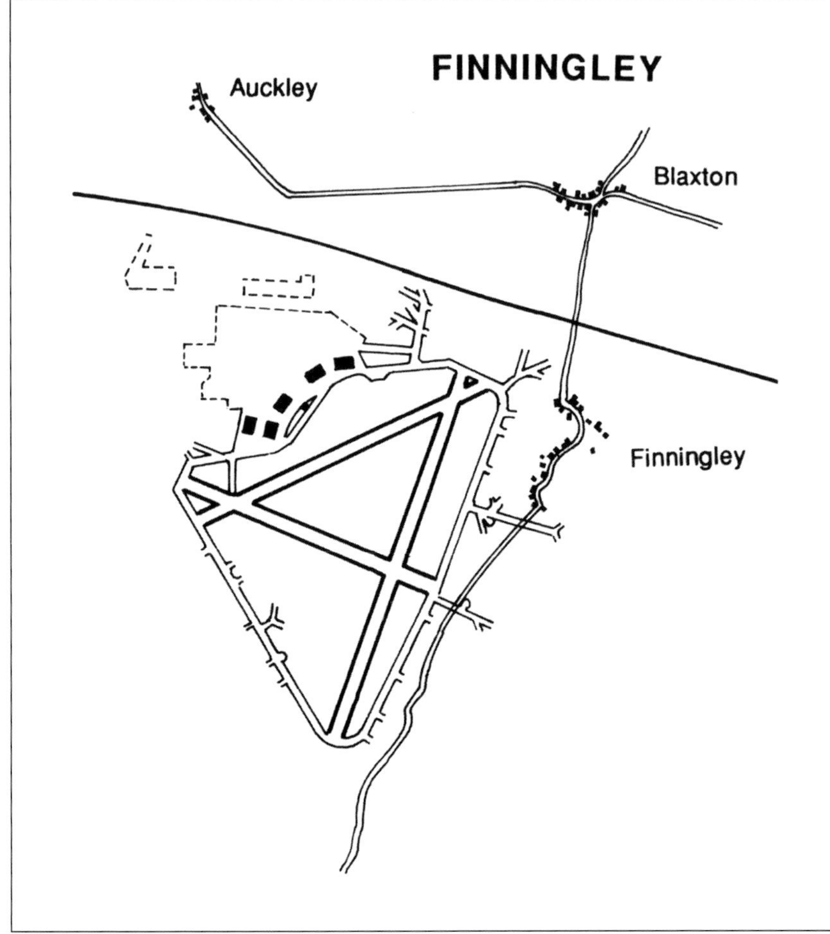

FINMERE, Bucks

LOCATION: 3½m W of Buckingham
OPENED: 08/42
CLOSED: 07/45. Agriculture (2011)
ELEVATION: 390ft
PUNDIT CODE: FI
FORMATIONS: 9, 12 Grp Fighter Command; 92 (OTU) Grp Bomber Command
MAIN CONTRACTOR: Various
RUNWAYS: 3 concrete
HANGARS: B1 (1), T2 (1)
USER SQNS/UNITS:

13 OTU
08/42–11/43
Blenheim I, IV; Mitchell II; Boston IIIa; Mosquito

307 FTU
18/03–05/43
Havoc; Boston

Satellite to Bicester, 08/42
Transferred to Flying Training Command control, 11/43

FINNINGLEY, Yorks

LOCATION: 7½m SE of Doncaster
OPENED: 09/36
CLOSED: 1996. Robin Hood Airport Doncaster Sheffield (2011)
ELEVATION: 28ft
PUNDIT CODE: FV
FORMATIONS: 2, 5, 6 (T), 7 (T), 93 (OTU) Grp Bomber Command
MAIN CONTRACTOR: Various
RUNWAYS: 3 concrete/Tarmac
HANGARS: C Type (5)
USER SQNS/UNITS:

7 Sqn
30/04–20/05/40
15–23/09/40
Hampden

12 Sqn
16/06–03/07/40
Battle

76 Sqn
12/04/37–23/09/39
Hampden; Anson

98 Sqn
19/03–16/04/40
Battle

106 Sqn
06/10/39–22/02/41
Hampden

18 OTU
07/03/43–01/45
Wellington III, X

25 OTU
01/03/41–07/01/43
Hampden; Manchester; Wellington

Bomber Command Instructors' School (BCIS)
05/12/44–22/01/47
Wellington X; Lancaster I, III; Halifax III; Spitfire; Master; Oxford

Opened in Bomber Command as parent station, 09/36

FISKERTON, Lincs

LOCATION: 4½m E of Lincoln
OPENED: 01/43
CLOSED: 12/45. Agriculture/poultry farming/oil extraction (2011)
ELEVATION: 50ft
PUNDIT CODE: FN
FORMATIONS: 1, 5 Grp Bomber Command
MAIN CONTRACTOR: Various
RUNWAYS: 3 concrete/Tarmac
HANGARS: T2 (2), B1 (1)
USER SQNS/UNITS:

49 Sqn
02/01/43–16/10/44
Lancaster I, III

150 Sqn
01–23/11/44
Lancaster I, III

576 Sqn
31/10/44–13/09/45
Lancaster I, III

Opened in Bomber Command as 52 Base substation, 01/43

FORD, Sussex

LOCATION: 2¼m NW of Littlehampton
OPENED: 1918
CLOSED: 11/58. HMP Ford (2011)

ELEVATION: 23ft
PUNDIT CODE: FD
FORMATIONS: 11 Grp Fighter Command; 83, 84 Grp 2 TAF
MAIN CONTRACTOR: Various
RUNWAYS: 2 Tarmac
HANGARS: Blister (20), Bellman (5), GRP (1)
USER SQNS/UNITS:

19 Sqn
15/04–12/05/44
15–25/06/44
Mustang III

23 Sqn
12/09/40–06/08/42
Blenheim If; Havoc I; Boston III; Mosquito II

29 Sqn
03/09/43–01/03/44
Mosquito XII, XIII

65 Sqn
15/04–14/05/44
Mustang III

66 Sqn
12–20/08/44
Spitfire LFIXb

96 Sqn
20/06–24/09/44
Mosquito XIII

122 Sqn
15/04–14/05/44
15–26/06/44
Mustang III

127 Sqn
12–20/08/44
Spitfire HFIX

129 Sqn
24/06–08/07/44
Mustang III

132 Sqn
18/04–25/06/44
Spitfire IXb

141 Sqn
10/08/42–18/02/43
Beaufighter If

256 Sqn
24/04–25/08/43
Beaufighter VIf; Mosquito XII

302 (Polish) Sqn
16/07–04/08/44
Spitfire IXe

306 (Polish) Sqn
27/06–08/07/44
Mustang III

308 (Polish) Sqn
16/07–04/08/44
Spitfire IX

315 (Polish) Sqn
25/06–10/07/44
Mustang III

317 (Polish) Sqn
16/07–04/08/44
Spitfire IX

331 (Norwegian) Sqn
13–30/08/44
Spitfire IXb

332 (Norwegian) Sqn
12–20/08/44
Spitfire IXb

418 (Canadian) Sqn
15/03/43–08/04/44
Boston III; Mosquito II

ABOVE: Flg Off Lee Howard and Sqn Ldr Charles Patterson of the RAF Film Production Unit prepare for a filming sortie over enemy territory from Ford airfield, Sussex, in June 1944. The aircraft is Mosquito Mk IV, DZ414, 'O', which had been specially modified for film work. (IWM FLM 2303)

441 (Canadian) Sqn
13/05–15/06/44
Spitfire IXb
442 (Canadian) Sqn
15/05–15/06/44
Spitfire IXb
443 (Canadian) Sqn
15/05–15/06/44
Spitfire IXb
453 (Australian) Sqn
18/04–25/06/44
Spitfire IXb
456 (Australian) Sqn
29/02–31/12/44
Mosquito II, XVII
602 (AAF) Sqn
18/04–25/06/44
Spitfire IXb
604 (AAF) Sqn
18/02–24/03/43
Beaufighter If
605 (AAF) Sqn
07/06/42–15/03/43
Havoc I, II; Boston III; Mosquito II
Fighter Interception Unit (FIU)
01/02/41–03/04/44
Fighter Interception Development Squadron (FIDS)/
Night Fighter Development Wing (NFDW)
23/08/44–07/45
Blenheim; Beaufighter; Mosquito
Under RN as HMS Peregrine, 09/39
To 11 Grp Fighter Command, 10/40
To 2 TAF, 04/44
To 11 Grp Fighter Command, 10/44

FORRES, Morayshire

LOCATION: 13m WSW of Elgin
OPENED: 04/40
CLOSED: 10/44. Agriculture (2011)
ELEVATION: 50ft
PUNDIT CODE: Not known
FORMATIONS: 6 (T), 91 (OTU) Grp Bomber Command
MAIN CONTRACTOR: Various
RUNWAYS: 2 grass
HANGARS: T2 (1)
USER SQNS/UNITS:
19 OTU
27/04/40–22/10/44
Whitley
Opened in Bomber Command as satellite to Lossiemouth, 04/40

FOULSHAM, Norfolk

LOCATION: 8m NE of Dereham
OPENED: 05/42
CLOSED: 1945. Agriculture (2011)
ELEVATION: 173ft
PUNDIT CODE: FU
FORMATIONS: 2, 3, 100 (BS) Grp Bomber Command
MAIN CONTRACTOR: Kirk & Kirk Ltd
RUNWAYS: 3 Tarmac, FIDO-equipped
HANGARS: T2 (9), B1 (1)
USER SQNS/UNITS:
98 Sqn
15/10/42–18/08/43
Mitchell II
180 Sqn
19/10/42–18/08/43
Mitchell II
192 Sqn
25/11/43–22/08/45
Halifax III, V; Mosquito XVI; Wellington X
462 (Australian) Sqn
22/12/44–24/09/45
Halifax III
514 Sqn
01/09–23/11/43
Lancaster II
1678 HCU
16/09–23/11/43
Lancaster II
Opened in Bomber Command as parent station, 05/42

FOWLMERE, Cambs

LOCATION: 3½m NE of Royston
OPENED: 06/40
CLOSED: 10/45. Agriculture (2011)
ELEVATION: 100ft
PUNDIT CODE: FW
FORMATION: 12 Grp Fighter Command
MAIN CONTRACTOR: Various
RUNWAYS: 2 steel matting
HANGARS: Blister (7), T2 (1)
USER SQNS/UNITS:
19 Sqn
25/06–03/07/40
24/07–01/11/40
Spitfire I, Ib, IIa
111 Sqn
27/09–20/10/42
Spitfire Vb
133 Sqn
03–08/10/41
Hurricane IIb
154 Sqn
17/11/41–12/03/42
05/04–07/05/42
Spitfire IIa, IIb, Va, Vb
174 Sqn
09–12/07/42
Hurricane IIb
264 Sqn
03–23/07/40
Defiant I
411 (Canadian) Sqn
05–12/03/43
Spitfire Vb
Opened in Fighter Command as satellite to Duxford, 06/40
To USAAF as Station AAF-378, 04/44

FRASERBURGH, Aberdeenshire

LOCATION: 17½m NW of Peterhead
OPENED: 1941
CLOSED: 06/1945. Agriculture (2011)
ELEVATION: 52ft
FORMATIONS: 13 Grp Fighter Command; 18 Grp Coastal Command
RUNWAYS: 3 Tarmac
HANGARS: T2 (1), Double Blister (6)
USER SQNS/UNITS:
279 Sqn (det)
26/12/44–07/45
Warwick I; Hurricane IIc
8 OTU
18/05/42–09/03/43
Spitfire; Mosquito
14 (P) AFU
25/05/43–01/09/44
Oxford
823 NAS
12/41–01/42
Swordfish

838 NAS
10–11/44
Swordfish
883 NAS
02/42
Sea Hurricane
Opened in Fighter Command as satellite to Peterhead, 06/12/41
To Coastal Command, 18/05/42
To 21 Grp Flying Training Command, 06/04/43
To Coastal Command as satellite to Banff, 09/44

FRISTON, Sussex
LOCATION: 5m WSW of Eastbourne
OPENED: 05/40
CLOSED: 04/46. Agriculture (2011)
ELEVATION: 355ft
PUNDIT CODE: FX
FORMATION: 11 Grp Fighter Command
MAIN CONTRACTOR: Various
RUNWAYS: 2 grass
HANGARS: Blister (2)
USER SQNS/UNITS:
32 Sqn
14/06–07/07/42
14–20/08/42
Hurricane I, Ib, IIc
41 Sqn
28/05–21/06/43
11/03–29/04/44
Spitfire XII
64 Sqn
06–19/08/43
Spitfire Vb
131 Sqn
28/08–31/10/44
Spitfire VII
253 Sqn
14/06–07/07/42
16–20/08/42
Hurricane I, IIa, IIb, IIc
306 (Polish) Sqn
19/08–22/09/43
Spitfire Vb
316 (Polish) Sqn
11/07–27/08/44
Mustang III
349 (Belgian) Sqn
22–26/10/43
10/11/43–11/03/44
Spitfire LFVb, Vc, LFIXe
350 (Belgian) Sqn
25/04–03/07/44
Spitfire Vb, Vc
412 (Canadian) Sqn
21/06–14/07/43
Spitfire Vb
501 (AAF) Sqn
30/04–02/07/44
Spitfire Vb
610 (AAF) Sqn
02/07–12/09/44
Spitfire XIV
Designated as 11 Grp Fighter Command Emergency Landing Ground (ELG) for Kenley, 05/40
Upgraded as satellite to Kenley, 05/41
Satellite to Tangmere, 04/44
Downgraded to ELG, 11/44

FULBECK, Lincs
LOCATION: 6½m ESE of Newark-on-Trent
OPENED: 1940
CLOSED: 1970. Military training area (2011)
ELEVATION: 50ft
PUNDIT CODE: FK
FORMATION: 5 Grp Bomber Command
MAIN CONTRACTOR: Various
RUNWAYS: 3 concrete/Tarmac
HANGARS: T2 (5)
USER SQNS/UNITS:
49 Sqn
16/10/44–22/04/45
Lancaster I, III
189 Sqn
02/11/44–08/04/45
Lancaster I, III
Opened in Bomber Command as satellite to Syerston, 1940
To USAAF as Station AAF-488, 01/10/43
To RAF as 56 Base substation, 17/10/44

FULL SUTTON, Yorks
LOCATION: 8m E of York
OPENED: 05/44
CLOSED: 04/63. Light aviation/HMP Full Sutton (2011)
ELEVATION: 86ft
PUNDIT CODE: FS
FORMATION: 4 Grp Bomber Command
MAIN CONTRACTOR: Various
RUNWAYS: 3 concrete/Tarmac
HANGARS: T2 (2), B1 (1)
USER SQNS/UNITS:
77 Sqn
15/05/44–31/08/45
Halifax II, III, V, VI
Opened in Bomber Command as 42 Base substation, 05/44

FUNTINGTON, Sussex
LOCATION: 5m W of Chichester
OPENED: 09/43
CLOSED: 13/12/44. Agriculture/QinetiQ (2011)
ELEVATION: 115ft
PUNDIT CODE: FJ
FORMATIONS: 11 Grp Fighter Command; 83, 84 Grp 2 TAF
MAIN CONTRACTOR: Various
RUNWAYS: 2 steel matting
HANGARS: Blister (4)
USER SQNS/UNITS:
4 Sqn
15/09–06/10/43
Mustang I
19 Sqn
20/05–15/06/44
Mustang III
33 Sqn
17/07–06/08/44
Spitfire LFIXe
65 Sqn
14–28/05/44
04–15/06/44
Mustang III
66 Sqn
06–12/08/44
Spitfire LFIXb
122 Sqn
14–21/05/44
28/05–15/06/44

Mustang III
127 Sqn
06–12/08/44
Spitfire LFIXe
164 Sqn
18–22/06/44
Typhoon Ib
183 Sqn
18/06–01/07/44
Typhoon Ib
198 Sqn
18–22/06/44
Typhoon Ib
222 Sqn
04/07–06/08/44
Spitfire LFIXb
329 (French) Sqn
22/06–01/07/44
Spitfire IX
331 (Norwegian) Sqn
06–13/08/44
Spitfire IXb
332 (Norwegian) Sqn
06–12/08/44
Spitfire IXb
340 (French) Sqn
22/06–01/07/44
Spitfire IXb
341 (French) Sqn
22/06–01/07/44
Spitfire IXb
349 (Belgian) Sqn
04/07–06/08/44
Spitfire LFIXe
438 (Canadian) Sqn
03–19/04/44
Hurricane IV; Typhoon Ib
439 (Canadian) Sqn
02–19/04/44
Hurricane IV; Typhoon Ib
440 (Canadian) Sqn
03–20/04/44
Typhoon Ib
441 (Canadian) Sqn
23/04–13/05/44
Spitfire IXb
442 (Canadian) Sqn
23–25/04/44
01–15/05/44
Spitfire IXb
443 (Canadian) Sqn
22/04–15/05/44
Spitfire IXb
485 (New Zealand) Sqn
03/07–07/08/44
Spitfire IXe
609 (AAF) Sqn
18/06–01/07/44
Typhoon Ib
Advanced Landing Ground (ALG)

GAMSTON, Notts
LOCATION: 2m S of Retford
OPENED: 12/42
CLOSED: 1957. Agriculture/Retford Airport (2011)
ELEVATION: 90ft
PUNDIT CODE: GB
FORMATIONS: 91 (OTU), 93 (OTU) Grp Bomber Command
MAIN CONTRACTOR: Various
RUNWAYS: 3 concrete/Tarmac
HANGARS: T2 (4), B1 (1)
USER SQNS/UNITS:
30 OTU
02–06/45
Wellington III, X
82 OTU
01/06/43–01/06/44
Wellington III, X
86 OTU
01/06–10/44
Wellington III, X
Opened in Flying Training Command as satellite to Ossington, 12/42
To 93 (OTU) Grp Bomber Command as satellite to Ossington, 05/43
To 7 Grp Bomber Command, 11/44
To 91 (OTU) Grp Bomber Command, 02/45

GATWICK, Surrey
LOCATION: 6m SSE of Reigate
OPENED: 08/30
CLOSED: London Gatwick Airport (2011)
ELEVATION: 205ft
PUNDIT CODE: GK
FORMATIONS: 11 Grp Fighter Command; 2 TAF
MAIN CONTRACTOR: Various
RUNWAYS: Steel matting/grass
HANGARS: Bellman (1), Blister (6)
USER SQNS/UNITS:
2 Sqn
04/04–27/06/44
Mustang
4 Sqn
04/04–27/06/44
Spitfire PRXI;
Mosquito PRXVI
19 Sqn
15–24/10/43
Spitfire IX
26 (South African) Sqn
06/43
Mustang I
65 Sqn
15–24/10/43
Spitfire IX
80 Sqn
27/06–05/07/44
Spitfire IX
141 Sqn
22/10–03/11/40
Defiant I
168 Sqn
06–31/03/44
Mustang I
175 Sqn
09/12/42–14/01/43
Hurricane IIb
183 Sqn
08/04–03/05/43
Typhoon Ib
229 Sqn
28/06–01/07/44
Spitfire IX
274 Sqn
28/06–05/07/44
Spitfire IX
Under control of 11 Grp Fighter Command, 09/39
To 71 Grp Army Co-operation Command, 01/41
To 11 Grp Fighter Command as satellite to Biggin Hill, 06/43
To 2 TAF, 04/44
To 11 Grp Fighter Command, 11/44

GAYDON, Warks

LOCATION: 10¾m NW of Banbury
OPENED: 13/06/42
CLOSED: 31/10/74. Heritage Motor Centre/Jaguar Land Rover test facility (2011)
ELEVATION: 41ft
PUNDIT CODE: GP
FORMATION: 91 (OTU) Grp Bomber Command
MAIN CONTRACTOR: John Laing & Son Ltd
RUNWAYS: 3 concrete/Tarmac
HANGARS: T2 (1), B1 (1)
USER SQNS/UNITS:
12 OTU
13/06–01/09/42
Wellington I, III, X
22 OTU
01/09/42–01/07/45
Wellington I, III, X
Opened in Bomber Command as satellite to Chipping Warden, 13/06/42
Became satellite to Wellesbourne Mountford, 01/09/42

GOSPORT, Hants

LOCATION: 4m W of Portsmouth
OPENED: 1914
CLOSED: 1956. Housing (2011)
ELEVATION: 24ft
FORMATIONS: 16, 17 Grp Coastal Command
RUNWAYS: 1 Tarmac, 3 grass
HANGARS: C Type (1), A Type (4), Bellman (2), Bessonneau (1), EO Blister (5)
USER SQNS/UNITS:
48 Sqn
30/11–23/12/42
Hudson III
86 Sqn
06/12/40–02/02/41
Blenheim IV
608 Sqn
27/08–09/11/42
Hudson V
667 Sqn
01/12/43–20/12/45
Defiant I, III; Hurricane IIc; Barracuda II; Oxford; Vengeance IV; Spitfire XVI
Torpedo Development Unit > Air Torpedo Development Unit
11/38–03/40; 03/40–01/56
Botha; Beaufort; Beaufighter; Swordfish; Albacore; Hampden; Wellington
HQ 17 Grp Coastal Command, 05/38

GOXHILL, Lincs

LOCATION: 5m E of Barrow on Humber
OPENED: 06/41
CLOSED: 12/53. Agriculture (2011)
ELEVATION: 20ft
PUNDIT CODE: GX
FORMATION: 12 Grp Fighter Command
MAIN CONTRACTOR: John Laing & Son Ltd
RUNWAYS: 3 Tarmac
HANGARS: Blister (4), J Type (1), T2 (2)
USER SQNS/UNITS:
Nominally under control of Fighter Command, but no flying units based
Opened in 1 Grp Bomber Command, 06/41
To 12 Grp Fighter Command, 12/41
To USAAF as Station AAF-345, 06/42
To 12 Grp Fighter Command, 01/45

GRANGEMOUTH, Stirlingshire

LOCATION: 3m NE of Falkirk
OPENED: 05/39
CLOSED: 1945. Industry/oil refinery/housing (2011)
ELEVATION: 13ft
PUNDIT CODE: GW
FORMATIONS: 9, 13, 14, 81 (OTU) Grp Fighter Command
MAIN CONTRACTOR: Various
RUNWAYS: 2 Tarmac
HANGARS: Blister (8)
USER SQNS/UNITS:
141 Sqn
19/10/39–13/02/40
22/02–28/06/40
Gladiator I; Blenheim If; Defiant I
263 Sqn
28/06–02/09/40
Hurricane I; Whirlwind I
602 (AAF) Sqn
07–13/10/39
Spitfire I
58 OTU > 2 Tactical Exercise Unit (TEU)
02/12/40 (17/10/43)–25/06/44
Spitfire I, II, V
Parent station in 13 Grp Fighter Command, 09/39

GRANSDEN LODGE, Beds

LOCATION: 10m W of Cambridge
OPENED: 04/42
CLOSED: 1955. Agriculture/gliding (2011)
ELEVATION: 70ft
PUNDIT CODE: GL
FORMATIONS: 3, 5, 8 (PFF) Grp Bomber Command
MAIN CONTRACTOR: John Laing & Son Ltd
RUNWAYS: 3 concrete
HANGARS: T2 (2), B1 (1)
USER SQNS/UNITS:
97 Sqn
08–09/43
Lancaster I, III
142 Sqn (LNSF)
25/10/44–28/09/45
Mosquito XVI, XXV, B35
192 Sqn
04/01–05/04/43
Wellington I, III, X; Mosquito IV
405 (Canadian) Sqn
19/04/43–26/05/45
Halifax II; Lancaster I, III
1418 Flt
08/04–20/07/42
Wellington
1474 Flt
04/07/42–04/01/43
Wellington
No 1 Bombing Development Unit (BDU)
20/07/42–04/43
Stirling; Lancaster; Halifax; Wellington III; Proctor
PFF Navigation Training Unit (NTU)
04–06/43
Halifax II
Opened in Bomber Command as

satellite to Tempsford, 04/42
Became satellite to Oakington, 04/43
Achieved parent station status, 06/43

GRAVELEY, Hunts

LOCATION: 5m S of Huntingdon
OPENED: 03/42
CLOSED: 12/68. Agriculture/light industry (2011)
ELEVATION: 177ft
PUNDIT CODE: GR
FORMATIONS: 3, 8 (PFF) Grp Bomber Command
MAIN CONTRACTOR: Various
RUNWAYS: 3 concrete, FIDO-equipped
HANGARS: T2 (3), B1 (1)
USER SQNS/UNITS:

35 Sqn
15/08/42–16/09/46
Halifax II, III; Lancaster I, III

161 Sqn
01/03–08/04/42
Lysander IIIa; Hudson I; Whitley V

571 Sqn (LNSF)
05–24/04/44
Mosquito XVI

692 Sqn (LNSF)
01/01/44–04/06/45
Mosquito IV, XVI

Opened in Bomber Command as satellite to Tempsford, 03/42
Became satellite to Wyton, 08/42
Achieved parent station status, 05/43

GRAVESEND, Kent

LOCATION: 2m SE of Gravesend
OPENED: 10/32
CLOSED: 06/56. Housing/leisure (2011)
ELEVATION: 240ft
PUNDIT CODE: GN
FORMATIONS: 11 Grp Fighter Command; 2 TAF; ADGB
MAIN CONTRACTOR: Various
RUNWAYS: 2 grass
HANGARS: Blister (8), T1 (1)
USER SQNS/UNITS:

2 Sqn
16/04–07/08/43
Mustang I

19 Sqn
06–20/06/43
24/10/43–15/04/44
Spitfire Vb; Mustang III

21 Sqn
17/04–18/06/44
Mosquito VI

32 Sqn
03/01–08/03/40
22–27/03/40
Hurricane I

64 Sqn
19/08–06/09/43
Spitfire Vb

65 Sqn
29/07–14/08/42
20/08–26/09/42
24/10/43–15/04/44
Spitfire Vb, IX; Mustang III

66 Sqn
10/09–30/10/40
Spitfire I

71 Sqn
14–20/08/42
Spitfire Vb

72 Sqn
01–05/06/40
08–26/07/41
20/10/41–22/03/42
Spitfire I, IIa, IIb, Vb

85 Sqn
23/11/40–01/01/41
Hurricane I

92 Sqn
24/09–20/10/41
Spitfire Vb

111 Sqn
30/06–07/07/42
Spitfire Vb

122 Sqn
03/11/43–15/04/44
Spitfire IX; Mustang III

124 Sqn
03/05–30/06/42
13–29/07/42
Spitfire Vb, VI

132 Sqn
20/06–03/07/43
Spitfire Vb, Vc

133 Sqn
31/07–17/08/42
Spitfire Vb

141 Sqn
03/11/40–29/04/41
Defiant I

165 Sqn

ABOVE: Gravesend, September 1940. Spitfire Mk IA, R6800, 'N', was the personal mount of No 66 Squadron's CO, Sqn Ldr R.H.A. 'Lucky' Leigh. In the background can be seen another No 66 Squadron Spitfire coming in to land, and a Hurricane, 'U', of No 501 Squadron. In the distance is the Thames estuary, with shipping clearly visible.

ABOVE: Ground staff at work on No 620 Squadron's Stirling Mk IV, 'Yorkshire Rose II', at Great Dunmow in 1944. (Noel Chaffey)

20/08–02/11/42
Spitfire Vb
174 Sqn
05/04–12/06/43
Typhoon Ib
181 Sqn
24/03–05/04/43
Typhoon Ib
193 Sqn
17/08–18/09/43
Typhoon Ib
232 Sqn
14–20/08/42
Spitfire Vb
245 Sqn
30/03–28/05/43
Typhoon Ib
247 Sqn
29/05–04/06/43
Typhoon Ib
257 Sqn
12/08–17/09/43
Typhoon Ib
264 Sqn
31/12/40–11/01/41
Defiant I
266 Sqn
07–10/09/43
Typhoon Ib
306 (Polish) Sqn
11–19/08/43
Spitfire Vb
350 (Belgian) Sqn
30/06–07/07/42
Spitfire Vb
401 (Canadian) Sqn
19/03–03/07/42
Spitfire Vb
501 (AAF) Sqn
25/07–10/09/40
Hurricane I
604 (AAF) Sqn
03–27/07/40
Blenheim If
609 (AAF) Sqn
28/07–24/09/41
Spitfire Vb
610 (AAF) Sqn
27/05–08/07/40
Spitfire I
421 Flt
07–30/10/43
Hurricane II
Fighter Command satellite to Biggin Hill, 09/39
Upgraded to parent station, 11/40

GREAT DUNMOW, Essex

LOCATION: 6½m E of Bishop's Stortford
OPENED: 07/43
CLOSED: 04/58. Agriculture (2011)
ELEVATION: 324ft
PUNDIT CODE: GD
FORMATION: 38 Grp Fighter Command
MAIN CONTRACTOR: US Army

ABOVE: Flt Sgt 'Nick' Nicholls of No 107 Squadron was awarded the DFM for bringing home his damaged Boston III from the daylight raid on the Philips works at Eindhoven in Holland, on 6 December 1941. Nicholls brought AL754, 'D', home to its Norfolk base on one engine for a wheels-up landing in which the bomber overshot the airfield and was written off. The crew escaped with minor bruising. (Author)

RUNWAYS: 3 concrete
HANGARS: Blister (1), T2 (2)
USER SQNS/UNITS:
190 Sqn
14/10/44–21/01/46
Stirling IV; Halifax III, VII
620 Sqn
18/10/44–15/01/46
Stirling IV; Halifax VII
Opened as USAAF Station AAF-164, 07/43
To 38 Grp RAF Fighter Command, 10/44

GREAT MASSINGHAM, Norfolk

LOCATION: 10m E of King's Lynn
OPENED: 09/40
CLOSED: 04/58. Agriculture/light aviation (2011)
ELEVATION: 295ft
PUNDIT CODE: GM
FORMATIONS: 2, 100 (BS) Grp Bomber Command
MAIN CONTRACTOR: Unit Construction Co Ltd
RUNWAYS: 3 concrete
HANGARS: T2 (4), B1 (1)
USER SQNS/UNITS:
18 Sqn
09/09/40–03/04/41
Blenheim IV
90 Sqn
15/05–30/08/41
Fortress I
98 Sqn
12/09–19/10/42
Mitchell II, III
107 Sqn
11/05/41–20/08/43
Blenheim IV; Boston III, IIIa
169 Sqn
04/06/44–10/08/45
Mosquito II, VI, XIX
342 (French) Sqn
19/07–06/09/43
Boston IIIa
1692 Bomber Support Training Unit (BSTU)
22/05/44–15/06/45
Beaufighter; Mosquito VI; Wellington XVIII; Anson; Oxford
Opened in Bomber Command as satellite to West Raynham, 09/40
Upgraded to parent station, 03/06/44

GREAT ORTON, Cumberland

LOCATION: 1¼m S of Kirkbampton
OPENED: 06/43
CLOSED: 1952. Restricted access – Foot-and-mouth disease animal burial site (2011)
ELEVATION: 241ft
PUNDIT CODE: GE
FORMATION: 9 Grp Fighter Command
MAIN CONTRACTOR: Various
RUNWAYS: 3 concrete/Tarmac
HANGARS: Blister (3)
USER SQNS/UNITS:
281 Sqn (det)
04–09/44
11/44–01/45
Warwick I
282 Sqn (det)

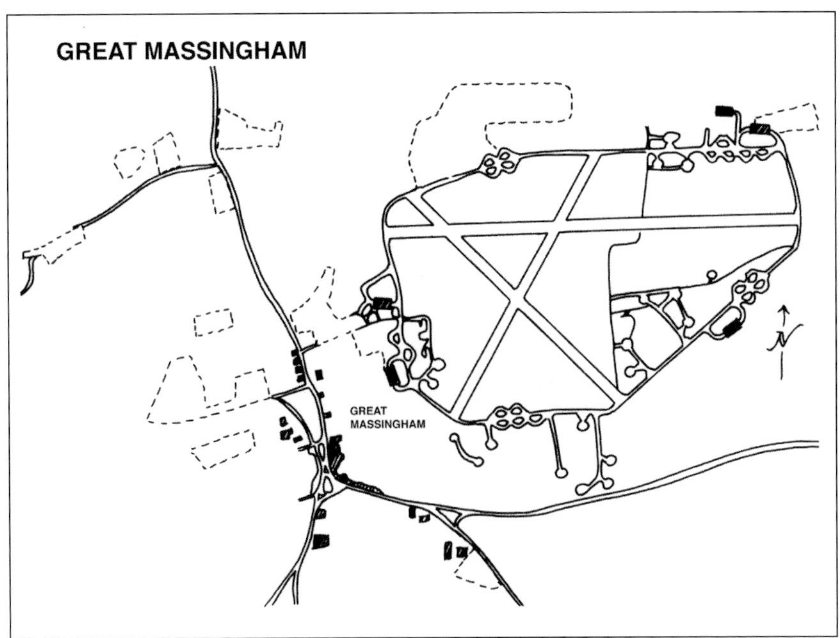

09–11/44
Warwick I
6 OTU
06/43–04/45
Wellington
55 OTU > 4 TEU > 3 TEU
20/10/43 (26/01/44)–28/03/44
07/04–10/05/44
Hurricane I, II; Typhoon I; Master I, II, III
1674 HCU (det)
11–12/43
Wellington
Opened in Fighter Command as satellite to Annan, 06/43

GREAT SAMPFORD, Essex

LOCATION: 7m SE of Saffron Walden
OPENED: 04/42
CLOSED: 08/44. Agriculture (2011)
ELEVATION: 342ft
PUNDIT CODE: GS
FORMATION: 11 Grp Fighter Command
MAIN CONTRACTOR: Various
RUNWAYS: 2 steel matting
HANGARS: Blister (4)
USER SQNS/UNITS:
65 Sqn
14/04–09/06/42
15–30/06/42
07–29/07/42
Spitfire Vb
133 Sqn
23–29/09/42
Spitfire Vb
676 Sqn
29/07–14/08/42
20/08–01/09/42
07–23/09/42
Spitfire Vb, VI
Opened in Fighter Command as satellite to Debden, 04/42

GRIMSBY/WALTHAM, Lincs

LOCATION: 9m S of Grimsby
OPENED: 11/41
CLOSED: 1946. Agriculture (2011)
ELEVATION: 67ft
PUNDIT CODE: GY
FORMATION: 1 Grp Bomber Command
MAIN CONTRACTOR: John Laing & Son Ltd
RUNWAYS: 3 concrete/Tarmac
HANGARS: T2 (2), B1 (1)
USER SQNS/UNITS:
100 Sqn
15/12/42–01/04/45
Lancaster I, III
142 Sqn
26/11/41–19/12/42
Wellington II, III
550 Sqn
20/10/43–03/01/44
Lancaster I, III
Opened in Bomber Command as satellite to Binbrook, 11/41
Became 12 Base substation, 1943

GRIMSETTER (KIRKWALL), Orkney

LOCATION: SE portion of mainland Orkney
OPENED: 10/40
CLOSED: Kirkwall Airport (2011)
ELEVATION: 30ft
PUNDIT CODE: Not known
FORMATION: 14 Grp Fighter Command
MAIN CONTRACTOR: Various
RUNWAYS: 3 concrete
HANGARS: Various (14)
USER SQNS/UNITS:
129 Sqn
25/09/42–19/01/43
Spitfire Vb
132 Sqn
11/06–23/09/42
Spitfire Vb
234 Sqn
19/01–24/04/43
Spitfire Vb, IV, VI
Opened in Fighter Command as a satellite of Skeabrae
Fighter Sector Station, 10/40
To RN as HMS Robin, 07/43

HAMPSTEAD NORRIS, Berks

LOCATION: 11m WNW of Reading
OPENED: 09/40
CLOSED: 1945. Agriculture (2011)
ELEVATION: 376ft
PUNDIT CODE: HN
FORMATIONS: 6 (T), 91 (OTU) Grp Bomber Command; 38 Grp Fighter Command
MAIN CONTRACTOR: George Wimpey & Co Ltd
RUNWAYS: 3 concrete/Tarmac
HANGARS: T2 (1), B1 (1), Bessonneau (1)
USER SQNS/UNITS:
Operational Refresher Training Unit (ORTU)
01/03/44–27/02/45

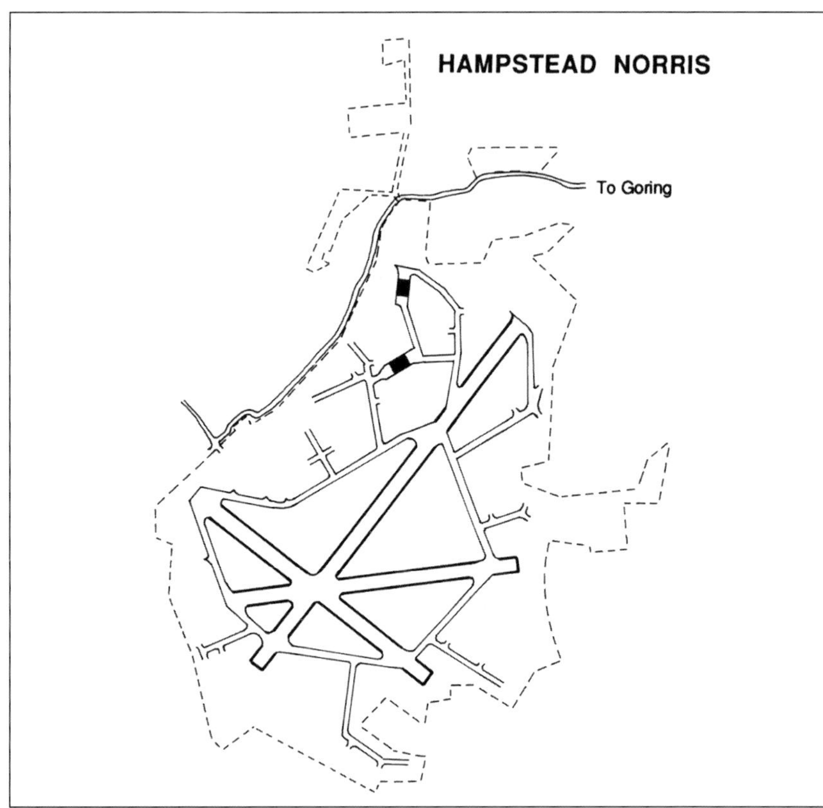

Whitley; Albemarle; Tiger Moth; Horsa

13 OTU
15/03–22/07/45
Mosquito II, III

15 OTU
09/40–03/44
Wellington I, III, X

Opened in 6 (T) Grp Bomber Command as satellite to Harwell, 09/40

To 38 Grp Fighter Command and upgraded to parent station, 03/44

Became satellite to Harwell, 02/45

HARRINGTON, Northants

LOCATION: 5m W of Kettering
OPENED: 09/11/43
CLOSED: 23/01/63. Agriculture/aviation museum (2011)
ELEVATION: 520ft
PUNDIT CODE: HR
FORMATION: 92 (OTU) Grp Bomber Command
MAIN CONTRACTOR: 826th and 852nd Engineer Battalions, US Army
RUNWAYS: 3 concrete
HANGARS: T2 (4)
USER SQNS/UNITS: none

Opened in Bomber Command as satellite to Desborough, 09/11/43

To USAAF as Station AAF-179, 28/03/44

HARROWBEER, Devon

LOCATION: 9m NNE of Plymouth
OPENED: 08/41
CLOSED: 1950. Agriculture (2011)
ELEVATION: 650ft
PUNDIT CODE: QB
FORMATION: 10 Grp Fighter Command
MAIN CONTRACTOR: Various
RUNWAYS: 3 asphalt
HANGARS: Bellman (2), Blister (8)
USER SQNS/UNITS:

1 Sqn
20–22/06/44
Spitfire IXb

64 Sqn
26/06–30/08/44
Spitfire Vc, IX

126 Sqn
03/07–30/08/44
Spitfire IXb

130 Sqn
25/10–30/11/41
Spitfire IIa, Vb, Vc

131 Sqn
24/03–24/05/44
Spitfire VII

165 Sqn
20–22/06/44
Spitfire IXb

175 Sqn
10/10–09/12/42
Hurricane IIb

183 Sqn
05/06–04/08/43
Typhoon Ib

193 Sqn
18/12/42–17/08/43
18/09/43–20/02/44
Hurricane II; Typhoon Ib

263 Sqn
20/02–15/03/43
19/03–19/06/44
Whirlwind I; Typhoon Ib

266 Sqn
07–10/09/43
21/09/43–07/03/44
12–15/03/44
Typhoon Ib

302 (Polish) Sqn
01/11/41–27/04/42
Spitfire Vb

312 (Czech) Sqn
02–19/05/42
31/05–01/07/42
08/07–16/08/42
20/08–10/10/42
Spitfire Vb, Vc

610 (AAF) Sqn
24/05–19/06/44
Spitfire XIV

611 (AAF) Sqn
24/06–03/07/44
Spitfire LFVb

Opened in Fighter Command as a satellite to Exeter, 08/41

To C&M, 08/44

Reopened as parent station in 10 Grp, 01/45

ABOVE: The personnel and aircraft of No 276 Squadron were assembled on 21 March 1943 at Harrowbeer to demonstrate the resources needed to mount a single air-sea rescue sortie. In the foreground is an Avro Anson, behind to its right is a Spitfire and at the rear, a Supermarine Walrus. The Commanding Officer, Squadron Leader Ronnie Hamlyn DFM, stands in the foreground. As a Spitfire pilot with No 610 Squadron in the Battle of Britain Hamlyn claimed five victories in one day, on 24 August. He went on to serve with No 242 Squadron flying Hurricanes and finished the war with 10 confirmed aerial victories. (IWM CH9017)

HARWELL, Berks

LOCATION: 6m S of Abingdon
OPENED: 02/37
CLOSED: UK Atomic Energy Research Establishment (2011)
ELEVATION: 384ft
PUNDIT CODE: HW
FORMATIONS: 6 (T), 91 (OTU) Grp Bomber Command; 12, 38 Grp Fighter Command
MAIN CONTRACTOR: John Laing & Son Ltd
RUNWAYS: 3 concrete
HANGARS: C Type (4)
USER SQNS/UNITS:

75 (New Zealand) Sqn
17/09/39–04/04/40
Wellington I

148 Sqn
17/09/39–08/04/40
Wellington I

295 Sqn
15/03–11/10/44
Albemarle I, V; Stirling IV

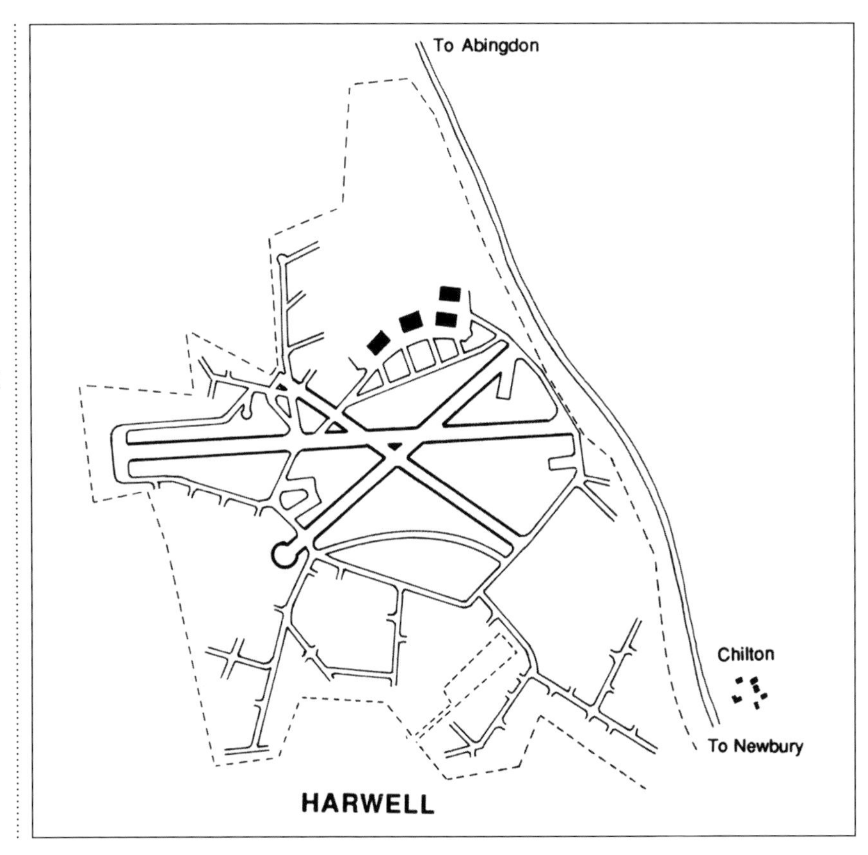

ABOVE: Spitfire Mk IA, X4595, JZ-D, was a presentation aircraft called 'Tamilnad' when she served with No 72 Squadron towards the end of the Battle of Britain. On 2 May 1941 she was handed down to No 57 OTU at Hawarden for pilot training, and in whose markings she is pictured. The unit moved north to RAF Eshott in Northumberland during 1942. On 17 March 1944, X4595 was being flown by Flt Sgt William Lynn when he was involved in a mid-air collision during formation flying practice with Spitfire Mk IA, R6596, piloted by Plt Off James Flood, also of No 57 OTU. Lynn was killed after X4595 crashed at Hepburn Moor, Northumberland. Flood survived to make an emergency landing. (Author)

570 Sqn
14/03–08/10/44
Albemarle I, II, V; Stirling IV
13 OTU
12/10/44–01/03/45
Mosquito I, III
15 OTU
08/04/40–03/03/44
Wellington I, X
Opened in Bomber Command as parent station, 02/37
To 38 Grp Fighter Command, 04/44
To 12 Grp Fighter Command, 10/44
To 2 Grp Bomber Command, 03/45

HAVERFORDWEST, Pembrokeshire

LOCATION: 2m W of Haverfordwest
OPENED: 1943
CLOSED: 1945. Private flying (2011)
ELEVATION: 163ft
FORMATION: 17 (T) Grp Coastal Command
RUNWAYS: 3 concrete and Tarmac
HANGARS: T2 (2)
USER SQNS/UNITS:
3 OTU
06/43–01/44
Whitley; Wellington; Anson
7 OTU > 4 Refresher Flying Unit (RFU)
01/44 (05/44)–09/44
Wellington
8 OTU
01–06/45
Spitfire; Mosquito

HAWARDEN, Flintshire

LOCATION: 4½m WSW of Chester
OPENED: 1939
CLOSED: BAE Systems (2011)
ELEVATION: 15ft
PUNDIT CODE: HK
FORMATIONS: 9, 12, 70 (OTU), 81 (OTU) Grp Fighter Command
MAIN CONTRACTOR: Various and Gerrard Ltd
RUNWAYS: 3 concrete
HANGARS: J Type (1), K Type (3), L Type (6), T2 (6)
USER SQNS/UNITS:
7 OTU > 57 OTU
15/06/40 (28/12/40)–10/11/42
Spitfire
41 OTU
14/11/42–23/03/45
Mustang I
Opened in Fighter Command as parent station, 1939

HAWKINGE, Kent

LOCATION: 2m N of Folkestone
OPENED: 1915
CLOSED: 01/62. Housing/Kent Battle of Britain Museum (2011)

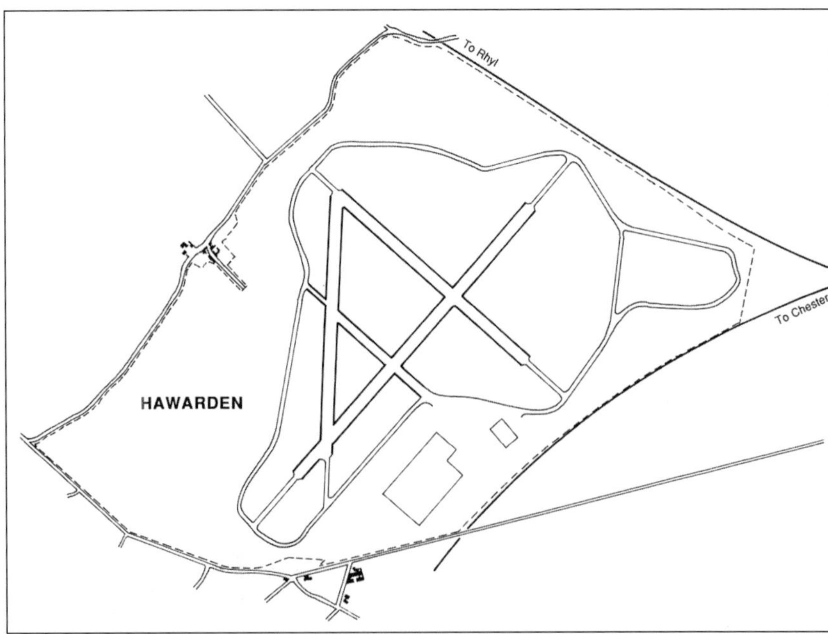

ELEVATION: 540ft
PUNDIT CODE: VK
FORMATION: 11 Grp Fighter Command
MAIN CONTRACTOR: Various
RUNWAYS: 3 grass
HANGARS: Blister (6), GS (4)
USER SQNS/UNITS:

17 Sqn
07–22/05/40
Hurricane I

25 Sqn
10–12/05/40
Blenheim If

41 Sqn
30/06–08/07/42
12/04–21/05/43
Spitfire XII

65 Sqn
30/06–07/07/42
Spitfire Vb

79 Sqn
01–11/07/40
Hurricane I

91 Sqn
09/01/41–02/10/42
09/10–23/11/42
11/01–20/04/43
21/05–28/06/43
Spitfire IIa, Vb, XII

124 Sqn
07–10/04/45
Spitfire HFIXe

313 (Czech) Sqn
21/08–18/09/43
Spitfire Vb

322 (Dutch) Sqn
31/12/43–25/02/44
01–10/03/44
Spitfire Vb, Vc

350 (Belgian) Sqn
01–12/10/43
31/10–30/12/43
10–14/03/44
08/08–29/09/44
Spitfire Vb, Vc, IXb, XIV

402 (Canadian) Sqn
08/08–30/09/44
Spitfire IX, XIVe

416 (Canadian) Sqn
14–20/08/42
Spitfire Vb

441 (Canadian) Sqn
01/10–30/12/44
Spitfire IXb

451 (Australian) Sqn
02/12/44–11/02/45
03–17/05/45
Spitfire IXb, XVI

453 (Australian) Sqn
02/05–14/06/45
Spitfire LFXVI

501 (AAF) Sqn
21/06/43–21/01/44
04/02–30/04/44
Spitfire Vb, IX

504 (AAF) Sqn
25–26/02/45
28/02–28/03/45
Spitfire IXe

605 (AAF) Sqn
21–28/05/40
Hurricane I

611 (AAF) Sqn
31/12/44–03/03/45
Spitfire IX

616 (AAF) Sqn
14–20/08/42
Spitfire VI

421 Flt
15/11/40–09/01/41
Spitfire IIa

To 11 Grp Fighter Command, 02/40

HEADCORN (Lashenden), Kent

LOCATION: 8m WSW of Ashford
OPENED: 07/43
CLOSED: 09/44. Agriculture/general aviation/Lashenden Air Warfare Museum (2011)
ELEVATION: 107ft
PUNDIT CODE: ED
FORMATION: 11 Grp Fighter Command
MAIN CONTRACTOR: RAF 511013 and 511014 ACS
RUNWAYS: 2 steel matting
HANGARS: None
USER SQNS/UNITS:

403 (Canadian) Sqn
20/08–14/10/43
Spitfire IXb

421 (Canadian) Sqn
20/08–14/10/43
Spitfire IX

Advanced Landing Ground (ALG)
Opened as HQ, 17 Fighter Wing, RCAF, 07/43
To USAAF as Station AAF-410, 10/43

HEMSWELL, Lincs

LOCATION: 7m E of Gainsborough
OPENED: 01/37
CLOSED: 1967. Agriculture/light industry/antiques centre (2011)

ELEVATION: 180ft
PUNDIT CODE: HL
FORMATIONS: 1, 5 Grp Bomber Command
MAIN CONTRACTOR: Various
RUNWAYS: 3 concrete/Tarmac
HANGARS: C Type (4), T2 (1)
USER SQNS/UNITS:

61 Sqn
08/03/37–17/07/41
Anson; Audax; Blenheim I; Hampden; Manchester

83 Sqn
18/04/44–01/01/56
Lancaster I, III; Lincoln

144 Sqn
09/03/37–17/07/41
Anson; Audax; Blenheim I; Hampden

150 Sqn
22/11/44–07/11/45
Lancaster I, III

170 Sqn
29/11/44–14/11/45
Lancaster I, III

300 (Polish) Sqn
18/07/41–18/05/42
31/01–22/06/43
Wellington I, III, IV, X

301 (Polish) Sqn
18/07/41–07/04/43
Wellington I, IV

305 (Polish) Sqn
22/07/42–22/06/43
Wellington II, IV, X

1 LFS
01–11/44
Lancaster I, III

Opened in Bomber Command as parent station, 01/37
Became 13 Base substation, 10/44

HESTON, Middx

LOCATION: 1¼m SSW of Southall
OPENED: 07/29
CLOSED: 1946. M4 motorway/industry/housing (2011)
ELEVATION: 100ft
PUNDIT CODE: HS
FORMATIONS: 11, 81 (OTU) Grp Fighter Command
MAIN CONTRACTOR: Various
RUNWAYS: 2 grass
HANGARS: Blister (6), T2 (6)
USER SQNS/UNITS:

129 Sqn
16–30/03/44
Spitfire IX; Mustang III

302 (Polish) Sqn
07/07–21/09/42
29/09/42–01/02/43
01–20/06/43
Spitfire Vb

303 (Polish) Sqn
05/02–05/03/43
12–26/03/43
08/04–01/06/43
Spitfire Vb

306 (Polish) Sqn
22/09–19/12/43
01/01–15/03/44
20/03–01/04/44
Spitfire Vb

308 (Polish) Sqn
30/07–15/09/42
21/09–29/10/42
21/09–11/11/43
Spitfire Vb

315 (Polish) Sqn
13/11–19/12/43
01/01–24/03/44
28/03–01/04/44
Spitfire Vb; Mustang III

316 (Polish) Sqn
23/04–30/07/42
Spitfire Vb

317 (Polish) Sqn
01–21/06/43
Spitfire Vb

350 (Belgian) Sqn
01–05/03/43
Spitfire Vb, Vc

515 Sqn
29/10/42–01/06/43
Defiant II

53 OTU
18/02–01/07/41
Spitfire I, II; Master III

61 OTU
01/07/41–15/04/42
Spitfire

Heston Flight (22/03/39) > 2 Camouflage Unit (01/11/39) > Photographic Development Unit (10/01/40) > Photographic Reconnaissance Unit (1 PRU, 18/07/40)
Blenheim IV; Lockheed 12A; Beechcraft C17; Spitfire I; Hudson I

1422 (Turbinlite) Flt
12/05/41–25/01/43
Boston; Havoc; Spitfire; Hurricane

Fighter Command satellite to Northolt, 09/39
To 81 (OTU) Grp, 12/40
To 11 Grp, 04/42
Forward Airfield in Tangmere Sector, 02/44
Satellite to Northolt, 06/44
To Ministry of Aircraft Production, 01/45

HIBALDSTOW, Lincs

LOCATION: 3m SW of Brigg
OPENED: 05/41
CLOSED: 05/45. Civilian parachute centre (2011)
ELEVATION: 33ft
PUNDIT CODE: HE
FORMATIONS: 9, 12, 81 (OTU) Grp Fighter Command
MAIN CONTRACTOR: Various
RUNWAYS: 3 Tarmac
HANGARS: Bellman (1), Blister (12)
USER SQNS/UNITS:

253 Sqn
21/09/41–24/05/42
30/05–14/06/42
07/07–16/08/42
20/08–13/11/42
Hurricane IIa, IIb, IIc, I

255 Sqn
15/05–20/09/41
Defiant I; Hurricane I; Beaufighter IIf

532 Sqn
09/11/42–25/01/43
Havoc I (Turbinlite); Boston III (Turbinlite)

1459 Flt > 538 Sqn
09/41 (02/09/42)–25/01/43
Havoc I, II (Turbinlite); Boston III (Turbinlite)

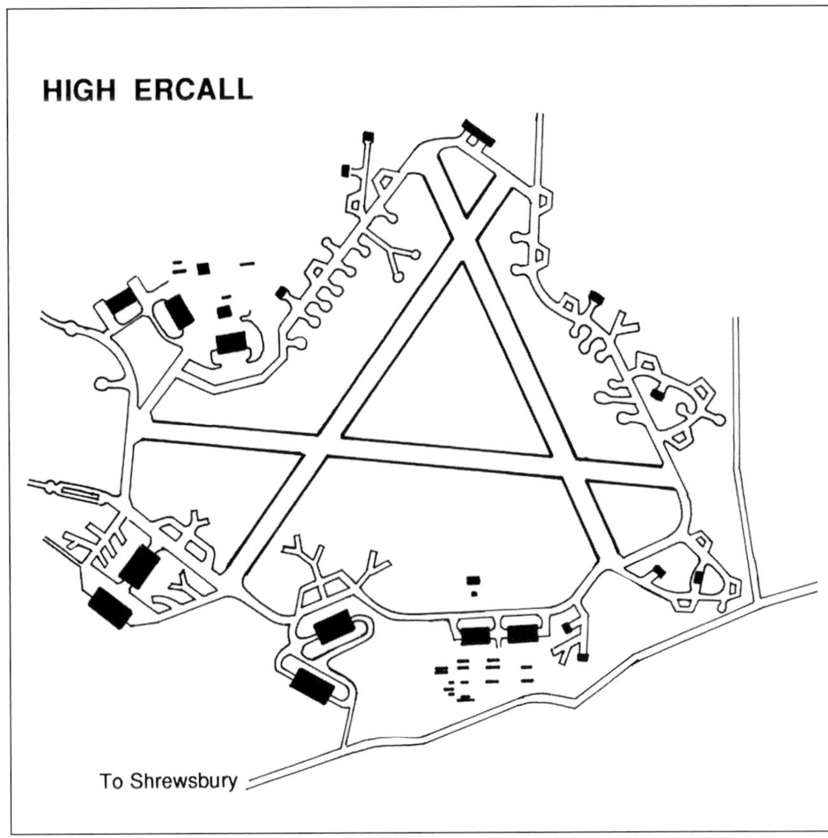

53 OTU
09/05/43–15/05/45
Spitfire I, II, V, IX; Master III

Opened in Fighter Command as satellite to Kirton-in-Lindsey, 05/41

To 81 (OTU) Grp as RLG for Kirton-in-Lindsey, 05/43

HIGH ERCALL, Salop

LOCATION: 5¼m NNW of Wellington
OPENED: 04/41
CLOSED: 02/62. Agriculture/storage (2011)
ELEVATION: 220ft
PUNDIT CODE: HC
FORMATIONS: 9, 81 (OTU) Grp Fighter Command
MAIN CONTRACTOR: G. Walker & Slater Ltd
RUNWAYS: 3 concrete
HANGARS: Blister (12), J Type (1), K Type (3), L Type (8), T2 (2)
USER SQNS/UNITS:

41 Sqn
25/02–12/04/43
Spitfire Vb, XII

68 Sqn
23/04/41–08/03/42
Blenheim If; Beaufighter If

247 Sqn
21/09/42–28/02/43
Hurricane IIb; Typhoon Ib

255 Sqn
02/03–06/06/42
Beaufighter IIf, VIf

257 Sqn
06/06–21/09/42
Hurricane IIb, IIa, IIc, I; Typhoon Ia, Ib

1456 Flt > 535 Sqn
00/06/42 (02/09)–25/01/43
Havoc I, II (Turbinlite); Boston III (Turbinlite)

60 OTU
17/05/43–11/03/45
Mosquito II, III

Opened in Fighter Command as parent station, 04/41

Upgraded to Sector Station, 05/43

To Maintenance Command, 03/45

HINTON-IN-THE-HEDGES, Northants

LOCATION: 6m ESE of Banbury
OPENED: 11/40
CLOSED: 07/45. Light aviation/gliding/skydiving (2011)
ELEVATION: 505ft
PUNDIT CODE: HI
FORMATIONS: 7 (T), 26 (Sig), 92 (OTU) Grp Bomber Command
MAIN CONTRACTOR: Various
RUNWAYS: 3 concrete/Tarmac
HANGARS: B1 (1), T1 (1)
USER SQNS/UNITS:

13 OTU
11/40–07/42
Blenheim

16 OTU
07/42–04/43
Wellington I

1478 Flt
15/04/43–07/44
Whitley V

Signals Development Unit (SDU)
06/43–07/44
Oxford; Anson; Master

Opened in Bomber Command as satellite to Bicester, 11/40

Satellite to Upper Heyford, 07/42

HIXON, Staffs

LOCATION: 7m NE of Stafford
OPENED: 05/42
CLOSED: 11/57. Agriculture/light industry (2011)
ELEVATION: 267ft
PUNDIT CODE: HX
FORMATION: 93 (OTU) Grp Bomber Command
MAIN CONTRACTOR: Various
RUNWAYS: 3 concrete/Tarmac
HANGARS: T2 (4), B1 (1)
USER SQNS/UNITS:

30 OTU
28/06/42–02/02/45
Wellington III, X

Opened in Bomber Command as satellite to Lichfield, 05/42

Upgraded to parent station, 07/42

HOLME-ON-SPALDING MOOR, Yorks

LOCATION: 5m SW of Market Weighton
OPENED: 08/41
CLOSED: 1954. Agriculture/light industry (2011)
ELEVATION: 12ft
PUNDIT CODE: HM
FORMATIONS: 1, 4 Grp Bomber Command
MAIN CONTRACTOR: Various
RUNWAYS: 3 Tarmac
HANGARS: J Type (1), T2 (5)
USER SQNS/UNITS:

76 Sqn
16/06/43–08/08/45
Halifax III, V, VI

101 Sqn
29/09/42–15/06/43
Wellington III; Lancaster I, III

458 (Australian) Sqn
25/08/41–23/03/42
Wellington I, IV

Opened in Bomber Command as parent station, 08/41
Became 44 Base HQ, 06/43
To Transport Command, 07/05/45

HOLMSLEY SOUTH, Hants

LOCATION: 6m NE of Christchurch
OPENED: 09/42
CLOSED: 10/46. Forestry Commission (2011)
ELEVATION: 20ft
PUNDIT CODE: Not known
FORMATION: 10 Grp Fighter Command
MAIN CONTRACTOR: John Laing & Son Ltd
RUNWAYS: 3 Tarmac
HANGARS: T2 (5)
USER SQNS/UNITS:

129 Sqn
22–24/06/44
Mustang III

174 Sqn
01/04–17/06/44
Typhoon Ib

175 Sqn
01/04–20/06/44
Typhoon Ib

182 Sqn
22/06–03/07/44
Typhoon Ib

184 Sqn
14–20/05/44
17–27/06/44
Typhoon Ib

ABOVE: After their pre-op briefing, Halifax crews of No 76 Squadron climb onboard their transports at Holme in the late afternoon of 22 October 1943, to be driven to their waiting aircraft at the dispersals. The target for tonight? Kassel. (IWM CH11401)

245 Sqn
01–25/04/44
30/04–12/05/44
22/05–27/06/44
Typhoon Ib
306 (Polish) Sqn
22–27/06/44
Mustang III
315 (Polish) Sqn
22–25/06/44
Mustang III
418 (Canadian) Sqn
08/04–14/07/44
Mosquito II
441 (Canadian) Sqn
18/03–01/04/44
Spitfire IXb
442 (Canadian) Sqn
18/03–01/04/44
Spitfire IXb
443 (Canadian) Sqn
18–27/03/44
Spitfire IXb
Opened in Coastal Command, 09/42
To 10 Grp Fighter Command, 01/44
To USAAF as Station AAF-455, 06/44
To 116 Wing RAF Transport Command, 10/44

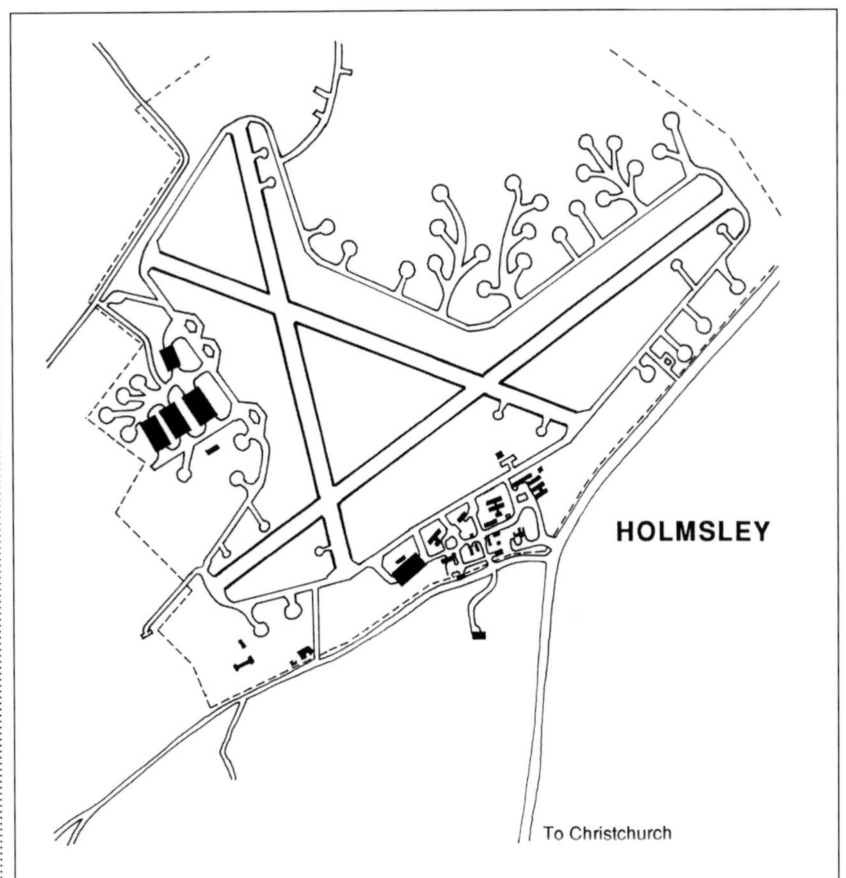

HONEYBOURNE, Worcs

LOCATION: 5m E of Evesham
OPENED: 10/41
CLOSED: 01/46. Agriculture/light industry (2011)
ELEVATION: 178ft
PUNDIT CODE: HQ
FORMATIONS: 6 (T), 91 (OTU) Grp Bomber Command
MAIN CONTRACTOR: John Laing & Son Ltd
RUNWAYS: 3 concrete
HANGARS: J Type (1), T2 (4)
USER SQNS/UNITS:
24 OTU
15/03/42–24/07/45
Whitley V, VII; Wellington III, X; Anson
Opened in Ferry Command as parent station, 10/41
To Bomber Command, 03/42

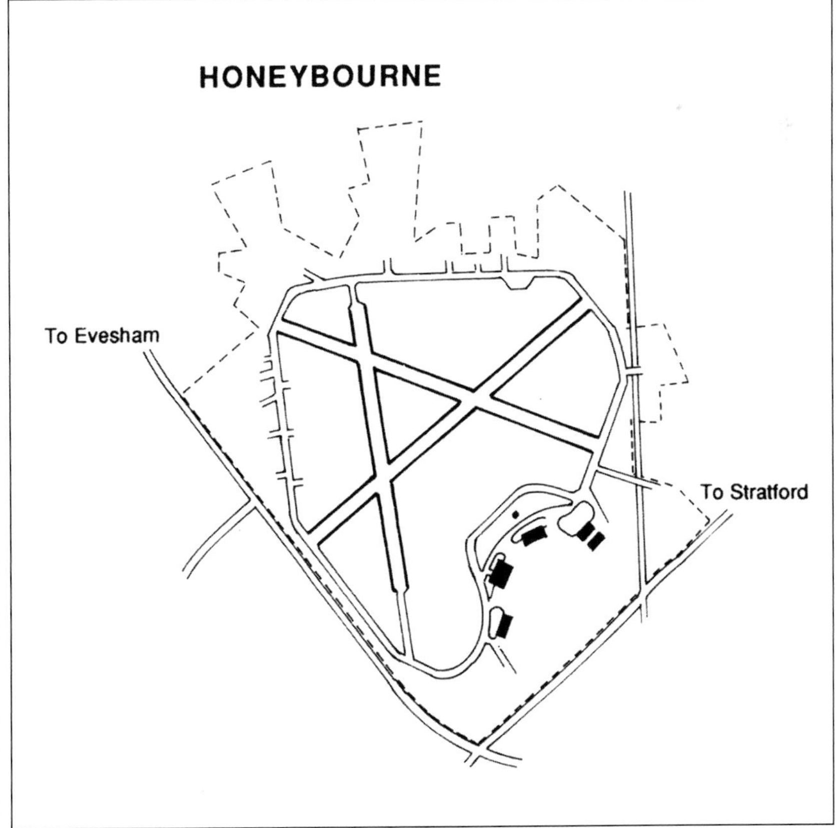

HONILEY, Warks

LOCATION: 7m SW of Coventry
OPENED: 08/41
CLOSED: 03/58. Vehicle test track (2011)
ELEVATION: 426ft
PUNDIT CODE: HY
FORMATIONS: 9 Grp Fighter Command; 26 Grp Bomber Command
MAIN CONTRACTOR: John Laing & Son Ltd
RUNWAYS: 3 Tarmac
HANGARS: Blister (12), Bellman (3)
USER SQNS/UNITS:

32 Sqn
10/09–19/10/42
Hurricane IIb, IIc

91 Sqn
20/04–09/05/43
Spitfire Vb, XII

96 Sqn
20/10/42–06/08/43
Beaufighter IIf, VIf

Signals Flying Unit
07/44–06/46
Anson; Beaufighter; Wellington; Oxford

135 Sqn
04/09–10/11/41
Hurricane IIa

219 Sqn
15–26/03/44
Mosquito XVII

234 Sqn
08/07–05/08/43
Spitfire Vb

255 Sqn
06/06–15/11/42
Beaufighter VIf

257 Sqn
07/11/41–06/06/42
Hurricane IIa, IIb, IIc, I; Spitfire Vb

605 (AAF) Sqn
04/09–01/11/41
Hurricane IIb

1456 Flt
24/11/41–06/42
Havoc I, II (Turbinlite); Boston III (Turbinlite)

63 OTU (AI Training)
17/08/43–21/03/44
Beaufighter II; Beaufort II; Blenheim V; Wellington XI

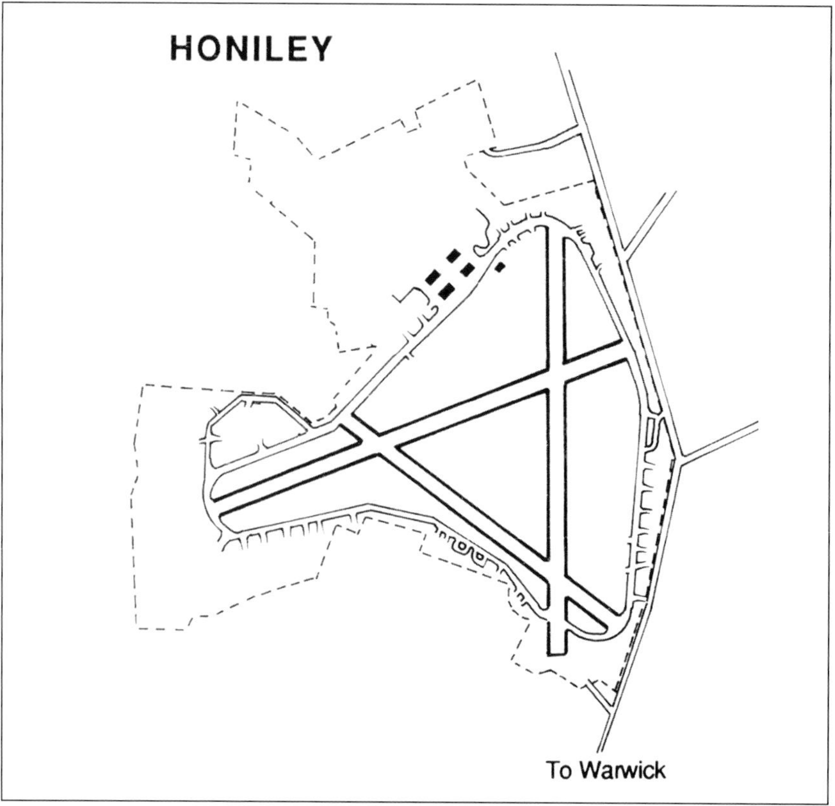

Opened in Fighter Command as Sector Station, 08/41
To 26 (Signals) Grp Bomber Command, 07/44

HONINGTON, Suffolk

LOCATION: 6m S of Thetford
OPENED: 03/05/37
CLOSED: RAF Regiment/Army (2011)
ELEVATION: 174ft
PUNDIT CODE: HT
FORMATIONS: 2, 3 Grp Bomber Command
MAIN CONTRACTOR: John Laing & Son Ltd
RUNWAYS: 3 grass
HANGARS: C Type (4)
USER SQNS/UNITS:

9 Sqn
15/07/39–08/08/42
Wellington I, II, III

103 Sqn
18/06–03/07/40
Battle

105 Sqn
14/06–10/07/40
Blenheim IV

214 Sqn
05–12/01/42
Wellington I

311 (Czech) Sqn
29/07–16/09/40
Wellington I

Opened in Bomber Command as parent station, 05/37
To USAAF, 09/42

HORNCHURCH, Essex

LOCATION: 2m SE of Romford
OPENED: 04/28
CLOSED: 07/62. Country park/housing (2011)
ELEVATION: 60ft
PUNDIT CODE: HO
FORMATION: 11 Grp Fighter Command
MAIN CONTRACTOR: Various
RUNWAYS: 3 grass
HANGARS: Blister (12), A Type (2), C Type (1)
USER SQNS/UNITS:

19 Sqn
25/05–05/06/40
Spitfire I

41 Sqn
28/05–17/06/40
26/07–08/08/40
03/09/40–23/02/41
Spitfire I, IIa

54 Sqn
15/01/30–28/10/39
03–17/11/39
02–16/12/39
29/12/39–16/01/40
14/02–23/03/40
20/04–28/05/40
04–25/06/40
24–28/07/40
08/08–03/09/40
23/02–31/03/41
20/05–11/06/41
13/06–04/08/41
25/08–17/11/41
Siskin IIIa; Bulldog IIa; Gauntlet II; Gladiator I; Spitfire I, IIa, Va, Vb

64 Sqn
11/11/40–27/01/41
31/03–09/05/41
15–16/05/41
16/11/41–06/02/42
22/02–31/03/42
01/05–19/07/42
27/07–08/09/42
14/11–09/12/42
15–28/03/43
Spitfire I, IIa, Vb, IX

65 Sqn
01/08/34–02/10/39
28/03–28/05/40
05/06–27/08/40
Demon; Gauntlet II; Gladiator I; Spitfire I

66 Sqn
08–16/11/43
01/12/43–22/02/44
Spitfire Vb, Vc, LFIXb

74 Sqn
21/09/36–22/10/39
29/10–03/11/39
14/11–02/12/39
16–29/12/39
16/01–14/02/40
23/03–20/04/40
26/06–14/08/40
Demon; Gauntlet II; Spitfire I, IIa

80 Sqn
05–19/05/44
Spitfire IX

81 Sqn
14/05–17/07/42
Spitfire Vb

92 Sqn
09–18/06/40
Spitfire I

122 Sqn
01/04–08/06/42
17/07–29/09/42
03/10–16/11/42
09/12/42–18/05/43
Spitfire Vb, IX

129 Sqn
28/06/43–17/01/44
Spitfire IX

132 Sqn
02–09/10/42
Spitfire Vb

154 Sqn
07/06–27/07/42
Spitfire Vb

167 Sqn
18–21/05/43
Spitfire Vb, Vc

222 Sqn
28/05–04/06/40
29/08–11/11/40
29/04–20/12/43
27–30/12/43
10/03–04/04/44
Spitfire I, Vb, IX, LFIXb

229 Sqn
24/04–19/05/44
Spitfire IX

239 Sqn
15/08–30/09/43
Mustang I

264 Sqn
22–29/08/40
Defiant I

266 Sqn
14–21/08/40
Spitfire I

274 Sqn
24/04–19/05/44
Spitfire IX

313 (Czech) Sqn
15/12/41–06/02/42
07/03–29/04/42
Spitfire Vb

340 (French) Sqn
28/07–23/09/42
Spitfire Vb

349 (Belgian) Sqn
11/03–06/04/44
Spitfire LFIXe

350 (Belgian) Sqn
07/12/42–01/03/43
13–15/03/43
19/02–10/03/44
Spitfire Vb, Vc, IXb

403 (Canadian) Sqn
04–25/08/41
Spitfire IIa, Vb

411 (Canadian) Sqn
19/11/41–07/03/42
Spitfire Vb

453 (Australian) Sqn
25/09–02/10/42
27/03–28/06/43
Spitfire Vb, IXb

485 (New Zealand) Sqn
18/10–21/11/43
28/02–21/03/44
07/04–07/05/44
Spitfire IXb

504 (AAF) Sqn
19–28/01/44
04/02–10/03/44
Spitfire IXb

600 (AAF) Sqn
02–16/10/39
20/10–27/12/39
24/08–12/09/40
Blenheim If, IV

603 (AAF) Sqn
28/08–03/12/40
16/05–16/06/41
09/07–12/11/41
Spitfire I, IIa, Va, Vb

611 (AAF) Sqn
27/01–20/05/41
14/06–12/11/41
Spitfire I, IIa, Va, Vb

Opened as parent station, 04/28
De-commissioned as fighter Sector Station, 06/44

HORNE, Surrey

LOCATION: 6½m SE of Redhill
OPENED: 04/44
CLOSED: 07/44. Agriculture (2011)
ELEVATION: 190ft
PUNDIT CODE: OR
FORMATION: 11 Grp Fighter Command
MAIN CONTRACTOR: RAFACS
RUNWAYS: 2 steel matting
HANGARS: Blister (4)
USER SQNS/UNITS:

130 Sqn
30/04–19/06/44
Spitfire Vb

303 (Polish) Sqn
30/04–19/06/44
Spitfire LFVb

402 (Canadian) Sqn
30/04–19/06/44
Spitfire Vb, Vc

Advanced Landing Ground (ALG)
Used by ADGB squadrons

HORSHAM ST FAITH, Norfolk

LOCATION: 4m N of Norwich
OPENED: 05/40
CLOSED: 1963. Norwich International Airport (2011)
ELEVATION: 102ft
PUNDIT CODE: HF
FORMATION: 2 Grp Bomber Command
MAIN CONTRACTOR: Various
RUNWAYS: 3 concrete
HANGARS: C Type (5)
USER SQNS/UNITS:

18 Sqn
13/07–05/11/41
05–09/12/41
Blenheim IV

105 Sqn
09/12/41–22/09/42
Mosquito IV

114 Sqn
10/06–10/08/40
Blenheim IV

139 Sqn
10/06/40–13/07/41
23/10–09/12/41
Blenheim IV

Opened in Bomber Command as parent station, 05/40
To USAAF as Station AAF-123, 09/42

HUCKNALL, Notts

LOCATION: 5¾m NW of Nottingham
OPENED: 1916
CLOSED: 1971. General aviation (2011)
ELEVATION: 300ft
PUNDIT CODE: Not known
FORMATION: 12 Grp Fighter Command; 1 Grp Bomber Command
MAIN CONTRACTOR: John Laing & Son Ltd
RUNWAYS: 2 grass
HANGARS: Blister (5); Various (6)
USER SQNS/UNITS:

98 Sqn
21/08/36–02/03/40
Hind; Battle

12 Grp Fighter Command, 09/39
To 1 Grp Bomber Command, 06/40

HUNSDON, Herts

LOCATION: 4m ESE of Ware
OPENED: 02/41
CLOSED: 07/47. Agriculture (2011)
ELEVATION: 254ft
PUNDIT CODE: HD
FORMATIONS: 11 Grp Fighter Command; 85 Grp 2 TAF; ADGB
MAIN CONTRACTOR: Various
RUNWAYS: 2 asphalt
HANGARS: Bellman (1), Blister (16)
USER SQNS/UNITS:

3 Sqn
09/08/41–14/05/43
Hurricane IIb, IIc; Typhoon Ib

21 Sqn
31/12/43–17/04/44
Mosquito VI

29 Sqn
19/06/44–22/02/45
Mosquito XIII, XXX

85 Sqn
03/05/41–13/05/43
Havoc I, II; Mosquito II, XV, XII

151 Sqn
19/11/44–01/03/45
Mosquito XXX

154 Sqn
01–19/03/45
Mustang IV

157 Sqn
13/05–09/11/43
Mosquito II, VI

219 Sqn
29/08–10/10/44
Mosquito XVII, XXX

264 Sqn
26/07–11/08/44
Mosquito XIII

409 (Canadian) Sqn
01/03–14/05/44
19/06–25/08/44
Beaufighter VIf; Mosquito XIII

410 (Canadian) Sqn
08/11–30/12/43
29/04–18/06/44
09–22/09/44
Mosquito II, VI, XIII, XXX

418 (Canadian) Sqn
28/08–21/11/44
Mosquito II

441 (Canadian) Sqn
29/04–17/05/45
Spitfire IX; Mustang III

442 (Canadian) Sqn
23/03–17/05/45
Mustang III

464 (Australian) Sqn
31/12/43–25/03/44
09–17/04/44
Mosquito VI

487 (New Zealand) Sqn
31/12/43–18/04/44
Mosquito VI

488 (New Zealand) Sqn
09/10–15/11/44
Mosquito XXX

501 (AAF) Sqn
03/03–20/04/45
Tempest V

515 Sqn
01/06–15/12/43
Defiant II; Beaufighter IIf

1451 Flt > 530 Sqn
22/05/41 (08/09/42)–25/01/43
Havoc II (Turbinlite); Boston III (Turbinlite)

ABOVE: Grp Capt P.C. 'Pick' Pickard (centre), Commander of No 140 Wing, No 2 Group, is flanked by Wg Cdr I.G.E. 'Daddy' Dale, Commanding Officer of No 21 Squadron (to Pickard's right), and Wg Cdr A.G. 'Willie' Wilson, Commanding Officer of No 487 (New Zealand) Squadron, during a visit to No 464 (Australian) Squadron at Hunsdon, Hertfordshire, in February 1944, prior to a daylight raid against flying-bomb sites in the Pas-de-Calais. No 464's de Havilland Mosquito FB VIs have been loaded with 250lb MC bombs for the operation. HX913, 'N', which can be seen in the background, was destroyed in an accident when it flew into the ground on Portland Bill during a night navigation exercise on 21 July 1944. This was one of the last photographs ever taken of Pickard: he was killed in action days later on 18 February during the famous Amiens prison raid. Dale was killed in action on 2 February 1945 when his Mosquito was shot down by flak. (IWM HU81335)

611 (AAF) Sqn
03/03–07/05/45
Mustang IV
Opened in Fighter Command as parent station, 02/41

HURN, Hants
LOCATION: 4m NE of Christchurch
OPENED: 07/41
CLOSED: Bournemouth Airport (2011)
ELEVATION: 34ft
PUNDIT CODE: KU
FORMATION: 11 Grp Fighter Command
MAIN CONTRACTOR: Various
RUNWAYS: 3 concrete
HANGARS: Bellman (3), Blister (10), T2 (4)
USER SQNS/UNITS:

125 Sqn
25/03–31/07/44
Mosquito XVII
164 Sqn
22/06–17/07/44
Typhoon Ib
181 Sqn
01/04–20/06/44
22–27/06/44
Typhoon Ib
182 Sqn
01/04–20/06/44
Typhoon Ib
183 Sqn
01–14/07/44
Typhoon Ib
193 Sqn
03–11/07/44
Typhoon Ib
197 Sqn
03–20/07/44
Typhoon Ib
198 Sqn
22/06–01/07/44
Typhoon Ib
247 Sqn
24/04–20/06/44
Typhoon Ib
257 Sqn
02–08/07/44
Typhoon Ib
263 Sqn
10–23/07/44
Typhoon Ib
266 Sqn
13–20/07/44
Typhoon Ib

412 (Canadian) Sqn
01–06/03/43
Spitfire Vb
418 (Canadian) Sqn
14–29/07/44
Mosquito II
438 (Canadian) Sqn
18/03–03/04/44
19/04–27/06/44
Hurricane IV; Typhoon Ib
439 (Canadian) Sqn
18/03–02/04/44
19/04–11/05/44
20/05–27/06/44
Hurricane IV; Typhoon Ib
440 (Canadian) Sqn
18/03–03/04/44
20/04–28/06/44
Hurricane IV; Typhoon Ib
604 (AAF) Sqn
03/05–13/07/44
Mosquito XIII
Opened in Fighter Command as a satellite to Ibsley, 07/41
To 38 Wing, 06/42
To 11 Grp, 03/44
To USAAF as Station AAF-492, 08/44
To BOAC, 10/44

HUSBANDS BOSWORTH, Leics

LOCATION: 10m NE of Rugby
OPENED: 1943
CLOSED: 1956. Agriculture/gliding (2011)
ELEVATION: 510ft
PUNDIT CODE: HZ
FORMATION: 92 (OTU) Grp Bomber Command
MAIN CONTRACTOR: Various
RUNWAYS: 3 concrete
HANGARS: T2 (4)
USER SQNS/UNITS:
14 OTU
08/43–15/06/44
Wellington III, X
85 OTU
06/44–07/45
Wellington III, X
Opened in Bomber Command as satellite to Market Harborough, 08/43

HUTTON CRANSWICK, Yorks

LOCATION: 4m SSW of Driffield
OPENED: 01/42
CLOSED: 06/46. Agriculture/industrial estate (2011)
ELEVATION: 107ft
PUNDIT CODE: CK
FORMATION: 12 Grp Fighter Command
MAIN CONTRACTOR: Various
RUNWAYS: 3 Tarmac
HANGARS: Blister (8), T Type (1)

BELOW: An AI Mk VIII radar-equipped Mosquito NF Mk XIII of No 604 Squadron takes off from Hurn during June 1944. In the background can be seen Typhoons of No 183 Squadron. (Author)

USER SQNS/UNITS:

19 Sqn
04/04–06/05/42
Spitfire Vb

91 Sqn
08–20/02/44
Spitfire XII

124 Sqn
10/04–15/07/45
Spitfire HFIXe

168 Sqn
20/09–10/10/43
Mustang Ia

170 Sqn
20/09–11/10/43
Mustang Ia

195 Sqn
19/11/42–12/02/43
Typhoon Ib

234 Sqn
15/10–31/12/43
Spitfire Vb

306 (Polish) Sqn
12/03–30/05/43
Spitfire Vb

308 (Polish) Sqn
07/05–01/07/42
07–30/07/42
05/07–07/09/43
13–21/09/43
02–18/12/43
Spitfire Vb, IX

310 (Czech) Sqn
21–25/02/44
Spitfire Vc

315 (Polish) Sqn
02/06–06/07/43
Spitfire Vb

316 (Polish) Sqn
30/07/42–12/03/43
Spitfire Vb

403 (Canadian) Sqn
24–29/02/44
Spitfire IXb

412 (Canadian) Sqn
05–20/01/44
Spitfire IXb

439 (Canadian) Sqn
11–20/05/44
Typhoon Ib

441 (Canadian) Sqn
12–23/04/44
Spitfire IXb

442 (Canadian) Sqn
25/04–01/05/44
Spitfire IXb

443 (Canadian) Sqn
27/03–08/04/44
Spitfire IXb

610 (AAF) Sqn
14/01–04/04/42
Spitfire Vb

Opened in Fighter Command as parent station, 01/42

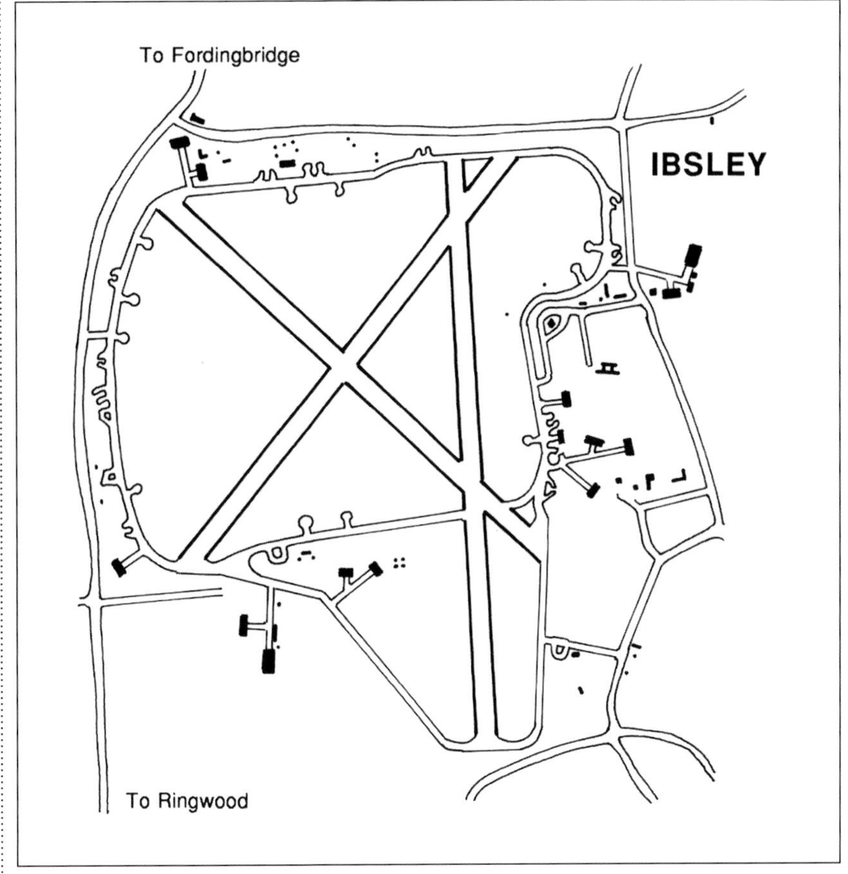

IBSLEY, Hants

LOCATION: 3m N of Ringwood
OPENED: 02/41
CLOSED: 1947. Gravel pits/landscaped lakes (2011)
ELEVATION: 80ft
PUNDIT CODE: IB
FORMATIONS: 10, 11 Grp Fighter Command
MAIN CONTRACTOR: Various
RUNWAYS: 3 Tarmac
HANGARS: Bellman (2), Blister (12)
USER SQNS/UNITS:

32 Sqn
16/02–17/04/41
Hurricane I

66 Sqn
27/04–03/07/42
07/07–16/08/42
20–24/08/42
23/12/42–09/02/43
Spitfire Vb, Vc

118 Sqn
18/04/41–23/02/42
07/03–03/07/42
07/07–16/08/42
23/12/42–03/01/43
Spitfire IIa, IIb, Vb

129 Sqn
13–28/02/43
13/03–28/06/43
Spitfire Vb

165 Sqn
30/06–30/07/43
Spitfire Vb, Vc

234 Sqn
05–24/11/41
31/12/41–23/03/42
04–27/04/42
Spitfire Vb
263 Sqn
05/12/43–05/01/44
Typhoon Ib
302 (Polish) Sqn
11/10–01/11/41
Spitfire IIa, Vb
310 (Czech) Sqn
19/09–02/12/43
Spitfire Vb, Vc
312 (Czech) Sqn
21/09–02/12/43
18/12/43–19/02/44
Spitfire Vc, LFIXb
313 (Czech) Sqn
18/09/43–06/01/44
20/01–20/02/44
Spitfire Vb, Vc, IX
421 (Canadian) Sqn
16–22/08/42
Spitfire Vb
453 (Australian) Sqn
28/06–20/08/43
Spitfire Vb, Vc
501 (AAF) Sqn
05/08/41–25/01/42
07/02–03/07/42
07/07–24/08/42
Spitfire IIa, Vb, Vc
504 (AAF) Sqn
30/12/42–30/06/43
Spitfire Vb
616 (AAF) Sqn
02/01–15/03/43
18/03–17/09/43
Spitfire VI

Opened in Fighter Command as a satellite to Middle Wallop, 02/41
To USAAF as Station AAF-347, 06/42
To 10 Grp RAF Fighter Command, 12/42
To USAAF as Station AAF-347, 01/44
To 11 Grp RAF Fighter Command, 10/44
To 46 Grp Transport Command, 03/45

INGHAM (CAMMERINGHAM), Lincs

LOCATION: 8m NW of Lincoln
OPENED: 05/42
CLOSED: 01/45. Agriculture (2011)
ELEVATION: 200ft
PUNDIT CODE: Not known
FORMATION: 1 Grp Bomber Command
MAIN CONTRACTOR: Various
RUNWAYS: 3 grass
HANGARS: T2 (2), B1 (1)
USER SQNS/UNITS:
199 Sqn
03/02–21/06/43
Wellington III, X
300 (Polish) Sqn
05/42–01/43
22/06/43–01/03/44
Wellington III, X
305 (Polish) Sqn
22/06–05/09/43
Wellington III, X

Opened in Bomber Command as satellite to Hemswell, 05/42
Became 13 Base substation, 03/44

ABOVE: No 299 Squadron's Stirling Mk IV, EF267, 'The Saint', was flown by Plt Off Den Hardwick and his crew from Keevil to Normandy on the eve of D-Day, 5/6 June 1944. The squadron carried paratroops of the 6th British Airborne Division's 5th Parachute Brigade to the eastern banks of the River Orne in Phase 1 of Operation 'Tonga'. Hardwick's crew successfully delivered 20 troops from 225 Parachute Field Ambulance, RAMC, and nine equipment containers. (D. Hardwick)

ABOVE: Keevil airfield remains in use in the 21st century by the RAF for occasional flying exercises and for civilian gliding. The watchtower is still used and is pictured here in May 1990. (Author)

IPSWICH, Suffolk

LOCATION: SE boundary of Ipswich
OPENED: 06/30
CLOSED: 1996. Housing (2011)
ELEVATION: 123ft
FORMATION: 12 Grp Fighter Command
MAIN CONTRACTOR: Various
RUNWAYS: 2 grass
HANGARS: Not known
USER SQNS/UNITS:

340 (French) Sqn
20–26/07/42
Spitfire Vb

Under control of Bomber Command, 09/39
To 12 Grp Fighter Command as satellite to Martlesham Heath, 03/42
Upgraded to parent station and transferred to 70 (T) Grp Army Co-operation Command, 03/43

KEEVIL, Wilts

LOCATION: 4½m E of Trowbridge
OPENED: 07/42
CLOSED: 1965. Army/RAF night flying training/gliding (2011)
ELEVATION: 188ft
PUNDIT CODE: KV
FORMATION: 38 Grp Fighter Command
MAIN CONTRACTOR: Various
RUNWAYS: 3 concrete
HANGARS: Blister (9), T2 (2)
USER SQNS/UNITS:

196 Sqn
14/03–09/10/44
Stirling IV

299 Sqn
15/03–09/10/44
Stirling IV

Opened in Army Co-operation Command as parent station, 07/42

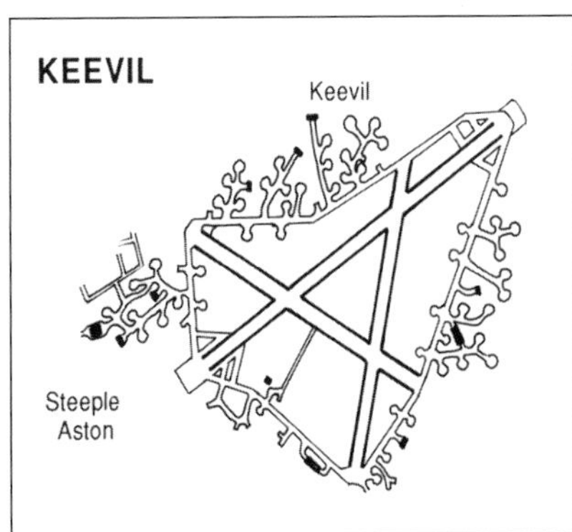

To USAAF as Station AAF-471, 09/42; 08/43
To 70 (AC) Grp RAF, 11/42
To USAAF as Station AAF-471, 08/43
To 38 Grp RAF Fighter Command, 02/44
To 23 Grp Flying Training Command, 10/44

KELSTERN, Lincs

LOCATION: 5m NW of Louth
OPENED: 09/43
CLOSED: 05/45. Agriculture (2011)
ELEVATION: 415ft
PUNDIT CODE: KS
FORMATION: 1 Grp Bomber Command
MAIN CONTRACTOR: Various
RUNWAYS: 3 concrete/Tarmac
HANGARS: T2 (2), B1 (1)
USER SQNS/UNITS:

170 Sqn
15–22/10/44
Lancaster I, III

625 Sqn
01/10/43–05/04/45
Lancaster I, III

Opened in Bomber Command as 12 Base substation, 09/43

KENLEY, Surrey

LOCATION: 4m S of Croydon
OPENED: 1917
CLOSED: 1959. Conservation area/ housing (2011)
ELEVATION: 524ft
PUNDIT CODE: KE
FORMATION: 11 Grp Fighter Command
MAIN CONTRACTOR: Constable, Hart & Co Ltd
RUNWAYS: 2 concrete
HANGARS: Belfast Truss (1), Blister (8)
USER SQNS/UNITS:

1 Sqn
05/01–07/04/41
01–14/06/41
Hurricane I, IIa, IIb

3 Sqn
28/01–10/05/40
20–30/05/40
Hurricane I

17 Sqn
25/05–08/06/40
Hurricane I

64 Sqn
16/05–19/08/40
Spitfire I

66 Sqn
03–10/09/40
13/08–17/09/43
Spitfire I, Vb, Vc

111 Sqn
28/07–21/09/42
Spitfire Vb

165 Sqn
08/08–17/09/43
Spitfire Vb, Vc

253 Sqn
08–24/05/40
29/08/40–03/01/41
Hurricane I

258 Sqn
22/04–01/06/41
14/06–10/07/41
Hurricane IIa

302 (Polish) Sqn
07/04–29/05/41
Hurricane IIa

312 (Czech) Sqn
29/05–20/07/41
Hurricane IIb

350 (Belgian) Sqn
16–31/07/42
Spitfire Vb

401 (Canadian) Sqn
24/09/42–23/01/43
Spitfire IX, Vb

402 (Canadian) Sqn
14–31/05/42
13/08/42–21/03/43
Spitfire Vb, IX

403 (Canadian) Sqn
23/01–07/08/43
14/10/43–24/02/44
29/02–18/04/44
Spitfire IXb

411 (Canadian) Sqn
22/03–08/04/43
Spitfire Vb

412 (Canadian) Sqn
02/11/42–29/01/43
Spitfire Vb

416 (Canadian) Sqn
01/02–29/05/43
12/02–17/04/44
Spitfire Vb, IXb

421 (Canadian) Sqn
06–11/10/42
29/01–01/03/43
13–23/03/43
17/05–06/08/43
14/10/43–02/03/44

ABOVE: During the first half of March 1943, Exercise 'Spartan' was held in southern and central England. With 10 Army divisions deployed on the ground, it was the largest offensive exercise ever conducted in Britain. 'Spartan' tested the efficiency of RAF tactical squadrons under mobile conditions and was effectively a rehearsal for the invasion and liberation of North West Europe. These Spitfire Mk Vs of Nos 416 and 421 (Canadian) Squadrons are pictured at Kenley. The white flashes on the fuselage sides denote the aircraft belonged to the 'Eastland' force. (Public Archives of Canada PL-15556)

08/03–18/04/44
Spitfire Vb, IX, IXb
452 (Australian) Sqn
21/07–21/10/41
14/01–23/03/42
Spitfire IIa, Vb
485 (New Zealand) Sqn
21/10/41–08/07/42
Spitfire Vb
501 (AAF) Sqn
10/09–17/12/40
Hurricane I
602 (AAF) Sqn
10/07/41–14/01/42
04/03–13/05/42
Spitfire IIa, Vb
611 (AAF) Sqn
03/06–13/07/42
14–20/08/42
Spitfire Vb, IX
615 (AAF) Sqn
22/05–29/08/40
16/12/40–21/04/41
Hurricane I, IIa
616 (AAF) Sqn
19/08–03/09/40
08–29/07/42
Spitfire I, VI
Fighter Command Sector Station, 09/39
Reduced to non-operational status, 04/44

KILLADEAS, Co Fermanagh, NI

LOCATION: 10m NW of Enniskillen
OPENED: 06/42
CLOSED: 1945. Lough Erne Yacht Club/ RNLI station (2011)
ELEVATION: 0ft
FORMATION: 17 (T) Grp Coastal Command
RUNWAYS: none. Alighting area in Gublusk Bay
HANGARS: Yes
USER SQNS/UNITS:
240 Sqn
28/03–23/08/41
Stranraer; Catalina I
131 (C) OTU
20/07/42–01/07/45
Catalina; Sunderland
302 FTU
15/04–01/07/45
Sunderland

KIMBOLTON, Hunts

LOCATION: 8m W of Huntingdon
OPENED: 11/41
CLOSED: 1946. Agriculture/industrial park (2011)
ELEVATION: 241ft
PUNDIT CODE: KI
FORMATION: 1 Grp Bomber Command
MAIN CONTRACTOR: Various
RUNWAYS: 3 concrete/asphalt
HANGARS: T2 (2)
USER SQNS/UNITS:
460 (Australian) Sqn
29/11/41–04/01/42
Wellington IV
Opened in Bomber Command as satellite to Molesworth, 11/41
To USAAF as Station AAF-117, 07/42

KINGS CLIFFE (Wansford), Northants

LOCATION: 12m W of Peterborough
OPENED: 10/41
CLOSED: 01/59. Agriculture (2011)
ELEVATION: 251ft
PUNDIT CODE: KO
FORMATION: 12 Grp Fighter Command
Main contractor. George Wimpey & Co Ltd
RUNWAYS: 3 concrete
HANGARS: Blister (4), T2 (2), other (8)
USER SQNS/UNITS:
93 Sqn
08/09–20/10/42
Spitfire Vb
266 Sqn
24/10/41–29/01/42
Spitfire IIa, Vb
349 (Belgian) Sqn
29/06–05/08/43
Spitfire Va
485 (New Zealand) Sqn
08/07–16/08/42
22/08–24/10/42
13/11/42–02/01/43
Spitfire Vb
676 Sqn
30/01–03/07/42
Spitfire Vb, VI
Opened in Fighter Command as satellite to Wittering, 10/41
To USAAF as Station AAF-367, 01/43
To RAF, 04/43
To USAAF as Station AAF-367, 09/43

KINGSNORTH, Kent

LOCATION: 2m S of Ashford
OPENED: 07/43
CLOSED: 01/45. Agriculture (2011)
ELEVATION: 125ft
PUNDIT CODE: IN
FORMATIONS: 83 Grp Fighter Command; 2 TAF
MAIN CONTRACTOR: RAFACS
RUNWAYS: 2 steel matting
HANGARS: Blister
USER SQNS/UNITS:
19 Sqn
18/07–30/09/43
Spitfire IX
65 Sqn
01/07–05/10/43
Spitfire Vb, IX
122 Sqn
01/07–05/10/43
Spitfire Vb, IX
184 Sqn
14–18/08/43
Hurricane IV
602 (AAF) Sqn
01/07–13/08/43
Spitfire Vb
Advanced Landing Ground (ALG)
Opened in Fighter Command, 07/43
To USAAF as Station AAF-418, 03/44

KINGSTON BAGPUIZE, Berks

LOCATION: 5m W of Abingdon
OPENED: 1942
CLOSED: 1954. Agriculture/business park (2011)
ELEVATION: 300ft
PUNDIT CODE: KB

FORMATION: Fighter Command
MAIN CONTRACTOR: Various
RUNWAYS: 2 steel matting
HANGARS: Butler (2), Blister (3), T2 (2)
USER SQNS/UNITS:
(uncertain)
Bomber Command satellite to Harwell

KINLOSS, Morayshire

LOCATION: 9m W of Elgin
OPENED: 1939
CLOSED: RAF base (2011)
ELEVATION: 19ft
PUNDIT CODE: KW
FORMATIONS: 7 (T), 91 (OTU) Grp Bomber Command
MAIN CONTRACTOR: Various
RUNWAYS: 3 concrete/Tarmac
HANGARS: K Type (2), L Type (9), Bellman (2)
USER SQNS/UNITS:
19 OTU
17/05/40–26/06/45
Whitley III, V; Wellington III, X
Opened in Flying Training Command as parent station, 1939
To Bomber Command, 04/40

KINNELL, Angus

LOCATION: 5½m S of Brechin
OPENED: 1942
CLOSED: 1945. Agriculture (2011)
ELEVATION: 150ft
PUNDIT CODE: KL
FORMATIONS: 9, 81 (OTU) Grp Fighter Command
MAIN CONTRACTOR: Various
RUNWAYS: 2 asphalt
HANGARS: Blister (4)
USER SQNS/UNITS:
56 OTU > 1 Combat Training Wing (CTW) > 1 Tactical Exercise Unit (TEU)
29/03/42 (05/10/43)–31/07/44
Hurricane; Spitfire
Opened in Fighter Command as satellite to Tealing, 1942
To Flying Training Command, 08/44

KIRKISTOWN, Co Down, NI

LOCATION: 2½m S of Ballyhalbert
OPENED: 07/41
CLOSED: 1952. Disused/motor racing track (2011)
ELEVATION: 20ft
PUNDIT CODE: IK
FORMATIONS: 13, 82 (OTU) Grp Fighter Command
MAIN CONTRACTOR: Various
RUNWAYS: 3 Tarmac
HANGARS: Blister (4)
USER SQNS/UNITS:
485 (New Zealand) Sqn
24/10–05/11/42
Spitfire Vb
504 (AAF) Sqn
12/01–19/06/42
Spitfire IIa, IIb, Vb
Opened in Fighter Command as satellite to Ballyhalbert, 07/41
To RAF Northern Ireland, 03/44

KIRMINGTON, Lincs

LOCATION: 6m NE of Brigg
OPENED: 10/42
CLOSED: 02/46. Humberside International Airport (2011)
ELEVATION: 86ft
PUNDIT CODE: KG
FORMATION: 1 Grp Bomber Command
MAIN CONTRACTOR: Various
RUNWAYS: 3 concrete/Tarmac
HANGARS: T2 (2), B1 (1)
USER SQNS/UNITS:
142 Sqn
19/12/42–27/01/43
Wellington III
150 Sqn
10–12/42
Wellington I, III
153 Sqn
07–15/10/44
Lancaster I, III
166 Sqn
27/01/43–18/11/45
Lancaster I, III
Opened in Bomber Command as satellite to Elsham Wolds, 10/42
Became 13 Base substation, 1943

KIRTON-IN-LINDSEY, Lincs

LOCATION: 16m N of Lincoln
OPENED: 05/40
CLOSED: RAF base, non-flying (2011)
ELEVATION: 200ft
PUNDIT CODE: Not known
FORMATIONS: 9, 12, 81 (OTU) Grp Fighter Command
MAIN CONTRACTOR: John Laing & Son Ltd
RUNWAYS: 2 grass
HANGARS: Blister (4), C Type (3)
USER SQNS/UNITS:
43 Sqn
01/09–28/10/42
Hurricane IIc
65 Sqn
28/05–05/06/40
26/02–28/09/41
03–07/10/41
Spitfire I, IIa, IIb
77 Sqn
23/11/40–05/04/41
Hurricane I, IIa
74 Sqn
21/08–09/09/40
Spitfire I, IIa
85 Sqn
23/10–23/11/40
Hurricane I
121 Sqn
05/05–28/09/41
03/10–16/12/41
Hurricane I, IIb; Spitfire IIa, Vb
133 Sqn
02/01–03/05/42
Spitfire Va, Vb
136 Sqn
20/08–09/11/41
Hurricane IIa, IIb
222 Sqn
23–28/05/40
28/05–04/06/40
Spitfire I
253 Sqn
24/05–21/07/40
Hurricane I
255 Sqn
23/11/40–15/05/41
Defiant I; Hurricane I
264 Sqn
23/07–22/08/40

29/08–29/10/40
Defiant I
302 (Polish) Sqn
01/02–17/04/43
Spitfire Vb
303 (Polish) Sqn
16/06–15/08/42
20/08/42–02/02/43
Spitfire Vb
306 (Polish) Sqn
03/05–16/06/42
Spitfire Vb
307 (Polish) Sqn
05/09–07/11/40
Defiant I
317 (Polish) Sqn
13/02–29/04/43
Spitfire Vb
452 (Australian) Sqn
08/04–21/07/41
Spitfire I, IIa
457 (Australian) Sqn
31/05–18/06/42
Spitfire Vb
486 (New Zealand) Sqn
03/03–09/04/42
Hurricane IIb
676 Sqn
09/09/40–26/02/41
06/10/41–30/01/42
Spitfire I, IIb, Vb
53 OTU
09/05/43–15/05/45
Spitfire I, II, V, IX; Master III
Opened in Fighter Command as Sector Station, 05/40
To USAAF as Station AAF-349, 1942
To RAF Training Command, 05/43

LAKENHEATH, Suffolk

LOCATION: 4½m SW of Brandon
OPENED: 06/41
CLOSED: USAF base (2011)
ELEVATION: 32ft
PUNDIT CODE: LK
FORMATIONS: 3, 6 (T), 91 (OTU) Grp Bomber Command
MAIN CONTRACTOR: Various
RUNWAYS: 3 concrete
HANGARS: T2 (2), B1 (1)
USER SQNS/UNITS:
20 OTU
24/11/41–12/01/42
Wellington I
149 Sqn
06/04/42–15/05/44
Stirling I, III
199 Sqn
21/06/43–01/05/44
Wellington III, X; Stirling III
Opened in Bomber Command as satellite to Mildenhall, 06/41
Became 31 Base substation, 12/42
Closed for rebuilding to Very Heavy Bomber (VHB) station standard, 05/44
*Flt Sgt R.H.Middleton, 149 Sqn, awarded posthumous VC, Turin, 28–29/11/42

LANGAR, Notts

LOCATION: 9m SE of Nottingham
OPENED: 09/42
CLOSED: 09/68. Parachute school/light industry (2011)
ELEVATION: 118ft
PUNDIT CODE: LA
FORMATIONS: 5, 7 (T) Grp Bomber Command
MAIN CONTRACTOR: George Wimpey & Co Ltd
RUNWAYS: 3 concrete/Tarmac
HANGARS: T2 (2)
USER SQNS/UNITS:
207 Sqn
20/09/42–12/10/43
Lancaster I, III
1669 HCU
11/44–03/45
Lancaster I, III; Halifax
Opened in Bomber Command as satellite to Bottesford, 09/42
To USAAF, 18/10/43
To RAF Bomber Command, 10/44
Became 72 Base substation, 11/44

LANGHAM, Norfolk

LOCATION: 5½m NW of Holt
OPENED: 1940
CLOSED: 1961. Agriculture (2011)
ELEVATION: 60ft
FORMATION: 16 Grp Coastal Command
RUNWAYS: 3 concrete and Tarmac
HANGARS: T2 (3), Blister (4)
USER SQNS/UNITS:
280 Sqn
30/07–05/11/42
06/09–30/10/44
Warwick I
407 (Canadian) Sqn (det)
14/04–09/05/45
Wellington XIV
455 (Australian) Sqn
14/04–20/10/44
Beaufighter X
489 (New Zealand) Sqn
08/04–24/10/44
Beaufighter X
521 Sqn
01/11/44–03/11/45
Gladiator II; Hudson VI; Ventura V; Hurricane II; Spitfire IX
524 Sqn
17/10/44–25/05/45
Wellington XIII, XIV
827 NAS
11/44–12/44
Barracuda
Opened in Coastal Command
To Care & Maintenance, 03/11/42
Reopened in 16 Grp, 22/02/44

LASHAM, Hants

LOCATION: 6m SSE of Basingstoke
OPENED: 11/42
CLOSED: 10/48. Agriculture/light industry/gliding (2011)
ELEVATION: 600ft
PUNDIT CODE: LQ
FORMATIONS: 10, 11 Grp Fighter Command; 2 Grp 2 TAF
MAIN CONTRACTOR: Sir Alfred McAlpine Ltd
RUNWAYS: 3 concrete
HANGARS: T2 (4)
USER SQNS/UNITS:
33 Sqn
15/12/44
Spitfire LFIXe

175 Sqn
11–13/03/43
29/05–02/06/43
Hurricane IIb; Typhoon Ib
181 Sqn
05/04–02/06/43
Typhoon Ib
182 Sqn
06/43
Typhoon Ib
183 Sqn
03–30/05/43
Typhoon Ib
412 (Canadian) Sqn
07/03–08/04/43
Spitfire Vb
602 (AAF) Sqn
14–29/04/43
Spitfire Vb
Opened in Army Co-operation Command, 11/42
To 10 Grp Fighter Command, 06/43
To 2 Grp, 2 TAF, 08/43
To 11 Grp Fighter Command, 11/44
Satellite to Blackbushe, 01/45

LECONFIELD, Yorks

LOCATION: 2¾m N of Beverley
OPENED: 12/36
CLOSED: 1977. Tri-Service Defence School of Transport; 202 Sqn RAF, SAR Flight (2011)
ELEVATION: 25ft
PUNDIT CODE: LC
FORMATIONS: 13 Grp Fighter Command; 4, 6 Grp Bomber Command
MAIN CONTRACTOR: Various
RUNWAYS: 3 concrete
HANGARS: C Type (5)
USER SQNS/UNITS:
51 Sqn
20/04–21/08/45
Halifax III; Stirling V
64 Sqn
19/08–13/10/40
Spitfire I
72 Sqn
17/10–01/11/39
12–13/01/40
13–20/10/40
Spitfire I
74 Sqn
27/05–06/06/40
Spitfire I
97 Sqn
07/01/37–17/09/39
Whitley II, III
129 Sqn
16/06–29/08/41
Spitfire I
134 Sqn
28/07–12/08/41
Hurricane IIb
196 Sqn
22/12/42–19/07/43
Wellington X
213 Sqn
29/11/40–15/01/41
Hurricane I
234 Sqn
30/10/39–22/05/40
Battle; Blenheim If; Gauntlet II; Spitfire I
245 Sqn
30/10/39–12/05/40
Blenheim If; Battle; Hurricane I
249 Sqn
17/05–08/07/40
Spitfire I; Hurricane I
253 Sqn
03/01–10/02/41
Hurricane I
258 Sqn
22/11–01/12/40
Hurricane I
302 (Polish) Sqn
13/07–11/10/40
Hurricane I

BELOW: Ground crew re-arm a No 489 (New Zealand) Squadron 'Torbeau' at Langham in Norfolk during the summer of 1944. This Kiwi Beaufighter squadron usually flew alongside neighbouring No 455 (Australian) Squadron on anti-shipping strikes, the latter unit acting in the anti-flak role. (IWM HU81248)

303 (Polish) Sqn
11/10/40–03/01/41
Hurricane I
313 (Czech) Sqn
01/07–26/08/41
Spitfire I
466 (Australian) Sqn
22/12/42–03/06/44
Wellington X; Halifax II, III
485 (New Zealand) Sqn
21/04–01/07/41
Spitfire I, IIa
610 (AAF) Sqn
29/08/41–14/01/42
Spitfire IIa, Vb
616 (AAF) Sqn
23/10/39–27/05/40
06/06–19/08/40
Gauntlet II; Battle; Spitfire I
640 Sqn
07/01/44–07/05/45
Halifax III, VI
60 OTU
28/04–04/06/41
Blenheim; Defiant; Oxford
Opened in Bomber Command as satellite to Driffield, 03/12/36
To 13 Grp Fighter Command, 10/39
Closed for runway building, 12/41
Reopened in 4 Grp Bomber Command, 02/12/42
Became 43 Base substation, 06/06/43

LEEMING, Yorks

LOCATION: 7m SW of Northallerton
OPENED: 06/40
CLOSED: RAF base (2011)
ELEVATION: 132ft
PUNDIT CODE: LG
FORMATIONS: 3, 4, 6 (RCAF) Grp Bomber Command
MAIN CONTRACTOR: Various
RUNWAYS: 3 concrete/Tarmac
HANGARS: C Type (5)
USER SQNS/UNITS:
7 Sqn
01/08–29/10/40
Stirling I
10 Sqn
08/07/40–19/08/42
Whitley V; Halifax
35 Sqn
20/11–05/12/40
Halifax I
77 Sqn
05/09/41–06/05/42
Whitley V
102 Sqn
25/08–01/09/40
Whitley V
405 (Canadian) Sqn
06/03–18/04/43
Halifax II
408 (Canadian) Sqn
14/09/42–26/08/43
Halifax V, II
419 (Canadian) Sqn
13–17/08/42
Wellington III
424 (Canadian) Sqn
07/04–02/05/43
Wellington III, X
427 (Canadian) Sqn
05/05/43–31/05/46
Halifax V, III; Lancaster III, X
429 (Canadian) Sqn
13/08/43–31/05/46
Halifax II, V, III; Lancaster III, X
1659 HCU
06/10/42–06/03/43
Halifax
Opened in Bomber Command as parent station, 06/40
Became 63 (RCAF) Base HQ, 01/01/43

LEICESTER EAST, Leics

LOCATION: 4m SE of Leicester
OPENED: 10/43
CLOSED: 12/47. Flying club (2011)
ELEVATION: 455ft
PUNDIT CODE: LE
FORMATION: 38 Grp Fighter Command
MAIN CONTRACTOR: Various
RUNWAYS: 3 concrete
HANGARS: T2 (4)
USER SQNS/UNITS:
190 Sqn
05/01–25/03/44
Stirling IV
196 Sqn
18/11/43–07/01/44
Stirling III, IV
620 Sqn
22/11/43–18/03/44
Stirling III
Opened in Fighter Command as parent station, 10/43
To Transport Command, 05/44

LEUCHARS, Fife

LOCATION: 4m NW of St Andrews
OPENED: 1918
CLOSED: RAF base, flying (2011)
ELEVATION: 38ft
FORMATION: 18 Grp Coastal Command
RUNWAYS: 2 concrete
HANGARS: C Type (4), Bellman (2), Aircraft sheds (4), EO Blister (9)
USER SQNS/UNITS:
42 Sqn
01/03/41–18/04/42
Beaufort I, II
72 Sqn
29/11–15/12/40
Spitfire I
107 Sqn
03/04–11/05/41
Blenheim IV
114 Sqn
13/05–19/07/41
Blenheim IV
144 Sqn
22/04/42–08/04/43
Hampden; Beaufighter VIc
206 Sqn
11/07/44–31/07/45
Liberator VI, VIII
224 Sqn
01/09/38–15/04/41
Hudson I, III
233 Sqn
01–28/09/38
10/10/38–03/08/40
14/09–08/12/40
Anson I; Hudson I; Blenheim IV

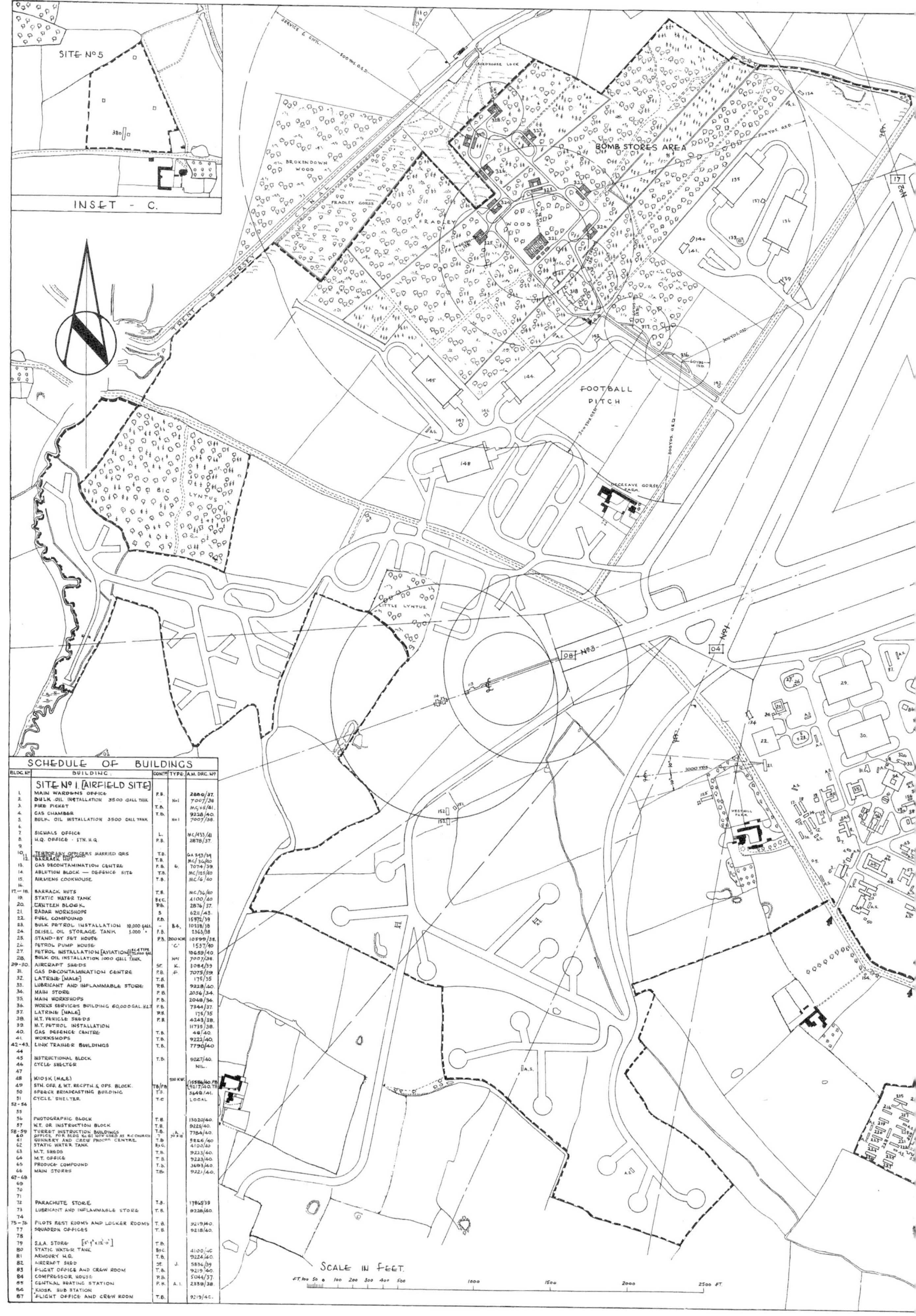

SCHEDULE OF BUILDINGS

BLDG. No	BUILDING	CONTR	TYPE.	A.M. DRG. No
	SITE No 1. [AIRFIELD SITE]			
1.	MAIN WARDENS OFFICE	P.B.		2880/37.
2.	BULK OIL INSTALLATION 3500 GALL TANK	–	No1	7007/38
3.	FIRE PICKET	T.B.		MC/65/41.
4.	GAS CHAMBER	T.B.		9228/40.
5.	BULK OIL INSTALLATION 3500 GALL TANK		No1	7007/38.
6.				
7.	SIGNALS OFFICE	L.		MC/433/41
8.	H.Q. OFFICE - STN. H.Q.	P.B.		2878/37.
9.				
10.	TEMPORARY OFFICERS MARRIED QRS	T.B.		GA 243/39
11.	CHURCH OF ENGLAND			
12.	BARRACK HUT	T.B.		MC/36/40
13.	GAS DECONTAMINATION CENTRE	P.B.	E.	7074/39.
14.	ABLUTION BLOCK — DEFENCE SITE	T.B.		MC/126/40
15.	AIRMENS COOKHOUSE	T.B.		MC/6/40
16.				
17.–18.	BARRACK HUTS	T.B.		MC/36/40
19.	STATIC WATER TANK	B&C.		4100/40
20.	CANTEEN BLOCK	P.B.		2876/37.
21.	RADAR WORKSHOPS	S		6211/43.
22.	FUEL COMPOUND	P.B.		15972/39
23.	BULK PETROL INSTALLATION 18,000 GALS.	–	B4.	10238/38
24.	DEISEL OIL STORAGE TANK 3.000 "	P.B.		2363/38
25.	STAND-BY SET HOUSE	P.B.	200 KW	10599/38.
26.	PETROL PUMP HOUSE		'C'	1537/40
27.	PETROL INSTALLATION [AVIATION] {SC4 TYPE 72,000 GAL			10659/40.
28.	BULK OIL INSTALLATION 1000 GALL TANK		No1	7007/38.
29-30.	AIRCRAFT SHEDS	ST.	K.	3084/39
31.	GAS DECONTAMINATION CENTRE	P.B.	F.	7075/39.
32.	LATRINE [MALE]	T.B.		175/35
33.	LUBRICANT AND INFLAMMABLE STORE	P.B.		9228/40.
34.	MAIN STORE	P.B.		2056/34.
35.	MAIN WORKSHOPS	P.B.		2048/34.
36.	WORKS SERVICES BUILDING 60,000 GAL. H.L.T	P.B.		7344/37.
37.	LATRINE [MALE]	P.B.		175/35
38.	M.T. VEHICLE SHEDS	P.B.		4243/38.
39.	M.T. PETROL INSTALLATION			11735/38.
40.	GAS DEFENCE CENTRE	T.B.		48/40.
41.	WORKSHOPS	T.B.		9222/40.
42-43.	LINK TRAINER BUILDINGS	T.B.		7790/40
44				
45	INSTRUCTIONAL BLOCK	T.B.		9227/40.
46	CYCLE SHELTER			NIL.
47				
48	KIOSK (M&E)		200 KW.	15586/40. PB
49	STN. OFF. & W.T. RECPTN. & OPS. BLOCK.	TB/PB		9217/40. TB
50	SPEECH BROADCASTING BUILDING	T.B.		5648/41.
51	CYCLE SHELTER	T.C		LOCAL
52-54				
55				
56	PHOTOGRAPHIC BLOCK	T.B.		13020/40.
57	W.T. OR INSTRUCTION BLOCK	T.B.		9225/40.
58-59	TURRET INSTRUCTION BUILDINGS	T.B.	A. 70'×18'	7784/40.
60	OFFICE FOR BLDG No 61 NOW USED AS R.C CHURCH	T		
61	GUNNERY AND CREW PROCSR CENTRE	T.B.		9226/40
62	STATIC WATER TANK	B&C.		4100/40
63	M.T. SHEDS	T.B.		9223/40.
64	M.T. OFFICE	T.B.		9223/40.
65	PRODUCE COMPOUND	T.B.		3693/40.
66	MAIN STORES	T.B.		9221/40.
67-68				
69				
70				
71				
72	PARACHUTE STORE	T.B.		17865/39
73	LUBRICANT AND INFLAMMABLE STORE	T.B.		9228/40.
74				
75-76	PILOTS REST ROOMS AND LOCKER ROOMS	T.B.		9219/40.
77	SQUADRON OFFICES	T.B.		9218/40.
78				
79	S.A.A. STORE [15'·9"×12'·0"]	T.B.		
80	STATIC WATER TANK	B&C.		4100/40
81	ARMOURY H.Q.	T.B.		9224/40.
82	AIRCRAFT SHED	ST.	J.	5836/39
83	FLIGHT OFFICE AND CREW ROOM	T.B.		9219/40.
84	COMPRESSOR HOUSE	P.B.		5044/37.
85	CENTRAL HEATING STATION	P.H.	A.1.	2338/38.
86	KIOSK SUB STATION			
87	FLIGHT OFFICE AND CREW ROOM	T.B.		9219/40.

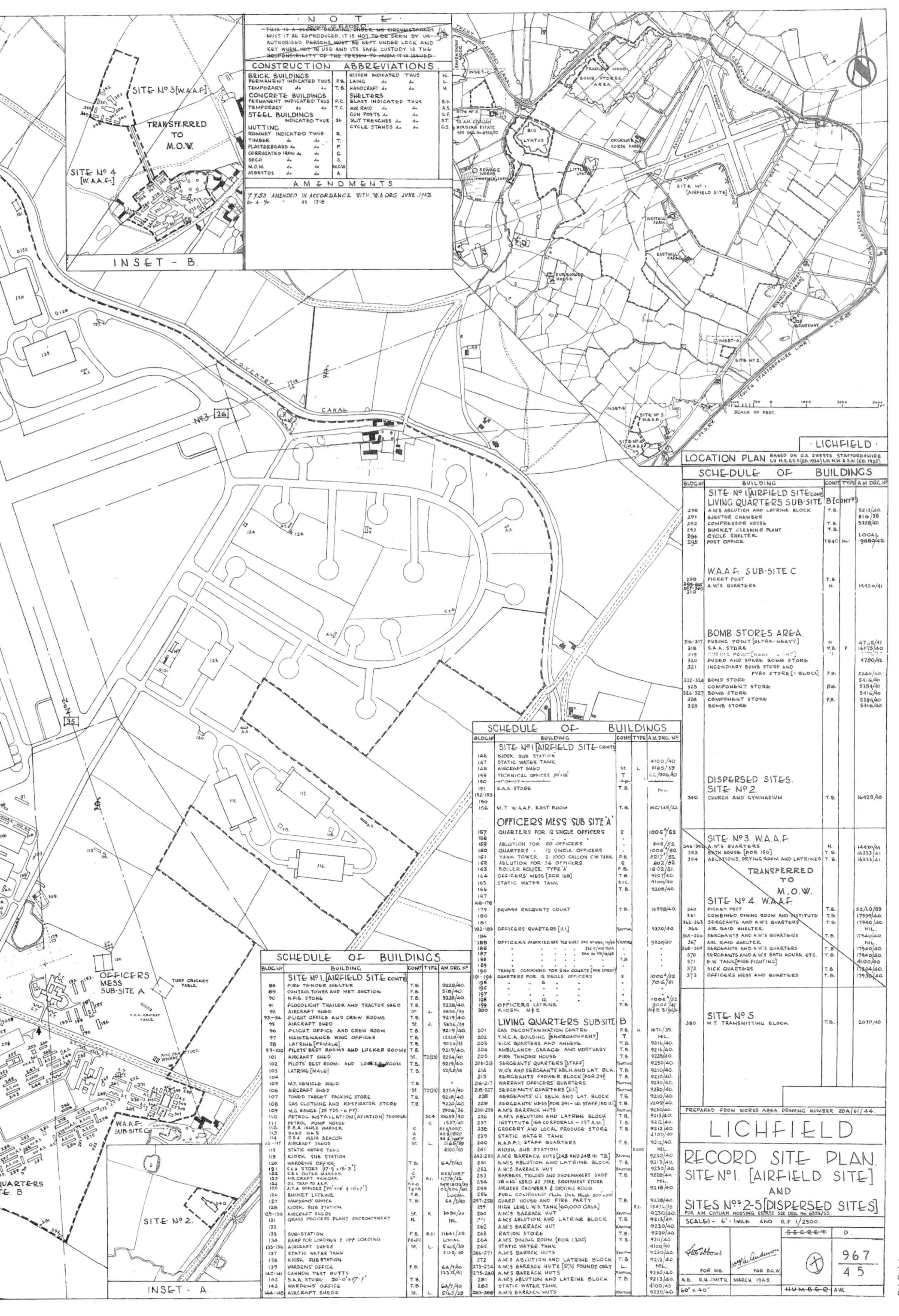

· N O T E ·

~~THIS IS A SECRET DRAWING. UNDER NO CIRCUMSTANCES~~ MUST IT BE REPRODUCED, IT IS NOT ~~TO BE~~ SEEN BY UNAUTHORISED PERSONS, ~~MUST BE~~ KEPT UNDER LOCK AND KEY WHEN ~~NOT IN~~ USE AND ITS SAFE CUSTODY IS THE ~~RESPONSIBILITY OF THE PERSON TO WHOM IT IS ISSUED~~

CONSTRUCTION ABBREVIATIONS.

BRICK BUILDINGS		NISSEN INDICATED THUS	N.
PERMANENT INDICATED THUS	P.B.	LAING do do	L.
TEMPORARY do do	T.B.	HANDCRAFT do do	H.
CONCRETE BUILDINGS		SHELTERS	
PERMANENT INDICATED THUS	P.C.	BLAST INDICATED THUS	B.S.
TEMPORARY do do	T.C.	AIR RAID do do	A.S.
STEEL BUILDINGS INDICATED THUS	St.	GUN POSTS do do	G.P.
HUTTING		SLIT TRENCHES do do	S.T.
ROMNEY INDICATED THUS	R.	CYCLE STANDS do do	C.S.
TIMBER do do	T.		
PLASTERBOARD do do	P.		
CORRUGATED IRON do do	C.		
SECO do do	S.		
M.O.W. do do	M.O.W.		
ASBESTOS do do	A.		

AMENDMENTS

7.7.53 AMENDED IN ACCORDANCE WITH W.A. DRG. JUNE 1953.
26.4.56 " as 1318

SCHEDULE OF BUILDINGS.

BLDG. No	BUILDING	CONST	TYPE	A.M. DRG. No
	SITE No 1. [AIRFIELD SITE CONTD]			
88	FIRE TENDER SHELTER	T.B.		9228/40.
89	CONTROL TOWER AND MET. SECTION	P.B.		518/40.
90	N.F.E. STORE	T.B.		9228/40.
91	FLOODLIGHT TRAILER AND TRACTOR SHED	T.B.		9228/40.
92	AIRCRAFT SHED	St.	J.	5836/39
93-94	FLIGHT OFFICE AND CREW ROOMS	T.B.		9219/40.
95	AIRCRAFT SHED	St.	J.	5836/39
96	FLIGHT OFFICE AND CREW ROOM	T.B.		9219/40.
97	MAINTENANCE WING OFFICES	T.B.		12330/40
98	LATRINE [FEMALE]	T.B.		9026/41
99-100	PILOTS' REST ROOMS AND LOCKER ROOMS	T.B.		9219/40.
101	AIRCRAFT SHED	St.	T2(23)	8254/40
102	PILOTS' REST ROOM AND LOCKER ROOM	T.B.		9219/40
103	LATRINE [MALE]	T.B.		52/LD/18
104				
105	M.T. VEHICLE SHED	T.B.		"
106	AIRCRAFT SHED	St.	T2(23)	8254/40
107	TOWED TARGET PACKING STORE	T.B.		9218/40.
108	GAS CLOTHING AND RESPIRATOR STORE	T.B.		9220/40
109	M.G. RANGE (25 YDS.-6 PT).			2904/36.
110	PETROL INSTALLATION (AVIATION) 72000 GL.		SC4	10659/40
111	PETROL PUMP HOUSE		C	1537/40
112	S.B.A INNER MARKER	C		RE 2/1057.
113	BABS MK 2	C		RE 2/1520
114	S.B.A MAIN BEACON	C		RE 2/1057
115-117	AIRCRAFT SHEDS	St.	L.	5165/39
118	STATIC WATER TANK			4100/40
119	KIOSK SUB STATION			
120	WARDENS OFFICE	T.B.		6A/7/40
121	S.A.A STORE [17'9" x 15'3"]	"		
122	S.B.A OUTER MARKER	C		RE2/1057
123	AIRCRAFT HANGAR	ST	B.1.	11776/42
124	OIL TRAP TO A.S.P.	R.C.C.		D of W 18132/39
125	A.T.A OFFICES [70' x 18' & 10' x 7']	T4 T.B		CE/206/40.
126	BUCKET LATRINE	T.B.		LOCAL.
127	WARDENS' OFFICE	T.B.		6A/7/40
128	KIOSK SUB STATION			
129-130	AIRCRAFT SHEDS	St.	K.	3084/39
131	GRASS PROCESS PLANT ENCROACHMENT	R		NIL.
132				
133	SUB-STATION	P.B.	B31	11641/39.
134	RAMP FOR LOADING & OFF LOADING	P.B.+P.C		LOCAL
135-136	AIRCRAFT SHEDS	St.	L.	5165/39
137	STATIC WATER TANK			4100/40
138	KIOSK SUB STATION			
139	WARDENS' OFFICE	P.B.		6A/7/40
140-141	CANNON TEST BUTTS			12312/41
142	S.A.A. STORE 20'-0" x 17'-9"	T.B.		
143	WARDENS' OFFICE	T.B.		6A/7/40
144-145	AIRCRAFT SHEDS	St.	L.	5165/39

SCHEDULE OF BUILDINGS

BLDG. No	BUILDING	CONST	TYPE	A.M. DRG. No
	SITE No 1 [AIRFIELD SITE CONTD]			
146	KIOSK SUB STATION			
147	STATIC WATER TANK			4100/40
148	AIRCRAFT SHED	ST.	L.	5165/39
149	TECHNICAL OFFICES 70' x 18'	T		CE/206/40
150	[illegible]			
151	S.A.A. STORE	T.B.		NIL.
152-153				
154				
156	M/T W.A.A.F. REST ROOM	T.B.		MC/145/42
	OFFICERS MESS SUB SITE 'A'			
157	QUARTERS FOR 12 SINGLE OFFICERS	S		1006A/52
158	" " " "	"		
159	ABLUTION FOR 60 OFFICERS	"		802/52
160	QUARTERS " 12 SINGLE OFFICERS	"		1006A/52
161	TANK TOWER 2-1000 GALLON C.W. TANK	P.B.		3217/52
162	ABLUTION FOR 36 OFFICERS	S.		802/52
163	BOILER HOUSE TYPE 'A'	P.B.		1802/51.
164	OFFICERS' MESS [FOR 168]	T.B.		9207/40.
165	STATIC WATER TANK	B.I.C.		4100/40
166		T.B.		9208/40.
167				
168-178				
179	SQUASH RACQUETS COURT	T.B.		16958/40.
180				
181				
182-183	OFFICERS' QUARTERS [U.I.]	Y HUTTING		9230/40.
184				
185	OFFICERS MARRIED QTR TEM BUILT DRG No WAG, 14/48	Y HUTTING		9230/40
186	" " " " " See C/WKS Sketch	"		"
187	" " " " " DRG No WAG/14/48	"		"
188	" " " " " " "	T.B		"
189	" " " " " " "	"		"
190	TENNIS COMPOUND FOR 2 No COURTS (NON UPKEEP)			
191-194	QUARTERS FOR 12 SINGLE OFFICERS	S		1006A/52
195	" " 6 " "	"		706/51
196	" " " " "	"		"
197	" " " " "	"		"
198	" " 12 " "	"		1006A/52
199	OFFICERS LATRINE	T.B		9026/41
200	KIOSK M&E			M&E 3194/50
	LIVING QUARTERS SUB-SITE B			
201	GAS DECONTAMINATION CENTRE	P.B.	H.	16711/39.
202	Y.M.C.A. BUILDING [ENCROACHMENT]	T		NIL.
203	SICK QUARTERS AND ANNEXE	T.B.		9216/40.
204	AMBULANCE, GARAGE AND MORTUARY	T.B.		9216/40.
205	FIRE TENDER HOUSE	T.B.		9228/40.
206-213	SERGEANTS' QUARTERS [STAFF]	Y HUTTING		9230/40.
214	W.O.'s AND SERGEANTS' ABLN. AND LAT. BLK.	T.B.		9210/40.
215	SERGEANTS SHOWER BLOCK [FOR 291]	T.B.		9210/40.
216-217	WARRANT OFFICERS' QUARTERS	Y HUTTING		9230/40.
218-227	SERGEANTS' QUARTERS [U.I.]	Y HUTTING		9230/40.
228	SERGEANTS' U.I. ABLN. AND LAT. BLOCK	T.B.		9210/40.
229	SERGEANTS' MESS [FOR 291 - 141 STAFF, 150 U.I.]	T.B.		9209/40.
230-235	A.M.'S BARRACK HUTS	X HUTTING		9230/40.
236	A.M.'S ABLUTION AND LATRINE BLOCK	T.B.		9213/40.
237	INSTITUTE [164 CORPORALS - 1137 A.M.]	T.B.		9212/40.
238	GROCERY AND LOCAL PRODUCE STORE	T.B.		9212/40.
239	STATIC WATER TANK			4100/40
240	N.A.A.F.I. STAFF QUARTERS	T.B.		9212/40.
241	KIOSK SUB STATION		11.000	NIL.
242-250	A.M.'S BARRACK HUTS [243 AND 248 IN T.B.]	X HUTTING		9230/40.
251	A.M.'S ABLUTION AND LATRINE BLOCK	T.B.		9213/40.
252	A.M.'S BARRACK HUT	X HUTTING		9230/40.
253	BARBERS, TAILORS AND SHOEMAKERS SHOP	T.B.		9228/40.
254	18' x 16' USED AS FIRE EQUIPMENT STORE			NIL.
255	AIRMENS SHOWERS & DRYING ROOM			9218/40.
256	FUEL COMPOUND Chain Link Mesh 200' x 100'			
257-258	GUARD HOUSE AND FIRE PARTY	T.B.		9228/40.
259	HIGH LEVEL W.S. TANK [60,000 GALS.]		P.S.	15872/39
260	A.M.'S BARRACK HUT	X HUTTING		9230/40.
261	A.M.'S ABLUTION AND LATRINE BLOCK	T.B.		9213/40.
262	A.M.'S BARRACK HUT	X HUTTING		9230/40.
263	RATION STORE	T.B.		9230/40.
264	A.M.'S DINING ROOM [FOR 1,300]	T.B.		9211/40.
265	STATIC WATER TANK			4100/40
266-271	A.M.'S BARRCK HUTS	X HUTTING		9230/40.
272	A.M.'S ABLUTION AND LATRINE BLOCK	T.B.		9213/40.
273-274	A.M.'S BARRACK HUTS [274 FOUNDS ONLY]	L.		NIL.
275-280	A.M.'S BARRACK HUTS	X HUTTING		9230/40.
281	A.M.'S ABLUTION AND LATRINE BLOCK	T.B.		9213/40.
282	STATIC WATER TANK			4100/40
283-288	A.M.'S BARRACK HUTS	X HUTTING		9230/40.

SCHEDULE OF BUILDINGS

BLDG. No	BUILDING	CONST	TYPE	A.M. DRG. No
	SITE No 1 [AIRFIELD SITE CONTD] LIVING QUARTERS SUB-SITE B [CONTD]			
290	A.M.'S ABLUTION AND LATRINE BLOCK	T.B.		9213/40
291	EJECTOR CHAMBER			1116/38
292	COMPRESSOR HOUSE	T.B.		9228/40
293	BUCKET CLEANING PLANT	T.B.		
294	CYCLE SHELTER			LOCAL
295	POST OFFICE	T.B.&C	No1	9889/42
	W.A.A.F. SUB-SITE C			
298	PICKET POST	T.B.		
299-305, 307-309, 310	A.W.'S QUARTERS	N.		14420/41
	BOMB STORES AREA.			
316-317	FUSING POINT [ULTRA-HEAVY]	N		[illegible]/41
318	S.A.A. STORE	P.B.	F	16075/40.
319	[illegible]			
320	FUSED AND SPARE BOMB STORE			4780/42
321	INCENDIARY BOMB STORE AND PYRO STORE [1 BLOCK]	P.B.		5244/40
322-324	BOMB STORE			5416/40
325	COMPONENT STORE	P.B.		5384/40
326-327	BOMB STORE			5416/40
328	COMPONENT STORE	P.B.		5384/40
329	BOMB STORE			5416/40
	DISPERSED SITES. SITE No 2.			
340	CHURCH AND GYMNASIUM	T.B.		16428/40
	SITE No 3. W.A.A.F.			
346-352	A.W.'S QUARTERS	N.		14420/41
353	BATH HOUSE [FOR 150]	T.B.		16333/41
354	ABLUTIONS, DRYING ROOM AND LATRINES	T.B.		16333/41.
	TRANSFERRED TO M.O.W.			
	SITE No 4. W.A.A.F.			
360	PICKET POST	T.B.		52/LD/89
361	COMBINED DINING ROOM AND INSTITUTE	T.B.		17939/40.
362-363	SERGEANTS AND A.W.'S QUARTERS	T.B.		17940/40.
364	AIR RAID SHELTER			NIL.
365-366	SERGEANTS AND A.W.'S QUARTERS	T.B.		17940/40.
367	AIR RAID SHELTER			NIL.
368-369	SERGEANTS AND A.W.'S QUARTERS	T.B.		17940/40.
370	SERGEANTS AND A.W.'S BATH HOUSE, ETC.	T.B.		17940/40.
371	E.W. TANK [FIRE FIGHTING]			4100/40
372	SICK QUARTERS	T.B.		17934/40.
373	OFFICERS MESS AND QUARTERS	T.B.		17938/40.
	SITE No 5.			
380	W.T. TRANSMITTING BLOCK	T.B.		2070/40

PREPARED FROM WORKS AREA DRAWING NUMBER 20A/61/44.

LICHFIELD

RECORD SITE PLAN. SITE No 1. [AIRFIELD SITE] AND SITES Nos 2-5 [DISPERSED SITES]

FOR A.M. CIVILIAN HOUSING ESTATE SEE DRG. No. 6525/52.

SCALES - 6" - 1 MILE AND R.F. 1/2500.

~~SECRET~~ D.

FOR W.B. FOR D.C.W.

A.B. R.H. SMITH. MARCH 1945.

967/45

~~NUMBER~~ AIR

60" x 40"

235 Sqn
21/01–29/08/43
Beaufighter VIc
320 (Dutch) Sqn
01/10/40–18/01/41
21/03/41–21/04/42
Hudson I, II, III, V
333 (Norwegian) Sqn (B Flt)
05/05/43–01/09/44
Catalina Ib, IV; Mosquito II, VI
415 (Canadian) Sqn
06/09–11/11/42
Hampden
455 (Australian) Sqn
28/04/42–14/04/44
Hampden; Beaufighter X
489 (New Zealand) Sqn
06/10/43–08/04/44
Beaufighter X
540 Sqn
19/10/42–29/02/44
Spitfire PRIV; Mosquito PRI, IV, VIII, IX
547 Sqn
01/10/44–04/06/45
Liberator VI, VIII
605 (AAF) Sqn
11–28/02/40
Hurricane I
10 BAT Flt > 1510 BAT Flt
01/41 (11/41)–08/44
Anson

LICHFIELD, Staffs

LOCATION: 3m NE of Lichfield
OPENED: 01/08/40
CLOSED: 04/58. Agriculture/light industry (2011)
ELEVATION: 220ft
PUNDIT CODE: LF
FORMATIONS: 6 (T), 91 (OTU), 93 (OTU) Grp Bomber Command
MAIN CONTRACTOR: Various
RUNWAYS: 3 Tarmac
HANGARS: J Type (3), K Type (4), L Type (8), B1 (1), T2 (2)
USER SQNS/UNITS:
27 OTU
23/04/41–08/07/45
Wellington III, X
Opened in Maintenance Command, 01/08/40
To Bomber Command as parent station, 05/41

LIMAVADY, Co Londonderry, NI

LOCATION: 2m N of Limavady
OPENED: 1940
CLOSED: 08/1945. Disused (2011)
ELEVATION: 65ft
FORMATIONS: 15, 17 (T) Grp Coastal Command
RUNWAYS: 3 concrete and Tarmac
HANGARS: T2 (2), Bellman (3), Blister (6)
USER SQNS/UNITS:
53 Sqn
17/12/41–18/02/42
Hudson V
143 Sqn
23/04–11/06/42
Blenheim IV
172 Sqn
01/09/44–04/06/45

ABOVE: Blenheim Mk IV, R3816, 'J', of No 107 Squadron, photographed at Leuchars during March 1941. For night fighter ops this aircraft's undersides have been painted black and it has toned down national insignia. (Andy Thomas)

Wellington XII/XIV

221 Sqn
02/05–29/09/41
Wellington Ic

224 Sqn
19/02–16/04/42
Hudson V

281 Sqn
31/03–13/08/45
Warwick I; Sea Otter

407 (Canadian) Sqn
29/01–28/04/44
Wellington XIV

502 (AAF) Sqn
27/01/41–10/01/42
Whitley V

612 (AAF) Sqn
26/01–01/03/44
09/09–19/12/44
Wellington XIII, XIV

7 OTU
01/04/42–01/44
Wellington; Anson

811 NAS
06/44
Swordfish

825 NAS
09–11/44
Swordfish; Sea Hurricane

846 NAS
06/44
Wildcat

850 NAS
08–11/44
Avenger

LINDHOLME, Yorks

LOCATION: 7m NE of Doncaster
OPENED: 01/06/40
CLOSED: 1985. Agriculture/HMP Lindholme (2011)
ELEVATION: 20ft
PUNDIT CODE: LB
FORMATIONS: 1, 5, 7 (T) Grp Bomber Command
MAIN CONTRACTOR: Various
RUNWAYS: 3 concrete/Tarmac
HANGARS: C Type (5)
USER SQNS/UNITS:

50 Sqn
10/07/40–20/07/41
Hampden

304 (Polish) Sqn
19/07/41–10/05/42
Wellington I

305 (Polish) Sqn
20/07/41–22/07/42
Wellington I

408 (Canadian) Sqn
24/06–19/07/41
Hampden

1656 HCU
10/42–11/45
Manchester; Halifax II, V; Lancaster I, III

1667 HCU
06–10/43
Lancaster I, III; Halifax II, V

1 LFS
11/43–01/44
Lancaster I, III

Opened in Bomber Command as parent station as Hatfield Woodhouse, 01/06/40
Name changed to Lindholme, 18/08/40
Became 11 (Training) Base HQ, 09/43
Became 71 (Training) Base HQ, 03/11/44

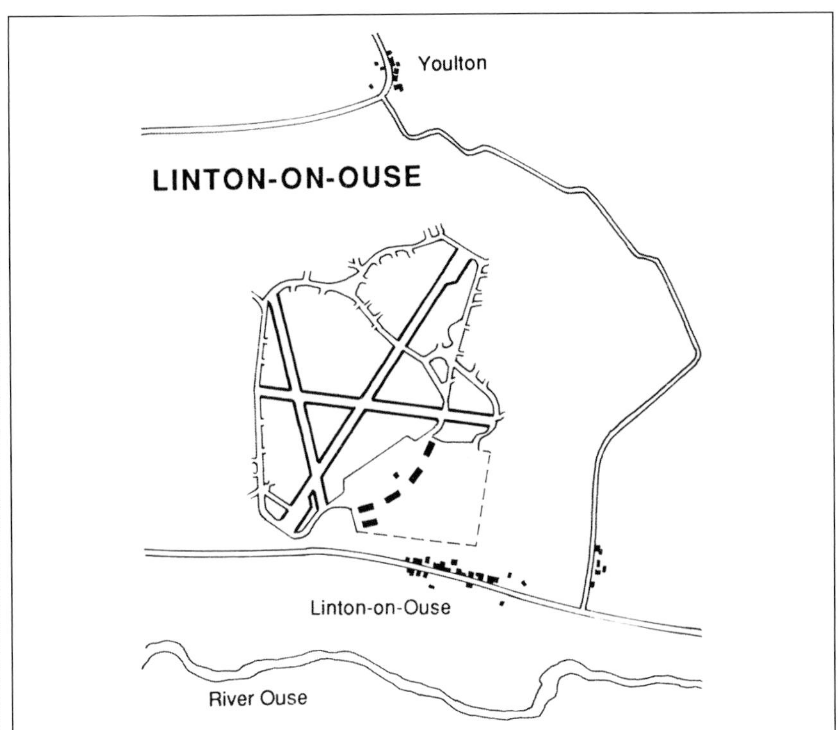

LINTON-ON-OUSE, Yorks

LOCATION: 8¾m NW of York
OPENED: 13/05/37
CLOSED: RAF base (2011)
ELEVATION: 53ft
PUNDIT CODE: LO
FORMATIONS: 4, 6 (RCAF) Grp Bomber Command
MAIN CONTRACTOR: Various
RUNWAYS: 3 concrete
HANGARS: C Type (5)
USER SQNS/UNITS:

35 Sqn
05/12/40–15/08/42
Halifax I, II

51 Sqn
20/04/38–09/12/39
Whitley II, III, IV

58 Sqn
20/04/38–30/09/39
14/02/40–08/04/42
Heyford III; Whitley II, III, V

76 Sqn
01/05–04/06/41
16/09/42–16/06/43
Halifax I, II, V

77 Sqn
28/08–05/10/40
Whitley V

ABOVE: The nose of No 408 (Canadian) Squadron's Lancaster Mk II, LL725, 'Z', seen at Linton-on-Ouse, is adorned with a painting that depicts a caped skeleton with a machine gun under one arm and a 4,000lb 'Cookie' under the other. The artwork is seen nearing completion on 7 April 1944 by its creator, rear gunner George Oliver, RCAF, who flew 22 of his 30-op tour in the 'Zombie'. The 'Zombie' and its crew were lost without trace in a raid on Hamburg on 28/29 July 1944, skippered by Plt Off John McCaffrey DFC, RCAF. George Oliver survived the war. (Public Archives of Canada PL-29074)

78 Sqn
13/12/39–16/07/40
16/09/42–16/06/43
Whitley V; Halifax II
102 Sqn
10/10–15/11/40
Whitley V
405 (Canadian) Sqn
26/05–16/06/45
Lancaster III, X
408 (Canadian) Sqn
27/08/43–14/06/45
Halifax II, III, VII; Lancaster II, X
426 (Canadian) Sqn
18/06/43–25/05/45
Lancaster II; Halifax III, VII
Opened in Bomber Command as parent station, 05/37
Became 62 (RCAF) Base HQ, 07/43

LISSETT, Yorks
LOCATION: 6m SSW of Bridlington
OPENED: 02/43
CLOSED: 08/45. Agriculture/wind farm (2011)
ELEVATION: 23ft
PUNDIT CODE: LT
FORMATION: 4 Grp Bomber Command
MAIN CONTRACTOR: Various
RUNWAYS: 3 concrete
HANGARS: T2 (2)
USER SQNS/UNITS:
158 Sqn
28/04/43–17/08/45
Halifax II, III, VI
640 Sqn
07/01/44–07/05/45
Halifax III, VI
Opened in Bomber Command as satellite to Driffield, 02/43
Became 43 Base substation, 06/06/43

LITTLE HORWOOD, Bucks
LOCATION: 2½m NE of Winslow
OPENED: 09/42
CLOSED: 11/47. Agriculture (2011)
ELEVATION: 385ft
PUNDIT CODE: LH
FORMATION: 92 (OTU) Grp Bomber Command
MAIN CONTRACTOR: Various
RUNWAYS: 3 concrete
HANGARS: T2 (1), B1 (1)
USER SQNS/UNITS:
26 OTU
09/42–26/08/44
10/44–03/46

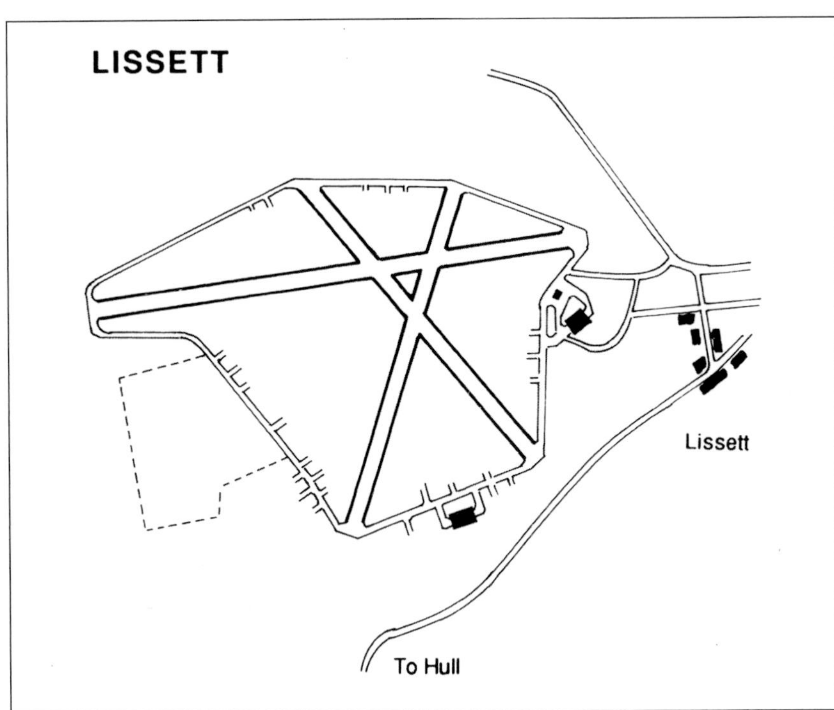

Wellington III, X
Opened in Bomber Command as satellite to Wing, 09/42

LITTLE SNORING, Norfolk

LOCATION: 3m NE of Fakenham
OPENED: 07/43
CLOSED: 10/58. Agriculture/light aviation (2011)
ELEVATION: 191ft
PUNDIT CODE: LS
FORMATIONS: 3, 100 (BS) Grp Bomber Command
MAIN CONTRACTOR: Taylor Woodrow Ltd
RUNWAYS: 3 concrete
HANGARS: T2 (2), B1 (1)
USER SQNS/UNITS:

23 Sqn
02/06/44–25/09/45
Mosquito VI, XXX

115 Sqn
06/08–26/11/43
Lancaster II

169 Sqn
07/12/43–04/06/44
Beaufighter VI; Defiant II; Mosquito II

515 Sqn
15/12/43–10/06/45
Beaufighter II; Blenheim V; Mosquito II

1678 HCU
08–09/43
Lancaster II

Opened in Bomber Command as a satellite to Foulsham, 07/43
Upgraded to parent station status, 08/43
To 100 (BS) Grp, 12/43

LITTLE STAUGHTON, Hunts

LOCATION: 8m NE of Bedford
OPENED: 12/42
CLOSED: 12/45. Agriculture/light industry/light aviation (2011)
ELEVATION: 225ft
PUNDIT CODE: LX
FORMATION: 8 (PFF) Grp Bomber Command
MAIN CONTRACTORS: AMWD, Llewellyn & Sons, Sindal, Wilmotts, Minter Ltd
RUNWAYS: 3 concrete/Tarmac
HANGARS: T2 (3), Robin (8)
USER SQNS/UNITS:

109 Sqn (PFF)
02/04/44–30/09/45
Mosquito XVI

582 Sqn (PFF)
01/04/44–10/09/45

ABOVE: 'Watch Office for All Commands 12779/41, with lower front windows to 343/43.' Although the watchtower at this former No 100 Group airfield is now a derelict shell (as seen here in 1991), Little Snoring is still used today by the occasional light aircraft. (Author)

ABOVE: Air and ground crews of A Flight, No 109 (PFF) Squadron, sit for the photographer in front of a Mosquito Mk IX in October 1944. (Author)

Lancaster I, III
Opened as USAAF Station AAF-127, 12/42
To RAF Bomber Command, 01/03/44
*Sqn Ldr R.A.M. Palmer DFC, 109 Sqn, posthumously awarded VC, Cologne, 23/12/44
*Capt E.E. Swales, 582 Sqn, posthumously awarded VC, Pforzheim, 23–24/02/45

LLANBEDR, Merionethshire

LOCATION: 3m SSW of Harlech
OPENED: 06/41
CLOSED: 2004. Disused (2011)
ELEVATION: 18ft
PUNDIT CODE: QD
FORMATION: 9 Grp Fighter Command
MAIN CONTRACTOR: Various
RUNWAYS: 2 concrete
HANGARS: Blister (4), T2 (2)
USER SQNS/UNITS:

41 Sqn
11–17/08/42
20/08–22/09/42
30/09–05/10/42
11/10/42–25/02/43
Spitfire Vb

66 Sqn
22/02–01/03/44
Spitfire LFIXb

74 Sqn
03/10/41–24/01/42
Spitfire IIa

129 Sqn
30/03–03/04/44
Spitfire IX; Mustang III

131 Sqn
09/02–04/03/42
16/04–14/05/42
Spitfire Vb

164 Sqn
11–22/04/44
Typhoon Ib

168 Sqn
21/01–04/02/44
Mustang I, Ia

193 Sqn
06–11/04/44
Typhoon Ib

232 Sqn
16/05–03/08/42
Spitfire Vb

302 (Polish) Sqn
01–07/03/44
Spitfire IX

306 (Polish) Sqn
19/12/43–01/01/44
15–20/03/44
Spitfire Vb

312 (Czech) Sqn
02–18/12/43
Spitfire Vc

331 (Norwegian) Sqn
05–21/01/44
Spitfire IXb

340 (French) Sqn
15–19/05/44
Spitfire IXb

609 (AAF) Sqn
22–30/04/44
Typhoon Ib

Opened in Fighter Command as satellite to Valley, 06/41

LLANDOW, Glamorgan

LOCATION: 14m W of Cardiff
OPENED: 1937
CLOSED: 1957. Agriculture/trading estate (2011)
ELEVATION: 290ft
PUNDIT CODE: Not known
FORMATION: 81 (OTU) Grp Fighter Command
MAIN CONTRACTOR: Various
RUNWAYS: 3 Tarmac
HANGARS: L Type (7), Super Robins (11), K Type (2), J Type (1), T2 (2), A1 (1), Blister (12)
USER SQNS/UNITS:

53 OTU
01/07/41–09/05/43
Spitfire I, II, V, IX; Master III

To Fighter Command, 07/41
To Maintenance Command, 07/43

LONG MARSTON, Warks

LOCATION: 3½m SW of Stratford-on-Avon
OPENED: 11/41
CLOSED: 1954. Agriculture/light aviation (2011)
ELEVATION: 145ft
PUNDIT CODE: JS
FORMATIONS: 6 (T), 91 (OTU) Grp Bomber Command
MAIN CONTRACTOR: John Laing & Son Ltd
RUNWAYS: 3 Tarmac
HANGARS: T2 (2), B1 (1)
USER SQNS/UNITS:

23 OTU
1943
Wellington III, X

24 OTU
03/42–07/45
Whitley; Wellington III, X

Became Bomber Command satellite to Honeybourne, 03/42

LONGTOWN, Cumberland

LOCATION: 8m N of Carlisle
OPENED: 07/41
CLOSED: 04/46. Disused (2011)
ELEVATION: 100ft
PUNDIT CODE: IO
FORMATIONS: 9, 13, 81 (OTU) Grp Fighter Command
MAIN CONTRACTOR: Various
RUNWAYS: 3 concrete
HANGARS: Blister (2), T2 (1)
USER SQNS/UNITS:

41 Sqn
01–11/08/42
Spitfire Vb

55 OTU
28/04/42–10/43
Hurricane I, II; Master I, II, III

59 OTU
07/41–08/42
Hurricane

Opened in 13 Grp Fighter Command as satellite to Crosby-on-Eden, 07/41
Satellite to Annan, 08/42
To 17 Grp Coastal Command, 10/43

LOSSIEMOUTH, Morayshire

LOCATION: 4½m N of Elgin
OPENED: 1939
CLOSED: RAF base (2011)
ELEVATION: 19ft
PUNDIT CODE: OL
FORMATIONS: 2, 6 (T), 91 (OTU) Grp Bomber Command
MAIN CONTRACTOR: Various
RUNWAYS: 3 concrete/Tarmac
HANGARS: C Type (3), J Type (1), K Type (4), L Type (7)
USER SQNS/UNITS:

21 Sqn
24/06–30/10/40
Blenheim IV

57 Sqn
23/06–14/08/40
Blenheim IV

20 OTU
27/05/40–07/45
Wellington III, X

Opened in Bomber Command as parent station, 1939

LUDFORD MAGNA, Lincs

LOCATION: 6m E of Market Rasen
OPENED: 06/43
CLOSED: 05/63. Agriculture (2011)
ELEVATION: 428ft
PUNDIT CODE: LM
FORMATION: 1 Grp Bomber Command
MAIN CONTRACTOR: George Wimpey & Co Ltd
RUNWAYS: 3 concrete

RIGHT: Ron Holmes' No 101 Squadron crew pose beside their Lancaster III, ME837, 'L', at Ludford Magna in the summer of 1944. Left to right, top to bottom: Sid Davison, wireless op; Norman Smith, rear gunner; Peter Holway, special operator; Stan Waind, flight engineer; Tom Wade, bomb-aimer; Charlie, radio technician; Alex Kabbash, navigator; 'Titch', ground crew; Ron Holmes, pilot; Bill, ground crew. (Peter Holway)

HANGARS: T2 (6), B1 (1)
USER SQNS/UNITS:
101 Sqn
15/06/43–01/10/45
Lancaster I, III
Opened in Bomber Command as parent station, 06/43
Became 14 Base HQ, 12/43

LUDHAM, Norfolk

LOCATION: 10m ENE of Norwich
OPENED: 10/41
CLOSED: 10/45. Agriculture/light aviation (2011)
ELEVATION: 40ft
PUNDIT CODE: LU
FORMATION: 12 Grp Fighter Command
MAIN CONTRACTOR: Richard Costain Ltd
RUNWAYS: 3 concrete/Tarmac
HANGARS: Blister (4), T2 (2)
USER SQNS/UNITS:
19 Sqn
01/12/41–04/04/42
Spitfire Vb
91 Sqn
08/04–14/07/45
Spitfire IXb, XXI
167 Sqn
14/10/42–01/03/43
13/03–13/05/43
Spitfire Vb, Vc
195 Sqn
13/05–31/07/43
Typhoon Ib
602 (AAF) Sqn
23/02–05/04/45
Spitfire XVI
603 (AAF) Sqn
24/02–05/04/45
Spitfire LFXVIe
610 (AAF) Sqn
04/04–16/08/42
21/08–15/10/42
Spitfire Vb, Vc
611 (AAF) Sqn
31/07–04/08/43
Spitfire LFVb
Opened in Fighter Command as a satellite to Coltishall, 10/41
To Air Ministry Works Directorate, 08/43
To RN, 08/44
To 12 Grp Fighter Command, 02/45

LYDD, Kent

LOCATION: 5½m NW of Dungeness
OPENED: 06/43
CLOSED: 01/45. London Ashford Airport (2011)
ELEVATION: 0ft
PUNDIT CODE: LD
FORMATION: 83 Grp 2 TAF
MAIN CONTRACTOR: RAFACS
RUNWAYS: 2 steel matting
HANGARS: Blister (5)
USER SQNS/UNITS:
174 Sqn
01/07–10/10/43
Typhoon Ib
175 Sqn
01/07–09/10/43
Typhoon Ib
245 Sqn
01/07–10/10/43
Typhoon Ib
Reserve Advanced Landing Ground (RALG)

LYMPNE, Kent

LOCATION: 2½m W of Hythe
OPENED: 1916
CLOSED: 05/45. Industrial estate (2011)
ELEVATION: 340ft
PUNDIT CODE: PY
FORMATIONS: 11 Grp Fighter Command; 2 TAF
MAIN CONTRACTOR: Various
RUNWAYS: 3 grass
HANGARS: Blister (4)
USER SQNS/UNITS:
1 Sqn
15/03/43–15/02/44
11/07–10/08/44
Typhoon Ib; Spitfire IXb
33 Sqn
17/05–03/07/44
Spitfire LFIXe
41 Sqn
11/07–05/12/44
Spitfire XXI, XIV
65 Sqn
02–11/10/42
Spitfire Vb
72 Sqn
30/06–07/07/42
Spitfire Vb
74 Sqn
15/05–03/07/44
Spitfire LFIXe
91 Sqn
02–09/10/42
23/11/42–11/01/43
Spitfire Vb
127 Sqn
16/05–04/07/44
Spitfire HFIX
130 Sqn
05–30/04/44
11/08–30/09/44
Spitfire Vb, XIV
133 Sqn
30/06–12/07/42
17–22/08/42
Spitfire Vb
137 Sqn
14/12/43–02/01/44
04/02–01/04/44
Hurricane IV; Typhoon Ib
165 Sqn
12/07–10/08/44
Spitfire IXb
310 (Czech) Sqn
01–11/07/44
Spitfire LFIX
312 (Czech) Sqn
04–11/07/44
Spitfire HFIX
313 (Czech) Sqn
04–11/07/44
Spitfire IX
350 (Belgian) Sqn
29/09–03/12/44
Spitfire XIV
401 (Canadian) Sqn
14–21/08/42
Spitfire IX
451 (Australian) Sqn
06/04–03/05/45
Spitfire XVI
453 (Australian) Sqn
06/04–02/05/45

Spitfire LFXVI
504 (AAF) Sqn
11–12/07/44
Spitfire Vb
609 (AAF) Sqn
18/08–14/12/43
Typhoon Ib
610 (AAF) Sqn
12/09–04/12/44
Spitfire XIV
Fighter Command forward satellite to Biggin Hill, 06/40
Upgraded to full satellite, 1942

MACMERRY, East Lothian

LOCATION: 14m E of Edinburgh
OPENED: 1929
CLOSED: 1953. Industrial estate (2011)
ELEVATION: 300ft
PUNDIT CODE: VC
FORMATIONS: 13, 81 (OTU) Grp Fighter Command
MAIN CONTRACTOR: Various
RUNWAYS: 3 grass
HANGARS: Blister (8), T2 (1)
USER SQNS/UNITS:
13 Sqn
01–10/08/42
Blenheim IV
63 Sqn
21/11/42–27/07/43
27/07–08/11/43 (det)
Mustang I
225 Sqn
19/05–31/08/42 (det)
31/08–30/10/42
Mustang I
607 (AAF) Sqn
16/01–02/03/41
Hurricane I
614 Sqn
05/03/4 –14/08/42
21–26/08/42
Lysander III; Blenheim IV
60 OTU
06/41–11/42
Defiant; Blenheim; Beaufighter; Oxford
To 13 Grp Fighter Command as satellite to Drem, 01/41
Occasional use as satellite to East Fortune, 1941–42
To RN, 01/45

MANSTON, Kent

LOCATION: 2¾m WNW of Ramsgate
OPENED: 1916
CLOSED: 1999. Kent International Airport/MOD Fire Training (2011)
ELEVATION: 150ft
PUNDIT CODE: MQ
FORMATION: 11 Grp Fighter Command
MAIN CONTRACTOR: Various and John Laing & Son Ltd
RUNWAYS: Single emergency runway, bitumen surface 3,000yd x 250yd, with 500yd overshoots at each end
HANGARS: Blister (7), Various (3)
USER SQNS/UNITS:
1 Sqn
18/12/44–08/04/45
Spitfire IXb
3 Sqn
11/06–28/12/43
14/02–06/03/44
Typhoon Ib; Tempest V
23 Sqn
06–14/08/42
21/08–13/10/42
Boston III; Mosquito II
32 Sqn
08–22/03/40
27/11/41–05/05/42
Hurricane I, IIb, IIc
56 Sqn
29/05–01/06/42
22/07–06/08/43
15–23/08/43
Typhoon Ia, Ib
74 Sqn
20/02–30/04/41
Spitfire IIa
79 Sqn
12/11/39–08/03/40
Hurricane I
80 Sqn
29/08–20/09/44
Tempest V
91 Sqn
29/10/44–08/04/45
Spitfire IXb, XXI
92 Sqn
09/01–20/02/41
Spitfire I
118 Sqn
25/09–15/12/44
Spitfire IXc
119 Sqn
19/07–09/08/44
Albacore
124 Sqn
25/09/44–10/02/45
Spitfire HFIXe
137 Sqn
17/09/42–12/06/43
08/08–14/12/43
01/04–14/08/44
Whirlwind I; Hurricane IV; Typhoon Ib
164 Sqn
06/08–22/09/43
Hurricane IV
174 Sqn
03/03–09/07/42
12/07–01/09/42
21/09–06/12/42
Hurricane IIb
183 Sqn
15/03–01/04/44
Typhoon Ib
184 Sqn
12/06–14/08/43
Hurricane IV
193 Sqn
08–12/09/44
Typhoon Ib
197 Sqn
15/03–01/04/44
03–11/09/44
Typhoon Ib
198 Sqn
24/03–15/05/43
22/08/43–16/03/44
Typhoon Ia, Ib
222 Sqn
01–19/07/41
30/06–07/07/42
Spitfire IIb, Vb
229 Sqn
25/09–22/10/44
Spitfire IX

242 Sqn
19/07–16/09/41
14–20/08/42
Hurricane IIb; Spitfire Vb
253 Sqn
20/10/39–14/02/40
Battle; Hurricane I
263 Sqn
07–10/09/43
06–11/09/44
Whirlwind I; Typhoon Ib
274 Sqn
17/08–20/09/44
Tempest V
310 (Czech) Sqn
27/02–07/08/45
Spitfire LFIX
312 (Czech) Sqn
27/02–07/08/45
Spitfire HFIX
313 (Czech) Sqn
27/02–07/08/45
Spitfire IX
331 (Norwegian) Sqn
30/06–07/07/42
14–20/08/42
02–09/10/42
Spitfire Vb
332 (Norwegian) Sqn
14–20/08/42
02–09/10/42
Spitfire Vb
403 (Canadian) Sqn
01–08/07/42
Spitfire Vb
406 (Canadian) Sqn
27/11/44–14/06/45
Mosquito XXX
451 (Australian) Sqn
11–23/02/45
Spitfire XVI
501 (AAF) Sqn
02/08–22/09/44
Tempest V
504 (AAF) Sqn
20–21/05/40
13/08/44–25/02/45
Hurricane I; Spitfire IXe
600 (AAF) Sqn
27/12/39–14/05/40
20/06–24/08/40
Blenheim If, IV
601 (AAF) Sqn
01/05–30/06/41
Hurricane IIb
604 (AAF) Sqn
15/05–20/06/40
Blenheim I; Gladiator I
605 (AAF) Sqn
07/04–21/11/44
Mosquito VI
609 (AAF) Sqn
02/11/42–22/07/43
04/12/43–06/02/44
20/02–16/03/44
Typhoon Ia, Ib
615 (AAF) Sqn
11/09–27/11/41
Hurricane IIb, IIc
616 (AAF) Sqn
21/07/44–17/01/45
Spitfire VII; Meteor I
To 11 Grp Fighter Command, 11/39
*FIDO-equipped Emergency Landing Ground (ELG)

MARHAM, Norfolk

LOCATION: 10m SE of King's Lynn
OPENED: 01/04/37
CLOSED: RAF base (2011)
ELEVATION: 70ft
PUNDIT CODE: MR
FORMATIONS: 2, 3, 8 (PFF) Grp Bomber Command
MAIN CONTRACTOR: Various
RUNWAYS: 3 concrete
HANGARS: C Type (5)
USER SQNS/UNITS:
38 Sqn
05/05/37–12/11/40
Hendon; Wellington I

ABOVE: Wing Commander Reg Reynolds (right), pilot and CO of No 139 Squadron, and his navigator, Flight Lieutenant Ted Sismore, in front of a Mosquito Mk IV at Marham in May 1943. On 31 January 1943, Reynolds and Sismore led the first Mosquito attack on Berlin, in daylight, when their bombs disrupted a live radio broadcast by Hermann Goering. (IWM CH10135)

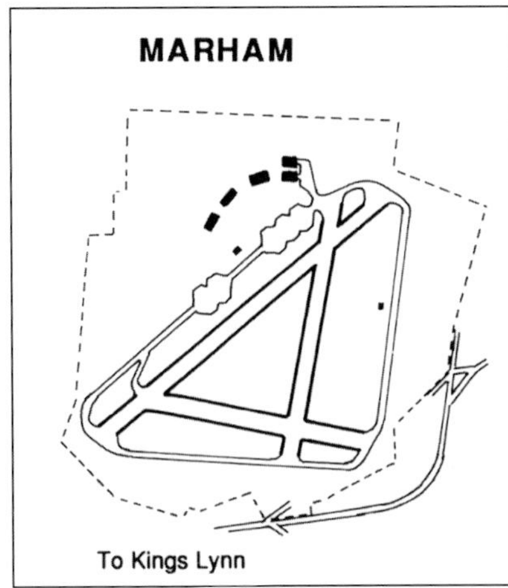

105 Sqn
29/09/42–23/03/44
Mosquito IV
115 Sqn
15/06/37–24/09/42
Harrow; Wellington I, III
139 Sqn
29/09/42–04/07/43
Blenheim V; Mosquito IV
218 Sqn
25/11/40–10/07/42
Wellington I; Stirling I
1418 Flt
06/01–01/03/42
Wellington III
1655 Mosquito Training Unit (MTU)
29/09/42–01/05/43
Blenheim; Mosquito
109 (PFF) Sqn
05/07/43–02/04/44
Mosquito IV, IX, XVI
Opened in Bomber Command as parent station, 01/04/37
Closed for redevelopment to VHB station standard, 03/44

MARKET HARBOROUGH, Leics

LOCATION: 2m NW of Market Harborough
OPENED: 05/43
CLOSED: 05/47. HMP Gartree (2011)
ELEVATION: 360ft
PUNDIT CODE: MB
FORMATION: 92 (OTU) Grp Bomber Command
MAIN CONTRACTOR: J. Mowlem & Co Ltd
RUNWAYS: 3 concrete/Tarmac
HANGARS: T2 (4), B1 (1)
USER SQNS/UNITS:
14 OTU
01/08/43–22/06/45
Wellington III, X
Opened in Bomber Command as parent station, 01/05/43

MARSTON MOOR, Yorks

LOCATION: 8½m W of York
OPENED: 20/11/41
CLOSED: 11/45. Agriculture/industry/housing (2011)
ELEVATION: 68ft
PUNDIT CODE: MA
FORMATIONS: 4, 7 (T) Grp Bomber Command
MAIN CONTRACTOR: John Laing & Son Ltd
RUNWAYS: 3 concrete
HANGARS: T2 (6), B1 (1)
USER SQNS/UNITS:
1652 HCU
03/01–07/42
08/42–25/06/45
Halifax I, II, III, V
Opened in Bomber Command as parent station, 20/11/41
Became 41 Base HQ, 09/43
Became 74 Base HQ, 12/44

MARTLESHAM HEATH, Suffolk

LOCATION: 1½m S of Woodbridge
OPENED: 01/17
CLOSED: 1963. Housing/retail/museum/BT research centre (2011)
ELEVATION: 90ft
PUNDIT CODE: MH
FORMATION: 11 Grp Fighter Command
MAIN CONTRACTOR: Various
RUNWAYS: 2 concrete/Tarmac
HANGARS: Blister (3), A Type (1), G Type (1), GS Type (1)
USER SQNS/UNITS:
1 Sqn
15/02–03/04/44
Typhoon Ib
3 Sqn
03/04–23/06/41
Hurricane IIb, IIc
17 Sqn
16–24/12/39
30/12/39–08/01/40
13–20/01/40
30/01–11/02/40
22–27/02/40
05–12/03/40
19–20/03/40
23–27/03/40
05–13/04/40
23–30/04/40
09/10/40–26/02/41
01–05/04/41
Hurricane I
25 Sqn
12/06–02/09/40
Blenheim If
41 Sqn
15–30/06/42
Spitfire Vb
54 Sqn
04–25/08/41
Spitfire Va
56 Sqn
22/10/39–28/02/40
23–26/06/41
06–15/08/43
04/10/43–15/02/44
Hurricane I, IIb; Typhoon Ib
65 Sqn
09–15/06/42
Spitfire Vb
77 Sqn
05/04–23/06/41
14/12/41–02/05/42
Hurricane I, IIa; Spitfire Vb
111 Sqn
21–27/09/42
Spitfire Vb
151 Sqn
20/05–29/08/40
Hurricane I
182 Sqn
25/08–07/12/42
30/01–01/03/43
Hurricane I; Typhoon Ia, Ib
198 Sqn
05/06–19/08/43
Typhoon Ib

ABOVE: 'Watch Office for All Commands, 343/43 with medium size front windows.' Little remains today of the busy airfield at Martlesham Heath, its runways and buildings torn up to make way for housing, supermarkets and the BT research centre. Thankfully, the watchtower has been preserved and is home to a flourishing aviation museum. (Author)

222 Sqn
01–29/04/43
Spitfire Vb

242 Sqn
16/12/40–09/04/41
Hurricane I, IIb

257 Sqn
05/09–08/10/40
07/11–16/12/40
Hurricane I

258 Sqn
10/07–03/10/41
Hurricane IIa

264 Sqn
07/12/39–10/05/40
Defiant I

266 Sqn
01/03–14/05/40
Battle; Spitfire I

303 (Polish) Sqn
26/03–08/04/43
Spitfire Vb

310 (Czech) Sqn
26/06–20/07/41
Hurricane IIa, IIb

312 (Czech) Sqn
20/07–19/08/41
Hurricane IIb

317 (Polish) Sqn
29/04–01/06/43
Spitfire Vb

350 (Belgian) Sqn
07–16/07/42
07–15/09/42
Spitfire Vb

401 (Canadian) Sqn
28/07–03/08/42
21–31/07/43
Spitfire Vb

402 (Canadian) Sqn
23/06–10/07/41
03–09/08/42
Hurricane IIa; Spitfire IX

403 (Canadian) Sqn
03/10–22/12/41
03–19/06/42
Spitfire Vb

412 (Canadian) Sqn
01/05–04/06/42
Spitfire Vb

416 (Canadian) Sqn
16/07–14/08/42
20/08–23/09/42
08–24/11/42
Spitfire Vb

453 (Australian) Sqn
24/11–07/12/42
Spitfire Vb

501 (AAF) Sqn
17/05–05/06/43
Spitfire Vb

504 (AAF) Sqn
24–30/12/39
08–13/01/40
20–30/01/40
11–22/02/40

27/02–05/03/40
12–18/03/40
27/03–04/04/40
13–23/04/40
30/04–07/05/40
Hurricane I

605 (AAF) Sqn
25/02–31/03/41
Hurricane IIa

607 (AAF) Sqn
20/08–10/10/41
Hurricane I, IIa, IIb

11 Grp Fighter Command, 09/39
To USAAF as Station AAF-369, 10/43

MATLASKE, Norfolk

LOCATION: 5½m SE of Holt
OPENED: 10/40
CLOSED: 10/45. Agriculture (2011)
ELEVATION: 165ft
PUNDIT CODE: MK
FORMATION: 12 Grp Fighter Command
MAIN CONTRACTOR: Various
RUNWAYS: 2 grass
HANGARS: Blister (5), T2 (1)
USER SQNS/UNITS:

3 Sqn
21–28/09/44
Tempest V

19 Sqn
16/08–01/12/41
04–20/06/43
28/09–14/10/44
Spitfire IIa, Vb; Mustang III

56 Sqn
24/08/42–22/07/43
23–28/09/44
Typhoon Ia, Ib; Tempest V

65 Sqn
29/09–03/10/44
04–14/10/44
Mustang III

122 Sqn
28/09–14/10/44
Mustang III

137 Sqn
30/11/41–02/08/42
11–24/08/42
Whirlwind I

195 Sqn
31/07–21/08/43
Typhoon Ib

222 Sqn
06/06–01/07/41
Spitfire IIb

229 Sqn
22/10–20/11/44
Spitfire IX

266 Sqn
02–11/08/42
Typhoon Ia, Ib

453 (Australian) Sqn

ABOVE: Typhoon Mk IB, EK183, 'A', was flown from Matlaske by the CO of No 56 Squadron, Sqn Ldr Thomas Pheloung, of Oamaru, New Zealand. On 20 June 1943, flying Typhoon Mk IB, EK184, Pheloung led an attack on an enemy convoy off the Hook of Holland, during which his aircraft was hit by fire from the ships. On the return flight his Typhoon was seen to make a sudden sharp diving turn and then crash into the sea. Pheloung was killed and his body was later washed up on the French coast. He is buried at Dunkirk. (Author)

18/10–20/11/44
15/03–06/04/45
Spitfire IXb, LFXVI
486 (New Zealand) Sqn
19–28/09/44
Tempest V
601 (AAF) Sqn
30/06–16/08/41
Hurricane IIb
602 (AAF) Sqn
18/10–20/11/44
Spitfire IXb
609 (AAF) Sqn
22/07–18/08/43
Typhoon Ib
611 (AAF) Sqn
01–31/07/43
Spitfire IX, LFVb
Opened in Fighter Command as a satellite to Coltishall, 10/40
To USAAF as Station AAF-178, 09/42–04/43; 08/43–09/44
Reopened in 12 Grp Fighter Command, 09/44

MAYDOWN, Co Londonderry, NI

LOCATION: 3m NE of Londonderry
OPENED: 07/42
CLOSED: 01/49. Agriculture/industry (2011)
ELEVATION: 50ft
PUNDIT CODE: Not known
FORMATION: 13 Grp Fighter Command
MAIN CONTRACTOR: Various
RUNWAYS: 2 concrete
HANGARS: Blister (9), T1 (1)
USER SQNS/UNITS:
No RAF flying units based
Opened as Fighter Command satellite to Eglinton, 07/42
Closed for rebuilding, 01/43
To RN as HMS *Shrike*, 05/43

MELBOURNE, Yorks

LOCATION: 12m SE of York
OPENED: 1940
CLOSED: 03/46. Agriculture (2011)
ELEVATION: 25ft
PUNDIT CODE: ME
FORMATION: 4 Grp Bomber Command
MAIN CONTRACTOR: Various
RUNWAYS: 3 concrete/Tarmac
HANGARS: T2 (2), B1 (1)
USER SQNS/UNITS:
10 Sqn
19/08/42–06/08/45
Halifax II, III
Opened in Bomber Command as satellite to Leeming, 1940
Became 44 Base substation, 06/43

MENDLESHAM, Suffolk

LOCATION: 5½m NE of Stowmarket
OPENED: 12/43
CLOSED: 06/54. Industrial estate/agriculture (2011)
ELEVATION: 210ft
PUNDIT CODE: MZ
FORMATION: 12 Grp Fighter Command
MAIN CONTRACTOR: Various
RUNWAYS: 3 concrete/Tarmac

ABOVE: Halifax B Mk II Series 1s of No 10 Squadron gain height in the failing evening light, outward bound from Melbourne for a raid on Turin, 8 December 1942. The squadron lost no aircraft that night. (IWM CH7900)

ABOVE: Four of Flt Sgt Doug Henley's No 75 (New Zealand) Squadron crew pose for the photographer at Mepal during the summer of 1943. Their Stirling Mk III, EE878, 'P', was attacked and fatally damaged by a night fighter over Berlin on 31 August. Henley nursed the wounded Stirling homewards but it crashed at Ahrbrüch in western Germany. Although four of the crew survived, Henley, the navigator and the bomb-aimer were killed. (Lew Parsons)

HANGARS: T2 (2)
USER SQNS/UNITS:
310 (Czech) Sqn
19–21/02/44
25/02–28/03/44
Spitfire LFIX
312 (Czech) Sqn
19–23/02/44
03/03–04/04/44
Spitfire LFIXb
313 (Czech) Sqn
20/02–14/03/44
20/03–04/04/44
Spitfire IX
Opened in Fighter Command as parent station, 12/43
To USAAF as Station AF-156, 04/44

MEPAL, Cambs
LOCATION: 6m W of Ely
OPENED: 06/43
CLOSED: 1963. Agriculture/light industry (2011)
ELEVATION: 80ft
PUNDIT CODE: MP
FORMATION: 3 Grp Bomber Command
MAIN CONTRACTOR: Various
RUNWAYS: 3 concrete
HANGARS: T2 (2), B1 (1)
USER SQNS/UNITS:
75 (New Zealand) Sqn
28/06/43–21/07/45
Stirling III; Lancaster I, III
Opened in Bomber Command as 33 Base substation, 06/43

MERRYFIELD, Somerset
LOCATION: 8m SE of Taunton
OPENED: 04/43
CLOSED: RN base (2011)
ELEVATION: 110ft
PUNDIT CODE: HI
FORMATION: 10 Grp Fighter Command
MAIN CONTRACTOR: John Laing & Son Ltd
RUNWAYS: 3 concrete/bitumen
HANGARS: T2 (2)
USER SQNS/UNITS:
No RAF flying units based
Opened in Army Co-operation Command as parent station, 04/43
To 10 Grp Fighter Command, 06/43
To USAAF as Station AAF-464, 02/44
To 10 Grp RAF ADGB, 08/44
To 47 Grp Transport Command, 11/44

MERSTON, Sussex
LOCATION: 2½m SE of Chichester
OPENED: 04/41
CLOSED: 11/45. Agriculture (2011)
ELEVATION: 50ft
PUNDIT CODE: XM
FORMATION: 11 Grp Fighter Command
MAIN CONTRACTOR: Various
RUNWAYS: 2 steel matting
HANGARS: Blister (6)
USER SQNS/UNITS:
41 Sqn
28/07–16/12/41
01/04–15/06/42
Spitfire I, IIa, Vb
118 Sqn
24/08–20/09/43
Spitfire Vb
130 Sqn
27/06–03/08/44

ABOVE: 'Here's Home', an unidentified Lancaster of No 106 Squadron, sits at its Metheringham dispersal in the summer of 1944. Note the exhaust staining on the engine nacelles caused by the heavily leaded fuel, and the US-made 500lb bombs in the left foreground. In the summer of 1944 these bombs were used by Bomber Command to make up for the shortage of British-made 500- and 1,000-pounders. They differed only in that they were built with two suspension lugs instead of one. No 106 Squadron was the sole occupant at Metheringham, where it was based from November 1943 until disbanded in February 1946. (Author)

Spitfire Vb
131 Sqn
14/05–22/08/42
Spitfire Vb
145 Sqn
28/05–28/07/41
Spitfire IIa, IIb
174 Sqn
12/06–01/07/43
Typhoon Ib
181 Sqn
08/10–31/12/43
13/01–06/02/44
21/02–01/04/44
Typhoon Ib
182 Sqn
12/10–31/12/43
23/01–01/04/44
Typhoon Ib
184 Sqn
31/05–12/06/43
Hurricane IV
229 Sqn
24–28/06/44
Spitfire IX
247 Sqn
11–31/10/43
05/11–31/12/43
13/01–01/04/44
Typhoon Ib
274 Sqn
22–28/06/44
Spitfire IX
303 (Polish) Sqn
27/06–09/08/44
Spitfire LFVb, IXc
329 (French) Sqn
17/04–19/05/44
23/05–22/06/44
Spitfire IX
340 (French) Sqn
17/04–15/05/44
19/05–22/06/44
Spitfire IXb
341 (French) Sqn
14/04–11/05/44
16/05–22/06/44
Spitfire IXb
402 (Canadian) Sqn
07/08–19/09/43
27/06–08/08/44
Spitfire Vc, IX
412 (Canadian) Sqn
19/06–24/08/42
Spitfire Vb
416 (Canadian) Sqn
09/08–19/09/43
Spitfire Vb
485 (New Zealand) Sqn
21/05–01/07/43
Spitfire Vb
Opened in Fighter Command as satellite to Tangmere, 04/41
To USAAF as Station AAF-356, 08/42
To 11 Grp Fighter Command, 05/43

METHERINGHAM, Lincs

LOCATION: 10m SE of Lincoln
OPENED: 10/43
CLOSED: 02/46. Agriculture/aviation museum (2011)
ELEVATION: 63ft
PUNDIT CODE: MN
FORMATION: 5 Grp Bomber Command
MAIN CONTRACTOR: Various
RUNWAYS: 3 concrete
HANGARS: T2 (2), B1 (1)
USER SQNS/UNITS:
106 Sqn
11/11/43–18/02/46
Lancaster I, III
Opened in Bomber Command as 54 Base substation, 10/43
*Sgt N.C. Jackson, 106 Sqn, awarded VC, Schweinfurt, 26–27/04/44

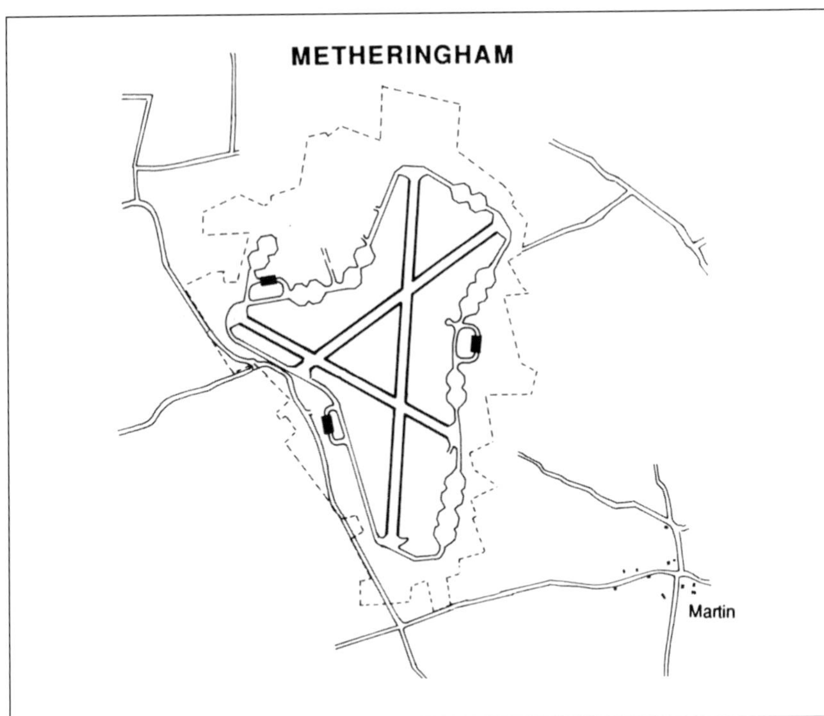

METHWOLD, Suffolk

LOCATION: 5m NW of Brandon
OPENED: 09/39
CLOSED: 06/58. Agriculture (2011)
ELEVATION: 50ft
PUNDIT CODE: ML
FORMATIONS: 2, 3 Grp Bomber Command
MAIN CONTRACTOR: Various
RUNWAYS: 3 concrete
HANGARS: T2 (4), B1 (1)
USER SQNS/UNITS:

21 Sqn
31/10/42–01/04/43
Ventura I, II

57 Sqn
01–09/42
Wellington I, III

149 Sqn
15/05/44–04/46
Stirling III; Lancaster I, III

ABOVE: No 149 Squadron's top-scoring Stirling Mk III, EF411, 'K', on her dispersal at Methwold in the summer of 1944. EF411 joined No 15 Squadron in May 1943 before passing to No 149 Squadron the following month, with which she completed at least 69 ops. She later served with No 1653 HCU and survived the war. (Author)

ABOVE: The Mosquito Mk II was a day and night fighter and intruder variant of the 'Wooden Wonder', armed with four 20mm Hispano cannon and four 0.303in machine guns. These Mk IIs belong to No 456 Squadron and are seen at Middle Wallop on 5 June 1943. (IWM CH10317)

214 Sqn
03/09/39–14/02/40
Wellington I
218 Sqn
04/08–05/12/44
Stirling III; Lancaster I, III
320 (Dutch) Sqn
15–30/03/43
Hudson VI
464 (Australian) Sqn
03/04–20/07/43
Ventura I, II
487 (New Zealand) Sqn
03/04–20/07/43
Ventura II
Opened in Bomber Command as satellite to Feltwell, 09/39
Became 31 Base substation, 07/43
*Sqn Ldr L.H. Trent, 487 (New Zealand) Sqn, awarded VC, Amsterdam power station, 03/05/43

MIDDLE WALLOP, Hants

LOCATION: 6m SW of Andover
OPENED: 04/40
CLOSED: Army base, flying (2011)
ELEVATION: 286ft
PUNDIT CODE: MW
FORMATIONS: 10, 11 Grp Fighter Command
MAIN CONTRACTOR: Higgs & Hill Ltd
RUNWAYS: 2 steel matting
HANGARS: Blister (4), C Type (5)
USER SQNS/UNITS:
1 (RCAF) Sqn
20/06–01/07/40
Hurricane I
19 Sqn
01–10/03/43
13/03–05/04/43
Spitfire Vb, Vc
32 Sqn
15/12/40–16/02/41
Hurricane I
56 Sqn
29/11–17/12/40
Hurricane I
420 Flt > 93 Sqn
09/40 (07/12/40)–18/11/41
Havoc I; Wellington Ic; Boston I
125 Sqn
31/07–18/10/44
Mosquito XVII
151 Sqn
16/08–17/11/43
Mosquito XII
164 Sqn
08/02–20/06/43
Hurricane IId, IV
182 Sqn
01/03–05/04/43
Typhoon Ib
234 Sqn
14/08–11/09/40
Spitfire I

TURBINLITE HAVOC FLIGHTS

Flight	Airfield	Sqn
1451	Hunsdon, Herts	3
1452	West Malling	264, 32
1453	Wittering	151, 486
1454	Charmy Down	87
1455	Tangmere	3, 1
1456	Honiley	257
1457	Colerne	47
1458	Middle Wallop	93, 245
1459	Hibaldstow	253
1460	Acklington	43

All 10 Turbinlite Flights were raised to full squadron status on 2 September 1942, being numbered Nos 530–539 Squadrons as follows:

530 Sqn (1451 Flt) Hunsdon
531 Sqn (1452 Flt) West Malling, Debden
532 Sqn (1453 Flt) Wittering, Hibaldstow
533 Sqn (1454 Flt) Charmy Down
534 Sqn (1455 Flt) Tangmere
535 Sqn (1456 Flt) High Ercall
536 Sqn (1457 Flt) Predannack, Fairwood Common
537 Sqn (1458 Flt) Middle Wallop
538 Sqn (1459 Flt) Hibaldstow
539 Sqn (1460 Flt) Acklington

All 10 Turbinlite squadrons were disbanded on 25 January 1943.

238 Sqn
20/06–14/08/40
Hurricane I
245 Sqn
19/12/41–26/10/42
Hurricane IIb, IIc
247 Sqn
28/02–05/04/43
Hurricane IIb; Typhoon Ib
406 (Canadian) Sqn
08/12/42–31/03/43
Beaufighter VIf
418 (Canadian) Sqn
29/07–28/08/44
Mosquito II
456 (Australian) Sqn
29/03–17/08/43
Mosquito II, VI
501 (AAF) Sqn
04–25/07/40
24/08–08/10/42
Hurricane I; Spitfire Vb, Vc
504 (AAF) Sqn
19/10–30/12/42
Spitfire Vb, Vc
1458 Flt > 537 Sqn
06/12/41 (08/09/42)–25/01/43
Havoc I (Turbinlite); Boston III (Turbinlite)
601 (AAF) Sqn
01–17/06/40
Hurricane I
604 (AAF) Sqn
27/07/40–12/08/42
23/08–07/12/42
Blenheim If; Beaufighter If
609 (AAF) Sqn
06/07–02/10/40
Spitfire I
Opened in Flying Training Command, 04/40
To 11 Grp Fighter Command, 06/40
To 10 Grp Fighter Command as Sector Station, 08/40
To USAAF as Station AAF-449, 12/43
To 10 Grp Fighter Command, 07/44
To RN as HMS *Flycatcher*, 02/45

MIDDLETON ST GEORGE, Co Durham

LOCATION: 5m E of Darlington
OPENED: 15/01/41
CLOSED: 1964. Durham Tees Valley Airport (2011)
ELEVATION: 115ft
PUNDIT CODE: MG
FORMATIONS: 4, 6 (RCAF) Grp Bomber Command
MAIN CONTRACTOR: Various
RUNWAYS: 3 Tarmac
HANGARS: C Type (1), B1 (1), J Type (1), T2 (2)
USER SQNS/UNITS:
76 Sqn
04/06/41–16/09/42
Halifax I, II
78 Sqn
07/04–20/10/41
10/06–16/09/42
Whitley V; Halifax II
419 (Canadian) Sqn
10/11/42–01/06/45
Halifax II; Lancaster X
420 (Canadian) Sqn
16/10/42–16/05/43
Wellington III
428 (Canadian) Sqn
04/06/43–31/05/45
Halifax V, II; Lancaster X
Opened in Bomber Command as parent station, 01/41
Became 64 (RCAF) Base HQ, 01/43
*Plt Off A.C. Mynarski, 419 (Canadian) Sqn, awarded posthumous VC, Cambrai, 12–13/06/44

MILDENHALL, Suffolk

LOCATION: 12m NW of Bury St Edmunds
OPENED: 16/10/34
CLOSED: USAF base (211)
ELEVATION: 15ft
PUNDIT CODE: MI
FORMATION: 3 Grp Bomber Command
MAIN CONTRACTOR: Various
RUNWAYS: 3 concrete
HANGARS: C Type (3), A Type (2), T2 (2)
USER SQNS/UNITS:
15 Sqn
14/04/43–19/08/46
Stirling III; Lancaster I, III
115 Sqn
24/09/42–08/11/42
Wellington III
149 Sqn
12/04/37–06/04/42
Heyford; Wellington I, II;
Stirling I

ABOVE: A Stirling crew of No 622 Squadron are debriefed by an intelligence officer at Mildenhall after returning from the major raid on Berlin of 22/23 November 1943. Some 764 aircraft took part in the attack, of which 50 were Stirlings (the last time they were sent to Germany). From left to right: Flt Lt R.D. Mackay (navigator), Flg Off G. Dunbar (interrogating officer), Sgt J. Towns (rear gunner, partly hidden by Dunbar), Plt Off K. Pollard (wireless operator), Flt Sgt C. Stevenson (second pilot, standing), Sqn Ldr J. Martin (captain and flight commander), Sgt W. Rigby (mid-upper gunner), Flg Off Grainger (bomb-aimer) and Sgt H. Fletching (flight engineer). (IWM CH11641)

419 (Canadian) Sqn
15/12/41–13/08/42
Wellington I, III
622 Sqn
10/08/43–15/08/45
Stirling III; Lancaster I, III
Opened in Bomber Command as parent station, 16/10/34
Became 32 Base HQ, 12/42
*Harry Watt's film Target for Tonight made here during 1941 by Crown Film Unit featuring Wellingtons and crews of 149 Sqn

MILFIELD, Northumberland

LOCATION: 4m NW of Wooler
OPENED: 08/42
CLOSED: 02/46. Disused/gliding (2011)
ELEVATION: 150ft
PUNDIT CODE: IL
FORMATIONS: 9, 81 (OTU) Grp Fighter Command
MAIN CONTRACTOR: Various
RUNWAYS: 3 concrete
HANGARS: Blister (8), T2 (2)
USER SQNS/UNITS:
56 OTU
15/12/44–14/02/46
Typhoon; Tempest; Hurricane; Master
59 OTU
06/08/42–26/01/44
Hurricane IV; Typhoon Ib
Fighter Leaders' School
26/01–27/12/44
Spitfire; Hurricane; Typhoon Ib
Opened in Fighter Command as parent station, 08/42

MILLTOWN, Morayshire

LOCATION: 4m NE of Elgin
OPENED: 1943
CLOSED: 1977. Radio research station (2011)
ELEVATION: 12ft
FORMATIONS: 17 (T), 18 Grp Coastal Command
RUNWAYS: 3 concrete and Tarmac
HANGARS: T2 (2), B1 (1)
USER SQNS/UNITS:
224 Sqn
11/09/44–20/07/45
Liberator V, VI, VII
20 OTU
06/43–09/44
Wellington
111 OTU
08/45–08/46
Liberator

MOLESWORTH, Hunts
LOCATION: 10½m WNW of Huntingdon
OPENED: 05/41
CLOSED: USAF base, non-flying (2011)
ELEVATION: 240ft
PUNDIT CODE: MX
FORMATION: 1 Grp Bomber Command
MAIN CONTRACTOR: Various
RUNWAYS: 3
HANGARS: T2 (2), J Type (1)
USER SQNS/UNITS:
460 (Australian) Sqn
15/11/41–04/01/42
Wellington IV
Opened in Bomber Command as parent station, 05/41
To USAAF as Station AAF-107, 06/42

MONTFORD BRIDGE, Salop
LOCATION: 4½m WNW of Shrewsbury
OPENED: 04/42
CLOSED: 12/45. Agriculture (2011)
ELEVATION: 265ft
PUNDIT CODE: MD
FORMATIONS: 81 (OTU), 9 Grp Fighter Command
MAIN CONTRACTOR: Various
RUNWAYS: 3 Tarmac
HANGARS: Bessonneau (7), Blister (4)
USER SQNS/UNITS:
61 OTU
04/42–06/45
Spitfire; Mustang III
Opened in Fighter Command as satellite to Rednal, 04/42

MORETON-IN-MARSH, Gloucs
LOCATION: 14m S of Stratford-on-Avon
OPENED: 01/41
CLOSED: Fire Service College (2011)
ELEVATION: 420ft
PUNDIT CODE: MO
FORMATIONS: 6 (T), 91 (OTU) Grp Bomber Command
MAIN CONTRACTOR: Various
RUNWAYS: 3 concrete/Tarmac
HANGARS: J Type (1), T2 (4)
USER SQNS/UNITS:
21 OTU
03/41–11/46
Wellington I, III, X
1446 Flt
05/42–01/05/43
Wellington
Opened in Bomber Command as parent station, 01/41

MORPETH, Northumberland
LOCATION: 3m SW of Morpeth
OPENED: 01/42
CLOSED: 07/48. Agriculture (2011)
ELEVATION: 363ft
PUNDIT CODE: EP
FORMATION: 13 Grp Fighter Command
MAIN CONTRACTOR: John Laing & Son Ltd
RUNWAYS: 3 Tarmac
HANGARS: Blister (17), T1 (3)
USER SQNS/UNITS:
72 Sqn
04–12/08/42
Spitfire Vb, Vc, IX
80 OTU
23/04–07/45
Spitfire; Master
Opened in Flying Training Command, 01/42
To 13 Grp Fighter Command, 04/45

MOUNT BATTEN, Devon
LOCATION: 1 mile S of Plymouth
OPENED: 1917
CLOSED: 1992. Industry (2011)
ELEVATION: 0ft
FORMATION: 19 Grp Coastal Command
RUNWAYS: No. Flying boat alighting area in Plymouth Sound and Batten Bay
HANGARS: T2 (2), B1 (1)
USER SQNS/UNITS:
10 (RAAF) Sqn
01/04/40–05/41
05/01/42–31/10/45
Sunderland
204 Sqn
05/08/36–02/04/40
London I, II; Sunderland I
461 (RAAF) Sqn
26/04–05/09/42
Sunderland II

MOUNT FARM, Oxon
LOCATION: 8m SE of Oxford
OPENED: 07/40
CLOSED: 1957. Agriculture/Berinsfield new village (2011)
ELEVATION: 180ft
PUNDIT CODE: MF
FORMATIONS: 6 (T) Grp Bomber Command; 106 (PR) Grp Coastal Command
MAIN CONTRACTOR: John Laing & Son Ltd
RUNWAYS: 3 concrete
HANGARS: Blister (8)
USER SQNS/UNITS:
140 Sqn
20/05/42–16/03/43
Spitfire Ia, Vg; Blenheim IV
12 OTU
07/40–07/41
Battle; Wellington I
Opened in Bomber Command as satellite to Benson, 07/40
Became satellite to Harwell, 07/41
Became satellite to Benson under Coastal Command control, 01/42
To USAAF, 02/43

MULLAGHMORE, Co Londonderry, NI
LOCATION: 4m W of Ballymoney
OPENED: 1942
CLOSED: 1945. Agriculture/racing circuit (2011)
ELEVATION: 35ft
FORMATION: 15 (T) Grp Coastal Command
RUNWAYS: 2 concrete and Tarmac
HANGARS: T2 (4)
USER SQNS/UNITS:
281 Sqn
27/02/44–07/02/45 (det)
07/02–31/03/45
Warwick I
7 OTU (det)
29/12/42–04/01/44
Wellington
104 OTU (det)
03/10/43–18/01/44
Wellington

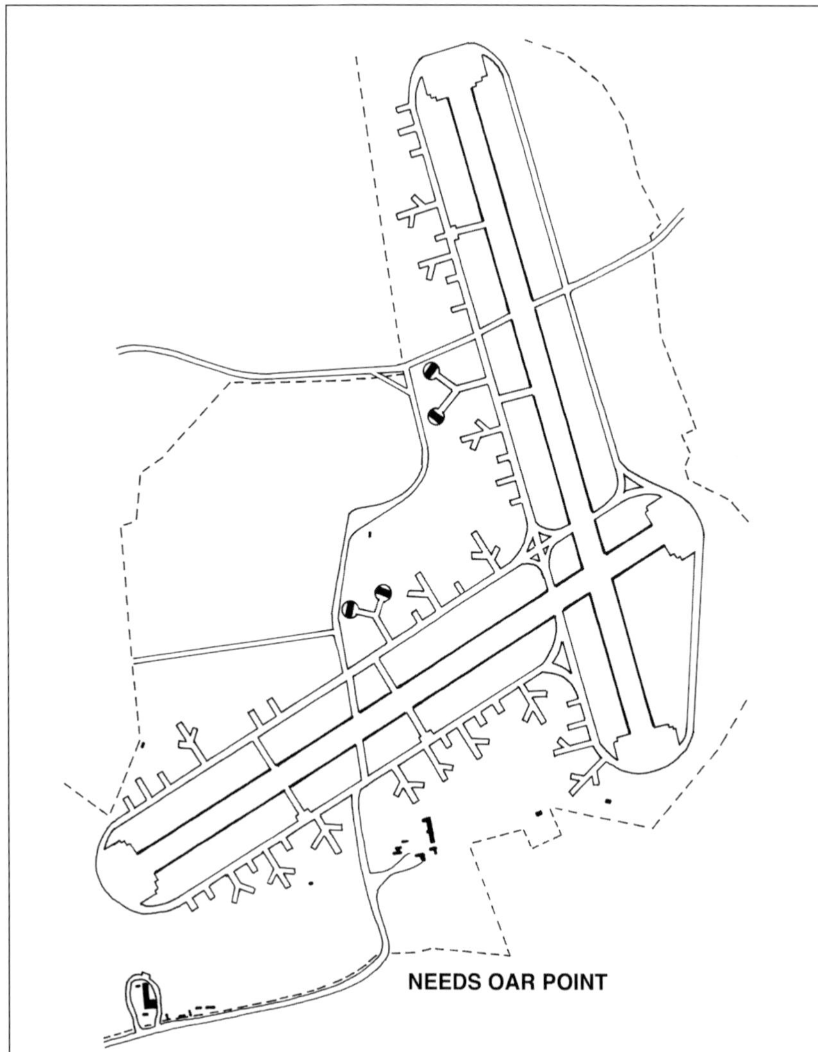

771 NAS
01–02/45
Firefly
824 NAS (det)
11/44
Avenger
825 NAS
11/44–03/45
Swordfish
850 NAS
11/44–03/45
Avenger
Loran Training Unit
08/44–03/45
Wellington XIII
Coastal Command satellite to Limavady
To USAAF as Station AAF-240, 12/43–05/44
To RAF Coastal Command, 05/44

NEEDSOAR POINT, Hants

LOCATION: 5m E of Lymington
OPENED: 04/44
CLOSED: 11/44. Agriculture (2011)
ELEVATION: 30ft
PUNDIT CODE: NI
FORMATION: 84 Grp 2 TAF
MAIN CONTRACTOR: RAF 5004 ACS
RUNWAYS: 2 steel matting
HANGARS: Blister (4)
USER SQNS/UNIT:
193 Sqn
11/04–03/07/44
Typhoon Ib
197 Sqn
10/04–03/07/44
Typhoon Ib
257 Sqn
10–11/04/44
12/04–02/07/44
Typhoon Ib
266 Sqn
10–27/04/44
06/05–29/06/44
Typhoon Ib
2 TAF Advanced Landing Ground (ALG)

NEW ROMNEY, Kent

LOCATION: 1½m N of New Romney
OPENED: 03/43
CLOSED: 12/44. Agriculture (2011)
ELEVATION: 10ft
PUNDIT CODE: XR
FORMATION: 83 Grp 2 TAF
MAIN CONTRACTOR: RAFACS
RUNWAYS: 2 steel matting
HANGARS: Blister (4)
USER SQNS/UNITS:
181 Sqn
03/07–08/10/43
Typhoon Ib
182 Sqn
02/07–12/10/43
22/09–12/10/43
Typhoon Ib
247 Sqn
10/07–07/08/43
13/08–11/10/43
Typhoon Ib
Became 2 TAF Reserve Advanced Landing Ground (RALG), 10/43

NEWCHURCH, Kent

LOCATION: 7m SSE of Ashford
OPENED: 07/43
CLOSED: 1945. Agriculture (2011)
ELEVATION: 0ft
PUNDIT CODE: XN
FORMATIONS: 83, 85 Grp 2 TAF
MAIN CONTRACTOR: RAFACS
RUNWAYS: 2 steel matting
HANGARS: Blister (4)
USER SQNS/UNITS:
3 Sqn
28/04–21/09/44
Tempest V

ABOVE: Pilots and squadron personnel from Newchurch-based No 486 (New Zealand) Squadron parade with a squadron Typhoon Mk IB at Tangmere in 1943. (R. Beeforth)

19 Sqn
02–18/07/43
Spitfire Vb, IX
56 Sqn
28/04–23/09/44
Typhoon Ib; Spitfire IX; Tempest V
132 Sqn
03/07–12/10/43
Spitfire Vb
184 Sqn
18/08–15/09/43
17/09–12/10/43
Hurricane IV
486 (New Zealand) Sqn
29/04–19/09/44
Tempest V
602 (AAF) Sqn
13/08–12/10/43
Spitfire Vb
Fighter Interception Unit (FIU) (det)
24/06–10/08/44
Hurricane; Beaufighter
2 TAF Advanced Landing Ground (ALG)

NEWMARKET, Suffolk

LOCATION: 1 ¼m W of Newmarket
OPENED: 1939
CLOSED: 05/45. Newmarket racecourse (2011)
ELEVATION: 96ft
PUNDIT CODE: NM
FORMATION: 3 Grp Bomber Command
MAIN CONTRACTOR: Various
RUNWAYS: 3 grass
HANGARS: B1 (3), T2 (3), Blister (3)
USER SQNS/UNITS:
7 Sqn
16/03–27/04/41
Stirling I
75 (New Zealand) Sqn
01/11/42–29/06/43
Wellington III; Stirling I, III
99 Sqn
01/09/39–08/03/41
Wellington I
138 Sqn
25/08–16/12/41
Lysander; Whitley V; Halifax II
161 Sqn
14/02–01/03/42
Lysander IIIa; Hudson I; Whitley V
215 Sqn
09/12/41–05/01/42
Wellington I
Bombing Development Unit (BDU)
11/09/43–25/02/45
Lancaster; Halifax; Stirling; Wellington; Spitfire; Mosquito; Beaufighter; Anson; Proctor
Opened in Bomber Command as satellite to Mildenhall, 09/39
Became 31 Base HQ, 12/42

NEWTON, Notts

LOCATION: 7m E of Nottingham
OPENED: 1937
CLOSED: 2001. Agriculture/industrial estate (2011)
ELEVATION: 151ft
PUNDIT CODE: NA
FORMATION: 1 Grp Bomber Command
MAIN CONTRACTOR: Various
RUNWAYS: 3 grass
HANGARS: C Type (5)
USER SQNS/UNITS:

103 Sqn
03/07/40–11/07/41
Battle; Wellington I

150 Sqn
03/07/40–10/07/41
Battle; Wellington I

Opened in Bomber Command as parent station, 07/40
To Flying Training Command, 07/41

NORTH COATES, Lincs

LOCATION: 6m SE of Grimsby
OPENED: 1918
CLOSED: 1990. Light aviation (2011)
ELEVATION: 17ft
FORMATION: 16 Grp Coastal Command
RUNWAYS: 1 concrete, 1 grass
HANGARS: Bellman (4), F Type (4)
USER SQNS/UNITS:

22 Sqn
08/04/40–25/06/41
Beaufort I

42 Sqn (det)
04/41
Beaufort I

53 Sqn
18/02–16/05/42
Hudson V

59 Sqn
17/01–29/08/42
Hudson V, VI

86 Sqn
15/05/41–10/01/42
Blenheim IV; Beaufort I

143 Sqn
27/08/42–28/08/43
Beaufighter IIf, XI

217 Sqn (det)
02/42
Beaufort II

235 Sqn
27/02–25/04/40
Blenheim If, IVF

236 Sqn
29/02–29/04/40
Blenheim If

248 Sqn
24/02–08/04/40
Blenheim If, IVf

254 Sqn
07/11/42–29/06/45
Beaufighter VI, X; Mosquito XVIII

278 Sqn (det)
10/41
4/42
Lysander IIIa; Walrus

407 (Canadian) Sqn
08/07/41–18/02/42
Hudson III, V

415 (Canadian) Sqn
05/06–05/08/42
Hampden

776 NAS
02/42
Roc

812 NAS
05/40
Swordfish I

816 NAS
05/41
Swordfish I

ABOVE: Beaufort Mk I, L4453, 'G', of No 22 Squadron, at North Coates early in 1940. This aircraft went missing off the Elbe during a mine-laying sortie on 9 May 1940. (Andy Thomas)

ABOVE: Air and ground crews of No 199 (RCM) Squadron's Stirling Mk III, LJ525, 'R', skippered by Flt Lt Noble, at North Creake in the summer of 1944. (R. Smith)

BELOW: Well-wishers beside the runway at North Killingholme wave to Flt Lt D.A. Shaw and his No 550 Squadron crew as they take off for a raid on Bochum on 4 November 1944. It was the 100th operational sortie for their Lancaster, ED905, F for Freddie. This Lanc survived the war to be struck off charge on 20 August 1945. (IWM CH14188)

NORTH CREAKE, Norfolk

LOCATION: 2m W of Little Walsingham
OPENED: 23/11/43
CLOSED: 09/47. Agriculture (2011)
ELEVATION: 240ft
PUNDIT CODE: NO
FORMATION: 100 (BS) Grp Bomber Command
MAIN CONTRACTORS: Taylor Woodrow Ltd, W. Lawrence & Son Ltd
RUNWAYS: 3 concrete
HANGARS: T2 (2), B1 (1)
USER SQNS/UNITS:

171 Sqn
08/09/44–27/07/45
Stirling III; Halifax III

199 Sqn
01/05/44–29/07/45
Stirling III; Halifax III

Opened in Bomber Command as satellite to Foulsham, 11/43
Upgraded to parent station, 04/44

NORTH KILLINGHOLME, Lincs

LOCATION: 10m NW of Grimsby
OPENED: 11/43
CLOSED: 10/45. Agriculture/light industry (2011)
ELEVATION: 31ft
PUNDIT CODE: NK
FORMATION: 1 Grp Bomber Command
MAIN CONTRACTOR: John Laing & Son Ltd
RUNWAYS: 3 concrete
HANGARS: T2 (2), B1 (1)
USER SQNS/UNITS:

550 Sqn
03/01/44–31/10/45
Lancaster I, III

Opened in Bomber Command as 13 Base substation, 11/43

NORTH LUFFENHAM, Rutland

LOCATION: 6m SW of Oakham
OPENED: 12/40
CLOSED: 1998.
ELEVATION: 350ft
PUNDIT CODE: NL
FORMATIONS: 5, 7 (HCU), 92 (OTU) Grp Bomber Command
MAIN CONTRACTOR: John Laing & Son Ltd
RUNWAYS: 3 concrete
HANGARS: B1 (1), J Type (2), T2 (3)
USER SQNS/UNITS:

61 Sqn
07–09/41
Hampden; Manchester

144 Sqn
17/07/41–22/04/42
Hampden

29 OTU
25/04/42–07/43
Wellington I, III

1653 HCU
27/11/44–28/10/45
Lancaster I, III; Stirling III; Beaufighter VI; Mosquito XIX

Opened in Bomber Command as parent station, 12/40
To Flying Training Command, 04/44
To Bomber Command as 73 Base HQ, 11/44

NORTH WEALD, Essex

LOCATION: 2½m NE of Epping
OPENED: 1916
CLOSED: 09/64. General aviation/museum (2011)
ELEVATION: 270ft
PUNDIT CODE: NQ
FORMATION: 11 Grp Fighter Command
MAIN CONTRACTOR: Various
RUNWAYS: 2 Tarmac
HANGARS: Blister (12), A Type (2)
USER SQNS/UNITS:

1 Sqn
03–22/04/44
Typhoon Ib; Spitfire IXb

2 Sqn
14–30/11/43
22/01–29/02/44
Mustang I

4 Sqn
14–30/11/43
Mustang I

17 Sqn
23/05–02/09/39
Hurricane I

25 Sqn
16/01–10/05/40
12/05–19/06/40
02/09–08/10/40
Blenheim If; Beaufighter If

33 Sqn
23/04–17/05/44
Spitfire LFIXe

46 Sqn
08/11–14/12/40
Hurricane I

56 Sqn
12/10/27–22/10/39
22/02–31/05/40
05/06–01/09/40
17/12/40–23/06/41
Hurricane I, IIb

63 Sqn
30/11/43–22/01/44
04/11/44–01/02/45
Mustang Ia; Spitfire Vb

66 Sqn
01–31/03/44
Spitfire LFIXb

71 Sqn
23/06–14/12/41
Hurricane IIa; Spitfire IIa, Vb

74 Sqn
24/04–15/05/44
Spitfire IX

111 Sqn
30/05–04/06/40
20/07–01/11/41
15–22/12/41
Hurricane I; Spitfire I, IIa, Vb

121 Sqn
16/12/41–03/06/42
Spitfire Vb

124 Sqn
07/11–07/12/42
21–29/12/42
21/01–01/03/43
12/03–26/07/43
Spitfire VI, IX, Vb, VII

127 Sqn
23/04–16/05/44
Spitfire HFIX

151 Sqn
04/08/36–13/05/40
20/05–29/08/40
Gauntlet II; Hurricane I

ABOVE: At the end of 1941 No 111 Squadron pilots, flying black-painted Spitfire Mk VBs, were trained in night-interception tactics in anticipation of a resumed Luftwaffe night offensive over Britain. This is JU-H in its sandbagged dispersal at North Weald. (Alfred Price)

168 Sqn
30/11/43–21/01/44
04–21/02/44
Mustang I, Ia

222 Sqn
18/08/41–30/06/42
07/07–04/08/42
Spitfire Vb

234 Sqn
28/08–17/12/44
Spitfire Vb; Mustang III

242 Sqn
22/05–19/07/41
11–14/08/42
20/08–01/09/42
Hurricane IIb; Spitfire Vb

249 Sqn
01/09/40–21/05/41
Hurricane I, IIa

257 Sqn
08/10–07/11/40
Hurricane I

285 Sqn
04/01–20/06/45
Hurricane IIc; Mustang I

310 (Czech) Sqn
28/08–29/12/44
Spitfire Vb, LFIX

312 (Czech) Sqn
27/08–03/10/44
Spitfire HFIX

313 (Czech) Sqn
04/10–29/12/44
Spitfire IX

331 (Norwegian) Sqn
04/05–30/06/42
07/07–14/08/42
20/08–07/09/42
14/09–02/10/42
09/10/42–05/01/44
21/01–05/03/44
13–31/03/44
Spitfire Vb, IXb

332 (Norwegian) Sqn
19/06–14/08/42
20/08–01/09/42
06/09–02/10/42
09/10/42–05/01/44
21/01–21/03/44
27–31/03/44
Spitfire Vb, IXb

403 (Canadian) Sqn
22/12/41–02/05/42
Spitfire Vb

412 (Canadian) Sqn
04–19/06/42
Spitfire Vb

486 (New Zealand) Sqn
27/09–10/10/42
Typhoon Ib

604 (AAF) Sqn
02/09/39–16/01/40
Blenheim I

Fighter Command Sector Station,
09/39

ABOVE: These Spitfire pilots of No 609 Squadron at Northolt are seen at readiness between sorties in early September 1940. None survived the war. From left to right: Plt Off 'Shorty' Keough (American, killed in action 15 February 1941), Plt Off Geoffrey Gaunt (killed in action a few days after this picture was taken, on 15 September), and Plt Off David Crook (killed in a flying accident on 18 December 1944). (Crown Copyright)

NORTHOLT, Middx

LOCATION: 3m E of Uxbridge
OPENED: 1915
CLOSED: RAF base, flying (2011)
ELEVATION: 120ft
PUNDIT CODE: NH
FORMATIONS: 11 Grp Fighter Command; 84 Grp 2 TAF
MAIN CONTRACTOR: Various and John Laing & Son Ltd
RUNWAYS: 3 asphalt
HANGARS: Belfast Truss (1), C1 (2)
USER SQNS/UNITS:

1 Sqn
18/06–23/07/40
01/08–09/09/40
15/12/40–05/01/41
Hurricane I

1 (RCAF) Sqn
00/08–09/10/40
Hurricane I

16 Sqn
16/04–04/09/44
Spitfire PRIX, XI

17 Sqn
26/08–02/09/40
Hurricane I

25 Sqn
22/08–15/09/39
04/10/39–16/01/40
Blenheim If

65 Sqn
02/10/39–28/03/40
Spitfire I

69 Sqn
05/05–04/09/44
Wellington XIII

92 Sqn
09/05–09/06/40
Spitfire I

111 Sqn
12/07/34–27/10/39
13–21/05/40
Bulldog IIa; Gauntlet I, II; Hurricane I

124 Sqn
26/07–20/09/43
Spitfire VII

140 Sqn
07/04–03/09/44
Mosquito XVI

229 Sqn
09/09–15/12/40
Hurricane I

253 Sqn
14/02–08/05/40
Battle; Hurricane I

257 Sqn
04/07–15/08/40
Hurricane I

302 (Polish) Sqn
11/10–23/11/40
21/09–02/12/43
19/12/43–01/03/44
07/03–01/04/44
Hurricane I; Spitfire IX

303 (Polish) Sqn
22/07–11/10/40
03/01–15/07/41
07/10/41–16/06/42
02–05/02/43
01/06–12/11/43
Hurricane I; Spitfire I, IIa, Vb, IXc

306 (Polish) Sqn
03/04–07/10/41
16/06/42–12/03/43
Hurricane IIa; Spitfire IIb, Vb, IXb

308 (Polish) Sqn
24/06–12/12/41
29/10/42–29/04/43
11/11–02/12/43
18/12/43–08/03/44
15/03–01/04/44
Spitfire IIa, Vb, IX

315 (Polish) Sqn
14/07/41–01/04/42
05/09/42–02/06/43
Spitfire IIa, IIb, Vb, IX

316 (Polish) Sqn
13/12/41–23/04/42
12/03–22/09/43
Spitfire Vb, IX

317 (Polish) Sqn
01/04–30/06/42
07/07–05/09/42
18/12/43–01/04/44
Spitfire Vb, IX

515 Sqn
01–29/10/42
Defiant II

600 (AAF) Sqn
25/08–02/10/39
14/05–20/06/40
Blenheim If, IV

601 (AAF) Sqn
17/12/40–01/05/41
Hurricane I, IIb

604 (AAF) Sqn
16/01–15/05/40
20/06–03/07/40
Blenheim I; Gladiator I

615 (AAF) Sqn
10/10–16/12/40
Hurricane I

Fighter Command Sector Station, 09/39

NUNEATON, Leics

LOCATION: 4½m NNE of Nuneaton
OPENED: 02/43
CLOSED: 09/46
ELEVATION: 323ft
PUNDIT CODE: NU
FORMATION: 93 (OTU) Grp Bomber Command
MAIN CONTRACTOR: Various
RUNWAYS: 3 concrete
HANGARS: T2 (1)
USER SQNS/UNITS:

18 OTU
02–03/43
Wellington I, III

Opened in Bomber Command as satellite to Bramcote, 02/43
To Transport Command, 04/43

NUTTS CORNER, Co Antrim, NI

LOCATION: 2m E of Crumlin
OPENED: 1941
CLOSED: 1963. Stock car and karting circuit (2011)
ELEVATION: 350ft
FORMATIONS: 15 (T) Grp Coastal Command; 44 Grp Ferry Command
RUNWAYS: 3 Tarmac
HANGARS: T1 (2), T2 (2)
USER SQNS/UNITS:

44 Sqn (det)
12/41–05/43
Lancaster I, III

120 Sqn
02/06/41–21/07/42
Liberator I
160 Sqn
07–30/05/42
Liberator II
220 Sqn
09/01–02/05/42
Fortress I
231 Sqn
02/01–21/03/43
Lysander III; Tomahawk I, II
1332 CU
07/10/44–27/04/45
To 44 Grp Ferry Command, 01/43

OAKINGTON, Cambs

LOCATION: 5m NW of Cambridge
OPENED: 01/07/40
CLOSED: Army Air Corps (2011)
ELEVATION: 40ft
PUNDIT CODE: OA
FORMATIONS: 3, 8 (PFF) Grp Bomber Command
MAIN CONTRACTOR: Various
RUNWAYS: 3 concrete/Tarmac
HANGARS: B1 (1), J Type (2), T2 (2)
USER SQNS/UNITS:
7 Sqn
29/10/40–24/07/45
Stirling I, III; Lancaster I, III
101 Sqn
06/07/41–11/02/42
Wellington I
218 Sqn
14/07–25/11/40
Blenheim IV
571 Sqn (LNSF)
24/04/44–29/07/45
Mosquito XVI
627 Sqn (LNSF)
12/11/43–15/04/44
Mosquito IV
3 PRU
16/11/40–07/41
Spitfire; Wellington

ABOVE: Here is a close-up view of the nose of a Sunderland of No 210 Squadron at Oban, in August 1940. A compartment inside the nose of the Sunderland contained an anchor, a winch, a boat-hook and a ladder, for the purposes of mooring the flying boat. The front turret was designed to slide back, thereby enabling the crew to secure the aircraft to a buoy, as demonstrated here. The circle painted on the fuselage just below the cockpit is a gas-detection patch. (IWM CH847)

1409 Met Flt
01/04/43–08/01/44
Mosquito IV, IX
Navigation Training Unit (NTU)
03–06/43
Lancaster I, III
Opened in Bomber Command as parent station, 01/07/40

OAKLEY, Bucks

LOCATION: 11½m WSW of Aylesbury
OPENED: 27/05/42
CLOSED: 08/45. Disused (2011)
ELEVATION: 233ft
PUNDIT CODE: OY
FORMATION: 92 (OTU) Grp Bomber Command
MAIN CONTRACTOR: John Laing & Son Ltd
RUNWAYS: 3 concrete
HANGARS: B1 (1), T2 (1)
User sqns/units:.
11 OTU
08/42–08/45
Wellington I, III, X
Opened in Bomber Command as satellite to Bicester, 27/05/42
Became satellite to Westcott, 08/42

OBAN, Argyllshire

LOCATION: Oban Bay
OPENED: 1939
CLOSED: 1945. Housing/harbour (2011)
ELEVATION: 24ft
FORMATIONS: 15, 17 Grp Coastal Command
RUNWAYS: none. Alighting area
HANGARS: none. Maintenance at Ganavan Sands
USER SQNS/UNITS:
209 Sqn
07/10/39–12/07/40
Stranraer; Lerwick I
210 Sqn
13/07/40–28/02/42
Sunderland I; Catalina I
228 Sqn
10/03–11/12/42
Sunderland I, II, III
330 (Norwegian) Sqn
28/01–12/07/43
Northrop N3P-B; Sunderland II, III
422 (Canadian) Sqn
05/11/42–08/05/43
Sunderland III
423 (Canadian) Sqn
18/05–02/11/42
Sunderland II, III
302 FTU
07/43–04/45
Catalina; Sunderland
524 Sqn
20/10–07/12/43
Mariner I

ODIHAM, Hants

LOCATION: 6½m ESE of Basingstoke
OPENED: 12/36
CLOSED: RAF base, flying (2011)
ELEVATION: 400ft
PUNDIT CODE: OI
FORMATIONS: 11 Grp Fighter Command; 84 Grp 2 TAF
MAIN CONTRACTOR: Lindsay Parkinson Ltd
RUNWAYS: 2 concrete
HANGARS: Blister (6), C Type (3)
USER SQNS/UNITS:
2 Sqn
07/08–14/11/43
27/06–29/07/44
Mustang I
4 Sqn
07/08–15/09/43
06/10–14/11/43
27/06–16/08/44
Mustang I; Mosquito XVI; Spitfire XI
96 Sqn
24/09–12/12/44
Mosquito XIII
168 Sqn
06/43
21/02–06/03/44
31/03–29/06/44
Mustang I, Ia
170 Sqn
06/43
Mustang I
174 Sqn
06/12/42–01/03/43
Hurricane IIb
175 Sqn
14/01–01/03/43
13–19/03/43
Hurricane IIb
181 Sqn
31/12/43–13/01/44
Typhoon Ib
182 Sqn
31/12/43–05/01/44
Typhoon Ib
184 Sqn
06–11/03/44
03–23/04/44
Hurricane IV; Typhoon Ib
247 Sqn
31/12/43–13/01/44
Typhoon Ib
264 Sqn
01/12/44–09/01/45
Mosquito XIII
604 (AAF) Sqn
05–31/12/44
Mosquito XIII
Opened in Fighter Command as parent station, 12/36
To 11 Grp Fighter Command, 06/43

OSSINGTON, Notts

LOCATION: 8m NNW of Newark-on-Trent
OPENED: 01/42
CLOSED: 08/46. Agriculture (2011)
ELEVATION: 180ft
PUNDIT CODE: ON
FORMATION: 93 (OTU) Grp Bomber Command
MAIN CONTRACTOR: Various
RUNWAYS: 3 concrete
HANGARS: T2 (4)
USER SQNS/UNITS:
82 OTU
01/06/43–09/01/45
Wellington III, X
6 LFS
01/01/44–01/11/45
Lancaster
Opened in Bomber Command as parent station, 01/42

ABOVE: This Focke Wulf Fw190A-3 of 7./JG2 landed in error at RAF Pembrey on 23 June 1942 after combat with RAF fighters over the southwest of England. (Crown Copyright)

To Flying Training Command, 01/42
To Bomber Command, 05/43
Transport Command 011/45

OULTON, Norfolk

LOCATION: 3m W of Aylsham
OPENED: 31/07/40
CLOSED: 11/47. Agriculture (2011)
ELEVATION: 157ft
PUNDIT CODE: OU
FORMATIONS: 2, 100 (BS) Grp Bomber Command; 2 TAF
MAIN CONTRACTOR: Prestige & Co Ltd
RUNWAYS: 3 concrete
HANGARS: T2 (4)
USER SQNS/UNITS:

18 Sqn
03/04–13/07/41
05/11–05/12/41
Blenheim IV

21 Sqn
01/04–19/08/43
Ventura I, II; Mitchell

88 Sqn
29/09/42–30/03/43
Boston III, IIIa

114 Sqn
10/08/40–02/03/41
Blenheim IV

139 Sqn
13/07–23/10/41
09/12/41–01/42
Blenheim IV; Hudson II

214 Sqn
16/05/44–27/07/45
Fortress II, III

223 Sqn
23/08/44–29/07/45
Liberator IV, VI; Fortress II, III

1699 CU
05/44–07/45
Fortress II, III; Liberator IV

Opened in Bomber Command as satellite to Horsham St Faith, 07/40
Became satellite to Swanton Morley, 09/42
Became satellite to Foulsham, 09/43

OUSTON, Northumberland

LOCATION: 1m S of Stamfordham
OPENED: 03/41
CLOSED: 1974. Army base (2011)
ELEVATION: 450ft
PUNDIT CODE: OS
FORMATIONS: 9, 12, 13 Grp Fighter Command
MAIN CONTRACTOR: Various
RUNWAYS: 3 Tarmac
HANGARS: Blister (8), J Type (1)
USER SQNS/UNITS:

72 Sqn
26/09–08/11/42
Spitfire Vb, Vc

81 Sqn
06/01–14/02/42
15–29/03/42
13/04–14/05/42
Spitfire Va, Vb

122 Sqn
26/06–31/08/41
Spitfire I

131 Sqn
30/06–10/07/41
Spitfire Ia
198 Sqn
23/01–09/02/43
Typhoon Ia, Ib
232 Sqn
21/07–11/11/41
Hurricane I, IIb
242 Sqn
15/05–01/06/42
Spitfire Vb
243 Sqn
01/06–02/09/42
Spitfire Vb
317 (Polish) Sqn
29/04–26/06/41
Hurricane I
350 (Belgian) Sqn
08/06–20/07/43
Spitfire Vb
55 OTU
04/41–04/42
Hurricane
62 OTU
21/06/43–06/06/45
Anson; Wellington
Opened in Fighter Command as Sector Station, 03/41
Satellite to Usworth, 04/41–04/42

PEMBREY, Carmarthenshire

LOCATION: 6m WNW of Llanelli
OPENED: 05/40
CLOSED: 1957. West Wales International Airport (2011)
ELEVATION: 17ft
PUNDIT CODE: Not known
FORMATION: 10 Grp Fighter Command
MAIN CONTRACTOR: Various
RUNWAYS: 3 concrete/Tarmac
HANGARS: Blister (13), Cranwell (2), F Type (4), VR1 Type (3)
USER SQNS/UNITS:
32 Sqn
17/04–01/06/41
Hurricane I
92 Sqn
18/06–08/09/40
Spitfire I
238 Sqn
01–16/04/41
Hurricane IIa
256 Sqn
04/01–06/02/41
Defiant I
316 (Polish) Sqn
12/02–18/06/41
Hurricane I
Opened in Fighter Command as Sector Station, 05/40
To Flying Training Command, 06/41

PEMBROKE DOCK, Pembrokeshire

LOCATION: close to town centre
OPENED: 1930
CLOSED: 1959. Dock/museum (2011)
ELEVATION: 0ft
FORMATION: 19 Grp Coastal Command
RUNWAYS: none. Alighting area
HANGARS: B Type (2), T2 (1)
USER SQNS/UNITS:
201 Sqn
08/04–03/11/44

ABOVE: At one point during World War 2, RAF Pembroke Dock was the busiest flying boat base in the world. Here Sunderland Mk III, ML747, 'N', of No 461 (Australian) Squadron, takes off from the South Wales base during 1944. (RAF Museum P958 via Andy Thomas)

02/08/45–01/04/46
Sunderland III, V
210 Sqn
08/10/38–23/10/39
06–24/11/39
21/05–13/07/40
Sunderland I
228 Sqn
09/10/38–05/06/39
10/09/39–10/06/40
Stranraer; Sunderland I
461 (Australian) Sqn
20/04/43–04/06/45
Sunderland II, III, V
VP-63 (US Navy)
20/07–15/12/43
Catalina

PEPLOW (CHILD'S ERCALL), Salop

LOCATION: 7m S of Market Drayton
OPENED: 07/43
CLOSED: 12/49. Agriculture/light industry (2011)
ELEVATION: 230ft
PUNDIT CODE: CE
FORMATION: 93 (OTU) Grp Bomber Command
MAIN CONTRACTOR: Various
RUNWAYS: 3 concrete
HANGARS: B1 (1), T2 (4)
USER SQNS/UNITS:
83 OTU
07/43–28/10/44
Wellington III, X
Flying Training Command RLG for Tern Hill, 1941
To Bomber Command as parent station, 07/43
To Flying Training Command, 01/45

PERRANPORTH, Cornwall

LOCATION: 7m SSW of Newquay
OPENED: 04/41
CLOSED: 04/46. Light aviation/parachuting (2011)
ELEVATION: 320ft
PUNDIT CODE: PP
FORMATIONS: 10 Grp Fighter Command; 19 Grp Coastal Command; 46 Grp Transport Command
MAIN CONTRACTOR: Various
RUNWAYS: 3 Tarmac
HANGARS: Blister (6), Teesside (1)
USER SQNS/UNITS:
19 Sqn
06/05–01/06/42
14/06–01/07/42
07–23/07/42
31/07–16/08/42
20/08/42–01/03/43
Spitfire Vb, Vc
65 Sqn
29/03–18/05/43
Spitfire Vb
66 Sqn
27/04–14/12/41
17/09–08/11/43
Spitfire IIa, Vb, Vc
130 Sqn
05/12/41–12/07/42
17/07–04/08/42
20/08–21/10/42
31/10/42–30/03/43
Spitfire Vb, Vc
132 Sqn
18/05–20/06/43
Spitfire Vb, Vc
183 Sqn
18/09–14/10/43
Typhoon Ib
234 Sqn
28/10–26/11/42
26/12/42–19/01/43
Spitfire Vb, IV
310 (Czech) Sqn
24/12/41–09/02/42
11/02–08/03/42
21/03–07/05/42
Spitfire IIa, Vb
317 (Polish) Sqn
21/06–21/08/43
Spitfire Vb
329 (French) Sqn
22/01–16/03/44
24/03–17/04/44
Spitfire Vb, Vc, IX
340 (French) Sqn
09/11/43–17/04/44
Spitfire Vb, IXb
341 (French) Sqn
11/10/43–14/04/44
Spitfire Vb, IXb
412 (Canadian) Sqn
13/04–21/06/43
Spitfire Vb
453 (Australian) Sqn
20/08–15/10/43
Spitfire Vb, Vc
602 (AAF) Sqn
20/01–14/04/43
Spitfire Vb, Vc
610 (AAF) Sqn
30/04–26/06/43
Spitfire Vc
Opened in Fighter Command as a satellite to Portreath, 04/41
To Coastal Command, 04/44
To Transport Command, 11/44

PERSHORE, Worcs

LOCATION: 8m ESE of Worcester
OPENED: 02/41
CLOSED: 1978. Agriculture/MOD (2011)
ELEVATION: 123ft
PUNDIT CODE: PR
FORMATIONS: 6 (T), 91 (OTU) Grp Bomber Command
MAIN CONTRACTOR: Various
RUNWAYS: 3 concrete/asphalt
HANGARS: J Type (1), T2 (4)
USER SQNS/UNITS:
23 OTU
01/04/41–15/03/44
Wellington I, III
Opened in Bomber Command as parent station, 02/41
To Ferry Command, 03/44

PETERHEAD, Aberdeenshire

LOCATION: 3m W of Peterhead
OPENED: 07/41
CLOSED: 08/45. Light aviation (2011)
ELEVATION: 150ft
PUNDIT CODE: PH
FORMATIONS: 13, 14 Grp Fighter Command
MAIN CONTRACTOR: Various
RUNWAYS: 3 Tarmac

HANGARS: Blister (8), Teeside (5)
USER SQNS/UNITS:
19 Sqn
13/02–23/05/45
Mustang III, IV
65 Sqn
03–04/10/44
16–28/01/45
01/02–06/05/45
Mustang III, IV
118 Sqn
20/09–19/10/43
23/01–05/02/44
09–29/08/44
Spitfire VI, IXc, Vb, VII
122 Sqn
01/05–03/07/45
Mustang IV
129 Sqn
17/01–16/03/44
Spitfire IX
132 Sqn
07/07/41–16/02/42
Spitfire I, IIb
164 Sqn
06/04–05/05/42
10/09/42–29/01/43
Spitfire Va, Vb
165 Sqn
29/03–30/06/43
Spitfire Vb
234 Sqn
01/05–03/07/45
Mustang IV
245 Sqn
29/01–30/03/43
Typhoon Ib
313 (Czech) Sqn
28/06–21/08/43
Spitfire Vb, Vc, VI
315 (Polish) Sqn
01/11/44–16/01/45
Mustang III
350 (Belgian) Sqn
14/03–25/04/44
Spitfire Vb, Vc
416 (Canadian) Sqn
22/11/41–14/03/42
03/04–25/06/42
07–16/07/42
Spitfire IIa, Vb
504 (AAF) Sqn
18/10/43–19/01/44
Spitfire Vb, VI, IXb
602 (AAF) Sqn
17/07–16/08/42
20/08–10/09/42
Spitfire Vb
603 (AAF) Sqn
14/03–13/04/42
Spitfire Vb
Opened in Fighter Command as Sector Station, 07/41

POCKLINGTON, Yorks

LOCATION: 12m ESE of York
OPENED: 06/41
CLOSED: 09/46. Gliding club/light industry (2011)
ELEVATION: 84ft
PUNDIT CODE: PO
FORMATION: 4 Grp Bomber Command
MAIN CONTRACTOR: Various

ABOVE: Flt Lt A. Carey and his No 102 Squadron Halifax Mk II crew walk to the transports at Pocklington on their return from a night raid on Frankfurt, 5 October 1943. This was the first serious attack on Frankfurt, causing widespread destruction in the eastern half of the city and in the docks on the River Main. (IWM CH11234)

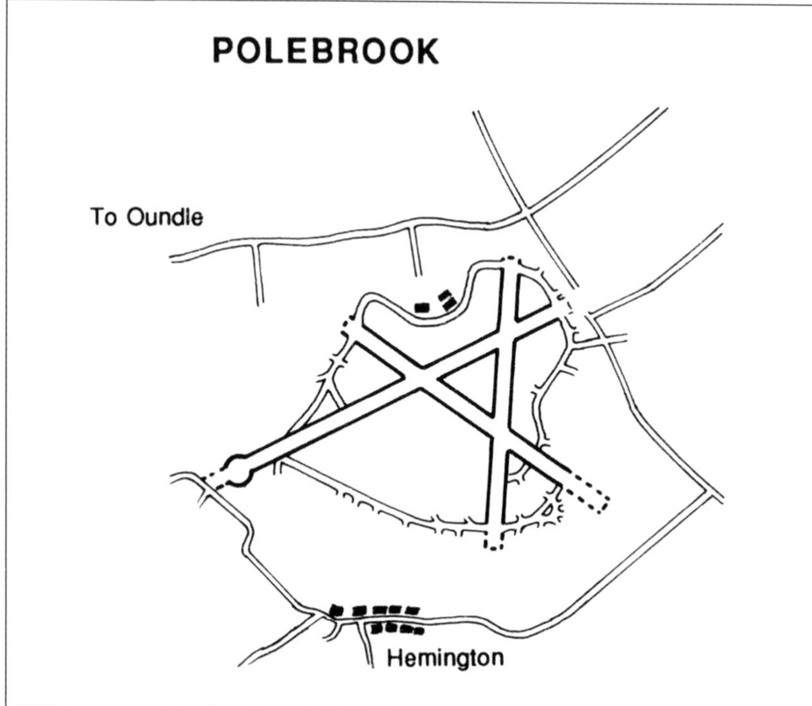

ABOVE: Aircrew of a No 90 Squadron Boeing Fortress Mk I board their aircraft at Polebrook for an attack on the German battle cruiser Gneisenau at Brest, on 24 July 1941. The Fortress proved unsuitable in Bomber Command service and was phased out by the end of 1941. Coastal Command, however, successfully used later marks of the Fort on maritime patrol duties. (IWM CH3084)

RUNWAYS: 3 concrete/Tarmac
HANGARS: B1 (1), J Type (1), T2 (4)
USER SQNS/UNITS:
102 Sqn
07/08/42–08/09/45
Halifax II, III, VI
405 (Canadian) Sqn
20/06/41–07/08/42
Wellington II; Halifax II
Opened in Bomber Command as parent station, 06/41
Became 42 Base HQ, 1943

POLEBROOK, Northants

LOCATION: 3½m ESE of Oundle
OPENED: 05/41
CLOSED: 01/67. Agriculture (2011)
ELEVATION: 234ft
PUNDIT CODE: PK
FORMATIONS: 3, 7 (T) Grp Bomber Command
MAIN CONTRACTOR: Various
HANGARS: J Type (1), T2 (1)
USER SQNS/UNITS:
90 Sqn
30/08/41–10/02/42
Fortress I; Blenheim IV
17 OTU
12/40–09/41
Blenheim I, IV
1653 HCU
01–06/42
Liberator II
Bomber Command satellite to Upwood, 12/40
Upgraded to parent station, 05/41

PORT ELLEN, Argyllshire

LOCATION: 4m NNW of Port Ellen, Isle of Islay
OPENED: 1940
CLOSED: 1947. Port Ellen (Glenegedale) Airport (2011)
ELEVATION: 46ft
FORMATION: 15 (T) Grp Coastal Command
RUNWAYS: 3 bitumen
HANGARS: ½ T2 (5), Callendar Hamilton (1)

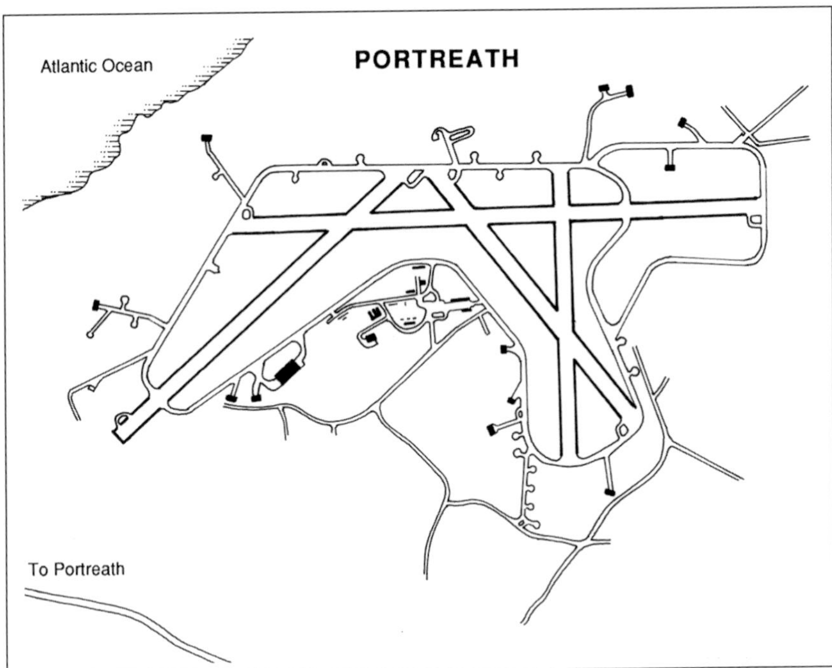

USER SQNS/UNITS:

304 FTU

05/02/43–08/01/44

Beaufort; Beaufighter

PORTREATH, Cornwall

LOCATION: 3½m N of Redruth

OPENED: 03/41

CLOSED: Military radar reporting post (2011)

ELEVATION: 295ft

PUNDIT CODE: PA

FORMATION: 10 Grp Fighter Command

MAIN CONTRACTOR: Richard Costain Ltd

RUNWAYS: 4 Tarmac

HANGARS: Blister (8), T2 (4)

USER SQNS/UNITS:

66 Sqn

14/12/41–08/02/42

22/02–27/04/42

Spitfire IIa, Va, Vb, Vc

130 Sqn

16/06–25/10/41

Spitfire IIa

152 Sqn

09/04–25/08/41

Spitfire IIa

153 Sqn

18–20/12/42

Beaufighter If, VIf

234 Sqn

27/04–23/08/42

30/08–28/10/42

26/11–26/12/42

Spitfire Vb, IV

247 Sqn

10/05–18/06/41

Hurricane I, IIa

263 Sqn

18/03–10/04/41

Whirlwind I

313 (Czech) Sqn

26/08–23/11/41

29/11–15/12/41

Spitfire IIa, Vb

Opened in Fighter Command as parent station, 03/41

Became 10 Grp Sector Station, 05/41

To 44 Grp Transport Command, 05/45

POULTON, Cheshire

LOCATION: 4½m S of Chester

OPENED: 03/43

CLOSED: 08/45. Disused (2011)

ELEVATION: 50ft

PUNDIT CODE: PU

FORMATIONS: 81 (OTU), 9 Grp Fighter Command

MAIN CONTRACTOR: George Wimpey & Co Ltd

RUNWAYS: 3 concrete

HANGARS: Bessonneau (1), Blister (8)

USER SQNS/UNITS:

41 OTU

01/03/43–03/45

Hurricane II; Harvard

3 TEU

11/43–28/03/44

Hurricane

Opened in Fighter Command as satellite to Hawarden, 03/43

PREDANNACK, Cornwall

LOCATION: 7½m S of Helston

OPENED: 05/41

CLOSED: RN base, flying (2011)

ELEVATION: 293ft

PUNDIT CODE: PD

FORMATION: 10 Grp Fighter Command

MAIN CONTRACTOR: Various

RUNWAYS: 4 Tarmac

HANGARS: Bellman (1), Blister (12)

USER SQNS/UNITS:

1 Sqn

29/04–20/06/44

Spitfire IXb

33 Sqn

15/12/44–21/02/45

Spitfire LFIXe; Tempest V

64 Sqn

09/12/42–02/01/43

Spitfire IX

141 Sqn

18/02–30/04/43

Beaufighter If

151 Sqn

25/03–08/10/44

Mosquito VI, XIII, XXX

157 Sqn

09/11/43–26/03/44

Mosquito II, VI

165 Sqn

02/04–20/06/44

Spitfire IXb

183 Sqn

14/10/43–01/02/44

Typhoon Ib

222 Sqn

15/12/44–21/02/45

Spitfire LFIXb; Tempest V

ABOVE: Facilities for personnel at Portreath in Cornwall were fairly rudimentary, as can be seen in this photograph of Spitfire pilots Sgt Anderson and Sgt Howard Marsh of No 152 Squadron in an off-duty moment during 1941. (W. Johnston)

234 Sqn
19/06–28/08/44
Spitfire Vb
247 Sqn
18/06/41–17/05/42
Hurricane I, IIa, IIb, IIc
264 Sqn
30/04–07/08/43
12/08–07/11/43
25/09–30/11/44
Mosquito II, VI, XIII
307 (Polish) Sqn
07/08–09/11/43
Mosquito II, VI
349 (Belgian) Sqn
16/02–19/04/45
Tempest V
406 (Canadian) Sqn
04/09–08/12/42
Beaufighter VIf
485 (New Zealand) Sqn
25/02–19/04/45
Tempest V; Typhoon Ib
1457 Flt > 536 Sqn
11/41 (08/09/42)–27/10/42
Havoc II (Turbinlite)
600 (AAF) Sqn
06/10/41–02/09/42
Beaufighter IIf, VIf
604 (AAF) Sqn
07/12/42–18/02/43
24/09–05/12/44
Beaufighter If; Mosquito XIII
677 Sqn
03–17/07/44
Spitfire LFVb, IX
Opened in Fighter Command as a satellite to Portreath, 05/41

PRESTWICK, Ayrshire

LOCATION: 3m NNE of Ayr
OPENED: 02/36
CLOSED: Prestwick Airport (2011)
ELEVATION: 35ft
PUNDIT CODE: PW
FORMATIONS: 13 Grp Fighter Command; 44 Grp Ferry Command
MAIN CONTRACTOR: Various
RUNWAYS: 2 concrete
HANGARS: Bellman (2), B1 (4)
USER SQNS/UNITS:
1 (RCAF) Sqn
09/10–08/12/40
Hurricane I
141 Sqn
13–22/02/40
25/07–22/08/40
Gladiator I; Blenheim If; Defiant I
253 Sqn
23–29/08/40
Hurricane I
602 (AAF) Sqn
17/12/40–15/04/41
Spitfire I
603 (AAF) Sqn
16/12/39–17/01/40
Spitfire I
610 (AAF) Sqn
04/04–10/05/40
Spitfire I
Temporary Fighter Command Forward Airfield in Turnhouse Sector, 12/39
To 44 Grp Ferry Command, 04/41

REDHILL, Surrey

LOCATION: 2m SE of Redhill
OPENED: 07/37
CLOSED: Light aviation (2011)
ELEVATION: 205ft
PUNDIT CODE: RI
FORMATION: 11 Grp Fighter Command
MAIN CONTRACTOR: Various
RUNWAYS: 2 steel matting
HANGARS: Blister (8)
USER SQNS/UNITS:
1 Sqn
01/05–01/06/41
14/06–01/07/41
Hurricane IIa, IIb
66 Sqn
10–13/08/43
Spitfire Vb, Vc
131 Sqn
16/08–17/09/43
Spitfire Vb, Vc
219 Sqn
12/10–10/12/40
Blenheim If; Beaufighter If
258 Sqn
01–15/06/41
Hurricane IIa
303 (Polish) Sqn
15–20/08/42
Spitfire Vb
308 (Polish) Sqn
01–07/07/42
Spitfire Vb
310 (Czech) Sqn
01–07/07/42
16–20/08/42
Spitfire Vb, Vc
312 (Czech) Sqn
01–08/07/42
16–20/08/42
Spitfire Vb
340 (French) Sqn
01–07/04/42
Spitfire Vb
350 (Belgian) Sqn
31/07–07/09/42
15–23/09/42
Spitfire Vb
402 (Canadian) Sqn
31/05–29/06/42
01/07–03/08/42
09–13/08/42
Spitfire Vb, IX
407 (Canadian) Sqn
29/05–21/07/43
31/07–07/08/43
Spitfire Vb
411 (Canadian) Sqn
08/04–07/08/43
Spitfire Vb
412 (Canadian) Sqn
23/09–01/11/42
14/07–08/08/43
Spitfire Vb
416 (Canadian) Sqn
23/09–08/11/42
24/11/42–01/02/43
Spitfire Vb
421 Sqn
23/03–10/04/43
22/04–17/05/43
Spitfire Vb
452 (Australian) Sqn
21/10/41–14/01/42
Spitfire Vb

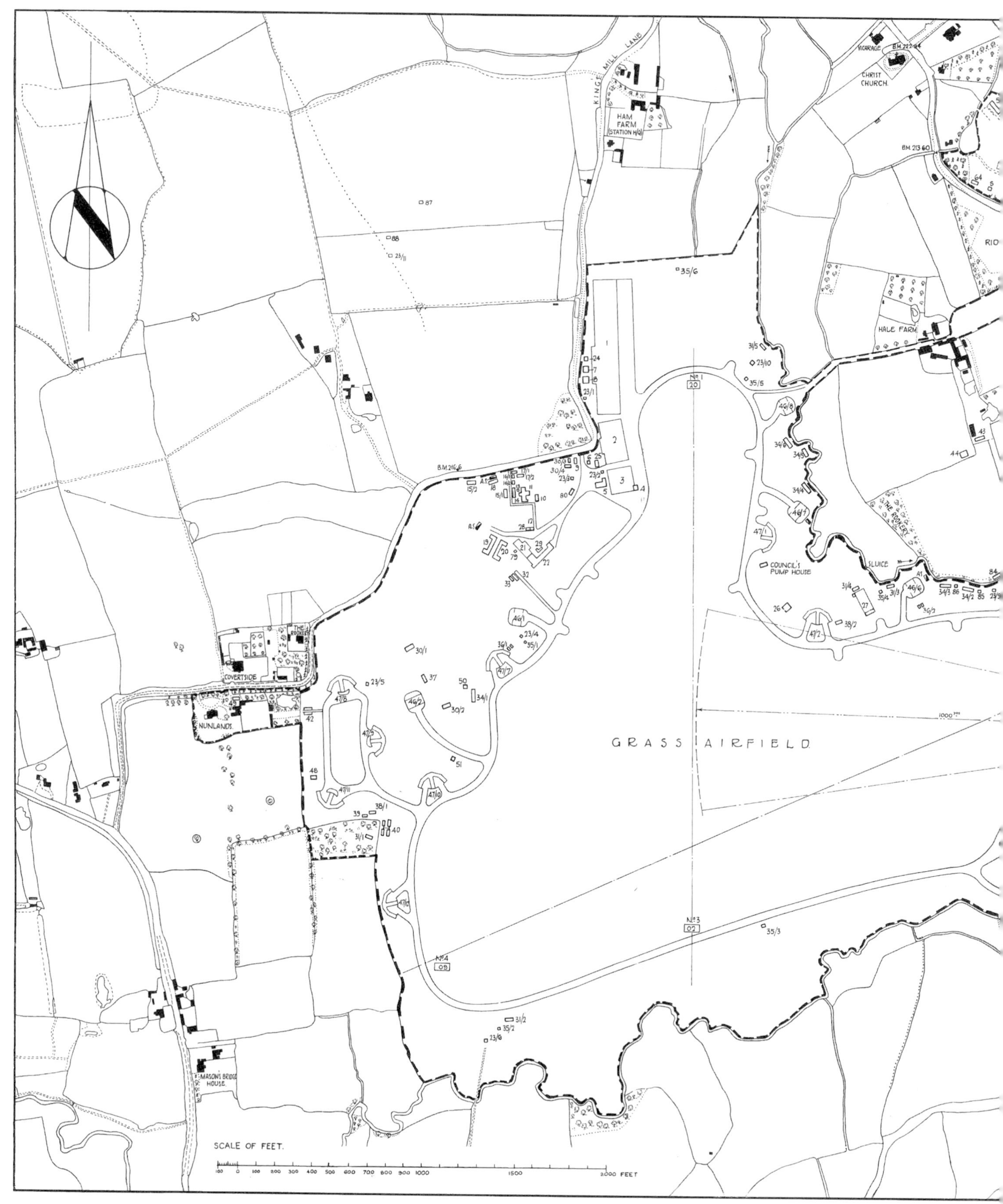

KINGS MILL LANE
HAM FARM (STATION H/Q)
VICARAGE
CHRIST CHURCH
HALE FARM
THE ROOKERY
SLUICE
COUNCIL'S PUMP HOUSE
COVERTSIDE
NUNLANDS
MASON'S BRIDGE HOUSE
GRASS AIRFIELD
SCALE OF FEET.
100 0 100 200 300 400 500 600 700 800 900 1000 1500 2000 FEET

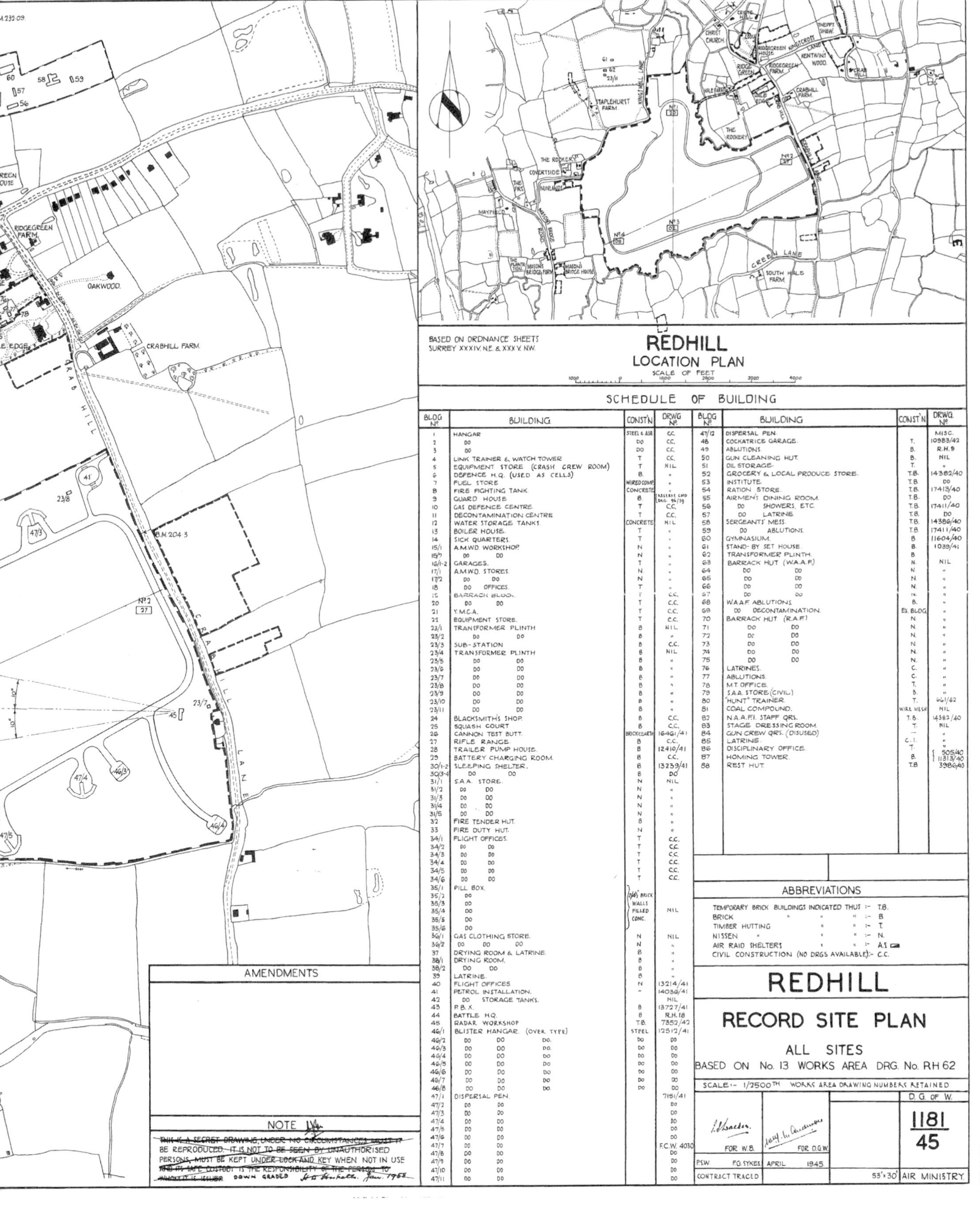

BASED ON ORDNANCE SHEETS
SURREY XXXIV. N.E. & XXX V. NW.

REDHILL

LOCATION PLAN

SCALE OF FEET
1000 0 1000 2000 3000 4000

SCHEDULE OF BUILDING

BLDG No	BUILDING	CONST'N	DRWG No
1	HANGAR	STEEL & ASB.	C.C.
2	DO	DO	C.C.
3	DO	DO	C.C.
4	LINK TRAINER & WATCH TOWER	T	C.C.
5	EQUIPMENT STORE (CRASH CREW ROOM)	T	NIL
6	DEFENCE H.Q. (USED AS CELLS)	B.	"
7	FUEL STORE	WIRED COMP.	"
8	FIRE FIGHTING TANK.	CONCRETE	"
9	GUARD HOUSE	B.	RESERVE CMD DRG. 96/39
10	GAS DEFENCE CENTRE.	T	C.C.
11	DECONTAMINATION CENTRE	T	C.C.
12	WATER STORAGE TANKS.	CONCRETE	NIL
13	BOILER HOUSE.	T	"
14	SICK QUARTERS.	T	"
15/1	A.M.W.D. WORKSHOP.	N	"
15/2	DO DO	N	"
16/1-2	GARAGES.	T	"
17/1	A.M.W.D. STORES.	N.	"
17/2	DO DO	N	"
18	DO OFFICES.	T	"
19	BARRACK BLOCK.	T	C.C.
20	DO DO	T	C.C.
21	Y.M.C.A.	T	C.C.
22	EQUIPMENT STORE.	T	C.C.
23/1	TRANSFORMER PLINTH	B	NIL
23/2	DO DO	B	"
23/3	SUB-STATION	B	C.C.
23/4	TRANSFORMER PLINTH	B	NIL
23/5	DO DO	B	"
23/6	DO DO	B	"
23/7	DO DO	B	"
23/8	DO DO	B	"
23/9	DO DO	B	"
23/10	DO DO	B	"
23/11	DO DO	B	"
24	BLACKSMITH'S SHOP.	B	C.C.
25	SQUASH COURT	B	C.C.
26	CANNON TEST BUTT.	BRICK & EARTH	16461/41
27	RIFLE RANGE.	B	C.C.
28	TRAILER PUMP HOUSE.	B	12410/41
29	BATTERY CHARGING ROOM.	B	C.C.
30/1-2	SLEEPING SHELTER.	B	13239/41
30/3-4	DO DO	B	DO
31/1	S.A.A. STORE.	N	NIL
31/2	DO DO	N	"
31/3	DO DO	N	"
31/4	DO DO	N	"
31/5	DO DO	N	"
32	FIRE TENDER HUT.	B	"
33	FIRE DUTY HUT.	N	"
34/1	FLIGHT OFFICES.	T	C.C.
34/2	DO DO	T	C.C.
34/3	DO DO	T	C.C.
34/4	DO DO	T	C.C.
34/5	DO DO	T	C.C.
34/6	DO DO	T	C.C.
35/1	PILL BOX.	2/4½" BRICK WALLS FILLED CONC.	NIL
35/2	DO		
35/3	DO		
35/4	DO		
35/5	DO		
35/6	DO		
36/1	GAS CLOTHING STORE.	N	NIL
36/2	DO DO DO	N	"
37	DRYING ROOM & LATRINE.	B	"
38/1	DRYING ROOM.	B	"
38/2	DO DO	B	"
39	LATRINE.	B	"
40	FLIGHT OFFICES.	N	13214/41
41	PETROL INSTALLATION.	-	14036/41
42	DO STORAGE TANKS.		NIL
43	P.B.X.	B	13727/41
44	BATTLE H.Q.	B	R.H. 18
45	RADAR WORKSHOP	T.B.	7352/42
46/1	BLISTER HANGAR. (OVER TYPE)	STEEL	12512/41
46/2	DO DO DO.	DO	DO
46/3	DO DO DO.	DO	DO
46/4	DO DO DO	DO	DO
46/5	DO DO DO	DO	DO
46/6	DO DO DO	DO	DO
46/7	DO DO DO	DO	DO
46/8	DO DO DO.	DO	DO
47/1	DISPERSAL PEN.		7151/41
47/2	DO DO		DO
47/3	DO DO		DO
47/4	DO DO		DO
47/5	DO DO		DO
47/6	DO DO		DO
47/7	DO DO		F.C.W. 4030
47/8	DO DO		DO
47/9	DO DO		DO
47/10	DO DO		DO
47/11	DO DO		DO
47/12	DISPERSAL PEN.		MISC.
48	COCKATRICE GARAGE.	T.	10983/42
49	ABLUTIONS.	B.	R.H. 9
50	GUN CLEANING HUT.	B.	NIL
51	OIL STORAGE.	T.	"
52	GROCERY & LOCAL PRODUCE STORE.	T.B.	14382/40
53	INSTITUTE.	T.B.	DO
54	RATION STORE.	T.B.	17413/40
55	AIRMEN'S DINING ROOM.	T.B.	DO
56	DO SHOWERS, ETC.	T.B.	17411/40
57	DO LATRINE	T.B.	DO
58	SERGEANTS' MESS.	T.B.	14386/40
59	DO ABLUTIONS.	T.B.	17411/40
60	GYMNASIUM.	B.	11604/40
61	STAND-BY SET HOUSE.	B.	1039/41
62	TRANSFORMER PLINTH.	B	
63	BARRACK HUT (W.A.A.F.)	N.	NIL
64	DO DO	N.	"
65	DO DO	N.	"
66	DO DO	N.	"
67	DO DO	N.	"
68	W.A.A.F. ABLUTIONS.	B.	"
69	DO DECONTAMINATION.	EX. BLDG.	"
70	BARRACK HUT (R.A.F.)	N.	"
71	DO DO	N.	"
72	DO DO	N.	"
73	DO DO	N.	"
74	DO DO	N.	"
75	DO DO	N.	"
76	LATRINES.	C.	"
77	ABLUTIONS.	C.	"
78	M.T. OFFICE.	T.	"
79	S.A.A. STORE (CIVIL)	B.	"
80	"HUNT" TRAINER.	T.	661/42
81	COAL COMPOUND.	WIRE MESH	NIL
82	N.A.A.F.I. STAFF QRS.	T.B.	14382/40
83	STAGE DRESSING ROOM.	T.	NIL
84	GUN CREW QRS. (DISUSED)	—	"
85	LATRINE.	C.I.	"
86	DISCIPLINARY OFFICE.	T.	"
87	HOMING TOWER.	B.	505/40, 11313/40
88	REST HUT.	T.B.	3986/40

ABBREVIATIONS

TEMPORARY BRICK BUILDINGS INDICATED THUS :- T.B.
BRICK " " " :- B
TIMBER HUTTING " " :- T.
NISSEN " " :- N.
AIR RAID SHELTERS " " :- A.S.
CIVIL CONSTRUCTION (NO DRGS AVAILABLE):- C.C.

AMENDMENTS

NOTE

~~THIS IS A SECRET DRAWING, UNDER NO CIRCUMSTANCES MUST IT~~ BE REPRODUCED. ~~IT IS NOT TO BE SEEN BY UNAUTHORISED~~ PERSONS, ~~MUST BE~~ KEPT UNDER ~~LOCK AND~~ KEY WHEN NOT IN USE ~~AND ITS SAFE CUSTODY IS THE RESPONSIBILITY OF THE PERSON TO WHOM IT IS ISSUED~~ DOWN GRADED Jan. 1953

REDHILL

RECORD SITE PLAN

ALL SITES

BASED ON No. 13 WORKS AREA DRG. No. RH 62

SCALE:- 1/2500TH WORKS AREA DRAWING NUMBERS RETAINED

D.G. OF W.

FOR W.B. FOR D.G.W.

1181
45

P.S.W. F.G. SYKES APRIL 1945

CONTRACT TRACED 53"×30" AIR MINISTRY

457 (Australian) Sqn
23/03–31/05/42
Spitfire Vb
485 (New Zealand) Sqn
01/07–21/10/41
Spitfire IIa, Vb
504 (AAF) Sqn
14/08–19/09/43
Spitfire Vb, Vc
600 (AAF) Sqn
12/09–12/10/40
Blenheim If; Beaufighter If
602 (AAF) Sqn
14/01–04/03/42
13/05–17/07/42
Spitfire Vb
677 Sqn
20–27/07/42
01–14/08/42
20/08–23/09/42
Spitfire Vb, IX
To Fighter Command as a satellite to Biggin Hill, 06/40

REDNAL, Salop

LOCATION: 12m NW of Shrewsbury
OPENED: 04/42
CLOSED: 1945. Agriculture/industry (2011)
ELEVATION: 300ft
FORMATIONS: 81 (OTU), 9 Grp Fighter Command
MAIN CONTRACTOR: Various
RUNWAYS: 3 Tarmac
HANGARS: Bellman (3), Blister (8)
USER SQNS/UNITS:
61 OTU
15/04/42–16/06/45
Spitfire; Mustang III
Opened in Fighter Command as parent station, 04/42

RHOOSE, Glamorgan

LOCATION: 3m W of Barry
OPENED: 04/42
CLOSED: Cardiff International Airport (2011)
ELEVATION: 280ft
PUNDIT CODE: RH
FORMATION: 81 (OTU) Grp Fighter Command
MAIN CONTRACTOR: Various
RUNWAYS: 2 Tarmac
HANGARS: Blister (4)
USER SQNS/UNITS:
53 OTU
07/04/42–09/05/43
Spitfire I, II, V; Master III
Opened in Fighter Command as a satellite to Llandow, 04/42
To Flying Training Command, 02/44
To 57 Wing, Maintenance Command, 11/44

RICCALL, Yorks

LOCATION: 10m S of York
OPENED: 09/42
CLOSED: 1946. Agriculture (2011)
ELEVATION: 35ft
PUNDIT CODE: RC
FORMATIONS: 4, 7 (HCU) Grp Bomber Command
MAIN CONTRACTOR: Various
RUNWAYS: 3 concrete/asphalt
HANGARS: B1 (1); T2 (6)
USER SQNS/UNITS:
1658 HCU
07/10/42–13/04/45
Halifax II, III
Opened in Bomber Command as satellite to Marston Moor, 09/42
Became 41 Base substation, 09/43
Became 74 Base substation, 11/44
To Transport Command, 04/45

RIDGEWELL, Essex

LOCATION: 7½m NNW of Halstead
OPENED: 12/42
CLOSED: 03/57. Agriculture/gliding club (2011)
ELEVATION: 260ft
PUNDIT CODE: RD
FORMATION: 3 Grp Bomber Command
MAIN CONTRACTOR: Various
RUNWAYS: 3 concrete
HANGARS: T2 (2)
USER SQNS/UNITS:
90 Sqn
29/12/42–31/05/43
Stirling I, III
Opened in Bomber Command as satellite to Stradishall, 12/42
To USAAF as Station AAF-167, 05/43

RINGWAY, Cheshire

LOCATION: 3½m SE of Altrincham
OPENED: 06/38
CLOSED: Manchester International Airport (2011)
ELEVATION: 235ft
FORMATION: 9 Grp Fighter Command
MAIN CONTRACTOR: Various
RUNWAYS: 3 concrete/Tarmac
HANGARS: Bellman (4), A1 (1)

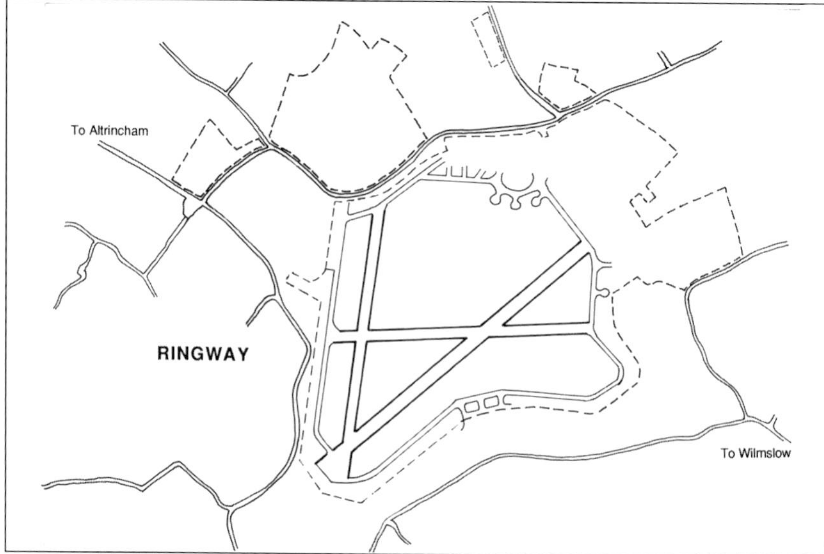

USER SQNS/UNITS:
Used for brief periods in 1940 by detachments from 64, 253 and 264 Sqns for air defence of Manchester

RIVENHALL, Essex

LOCATION: 1¾m N of Witham
OPENED: 12/44
CLOSED: 01/46. Agriculture/quarrying (2011)
ELEVATION: 168ft
PUNDIT CODE: RL
FORMATION: 38 Grp Fighter Command
MAIN CONTRACTORS: W. & C. French Ltd, Bovis Ltd
RUNWAYS: 3 concrete/Tarmac
HANGARS: Blister (1), T2 (2)
USER SQNS/UNITS:

295 Sqn
11/10/44–21/01/46
Albemarle I, II, V; Stirling IV

570 Sqn
08/10/44–28/12/45
Albemarle I, II, V; Stirling IV

Opened in USAAF as Station AAF-168, 12/43
To 38 Grp RAF Fighter Command, 10/44

ROBOROUGH, Devon

LOCATION: 4m NNE of Plymouth
OPENED: 07/31
CLOSED: Plymouth Airport (2011)
ELEVATION: 488ft
FORMATION: 10 Grp Fighter Command
MAIN CONTRACTOR: Various
RUNWAYS: 3 grass
HANGARS: Blister (1)
USER SQNS/UNITS:

247 Sqn
01/08/40–10/02/41
17/02–10/05/41
Gladiator II; Hurricane I

276 Sqn (det)
01/42–04/44
Hurricane I; Walrus; Lysander III; Spitfire IIa; Defiant I; Anson I; Sea Otter

691 Sqn
01/12/43–21/02/45
Martinet; Vengeance IV; Hurricane I, IIc; Oxford

Nominally under RN control but used by 10 Grp RAF Fighter Command for air defence of Devonport Dockyard 08/40–05/41

ROCHFORD (Southend), Essex

LOCATION: 2½m N of Southend
OPENED: 1914
CLOSED: Southend Airport (2011)
ELEVATION: 25ft
PUNDIT CODE: RO
FORMATION: 11 Grp Fighter Command
MAIN CONTRACTOR: Various
RUNWAYS: 2 grass
HANGARS: Bellman (2), Blister (4)
USER SQNS/UNITS:

19 Sqn
16–20/08/42
12–20/05/44
Spitfire Vb; Mustang III

54 Sqn
28/10–03/11/39
17/11–02/12/39
16–29/12/39
16/01–14/02/40
23/03–20/04/40
25/06–24/07/40
31/03–20/05/41
Spitfire I, IIa

64 Sqn
27/01–31/03/41
31/03–01/05/42
Spitfire I, IIa, Vb

74 Sqn
22–29/10/39
03–14/11/39
02–16/12/39
29/12/39–14/02/40
20/04–27/05/40
06–26/06/40
26/07–06/08/44
Spitfire I, LFIXe

127 Sqn
12–23/07/44
Spitfire IX

137 Sqn
12/06–08/08/43
Hurricane IV

222 Sqn
20–27/12/43
04–09/04/44
Spitfire LFIXb

234 Sqn
16/09–15/10/43
Spitfire Vb

264 Sqn
29/10–27/11/40
Defiant I

317 (Polish) Sqn
02–18/12/43
Spitfire IX

350 (Belgian) Sqn
23/09–07/12/42
12–31/10/43
Spitfire Vb, Vc

402 (Canadian) Sqn
19/08–06/11/41
Hurricane IIb

403 (Canadian) Sqn
02/05–03/06/42
Spitfire Vb

411 (Canadian) Sqn
07–30/03/42
Spitfire Vb

453 (Australian) Sqn
02/10–24/11/42
07/12/42–01/03/43
14–27/03/43
Spitfire Vb

603 (AAF) Sqn
03–13/12/40
16/06–09/07/41
Spitfire IIa, Va

611 (AAF) Sqn
13/12/40–27/01/41
20/05–14/06/41
06–13/09/43
Spitfire I, Va, LFVb

616 (AAF) Sqn
27/05–06/06/40
Spitfire I

To Fighter Command as forward satellite to Hornchurch, 10/39
Renamed Southend and upgraded to full satellite status, 10/40
Downgraded to forward satellite to Hornchurch, 09/44

ABOVE: During winter, air and ground crews often had to muck in together to clear aircraft, runways and taxiways of snow. This is the scene at Rufforth early in 1944 as personnel dig out No 1663 HCU's Halifax Mk III, OO-M, from a snow-bound dispersal. (IWM CH12431)

RUFFORTH, Yorks

LOCATION: 3½m W of York
OPENED: 11/42
CLOSED: 1974. Gliding club (2011)
ELEVATION: 64ft
PUNDIT CODE: RU
FORMATIONS: 4, 7 (HCU) Grp Bomber Command
MAIN CONTRACTOR: John Laing & Son Ltd
RUNWAYS: 3 Tarmac
HANGARS: B1 (1), T2 (2)
USER SQNS/UNITS:

158 Sqn
06/11/42–28/02/43
Halifax II

1663 HCU
01/03/43–28/05/45
Halifax II, III, V

Opened in Bomber Command as satellite to Marston Moor, 11/42
Became 41 Base substation, 09/43
Became 74 Base substation, 11/43

ST ANGELO, Co Fermanagh, NI

LOCATION: 3m N of Enniskillen
OPENED: 04/1941
CLOSED: 1947. Enniskillen Airport (2011)
ELEVATION: 155ft
FORMATION: 17 Grp Coastal Command
RUNWAYS: 2 concrete
HANGARS: T1 (3), Blister (8)
USER SQNS/UNITS:

153 Sqn (det)
03/42
Defiant I

235 Sqn
21/02–27/03/44
Beaufighter X

824 NAS
09–27/10/43
Swordfish

131 (C) OTU TT & Comms Flt
04/08/43–01/07/45
Catalina; Sunderland

12 (O) FIS > Coastal Command FIS
01/5/44 (23/02/45)–08/6/45
Wellington; Beaufort II; Mosquito III; Sunderland; Catalina; Buckmaster

Opened as 18 SLG Coastal Command in RAF Northern Ireland
To Coastal Command as satellite to Killadeas, 08/43

ST DAVIDS, Pembrokeshire

LOCATION: 12m NW of Haverfordwest
OPENED: 1943
CLOSED: 1945. Disused (2011)
ELEVATION: 250ft
FORMATION: 19 Grp Coastal Command
RUNWAYS: 3 concrete
HANGARS: T2 (3)
USER SQNS/UNITS:

53 Sqn
01/06–17/09/45
Liberator VI, VIII

58 Sqn
06/12/43–01/09/44
Halifax II

502 (AAF) Sqn
10/12/43–14/09/44
Halifax II

517 Sqn
25/11/43–01/02/44
Halifax V

ST EVAL, Cornwall

LOCATION: 6m NE of Newquay
OPENED: 10/1939
CLOSED: 1959. RAF communications base (2011)
ELEVATION: 340ft
FORMATION: 19 Grp Coastal Command
RUNWAYS: 3 concrete and Tarmac
HANGARS: C Type (3), T2 (2), Bellman (1), Blister (5)
USER SQNS/UNITS:

22 Sqn
08/40 (det)
28/10/41–01/02/42
Beaufort I

53 Sqn
11/40 (det)
20/03–03/07/41
20/10–17/12/41
16/05–03/07/42
Blenheim IV; Hudson V

58 Sqn
08/04–30/08/42
31/03–29/06/43
Whitley V, VII; Halifax II

86 Sqn
06/41 (det)
10/01–05/03/42
Beaufort I, II

179 Sqn
01/11/44–30/09/46
Warwick V; Lancaster ASR3

206 Sqn
03/40 (det)
30/05–12/08/41
12/04–11/07/44
Hudson I, II, III, IV; Liberator VI

217 Sqn
02/10/39–29/10/41
Beaufort I

224 Sqn
20/12/41–19/02/42
23/04/43–11/09/44
20/07/45–10/11/47
Hudson III; Liberator V, VI, VIII; Lancaster GR3

234 Sqn
18/06–14/08/40
11/09/40–24/02/41
Spitfire I

247 Sqn
08/40 (det)
10/02–10/05/41
Gladiator II; Hurricane I

263 Sqn
11/40 (det)
24/02–18/03/41
Whirlwind I

282 Sqn
19/09/44–09/07/45
Warwick I; Walrus; Sea Otter

304 (Polish) Sqn
06/03–09/07/45
Wellington XIV

502 (AAF) Sqn
01/41 (det)
01/42 (det)
22/02/42–02/03/43
25/03–30/06/43
Whitley V, VII; Halifax II

541 Sqn
12/42 (det)
Spitfire IX, XI

ABOVE: With the war almost at an end, this is the busy scene at the Coastal Command airfield of St Eval in Cornwall. A Vickers Wellington GR XIV of No 304 (Polish) Squadron runs up its engines against a backdrop of the familiar church tower and other squadron Wellingtons, 25 April 1945. (IWM MH2307)

547 Sqn
14/01–01/10/44
Liberator V, VI
10 OTU (det)
08/42–08/43
Whitley
1 PRU > A Flt 543 Sqn
19/10/42–19/10/43
Spitfire IV, XI
1st AS Sqn (Prov) USAAF
11/42–03/43
Liberator
4th AS Sqn USAAF
07–08/43
Liberator
19th AS Sqn USAAF
07–08/43
Liberator
409th BS USAAF
10–11/42
Liberator

ST MARY'S, Isles of Scilly

LOCATION: ¾m E of Hugh Town
OPENED: 1939
CLOSED: St Mary's Airport (2011)
ELEVATION: 100ft
PUNDIT CODE: Not known
FORMATION: 10 Grp Fighter Command
MAIN CONTRACTOR: Various
RUNWAYS: 3 grass
HANGARS: None
USER SQNS/UNITS:
87 Sqn (det)
19/05/41–04/42
Hurricane I, IIc
1449 Flt
04/42–17/09/44
Hurricane IIc

ST MAWGAN, Cornwall

LOCATION: 4m NE of Newquay
OPENED: 1933 (RAF 1939)
CLOSED: 2008. Newquay Airport (2011)
ELEVATION: 390ft
FORMATION: 19 Grp Coastal Command; Ferry Command
RUNWAYS: 3 concrete
HANGARS: T2 (2), B1 (2)
USER SQNS/UNITS:
264 Sqn (det)
05/42
Mosquito II
400 (Canadian) Sqn (det)
12/42–01/43
Mustang I
491st Base/Air Base Squadron, USAAF
06/43–08/45
B-17; B-24
RAF Ferry Command
07/43–08/45
Warwick
Originally RAF Trebelzue, satellite to St Eval

SALTBY, Leics

LOCATION: 8m NE of Melton Mowbray
OPENED: 08/41
CLOSED: 09/55. Gliding club (2011)
ELEVATION: 479ft
PUNDIT CODE: SY
FORMATIONS: 7 (T), 92 (OTU) Grp Bomber Command
MAIN CONTRACTOR: Various
RUNWAYS: 3 Tarmac
HANGARS: B1 (1), T2 (4)
USER SQNS/UNITS:
14 OTU
08/41–08/43
Hampden; Wellington
Opened in Bomber Command as satellite to Cottesmore, 08/41
To USAAF as Station AAF-538, 02/44

SANDTOFT, Lincs

LOCATION: 11¾m NE of Doncaster
OPENED: 02/44
CLOSED: 11/45. Commercial/light aviation/transport museum (2011)
ELEVATION: 8ft
PUNDIT CODE: SF
FORMATIONS: 1, 7 (HCU) Grp Bomber Command
MAIN CONTRACTOR: Various
RUNWAYS: 3 concrete/Tarmac
HANGARS: B1 (1), T2 (2)
USER SQNS/UNITS:
1667 HCU

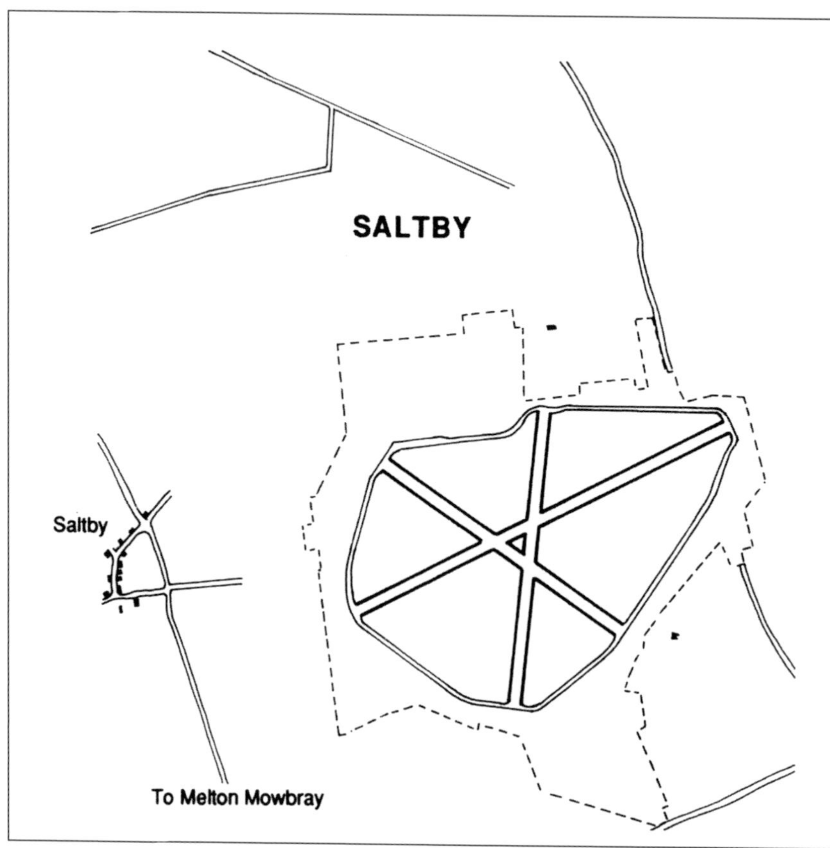

ABOVE: In a carefully choreographed press photograph, this is the crew of No 83 Squadron's Avro Manchester Mk IA, R5833, 'N', 'Ar hyd y nos' (which is Welsh for 'all through the night'), pictured at Scampton on 8 April 1942. From left to right the crew are: Sgt J. Bushby, Plt Off Billings, Sgt Dodsworth, Sgt Baines, Sgt Williams, and Warrant Officer Whitehead (pilot). 'Ar hyd y nos' failed to return from a mine-laying sortie on 6 June 1942, crashing near the Île de Quiberon. (Author)

20/02/44–10/11/45
Halifax II, V; Lancaster I, III
Opened in Bomber Command as 11 Base substation, 02/44
Became 71 Base substation, 11/44

SAWBRIDGEWORTH, Herts

LOCATION: 3m SW of Bishop's Stortford
OPENED: 1943
CLOSED: 1947 (2011)
ELEVATION: 320ft
FORMATIONS: 84 Grp 2 TAF
MAIN CONTRACTOR: Various
RUNWAYS: 3 steel matting
HANGARS: Blister (16), T2 (1)
USER SQNS/UNITS:

2 Sqn
30/11/43–22/01/44
29/02–11/03/44
24/03–04/04/44
Mustang I

4 Sqn
30/11/43–03/01/44
03/03–04/04/44
Spitfire PRVI;
Mosquito PRXVI

63 Sqn
12–30/11/43
Mustang Ia

80 Sqn
24/04–05/05/44
Spitfire IX

126 Sqn
30/04–22/05/44
Spitfire IXb

168 Sqn
12–30/11/43
Mustang Ia

170 Sqn
12/11/43–15/01/44 (disb)
Mustang Ia

182 Sqn
07/12/42–17/01/43
20–30/01/43
Typhoon Ia, Ib

239 Sqn (det)
22/10–18/11/42
Mustang I

268 Sqn
01–26/03/44
Mustang Ia

652 Sqn
20/02–28/03/43
Taylorcraft Plus C2; Auster I

SCAMPTON, Lincs

LOCATION: 5½m N of Lincoln
OPENED: 08/36
CLOSED: RAF base (2011)
ELEVATION: 195ft
PUNDIT CODE: SA
FORMATIONS: 1, 2, 5 Grp Bomber Command
MAIN CONTRACTOR: Various

RUNWAYS: 3 concrete/Tarmac
HANGARS: C2 Type (4), T1 (1)
USER SQNS/UNITS:
49 Sqn
14/03/38–02/01/43
Hampden; Manchester; Lancaster I, III
57 Sqn
04/09/42–28/08/43
Lancaster I, III
83 Sqn
14/03/38–15/08/42
Hampden; Manchester; Lancaster I, III
98 Sqn
02–19/03/40
Battle
153 Sqn
15/10/44–28/09/45
Lancaster I, III
467 (Australian) Sqn
07–22/11/42
Lancaster I
617 Sqn
21/03–30/08/43
Lancaster I, I (Special), III
625 Sqn
05/04–07/10/45
Lancaster I, III
1661 HCU
11–12/42
Halifax I, II
Opened in Bomber Command as parent station, 08/36
Became 52 Base HQ, 01/43
Became 15 Base HQ, 11/44
*Flt Lt R.A.B. Learoyd, 49 Sqn, awarded VC, Dortmund–Ems Canal, 12–13/08/40
*Sgt J. Hannah, 83 Sqn, awarded VC, Antwerp, 15–16/09/40
*Wg Cdr G.P. Gibson, DSO, DFC, 617 Sqn, awarded VC, Dams raid, 16–17/05/43

SCATSTA, Shetland

LOCATION: near Sullom Voe oil terminal
OPENED: 1940
CLOSED: 1946. Civil aviation (2011)
ELEVATION: 81ft
FORMATION: 18 Grp Coastal Command
RUNWAYS: 2
HANGARS: T2 (1)
USER SQNS/UNITS:
No flying units based
Satellite to Sullom Voe and Sumburgh

SCORTON, Yorks

LOCATION: 9m SSW of Darlington
OPENED: 10/39
CLOSED: 1945. Quarrying (2011)
ELEVATION: 200ft
PUNDIT CODE: SO
FORMATION: 13 Grp Fighter Command
MAIN CONTRACTOR: Various
RUNWAYS: 3 Tarmac
HANGARS: Blister (12)
USER SQNS/UNITS:
56 Sqn
15–23/02/44
07–30/03/44
07–28/04/44
Typhoon Ib
122 Sqn
06/10/41–01/04/42
Spitfire IIb, Vc
130 Sqn
10–16/11/43
04/01–13/02/44
Spitfire Vb, Vc
167 Sqn
06/04–01/06/42
Spitfire Vb
219 Sqn
04/10/39–12/10/40
21/10/42–25/04/43
Blenheim If; Beaufighter If
406 (Canadian) Sqn
16/06–04/09/42
Beaufighter IIf, VIf
410 (Canadian) Sqn
01/09–20/10/42
Beaufighter IIf
604 (AAF) Sqn
24/04/43–25/04/44
Beaufighter VIf; Mosquito XIII, XII
Opened in Fighter Command as satellite to Catterick, 10/39
To USAAF as Station AAF-425, 05/44

SCULTHORPE, Norfolk

LOCATION: 4m WNW of Fakenham
OPENED: 01/43
CLOSED: RAF base/Wicken Green new village/light industry (2011)
ELEVATION: 219ft
PUNDIT CODE: SP
FORMATIONS: 2, 100 (BS) Grp Bomber Command; 140 Wing 2 TAF
MAIN CONTRACTORS: Bovis Ltd; Constable, Hart & Co Ltd; John Laing & Son Ltd
RUNWAYS: 3 concrete
HANGARS: B1 (1), T2 (4)
USER SQNS/UNITS:
21 Sqn
27/09–31/12/43
Mosquito VI
214 Sqn
16/01–16/05/44
Fortress II
342 (French) Sqn
15/05–19/07/43
Boston III; Havoc
464 (Australian) Sqn
21/07–31/12/43
Ventura I, II; Mosquito IV
487 (New Zealand) Sqn
20/07–31/12/43
Ventura II; Mosquito IV
Opened in Bomber Command as satellite to West Raynham, 01/43
Achieved parent station status, 05/43
Closed for conversion to VHB station standard, 05/44

SEIGHFORD, Staffs

LOCATION:
OPENED: 01/43
CLOSED: 01/66. Agriculture/light industry/gliding club (2011)
ELEVATION: 308ft
PUNDIT CODE: YD
FORMATION: 93 (OTU) Grp Bomber Command
MAIN CONTRACTOR: Various
RUNWAYS: 3 concrete
HANGARS: B1 (1), T2 (2)
USER SQNS/UNITS:

ABOVE: This Stirling Mk IV of No 196 Squadron has been moved inside a T2 hangar for maintenance at Shepherds Grove in 1945. (via Alan Thomsett)

30 OTU
01/43–28/10/44
Wellington I, III
Opened in Bomber Command as satellite to Hixon, 01/43

SELSEY, Sussex

LOCATION: 5m S of Chichester
OPENED: 05/43
CLOSED: 05/45. Agriculture (2011)
ELEVATION: 20ft
PUNDIT CODE: ZS
FORMATIONS: 83, 84 Grp 2 TAF
MAIN CONTRACTOR: RAFACS
RUNWAYS: 2 steel matting
HANGARS: Blister (4)
USER SQNS/UNITS:

33 Sqn
06–10/08/44
18–19/08/44
Spitfire LFIXe

65 Sqn
31/05–01/07/43
Spitfire Vb

74 Sqn
17–26/07/44
Spitfire LFIXe

222 Sqn
09/04–30/06/44
06–19/08/44
Spitfire LFIXb

245 Sqn
02/06–01/07/43
Typhoon Ib

329 (French) Sqn
01/07–06/08/44
Spitfire IX

340 (French) Sqn
01/07–14/08/44
Spitfire IXb

341 (French) Sqn
01/07–06/08/44
Spitfire IXb

349 (Belgian) Sqn
11/04–30/06/44
06–19/08/44
Spitfire LFIXe

485 (New Zealand) Sqn
07/04–30/06/44
07–19/08/44
Spitfire IXb, IXe
2 TAF Advanced Landing Ground (ALG)

SHEPHERDS GROVE, Suffolk

LOCATION: 9m NE of Bury St Edmunds
OPENED: 04/44
CLOSED: 07/63. Industrial use (2011)
ELEVATION: 200ft
PUNDIT CODE: HP
FORMATION: 38 Grp Fighter Command
MAIN CONTRACTOR: Various
RUNWAYS: 3 concrete
HANGARS: T2 (2)
USER SQNS/UNITS:

196 Sqn
26/01/45–16/03/46
Stirling IV, V

299 Sqn
25/01/45–15/02/46
Stirling IV, V
Opened in Bomber Command as a satellite to Stradishall, 04/44
To 38 Grp Fighter Command with full station status, 01/45

SHERBURN-IN-ELMET, Yorks

LOCATION: 12½m E of Leeds
OPENED: 1917
CLOSED: 1945. Industry/light aviation (2011)
ELEVATION: 26ft
PUNDIT CODE: SH
FORMATION: 12 Grp Fighter Command
MAIN CONTRACTOR: Various
RUNWAYS: 1 concrete
HANGARS: Blister (5), Various (6)

USER SQNS/UNITS:

46 Sqn
01/03–20/05/41
Hurricane I

Brief use by Fighter Command, 09/39–05/41

SHOREHAM, Sussex

LOCATION: 1m N of Shoreham
OPENED: 02/11
CLOSED: Shoreham Airport (2011)
ELEVATION: 0ft
PUNDIT CODE: SQ
FORMATION: 11 Grp Fighter Command
MAIN CONTRACTOR: Various
RUNWAYS: 2 grass
HANGARS: Blister (4)
USER SQNS/UNITS:

253 Sqn
24–30/05/42
Hurricane I, IIa, IIb, IIc

345 (French) Sqn
26/04–16/08/44
Spitfire Vb

Fighter Interception Unit (FIU)
20/08/40–01/02/41
Beaufighter I; Blenheim I

422 Flt
14/10–18/12/40
Hurricane I

To Fighter Command as a satellite to Tangmere, 06/40

Satellite to Ford, 11/42

SILLOTH, Cumbria

LOCATION: ¾m E of Silloth
OPENED: 06/1939
CLOSED: 1960. Agriculture/industry (2011)
ELEVATION: 25ft
FORMATIONS: Maintenance Command; 17 (T) Grp Coastal Command
RUNWAYS: 3 concrete
HANGARS: C Type (3), D Type (4), E Type (6), L Type (4), A1 (1), Bellman (1), Robin (13), Super Robin (5)
USER SQNS/UNITS:

Coastal Command Group Pool > 1 OTU
11/39 (04/40)–03/43
Anson; Beaufort; Botha; Hudson

6 OTU
10/03/43–07/45
Wellington; Anson

SILVERSTONE, Northants

LOCATION: 4m S of Towcester
OPENED: 03/43
CLOSED: 11/46. Motor racing circuit (2011)
ELEVATION: 506ft
PUNDIT CODE: SV
FORMATION: 92 (OTU) Grp Bomber Command

ABOVE: Painted in the Fighter Command high altitude colour scheme of medium grey upper surfaces and PR blue undersides, this Spitfire Mk VII of No 312 (Czech) Squadron is seen on its dispersal at Skeabrae in the Orkneys. Note the double blast pen with crew rest shelter behind. (Alfred Price)

ABOVE: No 50 Squadron's Lancaster Mk I, R5689, 'V', was destroyed in a crash-landing at Skellingthorpe on 19 September 1942, returning from a mine-laying sortie. All but one of her crew survived the incident. (Author)

MAIN CONTRACTOR: J. Mowlem & Co Ltd
RUNWAYS: 3 concrete
HANGARS: B1 (1), T2 (4)
USER SQNS/UNITS:
17 OTU
10/04/43–11/46
Wellington I, III, X
Opened in Bomber Command as parent station, 03/43

SKEABRAE, Orkney

LOCATION: 12m NW of Kirkwall
OPENED: 08/40
CLOSED: 1945. Disused (2011)
ELEVATION: 60ft
PUNDIT CODE: KJ
FORMATIONS: 13, 14 Grp Fighter Command
MAIN CONTRACTOR: Various
RUNWAYS: 4 Tarmac
HANGARS: Callender-Hamilton (1), Teesside (12)
USER SQNS/UNITS:
3 Sqn
07/01–10/02/41
Hurricane I
66 Sqn
09/02–28/06/43
Spitfire Vb, Vc, VI
118 Sqn
10/03–12/07/44
Spitfire Vb, VII
129 Sqn
19/01–13/02/43
132 Sqn
16/02–11/06/42
Spitfire IIb, Vb
164 Sqn
05/05–10/09/42
Spitfire Va
234 Sqn
24/04–26/06/43
Spitfire Vb, VI
253 Sqn
10/02–21/09/41
Hurricane I, IIb
312 (Czech) Sqn
24/06–21/09/43
Spitfire Vb
313 (Czech) Sqn
11/07–04/10/44
Spitfire Vb, VII
329 (French) Sqn
03/04–25/05/45
Spitfire IX
331 (Norwegian) Sqn
21/09/41–04/05/42
Hurricane IIb; Spitfire IIa, Vb
441 (Canadian) Sqn
30/12/44–03/04/45
Spitfire IX, IXb
453 (Australian) Sqn
15/10/43–19/01/44
Spitfire Vb
602 (AAF) Sqn
10/09/42–20/01/43
17/01–12/03/44
Spitfire Va, VI, Vc, Vb, LFVb
611 (AAF) Sqn
03/10–31/12/44
Spitfire IX
Opened in Fighter Command as a satellite to Kirkwall, 08/40

SKELLINGTHORPE, Lincs

LOCATION: 3m W of Lincoln
OPENED: 10/41
CLOSED: 1952. Birchwood housing estate/A46 Lincoln bypass (2011)
ELEVATION: 60ft
PUNDIT CODE: SG
FORMATION: 5 Grp Bomber Command

MAIN CONTRACTOR: Various
RUNWAYS: 3 concrete/Tarmac
HANGARS: B1 (1), T2 (2)
USER SQNS/UNITS:
50 Sqn
26/11/41–20/06/42
17/10/42–15/06/45
Hampden; Manchester; Lancaster I, III
61 Sqn
16/11/43–12/01/44
15/04/44–16/06/45
Lancaster I, III
Opened in Bomber Command as satellite to Swinderby, 10/41
Became 53 Base substation, 11/42
*Flg Off L.T. Manser, 50 Sqn, awarded posthumous VC, Cologne, 30–31/05/42

SKIPTON-ON-SWALE, Yorks

LOCATION: 4m W of Thirsk
OPENED: 08/42
CLOSED: 10/45. Agriculture (2011)
ELEVATION: 90ft
PUNDIT CODE: SK
FORMATIONS: 4, 6 (RCAF) Grp Bomber Command
MAIN CONTRACTOR: Various
RUNWAYS: 3 Tarmac
HANGARS: B1 (1), T2 (2)
USER SQNS/UNITS:
420 (Canadian) Sqn
07/08–16/10/42
Hampden; Wellington III
424 (Canadian) Sqn
06/11/43–15/10/45
Halifax III; Lancaster I, III
432 (Canadian) Sqn
01/05–19/09/43
Wellington X
433 (Canadian) Sqn
25/09/43–15/10/45
Halifax III; Lancaster I, III
Opened in Bomber Command as satellite to Leeming, 08/42
Became 63 Base substation, 05/44

SKITTEN, Caithness

LOCATION: 4m NNW of Wick
OPENED: 12/40
CLOSED: 05/45. Agriculture/quarrying (2011)
ELEVATION: 65ft
PUNDIT CODE: NS
FORMATIONS: 14 Grp Fighter Command; 18 Grp Coastal Command
MAIN CONTRACTOR: Various
RUNWAYS: 3 Tarmac
HANGARS: Bellman (1), Blister Double EO (6), Standard (3)
USER SQNS/UNITS:
48 Sqn
20/10/41–06/01/42
Hudson III, V
86 Sqn
05/03–13/07/42
Beaufort II
172 Sqn (det)
08–09/43
Wellington XII, XIV
179 Sqn
01/09–18/11/42
Wellington VIII
217 Sqn (det)
11/41–03/42
Beaufort II
232 Sqn
13–24/10/40
11/11–04/12/40
Hurricane I
260 Sqn
05/12/40–07/01/41
10/02–16/04/41
Hurricane I
519 Sqn
10/12/43–28/11/44
Spitfire VI; Hudson III, IIIa; Ventura V; Fortress II
607 (AAF) Sqn
16/04–27/07/41
Hurricane I, IIa, IIb
618 Sqn
26/03/43–09/07/44
Mosquito IV, XVIII; Beaufighter II
Opened in Fighter Command as satellite to Castletown, 12/40
To 18 Grp Coastal Command, 07/41

SNAILWELL, Suffolk

LOCATION: 2m N of Newmarket
OPENED: 03/41
CLOSED: 1946. Agriculture (2011)
ELEVATION: 70ft
PUNDIT CODE: SW
FORMATION: 12 Grp Fighter Command
MAIN CONTRACTOR: Various
RUNWAYS: 3 grass
HANGARS: Bellman (1), Blister (10)
USER SQNS/UNITS:
56 Sqn
30/03–29/05/42
01/06–24/08/42
Hurricane IIb; Typhoon Ia, Ib
137 Sqn
24/08–17/09/42
Whirlwind I
152 Sqn
25–31/08/41
Spitfire IIa
181 Sqn
10/12/42–01/03/43
08–24/03/43
Hurricane I; Typhoon Ia, Ib
183 Sqn
08–12/03/43
Typhoon Ib
184 Sqn
15–17/09/43
Hurricane IV
Opened in Army Co-operation Command, but as a satellite to Duxford, 03/41
Upgraded to parent station, 07/41
To 12 Grp Fighter Command, 06/43
To 28 Grp Technical Training Command, 10/44
To USAAF as Station AAF-361

SNAITH, Yorks

LOCATION: 7m W of Goole
OPENED: 07/41
CLOSED: 04/46. Agriculture (2011)
ELEVATION: 33ft
PUNDIT CODE: SX
FORMATIONS: 1, 4 Grp Bomber Command
MAIN CONTRACTOR: Various
RUNWAYS: 3 Tarmac
HANGARS: J Type (1), T2 (2)

ABOVE: With the tension of the night's op now behind them, this smiling No 51 Squadron Halifax crew hand in their parachutes at Snaith on their return from a raid on the Ruhr in June 1943. (IWM CH10293)

USER SQNS/UNITS:
51 Sqn
27/10/42–20/04/45
Whitley V; Halifax II, III
150 Sqn
10/07/41–10/42
Wellington I, III
578 Sqn
14/01–06/02/44
Halifax III
Opened in Bomber Command as parent station, 07/41
Became 42 Base substation, 1943

SPEKE, Lancs

LOCATION: 5m SE of Liverpool
OPENED: 07/30
CLOSED: Liverpool John Lennon Airport (2011)
ELEVATION: 65ft
PUNDIT CODE: PZ
FORMATION: 9 Grp Fighter Command
MAIN CONTRACTOR: Various
RUNWAYS: 3 Tarmac
HANGARS: Bellman (2), Blister (4)
USER SQNS/UNITS:
229 Sqn
22/12/40–20/05/41
Hurricane I
303 (Polish) Sqn
15/07–07/10/41
Spitfire I, IIb; Hurricane I
306 (Polish) Sqn
07/10–12/12/41
Spitfire IIa
308 (Polish) Sqn
12–25/09/40
No aircraft
312 (Czech) Sqn
26/09/40–03/03/41
Hurricane I
315 (Polish) Sqn
13/03–14/07/41
Hurricane I
Fighter Command Sector Station, 09/40
To Directorate General of Civil Aviation, 07/44

SPILSBY, Lincs

LOCATION: 3m E of Spilsby
OPENED: 09/43
CLOSED: 03/58. Agriculture (2011)
ELEVATION: 27ft
PUNDIT CODE: SL
FORMATION: 5 Grp Bomber Command
MAIN CONTRACTOR: Various
RUNWAYS: 3 concrete

ABOVE: Armourers work on Hurricane Mk I, L1916, of No 312 (Czech) Squadron, at Speke in October 1940. This squadron was one of two Czech fighter squadrons that were operational during the Battle of Britain. (Author)

HANGARS: B1 (1), T2 (2)
USER SQNS/UNITS:
44 Sqn
30/09/44–21/07/45
Lancaster I, III
207 Sqn
12/10/43–21/07/45
Lancaster I, III
Opened in Bomber Command as 55 Base substation, 09/43

SQUIRES GATE, Lancashire

LOCATION: 1m SSE of Blackpool
OPENED: 1909
CLOSED: Blackpool Airport/industry/retail (2011)
ELEVATION: 33ft
FORMATION: 17 (T) Grp Coastal Command
RUNWAYS: 3 sand/bitumen
HANGARS: Bellman (4), Boulton Paul (2)
USER SQNS/UNITS:
63 Sqn
09/39–01/40
Battle; Anson I
75 Sqn (A Flt det)
10/39
Wellington
96 Sqn (det)
03–09/41
Hurricane I; Defiant I
215 Sqn
09/39–04/40
Wellington I; Anson I
3 School of General Reconnaissance
05–12/40
Anson; Botha

STANTON HARCOURT, Oxon

LOCATION: 5½m W of Oxford
OPENED: 03/09/40
CLOSED: 15/01/46. Gravel extraction/light industry (2011)
ELEVATION: 230ft
PUNDIT CODE: ST
FORMATIONS: 6 (T), 91 (OTU) Grp Bomber Command
MAIN CONTRACTOR: George Wimpey & Co Ltd
RUNWAYS: 3 Tarmac
HANGARS: B1 (1), T2 (1)
USER SQNS/UNITS:
10 OTU
03/09/40–01/45
Whitley V; Wellington X
Opened in Bomber Command as satellite to Abingdon, 03/09/40

STAPLEFORD TAWNEY, Essex

LOCATION: 5m N of Romford
OPENED: 06/34
CLOSED: 05/45. Stapleford Flight Centre (2011)
ELEVATION: 103ft
PUNDIT CODE: KZ

FORMATIONS: 11, 12 Grp Fighter Command
MAIN CONTRACTOR: Various
RUNWAYS: 2 grass
HANGARS: Blister (4)
USER SQNS/UNITS:

3 Sqn
23/06–09/08/41
Hurricane IIb, IIc

46 Sqn
01/09–08/11/40
Hurricane I

151 Sqn
29/08–01/09/40
Hurricane I

242 Sqn
09/04–22/05/41
Hurricane IIb

To 11 Grp Fighter Command as a satellite to North Weald, 01/40
To 34 Wing Army Co-operation Command, 03/43
To 12 Grp Fighter Command, 06/43

STAPLEHURST, Kent

LOCATION: 8m SSE of Maidstone
OPENED: 08/43
CLOSED: 01/45. Agriculture (2011)
ELEVATION: 100ft
PUNDIT CODE: XS
FORMATIONS: 83 Grp 2 TAF; 11 Grp Fighter Command
MAIN CONTRACTOR: Various
RUNWAYS: 2 steel matting
HANGARS: none
USER SQNS/UNITS:

401 (Canadian) Sqn
07/08–13/10/43
Spitfire Vb

411 (Canadian) Sqn
07/08–13/10/43
Spitfire Vb

412 (Canadian) Sqn
08/08–14/10/43
Spitfire Vb

2 TAF Advanced Landing Ground (ALG)
To USAAF as Station AAF-413, 04/44
To 11 Grp ADGB, 07/44

STEEPLE MORDEN, Cambs

LOCATION: 3½m W of Royston
OPENED: 09/40
CLOSED: 01/09/46. Agriculture (2011)
ELEVATION: 160ft
PUNDIT CODE: KR
FORMATIONS: 7 (T), 92 (OTU) Grp Bomber Comand
MAIN CONTRACTOR: Various
RUNWAYS: 3 concrete
HANGARS: T2 (1)
USER SQNS/UNITS:

11 OTU
09/40–09/42
Wellington I

17 OTU
13/01–04/05/43
Blenheim I, IV

Opened in Bomber Command as satellite to Bassingbourn, 09/40
To USAAF as Station AAF-122, 07/43

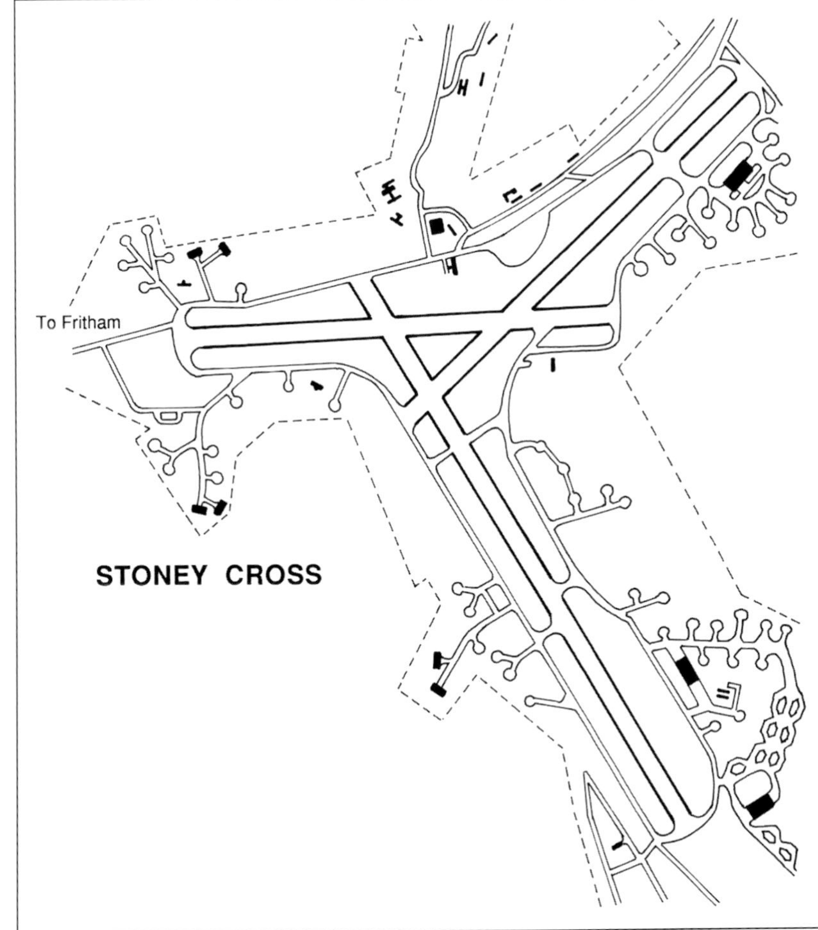

STONEY CROSS, Hants

LOCATION: 11m W of Southampton
OPENED: 11/43
CLOSED: 01/48. Forestry Commission (2011)
ELEVATION: 373ft
PUNDIT CODE: SS
FORMATION: 10 Grp Fighter Command
MAIN CONTRACTOR: George Wimpey & Co Ltd
RUNWAYS: 3 concrete
HANGARS: Blister (6), T2 (4)
USER SQNS/UNITS:

175 Sqn
19/03–08/04/43
Hurricane IIb

297 Sqn
25/08/43–14/03/44
Albemarle I, II

299 Sqn
04/11/43–15/03/44
Ventura I, II; Stirling IV

Opened in 38 Wing, Army Co-operation Command, 11/42

ABOVE: Wellington Mk IC, T2470, 'K', of No 214 Squadron is towed into a C-Type hangar at Stradishall during October 1940 for repairs after suffering damage on operations. She was destroyed in a crash the following month. (IWM CH1415)

To 10 Grp Fighter Command, 06/43
To USAAF as Station AAF-452, 03/44
To RAF Transport Command, 11/44

STORNOWAY, Hebrides

LOCATION: 2½m NE of Stornoway
OPENED: 1941
CLOSED: Stornoway Airport (2011)
FORMATION: 18 Grp Coastal Command
ELEVATION: 26ft
RUNWAYS: 4 Tarmac
HANGARS: T2 (10)
USER SQNS/UNITS:

48 Sqn
16/07/40–03/08/41 (det)
03/08–20/10/41
Hudson V, III

58 Sqn
30/08–02/12/42
01/09/44–25/05/45
Whitley V, VII; Halifax II, III

224 Sqn
19/02–16/04/42 (det)
Hudson V

500 Sqn
22/03–30/08/42
Hudson V

502 Sqn
14/09/44–25/05/45
Halifax II, III

518 Sqn
06/07–25/09/43
Halifax V

612 Sqn (det)
06/39–04/41
Hector; Anson I; Whitley V

STRADISHALL, Suffolk

LOCATION: 5m NE of Haverhill
OPENED: 03/02/38
CLOSED: 27/08/70. HMP Highpoint and HMP Edmunds Hill/MOD training site (2011)
ELEVATION: 382ft
Pundit: NX
FORMATIONS: 1, 2, 3, 7 (T) Grp Bomber Command
MAIN CONTRACTOR: Various
RUNWAYS: 3 concrete
HANGARS: C Type (5), T2 (3)
USER SQNS/UNITS:

75 (New Zealand) Sqn
13/07–14/09/39
Wellington I

101 Sqn
11/08–29/09/42
Wellington III

109 Sqn
06/04–06/08/42
Wellington I, IV, VI; Mosquito IV

138 Sqn
16/12/41–11/03/42
Lysander IIIa; Whitley V; Halifax II

148 Sqn
30/04–20/05/40
Wellington I

150 Sqn
18/06–03/07/40
Battle

186 Sqn
17/12/44–17/07/45
Lancaster I, II, III

214 Sqn
14/02/40–01/10/42
Wellington I, II; Stirling I
215 Sqn
05/01–12/02/42
Wellington I
1657 HCU
10/42–15/12/44
Stirling I
Opened in Bomber Command as parent station, 02/38
Became 31 Base HQ, 05/43

STRANRAER (Wig Bay), Wigtownshire

LOCATION: 5m N of Stranraer
OPENED: 1940
CLOSED: 1957. Sailing club (2011)
FORMATIONS: 15, 17 (T) Grp Coastal Command
ELEVATION: 0ft
RUNWAYS: Alighting area between Marian Port and St Mary's Croft.
HANGARS: B Type (2), T2 (1)
USER SQNS/UNITS:
209 Sqn
03/01–23/03/41
Lerwick I
228 Sqn
09/10/41–10/03/42
Sunderland I, II
240 Sqn
30/07/40–28/03/41
Stranraer
Flying Boat Training Sqn (FBTS)> 4 (C) OTU
01/06/40 (16/03/41)–06/41
03/42 (det)
Singapore; London; Stranraer; Lerwick; Catalina
302 FTU
01/12/42–21/07/43
Catalina

STRATFORD, Warks

LOCATION: 2¾m SSE of Stratford-on-Avon
OPENED: 12/07/41
CLOSED: 11/45. Agriculture (2011)
ELEVATION: 185ft
PUNDIT CODE: NF
FORMATIONS: 6 (T), 91 (OTU) Grp Bomber Command
MAIN CONTRACTOR: Various
RUNWAYS: 3 Tarmac
HANGARS: B1 (1), T2 (1)
USER SQNS/UNITS:
22 OTU
14/09/41–15/11/42
07/03–15/12/44
Wellington I, III, X
23 OTU
11/42–03/44
Wellington III, X
Opened in Bomber Command as satellite to Wellesbourne Mountford, 12/07/41
Became satellite to Pershore, 11/42
Reverted to satellite to Wellesbourne Mountford, 03/44

STRUBBY, Lincs

LOCATION: 3½m N of Alford
OPENED: 04/44
CLOSED: 09/72. Agriculture/light industry (2011)
ELEVATION: 35ft
PUNDIT CODE: NY
FORMATIONS: 5 Grp Bomber Command; 16 Grp Coastal Command
MAIN CONTRACTOR: William Moss & Sons
RUNWAYS: 3 concrete/Tarmac
HANGARS: B1 (1), T2 (2)

BELOW: Saro Lerwick I, L7265, 'Q', of No 209 Squadron at Stranraer, photographed up 'on the step'. This aircraft joined the squadron early in 1940 and was struck off charge at the end of the year with less than 200 flying hours on log. (Andy Thomas)

ABOVE: In what is probably the most famous Beaufighter action photograph of the war, 44 Beaufighter TF Mk Xs from four RAF squadrons (including No 144 Squadron from Strubby) attacked a German convoy off Schiermonnikoog in the Dutch Friesian Islands on 25 August 1944. In this photograph at least 14 aircraft can be seen attacking the convoy. (Crown Copyright)

USER SQNS/UNITS:

144 Sqn
01/07–03/09/44
Beaufighter X

227 Sqn
05/04–08/06/45
Lancaster I, III

280 Sqn
05–09/44
Warwick I

404 (Canadian) Sqn
01/07–03/09/44
Beaufighter X

619 Sqn
28/09/44–30/06/45
Lancaster I, III

Transferred from Coastal to Bomber Command as 55 Base substation, 07/44

STURGATE, Lincs

LOCATION: 4m ESE of Gainsborough
OPENED: 09/44
CLOSED: 1964. Light aviation (2011)
ELEVATION: 55ft
PUNDIT CODE: US
FORMATION: 5 Grp Bomber Command
MAIN CONTRACTOR: Various
RUNWAYS: 3 concrete/asphalt
HANGARS: B1 (1), T2 (2)
USER SQNS/UNITS:

50 Sqn
16/06/45–26/01/46
Lancaster I, III

61 Sqn
16/06/45–25/01/46
Lancaster I, III

Opened in Bomber Command as 71 Base substation, 09/44

SULLOM VOE, Shetland

LOCATION: 25m N of Lerwick
OPENED: 1939
CLOSED: 1946. Oil terminal (2011)
ELEVATION: 0ft
FORMATION: 18 Grp Coastal Command

RUNWAYS: none. Alighting area
HANGARS: none. Maintenance at Scatsta
USER SQNS/UNITS:

190 Sqn
17/02/43–01/01/44
Catalina Ib, IV

201 Sqn
09/08–06/11/39
26/05–09/10/41
London II; Sunderland I, II

204 Sqn
02/04/40–05/04/41
Sunderland I

210 Sqn
28/02–04/10/42
01/01/44–04/06/45
Catalina I, II, IV

240 Sqn
04/11/39–12/02/40
27/03–27/05/40
London II

330 (Norwegian) Sqn
12/07/43–14/06/45
Sunderland II, III, V

333 (Norwegian) Sqn (det)
01/05/43–01/09/44
Catalina Ib, IV; Mosquito II, VI

413 Sqn
01/10/41–02/04/42
Catalina I, IV

*The RAF's most northerly wartime base in the British Isles
*Flt Lt J.H. Cruikshank, 210 Sqn, awarded VC, U-boat patrol, 17/07/44

SUMBURGH, Shetlands

LOCATION: 1¼m NNW of Sumburgh Head
OPENED: 1933
CLOSED: Sumburgh Airport (2011)
ELEVATION: 2ft
PUNDIT CODE: UM
FORMATIONS: 13, 14 Grp Fighter Command; 18 Grp Coastal Command
MAIN CONTRACTOR: Various
RUNWAYS: 3 Tarmac
HANGARS: Bellman (3)
USER SQNS/UNITS:

48 Sqn
06/01–30/11/42
Hudson III, V

ABOVE: This is the crew of Consolidated Catalina Mk IV, 'X', of No 210 Squadron, who made the last attack of the war on a German submarine, standing by their aircraft at Sullom Voe, Shetland. In the early hours of 7 May 1945 they depth-charged the Type VIIC/41 submarine, U-320, west of Bergen, Norway. The U-boat was badly damaged and, despite an attempt at repairs by its crew, it sank off the Norwegian coast on 9 May. The Catalina's crew are, front row, left to right: Flg Off C. Humphrey (navigator), Flg Off F. Weston (3rd pilot), Flt Lt K. Murray (captain), Flt Lt W.C. Robertson (2nd pilot), Flt Sgt D. Fowler (1st wireless operator/air gunner). Back row, left to right: Flt Sgt G. Swift (air gunner), Flt Sgt P.G.A. Alway (flight mechanic), Flt Sgt L.W. Rose (wireless operator/mechanic) and Flt Sgt I.W. Evans (2nd wireless operator/air gunner). (IWM C5355)

118 Sqn (det)
03–07/44
Spitfire Vb, VII
125 Sqn (det)
09/42–04/43
Beaufighter VIf
143 Sqn
27/09–05/12/41
Beaufighter Ic
144 Sqn
04/42–04/43
Hampden; Beaufighter VIc
232 Sqn
17/07–18/09/40
Hurricane I
248 Sqn
14/07/40–06/01/41
30/05–09/42
Blenheim IVf; Beaufighter Ic, VIc
254 Sqn
16/05–02/08/40
07/01–29/05/41
Blenheim IVf
404 (Canadian) Sqn
09/10/41–26/03/42
05/08–24/09/42
Blenheim IVf
455 (Australian) Sqn (det)
04/42–04/44
Hampden; Beaufighter X
598 Sqn (det)
12/43–04/45
Oxford; Martinet; Hurricane IIc, IV
608 Sqn
29/07–27/08/42
Hudson III, IIIa, V
Sumburgh Fighter Flt
16/05–01/08/40
Gladiator II
To 13 Grp Fighter Command, 05/40
To 14 Grp, 07/40
To Coastal Command, 06/41

SUTTON BRIDGE, Lincs

LOCATION: 7m NNE of Wisbech
OPENED: 1926
CLOSED: 1958. Agriculture/power station (2011)
ELEVATION: 9ft
PUNDIT CODE: SB
FORMATIONS: 11, 81 (OTU) Grp Fighter Command
MAIN CONTRACTOR: Various
RUNWAYS: 1 grass, 2 steel matting
HANGARS: ARS (1), Bellman (2), Blister (12)
USER SQNS/UNITS:
6 OTU > 56 OTU
09/03–(01/11/40)–27/03/42
Hurricane I
254 Sqn
09/12/39–28/01/40
Blenheim If
264 Sqn
30/10–07/12/39
No aircraft
266 Sqn
30/10/39–01/03/40
Battle; Spitfire I
Central Gunnery School
1942–1945
Opened as temporary armament practice camp, 1926
To Flying Training Command, 1936
To 11 Grp Fighter Command, 09/39
To Flying Training Command, 04/42

SWANNINGTON, Norfolk

LOCATION: 3m SE of Reepham
OPENED: 01/04/44
CLOSED: 11/47. Agriculture/light industry (2011)
ELEVATION: 135ft
PUNDIT CODE: NG
FORMATION: 100 (BS) Grp Bomber Command
MAIN CONTRACTOR: Kent & Sussex Construction Co
RUNWAYS: 3 concrete
HANGARS: B1 (1), T2 (2)
USER SQNS/UNITS:
85 Sqn
01/05–21/04/44
29/08/44–27/06/45
Mosquito XII, XVII, XXX
157 Sqn
07/05–21/07/44
29/08/44–16/08/45
Mosquito XIX, XXX
Opened in Bomber Command as parent station, 04/44

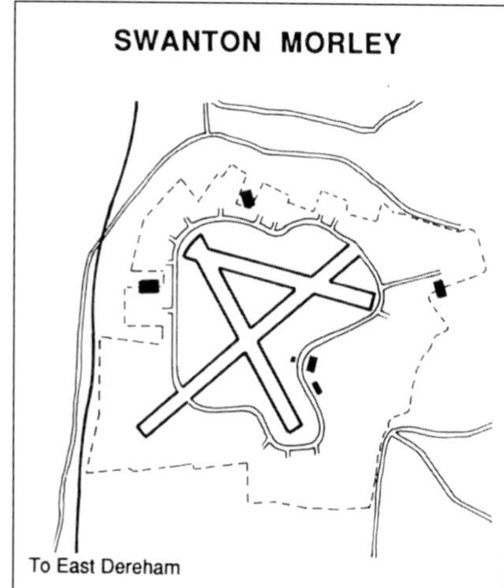

SWANTON MORLEY, Norfolk

LOCATION: 3½m N of East Dereham
OPENED: 09/40
CLOSED: 1995. Army base (2011)
ELEVATION: 150ft
PUNDIT CODE: SM
FORMATIONS: 1, 2, 100 (BS) Grp Bomber Command
MAIN CONTRACTOR: Richard Costain Ltd
RUNWAYS: 3 grass
HANGARS: Blister (4), J Type (1), T2 (4)
USER SQNS/UNITS:
88 Sqn
08/07–01/08/41
30/03–19/08/43
Blenheim I, V; Boston IIIa
98 Sqn
18/08/43–18/10/44
Mitchell II
105 Sqn
31/10/40–09/12/41
Blenheim IV; Mosquito IV
226 Sqn
09/12/41–13/02/44
Boston II, IIIa; Mitchell II
305 (Polish) Sqn
04/09–18/11/43
Mitchell II
2 Group Support Unit (GSU)
04–12/44
Mosquito III; Hurricane
BSDU
11/44–05/45
Lancaster I, III; Mosquito IX, XVI, XX; Beaufighter I; Spitfire V; Proctor; Anson

ABOVE: A snow-clearing machine helps to clear the main runway at Swinderby, Lincolnshire, after the heavy snowfalls of 5 March 1944. (IWM CH20521)

Opened in Bomber Command as parent station, 09/40

*Wg Cdr H.I. Edwards, DFC, 105 Sqn, awarded VC, Bremen, 04/07/41

SWINDERBY, Lincs

LOCATION: 9m SW of Lincoln

OPENED: 08/40

CLOSED: 1995. Agriculture/light industry/gravel extraction (2011)

ELEVATION: 69ft

PUNDIT CODE: NR

FORMATIONS: 1, 5, 7 (T) Grp Bomber Command

MAIN CONTRACTOR: John Laing & Son Ltd

RUNWAYS: 3 concrete

HANGARS: J Type (3), T2 (3)

USER SQNS/UNITS:

50 Sqn

20/07–26/11/41

20/06–16/10/42

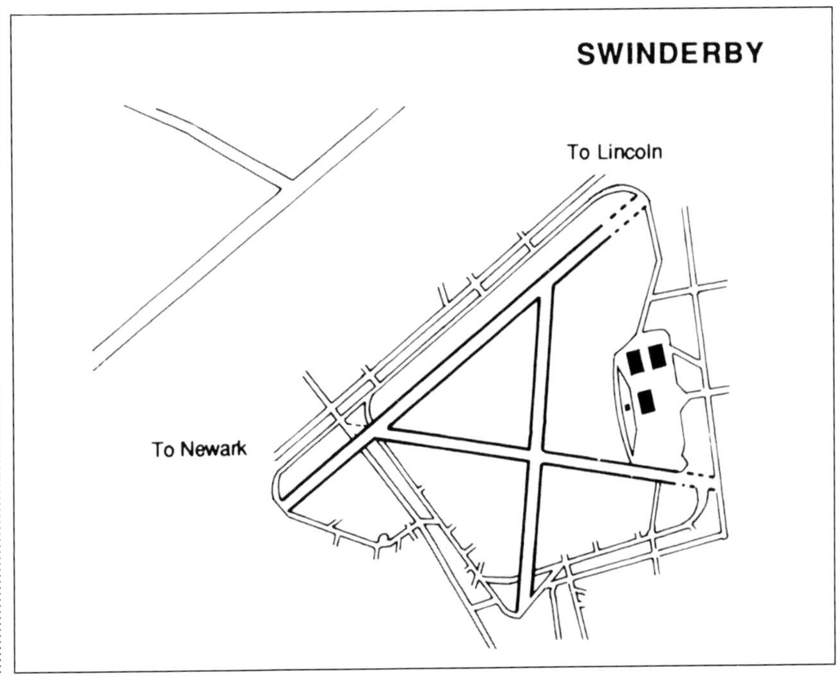

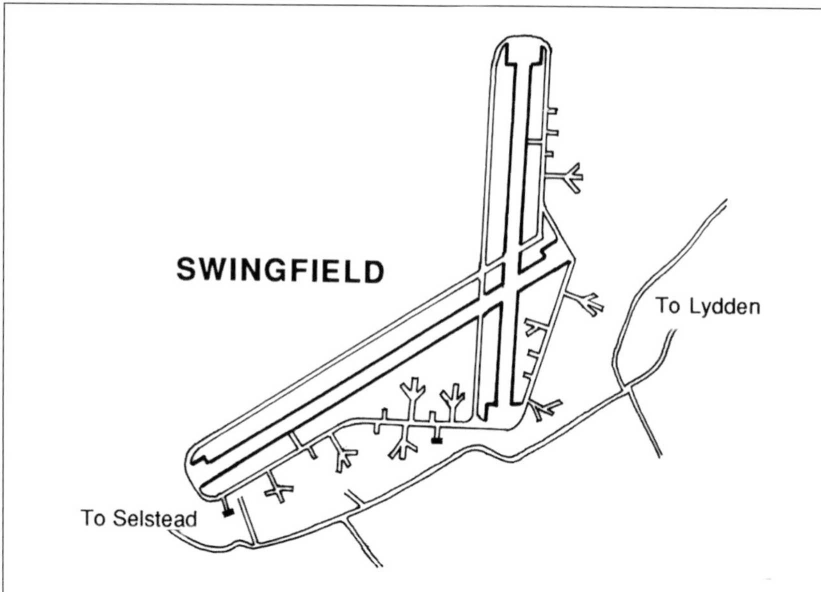

Hampden; Lancaster I, III

300 (Polish) Sqn
22/08/40–11/07/41
Battle; Wellington I

301 (Polish) Sqn
29/08/40–18/07/41
Battle; Wellington I

455 (Australian) Sqn
06/06/41–08/02/42
Hampden

1654 HCU
05–15/06/43
Stirling I, III

1660 HCU
10/42–11/46
Manchester; Halifax; Stirling I, III; Lancaster I, III

Opened in Bomber Command as satellite to Winthorpe, 08/40

Became 51 Base HQ, 03/43

Became 75 Base HQ, 11/44

SWINGFIELD, Kent

LOCATION: 5m NW of Dover
OPENED: 08/44
CLOSED: 04/45. Agriculture (2011)
ELEVATION: 460ft
PUNDIT CODE: IF
FORMATION: 11 Grp Fighter Command
MAIN CONTRACTOR: Royal Engineers Airfield Construction Group
RUNWAYS: 2 steel matting
HANGARS: Blister (4)
USER SQNS/UNITS:

Unused Advanced Landing Ground (ALG) in 11 Grp ADGB/Fighter Command. No RAF fighter units based

---

SYERSTON, Notts

LOCATION: 5½m SW of Newark-on-Trent
OPENED: 01/12/40
CLOSED: 1970. Gliding club (2011)
ELEVATION: 224ft
PUNDIT CODE: YN
FORMATIONS: 1, 5 Grp Bomber Command
MAIN CONTRACTOR: John Laing & Son Ltd
RUNWAYS: 3 concrete
HANGARS: B1 (1), J Type (2), T2 (6)
USER SQNS/UNITS:

49 Sqn
22/04–28/09/45
Lancaster I, III

61 Sqn
05/05/42–16/11/43
Manchester; Lancaster I, II, III

106 Sqn
01/10/42–11/11/43
Lancaster I, III

304 (Polish) Sqn
02/12/40–19/07/41
Wellington I

305 (Polish) Sqn
02/12/40–20/07/41
Wellington I

408 (Canadian) Sqn
20/07–08/12/41
Manchester; Lancaster I

Opened in Bomber Command as parent station, 01/12/40

Became 56 Base HQ, 10/44

*Flt Lt W. Reid, 61 Sqn, awarded VC, Düsseldorf, 03–04/11/43

TAIN, Ross-shire

LOCATION: 3½m E of Tain
OPENED: 09/41
CLOSED: 11/46. Agriculture (2011)
ELEVATION: 0ft
PUNDIT CODE: TN
FORMATIONS: 14 Grp Fighter Command; 18 Grp Coastal Command
MAIN CONTRACTOR: Various
RUNWAYS: 3 concrete
HANGARS: Bellman (3), Blister (8), T2 (2)
USER SQNS/UNITS:

17 Sqn
17/09–31/10/41
Hurricane IIa, I, IIb

76 Sqn (det)
03–04/42
Halifax I, II

86 Sqn
01/07/44–09/08/45
Liberator V, VIII

123 Sqn (det)
10/41–03/42
Spitfire IIa

186 Sqn
07/01–01/03/44
Typhoon Ib; Spitfire Vb

311 (Czech) Sqn
07/08/44–06/08/45
Liberator V, VI

801 NAS
03–04/42
Sea Hurricane

Coastal Command Development Unit
06/42–04/43

No 1 Torpedo Refresher School > Torpedo Training Unit

ABOVE: This No 144 Squadron Beaufighter Mk VI, photographed at Tain on 25 April 1943, is fitted with an 18in Mk XV torpedo using a purpose-built telescopic cradle. The torpedo is fitted with a Mk IV gyro-stabilised MAT (Monoplane Air Tail). (IWM CH9769)

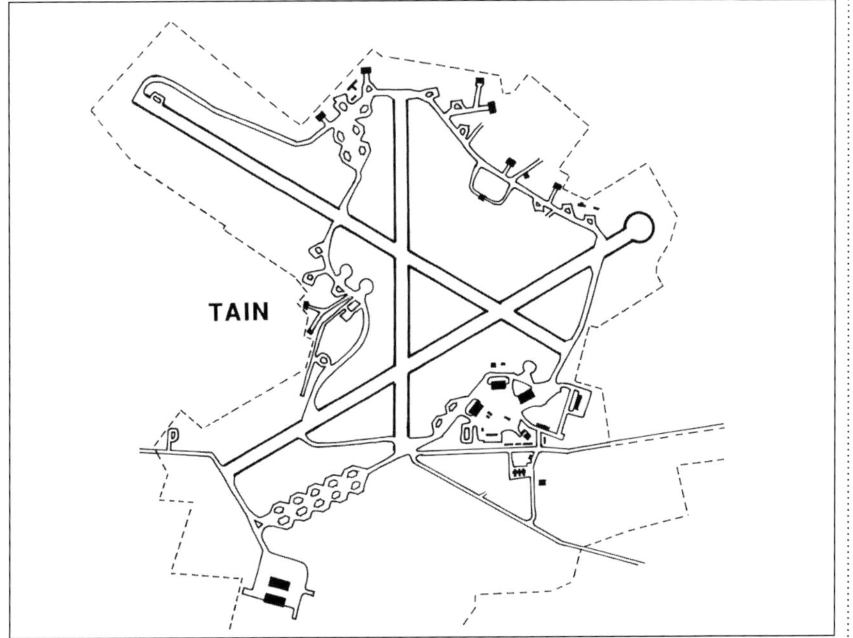

01/43–11/46

Opened in Fighter Command as Sector Station, 09/41

To 18 Grp Coastal Command, 02/43

TANGMERE, Sussex

LOCATION: 2½m E of Chichester

OPENED: 1918

CLOSED: 1970. Agriculture/Tangmere Military Aviation Museum (2011)

ELEVATION: 50ft

PUNDIT CODE: RN

FORMATIONS: 11 Grp Fighter Command; 84 Grp 2 TAF

MAIN CONTRACTOR: Various

RUNWAYS: 2 concrete

HANGARS: Bessonneau (2), Blister (16), T2 (1)

ABOVE: A Hurricane Mk I of No 601 Squadron at Tangmere is re-armed and refuelled in July 1940. (RAF Museum)

USER SQNS/UNITS:

1 Sqn
01/02/27–09/09/39
23/07–01/08/40
01/07/41–08/07/42
Siskin; Fury; Hurricane 1

17 Sqn
19/08–02/09/40
Hurricane I

33 Sqn
03–17/07/44
20–31/08/44
Spitfire LFIXe

41 Sqn
17–20/08/42
05–11/10/42
04/10/43–06/02/44
20/02–11/03/44
Spitfire Vb, XII

43 Sqn
12/12/26–18/11/39
31/05–08/09/40
16/06–01/09/42
Gamecock I; Siskin IIIa; Fury I;
Hurricane I, IIa, IIb, IIc

65 Sqn
29/11/40–26/02/41
Spitfire I

66 Sqn
03–07/07/42
16–20/08/42
22/06–06/08/44
Spitfire Vb, Vc, LFIXb

74 Sqn
03–17/07/44
06–20/08/44
Spitfire LFIXe

91 Sqn
04/10/43–08/02/44
20–29/02/44
Spitfire XII

118 Sqn
03–07/07/42
16–24/08/42
Spitfire Vb

124 Sqn
25/09–29/10/42
Spitfire VI

127 Sqn
04–12/07/44
23/07–06/08/44
Spitfire LFIXe

129 Sqn
28/02–13/03/43
Spitfire Vb

130 Sqn
03–11/08/44
Spitfire XIV
131 Sqn
22–24/08/42
31/08–24/09/42
Spitfire Vb
141 Sqn
23/06–10/08/42
Beaufighter If
145 Sqn
10/05–23/07/40
09/10/40–28/05/41
Spitfire I, IIa
165 Sqn
02/11/42–09/03/43
Spitfire Vb
183 Sqn
04/08–18/09/43
01/02–15/03/44
Typhoon Ib
197 Sqn
28/03/43–15/03/44
01–10/04/44
Typhoon Ib
198 Sqn
16–30/03/44
Typhoon Ib
213 Sqn
07/09–29/11/40
Hurricane I
219 Sqn
10/12/40–23/06/42
Blenheim If; Beaufighter If
222 Sqn
19–26/08/44
Spitfire LFIXb
229 Sqn
22–24/06/44
Spitfire IX
238 Sqn
16/05–20/06/40
Spitfire I
257 Sqn
03/02–10/04/44
Typhoon Ib
266 Sqn
23/03–10/04/44
Typhoon Ib
310 (Czech) Sqn
22–28/06/44
29/06–01/07/44
Spitfire LFIX
312 (Czech) Sqn
22–28/06/44
29/06–04/07/44
Spitfire HFIX
313 (Czech) Sqn
22–28/06/44
Spitfire IX
329 (French) Sqn
06–19/08/44
Spitfire IX
331 (Norwegian) Sqn
22/06–06/08/44
Spitfire IXb
332 (Norwegian) Sqn
21/06–06/08/44
Spitfire IXb
340 (French) Sqn
14–19/08/40
Spitfire IXb
341 (French) Sqn
06–19/08/44
Spitfire IXb
349 (Belgian) Sqn
19–26/08/44
Spitfire LFIXe
401 (Canadian) Sqn
18/04–18/06/44
Spitfire IXb
403 (Canadian) Sqn
18/04–16/06/44
Spitfire IXb
411 (Canadian) Sqn
16–17/04/44
22/04–19/06/44
Spitfire IXb
412 (Canadian) Sqn
24/08–23/09/42
15/04–18/06/44
Spitfire Vb, IXb
416 (Canadian) Sqn
17/04–16/06/44
Spitfire IXb
421 (Canadian) Sqn
18/04–16/06/44
Spitfire IXb
485 (New Zealand) Sqn
19–31/08/44
Spitfire IXe
486 (New Zealand) Sqn
29/10/42–31/01/44
Typhoon Ib
501 (AAF) Sqn
27/11/39–10/05/40
03–07/07/42
Hurricane I; Spitfire Vb, Vc
1455 Flt > 534 Sqn
07/07/41 (04/09/42)–25/01/43
Havoc I, II (Turbinlite); Boston I; Boston III (Turbinlite)
601 (AAF) Sqn
30/12/39–01/06/40
17/06–19/08/40
02–07/09/40
Blenheim If; Hurricane I
605 (AAF) Sqn
27/08/39–11/02/40
Gladiator I; Hurricane I
607 (AAF) Sqn
01/09–10/10/40
Hurricane I
609 (AAF) Sqn
16–21/03/44
Typhoon Ib
676 Sqn
26/02–09/05/41
23/09–29/10/42
Spitfire IIa, VI
Central Fighter Establishment (CFE)
01–10/45
Typhoon Ib; Tempest V
Fighter Interception Unit (FIU)
18/04–20/08/40
Blenheim; Beaufighter; Defiant
Fighter Command Sector Station, 09/39

TARRANT RUSHTON, Dorset

LOCATION: 4m E of Blandford
OPENED: 10/43
CLOSED: 09/80. Disused (2011)
ELEVATION: 255ft
PUNDIT CODE: TK
FORMATIONS: 38 Wing/38 Grp Fighter Command
MAIN CONTRACTOR: George Wimpey & Co Ltd
RUNWAYS: 3 concrete

ABOVE: The Secretary of State for Air, Sir Archibald Sinclair, pays an official visit to Tempsford on 4 April 1943. On the left of the picture is a Lysander Mk IIIA of No 161 Squadron. (H.G. Dublutt via Andy Thomas)

HANGARS: T2 (4)
USER SQNS/UNITS:
298 Sqn
04/11/43–05/07/45
Halifax V, III, VII
644 Sqn
23/02/44–01/12/45
Halifax V, III, VII
Opened in 38 Wing Fighter Command, 10/43

TEALING, Angus

LOCATION: 4m N of Dundee
OPENED: 03/42
CLOSED: 06/45. Agriculture (2011)
ELEVATION: 400ft
PUNDIT CODE: TG
FORMATIONS: 9, 81 (OTU) Grp Fighter Command
MAIN CONTRACTOR: Various
RUNWAYS: 2 concrete
HANGARS: Blister (8), T1 (3)
USER SQNS/UNITS:
56 OTU > 1 Combat Training Wing (CTW) > 1 Tactical Exercise Unit (TEU)
27/03/42 (05/10/43)–31/07/44
Hurricane; Master; Lysander; Typhoon; Spitfire
Opened in Fighter Command as parent station, 03/42
To Flying Training Command, 08/44

TEMPLETON, Pembrokeshire

LOCATION: 7m NNW of Tenby
OPENED: 1943
CLOSED: 1945. Agriculture (2011)
FORMATION: 17 Grp Coastal Command
ELEVATION: 350ft
RUNWAYS: 3 concrete
HANGARS: T2 (1)
USER SQNS/UNITS:
3 OTU
12/43
Anson
8 OTU (det)
01–02/45
Spitfire; Mosquito
306 FTU
01–06/43
Beaufort
Coastal Command satellite to Haverfordwest

TEMPSFORD, Beds

LOCATION: 9m ENE of Bedford
OPENED: 1941
CLOSED: 02/63. Agriculture (2011)
ELEVATION: 63ft
PUNDIT CODE: TE/TQ
FORMATIONS: 3, 7 (T), 92 (OTU) Grp Bomber Command
MAIN CONTRACTOR: John Laing & Son Ltd/Balfour Beatty
RUNWAYS: 3 concrete
HANGARS: B1 (1), T2 (6)
USER SQNS/UNITS:

109 Sqn
19/01–04/42
Wellington I, VI
138 Sqn
14/03/42–09/03/45
Whitley V; Halifax II, V; Stirling IV
161 Sqn
Whitley V; Halifax II, V; Stirling IV; Lysander IIIa; Hudson I
11 OTU
16/12/41–04/42
Wellington I
1418 Flt
03–04/42
Wellington III
Opened in Bomber Command as parent station, 1941

TERN HILL, Salop
LOCATION: 4m SW of Market Drayton
OPENED: 01/36
CLOSED: RAF base, flying (2011)
ELEVATION: 280ft
PUNDIT CODE: TR
FORMATION: 9 Grp Fighter Command
MAIN CONTRACTOR: Various
RUNWAYS: 2 concrete/Tarmac
HANGARS: C Type (4), Bellman (1), Blister (9)
USER SQNS/UNITS:
131 Sqn
06/08–27/09/41
Spitfire Ia
306 (Polish) Sqn
07/11/40–03/04/41
Hurricane I
403 (Canadian) Sqn
30/05–04/08/41
Spitfire I, IIa
605 (AAF) Sqn
31/03–30/05/41
Hurricane IIa
Fighter Command Sector Station, 08/40
To Flying Training Command, 10/41

THIRSK, Yorks
OPENED: —
CLOSED: —
ELEVATION: 85ft
PUNDIT CODE: None
FORMATION: 2 Grp Bomber Command
MAIN CONTRACTOR: Not known
HANGARS: None
USER SQNS/UNITS:
226 Sqn
18–27/06/40
Battle
Used occasionally as emergency landing ground for Topcliffe and Skipton

THOLTHORPE, Yorks
LOCATION: 12m NW of York
OPENED: 08/40
CLOSED: 09/45. Agriculture (2011)
ELEVATION: 60ft
PUNDIT CODE: TH

ABOVE: Ground crew attend to Halifax Mk V, LK640, 'Queenie', of No 431 Squadron, on its dispersal at Tholthorpe during the summer of 1943. Skippered by 27-year-old Flg Off Garnett Carefoot, RCAF, from Saskatchewan, she crashed in the sea returning from ops to Mannheim on 19 November. Burials of her crew took place on both sides of the Channel, with one crew member commemorated on the Runnymede Memorial. (Public Archives of Canada DND/UK PL-26140)

ABOVE: 'Watch Office for All Commands 343/43.' Pictured in 1997, the watchtower at Tholthorpe, the former home of Nos 420 and 425 (Canadian) Squadrons, no longer looks out towards the main runway, and its Halifaxes are long gone. It is now a private dwelling. (Author)

FORMATIONS: 4, 6 (RCAF) Grp Bomber Command
MAIN CONTRACTORS: Gerrards Ltd, Tarmac Ltd, Russells Ltd, Henry Boot Ltd
RUNWAYS: 3 concrete/Tarmac
HANGARS: B1 (1), T2 (2)
USER SQNS/UNITS:

77 Sqn
08–12/40
Whitley V

420 (Canadian) Sqn
12/12/43–12/06/45
Halifax III; Lancaster X

425 (Canadian) Sqn
10/12/43–13/06/45
Halifax III; Lancaster X

431 (Canadian) Sqn
15/07–10/12/43
Wellington X; Halifax V

434 (Canadian) Sqn
15/06–11/12/43
Halifax V

Opened in Bomber Command as satellite to Linton-on-Ouse, 08/40
Closed for rebuilding and runway laying, 12/40
Reopened as 62 Base substation, 07/43

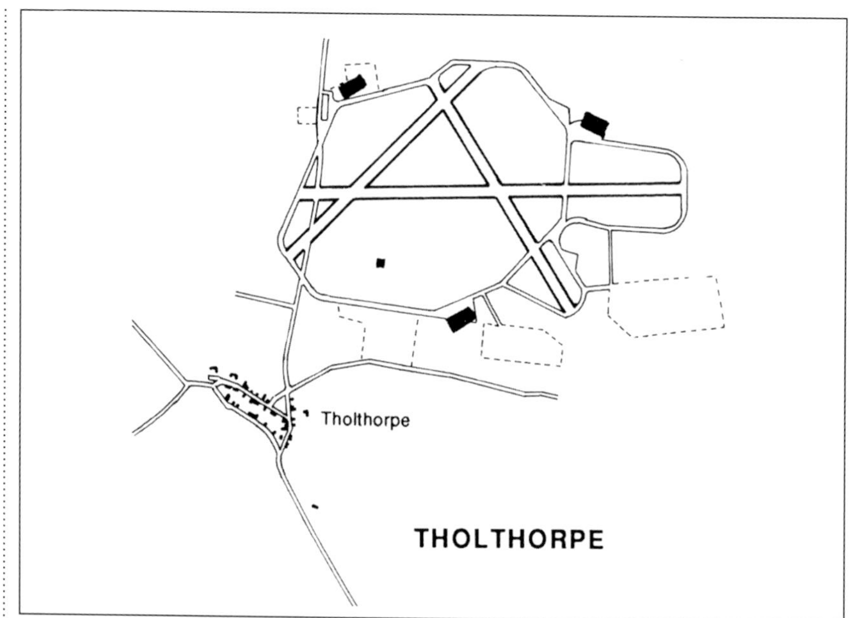

THORNABY, Yorkshire

LOCATION: 2m SW of Middlesbrough
OPENED: 1928
CLOSED: 1958. Housing/industry (2011)
FORMATIONS: 16, 18 Grp Coastal Command
ELEVATION: 60ft
RUNWAYS: 3 concrete
HANGARS: C Type (2), Bellman (1), Aeroplane (2), Blister (3)
USER SQNS/UNITS:

114 Sqn
02/03–13/05/41
Blenheim IV

143 Sqn
05/07–27/09/41
Beaufighter Ic

220 Sqn
21/08/39–28/04/41
Anson I; Hudson I, III, VI
279 Sqn
31/10/44–03/09/45
Hudson III, V, VI; Warwick I; Hurricane IIc; Sea Otter
280 Sqn
21/10/43–30/10/44
Anson I; Warwick I
281 Sqn
22/11/43–27/02/44
Warwick I
306 (Polish) Sqn (det)
05–08/43
Spitfire Vb
332 (Norwegian) Sqn (det)
01/42
Spitfire Va
401 (Canadian) Sqn (det)
25/01–27/05/43
Spitfire Vb
608 Sqn
17/03/30–02/01/42
Blenheim I, IV; Hudson III, V
1 (C) OTU
03–10/43
Hudson
ASR Training Unit
10–12/43
03–05/44
Warwick; Walrus; Lysander
6 (C) OTU
19/07/41–03/43
Hudson I, III, V
9 BAT Flt > 1509 BAT
01/41 (11/41)–06/04/42
Warwick Training Unit
21/11/43–06/44
Warwick

THORNEY ISLAND, Sussex

LOCATION: 2m S of Emsworth
OPENED: 02/38
CLOSED: Army base (2011)
ELEVATION: 0ft
PUNDIT CODE: TC
FORMATIONS: 16 Grp Coastal Command; 2, 84 Grp 2 TAF
MAIN CONTRACTOR: Various
RUNWAYS: 3 concrete
HANGARS: Blister (16), C Type (6)
USER SQNS/UNITS:
21 Sqn
18/06/44–06/02/45
Mosquito VI
22 Sqn
25/06–28/10/41
01–16/02/42
Beaufort I
42 Sqn
28/04–21/06/40
Beaufort I
48 Sqn
25/08/39–16/07/40
Anson I; Beaufort I
53 Sqn
24/11/40–20/03/41
29/04–25/09/43
Blenheim IV; Liberator Va
59 Sqn
03/07/40–23/06/41
22/07/41–17/01/42
29/08/42–06/02/43
27/03–11/05/43
Blenheim IV; Hudson III, V, VI; Liberator III, V; Fortress IIa
86 Sqn
01–03/42 (det)
01/08/42–18/03/43
Beaufort II; Liberator IIIa
129 Sqn
30/07–25/09/42
Spitfire Vb
130 Sqn
16–20/08/42
Spitfire Vb, Vc
131 Sqn
24/09–07/11/42
Spitfire Vb
164 Sqn
21/04–18/06/44
Typhoon Ib
183 Sqn
01–11/04/44
22/04–18/06/44
Typhoon Ib
193 Sqn
16/03–06/04/44
Typhoon Ib
198 Sqn
06–22/04/44
30/04–18/06/44
Typhoon Ib
217 Sqn
29/10/41–06/03/42
Beaufort I, II
235 Sqn
10–24/06/40
06/40–06/41 (det)
Blenheim IVf
236 Sqn
04/07–08/08/40
Blenheim IVf
280 Sqn
25/09–21/10/43
Anson I
404 (Canadian) Sqn
15/04–20/06/41
Blenheim IVf
407 (Canadian) Sqn
18/02–31/03/42
11/42–02/43 (det)
Hudson III, V
415 (Canadian) Sqn
20/08/41–11/04/42
16/05–05/06/42
11/02/42–15/11/43
11/43–07/44 (det)
Beaufort I; Hampden; Wellington XIII; Albacore
464 (Australian) Sqn
18/06/44–07/02/45
Mosquito VI
487 (New Zealand) Sqn
18/06/44–05/02/45
Mosquito VI
489 (New Zealand) Sqn
08/03–05/08/42
Hampden I
547 Sqn
25/10/43–14/01/44
Wellington XI, XIII; Liberator V
609 (AAF) Sqn
01–22/04/44
30/04–18/06/44
Typhoon Ib
612 (AAF) Sqn
18/08–23/09/42
Whitley VII

ABOVE: This Stirling Mk III, EF210, of No 1665 HCU, was flying circuits and bumps when it swung on landing in a strong cross-wind and careered onto the adjacent Whitchurch Road, but thankfully suffered only a few minor scrapes. (R.R. Glass)

810 NAS
02–04/45
Barracuda II, TRIII
816 NAS
12/42–02/43
Swordfish II
819 NAS
10/42
Swordfish I, II
822 NAS
02–06/45
Barracuda TRIII
833 NAS
02–07/43
Swordfish II; Seafire L.IIc
836 NAS
01–03/43
Swordfish I, II
838 NAS
11/44–02/45
Swordfish II, III
842 NAS
11/44–01/45
Swordfish II
848 NAS
06–07/44
Avenger I
854 NAS
05–07/44
Avenger II
855 NAS
05–09/44
Avenger II
Air-Sea Warfare Development Unit
04/45–1950
Avenger; Barracuda; Firefly; Sea Mosquito

Opened in Coastal Command, 02/38
To 84 Grp, 2 TAF, 03/44
To 2 Grp, 2 TAF, 06/44

TILSTOCK, Salop

LOCATION: 3m SSE of Whitchurch
OPENED: 01/08/42
CLOSED: 03/46. Agriculture/parachuting centre (2011)
ELEVATION: 308ft
PUNDIT CODE: OK
FORMATION: 93 (OTU) Grp Bomber Command
MAIN CONTRACTOR: Sir Alfred McAlpine
RUNWAYS: 3 concrete
HANGARS: T2 (4)
USER SQNS/UNITS:
81 OTU
01/09/42–01/01/44
Whitley; Wellington
1665 HCU
23/01/44–26/03/45
Stirling

Opened in Bomber Command as satellite to Hixon, 08/42
To 38 (Airborne Forces) Group, Fighter Command, 01/44

TIREE, Argyllshire

LOCATION: Isle of Tiree, Inner Hebrides, 5m W of E coast
OPENED: 1937
CLOSED: 01/07/1946. Agriculture/Tiree Airport (2011)
ELEVATION: 38ft

FORMATION: 15 (T) Grp Coastal Command
RUNWAYS: 3 concrete
HANGARS: ½ T2 (10)
USER SQNS/UNITS:

224 Sqn
16/04–10/09/42
Hudson V

281 Sqn
27/02/44–24/10/45
Warwick II, VI; Wellington XIII; Sea Otter

304 (Polish) Sqn
10/05–15/06/42
Wellington Ic

518 Sqn
25/09/43–18/09/45
Halifax V, III

Care and Maintenance, 10/42–09/43

TOPCLIFFE, Yorks

LOCATION: 2½m SW of Thirsk
OPENED: 09/40
CLOSED: RAF base/volunteer gliding squadron (2011)
ELEVATION: 92ft
PUNDIT CODE: TP
FORMATIONS: 4, 6 (RCAF), 7 (T) Grp Bomber Command
MAIN CONTRACTOR: Various
RUNWAYS: 3 concrete
HANGARS: C Type (5)
USER SQNS/UNITS:

77 Sqn
05/10/40–05/09/41
Whitley V

102 Sqn
15/11/40–15/11/41
Whitley V

405 (Canadian) Sqn
07/08–25/10/42
01–06/03/43
Halifax II

419 (Canadian) Sqn
18/08–01/10/42
Wellington II, III

424 (Canadian) Sqn
15/10/42–08/04/43
Wellington III, X

1659 HCU
03/43–09/45
Halifax III; Lancaster X

Opened in Bomber Command as parent station, 09/40
Closed for rebuilding, 11/41
Reopened, 06/42
Became 6 (RCAF) Training Base HQ, 01/43
Became 61 (RCAF) Training Base HQ, 09/43
Became 76 (RCAF) Training Base HQ, 11/44

TUDDENHAM, Suffolk

LOCATION: 7½m NW of Bury St Edmunds
OPENED: 10/43
CLOSED: 07/63. Agriculture (2011)
ELEVATION: 75ft
PUNDIT CODE: TD
FORMATION: 3 Grp Bomber Command
MAIN CONTRACTOR: M.J. Gleeson Ltd
RUNWAYS: 3 concrete
HANGARS: B1 (1), T2 (2)
USER SQNS/UNITS:

90 Sqn
13/10/43–11/11/46
Stirling III; Lancaster I, III

ABOVE: Whitley Mk V, T4261, 'S', Ceylon, of No 102 Squadron in snow at Topcliffe. Ceylon ditched off the Norfolk coast returning from a raid on Cologne on the night of 1/2 March 1941. Her pilot, Sqn Ldr C.E.F. Florigny, was last seen standing on the fuselage of the sinking bomber unable to reach the dinghy, which was being swept away by the gusting wind. (IWM CH2052)

ABOVE: Flt Sgt Jack Towers (third from left) and his No 90 Squadron Stirling crew at Tuddenham in March 1944. Within a month of this picture being taken Towers and two other crew members were dead, killed in two separate crash-landings returning from ops. (Bill Burns)

138 Sqn
09/03/45–12/11/46
Lancaster I, III
186 Sqn
05/10–17/12/44
Lancaster I, III
Opened in Bomber Command as 32 Base substation, 10/43

TURNBERRY, Ayrshire

LOCATION: 7m N of Girvan
OPENED: 1917
CLOSED: 1945. Golf course/light aviation (2011)
ELEVATION: 35ft
FORMATION: 17 (T) Grp Coastal Command
RUNWAYS: concrete/Tarmac
HANGARS: T2 (2), ½ T2 (2), Blister (24)
USER SQNS/UNITS:
618 Sqn (det)
05/43
Mosquito IV
Torpedo Training Unit
14/11/42–01/01/43
1 Torpedo Training Unit
01/01/43–22/05/44
01/08/45–10/12/47
5 (C) OTU
03/05–29/12/42
15/02/44–01/08/45
Beaufort; Hampden; Warwick I; Beaufighter Vic; Ventura; Hudson
Coastal Command Flying Instructors' School
09/06–13/10/45

TURNHOUSE, Midlothian

LOCATION: 5m W of Edinburgh
OPENED: 1916
CLOSED: Edinburgh Airport (2011)
ELEVATION: 100ft
PUNDIT CODE: TS
FORMATION: 13 Grp Fighter Command
MAIN CONTRACTOR: Various
RUNWAYS: 3 concrete
HANGARS: Blister (6), C Type (1)
USER SQNS/UNITS:
3 Sqn
14/09–13/10/40
Hurricane I
64 Sqn
16–17/05/41
06/08–04/10/41
Spitfire IIa
65 Sqn
27/08–29/11/40
Spitfire I
81 Sqn
06/12/41–06/01/42
14/02–15/03/42
Spitfire Va
122 Sqn
05/05–26/06/41
Spitfire I
123 Sqn
10/05–06/08/41
Spitfire I
141 Sqn
04–19/10/39

28/06–11/07/40
30/08–15/10/40
Gladiator I; Defiant I

232 Sqn
03–14/08/42
01/09–25/11/42
Spitfire Vb

242 Sqn
10/04–15/05/42
Spitfire Vb

243 Sqn
02/09–24/11/42
Spitfire Vb

245 Sqn
05/06–20/07/40
Hurricane I

253 Sqn
21/07–23/08/40
Hurricane I

329 (French) Sqn
09/03–03/04/45
Spitfire XVI

340 (French) Sqn
07/11–20/12/41
21/03–30/04/43
30/01–08/02/45
Spitfire IIa, Vb, IXb

341 (French) Sqn
18/01–21/03/43
01–09/02/45
Spitfire Vb, IXb

603 (AAF) Sqn
14/10/25–16/12/39
05/05–28/08/40
27/02–16/05/41
28/04–07/05/45
DH9A; Wapiti; Hart; Hind; Gladiator II; Spitfire I, IIa, LFXVIe

607 (AAF) Sqn
10/10–08/11/40
Hurricane I

Fighter Command Sector Station, 09/39

TURWESTON, Bucks

LOCATION: 9½m E of Aylesbury
OPENED: 23/11/42
CLOSED: 23/09/45. Light aviation/business park (2011)
ELEVATION: 448ft
PUNDIT CODE: TW
FORMATION: 92 (OTU) Grp Bomber Command
MAIN CONTRACTOR: Various
RUNWAYS: 3 concrete
HANGARS: T2 (1)
USER SQNS/UNITS:

12 OTU
23/11/42–04/43
Wellington I

13 OTU
30/04–08/43
Mitchell

17 OTU
08/43–07/45
Wellington III, X

Opened in Bomber Command as satellite to Chipping Warden, 23/11/42

Became satellite to Silverstone, 03/07/43

TWINWOOD FARM, Beds

LOCATION: 4m N of Bedford
OPENED: 04/42
CLOSED: 06/45. Concert arena/museum/agriculture (2011)
ELEVATION: 275ft
PUNDIT CODE: TF
FORMATIONS: 9, 81 (OTU) Grp Fighter Command
MAIN CONTRACTOR: Various
RUNWAYS: 3 concrete
HANGARS: Blister (6)
USER SQNS/UNITS:

164 Sqn
04–14/01/44
11/02–08/03/44
Hurricane IV; Typhoon Ib

51 OTU
19/04/42–14/06/45
Blenheim; Beaufighter; Beaufort; Havoc; Hudson; Wellington; Mosquito; Hurricane

Opened in Fighter Command as satellite to Cranfield, 04/42

UPOTTERY, Devon

LOCATION: 6m N of Honiton
OPENED: 1944
CLOSED: 1948. Agriculture (2011)
ELEVATION: 825ft
FORMATION: 19 Grp Coastal Command
RUNWAYS: 3 concrete/Tarmac
HANGARS: T2 (2)
USER SQNS/UNITS: none

Under Coastal Command control for only 4 days, 07–11/01/1945

UPPER HEYFORD, Oxon

LOCATION: 5m NW of Bicester
OPENED: 10/27
CLOSED: 1994. Automotive storage/police driving training (2011)
ELEVATION: 421ft
PUNDIT CODE: UH
FORMATIONS: 6 (T), 92 (OTU) Grp Bomber Command
MAIN CONTRACTOR: John Laing & Son Ltd
RUNWAYS: 3 concrete
HANGARS: A Type (6)
USER SQNS/UNITS:

7 Sqn
23/09/39–22/04/40
Hampden

18 Sqn
20/10/31–24/09/39
Hart; Hind; Blenheim I

57 Sqn
05/09/32–24/09/39
Hart; Hind; Blenheim I

76 Sqn
23/09/39–22/04/40
Hampden

16 OTU
22/04/40–03/46
Hampden; Hereford; Anson; Oxford; Wellington I, III, X

1473 Flt
10/07/42–01/43
Defiant; Lysander; Mosquito III, IV, VI, XX, XXV

Opened in Bomber Command as parent station, 10/27

ABOVE: Fairey Battle, K7602, 'B', of No 52 Squadron, is pictured in its prewar markings against the backdrop of one of Upwood's C-Type hangars. The squadron received its Battles in 1937 and shared the base with another Battle squadron, No 63. (Author)

UPWOOD, Hunts

LOCATION: 1¾m SW of Ramsey
OPENED: 01/37
CLOSED: 1994. USAF (non-flying)/light industry/gliding (2011)
ELEVATION: 76ft
PUNDIT CODE: UD
FORMATIONS: 6, 8 (PFF), 92 (OTU) Grp Bomber Command
MAIN CONTRACTOR: Various
RUNWAYS: 3 concrete/Tarmac
HANGARS: C Type (4)
USER SQNS/UNITS:

35 Sqn
01/02–08/04/40
Blenheim I, IV

90 Sqn
16/09/39–06/04/40
Blenheim I, IV

139 Sqn
01/02/44–04/02/46
Mosquito IX, XVI, XX, XXV

156 Sqn
05/03/44–27/06/45
Lancaster I, III

17 OTU
04/40–04/43
Blenheim; Wellington

PFF Navigation Training Unit (NTU)
06/43–03/44
Lancaster I, III

Opened in Bomber Command as parent station, 01/37

USWORTH, Co Durham

LOCATION: 3½m W of Sunderland
OPENED: 10/16
CLOSED: 1958. Nissan car factory/North East Aircraft Museum (2011)
ELEVATION: 120ft
PUNDIT CODE: Not known
FORMATIONS: 13, 81 (OTU) Grp Fighter Command
MAIN CONTRACTOR: Various and John Laing & Son Ltd
RUNWAYS: 2 concrete/Tarmac
HANGARS: Blister (3), Callender (1), Lemella (1)
USER SQNS/UNITS:

43 Sqn
08/09–12/12/40
Hurricane I

64 Sqn
01–16/05/40
Spitfire I

607 (AAF) Sqn
04/06–01/09/40
12/12/40–16/01/41
Hurricane I

55 OTU
14/03/41–28/04/42
Hurricane X

62 OTU
23/06/42–30/06/43
Anson

Fighter Command parent station, 09/39
To C&M, 04/44

VALLEY, Anglesey

LOCATION: 6m SE of Holyhead
OPENED: 02/41
CLOSED: RAF base, flying (2011)
ELEVATION: 26ft
PUNDIT CODE: VY
MAIN CONTRACTOR: Various
FORMATION: 9 Grp Fighter Command
RUNWAYS: 3 Tarmac
HANGARS: Bellman (3), T2 (3)
USER SQNS/UNITS:

125 Sqn
14/11/43–25/03/44
Beaufighter VIf; Mosquito XVII

131 Sqn
04/03–16/04/42
Spitfire Vb

157 Sqn
26/03–07/05/44
Mosquito II, VI

242 Sqn
16/09–01/11/41
Hurricane IIb

312 (Czech) Sqn
03/03–25/04/41
Hurricane I

350 (Belgian) Sqn
13/11/41–19/02/42
Spitfire IIa

406 (Canadian) Sqn
31/03–15/11/43
Beaufighter VIf

456 (Australian) Sqn
30/06/41–29/03/43
Defiant I; Beaufighter IIf, VIf; Mosquito II

615 (AAF) Sqn
21/04–11/09/41
Hurricane I, IIb, IIc

Opened in Fighter Command as a Sector Station, 02/41
Sector Station transferred to Woodvale, 11/43

WADDINGTON, Lincs

LOCATION: 4m S of Lincoln
OPENED: 11/16
CLOSED: RAF base, flying (2011)
ELEVATION: 235ft
PUNDIT CODE: WA
FORMATIONS: 1, 5 Grp Bomber Command
MAIN CONTRACTOR: Various
RUNWAYS: 3 concrete/Tarmac
HANGARS: C Type (5)
USER SQNS/UNITS:

9 Sqn
08/08/42–14/04/43
Lancaster I, III

44 Sqn
16/06/37–31/05/43
Hind; Blenheim I; Anson I; Hampden; Lancaster I, III

50 Sqn
03/05/37–10/07/40
Hind; Hampden

97 Sqn
25/02–10/03/41
Manchester

142 Sqn
15/06–03/07/40
Battle

207 Sqn
01/11/40–17/11/41
Manchester

BELOW: Hurricane Mk I, P2874, 'F', of No 607 Squadron, at Usworth during the summer of 1940. The aircraft was flown throughout the Battle of Britain by Flt Lt W.F. Blackadder DSO, 'A' Flight Commander, who led the squadron on 14 August against the Luftwaffe's attacks on northern England. (RAF Museum via Andy Thomas)

ABOVE: Lancasters of No 463 (Australian) Squadron, Waddington, attached to the Bomber Command Film Unit, were specially adapted to carry movie cameras and a cameraman for filming operational sorties. (IWM FLM 2229)

420 (Canadian) Sqn
19/12/41–07/08/42
Hampden
463 (Australian) Sqn
25/11/43–03/07/45
Lancaster I, III
467 (Australian) Sqn
13/11/43–15/06/45
Lancaster I, III
Opened as RFC Flying Training station, 11/16
Rebuilt to Expansion Scheme standard and reopened in Bomber Command as parent station, 05/37
Became 53 Base HQ, 11/43
*Sqn Ldr J.D. Nettleton, 44 Sqn, awarded VC, Augsburg, 17/04/42
*Avro Lancaster introduced into frontline service by 44 Sqn from Waddington

---

WARBOYS, Hunts

LOCATION: 5¾m NE of Huntingdon
OPENED: 09/41
CLOSED: 1963. Agriculture/light industry (2011)
ELEVATION: 90ft
PUNDIT CODE: WB
FORMATIONS: 3, 8 (PFF) Grp Bomber Command
MAIN CONTRACTOR: Various
RUNWAYS: 3 Tarmac
HANGARS: B1 (1), T2 (2)
USER SQNS/UNITS:
156 Sqn
15/08/42–05/03/44
Wellington III; Lancaster I, III
1655 MCU
03–12/44
Mosquito IV, XX; Oxford
PFF NTU
03/44–06/45
Halifax II; Lancaster I, III; Mosquito IV, XVI, XX, XXV
Opened in Bomber Command as satellite to Wyton, 09/41
Upgraded to parent station, 01/43

WARMWELL, Dorset

LOCATION: 4m E of Dorchester
OPENED: 05/37

ABOVE: A Whirlwind Mk I of No 263 Squadron, Warmwell, during October 1943. (263 Sqn records via Andy Thomas)

CLOSED: 11/45. Agriculture/quarrying (2011)
ELEVATION: 207ft
PUNDIT CODE: XW
FORMATION: 10 Grp Fighter Command
MAIN CONTRACTOR: Various
RUNWAYS: 3 grass
HANGARS: Bellman (2), Blister (8), T2 (2)
USER SQNS/UNITS:

19 Sqn
01–14/06/42
Spitfire Vb

41 Sqn
07–18/03/45
Spitfire XIV

118 Sqn
09–18/04/41
Spitfire I, IIa

130 Sqn
30/11–05/12/41
03–21/02/45
Spitfire IIa, Va, Vb, XIV

137 Sqn
07–19/03/45
Typhoon Ib

152 Sqn
12/07/40–09/04/41
Spitfire I, IIa

164 Sqn
20/06–06/08/43
Hurricane IV

174 Sqn
01–21/09/42
Hurricane IIb

175 Sqn
03/03–10/10/42
21/11–04/12/44
Hurricane IIb; Typhoon Ib

181 Sqn
12/01–03/02/45
Typhoon Ib

182 Sqn
03–21/02/45
Typhoon Ib

184 Sqn
04–18/12/44
07–28/05/45
Typhoon Ib

234 Sqn
24/02–05/11/41
23/03–04/04/42
Spitfire I, IIb, Vb

ABOVE: Operation 'Manna' was the air movement of food and supplies by the RAF and USAAF to the starving population of Holland in 1945. Here, ground crew at Waterbeach prepare to load sacks of food into the bomb-bay of a Lancaster of No 514 Squadron on 29 April 1945. (IWM CL2489)

245 Sqn
19/12/44–06/01/45
Typhoon Ib
247 Sqn
21/02–07/03/45
Typhoon Ib
257 Sqn
08/01–12/08/43
17/09/43–20/01/44
Typhoon Ib
263 Sqn
19–23/12/41
13/09/42–20/02/43
15/03–19/06/43
12/07–07/09/43
10/09–05/12/43
06–19/03/44
Whirlwind I; Typhoon Ib
266 Sqn
21/09/42–08/01/43
Typhoon Ib
302 (Polish) Sqn
05/09–11/10/41
27/04–01/05/42
Hurricane IIb;
Spitfire Vb
312 (Czech) Sqn
20–24/04/42
19–31/05/42
20/02–14/03/43
Spitfire Vb, Vc
350 (Belgian) Sqn
05–15/04/42
18/03–02/04/45
Spitfire IIa, Vb, XIV
401 (Canadian) Sqn
24/10–04/11/44
Spitfire IXb

402 (Canadian) Sqn
06/11/41–04/03/42
14/01–02/02/45
Hurricane IIb; Spitfire XIVe
403 (Canadian) Sqn
04–14/01/45
Spitfire XVI
411 (Canadian) Sqn
15–23/10/44
Spitfire IXe
438 (Canadian) Sqn
19/03–03/04/45
Typhoon Ib
439 (Canadian) Sqn
03–22/04/45
Typhoon Ib
440 (Canadian) Sqn
23/04–08/05/45
Typhoon Ib
443 (Canadian) Sqn
18/12/44–03/01/45
Spitfire IXb
609 (AAF) Sqn
02/10/40–24/02/41
Spitfire I
610 (AAF) Sqn
21/02–03/03/45
Spitfire XIV
Opened in Flying Training Command and known as Woodsford, 05/37
Renamed Warmwell, 07/38
To 10 Grp Fighter Command as satellite to Middle Wallop, 07/40
To USAAF as Station AAF-454, 03/44
To RAF, 08/44

WATERBEACH, Cambs

LOCATION: 5m N of Cambridge
OPENED: 11/01/41
CLOSED: Army base (2011)
ELEVATION: 17ft
PUNDIT CODE: WJ
FORMATION: 3 Grp Bomber Command
MAIN CONTRACTOR: Various
RUNWAYS: 3 concrete/Tarmac
HANGARS: B1 (1), J Type (2), T2 (3)
USER SQNS/UNITS:
99 Sqn
19/03/41–12/02/42
Wellington I, II
514 Sqn
23/11/43–22/08/45
Lancaster I, II, III
1651 HCU
02/01/42–21/11/43
Stirling I, III
1678 CF
11/43–12/06/44
Lancaster II
Bomber Command Film Unit
09/44–06/45
Lancaster I, III
Opened in Bomber Command as parent station, 11/01/41
Became 33 Base HQ, 09/43

WATTISHAM, Suffolk

LOCATION: 9m NW of Ipswich
OPENED: 03/39
CLOSED: Army Air Corps base (2011)
ELEVATION: 290ft
PUNDIT CODE: WT
FORMATION: 2 Grp Bomber Command
MAIN CONTRACTOR: Various
RUNWAYS: 3 concrete/Tarmac
HANGARS: L Type (4), T2 (4)
USER SQNS/UNITS:
18 Sqn
09/12/41–24/08/42
Blenheim IV
107 Sqn
03/05/39–11/05/41
Blenheim IV
110 Sqn
11/05/39–17/03/42
Blenheim I, IV
114 Sqn
31/05–10/06/40
Blenheim IV
226 Sqn
27/05–09/12/41
Blenheim IV
Opened in Bomber Command as parent station, 03/39
Transferred to USAAF, 09/42

WATTON, Suffolk

LOCATION: 11½m NE of Thetford
OPENED: 01/39
CLOSED: 1998. Army Air Corps base/gliding/housing (2011)
ELEVATION: 190ft
PUNDIT CODE: WN
FORMATIONS: 2, 3 Grp Bomber Command
MAIN CONTRACTOR: John Laing & Son Ltd
RUNWAYS: 3 concrete
HANGARS: B1 (2), Type C4 (4), T2 (3)
USER SQNS/UNITS:
18 Sqn
21–26/05/40
Blenheim I, IV
21 Sqn
02/03/39–24/06/40
30/10/40–25/12/41
Blenheim I, IV
82 Sqn
22/08/39–21/03/42
Blenheim I, IV
90 Sqn
03–15/05/41
Fortress I
105 Sqn
10/07–31/10/40
Blenheim IV
Opened in Bomber Command as parent station, 01/39
To USAAF as Station AAF-376, 05/43

WELLESBOURNE MOUNTFORD, Warks

LOCATION: 5m E of Stratford-on-Avon
OPENED: 04/41
CLOSED: 1964. General aviation/agriculture (2011)
ELEVATION: 154ft
PUNDIT CODE: WM
FORMATIONS: 6 (T), 91 (OTU) Grp Bomber Command
MAIN CONTRACTOR: John Laing & Son Ltd
RUNWAYS: 3 concrete/Tarmac
HANGARS: J Type (1), T2 (4)
USER SQNS/UNITS:
22 OTU
14/04/41–01/07/45
Wellington I, III, X
Opened in Bomber Command as parent station, 04/41

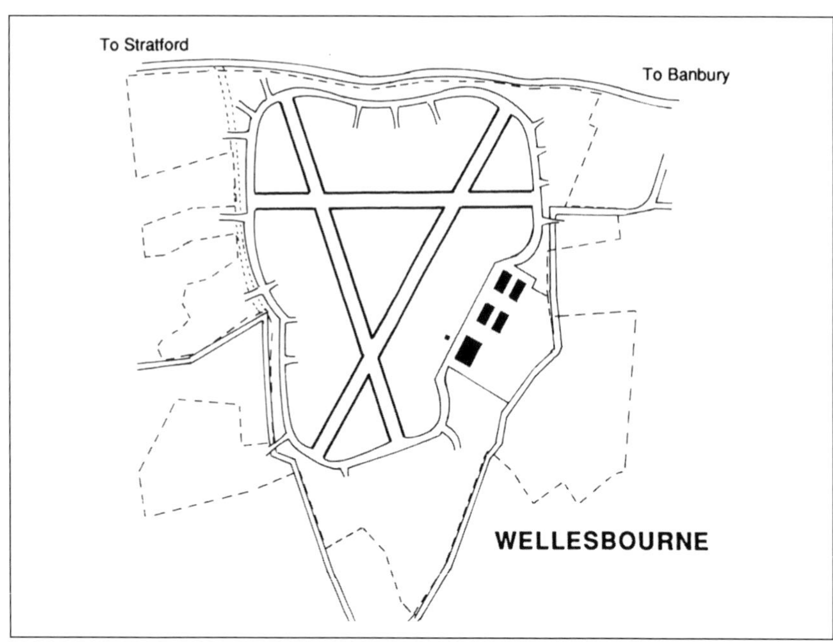

81 Sqn
01/09–30/10/42
Spitfire Vb
154 Sqn
01/09–01/11/42
Spitfire Vb, Vc
349 (Belgian) Sqn
05–16/08/43
Spitfire Va
402 (Canadian) Sqn
12/02–12/04/44
Spitfire Vb, Vc
412 (Canadian) Sqn
20/10/41–01/05/42
Spitfire IIa, Vb
416 (Canadian) Sqn
29/05–07/06/43
19/09–02/10/43
Spitfire IX, Vb
439 (Canadian) Sqn
01–08/01/44
Hurricane IV
To 12 Grp Fighter Command as RLG to Digby, 06/40
To Flying Training Command as RLG to Cranwell, 04/44

WELLINGORE, Lincs

LOCATION: 10½ m S of Lincoln
OPENED: 1935
CLOSED: 1945. Agriculture (2011)
ELEVATION: 260ft
PUNDIT CODE: JW
FORMATION: 12 Grp Fighter Command
MAIN CONTRACTOR: Various
RUNWAYS: 2 grass
HANGARS: Blister (8)
USER SQNS/UNITS:
29 Sqn
27/07/40–27/04/41
Blenheim If; Beaufighter If
54 Sqn
02–18/06/42
Spitfire Vb

ABOVE: Spitfire Mk VB, AD381, was a presentation aircraft, purchased by the workers of Plessey for the RAF. The 'Plessey Spitfire' entered service with No 412 (Canadian) Squadron on 16 December 1941 and then went on to serve with Nos 64, 453 (Australian), 129 and 313 (Czech) Squadrons, and the Fighter Leaders' School, before being destroyed in a crash on 23 June 1945. (Author)

WEST FREUGH, Wigtownshire

LOCATION: 5½m SE of Stranraer
OPENED: 01/37
CLOSED: 2001. QinetiQ missile test range (2011)
ELEVATION: 55ft
PUNDIT CODE: EW
FORMATION: 13 Grp Fighter Command
MAIN CONTRACTOR: Various
RUNWAYS: 2 Tarmac
HANGARS: Bessonneau (1), Bellman (7), Blister (8), F Type (1)
USER SQNS/UNITS:

130 Sqn
04–12/08/42
Spitfire Vb, Vc

Alternative emergency satellite to Ayr in 13 Grp Fighter Command, but never used for this purpose

WEST MALLING, Kent

LOCATION: 5m W of Maidstone
OPENED: 1930
CLOSED: 1969. Housing (2011)
ELEVATION: 308ft
PUNDIT CODE: VG
FORMATION: 11 Grp Fighter Command
MAIN CONTRACTOR: Various
RUNWAYS: 2 steel matting/concrete
HANGARS: Blister (16), J Type (1)
USER SQNS/UNITS:

3 Sqn
14/05–11/06/43
Typhoon Ib

29 Sqn
27/04/41–13/05/43
01/05–19/06/44
Blenheim If; Beaufighter If, VIf; Mosquito XIII

32 Sqn
05/05–14/06/42
07/07–20/08/42
Hurricane IIb, IIc, I

41 Sqn
19–28/06/44
Spitfire XII

ABOVE: This is Focke Wulf Fw190A-4/U8, Wk Nr 7155, of II/SKG10, pictured shortly after landing in error at RAF West Malling on 17 April 1943. The aircraft is painted overall in sooty black, except for the engine cowling. (Author)

64 Sqn
06–25/09/43
Spitfire Vc

66 Sqn
30/10–07/11/40
Spitfire I

80 Sqn
05/07–29/08/44
Spitfire IX

85 Sqn
13/05/43–01/05/44
21/07–29/08/44
Mosquito II, XV, XII, XIII, XVII

91 Sqn
23/04–21/07/44
Spitfire XIV

96 Sqn
08/11/43–20/06/44
Mosquito XIII

124 Sqn
20/09/43–05/01/44
18/01–18/03/44
Spitfire VII

130 Sqn
05/08–18/09/43
Spitfire Vb

141 Sqn
11–25/07/40
Defiant I

157 Sqn
21/07–29/08/44
Mosquito XIX

234 Sqn
05/08–16/09/43
Spitfire Vb

264 Sqn
14/04/41–01/05/42
Defiant I, II

274 Sqn
05/07–17/08/44
Spitfire IX

316 (Polish) Sqn
04–11/07/44
Mustang III

322 (Dutch) Sqn
20/06–21/07/44
Spitfire XIV

350 (Belgian) Sqn
07–19/09/43
Spitfire Vb

409 (Canadian) Sqn
14/05–19/06/44
Mosquito XIII

410 (Canadian) Sqn
20/10–08/11/43
Mosquito II

485 (New Zealand) Sqn
16–22/08/42
Spitfire Vb

BELOW: Spitfire Mk I, X4382, 'G', belonged to No 602 Squadron and is seen on the grass airfield at Westhampnett in September 1940. (Alfred Price)

486 (New Zealand) Sqn
10–29/10/42
Typhoon Ib
1452 Flt > 531 Sqn
07/07/41 (08/09/42)–02/10/42
09/10/42–25/01/43
Havoc I; Havoc I (Turbinlite); Boston III (Turbinlite)
610 (AAF) Sqn
16–21/08/42
19–27/06/44
Spitfire Vb, XIV
616 (AAF) Sqn
03–07/07/42
18/03–24/04/44
Spitfire VI, VII
421 Flt
10/40
Hurricane I
To 11 Grp Fighter Command as a satellite to Kenley, 06/40

WEST RAYNHAM, Norfolk

LOCATION: 5½m SW of Fakenham
OPENED: 05/39
CLOSED: Closed 1994. Housing/hotel (2011)
ELEVATION: 262ft
PUNDIT CODE: WR
FORMATIONS: 2, 6 (T), 100 (BS) Grp Bomber Command
MAIN CONTRACTOR: Allot Ltd
RUNWAYS: 2 concrete/Tarmac
HANGARS: C Type (4)
USER SQNS/UNITS:
18 Sqn
12/06–09/09/40
24/08–11/11/42
Blenheim IV, V
76 Sqn
30/04–20/05/40
Anson; Hampden
90 Sqn
11–14/09/39
15/05–30/08/41
Blenheim IV; Fortress I
98 Sqn
12/09–15/10/42
Mitchell II
101 Sqn
09/05/39–06/07/41
Blenheim I, IV; Wellington I
114 Sqn
06/07/41–13/11/42
Blenheim IV, V
139 Sqn
30/05–10/06/40
Blenheim IV
141 Sqn
04/12/43–03/07/45
Mosquito II, VI, XXX
180 Sqn
13/09–19/10/42
Mitchell II
239 Sqn
10/12/43–10/07/45
Mosquito II, VI, XXX; Beaufighter If
342 (French) Sqn
07/04–15/05/43
Boston IIIa
Opened in Bomber Command as parent station, 05/39

WESTCOTT, Bucks

LOCATION: 7m NW of Aylesbury
OPENED: 09/42
CLOSED: Currently in use by MOD
ELEVATION: 263ft
PUNDIT CODE: WX
FORMATIONS: 91 (OTU), 92 (OTU) Grp Bomber Command
MAIN CONTRACTOR: Various
RUNWAYS: 3 concrete
HANGARS: B1 (1), T2 (4)
USER SQNS/UNITS:
11 OTU
28/09/42–03/08/45
Wellington I III, X
Opened in Bomber Command as parent station, 09/42

WESTHAMPNETT, Sussex

LOCATION: 1½m NE of Chichester
OPENED: 07/40
CLOSED: 1946. Goodwood racing circuit/ Chichester Goodwood Airport (2011)
ELEVATION: 110ft
PUNDIT CODE: WQ
MAIN CONTRACTOR: Various
FORMATIONS: 11 Grp Fighter Command; 83 Grp 2 TAF
RUNWAYS: 3 grass
HANGARS: Blister (8), T1 (1)
USER SQNS/UNITS:
41 Sqn
16/12/41–01/04/42
21/06–04/10/43
28/06–03/07/44
Spitfire I, Vb, XII
65 Sqn
07/10–22/12/41
Spitfire IIb, Vb
91 Sqn
28/06–04/10/43
Spitfire XII
118 Sqn
15–24/08/43
29/08–25/09/44
Spitfire Vb, IXc
124 Sqn
29/10–07/11/42
09/08–25/09/44
Spitfire VI, HFIXe
129 Sqn
29/08–01/11/41
22/12/41–06/07/42
Spitfire IIa, Vb
130 Sqn
19–27/06/44
Spitfire Vb
131 Sqn
07/11/42–22/01/43
Spitfire Vb
145 Sqn
23/07–14/08/40
Hurricane I
167 Sqn
21/05–12/06/43
Spitfire Vb, Vc
174 Sqn
10/10/43–21/01/44
Typhoon Ib
175 Sqn
09/10/43–24/02/44
08/03–01/04/44
Typhoon Ib
184 Sqn
23/04–14/05/44

ABOVE: The wreckage of No 41 Squadron's Spitfire Mk XII, EN235, 'C', is examined by Luftwaffe personnel after it was shot down by Messerschmitt Bf109s on 18 July 1943 near Poix in northern France. Its pilot, Flg Off Bob Hogarth, was killed. (Author)

WESTHAMPNETT SPITFIRE DOWN

The clipped-wing Spitfire Mk XII was the first Rolls-Royce Griffon-engined version to enter service and was used primarily for home defence duties in the UK against tip-and-run Focke-Wulf Fw190s, although it was also used in the medium/low-level strike role in the Normandy area of France. Armed with two cannon and four 0.303in machine guns the Mk XII entered service early in 1943, but only two RAF fighter squadrons, Nos 41 and 91, were equipped with the version.

In the early evening of 18 July 1943, the Tangmere Wing (Nos 41 and 91 Squadrons) swept the Poix–Abbeville area as top cover for Typhoons of No 83 Group which were attacking the Luftwaffe fighter airfield at Abbeville. Some of the aircraft of No 41 Squadron were jumped by about 25 Messerschmitt Bf109s.

When Blue Section of No 41 Squadron was bounced, Flg Off Bob Hogarth in EN235 turned left into the enemy aircraft and in the ensuing combat he was shot down. His No 2 (Sgt J. Fisher) dived after him and got in two short bursts at a Bf109 but with little effect. Flying as Yellow 3, Flg Off Slack in EN233 was seen going down on the tail of a Bf109 but, unfortunately, he, too, was not seen again either.

The squadron diarist recorded: 'The squadron are very upset at the loss of Flg Off T.A. Slack and Flg Off R.H.W. Hogarth as they had been with the squadron a very long time and were two of our most experienced pilots – Slack with his lively wit and friendly nature was a great favourite with the pilots and ground crews; and Hogarth, with his shy but efficient manner, will be greatly missed.'

BELOW: Spitfire Mk XIIs of No 41 Squadron in starboard echelon in early 1944. The third aircraft from the camera, MB794, EB-H, failed to return from a beachhead patrol on D-Day +3, 9 June 1944. (Rolls-Royce)

ABOVE: These No 404 (Canadian) Squadron crews have just returned to Wick from a reconnaissance flight over the North Sea, and 'belly up' for tea and a wad from the Church of Scotland tea van. (Public Archives of Canada DND/UK PL19439)

20/05–17/06/44
Typhoon Ib

245 Sqn
10/10/43–01/04/44
Typhoon Ib

302 (Polish) Sqn
23/11/40–07/04/41
Hurricane I, IIa

303 (Polish) Sqn
19–27/06/44
09/08–25/09/44
Spitfire LFVB, IXc

340 (French) Sqn
07/04–20/07/42
26–28/07/42
Spitfire Vb

350 (Belgian) Sqn
03/07–08/08/44
Spitfire IX

402 (Canadian) Sqn
19–27/06/44
Spitfire Vb, Vc

416 (Canadian) Sqn
25/06–07/07/42
Spitfire Vb

441 (Canadian) Sqn
01–12/04/44
Spitfire IXb

442 (Canadian) Sqn
01–23/04/44
Spitfire IXb

443 (Canadian) Sqn
08–22/04/44
Spitfire IXb

485 (New Zealand) Sqn
02/01–21/05/43
Spitfire Vb

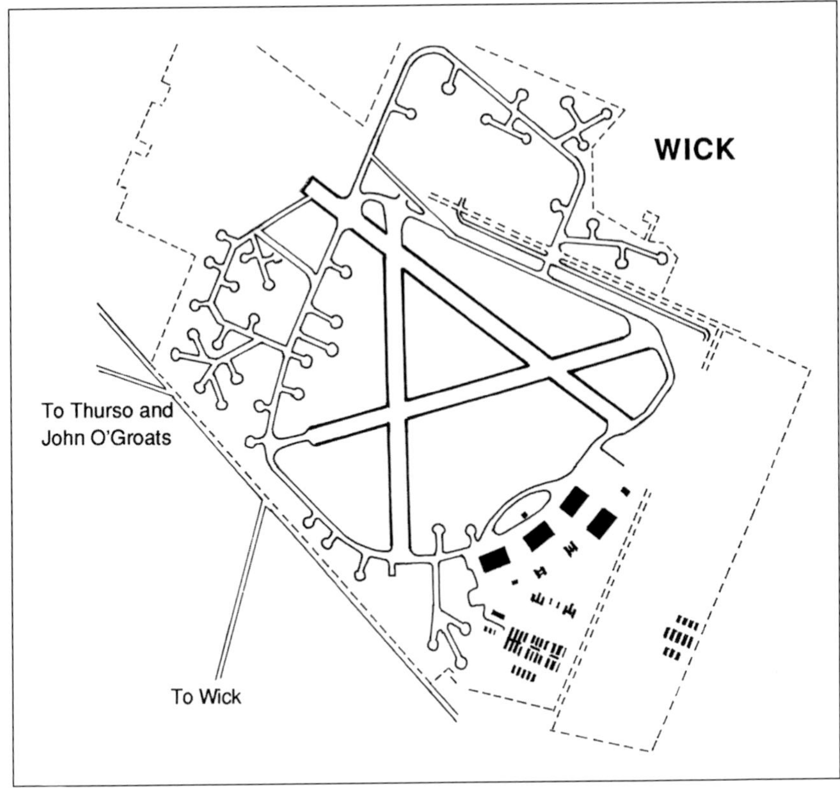

501 (AAF) Sqn
30/04–17/05/43
12–21/06/43
02/07–02/08/44
Spitfire Vb; Tempest V

602 (AAF) Sqn
13/08–17/12/40
Spitfire I

610 (AAF) Sqn
15/12/40–29/08/41
20/01–30/04/43
27/06–02/07/44
Spitfire I, IIa, Vb, XIV

676 Sqn
09/05–06/10/41
29/10/42–02/01/43
Spitfire IIa, Vb, VI

83 Grp Support Unit
04/11/44–22/02/45
Mustang; Spitfire

ELG in 11 Grp Fighter Command for Tangmere, 12/38
Upgraded to satellite to Tangmere, 07/40
To USAAF as Station AAF-352, 07/42
To 11 Grp RAF Fighter Command, 10/42
To Air Staff, SHAEF, 03/45

WESTON-ON-THE-GREEN, Oxon

LOCATION: 3½m SW of Bicester
OPENED: 07/18
CLOSED: RAF base (2011)
ELEVATION: 260ft
PUNDIT CODE: WG
FORMATIONS: 6 (T), 7 (T) Grp Bomber Command
MAIN CONTRACTOR: Various
RUNWAYS: 3 steel matting
HANGARS: Bessonneau (4), Blister (10), T2 (1)
USER SQNS/UNITS:

104 Sqn
09/39–04/40
Blenheim I, IV

108 Sqn
09/39–04/40
Blenheim I, IV

13 OTU
04–10/40
Blenheim I, IV

Used as Bomber Command satellite to Brize Norton, 09/39
Became satellite to Bicester, 10/40
To Flying Training Command, 11/40

WETHERSFIELD, Essex

LOCATION: 6m NNW of Braintree
OPENED: 01/44
CLOSED: 1993. HQ MOD Police (2011)
ELEVATION: 317ft
PUNDIT CODE: UW
FORMATION: 38 Grp Fighter Command
MAIN CONTRACTOR: Various
RUNWAYS: 3 concrete
HANGARS: T2 (2)
USER SQNS/UNITS:

196 Sqn
09/10/44–26/01/45
Stirling IV

299 Sqn
09/10/44–25/01/45
Stirling IV

Opened as USAAF Station AAF-170, 01/44
To 38 Grp RAF Fighter Command, 11/44
To USAAF as Station AAF-170, 03/45

WICK, Caithness

LOCATION: 1m N of Wick
OPENED: 09/39
CLOSED: 1978. Wick Airport (2011)
ELEVATION: 114ft
PUNDIT CODE: WC
MAIN CONTRACTOR: Various
FORMATIONS: 13 Grp Fighter Command; 18 Grp Coastal Command
RUNWAYS: 3 Tarmac
HANGARS: Bellman (2), C Type (4)
USER SQNS/UNITS:

3 Sqn
30/05–03/09/40
Hurricane I

41 Sqn
19–25/10/39
Spitfire I

42 Sqn
21/06/40–01/03/41
03/41–03/42 (det)
Beaufort I

43 Sqn
26/02–31/05/40
Hurricane I

48 Sqn
06/01–23/09/42
Hudson III, V

50 Sqn (det)
11–12/39
Hampden
61 Sqn (det)
11–12/39
Hampden
86 Sqn (det)
01–03/42
Beaufort I, II
111 Sqn
27/02–13/05/40
Hurricane I
144 Sqn
04/42–04/43 (det)
20/10/43–10/05/44
Hampden; Beaufighter VIc, X
220 Sqn
09/39–04/41 (det)
28/04–01/12/41
Hudson I, III, VI
269 Sqn
10/10/39–31/05/41
Hudson I
404 (Canadian) Sqn
20/04/43–08/05/44
Beaufighter X, XI
407 (Canadian) Sqn
24/08–11/11/44
Wellington XIV
489 (New Zealand) Sqn
24/09/42–06/10/43
Hampden I
504 (AAF) Sqn
22/05–21/06/40
Hurricane I
519 Sqn
07/08–10/12/43
28/11/44–17/08/45
Hampden; Hudson III, IIIa; Ventura V; Fortress II; Spitfire VI
605 (AAF) Sqn
28/02–21/05/40
Hurricane I
608 Sqn
02/01–29/07/42
Hudson III, V
612 (AAF) Sqn
01/04–15/12/41
23/09/42–18/04/43
Whitley V, VII; Wellington VIII, XIII
618 Sqn
04/43–07/44 (det)
09/07–21/08/44
Beaufighter II; Mosquito IV, VI, XVIII
803 NAS
09–11/39
Skua
1 PRU (det)
1940–41
Spitfire; Mosquito
1406 Met Flt > 519 Sqn
01/42 (15/08/43)
Hampden; Spitfire
Opened in Fighter Command as parent station, 09/39
Became Fighter Sector Station, 12/39
To Coastal Command, 10/40

WICKENBY, Lincs

LOCATION: 9½m NE of Lincoln
OPENED: 09/42
CLOSED: 1956. Agriculture/light aviation (2011)
ELEVATION: 86ft
PUNDIT CODE: UI
FORMATION: 1 Grp Bomber Command
MAIN CONTRACTOR: John Laing & Son Ltd
RUNWAYS: 3 concrete
HANGARS: B1 (1), T2 (2)
USER SQNS/UNITS:
12 Sqn
25/09/42–24/09/45
Wellington II, III; Lancaster I, III
626 Sqn
07/11/43–14/10/45
Lancaster I, III
Opened in Bomber Command as satellite to Ludford Magna, 09/42
Became 14 Base substation, 12/13

WIGSLEY, Notts

LOCATION: 7½m W of Lincoln
OPENED: 02/42
CLOSED: 07/58. Agriculture (2011)
ELEVATION: 23ft
PUNDIT CODE: UG
FORMATIONS: 5, 7 (HCU) Grp Bomber Command
MAIN CONTRACTOR: Sir Robert McAlpine & Sons Ltd
RUNWAYS: 3 concrete
HANGARS: B1 (1), T2 (2)
USER SQNS/UNITS:
455 (Australian) Sqn
08/02–28/04/42
Hampden
1654 HCU
15/06/42–08/45
Manchester; Halifax; Stirling; Lancaster
Opened in Bomber Command as satellite to Swinderby, 02/42
Became 75 Base substation, 11/44

WINFIELD, Berwickshire

LOCATION: 6m WSW of Berwick on Tweed
OPENED: 05/42
CLOSED: 05/45. Agriculture, private flying (2011)
ELEVATION: 170ft
PUNDIT CODE: IW
FORMATIONS: 9, 13, 81 (OTU) Grp Fighter Command
MAIN CONTRACTOR: James Miller & Partners Ltd
RUNWAYS: 2 Tarmac
HANGARS: Blister (4)
USER SQNS/UNITS:
222 Sqn
04–10/08/42
Spitfire Vb
54 OTU
01/05/42–31/10/45
Blenheim I, IV, V; Beaufort I; Beaufighter I, II, VI; Mosquito II, III, VI, XII, XIII, XVII, XIX, XXX; Wellington XVIII; Hurricane II
Opened in Fighter Command as satellite to Charter Hall, 05/42

WING, Bucks

LOCATION: 4m W of Leighton Buzzard
OPENED: 17/11/41
CLOSED: 04/60. Agriculture (2011)
ELEVATION: 450ft
PUNDIT CODE: UX
FORMATIONS: 7 (T), 92 (OTU) Grp Bomber Command

MAIN CONTRACTOR: Various
RUNWAYS: 3 concrete
HANGARS: B1 (1), T2 (4)
USER SQNS/UNITS:
26 OTU
15/01/42–04/03/46
Wellington I, III, X
Opened in Bomber Command as parent station, 17/11/41

WINKLEIGH, Devon

LOCATION: 9m N of Okehampton
OPENED: 01/43
CLOSED: 12/58. Agriculture/light industry (2011)
ELEVATION: 540ft
PUNDIT CODE: WK
FORMATION: 10 Grp Fighter Command
MAIN CONTRACTOR: Various
RUNWAYS: 2 concrete/Tarmac
HANGARS: Blister (8), T2 (1)
USER SQNS/UNITS:
406 (Canadian) Sqn
14/04–17/09/44
Beaufighter VIf; Mosquito XII, XXX
Opened in Fighter Command as a satellite to Exeter, 01/43
To USAAF as Station AAF-460, 10/43
To 10 Grp RAF Fighter Command, 04/44
To 23 Grp Flying Training Command, 11/44

WINKTON, Hants

LOCATION: 3m N of Christchurch
OPENED: 03/44
CLOSED: 01/45. Agriculture (2011)
ELEVATION: 40ft
PUNDIT CODE: XT
FORMATION: 11 Grp Fighter Command
MAIN CONTRACTOR: RAF 5005 ACS
RUNWAYS: 2 steel matting
HANGARS: Blister (4)
USER SQNS/UNITS:
Advanced Landing Ground (ALG) nominally under control of 11 Grp RAF Fighter Command
To USAAF as Station AAF-414, 04/44

WINTHORPE, Notts

LOCATION: 1½m NE of Newark-on-Trent
OPENED: 09/40
CLOSED: 07/59. Agricultural showground/Newark Air Museum/gliding (2011)
ELEVATION: 54ft
PUNDIT CODE: WE
FORMATIONS: 5, 7 (T) Grp Bomber Command
MAIN CONTRACTOR: Various
RUNWAYS: 3 concrete
HANGARS: B1 (1), T2 (2)
USER SQNS/UNITS:
1661 HCU
01/43–08/08/45
Manchester; Halifax: Stirling III; Lancaster I, III
Opened in Bomber Command as satellite to Swinderby, 09/40
Became satellite to Ossington, 11/41
Became satellite to Syerston, 02/42
Became 51 Base substation, 01/43
Became 75 Base substation, 11/44

WITCHFORD, Cambs

LOCATION: 2m SW of Ely
OPENED: 06/43
CLOSED: 03/46. Agriculture/industrial estate (2011)
ELEVATION: 47ft
PUNDIT CODE: EL
FORMATION: 3 Grp Bomber Command
MAIN CONTRACTOR: Various
RUNWAYS: 3 concrete
HANGARS: B1 (1), T2 (2)
USER SQNS/UNITS:
115 Sqn
26/11/43–28/09/45
Lancaster I, II, III
195 Sqn
01/10–13/11/44
Lancaster I, III
196 Sqn
19/07–18/11/43
Wellington X; Stirling III
513 Sqn
15/09–21/11/43
Stirling III
Opened in Bomber Command as 33 Base substation, 06/43

WITTERING, Northants

LOCATION: 3m SSE of Stamford
OPENED: 1916
CLOSED: RAF base, flying (2011)
ELEVATION: 250ft
PUNDIT CODE: WI
FORMATION: 12 Grp Fighter Command
MAIN CONTRACTOR: Various
RUNWAYS: 3 concrete
HANGARS: B1 (1), T2 (2)
USER SQNS/UNITS:
1 Sqn
09/09–15/12/40
Hurricane I
23 Sqn
16/05/38–31/05/40
16/08–12/09/40
Demon; Blenheim If
25 Sqn
27/12/40–16/01/42
Blenheim If; Beaufighter If; Havoc I
32 Sqn
26/05–04/06/40
Hurricane I
68 Sqn
08–27/02/45
Mosquito XXX
74 Sqn
14–21/08/40
Spitfire I
91 Sqn
09–21/05/43
Spitfire XII
118 Sqn
03–17/01/43
Spitfire Vb
141 Sqn
30/04–04/12/43
Beaufighter If, VIf; Mosquito II
151 Sqn
22/12/40–30/04/43
Defiant I, II; Hurricane IIc; Mosquito II
152 Sqn
30/09–10/11/42
Spitfire Vb
213 Sqn
18/05/38–09/06/40
Gauntlet II; Hurricane I
229 Sqn
26/06–09/09/40

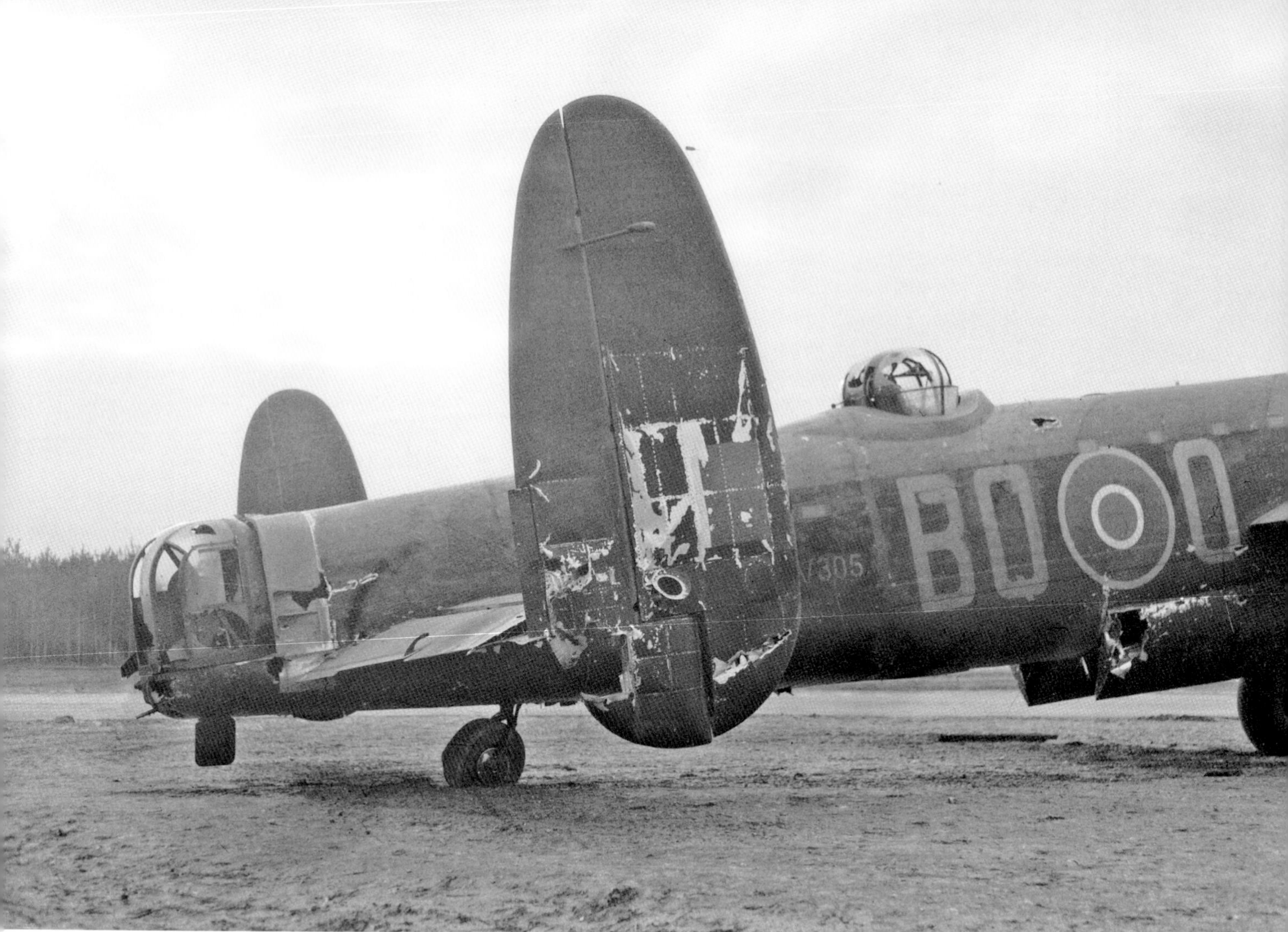

ABOVE: The rear section of Avro Lancaster Mk I, DV305, 'Q', of No 550 Squadron based at North Killingholme, Lincolnshire, is pictured at Woodbridge Emergency Landing Ground, Suffolk, after the severely damaged bomber crash-landed there following an attack by a German night fighter over Berlin on 30/31 January 1944. In the course of the attack both the rear and mid-upper gunners were killed, and the bomb-aimer baled out, having misunderstood orders. Without any navigation aids the pilot, Flg Off G.A. Morrison, managed to nurse the crippled Lanc back to a successful landing in England. (IWM CE121)

15–22/12/40
Hurricane I

266 Sqn
14/05–12/08/40
21/08/40–28/09/41
Spitfire I, IIa

349 (Belgian) Sqn
05–08/06/43
Spitfire Va

438 (Canadian) Sqn
19/12/43–10/01/44
Hurricane IV

486 (New Zealand) Sqn
09/04–27/09/42
Hurricane IIb; Typhoon Ib

1453 Flt > 532 Sqn
10/07/41 (02/09/42)–09/11/42
Havoc I (Turbinlite); Boston III; Boston III (Turbinlite)

610 (AAF) Sqn
10/10/39–04/04/40
Spitfire I

Fighter Interception Unit (FIU)
03/04–23/08/44
Beaufighter; Mosquito

To 12 Grp Fighter Command as Sector Station, 11/38

To 21 Grp Flying Training Command, 03/45

WOMBLETON, Yorks

LOCATION: 3m E of Helmsley
OPENED: 10/43
CLOSED: 1949. Agriculture (2011)
ELEVATION: 120ft
PUNDIT CODE: UN
FORMATIONS: 6 (T), 7 (T) Grp Bomber Command
MAIN CONTRACTOR: Various
RUNWAYS: 3 concrete
HANGARS: B1 (1), T2 (2)
USER SQNS/UNITS:

1666 HCU
21/10/43–03/08/45
Halifax II; Lancaster I, II, III

1679 HCU
13/12/43–27/01/44
Lancaster II

Opened in Bomber Command as 61 (RCAF) Training Base substation, 10/43

Became 76 (RCAF) Training Base substation, 11/44

WOODBRIDGE EMERGENCY LANDING GROUND

Between 15 November 1943 and 30 June 1945, 4,120 emergency landings had been made at Woodbridge. The following brief account, from official sources, is typical of the many dramatic incidents which were concluded at the airfield during the war years. It involves Lancaster ND763:W of 15 Squadron from nearby Mildenhall, skippered by Plt Off O. Brooks, RNZAF, which suffered extensive damage from heavy flak and a night fighter over Dusseldorf on 23/24 April 1944.

'The aircraft was hit by heavy flak and cannon shells from a night fighter as the bombs left the aircraft, causing fatal injuries to both the bomb-aimer, WO R. Gerrard, and the wireless operator, Flt Sgt Bob Barnes. Gerrard died within a few minutes and Barnes about half-an-hour before landing.

'The port inner engine was U/S, bomb doors failed to close, flaps, undercarriage, rear and mid-upper turrets were all U/S, as was also the elevator and rudder trim. Height was lost from 22,000ft over the target to 4,000ft over the enemy coast. A fire started in the rear of the aircraft and was extinguished by the mid-upper gunner, Sgt R. Wilson. Guns and other equipment were jettisoned to enable height to be maintained to reach the English coast, which was eventually crossed at 500ft. The navigator, Flt Sgt K. Pincott, acted as wireless operator, and Flt Lt J. Fabian DFC, the 'Y' Operator, rendered first aid to the injured men and assisted with the navigation.

'A crash-landing was effected at Woodbridge at 0355hrs.'

WOODBRIDGE, Suffolk

LOCATION: 11m ENE of Ipswich
OPENED: 15/11/43
CLOSED: 1993. Army base/MOD (2011)
ELEVATION: 70ft
PUNDIT CODE: OZ
FORMATION: 3 Grp Bomber Command
MAIN CONTRACTOR: Various
RUNWAYS: 1 bitumen/sand. 3,000yd x 250yd with undershoots and overshoots of 500yd each
HANGARS: Blister (1), B1 (1)
USER SQNS/UNITS:
None. FIDO-equipped Emergency Diversion Runway.

WOODCHURCH, Kent

LOCATION: 5m W of Ashford
OPENED: 07/43
CLOSED: 09/44. Agriculture (2011)
ELEVATION: 150ft
PUNDIT CODE: XO
MAIN CONTRACTOR: RAF 5003 ACS
FORMATION: 83 Grp 2 TAF
RUNWAYS: 2 steel matting
HANGARS: None
USER SQNS/UNITS:

231 Sqn
28/07–15/10/43
Mustang I

400 (Canadian) Sqn
28/07–15/10/43
Mustang I

2 TAF Advanced Landing Ground (ALG)
To USAAF as Station AAF-419, 04/44

WOODHALL SPA, Lincs

LOCATION: 6m SW of Horncastle
OPENED: 02/42
CLOSED: 1964. Agriculture/mineral extraction/RAF storage (2011)
ELEVATION: 45ft
PUNDIT CODE: WS
FORMATION: 5 Grp Bomber Command
MAIN CONTRACTOR: Various
RUNWAYS: 3 concrete
HANGARS: B1 (1), T2 (2)
USER SQNS/UNITS:

97 Sqn
02/03/42–18/04/43
Lancaster I, III

617 Sqn
10/01/44–17/06/45
Lancaster I, III

619 Sqn
18/04/43–09/01/44
Lancaster I, III

627 Sqn
15/04/44–30/09/45
Mosquito IV, XVI, XX, XXV

Opened in Bomber Command as satellite to Coningsby, 02/42
Became 54 Base substation, 08/43
*Wg Cdr G.L. Cheshire DSO DFC, 617 Sqn, awarded VC for numerous acts of courage on four tours of operations, 08/09/44

WOODVALE, Lancs

LOCATION: 12m NNW of Liverpool
OPENED: 12/41
CLOSED: RAF base (2011)
ELEVATION: 35ft
PUNDIT CODE: OD
MAIN CONTRACTOR: Various
FORMATIONS: 9, 12 Grp Fighter Command
RUNWAYS: 3 asphalt
HANGARS: Bellman (3), Blister (9)
USER SQNS/UNITS:

167 Sqn
12/06/43
(Disbanded, renumbered 322 (Dutch) Sqn)

195 Sqn
12/02–13/05/43
Typhoon Ib

198 Sqn
15/05–05/06/43
Typhoon Ia, Ib

ABOVE: Ground crew from No 1651 HCU strike a pose for the camera with one of their Lancasters as a backdrop, July 1944. (J. Hardman)

219 Sqn
27/02–15/03/44
Mosquito XVII
222 Sqn
30/12/43–14/02/44
Spitfire LFIXb
256 Sqn
01/06/42–24/04/43
25/08–25/09/43
Defiant II; Beaufighter If, VIf; Mosquito XII
308 (Polish) Sqn
12/12/41–01/04/42
Spitfire Vb, IIa
315 (Polish) Sqn
01/04–05/09/42
Spitfire Vb
316 (Polish) Sqn
15/02–28/04/44
Spitfire LFVb
317 (Polish) Sqn
05/09/42–13/02/43
Spitfire Vb
322 (Dutch) Sqn
12/06–15/11/43
30/11–31/12/43
Spitfire Vb
501 (AAF) Sqn
05–12/06/43
Spitfire Vb
Opened in Fighter Command as parent station, 12/41
To RN, 05/45

WOOLFOX LODGE, Rutland

LOCATION: 6m NW of Stamford
OPENED: 12/40
CLOSED: 01/66. Agriculture (2011)
ELEVATION: 344ft
PUNDIT CODE: WL
FORMATIONS: 3, 5, 7 (T) Grp Bomber Command
MAIN CONTRACTOR: John Mowlem
RUNWAYS: 3 Tarmac
HANGARS: B1 (1), T2 (4)
USER SQNS/UNITS:
61 Sqn
09/41–05/05/42
Manchester; Lancaster I, III
218 Sqn
07/03–04/08/44
Stirling III; Lancaster I, III
14 OTU
13/12/40–08/41
Hampden; Wellington
1429 (Czech) Operational Training Flight (OTF)
01/07–31/08/42
Wellington
1651 HCU
10/11/44–07/45
Lancaster I, III
1665 HCU
06/43–29/01/44
Stirling I, III
Opened in Bomber Command as RLG for Cottesmore, 12/40
Became satellite to North Luffenham, 10/41
Upgraded to parent station, 06/43
To USAAF, 09/44
To RAF as 73 Base substation, 10/44

WORKSOP, Notts

LOCATION: 4½m W of East Retford
OPENED: 11/43
CLOSED: 12/60. Agriculture (2011)
ELEVATION: 195ft
PUNDIT CODE: WP
FORMATION: 91 (OTU) Grp Bomber Command
MAIN CONTRACTOR: Wimpey & Carmichael
RUNWAYS: 3 concrete
HANGARS: T2 (2)
USER SQNS/UNITS:

18 OTU
11/11/43–01/45
Wellington III, X

Opened in Bomber Command as satellite to Finningley, 11/43

WRATTING COMMON, Cambs

LOCATION: 3¾m NNW of Haverhill
OPENED: 05/43
CLOSED: 04/46. Agriculture/light industry (2011)
ELEVATION: 390ft
PUNDIT CODE: WW
FORMATIONS: 3, 7 (T) Group Bomber Command
MAIN CONTRACTOR: Various
RUNWAYS: 3 concrete
HANGARS: B1 (1), T2 (4)
USER SQNS/UNITS:

90 Sqn
31/05–13/10/43
Stirling III; Lancaster I, III

195 Sqn
12/11/44–14/08/45
Lancaster I, III

1651 HCU
21/11/43–10/11/44
Stirling I, III

Opened in Bomber Command as 31 Base substation, West Wickham, 05/43
Renamed Wratting Common, 08/43

WREXHAM, Denbighshire

LOCATION: 9m SSW of Chester
OPENED: 06/41
CLOSED: 1945. Gravel extraction (2011)
ELEVATION: 220ft
PUNDIT CODE: RW
FORMATION: 9 Grp Fighter Command
MAIN CONTRACTOR: Sir Alfred McAlpine Ltd
RUNWAYS: 3 concrete
HANGARS: Bellman (1), Blister (11)
USER SQNS/UNITS:

96 Sqn
21/10/41–20/10/42
Defiant I, Ia, II; Beaufighter IIf, VIf

285 Sqn
01/12/41–29/10/42
Blenheim I; Hudson III; Lysander III; Oxford; Defiant I

577 Sqn (det)
01/12/43–15/06/46
Hurricane IIc, IV; Oxford; Beaufighter I; Spitfire Vb, XVI, Vengeance IV

595 Sqn (det)
01/12/43–27/04/46
Henley III; Hurricane IIc, IV; Martinet; Oxford; Vengeance IV; Spitfire Vb, IX, XII, XVI

57 OTU (det)
05/06/41–11/42
Spitfire

Opened in Fighter Command, 06/41
To 21 Grp Flying Training Command, 02/43

WYMESWOLD, Leics

LOCATION: 3¾m ENE of Loughborough
OPENED: 05/42
CLOSED: 1957. Industrial estate/motor sport (2011)
ELEVATION: 272ft
PUNDIT CODE: WD
FORMATIONS: 7 (T), 93 (OTU) Grp Bomber Command
MAIN CONTRACTOR: Various
RUNWAYS: 3 concrete
HANGARS: B1 (1), T2 (4)
USER SQNS/UNITS:

28 OTU
05/42–10/44
Wellington III, X; Lancaster; Halifax; Stirling

Opened in Bomber Command as satellite to Castle Donington, 05/42
To 44 Grp Transport Command, 15/10/44

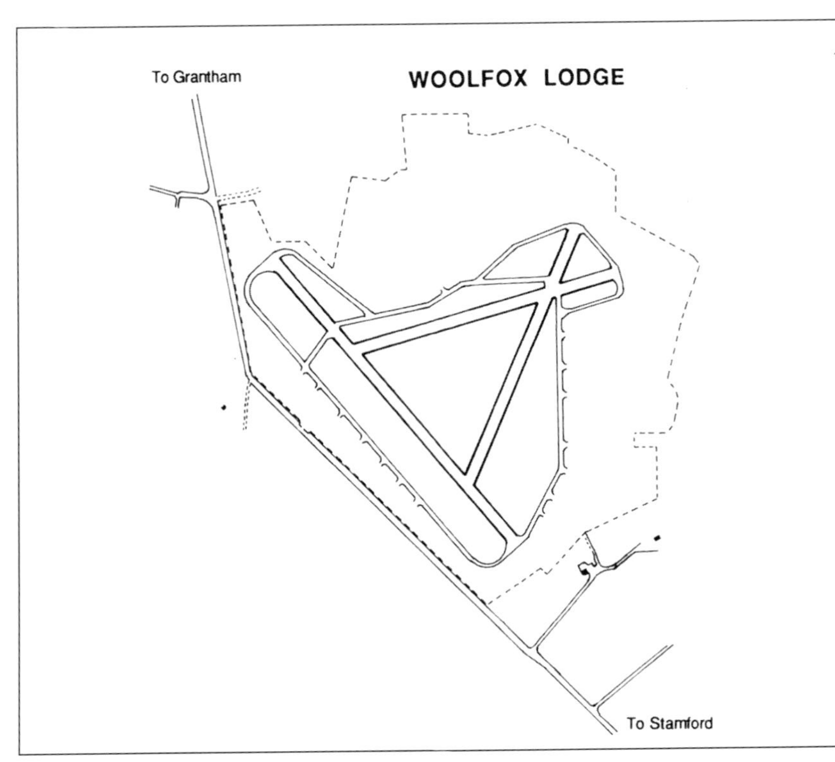

ABOVE: An aerial view of the Pathfinder airfield at Wyton. (Crown Copyright)

WYTON, Hunts
LOCATION: 3½m NE of Huntingdon
OPENED: 07/36
CLOSED: RAF base (2011)
ELEVATION: 132ft
PUNDIT CODE: WY
FORMATIONS: 2, 3, 8 (PFF) Grp Bomber Command
MAIN CONTRACTOR: Various
RUNWAYS: 3 concrete
HANGARS: C Type (4)
USER SQNS/UNITS:
15 Sqn
10/12/39–14/04/40
15/05/40–13/08/42
Battle; Blenheim IV; Wellington I; Stirling I
40 Sqn
03/12/39–02/02/41
Battle; Blenheim IV; Wellington I
57 Sqn
22–29/05
11–23/06
06–20/11/40
Blenheim IV; Wellington I
83 Sqn
15/08/42–18/04/44
Lancaster I, III
109 (PFF) Sqn
06/08/42–04/07/43
Lancaster I; Mosquito IV, IX
114 Sqn
01/12/36–09/12/39
Hind; Audax; Blenheim I, IV
128 Sqn (LNSF)
15/09/44–05/45
Mosquito XVI
139 Sqn
03/09/36–01/12/39
Hind; Blenheim I
163 Sqn (LNSF)
25/01–19/08/45
Mosquito XVI, XXV
1409 Met Rec Flt
01/44–05/45
Mosquito
Opened in Bomber Command as parent station, 07/36

ABOVE: 'Watch Office for Night Fighter Stations 15684/41.' The watchtower on the former fighter base at Zeals in south Wiltshire has had a chequered history since the end of the war, having lain derelict for many years and then used as a hay barn. It has now been converted into a private home. (Author)

ZEALS, Wilts
LOCATION: 4m NNW of Gillingham
OPENED: 05/42
CLOSED: 01/46. Agriculture (2011)
ELEVATION: 550ft
PUNDIT CODE: ZL
FORMATION: 10 Grp Fighter Command
MAIN CONTRACTOR: Various
RUNWAYS: 3 grass
HANGARS: Blister (8), T1 (1)
USER SQNS/UNITS:
66 Sqn
24/08–26/09/42
29/09–08/10/42
09/10–01/11/42
14/11–23/12/42
Spitfire Vb, Vc
118 Sqn
24/08–23/12/42
Spitfire Vb
132 Sqn
28/02–05/04/43
Spitfire Vb
174 Sqn
12/03–05/04/43
Hurricane IIb
184 Sqn
12/03–05/04/43
Hurricane IId
263 Sqn
19/06–12/07/43
Whirlwind I
410 (Canadian) Sqn
18/06–28/07/44
Mosquito XIII
421 Sqn
01–14/11/42
Spitfire Vb
488 (New Zealand) Sqn
12/05–29/07/44
Mosquito XIII
604 (AAF) Sqn
25–28/07/44
Mosquito XIII
Opened in Fighter Command as Forward Operating Airfield, 05/42
To USAAF as Station AAF-450, 08/43
To 10 Grp RAF Fighter Command, 04/44
To FAA as HMS *Humming Bird*, 04/45

RAF AIRFIELDS – THE HUMAN DIMENSION

'Laughter, sorrow, hope and pain,
I shall never know these things again.
Emotions that I came to know
Of strange young men so long ago.'

From *Old Airfield* by W. Scott, ex-630 Squadron

The personal accounts that follow give insights into the human dimension of the RAF airfield story in World War 2. All those fighters and bombers, all those miles of concrete runways and clusters of hangars were only of use if they had people to use them. These stories range from firsthand eyewitness testimony to tales of individuals and events, based upon a wide range of archive sources. They include accounts by and about air and ground crews, from all three frontline wartime commands of the RAF.

LEFT: RAF Mount Batten, Plymouth, 28 November 1942. Flt Lt Graham Pockley DFC and Bar poses for a final photograph with his No 10 (RAAF) Squadron crew and their Sunderland, W3983, 'R', before returning to Australia. From top, left to right: LAC E.W. Lee; Sgt J.A. Macdonald; LAC F. Kerrison; Sgt J.H. Leach; LAC R.K. Scott DFM; Captain, Flt Lt G. Pockley DFC and Bar; A/Sgt H.D. Gerke; Flg Off M.K. McKenzie; Flg Off H.L. Swan; Flg Off K.G. Fry; LAC J.F. Cureton. All from this crew were to survive the war, except for Pockley (missing in action, 25 February 1945), Flt Lt Keith McKenzie (pilot, missing over the Bay of Biscay, shot down by a Ju88 of V/KG40, 17 May 1943) and Flt Lt Kenneth Fry, MID (pilot, missing, shot down by a U-boat, 1 August 1943). (Australian War Memorial AWM SUK10858A)

1: WAR OVER THE WEST

By late September 1940 the balance of power in the skies over the British Isles had at last begun to tip in favour of the hard-pressed pilots of RAF Fighter Command. Since early July the mounting fury of Luftwaffe attacks had pushed the endurance of the RAF's men and machines to their uttermost limits. Desperate duels fought high in the often cloudless summer skies of southern England were watched with awe and trepidation by those far below on the ground. West of the main conflict being fought over southeastern England, the counties in the southwest witnessed their fair share of dogfights, too. The aircraft factories of Westland's at Yeovil and the Bristol Aeroplane Co at Filton were significant targets, as were the docks at Avonmouth and across the Bristol Channel in South Wales. Furthermore, many stray German raiders limping south and homewards to bases in France after bombing targets in the Midlands and northwest England, damaged and with dead and injured on board, often fell to the guns of pursuing RAF fighters before they reached the south coast.

In order to beef up the air defences west of Southampton, the grass airfield of Warmwell near Dorchester in Dorset was transferred to No 10 Group Fighter Command in June 1940 as a Forward Airfield in the Middle Wallop 'Y' Sector. On 12 July No 152 Squadron and its Spitfires were posted in from Acklington, Northumberland, with the prime role of defending the naval base at Portland.

They were joined in their task by the Spitfires of No 609 Squadron from nearby Middle Wallop which were detached to Warmwell on a daily basis for operations.

ABOVE: This informal photograph of Kenneth Holland with feline friend was probably taken at the Cornwall home of his guardian, Major Hugh Ripley, in Camelford. (Author)

One of No 152 Squadron's Spitfire pilots was a 20-year-old Australian named Kenneth Holland from the Sydney beachside suburb of Bondi. During the 1920s and 30s Bondi had become the centre of Australia's fast-growing surf life-saving movement and in 1935 Kenneth became a part of it, joining the Tamarama Surf Life Saving Club as a junior. Later that year he travelled to England with Major Hugh Ripley, with whom he lived as a ward on his farm at Camelford on the north Cornwall coast. Kenneth enrolled on a three-year engineering course at the Airspeed Aeronautical College in Portsmouth, where he was given the nickname 'Dutchy' by his friends. During term time his guardian would occasionally make the journey to Portsmouth where he would take Kenneth and his friends out for lunch at the Royal Beach Hotel. Kenneth returned to Sydney for several months in late 1937 and rejoined the surf club, gaining his Bronze Medallion in Surf Life Saving. He never completed his course at Airspeed because on 12 July 1939 he joined the RAFVR and learned to fly with No 11 Elementary & Reserve Flying Training School at Perth in Scotland. Kenneth gained his wings in April 1940 and after further training at 6 FTS Little Rissington and 5 OTU Aston Down, in Gloucestershire, he joined No 152 Squadron at Warmwell on 18 August. It was a baptism of fire because soon afterwards he was flying operational sorties in defence of the West Country.

Kenneth's lamentably short career as an RAF fighter pilot is related below and, sadly, it is typical of several hundred other young RAF pilots who died in the service of their mother country in the high summer of 1940.

The following events, which cover 10 days in September 1940 – the height of the Battle of Britain – have been transcribed from Kenneth Holland's combat reports. The action of 25 September in which he met his death has been pieced together from a number of sources, details of which can be found in the Bibliography at the end of this book. Comments in square brackets are explanatory notes added by the author.

Sunday 15 September

'Six aircraft of B Flight on patrol sighted 30 He111s [Heinkel He111] at 15.40hrs, 7 miles SW of Portland at 15,000ft proceeding to the NW. E/A [enemy aircraft] turned to the SE after attacking Portland. Green Section's three aircraft attacked a straggler from the enemy formation. Green 1 [Plt Off P. O'Brien] made an astern attack, concentrating his fire on the starboard engine. It [E/A] broke away left and down. Green 3 [Sgt K.C. Holland] attacked with a 5 second burst from astern and above and black smoke poured from the starboard engine and E/A began to lose height. Green 2 [Plt Off Weston] attacked E/A... [the rest of the report is missing].'

B Flight claimed one He111 destroyed and one probable. The aircraft were possibly of Kampfgruppe 55 (KG55) based at Chartres.

Tuesday 17 September

'I was Blue 2 when Ju88 [Junkers Ju88] was sighted. I followed Blue 1 into attack from the starboard beam giving a burst of 2 seconds from 250–200yd. I continued to attack from varying positions and later chased E/A through clouds. E/A was taking evasive action by doing steep turns, diving, side-slipping and throttling back when attacked. I saw engines of E/A had stopped but lost sight of it in thick cloud. After circling round looking for it above cloud, my engine was becoming hot so I landed at Yatesbury [Wiltshire]. My A/C [aircraft] was hit by m/g [machine-gun] fire in 3 places. Rounds fired – 1,650 (very approx).'

Sgt Holland had delivered his attack against a Junkers Ju88A-1, Werke Nummer (Wk Nr) 3188 L1+XC of Stab II/LG1, at 17,000ft over the town of Shepton Mallet in Somerset. The Ju88 had been on an operation from its French base at Orléans/Bricy to bomb factories at Speke near Liverpool when it was attacked by Holland at 1.50pm. Ten minutes later it crash-landed 20 miles to the east at Ladywell Barn near Warminster, in the neighbouring county of Wiltshire. From its crew of four, one man was killed in the action and three captured, one of whom was Major Cramer, the Gruppe Kommandeur of LG1.

ABOVE: No 152 Squadron pilots and ground staff at Warmwell in August 1940. To emphasise just how desperate the fight for survival was in the summer of 1940, nine of the 20 pilots in this group were dead within two months of the picture being taken. Back row: ground crew; middle row, left to right, are: Sgt H.J. Akroyd (K 08/10/40), Sgt E. Shepperd (KIFA 18/10/40), Plt Off Richard Hogg (MIA 25/08/40), Intelligence Officer, Plt Off Ian Bayles, Plt Off A. Weston, Plt Off W. Beaumont (MIA 23/09/40), Plt Off C. Warren, Plt Off Eric Marrs (MIA 24/07/41), Plt Off F. Holmes, Sgt John Barker (KIA 04/09/40), Sgt L. Reddington (MIA 30/09/40); front row, left to right, are: Sgt Jack McBean Christie (KIA 26/09/40), Plt Off T. Wildblood (MIA 25/08/40), Adjutant, Flg Off Peter O'Brien, Flt Lt Derek Boitel-Gill (KIFA 08/41), Sqn Ldr Peter Devitt (CO), Flt Lt F. Thomas, Flg Off E. Hogg, Engineer Officer, Plt Off G. Cox, Sgt Ken Holland (KIA 25/09/40); The Hon Plt Off Pooch. (Alan White)

In the engagement Holland's Spitfire suffered damage to its hydraulic, glycol and oil systems, and a punctured starboard tyre. He claimed one-third of the Ju88 destroyed shared with Plt Offs Eric Marrs and Peter O'Brien of B Flight's Blue Section.

Thursday 19 September

'I was Green 2 ordered to patrol cloud base. R/T [radio telephone] of Green 1 was U/S [unserviceable] so I became Green 1. I was ordered to 15,000ft over Warmwell and was then vectored to Ju88. As there was cloud at 10,000ft, Green 2 went below the cloud and I went above the cloud at 11,500ft. When cloud broke I went down to given height and sighted Ju88 ahead on the right two miles away. Green 2 was left behind below cloud. I gave tally-ho, but Green 2 could not find me. I made alternate quarter attacks from left and right from 300 to 200yd, firing one burst of 4 seconds and five each of 2 seconds, aiming first at gunners' positions and then at each engine. E/A took slight evasive action heading for cloud on a southerly course. White returned fire after my second attack. I continued to attack and eventually the E/A, now at 8,000ft, dived vertically towards the sea with both engines on fire. As my ammunition was finished, I flew on a northerly course and came to the Isle of Wight. My engine was missing slightly so I made for Portsmouth aerodrome where I landed and after checking engine returned to base. Rounds fired – 2,800.'

This ground-controlled interception and engagement took place at 10,000ft over the English Channel at 4.20pm and involved a Junkers Ju88A-1, possibly of 1/KG51 or 3/KG51. Sgt Holland claimed this Ju88 as destroyed.

Wednesday 25 September

Shortly after 10.00am on the morning of Wednesday 25 September, 12 Spitfires of No 152 Squadron were patrolling the south coast area near Portland when they were directed by radar controllers at nearby Worth Matravers to intercept a large formation of He111s apparently making for Yeovil. No 10 Group HQ at Box, Wiltshire, had ordered a total of three fighter squadrons (Nos 152, 238 and 609) to the area but the bombers, which had crossed the coast at Chesil Beach, passed well to the east of Yeovil and headed for the Bristol Aeroplane & Engine Co works at Filton, north of Bristol. The force of 57 He111s of I, II and III Staffels of KG55, based in northern France at Dreux, Chartres and Villacoublay respectively, to the south and west of Paris, protected by a strong screen of Messerschmitt Bf110C-4 heavy fighters of Zerstörergeschwader 26 (ZG26) from Arques near Dieppe, proceeded to drop their deadly cargo of over 100 tons of bombs on the factories, causing 238 casualties among the workers. Having wrought havoc over the defenceless works with little interruption, the German raiders swung to the south and headed for home.

Sgt Kenneth Holland was flying at 20,000ft as Blue 2 with B Flight of No 152 Squadron led by the squadron's CO, Sqn Ldr Peter Devitt (Blue 1). Although Holland was flying almost four miles high, the cramped cockpit of his Spitfire was sweltering and filled with the din from the 12-cylinder Rolls-Royce Merlin engine running at full power just a few feet in front of him. The sound of his breath rasped into the microphone of his oxygen mask. Through the mushy crackle in his headphones came the matter-of-fact voice of the CO: '100-plus bandits below

RIGHT: High over Bath on 25 September, Plt Off Dudley Williams, Green Section leader, started the attack on Hauptmann Hellmuth Brandt's Heinkel He111P of 6 Staffel Kampfgruppe 55 (6./KG55) that would cause it to crash minutes later at Woolverton in Somerset. (Alan White)

FAR RIGHT: Fellow Australian Plt Off Ian Bayles joined Sgt Kenneth Holland and closed in for the kill on Brandt's disabled Heinkel. (Alan White)

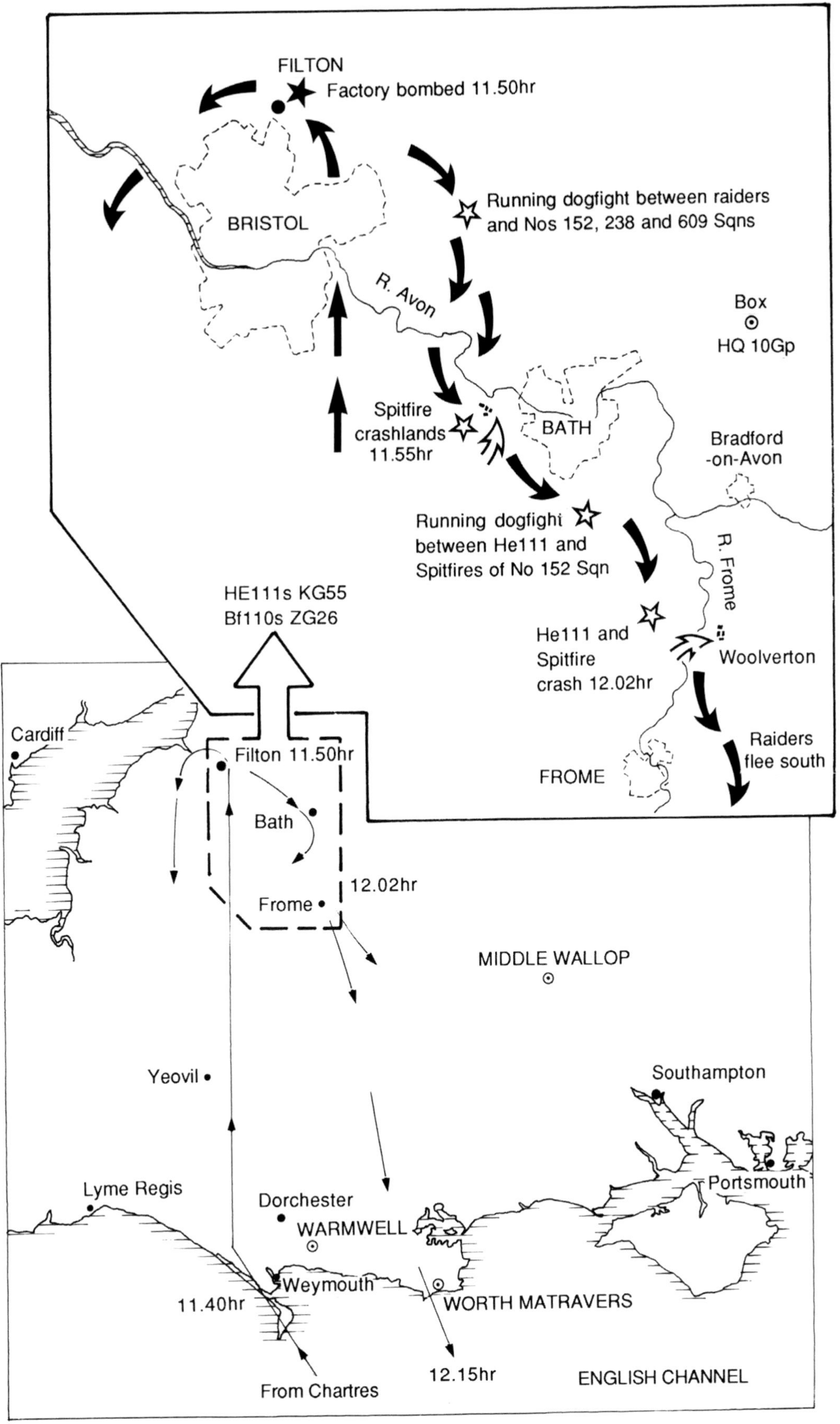

The action of 25 September 1940.

ABOVE: The shattered wreckage of Brandt's Heinkel He111P, G1+EP, lies spread over a field near Church Farm at Woolverton. (Alan White)

and to starboard. Let's go and sort them out. Tally-ho!' High over the winding River Avon and flying towards Bath, but some 5,000ft below them, the force of German fighters and bombers droned its way south.

One by one the squadron peeled off and dived towards the fleeing bombers. Blue 1 closed in fast on the port stern quarter of a vic of three He111s. With the safety catch off and the target in his sights he thumbed the fire button: bullets and tracer tore into one of the bombers. Devitt closed to 20yd but he was unable to observe the results of his attack when escaping petrol from his fuel tank, punctured by return fire from the He111, temporarily blinded him. Uninjured, he managed to force-land his Spitfire at Newton St Loe on the western outskirts of Bath at 11.55am.

Meanwhile, several thousand feet below over Bath, Plt Off Dudley Williams, leader of Green Section, jockeyed for position to attack an He111P, Wk Nr 1525, G1+EP, of II/KG55, which he had singled out for attention. This aircraft, based at Chartres, was flown by Hauptmann Helmut Brandt, Staffelkapitän of 6/KG55 (ie: 6th Staffel, or squadron, in the IInd Gruppe). Before being forced to break off his attack to help deal with the escorting Bf110s of ZG26, Williams succeeded in scoring hits in the engines of Brandt's Heinkel. He saw it drop out of formation and sideslip down and away with wisps of smoke trailing from its engines.

The action drifted south towards Frome, leaving the city of Bath beneath a fast-fading swirl of contrails in the sky. Brandt's disabled Heinkel was losing precious height and any chance he may have had of making it safely across the Channel to a crash-landing in France was by this stage very slim. Minutes later his hopes were completely dashed as four RAF fighters wheeled in to attack from out of the sun. The Spitfires of Sgt Kenneth Holland and Plt Off Ian Bayles (Black 1), along with two Hurricanes of No 238 Squadron from Middle Wallop, flown by Plt Off J. Urwin-Mann and Sgt R. Little, closed in for the kill.

Holland approached the Heinkel at great speed and overshot, banking into a tight turn before opening fire from about 400yd astern and slightly to port, raking it with the full force of his eight 0.303in Browning machine guns. Bullets smashed into the Heinkel's glazed cockpit, shattering the controls and injuring Brandt in the head, left eye, and all but severing the little finger of his right hand. Struggling along at 2,000ft the bomber rapidly lost height and Brandt, bleeding badly from his head wounds, decided to circle and search for somewhere to put his stricken aircraft down.

In the meantime, Holland had turned quickly and aligned his Spitfire on the Heinkel's tail for a second attack. However, Brandt's gunner, Gefreiter Rudolf Beck, had not been silenced in the first attack and was able to get in a well-aimed burst at close range with his 7.9mm machine gun. The bullets struck home with fatal results: Holland's Spitfire appeared to stop in mid-air before its nose swiftly dropped and the aircraft headed down towards the fields below at Church Farm, Woolverton, four miles north of Frome. Hauptman Brandt and two of his crew of four baled out of their wrecked aircraft, leaving it to crash and explode in an adjoining field at 12.02pm, some 400yd beyond where Holland's Spitfire had come down.

Brandt survived the ordeal but two of his crewmen who jumped too low were killed when their parachutes failed to

LEFT: Brandt's radio operator, Oberfeldwebel Rudi Kirchoff, from Brunswick, died in the crash. After the war the city of Bath was twinned with the German city of Brunswick. (Alan White)

ABOVE: At 12.10pm on 25 September, He111H, G1+BH, of 1./KG55, flown by Feldwebel Fritz Jürges, force-landed on Westfield Farm at Ballard Down, near Swanage, Dorset. It had been attacked by fighters of Nos 152, 238 and 609 Squadrons in a running fight after bombing Filton. Four of its crew of five survived the ordeal to become PoWs. The white bull on the fuselage side is the insignia of 1./KG55. (Alan White)

deploy in time. They were Oberfeldwebel Günter Wittkamp the observer, and Unteroffizier Hans Mertz, flight engineer. Both the radio operator Oberfeldwebel Rudi Kirchoff and the gunner Gefreiter Rudolf Beck, failed to get out of the aircraft and died in the ensuing inferno. Sgt Holland did not survive either – he was found dead by villagers in the cockpit of his Spitfire.

An eyewitness account by Tom Newman, who was in his teens at the time of the event, describes how Holland's Spitfire had crashed in a small field, coming to rest a few yards from the field wall, where it tipped on its nose with one wheel crumpled beneath it. It is likely Holland was semi-conscious for a short while after being hit because another eyewitness described how the Spitfire's undercarriage had been lowered and it looked as if Holland was going to follow the Heinkel down to the fields and land nearby. A single bullet – leaving a hole in the Spitfire's cockpit canopy, which was noted by several eyewitnesses after the crash – must have hit Holland in the head, with fatal results; he succumbed to his severe head injury after landing his aircraft in the field. The Heinkel had disintegrated when it hit the ground and lay in pieces all over the ploughed field.

As if to reinforce the notion that the past is in the present and forever with us, by a strange coincidence the author came across the dark-green cloth flying helmet belonging to Wittkamp the observer, and the Morse key reputedly from the Heinkel, in a bric-a-brac shop in the Somerset town of Glastonbury in September 1992. Inside the helmet, written in ink on one of the ear pieces, was the inscription 'Oberfw G.Wittkamp. 6.KG55'. On the outside, the thin metal covers to the ear pieces were dented and the paint chipped; the result of Wittkamp's fatal fall? The owner of the shop declared that both items had been salvaged in 1940 after the crash by the farmer, Mr Matthews, on whose land the Heinkel had come down. A few months before the author's visit, the farmer's family had passed them on to someone else who, in turn, had sold them to the bric-a-brac shop. Sadly, the price being asked for the helmet and Morse key together prevented their purchase by the author.

LEFT: A memorial stone was erected in the field where Kenneth Holland's Spitfire crashed, near to Church Farm. It was later moved to the edge of the field but was finally rescued and re-sited next to the village war memorial beside the A36 road, where it can be seen to this day. (Author)

2: THE EARLY DAYS

Sgt Jim Bowler was a Wellington pilot with No 99 Squadron, flying from Newmarket in Suffolk during the late summer and autumn of 1940. The 20-year-old from Coalville in Leicestershire was an avid letter writer to his fiancée, Frances, and the following excerpts are taken from the numerous letters he wrote her during his three-month period of duty with the squadron. It is interesting to note how free he is with details of the operations he flew. Despite the invasion fever that was sweeping the land in the summer of 1940, and a paranoia that Fifth Columnists were lurking at every street corner, there is no evidence of the censor having tampered with these letters.

On the night of 24/25 November 1940 when Jim Bowler went missing on a raid to Kiel, his crew were first pilot Flt Sgt Frank Swatton, MID, RAF, from Collyweston, Northants (27); observer Plt Off Robert Marsden, RAFVR; air gunner Sgt Raymond Powell, RAF, from Wolverhampton (19); front gunner and second wireless operator Sgt William 'Ginger' Dick, RAFVR, from Glasgow (23); and rear gunner Sgt Alistair MacNab, RAFVR (28).

ABOVE: When he was flying as a second pilot with No 99 Squadron from Newmarket, Sgt Jim Bowler failed to return from a raid on Kiel on the night of 25/26 November 1940. His Wellington ID, R1176, 'B', was shot down into the North Atlantic by flak. Jim and all his crew were lost without trace and are commemorated on the Runnymede Memorial. (Mrs F. Davies)

Tuesday 24 September 1940

'This is just more or less to tell you of a major flying episode! No doubt you have heard on the wireless today about the biggest raid of the war upon Berlin last night. We were there, dropping 500lb bombs and a six-hour delayed one, at one o'clock this morning; we left at 9.30pm last night and landed at 5 o'clock this morning to the accompaniment of German bombs dropping round the aerodrome! So while you were asleep (presumably) darling, we were trekking 1,200 miles or more to Berlin and back. We're now working fine as a crew, we five pals and Frank. Ted the navigator took us dead on to Berlin over cloud, and Jake the wireless operator, he's only nineteen, gets us home just like a veteran on radio. I'm hoping to become captain after about five more trips, it all depends on the report Frank gives of me to the CO when he is due for his rest.

'We bombed Berlin from 13,000ft. There were flares from other kites all over the place, scores of them on the job, and coming out we were chased by two fighters, but managed to keep them off and get rid of them. The temperature was minus 10 degrees and I was thankful for my Irvin-suit – fur-lined jacket and trousers (£24 a-time).

'You'll guess I'm pretty tired after only 3 hours' sleep, but I'm dossing down early tonight and everyone has all day off tomorrow. I asked if I could go home tonight for a day but it was impossible, worst luck, and I'll just have to wait for ordinary leave.'

Monday 30 September

'On Saturday night we went to Hanau, near Frankfurt in the Ruhr, to bomb a munitions factory. The trip was about 900 miles. We were up from 10.30pm to 4.30am Sunday, and landed in semi-fog. I was almost too tired to eat my meal when we landed! Next trip you will be crossing off the teens, darling, and before you know it you'll be off double figures on to singles. We aren't operating so often just at present, there's no moon out.

'We may be billeted out in big houses in the town before long we flying crews, although I'd rather be where I am for the winter.

'Frank had to make a press statement about our trip to Hanau, and though I didn't hear it I'm told it was given out on the wireless. He seems to think we're pretty good for a fairly new crew throughout, particularly as both Mac and Ginger the gunners never make a murmur when ack-ack is bursting all round us. Jake, our 19-year-old wireless operator, makes us really proud of him; he gets courses home and whatever we ask him for, like a veteran; and all the way out he listens in to German transmitters and checks up on our

ABOVE: Sgt Jim Bowler and his crew pictured during training at No 20 OTU, Lossiemouth, July–September 1940. Left to right: Sgt 'Ginger' Dick, front gunner and second wireless op; Sgt Alistair 'Mac' MacNab, rear gunner; Sgt Jake Linton, first wireless op; Sgt John Pascoe, first pilot; Sgt Jim Bowler, second pilot; Sgt J.E. 'Mac' Mackinley, observer. (Mrs F.M. Davies)

position. Ted (I may as well mention everyone) navigates us fine and bombs well, so we're happy all round. We were fired at all the way to Hanau and back, especially over Cologne coming back, so I had plenty of practice jinking. That was Frank's 23rd trip. He wants to stay on operations instead of going to an OTU, thinks it's an easier life!

'PS: I realised an ambition last Friday, to fly a Wimpy [Wellington] as only pilot on board. I went to Mildenhall to fetch our new aeroplane "B" for Berty, on my own. I flew back with 12 passengers on board: 4 officers and 8 airmen. Felt like an airliner pilot! Bragger!!'

Tuesday 8 October

'We went to Berlin again on Friday, took 7¾hrs, and to Boulogne last night, back by 10.00pm for a change! At Berlin we had a very hot reception, they let us drop our bombs in the city then caught us in the searchlights and sent up everything they had all the way across the city. Next morning there were about 15 holes in the machine and we took a distinctly dim view of Berlin hospitality, you can bet. Last night it was filthy weather for the take-off, an hour and a half late, and we were the only crew on the squadron who went through to our target and dropped our bombs. (Don't think I'm not bragging, because I am!)'

Thursday 31 October

'Just after I had scribbled Tuesday's note to you we had quite an exciting "welcome home to Newmarket". We were up at the house when some "Flying Pencils" [Dorniers] made a daylight attack on the aerodrome so we naturally dashed out to watch the fun and games. When we saw the German machine gunners firing tracer bullets all over the show, and heard them falling on the road, we started sheltering against a wall, dashing from one side to the other like idiots! We were down by it when one of them dropped a big stick of bombs quite close to us, so we promptly raced across a bone yard and some fields to see if we could be of any help, but luckily no-one was hurt, though two houses had very close shaves. One of the bombs fell about 20yds from that little stone bridge we used to go to, in the middle of the road! Some of their bombs hit the aerodrome and one of the bombs made an enormous crater smack in the middle of the race course in front of the grandstand!

'There was racing here yesterday on the other course, so we went across to watch and saw Gordon Richards win the Cesarewitch. He's a jockey, not a horse, if you've never heard of him, and he wasn't doing the running himself either (that's beaten you to it!)

'It's a queer game, the horses dash around a track miles away and all you see of them is when they come up for the finish past the stands. Mad, I call it! You should hear the bookmakers shouting one another down with the odds they're offering, just like Coalville market! (Break – wardens are bawling outside about our blackout.)'

Sunday 10 November

'This afternoon is a break in what has seemed like two days of rushing around getting "B" for Berty fit again after an inspection over at Mildenhall. We should have operated tonight, but apparently the weather is going to be bad and everyone has the afternoon and night off. It's very cold now and raining hard, so I'm pretty pleased we aren't going.

'Yesterday we had a little minor excitement after hearing Jerry overhead during the afternoon. He started dropping bombs by guess-work through the clouds, and they were quite near too, so we all bolted down the air-raid shelters for half-an-hour. He must have been scared to come down below the clouds. When the squadron operated last Friday night they were after the beer cellar at Munich where Hitler was supposed to be having a big pow-wow. Fletcher and his crew didn't come back, but don't worry, they only ran out of petrol and went down in the sea near Hastings. Coastal Command have picked them all up safe and sound; we're expecting to see them tomorrow.*

'Hope my last letter didn't make you feel dismal, darling, I don't know what was biting me when I wrote it, I'm sure. I love you just as much as ever, but sometimes this war makes everything seem so unreal compared with peacetime days, with hardly ever seeing you at all, and when all I have to represent you are letters. I suppose when it's all over I shall be able to settle my mind properly once more and my life will revolve around you, instead of round you and aeroplanes and bombs as it is doing at the moment. May the time soon come when I shall have something better to do in life than destroy things, though I don't mind in the least destroying what we are fighting against.

'I think I told you that now there are only Mac, Ginger and me left of the original No 2 crew from Lossiemouth. All

BELOW: In the early hours of 14 November 1940, No 99 Squadron's Wellington IC, R3167, 'B', skippered by Sgt Frank Swatton with Sgt Jim Bowler as second pilot, crashed onto houses at Hampton Court, Middlesex, after it became lost returning from Berlin in bad weather and ran out of fuel. (Mrs F.M. Davies)

Sgt Fletcher and crew, No 99 Squadron, ditched Wellington I, N2727, off Fairlight, Sussex. The aircraft was lost, broken up by the tides.

ABOVE: After baling out over West London in the dark and in a snowstorm on 13 November 1940, Sgt 'Ginger' Dick, Jim Bowler's second wireless op, landed in a tree at Hounslow Barracks where he hung for two hours before he was rescued. (Mrs F.M. Davies)

ABOVE: Sgt Alistair MacNab, rear gunner (pictured), and Jim Bowler visited the scene of 'B for Berty's' crash at Hampton Court the morning afterwards. Fortunately there were no civilian deaths, but two houses were destroyed and the aircraft was written off. (Mrs F.M. Davies)

being well, John, Ted and Jake will be by the Mediterranean sea before the week is out. Our new navigator seems like a good lad but I'm not very keen on the wireless operator. He may be OK but if he isn't we'll soon have him swapped.'

Thursday 14 November

'"B" for Berty has not yet been over your place and the one you flew in never will either! Last night we went to Berlin again for the third time. All was fine going out and on the target but coming back we ran into snow and had to fly blind. However, we found our coast OK and set course for home, still in snow and then we ran into a lot of static electricity which made the front guns and propellers glow blue and look weird and threw all the instruments haywire, finally burning the wireless set use. And we got completely lost, but eventually came to what seemed a very big place and looked round low, hoping to see an aerodrome. To cut a long story short, we were on our last drop of petrol and all had to do the wisest thing possible, leave the machine by parachute.

'I was in the seat at the time and wanted Frank to go out first, but as captain he naturally insisted upon being last, and persuaded me to go first to set an example to the others. We all went through the bottom door by which you entered, and went out at 3,000ft into the snow clouds, and gosh what a queer sensation it was. This was at 1.10am this morning, after 8½hrs in the air. I just dived through and got clear of the machine, pulled the rip-cord and in a second or two got a terrific jolt, then was swinging down in dead silence through snow. I didn't see the ground until about 200ft up, and a few seconds later landed on my back with a terrific bang, seeing stars, and the next thing I knew I was being dragged across the field I landed in at about 20mph, helpless to stop myself. Finally, the silk hit a hedge and I just shot forward head first into it! Then I detached the silk, was violently sick (shame!) and staggered into someone's back garden where I could get no answer to my knocks.

'Sorry darling, but I just can't carry on tonight. I feel ill and pretty well all-in. I'll carry on tomorrow.'

Friday 15 November

'Well, I feel a lot better now after a normal night's sleep. To continue the narrative, I staggered on a little further,

ABOVE: **Sgt Raymond Powell, RAF, air gunner (19).** (Mrs F.M. Davies)

ABOVE: **Sgt Frank Swatton, RAF, pilot.** (Mrs F.M. Davies)

knocked at another house and stood waiting in the snow, listening to a dog barking inside. Then a quavering female voice asked who was there. I told her and that I felt very ill and was in a shocking state, but she didn't trust me and wouldn't let me in, so I thanked her for her hospitality and staggered further on to a pill box at the side of the road where there were soldiers. After making sure who I was, they phoned the commanding officer at Heston aerodrome half-a-mile away and he fetched me in his car and put me to bed at the aerodrome in his pyjamas.

'So, we were in London! He was a fine fellow and took everything out of my hands and within half-an-hour I knew all the others were safe, though we were spread over 10 miles. "B" for Berty had hit a house in Hampton Court and was burnt out. Two people in the house had a miraculous escape and Mac and I went to see the wreck and ruins yesterday morning.

'I've never been so pleased in my life as I was when I knew everyone was safe. Mac landed on the edge of a gravel pit full of water at Hounslow and just missed drowning; Frank landed in a garden near the house; our new wireless op landed in a road; our new navigator landed on the hospital he's in, walked off the roof and sprained his ankle! But we got the biggest laugh over Ginger: he landed in a tree in Hounslow military barracks, and hung there for two hours in the snow! He bawled out for help, a soldier thought he was a Jerry and called out the guard. First they fetched a ladder which was too short, then another too short, and next thing Ginger heard was the Fire Brigade clanging its bell; and finally they got him down a fire escape and he spent the night in the hospital there.

'We got back here last night in two staff cars sent down for us, and in the morning we're fetching a brand new "B" for Berty over and I hope she lasts a long time. I'm OK now apart from bruises and stiff neck and shoulders.

'PS: I'm not in the slightest superstitious, but it's interesting to know it was my 13th operation, on the 13th of the month!'

Tuesday 19 November

'I suppose this will sound rather a tame letter after the last! Hope you were thrilled because I can assure you that I was when it all happened. We've been interviewed by quite a few of the "big boys" of the RAF, but none of them condemned what we did, they were all delighted to know we were all safe and didn't care a toss what had happened to the machine. You should see the new "B" for Berty which we have now: the other was a Ic, but this one is the very latest, a Mk Id with two extra guns just in case they're needed. We should have operated in her tonight, but the wireless isn't quite ready so our trip was scrubbed.

'You may like to tell your confederates about this. When the squadron last went to Munich, one of the crews took with them an umbrella with the words "You wouldn't listen to reason, you b.....s, now listen to these!" painted on it. Hope they translated it and I bet that would make them say "Ach" a few times!

'Our crew are now all members of the "Caterpillar Club". There are no membership privileges: membership means that you have saved your life by parachute. We shall all have a little solid gold caterpillar brooch with our names on from the Irvin Parachute Co. The idea of a caterpillar comes from the silkworm caterpillar "whose life hangs by a silken thread", as they put it.'

Sunday 24 November

'We took the new Berty on his/her maiden operation on Friday night and should have gone to a place in Germany on the Rhine, but Mac had some trouble with the rear gun turret just after take-off so rather than go through enemy fighter zones we went down to Ostend and bombed the docks there. Our substitute navigator was a young pilot officer on his first trip, about 6ft 7in tall, but he did some wizard bomb-aiming and we started some glorious fires with our incendiaries. When this navigator moved past me to do his bombing I saw his head go past, looked down about two minutes later and saw his legs just moving after him! S'true!

'As a contrast to the previous trip, there was not a cloud between the earth and the moon, beyond that I can't vouch for, and everything went perfectly. Hardly half a dozen shots were fired at us, not many searchlights were out, and the moon lit up the target like daytime. I said we went on Friday night, actually we took off at 3.00am Saturday morning and landed at 6.00am.

'Frank has been selected to represent the squadron by his looks and has got to sit for an oil painting for the Air Ministry. You should hear what he has to say about it. Quite a good choice, I think, don't you?

'I'm going to write a letter to the parachute firm after this to get our little gold caterpillars I told you about. Ginger seems to be dying to get his, he really is an excitable sort of lad.

'Our navigator who was hurt has returned today. He's hopping about with a stick and has one foot and ankle in Plaster of Paris. He seemed pretty shaken, too, by his experience. He told me he was sick as a dog all over his navigation table after I had told him to put on his parachute and take off his flying helmet. Poor little blighter, no doubt he will be going on a long leave. I almost wish I had broken a leg!! Some dirty "souvenir hunters" at the hospital in which he has been have stolen half his clothes, all his money, his watch, and his flying boots.

'Well, darling, once this month is over and that won't be long, it will soon come round to Christmas. It would be marvellous if it happened, but I'm afraid it's not even worth hoping I shall be at home for it. That glorious week we had together here might have happened a year ago, so long does it seem since I last saw you. However, it should be our ordinary turn soon, and on that reassuring note I think I may as well close down for tonight. Cheerio, dearest, write as often and as much as you can.

Your ever adoring, Jim. XXXXXXXXXXXX

On the following evening, Jim Bowler and his crew failed to return from a raid on Kiel in Wellington R1176, 'B', shot down into the North Sea by flak. Their bodies were never found.

3: SUMMER IN PARIS

'I shall never forget the astonishment of the crowds in the Paris streets, especially as we flew low over the Champs Elysées. The SS men on duty outside the old Admiralty Building were taken by surprise, and when our machine guns were fired, quickly vanished. What seemed to annoy the Hun more than anything we learned later, was the fact that they had planned a parade to take place a few minutes after . . . but the whole ceremony was abandoned because of the confusion we created!'

These words were penned in 1949 by Wg Cdr Ken Gatward, DSO, DFC and Bar, seven years after he flew one of the most daring missions of the war – dropping a French Tricolour on the Arc de Triomphe in central Paris on 12 June 1942 from his low-flying Bristol Beaufighter. His feat made headline news around the world.

In the spring of 1942, SOE agents in Paris had informed their London spy masters that German troops were known to parade every day down the most famous thoroughfare in the French capital, the Avenue des Champs Élysées, between 12.15 and 12.45pm. The Air Ministry was contacted and a hit-and-run spectacular was planned to coincide with the parade, its twin objectives being to boost French morale and create a public relations coup for the Allies.

Coastal Command's Commander-in-Chief, Air Chief Marshal Sir Philip Joubert de la Ferté, called the 28-year-old Beaufighter pilot from No 236 Squadron, Flt Lt Ken Gatward, into his office and asked him if he would volunteer for an 'unsafe' op. Gatward, a skilled and experienced pilot, accepted the challenge without actually knowing the task and so, too, did his navigator, Sgt George Fern.

Their brief was to fly at low level down the 1¼-mile length of the Champs- de la Ferté lysées, strafe the Nazi parade, and if that failed, attack the Gestapo HQ in the former Ministère de la Marine in the Place de la Concorde, at the eastern end of the Avenue.

Owing to the hazardous nature of the operation, cloud cover was needed for the Beaufighter crew's safety over certain parts of the route. Gatward had made three previous attempts at the operation in early June, but he had been forced to abandon each sortie through lack of cloud cover in France. But on 12 June the weather conditions were right. At 11.31am Gatward and Fern took off in Beaufighter Mk IC, T4800, 'C', from RAF Thorney Island on the edge of Chichester Harbour. They climbed away over the English Channel and in thick cloud and pouring rain set course for France. By the time the Beaufighter had crossed the coast near Fécamp at 11.58am the cloud had thinned and the rain had stopped. Forty miles on at Rouen the French countryside was bathed in sunlight.

ABOVE: Wg Cdr Ken Gatward in the cockpit of his Beaufighter TF Mk X, when he was CO of No 404 (Canadian) Squadron at Davidstow Moor in 1944. (IWM MH7660)

Flying at rooftop height, Gatward and Fern ran the risk of hitting high tension cables or suffering a bird strike, both of which could prove fatal to their aircraft. A surprised crow slammed into the Beaufighter's oil cooler radiator beneath an engine, causing the oil temperature to increase and the gauge in the cockpit to read erratically. But still Gatward and Fern pressed on.

In the by-now cloudless sky visibility was between 10 and 20 miles as the Beaufighter thundered low over the suburbs of Paris. For the first time some light flak was encountered.

At 12.27pm the pair spotted the Eiffel Tower sticking up out of the cityscape, which they circled. Gatward banked the aircraft to port and headed towards the Champs-Élysées. To his surprise there was no sign of the military parade. The usually reliable intelligence source had got the time wrong and the Beaufighter had arrived over central Paris a couple of minutes too early. This was no place to hang around at low level in broad daylight so

Gatward flew a circuit of the tower of the Église Saint-Augustin de Paris and then dropped a Tricolour over the Arc de Triomphe, after which he flew down along the Champs-Élysées at third-floor window level, but there was still no sign of any troops.

'I'll never forget the astonishment of the crowd in the Paris streets as we swept low at rooftop level. They had been taken completely by surprise,' he was to recall later. Parisians in the streets watched the British aircraft flying low across the centre of their city and many waved and cheered.

With the Ministère de la Marine building in the Place de la Concorde close by, Gatward flew south over the River Seine and returned to rake the Gestapo HQ with 20mm cannon shells. The gunfire terrified the SS troops who, much to Gatward's amusement, were seen running for their lives. Sgt Fern dropped a second Tricolour.

The Beaufighter cleared the roof of the Gestapo building before Gatward banked around and turned for home at 12.30pm, chased by coloured tracer fire. He retraced the track he had flown inward bound less than an hour earlier and crossed over the French coast for the second time, at 12.55pm. The windscreen of the aircraft was plastered with dead flies, which made visibility difficult, but luckily it began to rain as the Beaufighter headed out across the Channel, which cleared the mess.

The oil cooler radiator had held up in spite of its bird strike, and Gatward and Fern made a successful landing at RAF Northolt at 1.53pm.

Gatward had flown the entire sortie to Paris and back at the incredibly low height of between 20 and 30ft. Even though he had crossed over Rouen aerodrome at rooftop level he encountered no enemy opposition and the light flak over Paris had caused him no bother.

The mission was quite rightly milked by the Air Ministry for its publicity value and the amazing photographs taken during the sortie by Fern, some of which were released to the press.

For their skill and daring Ken Gatward was awarded an immediate DFC and his navigator George Fern was granted a commission. Both men survived the war. Grp Capt Alfred Kitchener 'Ken' Gatward, DSO, DFC and Bar, died at Colchester, Essex, on 19 November 1998 aged 84.

BELOW: Ken Gatward and George Fern flew their daring daylight mission to Paris on 12 June 1942 in this Beaufighter Mk IC, T4800, 'C', of No 236 Squadron. Taking off from Thorney Island, they flew at low level to Paris where they dropped a French Tricolour on the Arc de Triomphe and then attacked the Gestapo Headquarters in the Ministère de la Marine with cannon fire. (IWM C2733)

ABOVE: George Fern was busy with his camera recording their feat as the Beaufighter flashed over the rooftops of central Paris. In this photograph the Arc de Triomphe and the dome of the Église Saint-Augustin can be seen. (Author)

RIGHT: This wartime artist's impression shows the Beaufighter over Paris just as Fern drops the Tricolour onto the Arc de Triomphe. (Author)

ABOVE: Ken Gatward went on to command No 404 (Canadian) Squadron, leading many coastal sweeps and anti-shipping strikes. These photographs are three of a series taken on 14 August 1944 when the squadron had returned from an armed recce to the Gironde estuary. Here, Flg Off 'Red' McGrath, Flg Off Herb Hallett, Flg Off A.S. French and Wg Cdr Ken Gatward (jn the background, wiping his eye) are about to be debriefed by the squadron intelligence staff. (Public Archives of Canada PL-41054)

RIGHT: Gatward, his battledress stained with hydraulic fluid, wipes his smarting eyes. Returning from the shipping strike to the Gironde, Gatward's Beaufighter TF Mk X, NE800, was badly shot up attacking a German Sperrbrecher. He and his navigator, Flg Off 'Red' McGrath, had to jam the escape axe between the instrument panel and the control column to keep the aircraft from diving into the sea. Gatward was soaked by escaping hydraulic fluid, which splashed into his eyes and covered his clothing. Three hours later in the small hours they landed back at Davidstow, but Gatward had to be driven to debriefing because his eyesight had become impaired by the irritant effect of the hydraulic fluid. This was his last operational flight with 404. For his actions in leading the attack and bringing back his severely damaged aircraft he was awarded the Bar to his DFC. (Public Archives of Canada PL-41044)

BELOW: Gatward's navigator, Flg Off 'Red' McGrath, looks at the useless starboard aileron of their Beaufighter. (Public Archives of Canada PL-41042)

4: CHARMY DOWN – A DECAYING LEGACY

During World War 2, RAF Charmy Down was a busy satellite airfield to nearby RAF Colerne in Fighter Command's No 10 Group. Although Colerne has survived into the 21st century as a military base, albeit under the control of the Army, Charmy Down has fared less well.

Perched high on a hill to the north of the city of Bath, the former night fighter airfield is now derelict, its runways torn up and hangars torn down. The windowless watchtower and a clutch of ancillary buildings are all that remain, mute testimonies to the great things once achieved by the airfield, its men and machines.

BELOW: In this oblique aerial view, RAF Charmy Down near Bath in Somerset, can be seen from the south-south-west. Part of the village of Upper Swainswick can be seen at bottom centre. Charmy Down airfield was built in 1940 and opened in November of that year as a satellite of Colerne, across St Catherine's Valley. It was used in the defence of Bristol and Bath. No 87 Squadron with its night fighter Hawker Hurricanes (pictured on 20 June 1941) was based here from November 1940 until August 1941, and again from January to November 1942. A number of RAF and RCAF fighter squadrons spent their 'working-up' periods at the station between 1941 and 1943, before the Fighter Leaders' School arrived in February 1943. Fighter Command eventually relinquished Charmy Down in August 1943 when the airfield was transferred to the USAAF. (IWM HU93042)

LEFT: Ground crew re-arm the 20mm cannon of this night fighter Hurricane Mk IIC, BE500, of No 87 Squadron on a dispersal at Charmy Down in 1942. (RAF Museum)

BELOW: At more than 680ft above sea level, Charmy Down is virtually invisible from the busy A46 trunk road below, successfully concealing from prying eyes what little remains from its historic past. (Author)

ABOVE: On the northwest corner of the airfield stands the derelict brick watchtower (Watch Office for Night Fighter Stations, Type FCW 4514). For a short period after the war it was used as a private dwelling. During the late 1990s it was occupied for several years by so-called 'new age travellers', who did serious damage to the structure. (Author)

LEFT: Glassless windows in the empty ground floor of the watchtower gaze out towards long-gone runways. (Author)

ABOVE: Personnel in the watchtower could use this shelter in the event of an enemy air-raid. (Author)

ABOVE: These buildings on the domestic site are used today by a farmer for agricultural storage and as cattle barns. (Author)

LEFT: Most of the perimeter track is extant but is pitted and much reduced in width from its wartime days. (Author)

TOP RIGHT: A short stretch of a wartime runway remains in use today as a landing strip for light aircraft that operate from a small corner of the airfield. (Author)

BOTTOM RIGHT: The design and construction of the Decontamination Centre building was a highly specialised affair, where personnel who became casualties of a gas attack could receive first aid treatment and be decontaminated. (Author)

TOP LEFT: Charmy Down was built with a series of blast-proof twin-bay aircraft dispersal pens. (Author)

BOTTOM LEFT: Poking through the ground vegetation, these iron picket brackets are anchored into the concrete floors of the dispersal pens and were used for tying down aircraft. (Author)

ABOVE: This brick and concrete rest shelter behind a dispersal pen was used by air and ground crews when they were on standby. (Author)

5: POCKLEY THE U-BOAT MAGNET

'Sinking an armed German launch off the French coast, an attack on a U-boat in the Bay of Biscay, damaging of a 6,000-ton German supply ship, and two heavy attacks on Italian submarines, are the highlights of Flt Lt H. Graham Pockley's six months as captain of a Sunderland flying boat in Britain.' These effusive opening lines headed a report in the *Brisbane Courier-Mail* on 25 September 1942 about an Australian hero.

Coastal Command pilot Graham Pockley, DFC & Bar, from Sydney, was nicknamed 'the U-boat magnet' because submarines always seemed to come his way. In fact part of the Bay of Biscay was even named after him – unofficially. In No 10 (RAAF) Squadron's operations room at RAF Mount Batten in Plymouth his fellow pilots pencilled the words 'Pockley's Corner' on the wall-map, declaring this part of the Bay as 'out of bounds' for anyone else!

After the war, historians who wrote the RAAF's official account of the air war (in Australia and the War of 1939–1945) damned Pockley with faint praise: 'Pockley was overestimated by some of his contemporaries and under-estimated by others. His engagements were magnified in popular accounts until he assumed the status of "the U-boat magnet", while some of his fellows, perhaps influenced by his self-conscious itch for action, dismissed him as being lucky. Although not in all respects a great pilot, he was an outstanding captain of aircraft. He studied, and made his crew study, every aspect of the existing tactical and technical situation, and had one of the best-trained crews at that time serving in Coastal Command.'

Harold Graham Pockley was born on 5 February 1913 in Graceville, Queensland, and grew up in New Zealand and in the Randwick area of Sydney, Australia, where he attended Shore Grammar School. Making model aircraft was a childhood interest and before the war he learnt to fly full size aircraft at the Mascot Aero Club in New South Wales. His future wife, Joyce Price, used to go flying with him.

Pockley was an outdoors man and jackarooed in the Riverina for a time on his father's property, before trying his luck as a Ford salesman in Sydney. He took his 'A' flying licence in 1939 and was studying for his commercial pilot's licence when the first shots of World War 2 were fired in September 1939.

Pockley was caught up in the war fever after Britain declared war on Germany on 3 September 1939. He enlisted in the RAAF on 8 January 1940 and trained as a pilot, graduating from his course on 4 May with a distinguished pass and was commissioned into the RAAF.

ABOVE: Sqn Ldr Graham Pockley, DFC and Bar, RAAF – the 'U-boat magnet'. (Author)

He married Joyce on 13 July and embarked for overseas service on 27 December.

On 1 March 1941 Pockley reported to No 10 (RAAF) Squadron at Oban in Western Scotland where three weeks later he began his operational flying as a second pilot on Sunderland flying boats. He quickly made a name for himself as a courageous and capable pilot and became a crew captain the following year. Pockley recounted to the press one of his first combats as commander of a Sunderland:

'Dive-bombing the flak-ship in the Bay of Biscay was one of my most exciting encounters,' he said. 'Luckily for us, although it was an anti-aircraft ship – and I've never seen so much stuff hurled at any plane – not one hit was registered on my aircraft.

'They used multiple tracer pom-poms, a funny sort of ammunition. Looking down one could see dozens of trains of coloured objects, looking for all the world like strings of sausages, floating slowly up from the ship. They didn't travel so slowly when they got near to us.

'The boys in my crew marked their hits by painting swastikas or the Italian ensign on the side of our aircraft. In all our operations not one of my crew got even a scratch. But there were some miraculous escapes, like shrapnel knocking goggles off their helmets.'

On 28 May 1942 Pockley and his crew took part in a protracted attack on a fully surfaced Italian submarine in the Mediterranean. Pockley dived the Sunderland to attack, but was forced to take evasive action in the face of intense fire from the submarine, which turned sharply away to port but showed no intention of diving.

He made a second approach, his gunners hosing the submarine with machine-gun fire and then banked the Sunderland quickly to drop his depth-charges. Frustratingly, only four fell because the bomb circuit for the port bomb rack failed. The submarine made a sudden turn to port and the partial stick of depth-charges overshot.

While circling the still-surfaced enemy, Pockley instructed his crew to transfer the remaining depth-charges to the starboard rack. 'LAC Bob Scott of Melbourne, my armourer, did a wizard job transferring those bombs as we flew low to keep the submarine in sight. The submarine was a big fellow and he was throwing up flak all the time. We had over a hundred holes in the fuselage when we got back home.'

Pockley pursued the submarine for two hours while Scott toiled to transfer the bombs to the starboard side. When the armourer reported that everything was ready Pockley attempted to position the Sunderland for an attack, but the submarine zig-zagged to try and spoil the aim of the flying boat. From 2,000ft Pockley pushed the control yoke forward and dived steeply from dead astern in order to minimise the effect of any avoiding action. The submarine's helmsman again heeled the boat to port, but the Sunderland's depth-charges found their mark and straddled the vessel.

After the giant plumes of spray from the explosions had died away, the submarine could be seen holding an erratic course at greatly reduced speed. The depth-charges had ripped a large gash in its bow casing, and inflicted further damage to the decking forward of the conning tower.

'This attack took five and a half hours,' said Pockley. 'It was a long struggle. At times I had to dive so low over it, trying to dodge the sub's fire, that my keel just cleared the conning tower. They hit my Sunderland with a shell just before this, and apparently thought that I was going to crash right into the submarine. We could see them diving over the side to escape.'

The submarine's engines had stopped and she lay lifeless on the surface. Pockley and his crew then saw a great wave wash over the sub's deck casing, sweeping most of her crew

BELOW: Sunderland Mk II, W3983, 'R', was piloted on many occasions by Graham Pockley. Here the 'boat is about to be hauled out of the water and up the slipway at Pembroke Dock on 3 October 1941. (IWM CH16531)

ABOVE: The Italian submarine *Reginaldo Giuliani* under machine-gun attack in the Bay of Biscay from a Sunderland of No 10 (RAAF) Squadron, possibly that of Pockley, on 1 September 1942. Three Sunderlands were involved in the action but were ordered to continue their anti-shipping patrol before a concerted attack could take place. The submarine, which was sailing from Bordeaux for the Far East, was attacked on the following day by a Wellington of No 304 (Polish) Squadron and was forced to put into Santander, Spain, having sustained severe damage and a number of casualties. (IWM C3333)

into the sea. The Sunderland circled the crippled submarine until a Hudson arrived from Gibraltar to make a further attack. Pockley was credited with damage to this submarine, the first positive damage assessment achieved by No 10 (RAAF) Squadron in fifteen months.

Pockley was the first to acknowledge the contribution to his success made by his ground crew at Oban and later at Mount Batten. 'The squadron has certainly taken part in some great shows, but much of the credit must go to the maintenance personnel. They are the most wonderful blokes. Their mechanical skill is quite miraculous. They knock off when the job is finished, and not before. They are proud to keep the Sunderlands flying and what they do in days other men take weeks to do. There's no doubt that the record number of flying hours achieved by No 10 Squadron is due to the work of the maintenance boys,' said Pockley in a wartime press interview.

Another of Pockley's feats was when he and his crew played a part in the rescue of Plt Off Stan Sisney, RAAF – who at that time was wicket keeper for the Australian cricket team – when Sisney's No 202 Squadron Catalina (skippered by Flt Lt Bradley, RCAF, of which he was the second pilot) was shot down by Vichy French fighters off Algiers on 18 May 1942. Vichy Dewoitine fighters attacked

ABOVE: Sunderland Mk III, W4004, 'Z', of No 10 (RAAF) Squadron, Mount Batten, pictured in early 1942. This is the aircraft in which Flt Lt Keith McKenzie and his 12-man crew were shot down over the Bay of Biscay by a Ju88C-6 of KG40. (Andy Thomas)

Sisney's machine, which caused Bradley to make a forced landing on the sea.

Flt Lt Reginald Powell (also of No 202 Squadron, later Sqn Ldr, DFC and Bar) recalled: 'When attacked, Bradley flew close to the water. The French fighters came in on the beam firing into the sea and raising their sights when the splashes were right. Thus both pilots were hit but little else. Bradley had a cannon shell burst in his guts, but managed to put the Catalina down safely before he collapsed. Sisney had several bullets through his neck.'

Pockley, who was patrolling off Gibraltar, answered Bradley's SOS. 'I intercepted their SOS, got the direction, and re-transmitted the SOS and position to a destroyer while I flew on ahead.' He drove off the Vichy fighters and brought the destroyer HMS *Ithuriel* to the scene to rescue the Catalina's crew. (During Operation 'Pedestal' in the summer of 1942, HMS *Ithuriel* rammed and sank the Italian submarine *Cobalto* on 12 August.)

'When it [the destroyer] arrived seven fighters with French markings came over and started attacking it. So I climbed up to draw their attack on to me. We kept them busy while the destroyer got the men safely off their wrecked flying boat,' he recalled.

Bradley was picked up by Powell's Catalina and flown to hospital in Gibraltar. Both he and Sisney survived their ordeal.

On 1 September 1942, three Sunderlands – W3983 'R' and W3986 'U' of No 10 (RAAF) Squadron, and another of No 461 (RAAF) Squadron, armed not with depth-charges but with semi-armour-piercing bombs, were sent out on shipping strike duties. Flt Lt S.R.C. Wood DFC in 'U' spotted a surfaced Italian submarine, the 'Liuzzi' class *Reginaldo Giuliani*, commanded by Capitano di Corvette Vittore Raccanelli. He attacked from 400ft but his four bombs, although falling close to the submarine, failed to inflict any damage as they were fused to detonate only with a direct hit.

Pockley in 'R' made similar attacks from 1500ft with two bombs. His Sunderland met intense return fire from the Italian vessels and twice made diving attacks to silence the enemy gunners. He brought his flying boat in for a second attack with one bomb, which exploded astern of the submarine, but 'R' suffered flak damage from the boat's gunners.

Flt Lt B.L. Buls in the No 461 (RAAF) Squadron Sunderland, 'A', (killed in action on 21 January 1943) had joined the other two flying boats while they were circling, but just as they were about to launch a co-ordinated attack they were all ordered by Base to resume their original duty. A fourth Sunderland armed with depth-charges was sent to hunt this submarine but was unable to find it. The *Reginaldo Giuliani* came off badly from its encounter and suffered casualties amongst its crew. Its commander, Capitano di Corvette Vittore Raccanelli, was killed.

No further sightings came until 9 September, when Pockley and his crew intercepted a German U-boat through cloud on their ASV radar. Sighting it visually they climbed back into cloud to gain a better attacking position. When they broke cloud for the second time, the U-boat was fully surfaced 1 ½ miles ahead of the Sunderland which, at 400ft, was in a perfect position to achieve full surprise.

Pockley now made an important judgement call. Noticing there were men on the bridge and deck casing of the U-boat he estimated that it could not crash-dive immediately. In RAF circles at this time there were conflicting theories about the lethal effect of 250lb depth-charges when launched against surfaced targets. Preferring to make his attack while the U-boat was submerging, Pockley calmly climbed astern to 900ft and circled.

As the U-boat prepared to crash-dive, its bridge crew could be seen disappearing down inside the conning tower hatch. The U-boat's tanks were blown and she began her dive beneath the foaming water as the Sunderland approached and straddled the U-boat abaft the stem, three depth-charges falling on either side. The explosions from Pockley's textbook attack were particularly heavy and brought huge air and oil bubbles gushing to the surface, but the damaged U-boat did not expose itself to a second attack.

Shortly before the end of his tour with No 10 (RAAF) Squadron, Pockley took part in the support for Operation 'Torch', the Anglo-American invasion of Vichy French North Africa (Morocco and Algeria) on 8 November 1942. 'We started weeks before the convoy sailed, and continuously swept the area through which they would pass until they were beyond our range.

'All the time we didn't know why we were doing it, or for whom. Only a few of us even sighted the [invasion] convoy; most of the time we were hundreds of miles ahead. It wasn't at all exciting, as we were only part of the gigantic scheme of protection for the convoy. Hundreds of aircraft did hundreds of patrols, and flew thousands of hours on their task of preventing air, surface, or submarine attacks. The secrecy was amazing. Except for a few very exalted persons, not a soul in England knew that anything was about to happen, let alone when or where.'

Pockley flew his last operation with No 10 (RAAF) Squadron on 12 November 1942 before being posted home to Australia to join No 41 Squadron RAAF operating Martin Mariner flying boats. When he returned home he was one of the most publicised figures in the RAAF. He was promoted to acting squadron leader in August 1943 and given temporary command of No 41 Squadron briefly in May 1944, and again for several weeks in September.

In February 1945 Pockley was appointed to command the newly formed No 200 Flight (Special Duties) at Leyburn airfield near Toowoomba. They flew modified B-24 Liberator bombers to support M and Z Special Units operating in the Netherlands East Indies and Borneo.

On 25 February 1945 Pockley flew his first Special Forces mission – and what transpired to be his last – flying Liberator A72-191. He and his crew were posted missing in action after failing to return from a successful operation to insert Special Forces personnel and supplies into the jungles of Sarawak. Pockley's aircraft was last seen attacking an enemy merchant vessel off the coast of Borneo, which is believed to have shot his Liberator down. No trace of the aircraft or its crew was ever found.

Pockley's public image was certainly helped on its way during the war by the Air Ministry public relations machine and seized upon by the popular press in Britain and Australia. However, when the fighting was over, the politicians and official historians chose to re-write some aspects of the war, re-telling the story as they wanted the world to read it. Many British and Commonwealth war heroes became unwitting victims of this 'political correctness' (as we call it today). We have read earlier how the RAAF's official historians chose to downplay the 'effectiveness' of Pockley as a pilot.

In July 1942 Pockley had been awarded the DFC. His citation stated that 'his skill, tenacity and coolness under fire have set an inspiring example'. For his continuing success as a Coastal Command pilot and aircraft captain, a Bar to the DFC was awarded in November. 'This officer is an outstanding pilot and captain. These successes have been achieved as the result of sheer hard work, combined with great skill and determination.' His two DFCs were awarded for 'exceptional valour, courage or devotion to duty whilst flying in active operations against the enemy' and the citations speak for themselves.

Pockley was certainly a charismatic character. He must have been an inspirational figure to his crew as well as a PR godsend to the RAF in the Battle of the Atlantic, when the Allies sorely needed good fortune and good news. He was a brave man and a conscientious leader and he deserves to be remembered as such.

6: INTERNED IN PORTUGAL

'The enemy plane [a Junkers Ju88] had come on us before any of us, except the rear gunner, saw it. The first indication we got that anything was wrong was a correction from the rear gunner "hard right!"'

Sgt Lloyd French, a veteran of 15 ops over Germany and a passenger in the No 425 (Canadian) Squadron Wellington, caught the deadly effects of the Ju88's arsenal: 'I was sitting at the navigator's table. Next thing I knew I was hit. It fired both cannon and machine guns at us. I was hit in both knees and my right foot.' Twenty-two-year-old airframe mechanic LAC Raymond Larche, from Montreal, was hit in the buttocks by shrapnel, but was not seriously hurt.

The date was 3 June 1943. No 425 (Canadian) Squadron's Wellington Mk X, HE268, was one of twenty bombers that had taken off from the Fighter Command airfield at Portreath on the north Cornwall coast, bound for Gibraltar. The French-Canadian squadron was deploying to North Africa from its base in Yorkshire for bombing operations in the Mediterranean theatre.

After crossing the Bay of Biscay all the aircraft safely reached their destination of 'the Rock' with the exception of HE268, flown by 24-year-old Plt Off Rudolph J. Lacerte RCAF, from Edmonton, Alberta, which was intercepted by Ju88 heavy fighters of the Luftwaffe's long-range maritime fighter group, V Gruppe Kampfgeschwader 40 (V/KG40). In Lacerte's crew were Flg Off B.L. ('Bunny') Shaw, RAFVR (navigator), Sgt W.J. Brislan, RCAF (air gunner), Sgt F.W. Wright, RAFVR (wireless operator/air gunner), and three passengers – navigator Sgt Lloyd Gilbert French, RCAF, and ground crewmen LAC Raymond Larche, RCAF and LAC L.A. Dufresne, RCAF, who were hitching a ride in the Wellington to the squadron's new operating base.

About two and a half hours into their southbound flight they were attacked over the Bay of Biscay by long range

ABOVE: Flg Off Rudy Lacerte (far right) and his No 425 (Canadian) Squadron Wellington Mk IC crew were involved in a running fight with Junkers Ju88s of Kampfgruppe 40 (KG40) over the Bay of Biscay on 2/3 June 1943. With their bomber badly damaged and two crew members injured, Lacerte shook off the assailants and headed for Portugal. All of the crew successfully baled out and were interned for several months before repatriation to England. Left to right: Bill Brislan (USA); Lloyd French, RCAF, navigator; 'Bunny' Shaw, RCAF, bomb-aimer; Freddie Wright, RAFVR, wireless operator/AG; Rudy Lacerte, RCAF, pilot. (Mrs J. Yeomans)

ABOVE: No 425 (Canadian) Squadron's Wellington Mk X, HZ303, 'H', takes off from its base at Dishforth in September 1943. Formed in No 4 Group on 22 June 1942, the squadron operated Wellingtons from Dishforth until it transferred to the new No 6 (RCAF) Group in January 1943. It was then detached to the Middle East from June to November as part of No 331 Wing and on its return converted to Halifaxes at Tholthorpe, where it remained for the rest of the war. (Author)

Junkers Ju88C-6s of V/KG40. Lloyd French takes up the story again:

'I thought of many things – home and wife. I had been married just a month before. Our pilot shook off the attacker by getting into the clouds but our plane was badly damaged. We had only one motor. I was bandaged up in the plane then we were ordered to bale out two at a time.'

The Wellington had been badly mauled by machine-gun and cannon fire and was pouring fuel from its wing tanks, so pilot Rudy Lacerte made a bid to reach Portugal where the crew could bale out – which they did near the northern coastal towns of Espinho and Esmoriz.

French was in no shape to walk let alone bale out. He could only hobble to the escape hatch in the floor of the nose, and then tumble out and away from the doomed bomber. Bunny Shaw was the hero of the moment because he absolutely refused to leave French's side. When French jumped Shaw followed him. He kept as close as he could as they fell to earth, in order that he would be able to help his comrade when they reached the ground.

As the aircraft captain, Rudy Lacerte baled out last of all. Before he dropped through the escape hatch into the howling slipstream, he set the Wellington's automatic pilot so it would continue on its way and eventually crash into the sea – which it did.

'Shaw was a real guy,' French recalled. 'He went with me to look after me. We landed about a mile apart. We both had whistles. I blew. He blew an answer. It took him only about five minutes to reach my side. He ran all the way.'

French had parachuted into woodland where his chute had caught in a tree and there he hung, with his broken legs dangling. 'The pain wasn't enough to make me faint, but it was bad enough. I had lost a lot of blood,' he remembered. Pulling out the small escape knife tucked inside his flying boots he managed to cut through the nylon parachute shroud lines and he dropped to the ground, falling onto his injured legs.

People from a town a few miles away rushed to the scene. 'They had seen us coming down,' said French. 'We could see them coming toward us. Bunny started to carry me. Three fellows came out of the crowd and took over the job. Two of them made a swing for me with their hands and the other carried my feet. It took us two or three hours to make the town. They wanted us to have something to eat before I was taken to the hospital. A great crowd had gathered.' The two injured men were admitted to Oporto Military Hospital where they were to remain until 26 July.

The rest of the crew was taken to the ancient fortified town of Elvas where they were interned by the Portuguese authorities, within sight of the city of Badajoz, 7 miles away across the border with Spain.

Only two days before this incident, on 1 June, the KLM Douglas DC-3 airliner, G-AGBB, carrying the well-known English film star Leslie Howard home to England from a lecture tour of Spain and Portugal, was intercepted and attacked by eight Junkers Ju88C-6s of V/KG40 over the Bay of Biscay. The four crew and 13 passengers were all killed when the DC-3 ploughed into the sea and no trace of the aircraft or its occupants was ever found.

German U-boat tactics in the Bay of Biscay had changed on 3 June 1943 when U-boat commanders were ordered by their commander, Admiral Dönitz, to transit the Bay in groups of two or three boats when sailing to or from their bases along the Brittany coast and at Bordeaux. If intercepted and attacked by Allied aircraft they were to fight it out on the surface. In support of this change, on 1 June KG40 and its Ju88s intensified their operations over the Bay and it was a case of bad luck for those Allied civil and military aircraft that happened to be in the Bay at this time – including the KLM DC-3 and Rudy Lacerte's Wellington. KG40's Ju88C-6 fighters could certainly pack a deadly punch with their offensive fixed armament of three 7.9mm MG 17 machine guns and one 20mm MG FF cannon in the nose.

On 2 June a Sunderland flying boat of No 461 (RAAF) Squadron, EJ134, 'N', was attacked over the Bay at 7.00pm by eight Ju88s of V/KG40. In a vicious 45-minute combat three of the attackers were shot down. The Sunderland was severely damaged and its flight engineer killed, but in a superb feat of airmanship its crew, skippered by Flt Lt Walker RAAF, made it back to Cornwall where the flying boat was beached at Marazion, near St Michael's Mount.

The following excerpts are taken from two fascinating letters written by 'Bunny' Shaw, the Wellington crew's navigator, to his lady friend 'Sandy', from their internment camp in Elvas.

8 June 1943

'I guess a letter from me will shake you, especially coming from a neutral country! Well, lass, I fear it has happened at last, for we are all now interned after an unpleasant experience with Jerries.

'To cut a long story short (and also hoping that the Censors will not prevent the mailing of this epistle) we were badly shot up and Lloyd wounded in both legs. Everything was in a hell of a mess but I attended to his injuries myself and changed dressings frequently – by that I mean the kite was in a mess and not Lloyd. Frankly, one leg sustained a nasty cut but the other is definitely more nasty – maybe a stiff knee.

'I then decided to carry on and make Portugal which, by good fortune and lady luck, we did. Here we all baled out

ABOVE: Lloyd French with his future wife Mollie. David Lean and Noel Coward's classic British war film *In Which We Serve* is showing at the cinema behind the couple, which dates this photograph as probably late 1942. (Lloyd Holland)

and I left the plane with Lloyd so that when we landed I shouldn't be far away. The village peasants were very kind to us all and I eventually got him to a hospital. Meanwhile, you can easily imagine the excitement surrounding the local folk – believe me, I really felt like a curio! That's if I had any feelings left! My next job was to fetch over the British Consul and he sent a cable to Molly for me, stating Lloyd was safe. You see, I thought maybe those nasty telegrams would already have been delivered by the AM [Air Ministry].'

21 June

'Just a few lines to let you know we are all OK although gradually frying to death in a temperature of some 130 degrees F in the shade! I'll have to show you my sunburn tan when I get back, so hurry up and find out about the swimming baths!

'You will be very glad to hear that Lloyd has had his operation and they removed a piece of cannon shell from the knee. It must have given him merry hell you know, and yet I received such a jolly letter from him this week in which he assures us all is well and in fact he hopes to be up and about within three weeks!

'We are actually in a town called Elvas, which is in fact on the Spanish border. It is an old fortress with terrific walls around the whole town, but in its way that is most helpful for we are allowed to walk around so long as we don't wander out of the walls – what a joke!

'I have been made the CO of the Internee Camp, which means I really just hand out the mail (never heard of it!), pay them, give them their milk and tuck 'em in each night. Coming over?! I'm also supposed to be responsible for their behaviour, but as to that I have "mon droits".

'A major from the garrison has proved an excellent gentleman and four times weekly I roll up for sword fighting, gym and games. I'm glad I had some slight knowledge anyway of fencing, for these boys are really good and sword work with horse-riding is like eating bread and butter for them. It helps the time to pass anyway, for apart from this there is absolutely nothing to do. That may sound very nice, but after a couple of days it's nothing but a curse and with the heat makes the fellows difficult to check. We have a few books and a dart board, but the main interest seems to be wine and women! Good job I'm both a teetotaler and a good lad, methinks!

'If you have time, please drop me a few lines, Sandy, I'm hungry for mail and news of England.'

ABOVE: Dressed in 'civvies' during their internment in Portugal are (from left to right) Rudy Lacerte, Freddie Wright, Bunny Shaw, Bill Brislan and Dufresne, on 5 June 1943. (Lloyd Holland)

Lacerte, Shaw, Brislan, Wright and Dufresne were taken to Lisbon on 15 July and flown home to England on 18 July, where they arrived at Whitchurch Airport near Bristol.

Lloyd French and Raymond Larche remained in hospital in Oporto to recover from their injuries until they were considered medically fit to travel. They caught a train to Lisbon on 26 July and the following night boarded a BOAC Sunderland flying boat (G-AGES, ex-RAF serial JM661) for Ireland, with eighteen other passengers, seven crew and 30,000 letters from PoWs in Japanese prison camps in Java.

Lloyd and Ray must have thought they had been cursed, for on the final leg of their flight on the 28th, from Lisbon to Foynes in the Irish Republic, their Sunderland flew into high ground in thick fog at 2,000ft. The flying boat came down on the slopes of Mt Brandon at Slieveglass, above Brandon village on the Dingle peninsula, where it burst into flames. One of the crew escaped the carnage with only slight injuries and managed to reach a lonely cottage several miles from the scene of the crash and raise the alarm. Doctors and members of the Red Cross hurried to the scene, but could not reach the spot until 6 hours after the crash. Ten passengers and crew were killed, but there were 15 survivors including Lloyd and Ray. Perhaps they had charmed lives after all.

7: HOW TO BEND A LANC

Warrant Officer (WO) Ron Clark from Cumberland had joined No 100 Squadron at Grimsby from No 1651 HCU at Lindholme in May 1943 where the regular mount for him and his crew was Lancaster EE139, 'R', named the *Phantom of the Ruhr*. In the following account Ron Clark relates the terrifying ordeal suffered by him and his crew when they were coned by searchlights over the target, badly shot up by flak and then finally left for dead after being mauled by a night fighter.

'It was now September [1943] and the nights were getting longer. On the 23rd I felt a tingle inside at the briefing as the target was revealed: Mannheim and Ludwigshafen in southern Germany. We knew it was a tough proposition from our previous visit.

'There was no cancellation and out at the dispersal EE139 was bombed up and waiting. "Ben" Bennett, my flight engineer had long since painted her name below the cockpit window, the *Phantom of the Ruhr*, a ghoulish figure hurling down a thousand-pounder from each bony fist. There was also a neat row of miniature bombs including three red ones for the "Big City" and two yellow ice cream cornets for trips to Milan and Turin.

ABOVE: Ron Clark, skipper of *Phantom of the Ruhr*, as a pilot officer, DFC, with No 625 Squadron at Kelstern, where he finished his first tour. (Ron Clark)

'Being "top of the bill" we taxied out and took off first. We were soon overhead the bungalows in Waltham and climbing into the darkness. They never complained about the noise. There was not much conversation on the intercom except the odd irreverent remark from Geoff in the rear turret. He often addressed Doug the bomb-aimer by his surname to counter the Londoner's banter. Judging by the silence, Les in the mid-upper turret was now feeling even older than his 29 years. He sometimes got his fingers caught in the trigger guards of his twin .303in Brownings and we were quick to dub him "Trigger".

'Unserviceability of equipment at this point could be very inconvenient. With an engine out one would have to decide whether or not to go on to a nearby target like the Ruhr, or to drop the bomb load over the sea and return to base as would probably be the case with a distant target.

'We were now heading deep into Germany and by now we could judge our position by the areas of flak activity; there was always something going on. We checked the intercom regularly and kept a good look-out. As we approached the abrupt turning-in point to the target there were one or two radar-controlled searchlights probing purposefully. Far below, the River Neckar glinted from the light. By now the flak guns would be following our movements, our speed and height noted.

'We turned in towards the target and Doug tended his bomb-sight with the parachute pack under his belly as usual. I slid the heavy goggles over my face whilst Ben was mentally running through the engine fire drill. The barrage had started and everything the flak crews had was hurled up at us: weird scare flares, high explosive and illuminations. The night fighters were high up above with their navigation lights on, waiting for us to be silhouetted against the coming fires beneath.

'Suddenly a searchlight latched on to us and immediately all the others followed. A sharp evasive turn was not sufficient to escape their attentions. I called up Doug on the intercom to ask if he had seen the markers. There was no reply. He had been blinded by the monstrous glare and he knew like the rest of us that we were in mortal peril.

'It took about 15 seconds for the shells to reach us. Their fuses would probably be a little inaccurate as by now we had lost some height and increased our speed. There was a crunch behind me as a shell tore through the bomb bay and out through the roof to explode somewhere above us. We were hit again and the aircraft went into a steep spiraling turn.

ABOVE: With WO Ron Clark at the controls, No 100 Squadron's Lancaster III, EE139, 'R', *Phantom of the Ruhr*, survived flak and night fighter damage to return home safely after a raid on Mannheim-Ludwigshafen, 23/24 September 1943. (H. Bennett DFM)

'The searchlights were staring through the roof Perspex at times and the speed became excessive as we plunged towards the centre of Mannheim. Ben throttled the engines back and helped me wrench the aileron control free. This immediately set up a severe vibration but I was able to straighten her up and ease out of the dive, having by then lost about 10,000ft in altitude. We decided to jettison the bomb-load as a 15-second straight-and-level sequence seemed to be inappropriate under the circumstances. When the bombs went the Lancaster and the rest of us felt easier.

'We were now at 8,000ft, down from 19,000ft, where the searchlights seemed to be just outside the windscreen. But then my blood froze as I saw several streams of tracer fire pass very close and underneath us to meet at a point ahead like a series of tram lines. The spider had struck at us in its fatal web.

'Evasive action was imperative and I swung the suffering Lanc back into a steep diving turn. My mouth by then was so dry that I could only croak "Fighter!" into the intercom at the same time as "Lish" Easby, the wireless op, who was standing in the astrodome, shouted "Corkscrew!" We came back to straight and level and the aircraft was shaking like a leaf. As I couldn't focus my eyes on the vibrating instrument panel I shouted to Jim Siddell to tell me from the repeater compass at the navigator's position when I was on the outbound track. We were now well below the other bombers and flying through their falling bomb-loads. We found later that part of an incendiary bomb had lodged in one of the engine exhaust manifolds.

'I then realised that Ben was saying something to me. "The aileron control has been severed by the shell," he said.

'"What's that Ben?" Trimming wires were still attached to the tab on the aileron, I realised. It suddenly flashed through my mind that Ben had been coolly assessing the technical aspects of our predicament and was preparing to cut the trimming wires. I hurriedly told him to do as he thought best since the situation was desperate and there was no time for discussion.

'He got down by the throttle pedestal and somehow identified the trim wires to the starboard aileron which he then cut with his penknife. Inspiration was followed by a miracle and the aircraft immediately stopped shaking and became quite controllable with the half aileron control left to us. We were still very vulnerable to attack and the searchlights grimly hung on to us as we edged off the grotesque stage and into the enfolding darkness of the wings.

'The target began to recede and the searchlight beams seemed almost parallel to the ground as though the spotlights were lingering to welcome us back for an encore. We now had to take stock and gain some altitude. Miraculously no one was injured, the engines kept going and the systems seemed okay. Of course, we were uncertain about the extent of damage to the airframe and the possibility of fuel or engine coolant leaks. A voice asked me if I thought we'd make the coast to which I replied with some confidence "We're on our way home".

'Ben's superb coolness under fire and his airmanship coupled with his technical expertise had made a safe return to base a good possibility. He was to be awarded a well-deserved DFM.

'We flew back to Grimsby without further incident. I believe we were not attacked again because of our low altitude and our assailants probably assumed that we were a write-off. As we flew around the faint lights of the wartime Drem system at Grimsby we started the landing checks, but as 10 degrees of flap caused some vibration and rolling, I decided on a flapless landing. We didn't want a hydraulic leak at this stage and it was important to get the landing gear down. We were soon on the approach to the runway with the gear down and thankfully three green lights on the panel; no burst tyres we thought. It was difficult to keep the speed down without flaps but a little extra might be a good thing tonight, I thought. The runway loomed up and the Phantom was home again, rolling smoothly down the runway with brake pressure normal.

'Later that day, after we had got up, we went over to see our kite in the big hangar. Apart from the extensive damage caused by the direct hit, the flak damage on the tailplane and the night fighter cannon fire damage to the starboard wing flap, there had been distortion of the main wing

ABOVE : Lucky escape: over Mannheim a flak shell tore up through the Phantom's bomb-bay and out through the fuselage roof, missing wireless operator Sgt 'Lish' Easby by mere inches, to explode harmlessly in the sky above. (Ron Clark)

ABOVE: Flak damage to the Phantom's starboard horizontal stabiliser and elevator was sustained over the target. (Ron Clark)

structure. I took a photograph of "Lish" looking out of the shell hole and that was the end of our association with the *Phantom of the Ruhr*. It was a long time before she was nursed back to health and other hands were to guide her to her total of 120 operations. For me, it was business as usual. We were assigned a new aircraft and one week later we topped the bill once again on operations to Hagen.'

For their skill in getting the Phantom and its crew safely home against all the odds, WO Ron Clark was awarded the DFC, and the flight engineer, Sgt 'Ben' Bennett, the DFM.

Another alarming fact about this episode was discovered after the crew had inspected the Phantom in the hangar. Normally, when the aircraft stood on the ground the outer main planes had a slight dihedral, but now they noticed a pronounced anhedral. A working party from Avro (Woodford) confirmed on investigation that the wing root fittings had been subjected to abnormal stress loadings, resulting from the uncontrollable high-speed dive over the target and the subsequent pull-out. The Avro experts were astonished at what had happened and told an equally chastened crew they were extremely lucky not to have shed the wings completely.

Ron Clark and all but one of his original No 100 Squadron crew survived the war. Sadly, Jim Siddell, the navigator from Burnley, Lancashire (who by then was a

LEFT: Ron Clark and his crew pose for the camera in August 1943 with two ladies from Waltham village, whose bungalow lay just over the hedge from the Phantom's dispersal. From left to right: Sgt Geoff Green, rear gunner; WO Ron Clark, pilot; Sgt 'Trigger' Simpson, mid-upper gunner; Sgt 'Ben' Bennett, flight engineer; Sgt 'Lish' Easby, wireless operator. Not present in this group are Sgt Jim Siddell, navigator, and Sgt Doug Wheeler, bomb-aimer. (Ron Clark)

flying officer), went missing one night in October 1944 flying as navigator to Sqn Ldr Donald Wellings, DFC, in a No 613 Squadron Mosquito FBVI, HR362. Their Mossie hit a high tension cable and crashed at Voorthuizen in the Netherlands. The two men are buried side by side at Barneveld, near Arnhem.

ABOVE: On the morning after the raid, the Phantom received a damage assessment from the station's engineering staff and experts from Avro inside a T2 hangar at Grimsby/Waltham. (Ron Clark)

LEFT: The Phantom's air and ground crews get together for a group photograph. (Ron Clark)

8: WOMBLETON-ON-MUD

Bill Johnson was a ground crew engine fitter at Wombleton in Yorkshire, a No 6 (RCAF) Group station, from late in 1943 until the end of the war.

'When I first reported to Wombleton late in 1943, the civilian contractors were still at work. No 1666 HCU was in residence, later to be joined by No 1679 HCU, which moved away after a while leaving its aircraft with 1666, so we had a mixture of Halifax IIs and Lanc IIIs, all of them throw-outs from frontline squadrons. In most cases they were fit only for the breaker's yard but, nevertheless, we were expected to keep 'em flying. This we did to the best of our ability with the tools we had and the availability of spare parts. The most common snags we experienced on both [Merlin-engined] Halifax and Lanc were the everlasting glycol leaks and radiator changes, the latter caused by striking low-flying birds.

'It was only the youth of the ground staff that enabled them to do their jobs at all. The biggest enemy was the mud; drainage was something the contractors had forgotten. The mud was still there during the summer and wellies were the order of the day. Every day. The NAAFI, Mess hall and Nissen huts all had sludge tramped in.

'We dreaded the day an aircraft would come off the runway or perimeter track and sink deep into the mud. After we had put an air bag under the wing and inflated it with the aid of a small generator pump which took hours, it meant many more hours of digging, trying to get something solid under the wheels. Then came the problem of moving the aircraft by towing with tractors or any available fuel bowser. Once the job was complete there was just the problem of getting ourselves cleaned up, usually after a long walk from the 'drome to our billets via the Mess hall.

'That brought the next dreadful thought: ice-cold water in the ablutions. Hot water was available for about one hour most evenings on a first-come first-served basis. Those personnel who worked regular hours were the luckiest, while the late comers off the airfield had no chance and usually ended up having to heat water on the billet stove – if

ABOVE: Ground crew at Wombleton with one of their charges, a Halifax Mk II Series 1 (Special). (W. Johnson)

ABOVE: 'B' Flight ground crew from No 1666 HCU in mid-1944. Bill Johnson is second from the right. (W. Johnson)

it was in use. But most nights there was no coke even to provide that comfort and so cleanliness came as a luxury. That's why we occasionally took leave to get cleaned up.

'When the planes were airborne, those of us who worked out on the dispersals would spend our spare time servicing the different items used for our respective jobs: ladders, engine stands, trolley accumulators, chocks etc. We would also look for anything from which we could make some sort of shelter for ourselves, somewhere to store spares and toolboxes, and possibly make a work-bench to hold a vice. We also made quite a lot of our own tools as an improvement on those issued to us. We did anything possible to improve our lot.

'There's nowhere colder than the wide open spaces of an aerodrome. I've spent many an hour during the bitterly cold nights doing some work on an engine by the light of a torch so that the aircraft would be ready for the following morning. It's not the best of jobs in those conditions and the nearest living soul would be half-a-mile away; the only sound the dropping of a spanner from 15ft down on to the ground, with the resulting climb down from the engine stand to search for it. The torch batteries would then probably give up the ghost, just for a bonus.

'During the winter months, one of the amusing features of aerodrome life was the different sorts of clothing worn by the lads for a bit of extra warmth. All sorts of gear and, of course, the wellies. At times it caused a few laughs when one was asked by someone else – probably a desk type – if one was an airman before he could say what was on his mind. It was understandable, really, because Wombleton was an open airfield with country lanes running through it and the usual troupe of local villagers carried on their daily chores as if we weren't there. Anyone could go anywhere without question and any "Top Brass" would have to be

ABOVE: If an aircraft slithered off a taxiway into the mud, or bellied in after suffering damage on ops, the hard-pressed ground crews would be called upon to dig them out. This photograph was taken at Snaith on 21 December 1943 and shows badly damaged Halifax Mk III, HR868, 'B', of No 51 Squadron, which was attacked by a night fighter on its way to Frankfurt on the night of 20/21 December 1943. Amazingly, she was repaired and went on to serve with No 1656 HCU before being SOC on 25 January 1945. (IWM CE114)

very careful regarding saluting by airmen: it could be a farmer, or vice versa!

'Although the aircraft allocated to us were throw-outs from the squadrons, nevertheless they were used on occasions to create diversions from Main Force raids over enemy territory. The petrol loads were altered at times to try to ensure the planes had a chance to do this job. Sometimes we were told to leave certain tanks empty as a weight-saving exercise in order to make it possible for the aircraft to carry other things.

'Perhaps the best thing that happened to the lads at Wombleton was the eventual issue of bicycles, saving miles of walking and hours of time. But guess who had his bike nicked? Yours truly! I never did get it back and I had £5 deducted from my wages at 10 shillings (50p) each fortnight, which was a very painful sum to lose in those days.

'The next best thing was the issue of leather jerkins to give a bit of warmth and protection from the winds. I never did get the sleeves.

'One of the funniest things to happen to me was on one dark night at about 2 o'clock in the morning when I was wearily pedalling my way around the perimeter track after doing some work on one of the dispersals. I heard the sound of engines coming up behind me, and when I looked round I could just make out the shape of a Halifax. So I pedalled a bit faster and flashed the torch I was carrying to warn the pilot I was there. He obviously thought I was signalling him to follow me and increased his speed, and I mine. And so it went on, the only RAF bike to crash the sound barrier! After a few hundred yards I decided to abandon the bike and run across the mud alongside the track. The pilot eventually realised his mistake and stopped the aircraft while he sorted himself out. After all, he should have known to follow two lights and not one.

'The biggest mystery at Wombleton was when one of our Halifaxes circled the drome twice one night and prepared to land, but it never did. Instead, it flew off and away and was never seen or heard of again, although a farmer four miles away found tyre marks across his field, which faded out as if the pilot had either attempted to land and changed his mind, or he didn't realise how low he was and brushed the ground by accident. Whatever the reason, the aircraft is still unaccounted for to this day.'

ABOVE: General maintenance of an aircraft was undertaken by ground crew out of doors on the dispersal in all winds and weather, but a major overhaul meant the aircraft was returned to the hangars. (Ken Merrick)

ABOVE: Beneath the glare of the lights inside a T2 hangar at Rufforth, ground crew work on a Merlin XX-engine Halifax Mk V Series I A fitted with four-bladed Rotol propellers and Dowty undercarriage. No 6 (RCAF) Group, and Nos 77, 346 and 347 (French) Squadrons in No 4 Group, used this mark of Halifax on bomber operations for a limited period during 1943/44. This photograph was taken in December 1944. (IWM CH14222)

BELOW: This battered Halifax Mk II Series 1 (Special), ND-O, of No 1666 HCU, is pictured in June 1944 and bears testimony to the clapped-out condition of many aircraft used at bomber HCUs. (W. Johnson)

9: FLAK CLIPPED MY WINGS

Walter Johnston was born in Newcastle upon Tyne in 1920. His wartime flying career with Fighter Command was a comparatively long and eventful one. Inevitably known to his friends as 'Johnny', he gained his initial combat experience on Spitfires alongside some of the most famous names that the wartime Command produced. By the time he was grounded late in 1944 he had flown more than 500 hours on Spitfires and Mustangs from airfields in the UK.

Johnny's flying career began as a sergeant pilot on Spitfires with No 152 Squadron at Warmwell in Dorset during the dangerous autumn days of 1940. From there he was posted southwest with the squadron in April 1941 to Portreath in Cornwall, before moving east again later that year to join No 92 Squadron at Biggin Hill. There followed a break from operational flying with a spell of instructing at No 61 OTU, Rednal, and at the Central Gunnery School, Sutton Bridge. Then he joined No 234 Squadron at Deanland (an Advanced Landing Ground near Lewes in East Sussex) prior to D-Day for his second tour, flying in support of the Allied landings on 6 June 1944 and the subsequent breakout from the Normandy beachhead. Johnny survived a crash-landing in France after being shot down by flak on 14 June, hitching a ride home in Air Chief Marshal Sir Trafford Leigh-Mallory's personal Dakota. His last sortie was in November 1944 with No 234 Squadron from North Weald, flying a Mustang Mk III on bomber escort duty.

ABOVE: Towards the end of the Battle of Britain, Johnny Johnston joined No 152 Squadron as a sergeant pilot at RAF Warmwell near Dorchester. (W. Johnston)

Flying clipped-wing Spitfire Mk VBs from Deanland on D-Day, No 234 Squadron provided low cover over the Normandy beaches and escorted the Stirling, Halifax and Albemarle glider tugs of No 38 Group to their drop zones beside the River Orne. From 6 June onwards, the squadron flew a pattern of fairly uneventful fighter sweeps from Deanland over the Normandy beachhead with the task of preventing any low-level enemy air attacks on Allied ground forces. In common with the other squadrons similarly tasked, they were not authorised to make any 'freelance' low-level attacks on so-called soft targets, but on occasions the rules were bent to liven things up a little.

Johnny flew six beachhead patrols and cover sorties – including two dawn patrols – between 8 and 13 June. On D+8, 14 June, things suddenly became much more eventful for him flying his clipped-wing Spitfire Mk VB, BL415, 'B', as he recalls:

'We took off from Deanland at about 1.30pm to go over on beachhead cover and we started our patrol along a line roughly between Bayeux and Caen, just north of the main road, at a height of about 1,500ft. On the second run along the line someone reported on the R/T they had seen something below us that appeared to be different from on our first run. When we turned to come back on the westward leg we opened out a little bit so we could cover more ground.

'According to Operations back at Deanland (which was Army Intelligence), if anything came up we were to chase it because, in their words, we were "expendable" – which wasn't very nice to think. We thought that we were over our own lines at this time, and according to the map and with the marker of the road, we certainly were. We didn't see anything but quite suddenly, without any warning at all, I got hit.

'I assume it was a very near miss because it was from an 88mm ground battery and you don't get hit by one of those and stay airborne. The shell burst just underneath my starboard wingtip and blew the aircraft some 200ft upwards. I was flying a clipped-wing Mk VB and the burst took off another 2ft of wingtip, blowing the wing up from the exposed end like a paper bag, leaving the aileron dangling by a piece of wire.

'The aircraft was thrown bodily up into the air by the blast and I half-rolled it to port. While I was on my back I caught a split-second glimpse of the extent of the damage, but then almost immediately another burst caught me directly beneath the port wing close to the wing root, loosening the studs on the port and top engine cowlings and smashing the cockpit hood.

'The side door was forced open at the front of the runner, the Perspex was all smashed and the windscreen was starred. Something had grazed the right hand side of my flying helmet above the ear piece, but luckily without injuring me.

'By this time my prop had stopped and I was coming round in the roll. Then yet another burst took the radiator out along with a huge square of skin above it in the top of the port wing. I couldn't get out of the cockpit because the hood had jammed closed and I could only fly the aircraft with both hands and the stick right over to port as far as it would go. At one point I even cocked my leg over the stick to get the aircraft into the turn and keep it there.

'I was now coming down in a flat screaming turn. Funnily enough my pitot head was still working and I had about 200 on the clock. I had made a mental note of a flattish line on the ground from previous trips over the area, which I identified as a rough landing strip and now I aimed to try and put my aircraft down on it.

'All this time the aircraft was trying to tear itself back over to starboard and this proved very heavy on my arms as I tried to keep it pointing roughly in the direction of the flat strip I had seen. I overestimated my position a little but when I was over a hedgerow at the edge of the strip I allowed the controls to centralise a little before I thumped the Spit down on the ground at about 180 IAS and everything went haywire.

'The aircraft broke its back and my right hand shoulder strap snapped under the force of the impact, causing me to

ABOVE: A pilot's-eye view of the Normandy landing beaches in June 1944. (US National Archives)

ABOVE: This is what a low-flying RAF fighter pilot would have seen of the Normandy countryside in June 1944. The bucolic tranquility could be misleading, however, because mobile enemy flak batteries might be concealed in orchards and woodland and were capable of easily downing an Allied fighter at low level. (US National Archives)

thump forward into the gun sight – fortunately, of course, through the hood having been jammed, I still had my goggles down which saved me from a potentially serious facial injury. Amazingly, I didn't even get a black eye, but what I did have was the feeling of a lot of fluid pouring down over my face and for quite some minutes afterwards I thought that I'd lost my right eye.

'I got the shock of my life when, through my blurred vision, a crowd of people dressed in khaki battle dress arrived around my aircraft. They were wrenching away trying to get the hood open and finally tore the damned thing off, opened the door and hauled me out. It was then I heard a broad Geordie voice saying to me: "By Christ, man, ye haven't half been hit!"

'"God almighty," I thought, "I'm home or I'm dead." I struggled up from the cockpit and they helped me out and over the wing, frightened all the time that the aircraft would blow up.

'Two more pilots from the squadron, one from my flight, had also been hit by the salvo that had clobbered me, but they had been a little more fortunate. One of them, Flt Sgt Joe Fargher, brought his damaged aircraft in with its wheels down, although it did tip up on its nose and he grazed his forehead. The other aircraft, flown by Flg Off Bill Painter, came in on its wheels without too much trouble.

'The airfield we had landed on was at Coulombs, about 2 miles on the coast side of the Bayeux–Caen road along which we had been patrolling. It was occupied by a crowd from the Airfield Construction Unit to build what was eventually to be B6 Airfield [Coulombs/Cully]. The CO of the construction unit fixed a car for us, complete with driver and Bren gun sticking out of the top, and away we drove towards the coast.

'In some of the villages along our route, because of the colour of our uniforms, the locals mistook us for German prisoners under the supervision of the Army driver who was in khaki. One or two even spat at us as we drove past. We also had a few frights along the way because the airstrip we had landed at was at the extreme front of the Allied advance and virtually surrounded by Germans. At one

ABOVE: Although not Johnny's aircraft, this photograph of a downed No 412 (Canadian) Squadron Spitfire Mk IXC gives some idea of what happened to him on 14 June. This aircraft, MJ255, 'S', flown by Plt Off H.G. Garwood, suffered engine failure when on patrol over Normandy and crash-landed near Tilly-sur-Seulles on 11 June 1944 (three days before Johnny was shot down). The port wing (seen lying on the grass) was torn off when the Spitfire ground-looped. Garwood survived the war. The tanks are Shermans. (IWM B5660)

point in our journey there was an awful clanking sound and we weren't sure if there was something wrong with the car until, away to our right, a German halftrack emerged from a wood and drove across a field towards us. We slammed the brakes on and didn't know what to do until all of a sudden a figure, dressed in the uniform of a British paratrooper, emerged from the hedgerows beside the road and told us not to panic. He explained that he and his lads had just captured the halftrack after a firefight and were driving it away.

'Eventually we arrived at the map reference given to us earlier on by the Army at the airstrip. Here was a huge concentration of tents, vehicles and people milling around all over the place. A wood nearby concealed a battery of 4.5in guns firing away like mad and the noise was terrific. After asking for directions we eventually found a tent from where an Air Cdre Montgomery emerged. He was rather nonplussed to see three RAF pilots in an Army car, complete with parachutes, and he was even more intrigued when I told him our story. He said he couldn't help us or give us any transport (our Army driver was only allowed to take us this far) but with a quizzical look he offered to write out a form to help us on our way. We suggested that our Army driver go and get some food and while he was gone we re-fuelled the car and set off without him in the direction of the coast, taking it in turns to drive.

'We followed the directions given to us and in due course we arrived at a crossroads where we were waved across by SPs, bypassing huge convoys of trucks. Then we heard the unmistakable sound of aircraft. Quite suddenly, from driving along a country lane bordered by hedges, we emerged onto an airfield. There was a Dakota in front of us and a lot of people standing around it so we drove towards them. I was standing up on the seat of the car at this time, manning the Bren gun, and I noticed an awful lot of brass hats in evidence. There were Army and RAF Regiment personnel everywhere, armed to the teeth. I kicked Fargher to stop and then a burly figure detached himself from the group and walked over to us. He was absolutely furious and started to tear me off an awful strip, then he caught his

To. Flying Control B 2
or. 102 Sub Area HQ. 974849.

F/Lt. Johnston 234 Sqn. 149 Wing.
F/O Painter — " —
F/Sgt Fargher — " —

are returning to UK to rejoin their unit.
Please help.

A H Montgomery
A/Cdre.
AOA. 83 gp.
14 June.

RIGHT: Here is the handwritten pass given to Johnny to ease his journey back to the UK. (W. Johnston)

BELOW: Johnny's logbook page for the day he was shot down over Normandy. (W. Johnston)

Year 1944 Month	Date	Aircraft Type	Aircraft No.	Pilot, or 1st Pilot	2nd Pilot, Pupil or Passenger	Duty (Including Results and Remarks)	Single-Engine Day Dual (1)	Single-Engine Day Pilot (2)	Single-Engine Night Dual (3)	Single-Engine Night Pilot (4)	Multi-Engine Day Dual (5)	Multi-Engine Day 1st Pilot (6)	Multi-Engine Day 2nd Pilot (7)	Multi-Engine Night Dual (8)	Multi-Engine Night 1st Pilot (9)	Multi-Engine Night 2nd Pilot (10)	Passenger (11)	Instr/Cloud Flying Dual (12)	Instr/Cloud Flying Pilot (13)	
—	—	—	—	—	—	Totals Brought Forward	87.55	999.10	4.35	20.10	.10		1.20				9.45	15.20	49.30	
June	7	Spitfire VB	BL415 B	Self	—	Cannon test etc after inspection		.20												
..	8	..	..	..	-	Beach Head cover.		2.35												Low beach cover / assault area & inland
-	10		B	..	-	Beach head cover		2.25												& inland sweep.
..	-	-	B	..	-	Beach Head patrol.				1.45										Western beaches & Caen area
..	11	-	B	..	-	Beach Head cover		2.25												
.	12	-	B	..	-	Beach Head patrol		.40		1.30										Dawn
-	13	-	B	..	-	Beach Head patrol		.40		1.30										Dawn
-	14	-	B	.	..	Beach Head Cover.		1.10												Hit by flak (aileron - rad & oil) crash landed France (Coulombs)
..	15	Dakota	BJ 170	S/Ldr Jones.	Self	Lift back to England (with the Boss himself)											.50			Reached B2 a/f via Army HQ, 83 Gp HQ. (see line!)
-	16	Dominie	?	W/O Smith	Self etc.	From Thorney Island to Bearland.											.35			Home again
..	15	Spitfire	BM 417 B	Self	—	Beach Head Cover.		2.15												Not bad going - back home & over again in less than 24 hrs.
	16	..	-		-	Beach Head Cover - Freelance		2.30												
	..		-		-	Beach Head Cover - Freelance		2.35												
	17	-		-	-	Beach Head Cover.		2.10												
	-	-	-	-	-	Beach Head Cover.				2.10										Dusk? } Damned well black. Lost F/O Painter by own flak over Brighton 15
	18	-	J	-	-	Beach Head Cover		.40		1.10										Dawn?
	-	-	B	-	-	Beach Head Cover		2.40												
	19	..	B	-	..	To Predannock		1.30												Lost F/Sgt Henderson. 10
	21	-	B	..	-	Shipping Recce.		1.00												Weather u/s.
	23	..	B		-	Shipping Recco		1.30												
..	24	-	I	"	..	Patrol Charlie		1.20												
..	27	..	B	-	-	Rhubarb		1.45												Vannes etc - Fired at Bridge & two Radar Aerial.
	30	..	B	-	-	Shipping Recco (Bombs!)		1.10												Dropped 1x500 lbs on Radar Station in Ushant - MISSED IT!!
				Grand Total (Cols. (1) to (10)) 1152 Hrs. 45 Mins.		Totals Carried Forward	87.55	1030.30	4.35	28.15	.10		1.20				11.10	15.20	49.55	

ABOVE: American engineers construct the runway for an advanced landing ground in Normandy. (US National Archives)

breath and bawled: "Do you know who I am and do you know where you are?"

'I'd recognised him by this time and said: "Yes Sir, I know who you are. You're Harry Broadhurst."

'I forgot to give him his rank, which he didn't like [Air Vice-Marshal, AOC No 83 Group, 2 TAF], but he was gratified to learn that I actually knew who he was and for this reason he deemed us to be alright.

'It was at this point that another person detached himself from the group of brass hats and walked towards us with a retinue in tow. This, to my great surprise, was Sir Trafford Leigh-Mallory himself [Air Chief-Marshal Sir Trafford Leigh-Mallory, AOC-in-C Allied Expeditionary Air Force] who was extremely intrigued. He could see that Harry Broadhurst was losing his temper so he smoothed things over as we told him what had happened to us, and all that we wanted to do was to get the hell out of it and back to England. The Press corps was also there, which meant that this was too good a publicity opportunity to miss and Leigh-Mallory, seeing this, turned things to his advantage. We were taken over to stand outside the Dakota where photographs were taken of us and some beers thrust into our hands. Leigh-Mallory milked the situation for the publicity it generated – downed RAF fighter pilots simply itching to get back home to fly again. By this stage all we wanted to do was go home.

'We climbed on board the Dakota and it was not long afterwards that we were down at Thorney Island – not bad at all in the time we had been airborne, shot down, and so on. Once Leigh-Mallory and his entourage had left the aircraft they were whisked off back to London, and the attitude of all the administration people suddenly changed. They couldn't care less about us now.

'In the Officers' Mess at Thorney Island that evening, with Joe Fargher masquerading as a pilot officer, the three of us listened in to the news on the wireless that "three of our aircraft have been lost today, but the pilots are believed to be safe". Next morning we were ferried back to Deanland in a Dominie, where we told our story once again to the Intelligence people and by that afternoon, some 23 hours after I'd been shot down, I was back over France again. I looked down to see the wreckage of my aircraft that by now had been pushed to the edge of the airstrip beside a hedge.'

Flg Off Bill Painter was killed on 17 June by 'friendly' flak over Brighton, returning from a fighter sweep over the Normandy beachhead in the Bayeux area. He was 24. His body was washed up on the south coast several weeks later. He is buried at Brookwood Military Cemetery. Joe Fargher was shot down again over France the next month and escaped to England with the help of the Maquis, only to be shot down again several months later over the Channel flying a Mustang. He was fortunate to be rescued by an airborne lifeboat, which was dropped to him, and he survived the war.

Johnny Johnston spent his retirement years in Cornwall and died on 27 June 2009 aged 88.

BELOW: The Commander-in-Chief of the Allied Expeditionary Air Force, Air Chief Marshal Sir Trafford Leigh-Mallory, chats with Flt Sgt Joe Fargher at B2/Bazenville advanced landing ground in Normandy. Fargher was one of three No 234 Squadron Spitfire pilots (the other two were Johnny Johnston and Bill Painter) forced down in the Caen area on 14 June after being hit by anti-aircraft fire, to whom Leigh-Mallory offered a lift back to RAF Thorney Island in his personal Douglas Dakota, following a mid-morning visit to General Sir Bernard Montgomery. (IWM CL129)

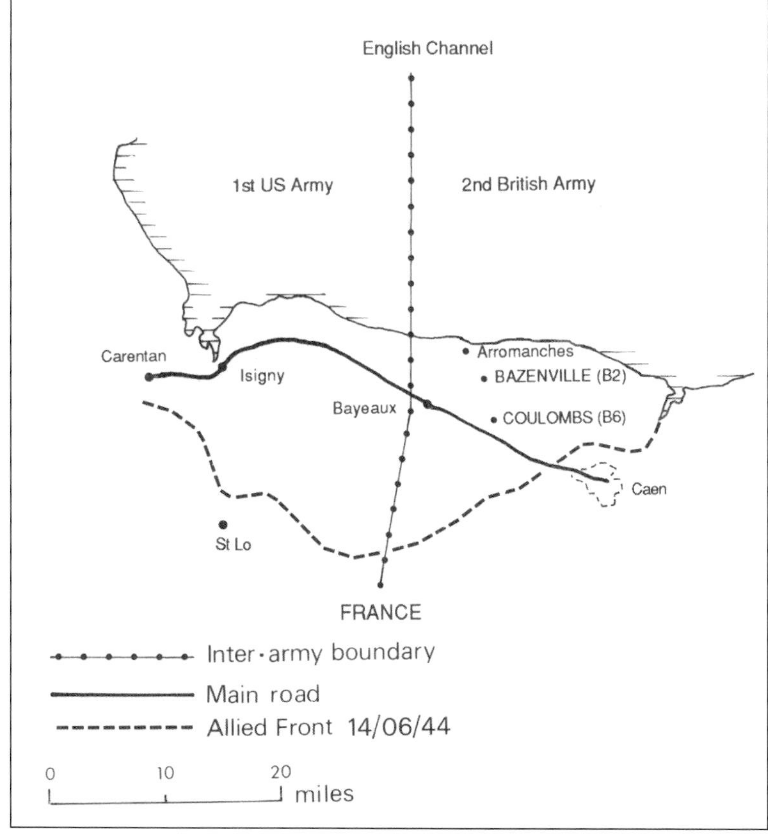

ABOVE: 'Shot down but safe.' Pictured here beside Leigh-Mallory's Dakota aircraft in France before being flown home are (from left to right): Flt Sgt Joe Fargher, Flg Off Bill Painter, Flt Lt Johnny Johnston. (W. Johnston)

LEFT: Map to illustrate the location of the events of 14 June 1944, as described by Johnny Johnston.

10: EVASION IN FRANCE

After joining No 57 Squadron at East Kirkby from 1660 HCU, Swinderby, in June 1944, Len Manning's wartime career as a Lancaster rear gunner was cut dangerously short on his third op. Flying in Lancaster III, JB318, 'O', he and his crew skippered by Flt Lt John Bulcraig DFM fell victim over northeastern France to the lethal upward-firing Schräge Musik 30mm cannon of a Messerschmitt Bf110G-4 flown by Oberfeldwebel Herbert Altner. Altner was a pilot with 8./NJG5, a Luftwaffe night fighter unit operating from Laon/Athies, 40 miles northwest of Reims. On the night of 18/19 July in the space of just 30 minutes he was responsible for downing five of the 27 Lancasters that were lost that night. Len Manning:

'At the end of June 1944 my crew joined No 57 Squadron at East Kirkby in Lincolnshire where we did several training flights on Lancasters before our first op on 15 July. This was a night attack on the railway yards at Nevers in central France.

'On the 18th we took part in the huge daylight raid on Caen by 942 bombers – Operation "Goodwood". As we turned for home I had a grandstand view from the rear turret; the whole area was covered in dust and smoke. It was simply amazing to see so many planes in the sky at one time. We had taken off for this raid at 4.00am and on our return to East Kirkby we were told, after debriefing, that we were to be on again that same night. This was to be my third – and last – op.

'On the evening of 18 July we took off for Revigny in northern France, which lies some 50 miles south-east of

BELOW: As dusk falls and the shadows lengthen, the bomber airfield assumes its true identity and comes to life. In this atmospheric photograph taken at Scampton, Lincolnshire, in February 1943, No 57 Squadron's Lancasters wait for their crews during the Battle of the Ruhr – and the target for tonight? Essen, Düsseldorf, maybe, or perhaps the Barmen/Elberfeld conurbation? (IWM H8785)

Reims. After crossing the French coast we were picked up by searchlights and during our evasive action we lost the protection of the bomber stream, which made us vulnerable to attack by enemy fighters. Having lost the searchlights we set a new course for the target.

'Soon after this there was an enormous explosion in the port wing: we had been hit by cannon fire from an enemy night fighter. Immediately, flames streamed past my turret which by now had seized up. This was because the hydraulic power it needed to function was drawn from the port engine, which had stopped working after the attack. I centralised the turret by hand, opened the rear doors and clambered back into the fuselage. Fred Taylor was already out of his mid-upper turret and clipping his chute on to his harness. He struggled to open the rear crew door, but once this was done he jumped out into the night.

'By this time the aircraft was in a steep dive and the fuselage a mass of flame and molten metal. My chute which was stowed on the port side had started to smoulder. I pulled it from its stowage and battled against the strong "G" forces to clip it on to my harness. With a supreme effort I just managed to fix the chute on to one of the clips, but the second clip eluded me. With everything about me burning I thought to myself "it's now or never" and leapt through the open door.

'As I fell, I pulled the rip cord and hoped the chute would open. It did with a crack, but I found myself hanging to one side. I felt something brush past my face. It was the intercom cord attached to my flying helmet which had been whipped off as the chute opened, becoming entangled in the silken shroud lines of my chute. I grabbed the cord and hung on. This probably saved my life as it helped to take my weight (I should have removed the flying helmet before jumping).

'When I looked up I could see the canopy smouldering and I hoped that I would reach the ground before it fell apart. On the way down I saw a terrific explosion which was the Lanc blowing up as it hit the ground with a full bomb-load.

'I hit the ground flat on my back which winded me. My chute had started to burn so I quickly smothered the flames and gathered it up, pushing it into a hedge before staggering off into the darkness. I lurched on for about eight miles before I collapsed exhausted into the doorway of a farmhouse. The farmer must have heard me moaning for by now the burns on my face were giving me great pain. He took me in and with the help of his wife put me to bed.

'The following morning I was given civilian clothes to replace my burnt flying suit and boots, and then moved to another farm in the same village, Sablonnière [45 miles SW of Reims]. I was again put to bed. Then to my amazement I was interrogated by members of the Resistance to ensure that I was not a German spy. This was all pretty frightening but having convinced them I was English they gave me a Sten gun, which I kept under the bed. Later, a doctor arrived to treat my burns, which he dusted with a white powder.

ABOVE: Sgt Len Manning (centre) was returning from only his third op as an air gunner with No 57 Squadron when his Lancaster was shot down over northeastern France on 18/19 July 1944 by a Messerschmitt Bf110 night fighter of 8.NJG/5, piloted by Oberfeldwebel Herbert Altner. Manning is pictured here with wireless op Sgt Tom Loughlin (left) and Flg Off E. Robson, bomb-aimer, both of whom lost their lives following the incident. (Len Manning)

'The Germans came looking for me at the farm, but the farmer convinced them that I had not been seen. In view of this the farmer decided to move me again. A member of the Resistance came for me and we travelled cross-country to dodge German patrols. At one stage my guide indicated that he was lost and would have to call at a house to ask the way. He pushed a Luger pistol into my hand and hid me in a hedge, telling me to shoot if he encountered any trouble

ABOVE: Herbert Altner was flying a Bf110 similar to this one when he intercepted and shot down Len Manning's Lancaster. This aircraft is equipped with Lichtenstein airborne interception radar and the deadly Schräge Musik upward-firing cannon that downed so many RAF heavy bombers without their crews ever seeing what had hit them. (Author)

LEFT: The hunter: a Messerschmitt Bf110 night fighter pilot climbs into the cockpit of his aircraft, silhouetted against the pale moonlight. (Author)

at the house. He returned shortly with directions and we continued on our way until we reached a small café in the village of La Trétoire. The café was owned by two elderly ladies, Louisette Beaujard and her mother. Although neither spoke English, I was made very welcome and given a room in their hotel across the courtyard. If the Germans came into the village I would have to move into the ladies' room over the café, I was told, because German officers used the hotel when in the village.

'Two young men, Albert Bertin and Jacque Gaignard, were also staying with the ladies at the hotel. They were on the run from the Germans who wanted to conscript them for forced labour in Germany. Later, another chap appeared named Maurice Leterne, and from time to time a young lady, Madeleine Foley-Godard, would bring us cigarettes and money from the Resistance.

'I had the run of the orchard behind the hotel, but the café was strictly out of bounds. I was warned to make myself scarce when the postman was about because he was suspected of being a collaborator. There was also a lot of furtive coming and going by members of the Resistance.

'One evening a group of Germans came into the café for drinks while we were having our evening meal in the back room. Madame Beaujard came in to fetch some change and one of the Germans followed her. He stood by the door and looked around the room at the four of us. Madame gave him his change and he turned and left the room without a word, much to our relief.

'Some days later we were told that German tanks were coming towards the village and once again I moved into the ladies' room over the café. The next morning I was roused by the noise of the tanks. Looking down from the window I saw that the courtyard was full of them; soldiers were standing about holding machine guns and some had grenades stuck inside the tops of their belts. This was

ABOVE: The remains of Canadian Flg Off Joe Hogan's No 57 Squadron Lancaster III, LM336, 'G', are cleared from the streets of central Paris. Returning from a raid on Mannheim on 23 September 1943, the bomber was badly damaged and set on fire by a flak battery at Pré-Saint-Gervais in the French capital. Losing height, the Lancaster crashed onto the roof of the Grands Magasins department store in the Rue St Honoré. Hogan and all his crew were killed. (Author)

another worrying time for me, but later that day the soldiers and their tanks moved out and this was the last time that I saw any Germans.

'After a few more weeks some jubilant young Resistance men arrived riding a captured German motorcycle combination. They told us that the Americans had arrived outside the village and were setting up a field hospital. The following day I went down and found an officer who offered me a lift to Paris. He gave me a good supply of coffee and tinned food for my French friends. That night there was a big party to celebrate the liberation and all the good wines were brought out of hiding. My charred battle dress also reappeared, darned and pressed.

'The next day I returned to the American camp after three months in France. I was driven to the Hotel Maurice in Paris where the RAF had set up a reception centre for evaders. The following day I was flown to England, arriving at RAF Hendon in north London, where I was interrogated once again to make sure I was not a German spy. I was then taken to a hotel at Marylebone where I made a full report to Bomber Command Intelligence. Telegrams were then sent home and I was sent on leave. Living as I did in London, I arrived home before the telegram so it was quite a shock for my parents to find me at the front door, having heard nothing of me since I was reported missing some three months earlier.'

Two other members of Len Manning's crew survived being shot down: Sgt Fred Taylor, the mid-upper gunner, also evaded capture; Flg Off 'Rusty' Ruston, the navigator, became a PoW. The rest of the crew were killed when their Lancaster crashed and exploded near the small village of Bassevelle, little more than a mile from the River Marne, and some five or so miles from La Trétoire. They were 24-year-old Flt Lt John Bulcraig DFM*, the pilot, a second-tourist, who had flown his

** Bulcraig had been a supporter of Oswald Mosley and the British Union of Fascists in the late 1930s, taking part in the anti-Semitic marches into London's East End.*

first tour in 1940-41 as a navigator with No 50 Squadron on Hampdens and was awarded the DFM in January 1941; Flg Off Edward 'Robby' Robson (20), bomb-aimer; Sgt Tom Loughlin (21), wireless operator; and Flt Sgt Norman Gale DFM (24), flight engineer. The four men are buried side by side at Bassevelle's small communal cemetery where, with four dead from World War 1, they are the only British burials.

Altner served with 5. and Stab./NJG3, and 8./NJG5, scoring his first kill (a Halifax) on 19 August 1942. He flew a two-seat Messerschmitt Me262 jet night fighter with II./NJG11 and on 3 April 1945 over Berlin he became the only pilot of a two-seat Me262 to score a Mosquito kill. He finished the war as a Leutnant with a total score of 21 kills.

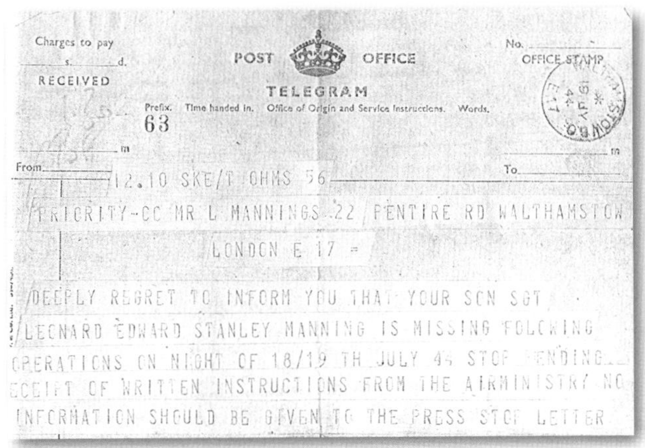

Charges to pay s. d.
RECEIVED

POST OFFICE
TELEGRAM

Prefix. Time handed in. Office of Origin and Service Instructions. Words.
63

No.
OFFICE STAMP

From. 12.10 SKE/T OHMS 56 To.

PRIORITY-CC MR L MANNINGS 22 PENTIRE RD WALTHAMSTOW
LONDON E 17 =

DEEPLY REGRET TO INFORM YOU THAT YOUR SON SGT
LEONARD EDWARD STANLEY MANNING IS MISSING FOLLOWING
OPERATIONS ON NIGHT OF 18/19 TH JULY 44 STOP PENDING
RECEIPT OF WRITTEN INSTRUCTIONS FROM THE AIRMINISTRY NO
INFORMATION SHOULD BE GIVEN TO THE PRESS STOP LETTER

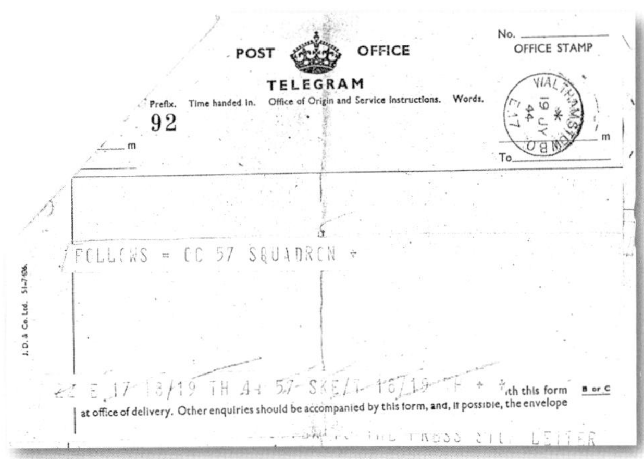

POST OFFICE
TELEGRAM

Prefix. Time handed in. Office of Origin and Service Instructions. Words.
92

No.
OFFICE STAMP
To.

FOLLOWS = CC 57 SQUADRON +

E 17 18/19 TH 44 57 SKE/T 18/19 F + ...th this form B or C
at office of delivery. Other enquiries should be accompanied by this form, and, if possible, the envelope

J.D.& Co. Ltd. 51-7406.

ABOVE LEFT AND RIGHT: The dreaded Post Office telegram that brought tidings of such great sorrow to so many families during the war years, opened with the heart-stopping line 'Deeply regret to inform you... '. (Len Manning)

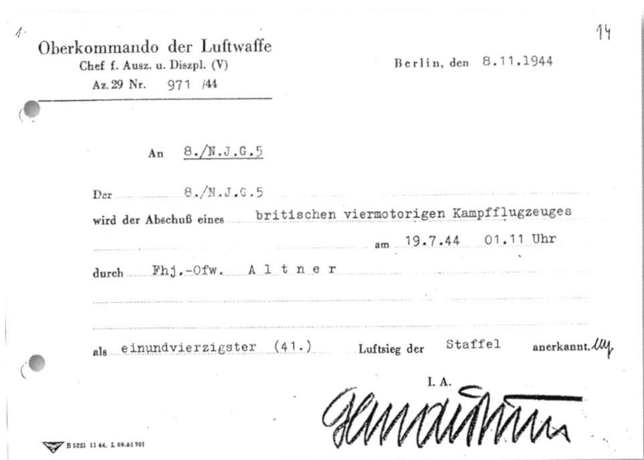

Oberkommando der Luftwaffe
Chef f. Ausz. u. Diszpl. (V)
Az. 29 Nr. 971 /44

Berlin, den 8.11.1944

14

An 8./N.J.G.5

Der 8./N.J.G.5
wird der Abschuß eines britischen viermotorigen Kampfflugzeuges
am 19.7.44 01.11 Uhr
durch Fhj.-Ofw. Altner

als einundvierzigster (41.) Luftsieg der Staffel anerkannt.

I. A.

B 5221 11 44. L 69.61 701

ABOVE: One of the five 'kill' certificates awarded to Altner, confirming his victories against 'Britischen viermotorigen Kampfflugzeuges' on the night of 18/19 July 1944. (Len Manning)

RIGHT: A grateful Len Manning poses for the camera with his 'rescuers', Louisette Beaujard and her mother, at La Trétoire, France, September 1944. (Len Manning)

11: MOSQUITO DOWN

In the summer of 1944, 36-year-old Aircraftman Harry Mott was an ambulance driver with No 140 Wing, 2nd Tactical Air Force, based at RAF Thorney Island in Sussex. The airfield is a remote place, situated on a dead flat isthmus of land that juts out into Chichester Harbour. On 19 June, three weeks after the D-Day landings, a massive storm blew up in the English Channel and raged for four days and nights. The 'Great Storm' lasted until 24 June, seriously hampering Allied operations and irreparably damaging the two Mulberry Harbours off the Normandy coast. At least 700 ships and smaller craft were run aground by the high seas and gale force winds.

Late in the evening of 22 June, Mosquito FBVI NS837, of No 21 Squadron, took off on a Night Ranger operation from its base at Thorney Island. At the controls was 22-year-old Flt Lt The Honourable Michael Benn DFC, with Flg Off W.A. Roe as navigator. Soon after take-off Michael discovered that the Mosquito's airspeed indicator was not working properly. Deciding to return to base, he was led in by another aircraft to make sure he was flying at the correct speed for landing. Even so, Michael's speed may have been too high on final approach as he overshot, touching down too far along the runway to stop in time. The aircraft smashed through the sea wall and came to rest on the mud flats in Chichester Harbour, at high tide. The Mosquito's undercarriage and tail plane were ripped off and the armour plate in the pilot's seat was forced forward with the sudden deceleration, breaking Michael's back. Roe escaped with minor injuries. (Later he crewed up with Flt Lt Lloyd. They were shot down on 7 August and became PoWs.)

Harry Mott, who was on duty with his ambulance that night, recalls the incident that claimed the life of the eldest son of Viscount Stansgate.

'It was a wild night and a high tide covered the mud flats round the island. I was standing apart from the ambulance, watching a Mosquito landing around about midnight. Suddenly I heard a crash – then silence. I yelled "crash!" to the fire crew and the watchtower, and then I belted like mad to the end of the runway. I could find no sign of a crash.

'The officer of the watch came down in a fast staff car. He was annoyed. "Rubbish," he said, "there's been no crash. Get back to your posts at once."

'But I was sure there had been a mishap. I drove along the barbed wire sea defences, stopped the engine and listened. Sure enough from the sea came the sound of a whistle (whistles were worn by aircrew on their tunics for just this kind of emergency). One man was shouting "Over here, in the sea. The plane is sinking, the pilot is injured. Double-up there!"

ABOVE: Flt Lt The Honourable Michael Wedgwood Benn DFC. (Tony Benn)

'This was no time for parade ground stuff. The coiled wire was nearly 20ft high so clearly we had to get help. I told George Biggs, the orderly, to get out the gear from the crash box while I climbed onto the roof of the ambulance cab and signalled the watchtower with two torches. It was enough, for the fire tender was soon back with us, but with only two men. The firemen had already jumped down from the tender, thinking the panic was over, but as the tender quickly turned around they were unable to get back on again.

'The driver was a big Scot from Glasgow, John McCluskey, who soon had a plan. "How many stretchers have you?" he said. I had six. "We must use them, at least five of them, to get over the wire. There's no time to cut through."

'George and I had started to cut through the wire but we soon realised how futile it was. Jock beat it down with a rolled up stretcher, so as to get a start with the first unrolled stretcher. I handed the first stretcher to him. Corporal Hargreaves (from Burnley) and George clambered about on them to keep them in some sort of order on the tough springy wire.

'One stretcher had to be saved for the injured pilot. We used five to get us across, and two or three blankets to enable us to drop down into the sea without getting caught up in the treacherous wire.

'Jock, being the tallest, went first. "I canna swim," he said, "so if I go under dinna foller, but go and get more help." Corporal Hargreaves went next, then George. Being the shortest I was last.

'The water came up over my shoulders and was bitterly cold. The two men in front carried the stretcher. The first three climbed onto the wing of the Mosquito; the wheels had broken off and the aircraft was floating. As I heaved myself onboard my numb fingers slipped and I fell back into the sea. I quickly recovered and joined the others.

'The navigator was not injured although he was suffering from shock. The cockpit cover was broken and Hargreaves sat astride the fuselage behind the pilot trying to lift him out. His feet were caught somewhere below the water level in the cockpit. I leaned over to try and free them. I looked up to his face as I struggled up to my shoulders in water. It was covered in blood. He sat very still. I said to the man beside me, "I believe he's gone."

'"Don't worry old chap," said the pilot. "I'll be quite alright if you can get me out of here. I'm numb with the cold."

'I was greatly relieved by these brave words. We got him out and onto the stretcher. Despite the desperate efforts to get to the wreck, George had not forgotten to bring the first aid satchel with him. While he was attending to the pilot I counted five doodlebugs over Portsmouth, one after the other. I also noticed how far we were from the shore – I reckoned about 100yds. I thought of King Henry's speech at Agincourt: "And gentlemen in England now a bed, shall think themselves accurs'd they were not here."

'I was comforted to see the junior MO arrive. Others were wading out too. Four of the tallest men carried the stretcher on their shoulders. We got him [the pilot] over the wire and into the ambulance. We hurried away to the station sick quarters where a quick examination showed he needed hospital treatment. In spite of my soaked condition I was told to drive as fast as possible to St Richard's Hospital at Chichester where, having carried in our casualty, I waited for further instructions as we had also taken the navigator there for a check-up.

'I fished a packet of cigarettes from my pocket. They were useless, having been soaked with sea water. The nurse who saw them asked if I had been in the sea. I told her how we had taken the pilot from the crashed aircraft in the sea off Thorney Island.

'The pilot died the next day. We learned then that he was the elder son of Lord Stansgate – to us [acting] Squadron Leader Michael Wedgwood Benn. We were sorry our efforts had been in vain. Lord Stansgate came to Thorney to hear the story first-hand from George Briggs (owing to censorship, detailed [press] reports were out of the question). George was the only one of the four of us involved. The other two and I had since gone to France with a large advance party [from the base].

'Soon after the MO recommended us for a special mention [in despatches], but the people who decide these things said we had done nothing beyond the call of duty. That may be so.

'I had to appear at the subsequent [Board of] Inquiry. I was questioned as to why I took so long to get to the injured man. After quite a lot of cross-examination I got angry and although I knew they were top brass I gave them answers without the questions. I told them straight. "The navigator had thought the plane was sinking and was shouting all the

ABOVE: The wreckage of Michael Benn's Mosquito FBVI, NS837, 'G', lies on the mud flats at the edge of Chichester Harbour, where it crashed after overshooting the runway at Thorney Island. (Les Bulmer)

ABOVE: RAF Thorney Island's crash tender crew played a key part in the rescue of Michael Benn and his navigator, Flg Off W.A. Roe. This is the crash crew from RAF Waterbeach pictured in 1943. The two airmen in the foreground wear bulky fireproof asbestos suits. When dressed in the suit with full-facial helmet, its wearer was protected from flames and heat when dealing with a burning aircraft. (H. Evans)

time for us to double up. It is understandable if he thought we were a long time."

'They kept nodding their heads, so I went on. "The island defences were put up to keep out German invaders, yet four of us broke out in less than half an hour."

'I told the senior MO what I had told the Board of Inquiry. He shrugged and said, "you may survive this war, but you'll get no medals I'll bet. Anyway, you are wanted in the yard – not Scotland Yard, the transport yard. If it's promotion and you take it, you'll have to give up the ambulance."

'I had been over two years with the sick quarters, it had become my life. I did not think I would fit anywhere else. If I did not wish to change I could decline promotion and indeed I had a feeling the MO didn't want me to go. We had had several different drivers, although none had stayed long enough to learn the job; in fact some were no use at all.

'I was off duty and lying in the shade one hot afternoon when I heard someone start up [the ambulance] and I ran to find out what was going on. The senior MO was trying to start the engine, muttering to himself, "Damned incompetence. There's been a crash, where is everybody?"

'I took a liberty and pushed him onto the other seat. "The way you're going it will never start at all," I said. With a flick of the starter it [the engine] roared away. I started off and nearly shot him off the seat.

'"Where to?" I asked.

'"On the runway, far end of the runway."

'As we went along he shivered. "You're not cold on a hot day like this are you?" I asked him.

'"No, it's these crashes that get me down."

'"You're a doctor in civvy street," I said. "I'm merely a van driver."

'"We seldom get such mutilations as we get here," he replied. I was reassured to hear that. I thought I was the only one who worried.'

Michael Julius Wedgwood Benn (b.1922) was the eldest son of William Wedgwood Benn, 1st Viscount Stansgate PC, DSO, DFC, the Liberal and Labour politician, and a former Secretary of State for India. Michael's younger brother is Tony Benn (b.1925), the well-known Labour party politician and former Cabinet minister.

Michael Benn joined the RAFVR in 1941 and trained as a pilot. He was posted to No 153 Squadron as a night fighter pilot and completed a first tour of operations in North Africa as a flying officer on Beaufighters, with Flt Sgt William Lunan RAFVR as his radar op. He scored 4 kills during this tour and was awarded the DFC (gazetted 20 August 1943). (Flying with No 239 Squadron, Lunan died in a landing accident at West Raynham on 10 September 1944.)

Michael joined No 21 Squadron in 1944 as a Mosquito FBVI fighter-bomber pilot for his second tour of ops and was one of the squadron's most experienced pilots.

RAF ambulanceman Harry Mott survived the war. He died at Bury St Edmunds, Suffolk, in 1993, aged 85.

12: ONE-WAY TICKET TO DUISBURG

Flg Off George 'Nobby' Clarke, RCAF, from Windsor, Ontario, and his No 429 (Canadian) Squadron Halifax crew had already flown 16 ops when their names were posted on the battle order at RAF Leeming for 30 November 1944, their target Duisburg in the Ruhr. Nobby Clarke's crew was Clarence 'Shorty' Short (navigator), Frank Manchip (bomb-aimer), Flt Sgt Les Fry (flight engineer), Jerry Paré (wireless operator/air gunner), Sgt 'Scotty' Ogilvie (mid-upper gunner), and Sgt Bobby Nimmo (rear gunner).

The precise chain of events on that fateful day and night will never be known for sure, but what follows is a detailed reconstruction based on original research by the author.

At some time before noon on the 30th briefing was announced for 2.00pm. For those whose churning stomachs could take it, a light lunch in the mess preceded a repeat of the performance earlier that morning before the station had been stood down.

With the formalities of briefing finally over, there was much scraping of benches on the concrete floor as the crews hurried to the locker rooms to change into flying kit. Valuables were handed in and 'chutes and escape kits collected. Amidst the usual babble of conversation and the jumble of parachutes, helmets and flying boots, 'Nobby' Clarke and his crew struggled into their unwieldy flying gear. Sandwiches and flasks of coffee for the return journey together with slabs of Fry's Sandwich chocolate and barley sugar sweets were handed out to each crew member from wrappings of newspaper.

ABOVE: Flg Off George 'Nobby' Clarke, RCAF, from Windsor, Ontario, skipper of No 429 (Canadian) Squadron's Halifax Mk III, NR193. (Author)

Outside the locker room the buses arrived to take the crews on the bumpy ride to their aircraft, dispersed around the perimeter of the airfield like huge crouching birds. A corporal stood at the open door shouting out the letters by which each aircraft was known. As space became available on a bus for that aircraft's crew, they climbed on board and were gone in to the night. Some crews sat around the dusty floor waiting. Others slouched against the wall, alone with their thoughts. Some paced up and down like caged tigers, unable to relax.

Because they were flying in Halifax Mk III, MZ314, 'W', once again, Nobby and his crew had to wait for transport until most of the other crews had left the locker room. When at last the bus came for them they clambered aboard, the rear door slammed shut after they had seated themselves on the slatted wooden seats, and with a thoughtful silence they rumbled off to dispersal.

Some 576 aircraft from four bomber groups were detailed for the night's raid on the German industrial city of Duisburg. These were as follows:

No 1 Group – 16 Lancasters
No 4 Group – 234 Halifaxes
No 6 Group – 52 Lancasters and 191 Halifaxes
No 8 Group – 25 Mosquitoes and 58 Lancasters

The target was to be marked by a mixed force of 83 Mosquitoes and Lancasters of the Pathfinder Force, and an airborne 'Mandrel' screen (electronic counter-measures) was also to be flown by 88 Stirlings, Halifaxes and Liberators of No 100 (SD) Group and the US 8th Air Force. Also, a diversionary force of 53 Mosquitoes was to attack Hamburg. (From the total of 576 despatched, 553 aircraft actually attacked the primary target, but 15 crews aborted over enemy territory en route, and eight over friendly territory.)

The bus drew up beneath one of the huge black wings of 'Whisky' and the seven boys piled out on to the concrete dispersal pan. A cold wind ruffled their hair and made their eyes smart after the smoky atmosphere of the locker room and crew bus.

The last streaks of sunlight had all but vanished from the western sky. Now, from around the vastness of the airfield, the sound of revving aero engines drifted across to them on the dusky air. The first aircraft were taxiing out to the take-off point. Bobby Nimmo and Scotty Ogilvie were now ensconced in their turrets checking on the movements of their guns. Clarence 'Shorty' Short the navigator was tucked away at his snug station in the nose of the aircraft beneath Nobby's position. At this point in the aircraft the fuselage was some 9ft deep. Having checked their guns, Bobby and Scotty climbed back out of the aircraft for a last-minute cigarette and a leak in the grass at the edge of the dispersal.

Nobby looked at his watch. He completed the formalities of signing the Form 700 for the ground crew corporal after a careful check of the control surfaces, wheel tyres and undercarriage oleo legs. Then they all climbed into the aft belly hatch of the aircraft: Les Fry (flight engineer, and the only Englishman in the crew of Canadians), Nobby, Frank Manchip (bomb-aimer) and Jerry Paré (wireless op) made their way up the fuselage to the nose, Bobby and Scotty to their turrets. Nobby stowed his 'chute and strapped himself into his seat. Outside, on the cold dark dispersal pan, the ground crew were moving the starter trolley into position under the port wing.

Les checked to see that all the fuel cocks below his instrument panel were in their correct positions, then he leant forward to Nobby and declared 'Ready for start-up, skip'.

'Okay, Les, see if they're ready outside.' Les looked out of the cockpit window and down to the ground beneath. He called back that the ground crew were ready to start the port inner and Nobby switched on the ignition.

'Contact!' yelled the fitter from down beneath the wing. Les pressed one of the four black starter buttons on his panel and the first of four Bristol Hercules radial engines coughed, spluttered and finally roared into life. The same procedure was repeated until all four engines were running. Nobby checked the intercom, opened up the engines to 1,000rpm and then allowed them to warm up to operating temperature.

Taxiing times for each individual aircraft had been set at briefing and 'Whisky's' time to taxi out for take-off had now arrived. Les was standing behind Nobby, keeping watch on the array of dials on his engineer's panel. Frank came up the two steps from the nose to assist Nobby at take-off.

With the wheel-chocks pulled away, Nobby gently opened the throttles and the great Halifax trundled and swayed forward, following the aircraft in front around the perimeter track in a stately procession towards the duty runway for the night. Nobby went through his final cockpit check. A green Aldis light from the control van winked through the darkness. 'Okay, boys, here we go!' called Nobby over the intercom.

At first the engines were opened up to 1,400rpm then up to the 'gate' as the machine accelerated down the runway. Seven men and 8,000lb of bombs headed skywards between the two lines of yellow flare-path lights and away into the darkness.

ABOVE: Sgt Les Fry, RAFVR, the author's cousin, was the flight engineer – and the only Englishman – in Clarke's Canadian crew. He is pictured with his brother, George. (Author)

Although the throttles were almost fully open, Nobby held 'Whisky's' nose down as she strained to leave the ground in order to build up as much speed as possible. Frank eased the throttles through the gate for full take-off power and slammed the clamp on to keep them from slipping back at the crucial moment through vibration. With both hands firmly grasping the control column, Nobby eased it back and the engine note changed as the big black bird clawed its way into the sky at 110mph, leaving the runway to slip away beneath. The wheel brake lever was nipped to stop the wheels turning before the main gear and tail wheel were retracted with a clunk. The red and green indicator lights went out on Nobby's instrument panel. W-Whisky was airborne at 4.43pm.

The No 4 Group station at RAF Burn, just over 40 miles south of Leeming, reverberated to the sound of its resident Halifax squadron, No 578, getting airborne. It,

ABOVE: An unidentified Halifax III, similar to the one flown by 'Nobby' Clarke and his crew on the night of 30 November/1 December 1944. (Public Archives of Canada PL-41623 via K. Merrick)

too, would be one of the No 4 Group's squadrons accompanying the Lancaster crews of No 1 Group and the Canadians of No 6 Group to bomb Duisburg.

At 5.10pm Halifax Mk III, NR193, 'V', was eased off the runway by her pilot, 28-year-old Plt Off Vincent Mathias from Christchurch, New Zealand, and was soon lost in the blackness of the night. For Mathias and his British crew this was their 16th op since joining the squadron from No 1652 HCU at Marston Moor on 18 August.

Meanwhile, Nobby continued in a shallow climb until the airspeed had built sufficiently for him to adjust the fuel mixture and engine revolutions to normal. Les eased the throttles back as the heavy bomber continued to climb. The flaps were now fully retracted and the power eased off again to suit the rate of climb selected. Shorty gave Nobby a course to steer and with the reassuring glow of the red and green navigation lights of the other aircraft in the sky all around them, they flew south in the climb towards their first checkpoint over Reading.

To prevent the Germans receiving early warning of their impending arrival the crews of Nos 1, 4 and 6 Groups which comprised the main attacking force, had been briefed to stay below a height of 6,000ft until they reached the town of Vervins at 0400 degrees E over Picardy. In fact, the Luftwaffe controllers concluded that the Main Force's southeasterly course threatened the Frankfurt area so one Gruppe of night fighters was sent to a beacon in that area to await the arrival of the bombers.

The three groups made rendezvous over Reading where one by one their navigation lights were turned out as the armada of bombers droned its way southeastwards at a speed of 200mph towards Beachy Head where it left the shores of England behind. Navigating with the aid of 'Gee', landfall in France was made over the Somme estuary in the inky blackness at 6.35pm. The force headed inland for 110 miles across the bygone killing fields of the Western Front until it reached Vervins and the latitude of 0400 degrees E.

At this point the bomber stream split into two diverging courses and climbed up through the thick covering of stratocumulus, heading northeastwards across Belgium in a long slow climb over a distance of 130 miles to the bombing height of 18,500–19,500ft. The aircraft broke through the cloud into the hazy light of a full moon, with broken patches of cirrus scudding high above them. Passing through the 10,000ft height band the order came from each aircraft's skipper for his crew members to switch on their personal oxygen supplies. In W-Whisky Les was busy keeping a log of the engine conditions and recording the state of the fuel load.

Confused by the strong 'Mandrel' screen, the Germans were kept guessing as to where the bombers would finally strike. By the time the two formations had crossed from Belgium into the Dutch province of Limburg, a major course change was imminent. At a point between Eindhoven and Weert the two separate formations turned eastwards onto parallel, but still separate, courses for the 50-mile run-in to the target. No 4 Group's Halifaxes were now slightly ahead of those from No 6 Group.

The tactical plan was for the two Main Force formations and a special 'Window' force comprising two Mosquitoes from No 608 Squadron, Downham Market, to converge on the Ruhr from different directions. The Pathfinder Force was timed to drop its markers between 7.58 and 8.06pm from a height of 16,800–18,500ft. With the Main Force attack, No 1 Group's Lancasters were timed to bomb between 8.00 and

ABOVE: Flg Off Vincent Mathias, RNZAF, and his No 578 Squadron crew, pictured at Burn during September 1944. Left to right: Robert Brown, wireless operator; Basil Hudspeth, mid-upper gunner; Roy Harvey, navigator; Vincent Mathias, pilot; Geoff Lovegrove, bomb-aimer; Oswald Parry, flight engineer; David Evans, rear gunner. (Author)

8.04pm; No 4 Group was to concentrate its aircraft over the target area in 3-minute waves between 8.00 and 8.06pm; No 6 Group similarly between 8.06 and 8.12pm. The whole raid was timed to last just 14 minutes, with 553 bombers being streamed over the target during this time.

At about 8.00pm over the Dutch town of Weert, Nobby had almost certainly just turned on to the final leg that ran into the target when something went very badly wrong. Frank the bomb-aimer had gone down into the nose to check his bomb sight and fusing panel; Les had gone aft beyond the cockpit bulkhead to check the master fuel cocks. Nobby called up the gunners for them to keep their eyes peeled for enemy fighters. Shorty's voice came over the intercom giving Nobby the ETA on target. Each member of the crew was busy at his station as the procession of aircraft in each formation began to converge for the final run-in to the target.

In the blacked-out towns and villages that dotted the flat Limburg countryside far below, the war-weary inhabitants were settling down for the evening. Two miles from the Belgian border in the tiny village of Altweerterheide the Blok family, tired after a hard day's work on their farm, were settling down for a well-earned rest in their farmhouse kitchen, having just put their youngest children to bed.

High over Weert disaster struck. Two fully loaded bombers collided. Nobby and his crew were in one of them, Vincent Mathias and his crew in the other. Violent explosions and gunfire in the night were sounds that the Bloks were all too familiar with, living as they did in a corner of Europe that for five years had witnessed the nightly procession of Allied bombers droning their way east towards the Ruhr. The gut-wrenching sound of rending metal high in the sky that night was nothing out of the ordinary for them. Not, that is, until shards of razor sharp metal, heavy engines, iron bombs and the pitiful remains of what moments before had been two four-engine bombers and 14 men, rained down about their farm in the meadow.

The two fatally damaged aircraft had become locked together by the force of the impact and had fallen 18,000ft to hit the ground two miles south of Weert, near Altweerterheide.

Wreckage from the two aircraft and the bodies of the 14 crew crashed to earth in a meadow bounded by three farms, close to a road leading towards the small town of Bocholt over the Belgian border nearby. It was a miracle indeed that the inhabitants of the village escaped injury since pieces of the falling aircraft narrowly missed smashing through the roof of the Bloks' farmhouse where the youngest members of the family lay sleeping. For some reason the wreckage did not catch fire despite the presence of a volatile cocktail of high octane fuel, bombs, ammunition and pressurised oxygen cylinders. But there were no survivors among the two crews.

The collision must have been severe enough to prevent all 14 men from baling out. With the terrific pressures exerted on their bodies by 'G' forces as both aircraft tumbled out of control, even if they had been struggling to reach the emergency hatches the effects of positive 'G' would have pinned them to the insides of the fuselages, rendering them completely helpless.

Meanwhile, up above, the rest of the bomber force droned its way inexorably eastwards towards Duisburg, some 40 miles distant, oblivious of the fate that had befallen the two crews.

Most of No 429 Squadron's aircraft had returned safely home by 11.00pm, the last aircraft touching down on Leeming's runway at 11.18pm. The attack on Duisburg

RIGHT: Salvaged aluminium wing sections from the crashed bombers are driven away on a lorry to be melted down for scrap. (Author)

LEFT: The starboard wing section from one of the Halifaxes lies in the field where it fell. The wing centre section has been torn away from the centre fuselage, and the engine bearers have been removed, exposing the front spar. There are holes in the alloy stressed skin surface of the upper mainplane. (Author)

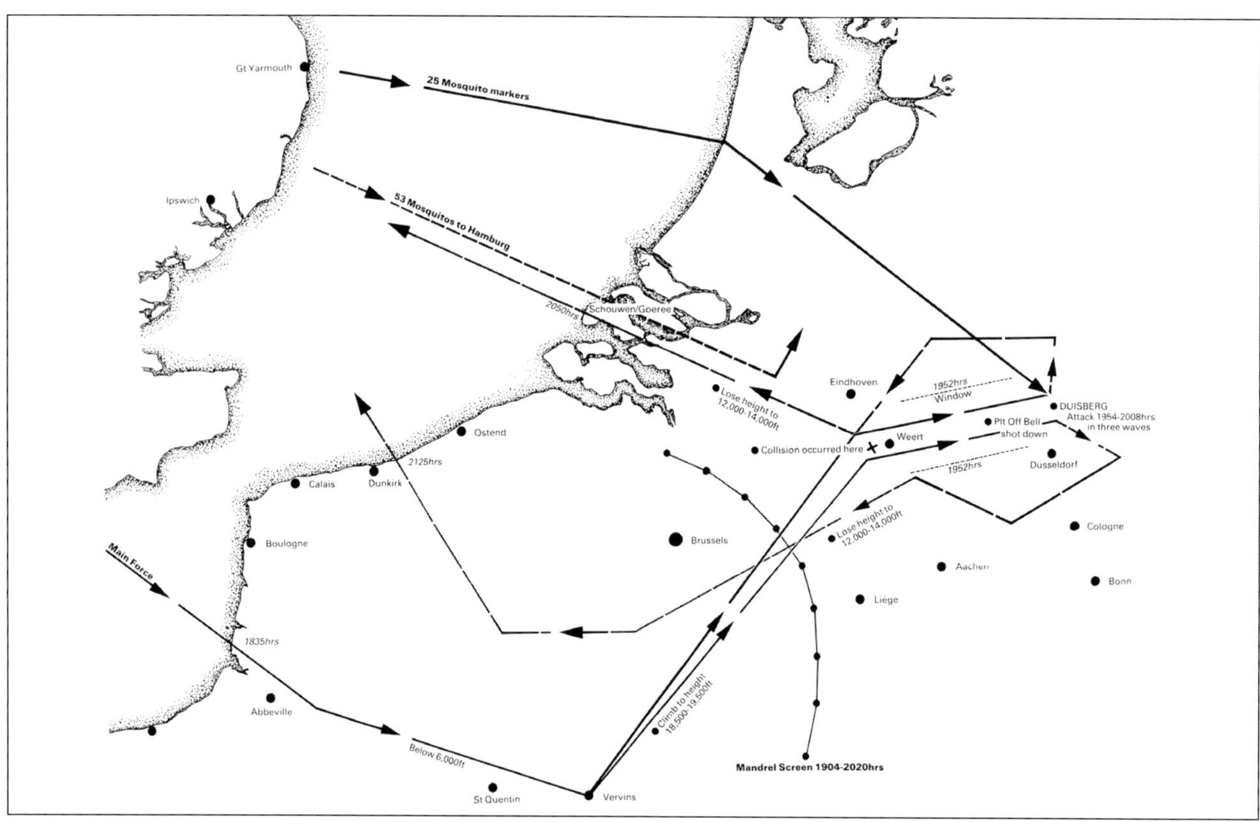

ABOVE: Bomber Command's air operations over North-West Europe, 30 November/1 December 1944. (Author)

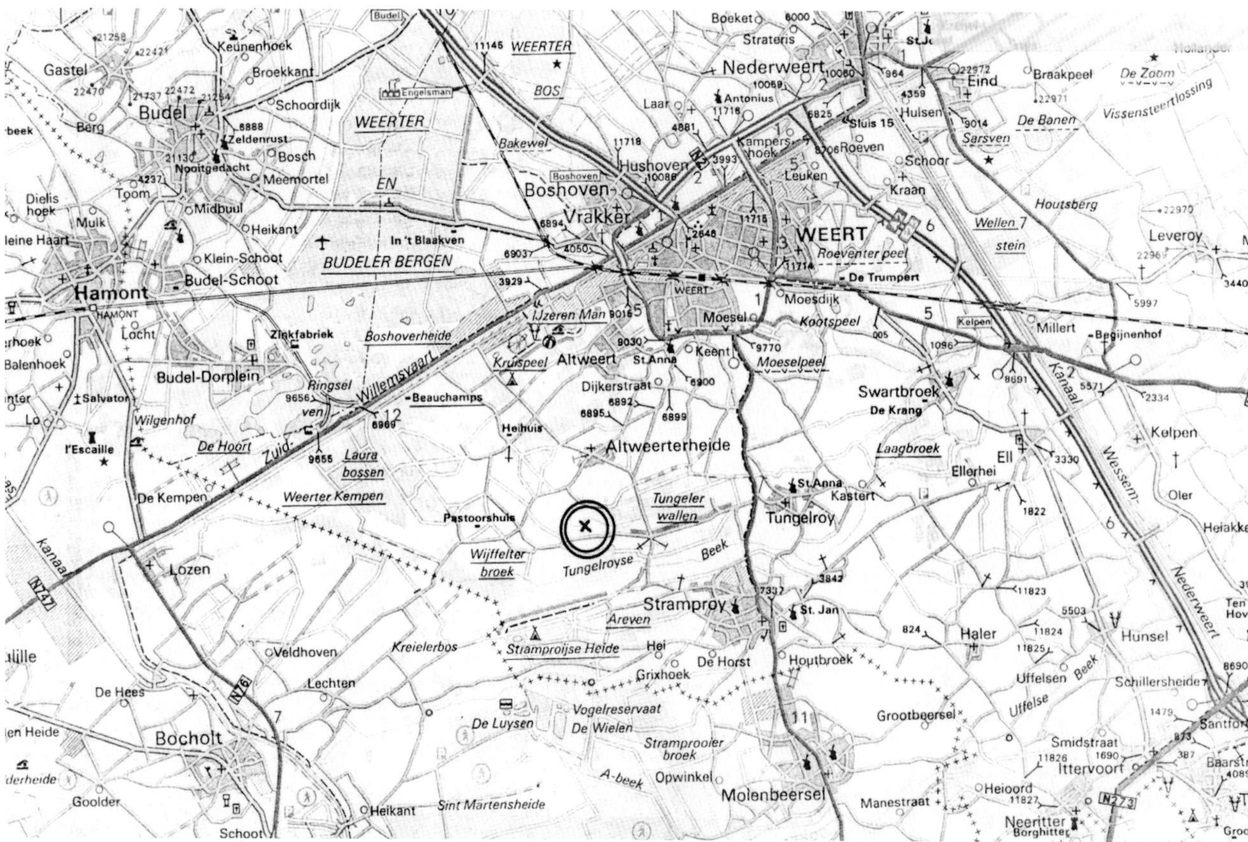

ABOVE: 'X' marks the location of the crash site at Altweerterheide, close to the town of Weert in eastern Holland. (Author)

ABOVE: The tangled remains of Halifaxes MZ314 and NR193 at Altweerterheide, photographed in July 1945 by the Blok family on whose farmland they crashed. In the foreground is a propeller from a Bristol Hercules engine and what appears to be part of an exhaust collector ring to the right of the propeller hub. To the left of the prop are oxygen bottles, control cables, what appears to be part of a throttle quadrant, part of the front wing spar, and another engine and propeller. (Author)

had not been concentrated but, nevertheless, much fresh damage had been caused to the city. Fires were visible from up to 60 miles away by homeward-bound crews. Some 528 houses were destroyed and 805 seriously damaged. Contemporary reports do not mention any damage to industrial premises, but 246 people were killed, including 55 foreign workers and 12 prisoners of war.

Altweerterheide was already in Allied hands at the time of the crash and had been so since the beginning of November. On the day after the crash, Friday 1 December 1944, British military authorities arrived at the scene to examine the wreckage and to collect the bodies of the 14 crew before their eventual burial in the nearby Cemetery Keent at Nederweert. One year later, the bodies of all 14 men were exhumed and reburied in the newly opened Canadian War Cemetery at Groesbeek near Nijmegen.

We shall never know for certain the precise chain of events which led these two bombers to collide over Holland with such tragic consequences. The spectre of mid-air collision was forever in the backs of the minds of the bomber crews and the raid planners at Bomber Command HQ, particularly during the huge massed raids that marked the culmination of the strategic air offensive from mid-1944 until the war's end. But, with many other factors more likely to pluck them from the skies, such as flak, fighters, the elements and fatigue, mid-air collision was just another part of the calculated risk of operational flying, particularly at night. Bomber Command lost approximately 112 aircraft through collision between July 1942 and May 1945: 2,278 to German fighters, 1,345 to flak, and 2,072 to unknown causes (probably one, or a combination of each, of the former).

BIBLIOGRAPHY

Primary Source Material

1: UNPUBLISHED
THE NATIONAL ARCHIVES, KEW

AIR 10 – Air Publications and Reports
AIR 10 3815-3838 Air Ministry Confidential Air Force Lists (Jun 39/Jun 45)

AIR 14 – Bomber Command Records

AIR 14/554 No 6 Group Summary of Events
AIR 14/1847 The Effect of Experience on Bomber Losses: Dec 1943–Aug 1946
AIR 14/2504 No 6 Group Analysis of Operations: Jan 1944–May 1945
AIR 14/2791 Missing Aircraft Register: Jan 1943–Jan 1945
AIR 14/3069 Group Summary of Operations: Sept 1944 – Day
AIR 14/3076 Group Summary of Operations: Dec 1944 – Night
AIR 14/3234 No 4 Group Raid Assessments and Flight Plans: Nov 1944–Feb 1945
AIR 14/3453 Bomber Command Quarterly Review No 10: Jul–Sep 1944
AIR 14/3454 Bomber Command Quarterly Review No 11: Oct–Dec 1944

AIR 24 – Air Ministry Records

AIR 24 – Bomber Command Operations Record Books (ORBs)
AIR 24/300 Bomber Command HQ ORB Vol 3: Intelligence Reports and Narrative of Operations – Nov 1944

AIR 27 – Squadrons ORBs

AIR 27/150-153 No 10 Squadron (RAAF): May 1941–May 1944
AIR 27/425 No 41 Squadron: Jan 1941–Dec 1943
AIR 27/1025 No 152 Squadron
AIR 27/1440 No 234 Squadron: Jan 1944–Aug 1946
AIR 27/1447 No 236 Squadron: Jan–Dec 1942
AIR 27/1853 No 429 Squadron: Jan 1943–Dec 1944
AIR 27/1858 No 431 Squadron: Jan 1944–May 1945
AIR 27/2050 No 578 Squadron
AIR 27/2155 No 635 Squadron

AIR 28 – Station ORBs

AIR 28/451 RCAF Station Leeming: Jan 1943–Dec 1944

AIR 50 – Combat Reports

AIR 50/64 No 152 Squadron Combat Reports

CIRCUMSTANTIAL REPORT

By Flt Lt Hudson, RAF Old Sarum: *Investigation into No 152 Squadron Spitfire crash following aerial engagement over Woolverton, Somerset, 25 September 1940*

JOHN LAING PLC – MILITARY CONTRACTS LISTING

Miscellaneous papers relating to individual airfield construction contracts

PUBLIC ARCHIVES OF CANADA, OTTAWA

RCAF Attestation Papers and Records of Service (various)
RCAF Casualty Notification – 27 Nov 1944
Circumstantial Report re: Halifax LW136 – 24 Sep 1944
Letter from AOC-in-C RCAF Overseas to Director General Graves Registration and Enquiries – 10 Aug 1945
RAF Form 551: Report on Accidental Injuries or Death – 15 Mar 1945

MINISTRY OF DEFENCE, NEW ZEALAND

Royal New Zealand Air Force – Record of Service

2: PUBLISHED

Sqn Ldr L. Harding (Ed), *Transport Command Flying Control Aircrew Manual* (Jan 1945)

Secondary Source Material

BOOKS

Air Historical Branch Monographs: *Works* (AP3236) (HMSO, 1956)
Anon, *Serving a Nation at War 1939–1945: A Review of the Building and Civil Engineering Work of John Laing & Son Ltd* (John Laing & Son, 1946)
Anon, *The History of Royal Air Force Finningley* (1969)
Ashworth, Chris, *Action Stations 9: Military Airfields of the Central South and South-East* (PSL, 1985)
Ashworth, Chris, *RAF Coastal Command 1936–1969* (PSL, 1992)
Bennett, AVM D.C.T., *Pathfinder* (Goodall Publications, 1988)
Bowyer, Chaz, *Fighter Command 1936–1968* (Dent, 1980)

Bowyer, Chaz, *Mosquito Squadrons of the Royal Air Force* (Ian Allan, 1984)

Bowyer, Michael J.F., *Action Stations 1: East Anglia (PSL, 1990)*

Bowyer, Michael J.F., *Action Stations 6: Cotswolds and the Central Midlands* (PSL, 1983)

Brogden, Stanley, *Sky Diggers: A Tribute to the RAAF* (Whitcombe & Tombs Pty Ltd, Melbourne, n.d., c.1944)

Brooks, Stephen, Bomber: *Strategic Air Power in Twentieth Century Conflict* (Imperial War Museum, 1983)

Brown, Robin A., *A Short History of No 234 Squadron RAF – 1917–1955* (234 Squadron, n.d.)

Collier, Basil, *The Defence of the United Kingdom* (HMSO, 1957)

Congdon, Philip, *Per Ardua Ad Astra: A Handbook of the Royal Air Force* (Airlife, 1987)

Copeman, Geoff D., *Silksheen: The History of East Kirkby Airfield* (Midland Counties Publications, 1989)

Davies, Ken, *Ninety Days to Normandy: The Advanced Landing Grounds of 1944* (Niche Publications, 1992)

Davies, Ken, *New Forest Airfields* (Niche Publications, 1992)

Donnelly, G.L. 'Larry', *The Whitley Boys: 4 Group Bomber Operations 1939–1940* (Air Research Publications, 1991)

Foreman, John, *Battle of Britain, the Forgotten Months: November and December 1940* (Air Research Publications, 1988)

Francis, Paul, *Military Airfield Architecture* (PSL, 1996)

Gelb, Norman, *Scramble: A Narrative History of the Battle of Britain* (Michael Joseph, 1986)

Gunn, Peter B., *RAF Great Massingham: A Norfolk Airfield at War* (Peter B. Gunn, 1990)

Halpenny, Bruce Barrymore, *Action Stations 2: Lincolnshire and the East Midlands* (PSL, 1981)

Halpenny, Bruce Barrymore, *Action Stations 4: Yorkshire* (PSL, 1984)

Halpenny, Bruce Barrymore, *Action Stations 8: Greater London* (PSL, 1984)

Hamlin, John F., *The Royal Air Force at Newmarket 1939–1947* (J.F. Hamlin, 1985)

Hammerton, Sir John (Ed), *ABC of the RAF* (The Amalgamated Press, 1941)

Hollis S. & Willis, B., *Military Airfields in the British Isles 1939–1945* (Omnibus Edition) (Enthusiast Publications, 1987)

Jefford, Wg Cdr C.G., *RAF Squadrons* (Airlife, 1988)

Mason, Francis K., *The Avro Lancaster* (Aston Publications, 1990)

Mason, Francis K., *The Hawker Typhoon & Tempest* (Aston Publications, 1988)

Mason, Francis K., *The Hawker Hurricane* (Aston Publications, 1990)

Moyes, Philip, *Bomber Squadrons of the RAF and their Aircraft* (Macdonald, 1964)

Neil, Wg Cdr T.F., *From the Cockpit: Spitfire* (Ian Allan, 1990)

Ramsey, Winston G. (Ed), *The Battle of Britain Then and Now* (After the Battle, 1980)

Rawlings, John, *Fighter Squadrons of the RAF and their Aircraft* (Macdonald & Jane's, 1969)

Richards, Denis & Saunders, Hilary St G., *Royal Air Force 1939–1945* (three volumes) (HMSO 1953, 1954)

Robinson, Anthony, *RAF Fighter Squadrons in the Battle of Britain* (Arms & Armour Press, 1987)

Sharp, C. Martin & Bowyer, Michael J.F., *Mosquito* (Faber & Faber, 1967)

Shores, Christopher F., *2nd Tactical Air Force* (Osprey, 1970)

Smith, David J., *Action Stations 3: Wales and the North-West* (PSL, 1990)

Smith, David J., *Action Stations 7: Scotland, the North-East and Northern Ireland* (PSL, 1989)

Smith, David J., *Britain's Military Airfields 1939–45* (PSL, 1989)

Spaight, J.M., *Air Power in the Next War* (Geoffrey Bles, 1938)

Verrier, Anthony, *The Bomber Offensive* (Pan, 1974)

Webster, Sir Charles & Frankland, Noble, *The Strategic Air Offensive Against Germany 1939 – 1945*, Vols I–IV (HMSO, 1961)

Wilmot, Chester, *The Struggle for Europe* (Collins, 1952)

JOURNAL ARTICLES

Uri Bialer, 'Humanisation of Air Warfare in British Foreign Policy on the Eve of World War Two', *Journal of Contemporary History*, Vol 13, No 1, 1978.

Malcolm Smith, 'A Matter of Faith: British Strategic Air Doctrine Before 1939', *Journal of Contemporary History*, Vol 15, No 3, 1980.

Chris Taylor, 'The life and times of Kenneth Holland, the Spitfire pilot from Waverley', 2010.

MAGAZINES AND PERIODICALS

Various editions/issues of *Aeroplane Monthly*, *Air Britain Digest*, *Air Ministry News Letter*, *Air Pictorial*, *Aviation News*, *FlyPast*.

APPENDICES

APPENDIX 1
RAF Fighter Command Headquarters and Air Officer Commanders-in-Chief 1939-45

HEADQUARTERS

Formed 14/07/36 at Bentley Priory, Stanmore, Middx.

Air Officer Commanders-in-Chief (with dates of appointment)

AM H.C.T Dowding – 14/07/36
AM W. Sholto Douglas – 25/11/40
AM T. Leigh-Mallory – 28/11/42
AM R.M Hill – 15/11/43
AM J.M Robb– 14/05/45
(Fighter Command was re-titled Air Defence of Great Britain (ADGB) wef 15/11/43; it was re-titled Fighter Command again wef 15/10/44)

No 9 GROUP HEADQUARTERS (NW Midlands)

Formed 09/08/40 at Barton Hall, Preston, Lancashire (disbanded summer 1944)

Air Officers Commanding (with dates of appointment)

AVM W.A McClaughry – 16/09/40
AVM J.W. Jones – 10/11/42
AVM L.N. Hollinghurst – 02/07/43
AVM D.F. Stevenson – 07/12/43

No 10 GROUP HEADQUARTERS (West)

Formed 01/06/40 at Rudloe Manor, Box, Wilts (disbanded 04/45)

Air Officers Commanding (with dates of appointment)

AVM C.J.Q. Brand – 15/06/40
AVM A.H. Orlebar – 22/07/41
AVM W.F. Dickson – 04/11/42
AVM C.R. Steele – 05/05/43
Air Cdre A.V. Harvey – 03/06/44
AVM J.B. Cole-Hamilton – 10/07/44

No 11 GROUP HEADQUARTERS (South)

Formed 14/07/36 at Hillingdon House, Uxbridge, Middx

Air Officers Commanding (with dates of appointment)

AVM P.B. Joubert de la Ferté – 14/07/36
AVM E.L. Gossage – 07/09/36
AVM K. Park – 20/04/40
AVM T. Leigh-Mallory – 18/12/40
AVM H.W.L. Saunders – 28/11/42
AVM J.B. Cole-Hamilton – 01/11/44

No 12 GROUP HEADQUARTERS (Midlands)

Formed 14/07/36 at Watnall, Notts

Air Officers Commanding (with dates of appointment)

AVM T. Leigh-Mallory – 04/12/37
AVM R.E. Saul – 17/12/40
AVM J.O. Andrews – 29/11/42
AVM R.M. Hill – 26/07/43
AVM M. Henderson – 22/11/43
AVM J.W. Baker – 01/01/45

No 13 GROUP HEADQUARTERS (North)

Formed 24/07/39 at Hucknall, Notts; Blakelaw Estate, Ponteland Rd, Newcastle upon Tyne; Drummossie Hotel, Inverness

Air Officers Commanding (with dates of appointment)

AVM R.E. Saul – 24/07/39
AVM J.O. Andrews – 04/02/41
AVM M. Henderson – 27/11/42
Air Cdre J.A. Boret – 26/01/44–07/05/45

No 14 GROUP HEADQUARTERS (Scotland, Orkneys, Shetlands)

Formed 20/07/40 at Drummossie Hotel, Inverness
(Later amalgamated with No 13 Group)

Air Officers Commanding (with dates of appointment)

AVM M. Henderson – 20/07/40
AVM J.H. D'Albiac – 10/02/41
AVM R. Collishaw – 21/03/42

APPENDIX 1 *continued*

No 22 (ARMY CO-OPERATION) GROUP HEADQUARTERS

Formed 01/07/36 at Farnborough, Hants (Became Army Co-operation Command on 20/11/40)

Air Officers Commanding (with dates of appointment)

AVM B.E. Sutton – 01/07/36
AM A.S. Barratt – 20/11/40

No 38 (AIRBORNE FORCES) GROUP HEADQUARTERS

Formed 15/01/42 at Netheravon, Salisbury, Wilts, as No 38 Wing under operational control of Army Co-operation Command;
06/43 – Transferred to Fighter Command control with disbandment of Army Co-operation Command;
10/43 – Re-formed as No 38 Group under ADGB control;
10/44 – Marks Hall, Coggeshall, Colchester, Essex

Air Officers Commanding (with dates of appointment)

Air Cdre N. Norman – 15/01/42
Air Cdre W.H. Primrose – 05/43
AVM L.N. Hollinghurst – 06/11/43
AVM J.R. Scarlett-Streatfield – 18/10/44

No 70 (TRAINING) GROUP HEADQUARTERS

Formed 11/42 at South Farnborough, Hants

Air Officers Commanding (with dates of appointment)

Gp Capt H.R. McL. Reid – 28/11/42 (SASO – acting as AOC)
Air Cdre H.B. Russell – 12/07/43

No 81 (OTU) GROUP HEADQUARTERS

Formed 12/40 at Autumn Avenue, Worcester
02/42 – Avening, Stroud, Glos (Disbanded 05/43 and OTU responsibilities assumed by No 9 Gp)

Air Officers Commanding (with dates of appointment)

Air Cdre F.J. Vincent – 16/12/40
Air Cdre W.H. Dunn – 29/07/42

No 82 GROUP HEADQUARTERS

Formed 21/07/41 at Belfast, NI
(Later amalgamated with No 9 Gp)

Air Officer Commanding (with date of appointment)

Air Cdre G.M. Lawson – 21/07/41

No 88 (FIGHTER) GROUP HEADQUARTERS

Formed 07/05/45 at Kinellan House, Murrayfield Road, Edinburgh

Air Officer Commanding (with date of appointment)

AVM J.A. Boret – 07/05/45

APPENDIX 2
2nd Tactical Air Force Headquarters and Air Officer Commanders-in-Chief

HEADQUARTERS
Formed 01/06/43 at Bracknell, Berks

Air Officer Commanders-in-Chief (**with dates of appointment**)

AM J.H. D'Albiac – 01/06/43
AM A. Coningham – 21/01/44

No 83 (COMPOSITE) GROUP HEADQUARTERS
Formed 05/43 at Gatton Park, Reigate, Surrey
06/44 – Gatwick, Surrey

Air Officers Commanding (**with dates of appointment**)

AVM W.F. Dickson – 05/43
AVM H. Broadhurst – 25/03/44

No 84 (COMPOSITE) GROUP HEADQUARTERS
Formed 09/43 at Cowley Barracks, Oxford
06/44 – Chichester

Air Officers Commanding (**with dates of appointment**)

AVM L.O. Brown – 10/11/43
AVM E.C. Hudleston – 10/11/44

No 85 (BASE) GROUP HEADQUARTERS
Formed 02/44 at Uxbridge, Middx

Air Officers Commanding (**with dates of appointment**)

AVM J.B. Cole-Hamilton – 13/02/44
AVM C.R. Steele – 10/07/44
AVM D.A. Boyle – 26/04/45

APPENDIX 3
RAF Fighter Command and Air Defence of Great Britain, Home-based Frontline Unit Strengths 1939–45

3 SEPTEMBER 1939
No 11 Group, HQ: Hillingdon House, Uxbridge, Middx

1 Sqn	Tangmere	Hurricane I
43 Sqn	Tangmere	Hurricane I
501 Sqn	Filton	Hurricane I
3 Sqn	Croydon	Hurricane I
17 Sqn	Croydon	Hurricane I
615 Sqn	Croydon	Gladiator I
601 Sqn	Biggin Hill	Blenheim If
54 Sqn	Hornchurch	Spitfire I
65 Sqn	Hornchurch	Spitfire I
74 Sqn	Hornchurch	Spitfire I
25 Sqn	Northolt	Blenheim If
111 Sqn	Northolt	Hurricane I
600 Sqn	Northolt	Blenheim If
56 Sqn	North Weald	Hurricane I
151 Sqn	North Weald	Hurricane I
604 Sqn	North Weald	Blenheim If
29 Sqn	Debden	Blenheim If
85 Sqn	Debden	Hurricane I
87 Sqn	Debden	Hurricane I

No 12 Group, HQ: Watnall, Notts

66 Sqn	Duxford	Spitfire I
611 Sqn	Duxford	Spitfire I
23 Sqn	Wittering	Blenheim If
213 Sqn	Wittering	Hurricane I
46 Sqn	Digby	Hurricane I
73 Sqn	Digby	Hurricane I
504 Sqn	Digby	Hurricane I
64 Sqn	Church Fenton	Blenheim If
72 Sqn	Church Fenton	Spitfire I

No 13 Group, HQ: Blakelaw Estate, Ponteland, Newcastle upon Tyne

41 Sqn	Catterick	Spitfire I
609 Sqn	Catterick	Spitfire I
603 Sqn	Turnhouse	Gladiator II; Spitfire I

15 SEPTEMBER 1940
No 9 Group, HQ: Preston, Lancs

308 Sqn	Speke	no a/c

APPENDIX 3 *continued*

No 10 Group, HQ: Rudloe Manor, Box, Wilts

79 Sqn	Pembrey	Hurricane I
87 Sqn	Exeter	Hurricane I
601 Sqn	Exeter	Hurricane I
247 Sqn	Roborough	Gladiator II
234 Sqn	Middle Wallop	Spitfire I
604 Sqn	Middle Wallop	Blenheim I; Beaufighter If
609 Sqn	Middle Wallop	Spitfire I
152 Sqn	Warmwell	Spitfire I

No 11 Group, HQ: Hillingdon House, Uxbridge, Middx

213 Sqn	Tangmere	Hurricane I
607 Sqn	Tangmere	Hurricane I
602 Sqn	Westhampnett	Spitfire I
501 Sqn	Kenley	Hurricane I
605 Sqn	Croydon	Hurricane I
72 Sqn	Biggin Hill	Spitfire I
92 Sqn	Biggin Hill	Spitfire I
600 Sqn	Redhill	Blenheim If; Beaufighter If
66 Sqn	Gravesend	Spitfire I
41 Sqn	Hornchurch	Spitfire I
222 Sqn	Hornchurch	Spitfire I
603 Sqn	Hornchurch	Spitfire I
1 (RCAF) Sqn	Northolt	Hurricane I
229 Sqn	Northolt	Hurricane I
303 Sqn	Northolt	Hurricane I
25 Sqn	North Weald	Blenheim If; Beaufighter If
249 Sqn	North Weald	Hurricane I
46 Sqn	Stapleford Tawney	Hurricane I
17 Sqn	Debden	Hurricane I
257 Sqn	Martlesham Heath	Hurricane I
23 Sqn	Ford	Blenheim If
73 Sqn	Castle Camps	Hurricane I

No 12 Group, HQ: Watnall, Notts

310 Sqn	Duxford	Hurricane I
312 Sqn	Duxford	Hurricane I
19 Sqn	Fowlmere	Spitfire I; IIa
74 Sqn	Coltishall	Spitfire I; IIa
242 Sqn	Coltishall	Hurricane I
1 Sqn	Wittering	Hurricane I
266 Sqn	Wittering	Spitfire IIa
611 Sqn	Digby	Spitfire I; IIa
29 Sqn	Wellingore	Blenheim If; Beaufighter If
264 Sqn	Kirton-in-Lindsey	Defiant I
307 Sqn	Kirton-in-Lindsey	Defiant I
616 Sqn	Kirton-in-Lindsey	Spitfire I
85 Sqn	Church Fenton	Hurricane I
306 Sqn	Church Fenton	Hurricane I

No 13 Group, HQ: Blakelaw Estate, Ponteland, Newcastle upon Tyne

54 Sqn	Catterick	Spitfire I
219 Sqn	Catterick	Blenheim If; Beaufighter If
64 Sqn	Leconfield	Spitfire I
302 Sqn	Leconfield	Hurricane I
32 Sqn	Acklington	Hurricane I
610 Sqn	Acklington	Spitfire I
43 Sqn	Usworth	Hurricane I
219 Sqn	Scorton	Blenheim If; Beaufighter If
3 Sqn	Turnhouse	Hurricane I
65 Sqn	Turnhouse	Spitfire I
141 Sqn	Turnhouse	Defiant I
615 Sqn	Prestwick	Hurricane I
111 Sqn	Drem	Hurricane I
263 Sqn	Drem	Hurricane I; Whirlwind I
245 Sqn	Aldergrove	Hurricane I

No 14 Group, HQ: Drummossie, Inverness

145 Sqn	Dyce	Hurricane I

1 JANUARY 1941

No 9 Group, HQ: Preston, Lancs

229 Sqn	Speke	Hurricane I
312 Sqn	Speke	Hurricane I
308 Sqn	Baginton	Hurricane I
306 Sqn	Tern Hill	Hurricane I
96 Sqn	Cranage	Hurricane I

No 10 Group, HQ: Rudloe Manor, Box, Wilts

79 Sqn	Pembrey	Hurricane I
263 Sqn	Exeter	Whirlwind I
504 Sqn	Exeter	Hurricane I
247 Sqn	Roborough	Gladiator II/Hurricane I
87 Sqn	Charmy Down	Hurricane I
501 Sqn	Filton	Hurricane I
32 Sqn	Middle Wallop	Hurricane I
93 Sqn	Middle Wallop	Harrow II; Havoc I
604 Sqn	Middle Wallop	Blenheim If; Beaufighter If

APPENDIX 3 *continued*

152 Sqn	Warmwell	Spitfire I
609 Sqn	Warmwell	Spitfire I
238 Sqn	Chilbolton	Hurricane I

No 11 Group, HQ: Hillingdon House, Uxbridge, Middx

65 Sqn	Tangmere	Spitfire I/IIa
145 Sqn	Tangmere	Hurricane I/Spitfire I
219 Sqn	Tangmere	Blenheim If; Beaufighter If
302 Sqn	Westhampnett	Hurricane I
610 Sqn	Westhampnett	Spitfire I
23 Sqn	Ford	Blenheim If
253 Sqn	Kenley	Hurricane I
615 Sqn	Kenley	Hurricane I
605 Sqn	Croydon	Hurricane IIa
66 Sqn	Biggin Hill	Spitfire IIa
74 Sqn	Biggin Hill	Spitfire IIa
92 Sqn	Biggin Hill	Spitfire I
141 Sqn	Gravesend	Defiant I
264 Sqn	Gravesend	Defiant I
41 Sqn	Hornchurch	Spitfire IIa
64 Sqn	Hornchurch	Spitfire I/IIa
611 Sqn	Southend	Spitfire I, IIa
1 Sqn	Northolt	Hurricane I
601 Sqn	Northolt	Hurricane I
56 Sqn	North Weald	Hurricane I
249 Sqn	North Weald	Hurricane I
85 Sqn	Debden	Hurricane I
17 Sqn	Martlesham Heath	Hurricane I
242 Sqn	Martlesham Heath	Hurricane I

No 12 Group, HQ: Watnall, Notts

19 Sqn	Duxford	Spitfire IIa
310 Sqn	Duxford	Hurricane I
222 Sqn	Coltishall	Spitfire I
257 Sqn	Coltishall	Hurricane I
25 Sqn	Wittering	Blenheim If/Beaufighter If
151 Sqn	Wittering	Defiant I
266 Sqn	Wittering	Spitfire I
2 (RCAF) Sqn	Digby	Hurricane I
46 Sqn	Digby	Hurricane I
29 Sqn	Wellingore	Blenheim If; Beaufighter If
71 Sqn	Kirton-in-Lindsey	Hurricane I
255 Sqn	Kirton-in-Lindsey	Defiant I
616 Sqn	Kirton-in-Lindsey	Spitfire I

No 13 Group, HQ: Blakelaw Estate, Ponteland, Newcastle upon Tyne

54 Sqn	Catterick	Spitfire I
256 Sqn	Catterick	Defiant I
600 Sqn	Catterick	Blenheim If; Beaufighter If
213 Sqn	Leconfield	Hurricane I
303 Sqn	Leconfield	Hurricane I
607 Sqn	Usworth	Hurricane I
72 Sqn	Acklington	Spitfire I
258 Sqn	Acklington	Hurricane I
43 Sqn	Drem	Hurricane I
603 Sqn	Drem	Spitfire IIa
602 Sqn	Prestwick	Spitfire I
245 Sqn	Aldergrove	Hurricane I

No 14 Group, HQ: Drummossie, Inverness

111 Sqn	Dyce	Hurricane I
1 (RCAF) Sqn	Castletown	Hurricane I
3 Sqn	Castletown	Hurricane I
260 Sqn	Skitten	Hurricane I

1 MAY 1942

No 9 Group, HQ: Preston, Lancs

232 Sqn	Atcham	Spitfire Vb
255 Sqn	High Ercall	Beaufighter IIf/VIf
257 Sqn	Honiley	Hurricane I, IIa, IIb, IIc; Spitfire Vb
131 Sqn	Llanbedr	Spitfire Vb
315 Sqn	Woodvale	Spitfire Vb

No 10 Group, HQ: Rudloe Manor, Box, Wilts

312 Sqn	Fairwood Common	Spitfire Vb
402 Sqn	Fairwood Common	Spitfire Vb
263 Sqn	Angle	Whirlwind I
234 Sqn	Portreath	Spitfire Vb
130 Sqn	Perranporth	Spitfire Vb, Vc
310 Sqn	Perranporth	Spitfire Vb
247 Sqn	Predannack	Hurricane I, IIc
600 Sqn	Predannack	Beaufighter VIf
1457 Flt	Predannack	Turbinlite Havoc
307 Sqn	Exeter	Beaufighter IIf/VIf
308 Sqn	Exeter	Spitfire Vb
306 Sqn	Culmhead	Spitfire Vb
125 Sqn	Colerne	Defiant I, II/Beaufighter IIf
1454 Flt	Colerne	Turbinlite Havoc

APPENDIX 3 *continued*

264 Sqn	Colerne	Defiant II/Mosquito II
87 Sqn	Charmy Down	Hurricane I, IIc
245 Sqn	Middle Wallop	Hurricane IIb, IIc
604 Sqn	Middle Wallop	Beaufighter If
1458 Flt	Middle Wallop	Turbinlite Havoc
175 Sqn	Warmwell	Hurricane IIb
302 Sqn	Warmwell	Spitfire Vb
66 Sqn	Ibsley	Spitfire Vb, Vc
118 Sqn	Ibsley	Spitfire Vb
501 Sqn	Ibsley	Spitfire Vb, Vc

No 11 Group, HQ: Hillingdon House, Uxbridge, Middx

1 Sqn	Tangmere	Hurricane I, IIc
219 Sqn	Tangmere	Beaufighter If
1455 Flt	Tangmere	Turbinlite Havoc
129 Sqn	Westhampnett	Spitfire Vb
340 Sqn	Westhampnett	Spitfire Vb
41 Sqn	Merston	Spitfire Vb
23 Sqn	Ford	Havoc I; Boston III
316 Sqn	Heston	Spitfire Vb
1422 Flt	Heston	Havoc
485 Sqn	Kenley	Spitfire Vb
602 Sqn	Kenley	Spitfire Vb
72 Sqn	Biggin Hill	Spitfire Vb
124 Sqn	Biggin Hill	Spitfire Vb
401 Sqn	Gravesend	Spitfire Vb
29 Sqn	West Malling	Beaufighter If
1452 Flt	West Malling	Turbinlite Havoc
457 Sqn	Redhill	Spitfire Vb
91 Sqn	Hawkinge	Spitfire Vb
64 Sqn	Hornchurch	Spitfire Vb
122 Sqn	Hornchurch	Spitfire Vb
303 Sqn	Northolt	Spitfire Vb
317 Sqn	Northolt	Spitfire Vb
121 Sqn	North Weald	Spitfire Vb
222 Sqn	North Weald	Spitfire Vb
403 Sqn	North Weald	Spitfire Vb
65 Sqn	Great Sampford	Spitfire Vb
313 Sqn	Fairlop	Spitfire Vb
32 Sqn	Manston	Hurricane I, IIb, IIc
174 Sqn	Manston	Hurricane IIb
418 Sqn	Bradwell Bay	Boston III
3 Sqn	Hunsdon	Hurricane IIc
85 Sqn	Hunsdon	Havoc II
1451 Flt	Hunsdon	Turbinlite Havoc
111 Sqn	Debden	Spitfire Vb
350 Sqn	Debden	Spitfire Vb
412 Sqn	Martlesham Heath	Spitfire Vb
157 Sqn	Castle Camps	Mosquito II

No 12 Group, HQ: Watnall, Notts

266 Sqn	Duxford	Spitfire Vb/Typhoon Ia, Ib
609 Sqn	Duxford	Spitfire Vb/Typhoon Ia, Ib
56 Sqn	Snailwell	Typhoon Ia, Ib
68 Sqn	Coltishall	Beaufighter If
137 Sqn	Matlaske	Whirlwind I
151 Sqn	Wittering	Defiant II/Mosquito II
486 Sqn	Wittering	Hurricane IIb
1453 Flt	Wittering	Turbinlite Havoc
411 Sqn	Digby	Spitfire Vb
421 Sqn	Digby	Spitfire Va/Vb
133 Sqn	Kirton-in-Lindsey	Spitfire Vb
253 Sqn	Hibaldstow	Hurricane I, IIa, IIb, IIc
1459 Flt	Hibaldstow	Turbinlite Havoc
19 Sqn	Hutton Cranswick	Spitfire Vb

No 13 Group, HQ: Blakelaw Estate, Ponteland, Newcastle upon Tyne

332 Sqn	Catterick	Spitfire Vb
81 Sqn	Ouston	Spitfire Vb
141 Sqn	Acklington	Beaufighter If
1460 Flt	Acklington	Turbinlite Havoc
242 Sqn	Turnhouse	Spitfire Vb
167 Sqn	Scorton	Spitfire Vb
416 Sqn	Peterhead	Spitfire Vb
410 Sqn	Drem	Defiant I/Beaufighter IIf
611 Sqn	Drem	Spitfire Vb
165 Sqn	Ayr	Spitfire Va/Vb
406 Sqn	Ayr	Beaufighter IIf

No 14 Group, HQ: Drummossie, Inverness

132 Sqn	Skeabrae	Spitfire Vb
331 Sqn	Skeabrae	Spitfire Vb

No 82 Group, HQ: (Northern Ireland)

25 Sqn	Ballyhalbert	Beaufighter If
153 Sqn	Ballyhalbert	Beaufighter If
152 Sqn	Eglinton	Spitfire IIa/Vb
504 Sqn	Kirkistown	Spitfire Vb

APPENDIX 3 *continued*

1 MARCH 1943

No 9 Group, HQ: Preston, Lancs

96 Sqn	Honiley	Beaufighter VIf
456 Sqn	Valley	Beaufighter IIf/Mosquito II
41 Sqn	High Ercall	Spitfire Vb/XII
195 Sqn	Woodvale	Typhoon Ib
219 Sqn	Scorton	Beaufighter If
256 Sqn	Woodvale	Beaufighter VIf

No 10 Group, HQ: Rudloe Manor, Box, Wilts

125 Sqn	Fairwood Common	Beaufighter VIf
130 Sqn	Perranporth	Spitfire Vc/Vb
602 Sqn	Perranporth	Spitfire Vc/Vb
141 Sqn	Predannack	Beaufighter If
266 Sqn	Exeter	Typhoon Ib
307 Sqn	Exeter	Mosquito II
310 Sqn	Exeter	Spitfire Vb, Vc
313 Sqn	Culmhead	Spitfire Vb, Vc
193 Sqn	Harrowbeer	Typhoon Ib
263 Sqn	Harrowbeer	Whirlwind I
264 Sqn	Colerne	Mosquito II
19 Sqn	Middle Wallop	Spitfire Vc/Vb
164 Sqn	Middle Wallop	Hurricane IId, IV
182 Sqn	Middle Wallop	Typhoon Ib
247 Sqn	Middle Wallop	Hurricane IIb/Typhoon Ib
406 Sqn	Middle Wallop	Beaufighter VIf
257 Sqn	Warmwell	Typhoon Ia, Ib
312 Sqn	Warmwell	Spitfire Vb, Vc
132 Sqn	Zeals	Spitfire Vb
504 Sqn	Ibsley	Spitfire Vb, Vc
616 Sqn	Ibsley	Spitfire VI
174 Sqn	Chilbolton	Hurricane IIb
175 Sqn	Stoney Cross	Hurricane IIb
184 Sqn	Chilbolton	Hurricane IId
412 Sqn	Hurn	Spitfire Vb

No 11 Group, HQ: Hillingdon House, Uxbridge, Middx

129 Sqn	Tangmere	Spitfire Vb
165 Sqn	Tangmere	Spitfire Vb
486 Sqn	Tangmere	Typhoon Ib
610 Sqn	Westhampnett	Spitfire Vb
604 Sqn		Beaufighter If
605 Sqn	Ford	Mosquito II
303 Sqn	Heston	Spitfire Vb
350 Sqn	Heston	Spitfire VC/Vb
515 Sqn	Heston	Defiant II
402 Sqn	Kenley	Spitfire IX/Vb
403 Sqn	Kenley	Spitfire IXb
416 Sqn	Kenley	Spitfire Vb/IX
421 Sqn	Kenley	Spitfire Vb
1 Sqn	Biggin Hill	Typhoon Ib
340 Sqn	Biggin Hill	Spitfire IXb
611 Sqn	Biggin Hill	Spitfire IX
29 Sqn	West Malling	Beaufighter If/VIf
91 Sqn	Hawkinge	Spitfire Vb
122 Sqn	Hornchurch	Spitfire IX
453 Sqn	Southend	Spitfire Vb
306 Sqn	Northolt	Spitfire IX/VB
308 Sqn	Northolt	Spitfire Vb
315 Sqn	Northolt	Spitfire IX, Vb
124 Sqn	North Weald	Spitfire VI, IX
331 Sqn	North Weald	Spitfire IXb
332 Sqn	North Weald	Spitfire IXb
64 Sqn	Fairlop	Spitfire IX/VB
137 Sqn	Manston	Whirlwind I
609 Sqn	Manston	Typhoon Ib
418 Sqn	Bradwell Bay	Boston III
3 Sqn	Hunsdon	Typhoon Ib
85 Sqn	Hunsdon	Mosquito II, XV, XII
157 Sqn	Castle Camps	Mosquito II

No 12 Group, HQ: Watnall, Notts

181 Sqn	Cranfield	Typhoon Ib
183 Sqn	Cranfield	Typhoon Ib
68 Sqn	Coltishall	Beaufighter VIf
118 Sqn	Coltishall	Spitfire Vb
56 Sqn	Matlaske	Typhoon Ib
151 Sqn	Wittering	Mosquito II
411 Sqn	Digby	Spitfire Vb
410 Sqn	Coleby Grange	Mosquito II
302 Sqn	Kirton-in-Lindsey	Spitfire Vb
317 Sqn	Kirton-in-Lindsey	Spitfire Vb
25 Sqn	Church Fenton	Mosquito II
316 Sqn	Hutton Cranswick	Spitfire Vb

APPENDIX 3 *continued*

No 13 Group, HQ: Blakelaw Estate, Ponteland, Newcastle upon Tyne

401 Sqn	Catterick	Spitfire Vb
198 Sqn	Acklington	Typhoon Ia/Ib
409 Sqn	Acklington	Beaufighter VIf
341 Sqn	Turnhouse	Spitfire Vb
65 Sqn	Drem	Spitfire Vb
197 Sqn	Drem	Typhoon Ib
222 Sqn	Ayr	Spitfire Vb
488 Sqn	Ayr	Beaufighter IIf/VIf

No 14 Group, HQ: Drummossie, Inverness

245 Sqn	Peterhead	Typhoon Ib
234 Sqn	Grimsetter	Spitfire IV, Vb, VI
66 Sqn	Skeabrae	Spitfire Vb, Vc
131 Sqn	Castletown	Spitfire Vb

No 82 Group, HQ: (Northern Ireland)

501 Sqn	Ballyhalbert	Spitfire Vb

APPENDIX 4
Allied Expeditionary Air Force: 2nd Tactical Air Force (2 TAF)

BATTLE ORDER – 5 JUNE 1944

Includes tactical/strike (83, 84 Grps) and air defence (85 Grp) elements; excludes No 2 Group squadrons, reconnaissance and AOP units.

No 83 Group

121 Wing	Holmsley South	174, 175, 245 Sqns	Typhoon Ib
122 Wing	Funtington	19, 65 122 Sqns	Mustang III
124 Wing	Hurn	181, 182, 247 Sqns	Typhoon Ib
125 Wing	Ford	132, 453, 602 Sqns	Spitfire IXb
126 Wing	Tangmere	401, 411, 412 Sqns	Spitfire IXb
127 Wing	Tangmere	403, 416, 421 Sqns	Spitfire IXb
129 Wing	Westhampnett	184 Sqn	Typhoon Ib
143 Wing	Hurn	438, 439, 440 Sqns	Typhoon Ib
144 Wing	Ford	441, 442, 443 Sqns	Spitfire IXb

No 84 Group

123 Wing	Thorney Island	198, 609 Sqns	Typhoon Ib
131 Wing	Chailey	302, 308, 317 Sqns	Spitfire IX, IXe
132 Wing	Bognor	66, 331, 332 Sqns	Spitfire IXb, LFIXb
133 Wing	Coolham	129, 306, 315 Sqns	Mustang III
134 Wing	Apuldram	310, 312, 313 Sqns	Spitfire IX, LFIX, LFIXb
135 Wing	Selsey	222, 349, 485 Sqns	Spitfire IXb, LFIXb, LFIXe
136 Wing	Thorney Island	164, 183 Sqns	Typhoon Ib
145 Wing	Merston	329, 340, 341 Sqns	Spitfire IX, IXb
146 Wing	Needs Ore Point	193, 197, 257, 266 Sqns	Typhoon Ib

APPENDIX 4 *continued*

No 85 Group

141 Wing	Hartfordbridge	264 Sqn	Mosquito XIII
		322 Sqn	Spitfire XIV
147 Wing	Zeals	488 Sqn	Mosquito XIII
148 Wing	West Malling	29, 409 Sqns	Mosquito XIII
		91 Sqn	Spitfire XIV
150 Wing	Newchurch	3, 486 Sqns	Tempest V
		56 Sqn	Spitfire IX
	Bradwell Bay	124 Sqn	Spitfire VII
	Hunsdon	410 Sqn	Mosquito XIII
	Hurn	604 Sqn	Mosquito XIII

Air Defence of Great Britain – units attached to 2 TAF

Shoreham	345 Sqn	Spitfire Vb
Friston	350 Sqn	Spitfire Vb, Vc
	501 Sqn	Spitfire Vb

APPENDIX 5
Air Defence of Great Britain

BATTLE ORDER – 5 JUNE 1944
No 10 Group. HQ: Rudloe Manor, Box, Wilts

1 Sqn	Predannack	Spitfire IXb
165 Sqn	Predannack	Spitfire IXb
152 Sqn	Predannack	Mosquito XIII
41 Sqn	Bolt Head	Spitfire XII
126 Sqn	Culmhead	Spitfire IXb
131 Sqn	Culmhead	Spitfire VII
616 Sqn	Culmhead	Spitfire VII
610 Sqn	Harrowbeer	Spitfire XIV
263 Sqn	Harrowbeer	Typhoon Ib
68 Sqn	Fairwood Common	Beaufighter VIf
406 Sqn	Winkleigh	Beaufighter VIf, Mosquito XII

No 11 Group, HQ: Hillingdon House, Uxbridge, Middx

33 Sqn	Lympne	Spitfire LF IXe
74 Sqn	Lympne	Spitfire LF IXe
127 Sqn	Lympne	Spitfiree HF IX
64 Sqn	Deanland	Spitfire Vc
234 Sqn	Deanland	Spitfire Vb
611 Sqn	Deanland	Spitfire LF Vb
80 Sqn	Detling	Spitfire IX
229 Sqn	Detling	Spitfire IX
274 Sqn	Detling	Spitfire IX
130 Sqn	Holme	Spitfire Vb
303 Sqn	Holme	Spitfire LF Vb
402 Sqn	Holme	Spitfire Vb, Vc
137 Sqn	Manston	Typhoon Ib
605 Sqn	Manston	Mosquito VI
96 Sqn	West Malling	Mosquito XIII
125 Sqn	Hurn	Mosquito XVII
219 Sqn	Bradwell Bay	Mosquito XVII
456 Sqn	Ford	Mosquito XVII
418 Sqn	Holmsley South	Mosquito XII

No 12 Group, HQ: Watnall, Notts

25 Sqn	Coltishall	Mosquito XVII
316 Sqn	Coltishall	Mustang III
307 Sqn	Church Fenton	Mosquito XII
504 Sqn	Digby (det at Acklington)	Spitfire Vb

APPENDIX 5 *continued*

No 13 Group, HQ: Blakelaw Estate, Ponteland, Newcastle upon Tyne

118 Sqn	Skeabrae (det at Sumburgh)	Spitfire Vb, VII
309 Sqn	Drem (det at Peterhead)	Hurricane IIc

1 JANUARY 1945

No 10 Group, HQ: Rudloe Manor, Box, Wilts

33 Sqn	Predannack	Tempest V
222 Sqn	Predannack	Tempest V
245 Sqn	Warmwell	Typhoon Ib
443 Sqn	Warmwell	Spitfire IXb

No 11 Group, HQ: Hillingdon House, Uxbridge, Middx

154 Sqn	Biggin Hill	Spitfire VII
322 Sqn	Biggin Hill	Spitfire LFXVIe
611 Sqn	Hawkinge	Spitfire IX
264 Sqn	Odiham	Mosquito XIII
418 Sqn	Blackbushe	Mosquito VI
605 Sqn	Blackbushe	Mosquito VI
1 Sqn	Manston	Spitfire IXb
91 Sqn	Manston	Spitfire IXb/XXI
124 Sqn	Manston	Spitfire HFIXe
406 Sqn	Manston	Mosquito XXX
504 Sqn	Manston	Spitfire IXe
616 Sqn	Manston	Meteor I
29 Sqn	Hunsdon	Mosquito XIII
151 Sqn	Hunsdon	Mosquito XXX
310 Sqn	Bradwell Bay	Spitfire LFIX
312 Sqn	Bradwell Bay	Spitfire HFIX
313 Sqn	Bradwell Bay	Spitfire IX
501 Sqn	Bradwell Bay	Tempest V
19 Sqn	Andrews Field	Mustang III
65 Sqn	Andrews Field	Mustang III
122 Sqn	Andrews Field	Mustang III
306 Sqn	Andrews Field	Mustang III
316 Sqn	Andrews Field	Mustang III
64 Sqn	Bentwaters	Mustang III
118 Sqn	Bentwaters	Spitfire IXc/Mustang III
126 Sqn	Bentwaters	Mustang III
129 Sqn	Bentwaters	Mustang III
165 Sqn	Bentwaters	Mustang III
234 Sqn	Bentwaters	Mustang III
25 Sqn	Castle Camps	Mosquito XXX, VI

No 12 Group, HQ: Watnall, Notts

68 Sqn	Coltishall	Mosquito XVII, XIX
125 Sqn	Coltishall	Mosquito XVII
229 Sqn	Coltishall	Spitfire LFXVIe
303 Sqn	Coltishall	Spitfire LFVb, IXc
307 Sqn	Church Fenton	Mosquito XII/XXX
456 Sqn	Church Fenton	Mosquito XVII, XXX

No 13 Group, HQ: Blakelaw Estate, Ponteland, Newcastle upon Tyne

315 Sqn	Peterhead	Mustang III
340 Sqn	Drem	Spitfire IXb
441 Sqn	Skeabrae	Spitfire IX

No 38 Group, HQ: Marks Hall, Earls Colne, Essex

298 Sqn	Tarrant Rushton	Halifax III
644 Sqn	Tarrant Rushton	Halifax III
296 Sqn	Earls Colne	Halifax V
297 Sqn	Earls Colne	Halifax V
196 Sqn	Wethersfield	Stirling IV
299 Sqn	Wethersfield	Stirling IV
295 Sqn	Rivenhall	Stirling IV
570 Sqn	Rivenhall	Stirling IV
190 Sqn	Great Dunmow	Stirling IV
620 Sqn	Great Dunmow	Stirling IV

APPENDIX 6
RAF Fighter Command Training Unit Strengths 1939–45

3 SEPTEMBER 1939

11 Grp Pool	St Athan	Hurricane
12 Grp Pool	Aston Down	Hurricane; Gladiator; Blenheim

Miscellaneous Units

Heston Special Flt	Heston	Blenheim; Spitfire; Hudson

15 SEPTEMBER 1940

5 OTU	Aston Down	Spitfire; Hurricane; Blenheim
6 OTU	Sutton Bridge	Hurricane
7 OTU	Hawarden	Spitfire

Miscellaneous Units

Fighter Interception Unit (FIU)		
	Shoreham	Beaufighter; Blenheim
No 1 Camouflage Unit		
	Baginton	Reliant; Blenheim; Spitfire
No 2 School of Army Co-operation		
	Andover	Blenheim; Anson

1 JANUARY 1941
No 81 (OTU) Group, HQ: Autumn Avenue, Worcester

54 OTU	Church Fenton	Blenheim; Beaufighter
55 OTU	Aston Down	Spitfire; Hurricane; Blenheim
56 OTU	Sutton Bridge	Hurricane
57 OTU	Hawarden	Spitfire
58 OTU	Grangemouth	Spitfire

Miscellaneous Units

FIU	Shoreham	Blenheim; Beaufighter
Air Fighting Development Unit (AFDU)		
	Duxford	Spitfire; Hurricane; various
No 1 Camouflage Unit		
	Baginton	Reliant; Blenheim; Spitfire
No 2 School of Army Co-operation		
	Andover	Blenheim; Anson

1 MAY 1942
No 81 (OTU) Group, HQ: Avening, Stroud, Glos

51 OTU	Cranfield; Twinwood Farm	Blenheim; Beaufighter
52 OTU	Aston Down	Spitfire
53 OTU	Llandow; Rhoose	Spitfire
54 OTU	Charter Hall; Winfield	Blenheim; Beaufighter
55 OTU	Annan; Longtown	Hurricane
56 OTU	Tealing; Kinnell	Hurricane
57 OTU	Hawarden	Spitfire
58 OTU	Grangemouth; Balado Bridge	Spitfire
59 OTU	Crosby-on-Eden; Longtown	Hurricane
60 OTU	East Fortune; Macmerry	Blenheim; Beaufighter
61 OTU	Rednal; Montford Bridge	Spitfire

Miscellaneous Units

FIU	Ford	Blenheim; Beaufighter
AFDU	Duxford	Spitfire; Hurricane; various

1 MARCH 1943
No 81 (OTU) Group, HQ: Avening, Stroud, Glos

41 OTU	Hawarden; Poulton	Mustang; Hurricane
51 OTU	Cranfield; Twinwood Farm	Blenheim; Beaufighter
52 OTU	Aston Down	Spitfire
53 OTU	Llandow; Rhoose	Spitfire
54 OTU	Charter Hall; Winfield	Blenheim; Beaufighter
55 OTU	Annan; Longtown	Hurricane
56 OTU	Tealing; Kinnell	Hurricane; Spitfire
57 OTU	Eshott; Boulmer	Spitfire
58 OTU	Grangemouth; Balado Bridge	Spitfire
59 OTU	Milfield; Brunton; Boulmer	Hurricane
61 OTU	Rednal; Montford Bridge	Spitfire
62 OTU	Usworth	Anson

Miscellaneous Units

FIU	Ford	Blenheim; Beaufighter; Mosquito
AFDU	Duxford	Spitfire; Hurricane; various
Fighter Leaders' School		
	Charmy Down	Spitfire

6 JUNE 1944
No 9 Group, HQ: Barton Hall, Preston, Lancs

13 OTU	Bicester; Finmere	Mosquito; Boston
41 OTU	Hawarden; Poulton	Mustang; Hurricane
42 OTU	Ashbourne; Darley Moor	Whitley, Oxford; Anson; Albemarle
51 OTU	Cranfield; Twinwood Farm	Mosquito
53 OTU	Kirton-in-Lindsey; Hibaldstow; Caistor	Spitfire
54 OTU	Charter Hall; Winfield	Beaufighter
57 OTU	Eshott; Boulmer	Spitfire
59 OTU	Boulmer	Hurricane; Typhoon

APPENDIX 6 *continued*

60 OTU	High Ercall	Mosquito
61 OTU	Rednal; Montford Bridge	Spitfire
62 OTU	Ouston	Anson; Wellington
1 TEU	Kinnell	Hurricane; Spitfire
2 TEU	Grangemouth; Balado Bridge	Spitfire
3 TEU	Annan	Typhoon; Hurricane

Miscellaneous Units

FIU	Wittering	Mosquito; various
Fighter Leaders' School	Milfield; Brunton	Spitfire; Typhoon; Hurricane
ORTU	Hampstead Norris	Albemarle; Tiger Moth; Whitley; Horsa
83 GSU	Redhill	Typhoon
84 GSU	Aston Down	Typhoon; Tempest; Spitfire; Mustang

1 JANUARY 1945
Nos 11, 12, 13 and 38 Groups

13 OTU	Harwell; Finmere	Mosquito
41 OTU	Hawarden; Poulton	Mustang; Hurricane
42 OTU	Ashbourne; Darley Moor	Albemarle; Oxford; Anson
51 OTU	Cranfield; Twinwood Farm	Mosquito
53 OTU	Kirton-in-Lindsey; Caistor; Hibaldstow	Spitfire
54 OTU	Charter Hall; Winfield	Mosquito
55 OTU	Aston Down; Chedworth	Typhoon; Hurricane
56 OTU	Milfield; Brunton	Typhoon; Tempest
57 OTU	Eshott; Boulmer	Spitfire
60 OTU	High Ercall	Mosquito
61 OTU	Rednal; Montford Bridge	Spitfire; Mustang
62 OTU	Ouston	Anson; Wellington

Miscellaneous Units

ORTU	Hampstead Norris	Albemarle; Tiger Moth; Whitley; Horsa
FIDS/NFDW	Ford	Mosquito; various
83 GSU	Westhampnett	Mustang; Spitfire
84 GSU	Lasham	Mustang; Spitfire

APPENDIX 7
RAF Bomber Command Headquarters and Air Officer Commanders-in-Chief 1939–45

Headquarters

Formed 14/07/36 at Hillingdon House, Uxbridge, Middx
08/39–03/40 – Richings Park, Langley, Bucks
03/40–04/69 – High Wycombe, Bucks

Air Officer Commanders-in-Chief (with dates of appointment)

ACM Sir Edgar Ludlow-Hewitt – 12/09/37
AM Sir Charles Portal – 03/04/40
AM Sir Richard Peirse – 05/10/40
AVM J.E.A. Baldwin (Acting AOC-in-C) 09/01/42
ACM Sir Arthur Harris 22/02/42–15/09/45

Senior Air Staff Officers (with dates of appointment)

Air Cdre N.H. Bottomley – 17/11/38
AVM R.H.M.S. Saundby – 21/11/40

No 1 GROUP HEADQUARTERS

Formed 01/05/36 at Abingdon, Berks
09/39 – Benson, Oxon
12/39 – Disbanded
06/40 – Re-formed Hucknall, Notts
07/41 – Bawtry Hall, Yorks

Air Officers Commanding (with dates of appointment)

AVM A.C. Wright – 03/09/39
Air Cdre J.J. Breen – 27/06/40
AVM R.D. Oxland – 27/11/40
AVM E.A.B. Rice – 24/02/43
AVM R.S. Blucke – 12/02/45

No 2 GROUP HEADQUARTERS

Formed 20/03/36 at Abingdon, Berks
05/38 – Wyton, Hunts
10/39 – Castlewood House, Hunts
05/43 – Bylaugh Hall, East Dereham, Norfolks
01/06/43 – No 2 Group joined 2 TAF and left Bomber Command control for duration of war

APPENDIX 7 *continued*

Air Officers Commanding (with dates of appointment)

AVM C.T. Maclean – 16/05/38
AVM J.M. Robb – 17/04/40
AVM D.F. Stevenson – 12/02/41
AVM A. Lees – 17/12/41
AVM J.H. D'Albiac – 29/12/42
AVM B.E. Embry – 01/06/43 (2 TAF)

No 3 GROUP HEADQUARTERS

Formed 01/05/36 at Andover, Hants
01/37 – Mildenhall, Suffolk
03/40 – Exning, Suffolk

Air Officers Commanding (with dates of appointment)

AVM J.E.A. Baldwin – 28/08/39
AVM The Hon R.A. Cochrane – 14/09/42
AVM R. Harrison – 27/02/43

No 4 GROUP HEADQUARTERS

Formed 01/04/37 at Mildenhall, Suffolk
06/37 – Linton-on-Ouse, Yorks
04/40 – Heslington Hall, Yorks
07/05/45 – to Transport Command

Air Officers Commanding (with dates of appointment)

AVM A. Coningham – 03/07/39
AVM C.R. Carr – 26/07/41
AVM J.R. Whitley – 12/02/45

No 5 GROUP HEADQUARTERS

Formed 01/09/37 at Mildenhall, Suffolk
10/37 – St Vincent's, Grantham, Lincs
11/43 – Moreton Hall, Swinderby, Lincs
12/45 – Disbanded

Air Officers Commanding (with dates of appointment)

Air Cdre W.B. Calloway – 17/08/37
AVM A.T. Harris – 11/09/39
AVM N.R. Bottomley – 22/11/40
AVM J.C. Slessor – 12/05/41
AVM W.A. Coryton – 25/04/42
AVM The Hon Sir R.A. Cochrane – 28/02/43
AVM H.A. Constantine – 16/02/45

No 6 (BOMBER) GROUP HEADQUARTERS

Formed 02/09/39 at Abingdon, Berks
09/39 – Abingdon, Berks
11/05/42 – No 6 (Bomber) Group became No 91 (OTU) Group

Air Officers Commanding (with dates of appointment)

Air Cdre W.F. McN. Foster – 02/09/39
Gp Capt H.S.P. Walmsley – 16/03/42

No 6 (RCAF) GROUP HEADQUARTERS

Formed 25/10/42 at Allerton Park, Yorks
08/45 – UK HQ disbanded

Air Officers Commanding (with dates of appointment)

AVM G.E. Brookes – 25/10/42
AVM C.M. McEwen – 29/02/44
Air Cdre J.L. Hurley – 19/06/45

No 8 (PATHFINDER) GROUP HEADQUARTERS

Formed 15/08/42 at Wyton, Hunts, as 'Pathfinder Force' and redesignated No 8 (PFF) Group at Wyton on 13/01/43
08/42 – Wyton, Hunts
06/43 – Castle Hill House, Hunts
12/45 – Disbanded

Air Officers Commanding (with dates of appointment)

AVM D.C.T. Bennett – 13/01/43 (Bennett, as an Air Cdre, had been appointed to command the PFF in 08/42)
AVM J.R. Whitley – 21/05/45

No 100 (SPECIAL DUTIES) GROUP HEADQUARTERS

Formed 23/11/43 at Radlett, Herts
23/11/43 – Radlett, Herts
03/12/43 – West Raynham, Norfolk
01/01/44 – Bylaugh Hall, East Dereham, Norfolk
12/45 – Disbanded

APPENDIX 7 *continued*

Air Officers Commanding (with date of appointment)

AVM E.B. Addison – 18/11/43

No 91 (OTU) GROUP HEADQUARTERS

Formed 11/05/42 at Abingdon, Berks

Air Officers Commanding (with dates of appointment)

Gp Capt H.S.P Walmsley – 16/03/42
AVM J.A. Gray – 08/02/44

No 92 (OTU) GROUP HEADQUARTERS

Formed 14/05/42 at Winslow Hall, Bucks

Air Officers Commanding (with dates of appointment)

Gp Capt H.A. Haines – 14/05/42
AVM H.K. Thorold – 17/03/43

NO 93 (OTU) GROUP HEADQUARTERS

Formed 15/06/42 at Egginton Hall, Derby

Air Officers Commanding (with dates of appointment)

Gp Capt C.E. Maitland – 15/06/42
Air Cdre A.P. Ritchie – 25/02/43
AVM O.T. Boyd – 24/02/44
AVM G.S. Hodson – 09/08/44

No 7 (HCU) GROUP HEADQUARTERS

Formed 01/11/44 at St Vincent's, Grantham, Lincs

Air Officer Commanding (with date of appointment)

AVM G.S. Hodson – 01/11/44

APPENDIX 8
RAF Bomber Command, Homebased Frontline Unit Strengths 1939–45

27 SEPTEMBER 1939
No 1 Group, HQ: Forming at Benson, Oxon

No 2 Group, HQ: Wyton, Cambs

21 Sqn	79 Wing Watton	Blenheim I, IV
82 Sqn		
114 Sqn	82 Wing Wyton	Blenheim I, IV
139 Sqn		
107 Sqn	83 Wing Wattisham	Blenheim I, IV
110 Sqn		
101 Sqn	West Raynham	Blenheim IV

No 3 Group, HQ: Mildenhall, Suffolk

9 Sqn	Honington	Wellington I
37 Sqn	Feltwell	Wellington I
38 Sqn	Marham	Wellington I
99 Sqn	Mildenhall	Wellington I
115 Sqn	Marham	Wellington I
149 Sqn	Mildenhall	Wellington I
214 Sqn	Feltwell	Wellington I
215 Sqn	Bassingbourn	Wellington I; Harrow

No 4 Group, HQ: Linton-on-Ouse, Yorks

10 Sqn	Dishforth	Whitley IV
51 Sqn	Linton-on-Ouse	Whitley II, III
58 Sqn	Linton-on-Ouse	Whitley III
77 Sqn	Driffield	Whitley III, V
78 Sqn	Dishforth	Whitley I, IV, V
102 Sqn	Driffield	Whitley III

No 5 Group, HQ: St Vincent's, Grantham, Lincs

44 Sqn	Waddington	Hampden
49 Sqn	Scampton	Hampden
50 Sqn	Waddington	Hampden
61 Sqn	Hemswell	Hampden
83 Sqn	Scampton	Hampden
106 Sqn	Cottesmore	Hampden
144 Sqn	Hemswell	Hampden
185 Sqn	Cottesmore	Hampden

FEBRUARY 1940
No 1 Group: in France as a part of AASF under control of HQ, AASF, Reims

No 2 Group, HQ: Castlewood House, Huntingdon

15 Sqn	Wyton	Blenheim IV
21 Sqn	Watton	Blenheim IV

APPENDIX 8 *continued*

40 Sqn	Wyton	Blenheim IV
82 Sqn	Watton	Blenheim IV
101 Sqn	West Raynham	Blenheim IV
107 Sqn	Wattisham	Blenheim IV
110 Sqn	Wattisham	Blenheim IV

No 3 Group, HQ: Exning, Suffolk

9 Sqn	Honington	Wellington I
37 Sqn	Feltwell	Wellington I
38 Sqn	Marham	Wellington I
99 Sqn	Newmarket	Wellington I
115 Sqn	Marham	Wellington I
149 Sqn	Mildenhall	Wellington I
214 Sqn	Methwold	Wellington I

No 4 Group, HQ: Linton-on-Ouse, Yorks

10 Sqn	Dishforth	Whitley IV
51 Sqn	Dishforth	Whitley III, IV, V
58 Sqn	Linton-on-Ouse	Whitley III
77 Sqn	Driffield	Whitley V
78 Sqn	Linton-on-Ouse	Whitley IV, V
102 Sqn	Driffield	Whitley V

No 5 Group, HQ: St Vincent's, Grantham, Lincs

44 Sqn	Waddington	Hampden
49 Sqn	Scampton	Hampden
50 Sqn	Waddington	Hampden
61 Sqn	Hemswell	Hampden
83 Sqn	Scampton	Hampden
106 Sqn	Finningley	Hampden
144 Sqn	Hemswell	Hampden

FEBRUARY 1941

No 1 Group, HQ: Hucknall, Notts

12 Sqn	Binbrook	Wellington II
103 Sqn	Newton	Wellington I
142 Sqn	Binbrook	Wellington II
150 Sqn	Newton	Wellington I
300 Sqn	Swinderby	Wellington I
301 Sqn	Swinderby	Wellington I
304 Sqn	Syerston	Wellington I
305 Sqn	Syerston	Wellington I

No 2 Group, HQ: Castlewood House, Huntingdon

18 Sqn	Great Massingham	Blenheim IV
21 Sqn	Watton	Blenheim IV
82 Sqn	Watton	Blenheim IV
101 Sqn	West Raynham	Blenheim IV
105 Sqn	Swanton Morley	Blenheim IV
107 Sqn	Wattisham	Blenheim IV
110 Sqn	Wattisham	Blenheim IV
114 Sqn	Oulton	Blenheim IV
139 Sqn	Horsham St Faith	Blenheim IV

No 3 Group, HQ: Exning, Suffolk

7 Sqn	Oakington	Stirling I
9 Sqn	Honington	Wellington I
15 Sqn	Wyton	Wellington I
40 Sqn	Wyton	Wellington I
57 Sqn	Feltwell	Wellington I
75 Sqn	Feltwell	Wellington I
99 Sqn	Newmarket	Wellington I
115 Sqn	Marham	Wellington I
149 Sqn	Mildenhall	Wellington I
214 Sqn	Stradishall	Wellington I
311 Sqn	East Wretham	Wellington I

No 4 Group, HQ: Heslington Hall, Yorks

10 Sqn	Leeming	Whitley V
35 Sqn	Linton-on-Ouse	Whitley V
51 Sqn	Dishforth	Whitley V
58 Sqn	Linton-on-Ouse	Whitley V
77 Sqn	Topcliffe	Whitley V
78 Sqn	Dishforth	Whitley V
102 Sqn	Topcliffe	Whitley V

No 5 Group, HQ: St Vincent's, Grantham, Lincs

44 Sqn	Waddington	Hampden
49 Sqn	Scampton	Hampden
57 Sqn	Methwold	Wellington I
61 Sqn	Hemswell	Hampden
83 Sqn	Scampton	Hampden
97 Sqn	Waddington	Manchester
106 Sqn	Coningsby	Hampden
144 Sqn	Hemswell	Hampden
207 Sqn	Waddington	Manchester

APPENDIX 8 *continued*

FEBRUARY 1942

No 1 Group, HQ: Bawtry Hall, Yorks

12 Sqn	Binbrook	Wellington I
101 Sqn	Bourn	Wellington I, III
142 Sqn	Grimsby/Waltham	Wellington IV
150 Sqn	Snaith	Wellington I
300 Sqn	Hemswell	Wellington IV
301 Sqn	Hemswell	Wellington IV
304 Sqn	Lindholme	Wellington I
305 Sqn	Lindholme	Wellington II
460 Sqn	Breighton	Wellington IV

No 2 Group, HQ: Castlewood House, Huntingdon

18 Sqn	Wattisham	Blenheim IV
82 Sqn	Watton	Blenheim IV
88 Sqn	Attlebridge	Blenheim IV/Boston III
98 Sqn	Foulsham	Mitchell II
105 Sqn	Horsham St Faith	Mosquito IV
107 Sqn	Great Massingham	Blenheim IV/Boston III
110 Sqn	Wattisham	Blenheim IV
139 Sqn	Oulton	Hudson III
226 Sqn	Swanton Morley	Boston III

No 3 Group, HQ: Exning, Suffolk

7 Sqn	Oakington	Stirling I
9 Sqn	Honington	Wellington III
15 Sqn	Wyton	Stirling I
40 Sqn	Alconbury	Wellington I
75 Sqn	Feltwell	Wellington III
90 Sqn	Polebrook	Fortress I/Blenheim IV
99 Sqn	Waterbeach	Wellington I
101 Sqn	Oakington	Wellington I
109 Sqn	Tempsford	Wellington I
115 Sqn	Marham	Wellington I, III
138 Sqn	Stradishall	Lysander IIIa; Whitley V; Halifax II
149 Sqn	Mildenhall	Stirling I
156 Sqn	Alconbury	Wellington I, III
161 Sqn	Newmarket	Lysander IIIa; Hudson I; Whitley V
214 Sqn	Stradishall	Wellington I
218 Sqn	Marham	Stirling I
311 Sqn	East Wretham	Wellington I
419 Sqn	Mildenhall	Wellington I, III

No 4 Group, HQ: Heslington Hall, Yorks

10 Sqn	Leeming	Halifax I, II
35 Sqn	Linton-on-Ouse	Halifax I, II
51 Sqn	Dishforth	Whitley V
58 Sqn	Linton-on-Ouse	Whitley V
76 Sqn	Middleton St George	Halifax I, II
77 Sqn	Leeming	Whitley V
102 Sqn	Dalton	Whitley V, Halifax II
104 Sqn	Driffield	Wellington II
158 Sqn	Driffield	Halifax II
405 Sqn	Pocklington	Wellington II
458 Sqn	Holme	Wellington I

No 5 Group, HQ: St Vincent's, Grantham, Lincs

44 Sqn	Waddington	Lancaster I
49 Sqn	Scampton	Hampden
50 Sqn	Skellingthorpe	Hampden
57 Sqn	Methwold	Wellington III
61 Sqn	Woolfox Lodge	Manchester
83 Sqn	Scampton	Manchester
97 Sqn	Coningsby	Manchester/Lancaster I
106 Sqn	Coningsby	Hampden/Manchester
207 Sqn	Bottesford	Manchester
408 Sqn	Balderton	Hampden
420 Sqn	Waddington	Hampden
455 Sqn	Wigsley	Hampden

FEBRUARY 1943

No 1 Group, HQ: Bawtry Hall, Yorks

12 Sqn	Wickenby	Lancaster I, III
101 Sqn	Holme	Lancaster I, III
103 Sqn	Elsham Wolds	Lancaster I, III
166 Sqn	Kirmington	Wellington III, X
199 Sqn	Ingham	Wellington III
300 Sqn	Hemswell	Wellington III
301 Sqn	Hemswell	Wellington IV
305 Sqn	Hemswell	Wellington IV
460 Sqn	Breighton	Lancaster I, III

No 2 Group, HQ: Castlewood House, Huntingdon

21 Sqn	Methwold	Ventura I, II
88 Sqn	Oulton	Boston III
98 Sqn	Foulsham	Mitchell II
105 Sqn	Marham	Mosquito IV

APPENDIX 8 *continued*

107 Sqn	Great Massingham	Boston III, IIIa
139 Sqn	Marham	Mosquito IV
180 Sqn	Foulsham	Mitchell II
226 Sqn	Swanton Morley	Boston III, IIIa
464 Sqn	Feltwell	Ventura I, II
487 Sqn	Feltwell	Ventura II

No 3 Group, HQ: Exning, Suffolk

15 Sqn	Bourn	Stirling I, III
75 Sqn	Newmarket	Stirling I
90 Sqn	Ridgewell	Stirling I
115 Sqn	East Wretham	Wellington III
138 Sqn	Tempsford	Halifax II, V
149 Sqn	Lakenheath	Stirling I, III
161 Sqn	Tempsford	Lysander; Halifax; Hudson; Havoc; Albemarle
192 Sqn	Gransden Lodge	Wellington I, III, X; Mosquito IV
214 Sqn	Chedburgh	Stirling I, III
218 Sqn	Downham Market	Stirling I, III

No 4 Group, HQ: Heslington Hall, Yorks

10 Sqn	Melbourne	Halifax II
51 Sqn	Snaith	Halifax II
76 Sqn	Linton-on-Ouse	Halifax II, V
77 Sqn	Elvington	Halifax II
78 Sqn	Linton-on-Ouse	Halifax II
102 Sqn	Pocklington	Halifax II
158 Sqn	Rufforth	Halifax II
196 Sqn	Leconfield	Wellington X
429 Sqn	East Moor	Wellington III, X
466 Sqn	Leconfield	Wellington X

No 5 Group, HQ: St Vincent's, Grantham, Lincs

9 Sqn	Waddington	Lancaster I, III
44 Sqn	Waddington	Lancaster I, III
49 Sqn	Fiskerton	Lancaster I, III
50 Sqn	Skellingthorpe	Lancaster I, III
57 Sqn	Scampton	Lancaster I, III
61 Sqn	Syerston	Lancaster I, III
97 Sqn	Woodhall Spa	Lancaster I, III
106 Sqn	Syerston	Lancaster I, III
207 Sqn	Langar	Lancaster I, III
467 Sqn	Bottesford	Lancaster I, III

No 6 (RCAF) Group, HQ: Allerton Park, Yorks

405 Sqn	det Beaulieu, Hants	Halifax II
408 Sqn	Leeming	Halifax II
419 Sqn	Middleton St George	Halifax II, X
420 Sqn	Middleton St George	Wellington III, X
424 Sqn	Topcliffe	Wellington III, X
425 Sqn	Dishforth	Wellington III
426 Sqn	Dishforth	Wellington III
427 Sqn	Croft	Wellington III, X
428 Sqn	Dalton	Wellington III

No 8 (PFF) Group, HQ: Wyton, Hunts

7 Sqn	Oakington	Stirling I, III
35 Sqn	Graveley	Halifax II
83 Sqn	Wyton	Lancaster I, III
109 Sqn	Wyton	Mosquito IV
156 Sqn	Warboys	Wellington III; Lancaster I, III

FEBRUARY 1944

No 1 Group, HQ: Bawtry Hall, Yorks

12 Sqn	Wickenby	Lancaster I, III
100 Sqn	Grimsby/Waltham	Lancaster I, III
101 Sqn	Ludford Magna	Lancaster I, III
103 Sqn	Elsham Wolds	Lancaster I, III
166 Sqn	Kirmington	Lancaster I, III
300 Sqn	Ingham	Wellington X
460 Sqn	Binbrook	Lancaster I, III
550 Sqn	North Killingholme	Lancaster I, III
576 Sqn	Elsham Wolds	Lancaster I, III
625 Sqn	Kelstern	Lancaster I, III
626 Sqn	Wickenby	Lancaster I, III

No 2 Group: under control of 2 TAF

No 3 Group, HQ: Exning, Suffolk

15 Sqn	Mildenhall	Lancaster I, III
75 Sqn	Mepal	Stirling III
90 Sqn	Tuddenham	Stirling III
115 Sqn	Witchford	Lancaster II
138 Sqn	Tempsford	Halifax II, V
149 Sqn	Lakenheath	Stirling III
161 Sqn	Tempsford	Halifax V; Hudson IIIa, V
199 Sqn	Lakenheath	Stirling III
218 Sqn	Downham Market	Stirling III
514 Sqn	Waterbeach	Lancaster II
622 Sqn	Mildenhall	Lancaster I, III

APPENDIX 8 *continued*

No 4 Group, HQ: Heslington Hall, Yorks

10 Sqn	Melbourne	Halifax II
51 Sqn	Snaith	Halifax III
76 Sqn	Holme	Halifax V, III
77 Sqn	Elvington	Halifax II
78 Sqn	Breighton	Halifax III
102 Sqn	Pocklington	Halifax II
158 Sqn	Lissett	Halifax III
466 Sqn	Leconfield	Halifax III
578 Sqn	Burn	Halifax III
640 Sqn	Leconfield	Halifax III

No 5 Group, HQ: Moreton Hall, Swinderby, Lincs

9 Sqn	Bardney	Lancaster I, III
44 Sqn	Dunholme Lodge	Lancaster I, III
49 Sqn	Fiskerton	Lancaster I, III
50 Sqn	Skellingthorpe	Lancaster I, III
57 Sqn	East Kirkby	Lancaster I, III
61 Sqn	Coningsby	Lancaster I, III
97 Sqn	Bourn	Lancaster I, III
106 Sqn	Metheringham	Lancaster I, III
207 Sqn	Spilsby	Lancaster I, III
463 Sqn	Waddington	Lancaster I, III
467 Sqn	Waddington	Lancaster I, III
617 Sqn	Woodhall Spa	Lancaster I, III
619 Sqn	Coningsby	Lancaster I, III
630 Sqn	East Kirkby	Lancaster I, III

No 6 (RCAF) Group, HQ: Allerton Park, Yorks

408 Sqn	Linton-on-Ouse	Lancaster II
419 Sqn	Middleton St George	Halifax II
420 Sqn	Tholthorpe	Halifax III
424 Sqn	Skipton-on-Swale	Halifax III
425 Sqn	Tholthorpe	Halifax III
426 Sqn	Linton-on-Ouse	Lancaster II
427 Sqn	Leeming	Halifax V, III
428 Sqn	Middleton St George	Halifax V, II
429 Sqn	Leeming	Halifax V
431 Sqn	Croft	Halifax V
432 Sqn	East Moor	Lancaster II; Halifax III
433 Sqn	Skipton-on-Swale	Halifax III
434 Sqn	Croft	Halifax V

No 8 (PFF) Group, HQ: Castle Hill House, Hunts

7 Sqn	Oakington	Lancaster I, III
35 Sqn	Graveley	Halifax III
83 Sqn	Wyton	Lancaster I, III
105 Sqn	Marham	Mosquito IV, IX
109 Sqn	Marham	Mosquito IV, IX
139 Sqn	Upwood	Mosquito IV, IX, XVI, XX
156 Sqn	Warboys	Lancaster I, III
405 Sqn	Gransden Lodge	Lancaster I, III
627 Sqn	Oakington	Mosquito IV
692 Sqn	Graveley	Mosquito IV

No 100 (SD) Group, HQ: Bylaugh Hall, East Dereham, Norfolk

141 Sqn	West Raynham	Mosquito II
169 Sqn	Little Snoring	Mosquito II
192 Sqn	Foulsham	Wellington X; Halifax V; Mosquito IV
214 Sqn	Sculthorpe	Stirling I; Fortress II
239 Sqn	West Raynham	Mosquito II
515 Sqn	Little Snoring	Beaufighter IIf; Mosquito II

22 MARCH 1945

No 1 Group, HQ: Bawtry Hall, Yorks

12 Sqn	Wickenby	Lancaster I, III
100 Sqn	Grimsby	Lancaster I, III
101 Sqn	Ludford Magna	Lancaster I, III
103 Sqn	Elsham Wolds	Lancaster I, III
150 Sqn	Hemswell	Lancaster I, III
153 Sqn	Scampton	Lancaster I, III
166 Sqn	Kirmington	Lancaster I, III
170 Sqn	Hemswell	Lancaster I, III
300 Sqn	Faldingworth	Lancaster I, III
460 Sqn	Binbrook	Lancaster I, III
550 Sqn	North Killingholme	Lancaster I, III
576 Sqn	Fiskerton	Lancaster I, III
625 Sqn	Kelstern	Lancaster I, III
626 Sqn	Wickenby	Lancaster I, III

No 3 Group, HQ: Exning, Suffolk

15 Sqn	Mildenhall	Lancaster I, III
75 Sqn	Mepal	Lancaster I, III
90 Sqn	Tuddenham	Lancaster I, III
115 Sqn	Witchford	Lancaster I, III
149 Sqn	Methwold	Lancaster I, III

APPENDIX 8 *continued*

186 Sqn	Stradishall	Lancaster I, III
195 Sqn	Wratting Common	Lancaster I, III
218 Sqn	Chedburgh	Lancaster I, III
514 Sqn	Waterbeach	Lancaster I, III
622 Sqn	Mildenhall	

No 4 Group, HQ: Heslington Hall, Yorks

10 Sqn	Melbourne	Halifax III
51 Sqn	Snaith	Halifax III
76 Sqn	Holme	Halifax III, VI
77 Sqn	Full Sutton	Halifax III, VI
78 Sqn	Breighton	Halifax III
102 Sqn	Pocklington	Halifax III, VI
158 Sqn	Lissett	Halifax III
346 Sqn	Elvington	Halifax III, VI
347 Sqn	Elvington	Halifax III, VI
466 Sqn	Driffield	Halifax III
640 Sqn	Leconfield	Halifax III, VI

No 5 Group, HQ: Moreton Hall, Swinderby, Lincs

9 Sqn	Bardney	Lancaster I, III
44 Sqn	Spilsby	Lancaster I, III
49 Sqn	Fulbeck	Lancaster I, III
50 Sqn	Skellingthorpe	Lancaster I, III
57 Sqn	East Kirkby	Lancaster I, III
61 Sqn	Skellingthorpe	Lancaster I, III
106 Sqn	Metheringham	Lancaster I, III
189 Sqn	Fulbeck	Lancaster I, III
207 Sqn	Spilsby	Lancaster I, III
227 Sqn	Balderton	Lancaster I, III
463 Sqn	Waddington	Lancaster I, III
467 Sqn	Waddington	Lancaster I, III
617 Sqn	Woodhall Spa	Lancaster I, III; Mosquito VI
619 Sqn	Strubby	Lancaster I, III
630 Sqn	East Kirkby	Lancaster I, III

On loan from No 8 (PFF) Group

83 Sqn (PFF) Coningsby	Lancaster I, III
97 Sqn (PFF) Coningsby	Lancaster I, III
627 Sqn (PFF) Woodhall Spa	Mosquito IV, IX, XVI, XX, XXV

No 6 (RCAF) Group, HQ: Allerton Park, Yorks

408 Sqn	Linton-on-Ouse	Halifax VII
415 Sqn	East Moor	Halifax III, VII
419 Sqn	Middleton St George	Lancaster X
420 Sqn	Tholthorpe	Halifax III
424 Sqn	Skipton-on-Swale	Lancaster I, III
425 Sqn	Tholthorpe	Halifax III
426 Sqn	Linton-on-Ouse	Halifax VII
427 Sqn	Leeming	Lancaster I, III; Halifax III
428 Sqn	Middleton St George	Lancaster X
431 Sqn	Croft	Lancaster X
432 Sqn	East Moor	Halifax VII
433 Sqn	Skipton-on-Swale	Lancaster I, III, Halifax III
434 Sqn	Croft	Lancaster I, III, X

No 8 (PFF) Group, HQ: Castle Hill House, Hunts

7 Sqn	Oakington	Lancaster I, III
35 Sqn	Graveley	Lancaster I, III
105 Sqn	Bourn	Mosquito IX, XVI
109 Sqn	Little Staughton	Mosquito IX, XVI
128 Sqn	Wyton	Mosquito XVI
139 Sqn	Upwood	Mosquito IX, XVI, XX, XXV
142 Sqn	Gransden Lodge	Mosquito XXV
156 Sqn	Upwood	Lancaster I, III
162 Sqn	Bourn	Mosquito XX, XXV
163 Sqn	Wyton	Mosquito XXV
405 Sqn	Gransden Lodge	Lancaster I, III
571 Sqn	Oakington	Mosquito XVI
582 Sqn	Little Staughton	Lancaster I, III
608 Sqn	Downham Market	Mosquito XX, XXV
635 Sqn	Downham Market	Lancaster I, III
692 Sqn	Graveley	Mosquito XVI

No 100 (SD) Group, HQ: Bylaugh Hall, East Dereham, Norfolk

23 Sqn	Little Snoring	Mosquito VI
85 Sqn	Swannington	Mosquito XXX
141 Sqn	West Raynham	Mosquito VI, XXX
157 Sqn	Swannington	Mosquito XIX, XXX
169 Sqn	Great Massingham	Mosquito VI, XIX
171 Sqn	North Creake	Halifax III
192 Sqn	Foulsham	Halifax III; Mosquito IV, XVI
199 Sqn	North Creake	Halifax III; Stirling III
214 Sqn	Oulton	Fortress III
223 Sqn	Oulton	Liberator IV
239 Sqn	West Raynham	Mosquito XXX
462 Sqn	Foulsham	Halifax III
515 Sqn	Little Snoring	Mosquito VI

APPENDIX 9
RAF Bomber Command Training Unit Strengths 1939-45

SEPTEMBER 1939
No 6 Group, HQ: Abingdon, Berks

97 Sqn	Abingdon	Whitley	(No 4 Group Pool)
166 Sqn			
104 Sqn	Bicester	Blenheim	(No 2 Group Pool)
108 Sqn			
90 Sqn	Upwood	Blenheim	(No 2 Group Pool)
52 Sqn	Benson	Battle	(No 1 Group Pool)
63 Sqn			
35 Sqn	Cranfield	Battle	(No 1 Group Pool)
207 Sqn			
98 Sqn	Hucknall	Battle	(No 1 Group Pool)
75 Sqn	Harwell	Wellington	(No 3 Group Pool)
148 Sqn			
7 Sqn	Upper Heyford	Hampden	(No 5 Group Pool)
76 Sqn			

JUNE 1940
No 6 Group, HQ: Abingdon, Berks

10 OTU	Abingdon	Whitley II, III, V
11 OTU	Bassingbourn	Wellington I
12 OTU	Benson	Battle
13 OTU	Bicester Weston-on-the-Green	Blenheim I, IV
14 OTU	Cottesmore	Hampden; Hereford
15 OTU	Harwell	Wellington I
16 OTU	Upper Heyford	Hampden; Hereford
17 OTU	Upwood	Blenheim I, IV
18 OTU	Bramcote	Wellington I, III
19 OTU	Kinloss	Whitley II, III, V
20 OTU	Lossiemouth Elgin	Wellington I

FEBRUARY 1941
No 6 Group, HQ: Abingdon, Berks

10 OTU	Abingdon Stanton Harcourt	Whitley III, V
12 OTU	Benson Mount Farm	Wellington I
15 OTU	Harwell Hampstead Norris	Wellington I
19 OTU	Kinloss Lossiemouth	Whitley III, V
20 OTU	Elgin	Wellington I

No 7 Group, HQ: Bicester

11 OTU	Bassingbourn Steeple Morden	Wellington I
13 OTU	Bicester Hinton-in-the-Hedges	Blenheim I, IV
14 OTU	Cottesmore Woolfox Lodge	Hampden; Hereford
16 OTU	Upper Heyford Croughton	Hampden; Hereford
17 OTU	Upwood	Blenheim I, IV
18 OTU	Bramcote	Wellington I

FEBRUARY 1942
No 1 Group, HQ: Bawtry Hall, Yorks

1653 HCU	Polebrook	Liberator III

No 3 Group, HQ: Exning, Suffolk

1651 HCU	Waterbeach	Stirling I

No 4 Group, HQ: Heslington Hall, Yorks

1652 HCU	Marston Moor	Halifax

No 6 Group, HQ: Abingdon, Berks

10 OTU	Abingdon	Whitley V
12 OTU	Chipping Warden	Wellington I
15 OTU	Harwell Hampstead Norris	Wellington I
19 OTU	Kinloss Forres	Whitley V
20 OTU	Lossiemouth Elgin	Wellington I
21 OTU	Moreton-in-Marsh Edgehill	Wellington I
22 OTU	Wellesbourne Mountford Stratford	Wellington I
23 OTU	Pershore	Wellington I

No 7 Group, HQ: Bicester

11 OTU	Bassingbourn Steeple Morden	Wellington
13 OTU	Bicester Hinton-in-the-Hedges	Blenheim I, IV
14 OTU	Cottesmore Saltby	Hampden; Hereford

APPENDIX 9 *continued*

16 OTU	Upper Heyford Croughton	Hampden
17 OTU	Upwood	Blenheim I, IV
18 OTU	Bramcode Bitteswell	Wellington I
25 OTU	Finningley	Wellington I
26 OTU	Wing	Wellington I
27 OTU	Lichfield Tatenhill	Wellington I

FEBRUARY 1943

No 1 Group, HQ: Bawtry Hall, Yorks

1662 HCU	Blyton	Halifax I, II; Lancaster I

No 3 Group, HQ: Exning, Suffolk

1651 HCU	Waterbeach	Stirling I
1657 HCU	Stradishall	Stirling I

No 4 Group. HQ: Heslington Hall, Yorks

1652 HCU	Marston Moor	Halifax I, II, V
1658 HCU	Riccall	Halifax I, II, V
1659 HCU	Leeming	Halifax I, II, V

No 5 Group, HQ: St Vincent's, Grantham, Lincs

1654 HCU	Wigsley	Manchester; Lancaster I; Halifax II, V
1656 HCU	Lindholme	Manchester; Lancaster I; Halifax V
1660 HCU	Swinderby	Manchester; Lancaster I; Halifax II, V
1661 HCU	Winthorpe	Lancaster I; Halifax I, II

No 91 Group, HQ: Abingdon, Berks

10 OTU	Abingdon Stanton Harcourt	Whitley V
15 OTU	Harwell Hampstead Norris	Wellington Ic
19 OTU	Kinloss Forres	Whitley V
20 OTU	Lossiemouth Elgin	Wellington I
21 OTU	Moreton-in-Marsh Edgehill	Wellington I
22 OTU	Wellesbourne Mountford Gaydon	Wellington I, III
23 OTU	Pershore Stratford	Wellington I
24 OTU	Honeybourne Long Marston	Whitley V

No 92 Group, HQ: Winslow, Bucks

11 OTU	Westcott Oakley	Wellington I
12 OTU	Chipping Warden Turweston	Wellington
13 OTU	Bicester Finmere	Blenheim I, IV
14 OTU	Cottesmore Saltby	Wellington I
16 OTU	Upper Heyford Hinton-in-the-Hedges	Wellington I, III
17 OTU	Upwood	Blenheim I, IV
26 OTU	Wing Little Horwood	Wellington I, III
29 OTU	North Luffenham	Wellington I, III
81 OTU	Tilstock	Whitley V

No 93 Group, HQ: Egginton Hall, Derby

18 OTU	Bramcote Bitteswell	Wellington I, III
27 OTU	Lichfield Church Broughton	Wellington I, III
28 OTU	Wymeswold Castle Donington	Wellington I, III
30 OTU	Hixon Seighford	Wellington III, X

FEBRUARY 1944

No 1 Group, HQ: Bawtry Hall, Yorks

1662 HCU	Blyton	Halifax I, II, V
1667 HCU	Sandtoft	Halifax II, V
1 LFS	Hemswell	Lancaster I, III

No 3 Group, HQ: Exning, Suffolk

1651 HCU	Wratting Common	Stirling I, III
1653 HCU	Chedburgh	Stirling I, III
1657 HCU	Stradishall	Stirling I, III
3 LFS	Feltwell	Lancaster I, III

APPENDIX 9 *continued*

No 4 Group, HQ: Heslington Hall, Yorks

1652 HCU	Marston Moor	Halifax I, II, V; Stirling III
1658 HCU	Riccall	Halifax I, II, V
1663 HCU	Rufforth	Halifax II

No 5 Group, HQ: Moreton Hall, Swinderby, Lincs

1654 HCU	Wigsley	Stirling III; Lancaster I, III
1656 HCU	Lindholme	Halifax V; Lancaster I, III
1660 HCU	Swinderby	Stirling I, III
1661 HCU	Winthorpe	Stirling III
5 LFS	Syerston	Lancaster I, III

No 6 (RCAF) Group, HQ: Allerton Park, Yorks

1664 HCU	Dishforth	Halifax II, V
1666 HCU	Wombleton	Halifax II; Lancaster I, II

No 8 (PFF) Group, HQ: Castle Hill House, Hunts

PFF Navigation Training Unit		
	Upwood	Lancaster; Mosquito

No 91 Group, HQ: Abingdon, Berks

10 OTU	Abingdon Stanton Harcourt	Whitley V, VII
15 OTU	Harwell Hampstead Norris	Wellington III, X
19 OTU	Kinloss Forres	Wellington III, X
20 OTU	Lossiemouth Elgin	Wellington III, X
21 OTU	Moreton-in-Marsh Enstone	Wellington III, X
22 OTU	Wellesbourne Mounford	
	Gaydon	Wellington III, X
23 OTU	Pershore Stratford	Wellington III, X
24 OTU	Honeybourne Long Marston	Wellington III, X

No 92 Group, HQ: Winslow, Bucks

11 OTU	Westcott Oakley	Wellington III, X
12 OTU	Chipping Warden Edgehill	Wellington III, X
14 OTU	Market Harborough Husbands Bosworth	Wellington III, X
16 OTU	Upper Heyford Barford St John	Wellington III, X
17 OTU	Silverstone Turweston	Wellington III, X
26 OTU	Wing Little Horwood	Wellington III, X
28 OTU	Wymeswold Castle Donington	Wellington III, X
29 OTU	Bruntingthorpe Bitteswell	Wellington III, X
84 OTU	Desborough	Wellington III, X

No 93 Group, HQ: Egginton Hall, Derby

18 OTU	Finningley Doncaster	Wellington III, X
27 OTU	Lichfield Church Broughton	Wellington III, X
30 OTU	Hixon Seighford	Wellington III, X
82 OTU	Ossington Gamston	Wellington III, X
83 OTU	Peplow Wellington	Wellington III, X

FEBRUARY 1945

No 7 Group, HQ: St Vincent's, Grantham, Lincs

1651 HCU	Woolfox Lodge	Lancaster I, III
1652 HCU	Marston Moor	Halifax II, V, III
1653 HCU	North Luffenham	Lancaster I, III
1654 HCU	Wigsley	Stirling III; Lancaster I, III
1656 HCU	Lindholme	Halifax V; Lancaster I, III
1658 HCU	Riccall	Halifax II, V, III
1659 HCU	Topcliffe	Halifax V, III; Lancaster I, III
1660 HCU	Swinderby	Stirling III; Lancaster I, III
1661 HCU	Winthorpe	Stirling III; Lancaster I, III
1662 HCU	Blyton	Lancaster I, III
1663 HCU	Rufforth	Halifax III
1664 HCU	Dishforth	Halifax II, V; Lancaster I, III, X
1666 HCU	Wombleton	Lancaster I, III, X
1667 HCU	Sandtoft	Halifax V; Lancaster I, III
1668 HCU	Bottesford	Lancaster I, III
1669 HCU	Langar	Halifax II, V; Lancaster I, III
Bomber Instructors' School, Finningley		
		Wellington X; Halifax; Lancaster I, III

APPENDIX 9 *continued*

No 91 Group, HQ: Abingdon, Berks

10 OTU	Abingdon	Wellington X
19 OTU	Kinloss	Wellington X
20 OTU	Lossiemouth	Wellington X
	Elgin	
21 OTU	Moreton-in-Marsh	Wellington X
	Enstone	
22 OTU	Wellesbourne Mountford	Wellington III, X
	Gaydon	
24 OTU	Honeybourne	Wellington X
	Long Marston	
27 OTU	Lichfield	Wellington X
	Church Broughton	
30 OTU	Gamston	Wellington III, X
	Hixon	

No 92 OTU, HQ: Winslow, Bucks

11 OTU	Westcott	Wellington X
	Oakley	
12 OTU	Chipping Warden	Wellington X
	Edgehill	
14 OTU	Market Harborough	Wellington X
16 OTU	Upper Heyford	Wellington X; Mosquito III, IV, VI
	Barford St John	
17 OTU	Silverstone	Wellington X
	Turweston	
26 OTU	Wing	Wellington III, X
	Little Horwood	
29 OTU	Bruntingthorpe	Wellington X
84 OTU	Desborough	Wellington X
85 OTU	Husbands Bosworth	Wellington X

No 8 (PFF) Group, HQ: Castle Hill House, Hunts

PFF Navigation Training Unit		
	Warboys	Lancaster I, III; Mosquito IV, XVI, XX, XXV

No 100 Group, HQ: Bylaugh Hall, East Dereham, Norfolk

1699 HCU	Oulton	Fortress II, III; Liberator IV

APPENDIX 10
RAF Coastal Command Headquarters and Air Officer Commanders-in-Chief 1939–45

HEADQUARTERS

Formed 14/07/36 at Northwood, Middx.
08/39–03/40 – Richings Park, Langley, Bucks
03/40–04/69 – High Wycombe, Bucks

Air Officer Commanders-in-Chief (with dates of appointment)

08/37 – AM Sir F. Bowhill
06/41 – ACM Sir P. Joubert de la Ferté
02/43 – AM Sir John Slessor
01/44 – ACM Sir W. Sholto Douglas
06/45 – AM Sir L. Slatter

RAF Coastal Command Frontline and Training Groups, Headquarters and Air Officers Commanding

No 15 Group

Formed 15 March 1939 at Lee-on-Solent, Hants

Air Officers Commanding (with dates of appointment)

06/39 – Air Cdre R.G. Parry
02/41 – AVM J.M. Robb
04/42 – AVM D. Colyer
11/42 – AVM T.A. Langford-Sainsbury
02/43 – AVM Sir L. Slatter

No 16 Group

Formed 1 December 1936 at Wykeham Hall, Lee-on-Solent, Hants

Air Officers Commanding (with dates of appointment)

08/39 – Air Cdre R.L.G. Marix
01/40 – AVM J.H.S. Tyssen
02/42 – Air Cdre I.T. Lloyd
07/42 – AVM B.E. Baker
07/43 – AVM F.L. Hopps

No 17 (T) Group

Formed 1 December 1936 at Wykeham Hall, Lee-on-Solent, Hants.

APPENDIX 10 *continued*

Air Officers Commanding (with dates of appointment)

11/38 – Air Cdre T.E.B. Howe
11/41 – Air Cdre H.G. Smart

No 18 Group

Formed 1 September 1938 at Lee-on-Solent, Hants.

HQ: Pitreavie Castle

Air Officers Commanding (with dates of appointment)

09/38 – Air Commodore C.D. Breese
03/41 – Air Vice-Marshal R.L.G. Marix
02/42 – Air Vice-Marshal A. Durston
01/43 – Air Vice-Marshal A.B. Ellwood
02/44 – Air Vice-Marshal S.P. Simpson

No 19 Group

Formed January 1941 at Mount Wise, Plymouth, Devon.

Air Officers Commanding (with dates of appointment)

02/41 – Air Cdre G.H. Boyce
09/41 – AVM G.R. Bromet
07/43 – AVM B.E. Baker
12/44 – AVM F.H.M. Maynard
09/45 – AVM C.B.S. Spackman

No 106 (PR) Group

Formed 14 April 1944 at Benson, Oxon.
04/44 – Air Cdre J.N. Boothman
06/45 – Air Cdre A.W.B. McDonald

APPENDIX 11
Coastal Command, Homebased Frontline Unit Strengths 1939–45

3 SEPTEMBER 1939
No 15 Group

HQ: Mount Wise, Plymouth, Devon

204 Sqn	Mount Batten	Sunderland
210 Sqn	Pembroke Dock	Sunderland
217 Sqn	Warmwell	Anson
228 Sqn	Pembroke Dock	Sunderland
502 Sqn	Aldergrove	Anson

No 16 Group

HQ: Chatham, Kent

22 Sqn	Thorney Island	Vildebeeste
42 Sqn	Bircham Newton	Vildebeeste
48 Sqn	Thorney Island	Anson
206 Sqn	Bircham Newton	Anson
500 Sqn	Detling	Anson

No 17 Group (T)

HQ: Fort Grange, Gosport, Hants

Torpedo Training School	Gosport	N/A
School of General Reconnaissance	Thorney Island	N/A
Seaplane Training Sqn	Calshot	N/A

No 18 Group

HQ: Pitreavie Castle, Dunfermline

201 Sqn	Sullom Voe	London
209 Sqn	Invergordon	Stranraer
220 Sqn	Thorney Island	Anson
224 Sqn	Leuchars	Hudson
233 Sqn	Leuchars	Hudson
240 Sqn	Invergordon	London
269 Sqn	Montrose	Anson
608 Sqn	Thornaby	Anson
612 Sqn	Dyce	Anson

1 NOVEMBER 1940
No 15 Group

HQ: Egg Buckland Keep, Plymouth, Devon

48 Sqn	Hooton Park	Vildebeest (or Anson)
209 Sqn	Pembroke Dock	Anson, Beaufort (or Lerwick)
217 Sqn	St Eval	Blenheim (or Anson, Beaufort)
236 Sqn	St Eval	Anson (or Blenheim IVF)
321 Sqn	Carew Cheriton	Anson

APPENDIX 11 *continued*

502 Sqn	Aldergrove	Whitley (+Botha?)
10 (RAAF) Sqn	Pembroke Dock	Sunderland

No 16 Group

HQ: Chatham, Kent

53 Sqn	Detling	Blenheim IV
59 Sqn	Thorney Island	Blenheim IV
206 Sqn	Bircham Newton	Hudson
220 Sqn	Thorney Island (or Thornaby?)	Hudson
235 Sqn	Bircham Newton	Blenheim IVF
500 Sqn	Detling	Anson
608 Sqn	Thorney Island	Anson (+ Botha?)

No 18 Group

HQ: Pitreavie Castle, Dunfermline

42 Sqn	Wick	Beaufort
98 Sqn	Kaldadarnes	Battle
201 Sqn	Sullom Voe	Sunderland
204 Sqn	Sullom Voe	Sunderland
210 Sqn	Oban	Sunderland
224 Sqn	Leuchars	Hudson
233 Sqn	Leuchars	Hudson
240 Sqn	Stranraer	Stranraer
248 Sqn	Dyce	Blenheim IVF
254 Sqn	Dyce	Blenheim IVF
320 Sqn	Leuchars	Anson, Hudson
612 Sqn	Dyce	Anson

12 FEBRUARY 1942

No 15 Group

HQ: Derby House, Liverpool

53 Sqn	Limavady	Hudson
120 Sqn	Nutts Corner	Liberator
143 Sqn	Aldergrove	Blenheim IV
201 Sqn	Castle Archdale	Sunderland
206 Sqn	Aldergrove	Hudson
210 Sqn	Oban	Catalina
220 Sqn	Nutts Corner	Flying Fortress
228 Sqn	Stranraer	Sunderland
240 Sqn	Castle Archdale	Catalina
1402 (Met) Flt	Aldergrove	Spitfire, Gladiator
1405 (Met) Flt	Aldergrove	Blenheim, Hudson

No 16 Group

HQ: Chatham, Kent

22 Sqn	Thorney Island	Beaufort, Hudson
59 Sqn	North Coates	Hudson
217 Sqn	Thorney Island	Beaufort
233 Sqn	Thorney Island	Hudson
248 Sqn	Bircham Newton	Beaufighter
279 Sqn	Bircham Newton	Hudson
280 Sqn	Detling	Anson
407 (RCAF) Sqn	North Coates	Hudson
415 (RCAF) Sqn	Bircham Newton	Catalina
500 (AuxAF) Sqn	Bircham Newton	Hudson
502 (AuxAF) Sqn	Bircham Newton	Whitley
1401 (Met) Flt	Bircham Newton	Blenheim
Photographic Reconnaissance Unit	Benson	Spitfire

No. 18 Group

HQ: Pitreavie Castle, Dunfermline

42 Sqn	Leuchars	Beaufort
48 Sqn	Wick	Hudson
235 Sqn	Dyce	Beaufighter
320 (Dutch) Sqn	Leuchars	Hudson
404 (RCAF) Sqn	Sumburgh	Blenheim IV
413 (RCAF) Sqn	Sullom Voe	Catalina
489 (NZ) Sqn	Leuchars	Blenheim IV
608 (AuxAF) Sqn	Wick	Hudson
1406 (Met) Flt	Wick	Blenheim
1408 (Met) Flt	Wick	Hudson

No. 19 Group

HQ: Mount Wise, Plymouth, Devon

22 Sqn	St Eval	Beaufort
86 Sqn	St Eval	Beaufort
209 Sqn	Pembroke Dock	Catalina
217 Sqn	St Eval	Beaufort
224 Sqn	St Eval	Hudson
254 Sqn	Carew Cheriton	Blenheim IVF
502 Sqn	St Eval	Whitley
10 (RAAF) Sqn	Mount Batten	Sunderland
1404 (Met) Flt	St Eval	Hudson
1417 (Leigh Light Trials) Flt	Chivenor	Wellington
Photographic Reconnaissance Unit	St Eval	Spitfire

APPENDIX 11 *continued*

15 FEBRUARY 1943

No 15 Group

HQ: Derby House, Liverpool

59 Sqn	Aldergrove	Liberator V
86 Sqn	Aldergrove	Liberator V, IIIA
120 Sqn	Aldergrove (det Keflavik)	Liberator
201 Sqn	Castle Archdale	Sunderland III
206 Sqn	Benbecula	Fortress IIA
220 Sqn	Aldergrove	Fortress IIA
228 Sqn	Castle Archdale	Sunderland
246 Sqn	Bowmore	Sunderland
422 (RCAF) Sqn	Oban	Sunderland
423 (RCAF) Sqn	Castle Archdale	Sunderland III
1402 Flt	Aldergrove	Spitfire, Gladiator, Hudson

No 16 Group

HQ: Chatham, Kent

53 Sqn	Docking	Hudson
86 Sqn	Thorney Island	Liberator
143 Sqn	North Coates	Beaufighter XIC
236 Sqn	North Coates	Beaufighter X
254 Sqn	North Coates	Beaufighter X
320 Sqn	Bircham Newton	Hudson
407 (RCAF) Sqn	Docking	Hudson
521 Sqn	Bircham Newton	Spitfire, Hudson, Mosquito, Gladiator
540 Sqn	Benson	Mosquito
541 Sqn	Benson	Spitfire
542 Sqn	Benson	Spitfire
543 Sqn	Benson	Spitfire
544 Sqn	Benson	Wellington, Spitfire, Anson
833 (FAA) Sqn	Thorney Island	Swordfish
836 (FAA) Sqn	Thorney Island	Swordfish

No 18 Group

HQ: Pitreavie Castle, Dunfermline

144 Sqn	Leuchars	Beaufighter X
190 Sqn	Sullom Voe	Catalina IB
235 Sqn	Leuchars	Beaufighter X
455 (RAAF) Sqn	Leuchars	Hampden I
489 (RNZAF) Sqn	Wick	Hampden I
540 Sqn (det)	Leuchars	Mosquito
547 Sqn	Tain	Wellington
612 Sqn	Wick	Whitley
1406 (Met) Flt	Wick	Spitfire, Hudson
1408 (Met) Flt	Wick	Hampden
1477 Flt	Woodhaven	Catalina

No 19 Group

HQ: Mount Wise, Plymouth, Devon

10 (RAAF) Sqn	Mount Batten	Sunderland
58 Sqn	Holmsley South	Whitley, Halifax II
59 Sqn	Chivenor	Fortress
119 Sqn	Pembroke Dock	Sunderland
172 Sqn	Chivenor	Wellington XII
179 Sqn (det)	??	Wellington
210 Sqn	Pembroke Dock	Catalina IB
224 Sqn	Beaulieu	Liberator V
248 Sqn	Predannack	Beaufighter X
304 (Polish) Sqn	Dale	Wellington XIII
311 (Czech) Sqn	Talbenny	Wellington
404 Sqn	Chivenor	Beaufighter
405 Sqn	Beaulieu	Halifax
461 (RAAF) Sqn	Hamworthy	Sunderland III
502 Sqn	St Eval	Whitley
543 Sqn (det)	St Eval	Spitfire
1404 (Met) Flt	St Eval	Hudson, Ventura
1 (USAAF) AS Sqn	St Eval	B-24 Liberator
2 (USAAF) AS Sqn	St Eval	B-24 Liberator

1 MAY 1945

No. 15 Group

HQ: Derby House, Liverpool

36 Sqn	Benbecula	Wellington XIV
59 Sqn	Ballykelly	Liberator VIII
120 Sqn	Ballykelly	Liberator VIII
172 Sqn	Limavady	Wellington XIV
201 Sqn	Castle Archdale	Sunderland III, V
202 Sqn	Castle Archdale	Catalina IVA
423 (RCAF) Sqn	Castle Archdale	Sunderland III, V

No. 16 Group

HQ: Chatham, Kent

236 Sqn	North Coates	Beaufighter X
254 Sqn	North Coates	Beaufighter X
254 Sqn	North Coates	Mosquito XVIII

APPENDIX 11 *continued*

407 (RCAF) Sqn (det)		
	Langham	Wellington XIV
524 Sqn	Langham	Wellington XIV
612 Sqn	Langham	Wellington XIV
810 (FAA) Sqn	Beccles	Barracuda
822 (FAA) Sqn	Manston	Barracuda

No. 18 Group

HQ: Pitreavie Castle, Dunfermline

58 Sqn	Stornoway	Halifax II, III
86 Sqn	Tain	Liberator VIII
143 Sqn	Banff	Mosquito VI
144 Sqn	Dallachy	Beaufighter X
206 Sqn	Leuchars	Liberator VIII
210 Sqn	Sullom Voe	Catalina IVA
224 Sqn	Milltown	Liberator VIII
235 Sqn	Banff	Mosquito VI
248 Sqn	Banff	Mosquito VI
311 (Czech) Sqn	Tain	Liberator VI
330 (Norge) Sqn	Sullom Voe	Sunderland III
333 (Norge) Flt	Banff	Mosquito VI
333 (Norge) Flt	Woodhaven	Catalina IVA
404 (RCAF) Sqn	Banff	Mosquito VI
455 (RAAF) Sqn	Dallachy	Beaufighter X
489 (RNZAF) Sqn	Dallachy	Beaufighter X
502 Sqn	Stornoway	Halifax II, III
547 Sqn	Leuchars	Liberator VI, VIII
1693 Flt	Sumburgh	Anson I

No 19 Group

HQ: Mount Wise, Plymouth, Devon

10 (RAAF) Sqn	Mount Batten	Sunderland III
14 Sqn	Chivenor	Wellington XIV
63 (USN) Sqn	Upottery (det)	Catalina (PB4Y) (on loan)
103 (USN) Sqn	Dunkeswell	Liberator (PB4Y) (on loan)
105 (USN) Sqn	Dunkeswell	Liberator (PB4Y) (on loan)
107 (USN) Sqn	Upottery	Liberator (PB4Y) (on loan)
110 (USN) Sqn	Dunkeswell	Liberator (PB4Y) (on loan)
112 (USN) Sqn	Upottery	Liberator (PB4Y) (on loan)
179 Sqn	St Eval	Warwick V
228 Sqn	Pembroke Dock	Sunderland III, V
304 (Polish) Sqn	St Eval	Wellington XIV
407 (RCAF) Sqn	Chivenor	Wellington XIV (det Langham)
422 (RCAF) Sqn	Pembroke Dock	Sunderland III
461 (RAAF) Sqn	Pembroke Dock	Sunderland III, V

Photographic Reconnaissance

541 Sqn	Benson	Spitfire X, XI, XIX, Mustang III
542 Sqn	Benson	Spitfire X, XI, XIX
544 Sqn	Benson	Mosquito VI, XVI (det Leuchars)

Air-Sea Rescue

278 Sqn	Beccles	Walrus, Sea Otter (dets Thorney Island, Hawkinge)
279 Sqn	Banff	Warwick I, Sea Otter,

ABOVE: Wellington GR Mk XIVs pictured at Chivenor, North Devon, during the summer of 1943. MP774 'P' in the foreground is a visitor from No 179 Squadron, while the other aircraft belong to No 407 (Canadian) Squadron, which was based at Chivenor for much of the war from April 1943. (IWM FLM1995)

		Hurricane IIC (dets Thornaby, Wick)
280 Sqn	Beccles	Warwick I
281 Sqn	Tiree	Warwick I, Sea Otter (dets Limavady, Valley)
282 Sqn	St Eval	Warwick I, Sea Otter (det Exeter)

Meteorological

517 Sqn	Brawdy	Halifax III, V
518 Sqn	Tiree	Halifax III, V
519 Sqn	Wick	Fortress II, IIA, Spitfire VII
521 Sqn	Langham	Fortress II, IIA, Hurricane IIC
1402 Flt	Ballyhalbert	Spitfire VII, Hurricane IIC

APPENDIX 12
RAF Coastal Command Training Units 1939–45

1 NOVEMBER 1940
No 17 Group

1 OTU	Silloth	Hudson, Blenheim, Beaufort, Wellington, Whitley, Oxford
2 OTU	Catfoss	Blenheim, Anson, Beaufighter, Oxford, Beaufort, Lysander, Martinet

12 FEBRUARY 1942
No 17 Group

HQ: Mackenzie's Hotel, Edinburgh

1 OTU	Silloth	Hudson, Blenheim, Beaufort, Wellington, Whitley, Oxford
2 OTU	Catfoss	Blenheim, Anson, Beaufighter, Oxford, Beaufort, Lysander, Martinet
3 OTU	Chivenor	Anson, Beaufort, Whitley, Oxford, Wellington
4 OTU	Invergordon (det Stranraer)	Singapore III, Stranraer, London, Lerwick, Catalina
5 OTU	Chivenor	Beaufort, Anson, Oxford
6 OTU	Thornaby	Hudson, Anson, Oxford, Wellington

15 FEBRUARY 1943
No 17 Group

HQ: Mackenzie's Hotel, Edinburgh

1 OTU	Silloth	Fortress, Halifax, Liberator, Hudson, Blenheim, Beaufort, Wellington, Whitley, Oxford
2 OTU	Catfoss	Blenheim, Anson, Beaufighter, Oxford, Beaufort, Lysander, Martinet
3 OTU	Chivenor	Anson, Beaufort, Whitley, Oxford, Wellington
4 OTU	Alness	Singapore III, Stranraer, London, Lerwick, Catalina
5 OTU	Long Kesh	Ventura, Hudson
7 OTU	Limavady	Wellington, Anson, Oxford, Lysander, Martinet
8 OTU	Dyce	Spitfire, Mosquito, Master, Oxford, Anson
9 OTU	Crosby-on-Eden	Lysander, Martinet
131 OTU	Killadeas	Catalina, Sunderland, Oxford, Martinet, Hurricane
132 OTU	East Fortune (formed from 60 OTU)	Beaufighter, Oxford, Blenheim, Beaufort
132 OTU	Macmerry (satellite)	

No 19 Group

HQ: Mountwise, Plymouth, Devon

10 OTU	St Eval (ex-Bomber Command)	Whitley

6 JUNE 1944
No 17 Group

HQ: Mackenzie's Hotel, Edinburgh

5 OTU	Turnberry	Beaufighter, Warwick, Wellington
6 OTU	Silloth	Martinet
8 OTU	Fraserburgh	Spitfire, Mosquito, Master, Oxford, Anson
9 OTU	Crosby-on-Eden	Lysander, Martinet
131 OTU	Killadeas	Catalina, Sunderland, Oxford, Martinet, Hurricane
131 OTU	Boa Island/Rock Bay (det)	
132 OTU	East Fortune (formed from 60 OTU)	Beaufighter, Oxford, Blenheim, Beaufort
132 OTU	Macmerry (satellite)	

1 JANUARY 1945
No 17 Group

HQ: Mackenzie's Hotel, Edinburgh

4 OTU (det)	Tain	Target Towing
6 OTU	Kinloss	Warwick
8 OTU	Haverfordwest	Spitfire, Mosquito, Master, Oxford, Anson
8 OTU	Mount Farm	Spitfire, Mosquito, Master, Oxford, Anson
131 OTU	Killadeas	Catalina, Sunderland, Oxford, Martinet, Hurricane
131 OTU (det)	Boa Island/Rock Bay	
132 OTU	East Fortune (formed from 60 OTU)	Beaufighter, Oxford, Blenheim, Beaufort
132 OTU	Macmerry (satellite)	
132 OTU	Haverfordwest (det)	Mosquito